A COMPANION
TO LATIN
LITERATURE

BLACKWELL COMPANIONS TO THE ANCIENT WORLD

This series provides sophisticated and authoritative overviews of periods of ancient history, genres of classical literature, and the most important themes in ancient culture. Each volume comprises between twenty-five and forty concise essays written by individual scholars within their area of specialization. The essays are written in a clear, provocative, and lively manner, designed for an international audience of scholars, students, and general readers.

ANCIENT HISTORY

Published

A Companion to the Roman Army
Edited by Paul Erdkamp

A Companion to the Roman Republic
Edited by Nathan Rosenstein and Robert Morstein-Marx

A Companion to the Roman Empire
Edited by David S. Potter

A Companion to the Classical Greek World
Edited by Konrad H. Kinzl

A Companion to the Ancient Near East
Edited by Daniel C. Snell

A Companion to the Hellenistic World
Edited by Andrew Erskine

In preparation

A Companion to Ancient History
Edited by Andrew Erskine

A Companion to Archaic Greece
Edited by Kurt A. Raaflaub and Hans van Wees

A Companion to Julius Caesar
Edited by Miriam Griffin

A Companion to Late Antiquity
Edited by Philip Rousseau

A Companion to Byzantium
Edited by Elizabeth James

LITERATURE AND CULTURE

Published

A Companion to Greek and Roman Historiography
Edited by John Marincola

A Companion to Catullus
Edited by Marilyn B. Skinner

A Companion to Roman Religion
Edited by Jörg Rüpke

A Companion to Greek Religion
Edited by Daniel Ogden

A Companion to Classical Tradition
Edited by Craig W. Kallendorf

A Companion to Roman Rhetoric
Edited by William Dominik and Jon Hall

A Companion to Greek Rhetoric
Edited by Ian Worthington

A Companion to Ancient Epic
Edited by John Miles Foley

A Companion to Greek Tragedy
Edited by Justina Gregory

A Companion to Latin Literature
Edited by Stephen Harrison

In preparation

A Companion to Classical Receptions
Edited by Lorna Hardwick

A Companion to Ancient Political Thought
Edited by Ryan K. Balot

A Companion to Classical Studies
Edited by Kai Brodersen

A Companion to Classical Mythology
Edited by Ken Dowden and Niall Livingstone

A Companion to the Ancient Greek Language
Edited by Egbert Bakker

A Companion to Hellenistic Literature
Edited by Martine Cuypers and James J. Clauss

A Companion to Ovid
Edited by Peter Knox

A Companion to Horace
Edited by N. Gregson Davis

A COMPANION TO LATIN LITERATURE

Edited by

Stephen Harrison

Blackwell
Publishing

© 2005, 2007 by Blackwell Publishing Ltd

BLACKWELL PUBLISHING
350 Main Street, Malden, MA 02148-5020, USA
9600 Garsington Road, Oxford OX4 2DQ, UK
550 Swanston Street, Carlton, Victoria 3053, Australia

The right of Stephen Harrison to be identified as the Author of the Editorial Material in this Work has been asserted in accordance with the UK Copyright, Designs, and Patents Act 1988.

First published 2005 by Blackwell Publishing Ltd
First published in paperback 2007 by Blackwell Publishing Ltd

1 2007

Library of Congress Cataloging-in-Publication Data

A companion to Latin literature / edited by Stephen Harrison.
    p. cm. — (Blackwell companions to the ancient world. Ancient history)
Includes bibliographical references and index.
ISBN 0-631-23529-9 (alk. paper)
1. Latin literature—History and criticism—Handbooks, manuals, etc. 2. Latin literature—Themes, motives—Handbooks, manuals, etc. 3. Authors, Latin—Biography—Handbooks, manuals, etc.
4. Rome—Intellectual life—Handbooks, manuals, etc. 5. Rome—In literature—Handbooks, manuals, etc.
I. Harrison, S. J. II. Series.

PA6004.C66 2004
870.9′001—dc22

2004005855

ISBN-13: 978-0-631-23529-3 (alk. paper)
ISBN-13: 978-1-4051-6131-2 (pbk: alk. paper)
ISBN-10:1-4051-6131-0 (pbk: alk. paper)

A catalogue record for this title is available from the British Library.

Set in 10.5/13 Galliard
by Kolam Information Services Pvt. Ltd, Pondicherry, India
Printed and bound in the United Kingdom
by TJ International Ltd, Padstow, Cornwall

The publisher's policy is to use permanent paper from mills that operate a sustainable forestry policy, and which has been manufactured from pulp processed using acid-free and elementary chlorine-free practices. Furthermore, the publisher ensures that the text paper and cover board used have met acceptable environmental accreditation standards.

For further information on
Blackwell Publishing, visit our website:
www.blackwellpublishing.com

Contents

Figures

Chronological Table of Important Dates in Latin Literature and History to AD 200

Full descriptions of the works of authors referred to here only by name are to be found in the 'General Resources and Author Bibliographies' section in the introduction (pp. 3–12). Dates given are usually consistent with the information in the *Oxford Classical Dictionary* (1996). 'Caesar' is the term used for the future Augustus between his adoption in Julius Caesar's will (44) and his assumption of the name 'Augustus' in 27, rather than 'Octavian', a name he never used. Full accounts of the historical periods covered here are to be found in volumes 8–11 of the *Cambridge Ancient History* (1989–2000).

The Early Republican period (beginnings to 90 BC)

	Key literary events		*Key historical events*
c. 240–after 207 BC	Livius Andronicus active as poet/dramatist	264–41	First Punic War (Rome wins)
		218–201	Second Punic War (Rome wins)
c. 235–204	Naevius active as poet/dramatist	200–146	Rome conquers Greece; Greek cultural influence on Rome
c. 205–184	Plautus active as dramatist	149–146	Third and final Punic War (Rome conquers Carthage)
204–169	Ennius active as poet/dramatist		
?200	Fabius Pictor's first history of Rome (in Greek)	122–106	War against Jugurtha in North Africa (Rome wins)
c. 190–149	Literary career of Cato	91–88	Social War in Italy (over issue of full Roman citizenship for Latin communities)
166–159	Plays of Terence produced		
125–100	Lucilius active as satirist		

The late Republican/Triumviral period (90–40 BC)

Key literary events	Key historical events
81 BC Cicero's first preserved speech (*Pro Quinctio*); literary career continues until death in 43 BC	88–80 Civil wars between Sulla and Marius; dictatorship of Sulla
	73–1 Revolt of Spartacus
	58–49 Julius Caesar's Gallic campaigns
	49–45 Civil War between Julius Caesar and Pompey
50s BC Poetry of Lucretius and Catullus; Caesar's *Gallic Wars*	44 Assassination of Julius Caesar
	43 Caesar becomes consul
40s BC Work of Sallust (dies *c*. 35); Gallus begins poetical career	43–40 Sporadic civil war in Italy
	42 Defeat of Julius Caesar's assassins at Philippi

The Augustan period (40 BC–14 AD)

Key literary events	Key historical events
?38 BC Virgil's *Eclogues* published	38–36 Renewed civil war against S. Pompey
35 BC Horace, *Satires* 1 published	32–30 Caesar fights and defeats Antony and
30 BC Horace, *Satires* 2 and *Epodes* published	Cleopatra at Actium and Alexandria
	29 Triple triumph of Caesar
30s–AD 17 Livy's history published	27 'Restoration of republic': Caesar
29 BC Virgil, *Georgics* published	assumes title of 'Augustus'
20s BC Earliest elegies of Propertius, Tibullus and (later) Ovid published	18–17 Moral legislation of Augustus
	17 Augustus celebrates Saecular Games
?23 BC Horace, *Odes* 1–3 published	12 Augustus becomes *pontifex* *maximus* (head of state religion)
?19 BC Deaths of Virgil and Tibullus	AD 4 Tiberius becomes final heir of Augustus
?16 BC Propertius, Book 4 published	AD 14 Death of Augustus, succession of Tiberius
13 BC Horace, *Odes* 4 published	
8 BC Death of Horace	
AD 8 Ovid banished to Romania	
Before and after AD 14 Manilius active	

The early Empire (14–68 AD)

Key literary events		Key historical events	
AD 17	Deaths of Ovid and Livy	AD 37	Death of Tiberius; accession of Gaius (Caligula)
20s/30s	Phaedrus and Velleius active		
c. 41–65	Literary career of younger Seneca	41	Assassination of Gaius; accession of Claudius
c. 51–79	Literary career of elder Pliny		
60s	Persius, Lucan, Petronius, Calpurnius Siculus active	54	Death of Claudius; accession of Nero
		65	'Pisonian' conspiracy against Nero unsuccessful
65	Seneca and Lucan forced to suicide		
		68	Death of Nero
66	Petronius forced to suicide		

The high Empire (69–200 AD)

Key literary events		Key historical events	
AD 70–102	Valerius Flaccus, Silius, Statius, Quintilian and Martial active	AD 69	The year of the four emperors (Galba, Otho, Vitellius, Vespasian)
		79	Death of Vespasian; accession of Titus
		81	Death of Titus; accession of Domitian
		96	Assassination of Domitian; accession of Nerva
96–138	Younger Pliny, Tacitus, Juvenal and Suetonius active	98	Death of Nerva; accession of Trajan
		101–117	Wide conquests of Trajan
		117	Death of Trajan; accession of Hadrian
		138	Death of Hadrian; accession of Antoninus Pius
140s–180s	Fronto, Gellius and Apuleius active	161	Death of Antoninus Pius; accession of Marcus Aurelius
		180	Death of Marcus Aurelius; accession of Commodus
		192	Assassination of Commodus
		193–211	Reign of Septimius Severus

Notes on Contributors

Alessandro Barchiesi is Professor of Latin at the University of Siena at Arezzo and also teaches at Stanford University. He is the author of books on Virgil and Ovid, including *The Poet and the Prince* (Berkeley, 1997) and *Speaking Volumes* (London, 2001), of a commentary on Ovid *Heroides* 1–3, and of many articles on Latin literature.

D. H. Berry is Senior Lecturer in Classics at the University of Edinburgh. He is the author of a commentary on Cicero *Pro Sulla* (Cambridge, 1996) and translator of Cicero *Defence Speeches* (Oxford, 2000) and Cicero *Political Speeches* (Oxford, 2006). He has also revised M. L.Clarke's *Rhetoric at Rome: a Historical Survey* (London, 1996).

Catharine Edwards is Senior Lecturer in ancient history at Birkbeck College, University of London. Her publications include *The Politics of Immorality in Ancient Rome* (Cambridge, 1993) and *Writing Rome: Textual Approaches to the City* (Cambridge, 1996), as well as several articles on Seneca's Letters.

Jaś Elsner is Humfry Payne Senior Research Fellow in Classical Archaeology at Corpus Christi College, Oxford. He works especially on Roman and late antique art and their relations to literature. Among his books are *Art and the Roman Viewer* (Cambridge, 1995), *Art and Text in Roman Culture* (Cambridge, 1996, editor) and *Imperial Rome and Christian Triumph* (Oxford, 1998).

Elaine Fantham is Giger Professor of Latin Emerita at Princeton University. She is author of several commentaries on Latin poetry, Seneca's *Trojan Women* (Princeton, 1982), Lucan *Civil War* Bk 2 (Cambridge, 1992) and Ovid *Fasti* Book 4 (Cambridge, 1998), many articles on Roman literature, and the monograph *Roman Literary Culture from Cicero to Apuleius* (Baltimore, 1996).

Joseph Farrell is Professor of Classical Studies at the University of Pennsylvania. He is, most recently, author of *Latin Language and Latin Culture from Ancient to Modern Times* (Cambridge, 2001).

Monica Gale is Lecturer in Classics at Trinity College, Dublin. She is the author of *Myth and Poetry in Lucretius* (Cambridge, 1994), *Virgil on the Nature of Things* (Cambridge, 2000) and *Lucretius and the Didactic Epic* (London, 2001).

Bruce Gibson is Lecturer in Classics at the University of Liverpool. His text, translation and commentary on Statius, *Silvae* 5, is forthcoming with Oxford University Press; publications to date include articles on Ovid, Statius, Tacitus and Apuleius. He is working on Pliny's *Panegyricus*.

Roy Gibson teaches Classics at the University of Manchester, and is the author of *Ovid: Ars Amatoria Book 3* (Cambridge, 2003), and the co-editor, with Christina Shuttleworth Kraus, of *The Classical Commentary: Histories, Practices, Theory* (Leiden, 2002), and with Ruth Morello of *Re-Imagining Pliny the Younger* (*Arethusa* 36, 2003).

Sander M. Goldberg is Professor of Classics at the University of California, Los Angeles. He is the author of *The Making of Menander's Comedy* (London, 1980), *Understanding Terence* (Princeton, 1986) and *Epic in Republican Rome* (Oxford, 1995), and a past editor of the *Transactions of the American Philological Association*.

Thomas Habinek is Professor of Classics at the University of Southern California. He is the author of *The Colometry of Latin Prose* (Berkeley, 1985) and *The Politics of Latin Literature* (Princeton, 1998) and co-editor of *The Roman Cultural Revolution* (Cambridge, 1997). He is completing a study entitled *Song and Society in Archaic and Classical Rome*.

Philip Hardie is Senior Research Fellow in Latin Literature at the University of Cambridge. His books include *Virgil's Aeneid: Cosmos and Imperium* (Oxford, 1986) and *Ovid's Poetics of Illusion* (Cambridge, 2002).

Stephen Harrison is Fellow and Tutor in Classics at Corpus Christi College, Oxford, and Professor of Classical Languages and Literature in the University of Oxford. He is the author of a commentary on Vergil *Aeneid* 10 (Oxford, 1991) and of *Apuleius: A Latin Sophist* (Oxford, 2000), and editor of several volumes including *Texts, Ideas and the Classics* (Oxford, 2001).

Stephen Heyworth is Bowra Fellow & Tutor in Classics at Wadham College, Oxford. He was editor of *Classical Quarterly* from 1993 to 1998, and is producing a new Oxford Classical Text of Propertius.

Robert A. Kaster is Professor of Classics and Kennedy Foundation Professor of Latin Language and Literature at Princeton University. He is the author of *Guardians of Language: the Grammarian and Society in Late Antiquity* (Berkeley, 1988), a commentary on Suetonius' *De Grammaticis et Rhetoribus* (Oxford, 1995), and articles on Roman literature and culture.

A. M. Keith is Professor of Classics and Women's Studies, and Fellow of Victoria College, at the University of Toronto. She is the author of *The Play of Fictions: Studies in Ovid's Metamorphoses Book 2* (Ann Arbor 1992) and *Engendering Rome: Women in Latin Epic* (Cambridge 2000).

David Konstan is the John Rowe Workman Distinguished Professor of Classics and Professor of Comparative Literature at Brown University. Among his recent publications are *Sexual Symmetry: Love in the Ancient Novel and Related Genres* (Princeton, 1994); *Greek Comedy and Ideology* (Oxford, 1995); *Friendship in the Classical World* (Cambridge, 1997); and *Pity Transformed* (Duckworth, 2001). He is currently working on a book entitled *The Emotions of the Ancient Greeks*.

Christina Shuttleworth Kraus is Professor of Classics at Yale University. She has written articles on Greek tragic narrative and on Latin historiographical prose, and is the author of a commentary on Livy, *Ab Vrbe Condita* VI (Cambridge, 1994) and (with A. J. Woodman) of a *Greece & Rome* New Survey in the Classics on *Latin Historians* (Oxford, 1997). She has edited *The Limits of Historiography: Genre and Narrative in Ancient Historical Texts* (Leiden, 1999) and (with R. K. Gibson) *The Classical Commentary: Histories, Practices, Theory* (Leiden, 2002).

D. S. Levene is Professor of Classics at New York University. He has published a variety of works on Latin historiography and rhetoric, including *Religion in Livy* (Leiden, 1993).

Roland Mayer is a Professor of Classics in the University of London. He has written widely on a number of Roman authors and literary issues, focused mainly on the period of the early Principate.

Llewelyn Morgan is Fellow and Tutor in Classics at Brasenose College, Oxford, and Lecturer in Classical Languages and Literature in the University of Oxford. He is the author of *Patterns of Redemption in Virgil's Georgics* (Cambridge, 1999) and of a number of articles on Roman literature.

Costas Panayotakis is Senior Lecturer in Classics at the University of Glasgow. He is the author of *Theatrum Arbitri: Theatrical Elements in the Satyrica of Petronius* (Brill, 1995), and of annotated translations into Modern Greek of Publilius Syrus, and of selected plays of Plautus, and Terence. He is preparing an edition of the fragments of the Roman mimographers.

J. G. F. Powell is Professor of Latin at Royal Holloway, University of London. He has published editions of Cicero's *Cato/De Senectute* and *Laelius/De Amicitia*, has edited *Cicero the Philosopher* (Oxford, 1997) and *Cicero the Advocate* (Oxford, forthcoming), and is completing a new edition of Cicero *De Re Publica* and *De Legibus* for the Oxford Classical Texts series.

Yasmin Syed has been Assistant Professor of Classics at Stanford University and Visiting Assistant Professor of Classics at the University of California, Berkeley. She is the author of *Vergil's Aeneid and the Roman Self: Subject and Nation in Literary Discourse* (Ann Arbor, 2004).

Susan Treggiari is Anne T. and Robert M. Bass Professor Emeritus in the School of Humanities, Stanford University. Her publications include *Roman Freedmen during the Late Republic* (Oxford, 1969, 2000), *Roman Marriage: Iusti Coniuges from the Time of Cicero to the Time of Ulpian* (Oxford, 1991) and *Roman Social History* (London, 2002).

Lindsay C. Watson is a Senior Lecturer in Classics at the University of Sydney. He is the author of *Arae: the Curse Poetry of Antiquity* (Leeds, 1991), *A Commentary on Horace's Epodes* (Oxford, 2003) and, with P. Watson, *Martial: Select Epigrams* (Cambridge, 2003). He continues to view himself as an active researcher despite a governmental and university diktat that those whose research is not externally funded cannot be so regarded.

Preface

I would like to thank all the contributors most warmly for participating in this project and for their tolerance of editorial foibles. Thanks go too to Al Bertrand at Blackwell for commissioning this volume and guiding it to completion, to his colleague Angela Cohen for practical and editorial help, to Janey Fisher for her editorial work and to Eldo Barhuizen for his copy-editing expertise.

As editor I have allowed contributors to use either BC/BCE or AD/CE for dates, according to personal taste. Abbreviations of the titles of ancient texts are those to be found in *The Oxford Classical Dictionary* (3rd edition) [Hornblower and Spawforth 1996] and in *The Oxford Latin Dictionary*.

Stephen Harrison
Corpus Christi College, Oxford, March 2004

Reference Works: Abbreviations

AAWM	Abhandlungen der Akademie der Wissenschaften und Literatur, Mainz
AJP	American Journal of Philology
ANRW	Aufstieg und Niedergang der römischen Welt
APA	American Journal of Philology
A&A	Antike und Abendland
BICS	Bulletin of the Institute of Classical Studies
BMCR	Bryn Mawr Classical Review
CJ	Classical Journal
ClAnt	Classical Antiquity
CPh	Classical Philology
CQ	Classical Quarterly
CR	Classical Review
CW	Classical World
DArch	Dialogi di Archeologia
EMC/CV	Echos du monde classique/Classical Views
G&R	Greece and Rome
GCN	Groningen Colloquia on the Novel
GRBS	Greek, Roman and Byzantine Studies
HSCP	Harvard Studies in Classical Philology
ICS	Illinois Classical Studies
JKPh	Jahrbuch für Klassischen Philologie
JRS	Journal of Roman Studies
LCM	Liverpool Classical Monthly
MD	Materiali e discussioni per l'analisi dei testi classici
MH	Museum Helveticum
PACA	Proceedings of the African Classical Association
PBSR	Proceedings of the British School at Rome

PCPhS	*Proceedings of the Cambridge Philological Society*
PLLS	*Proceedings of the Liverpool Latin Seminar*
PVS	*Proceedings of the Virgil Society*
RAC	*Reallexikon der Antike und Christentum*
RE	*Real-Encyclopädie der Altertumswissenschaft*
REL	*Revue des Etudes latines*
RFIC	*Rivista di Filologia e Istruzione Classica*
RhM	*Rheinisches Museum*
SO	*Symbolae Osloenses*
TAPA	*Transactions of the American Philological Association*
WJA	*Würzburger Jahrbücher der Altertumswissenschaft*
WS	*Wiener Studien*
YCS	*Yale Classical Studies*
ZPE	*Zeitschrift für Papyrologie und Epigraphik*

Introduction: Constructing Latin Literature

Stephen Harrison

1 Rationale of This Volume

The editing of *A Companion to Latin Literature* necessarily requires ideological and pragmatic choices on the part of the editor as well as by the contributors. This volume is aimed at university students of Latin literature and their teachers, and at scholarly colleagues in other subjects who need orientation in Latin literature, though I hope that it will also be of use to those studying Latin texts in the last years of school. It has been designed to be usable by those who read their Latin literature in translation as well as by those able to read the originals; all major Latin passages are translated, and modern English translations for key authors are listed in the 'General Resources and Author Bibliographies' section at the end of this introduction. In general, it seeks to combine the form of a reliable literary history with work by leading-edge scholars in particular areas, while also acting as a general reference book through its list of resources and extensive bibliography.

The contributors to this volume range quite widely in their approaches to Latin literature, and there was no ideological 'line' imposed by the editor for their contributions. Nevertheless, I would like to point out the increasing importance of the application of literary theory in the study of classical literature (see my introduction to Harrison 2001c), and to suggest that some of the most stimulating and provocative recent readings of Latin literature are informed by such ideas (see e.g. Conte 1986 and 1994a; Hardie 1993; Henderson 1998a and 1999; Fowler 2000).

In deciding the format of this volume I wanted to avoid the standard listing by author to be found in many literary histories, and which is already available in good up-to-date reference works such as the *Oxford Classical Dictionary* (1996); some concession is, however, made to this traditional mode of reference by including a list of bibliographical resources for twenty of the most important authors in the 'General Resources and Author Bibliographies' section at the end of this introduction.

The ordering of the main chapters is threefold. The first section gives accounts of the five major periods of literature within the chronological scope of the book (*c.* 250 BC to *c.* AD 200); the second and most substantial focuses on particular literary genres and their development across these periods; and the third picks out some topics of particular interest within Roman literature and its backgrounds. Like the stimulating Braund (2002), whose topics in many ways complement those selected for this volume, I think that a topical approach to Latin literature has considerable benefits, highlighting areas of particular cultural specificity and difference; like the impressive Conte (1994b), I also think that historical ordering and generic grouping have an important function, showing what kinds of literature flourished at Rome, when and (perhaps) why.

The chronological scope of the book does not imply a derogatory exclusion or lower valuing of post-200 Latin literature, whether pagan or Christian, and I greatly admire literary histories of Rome such as that of Conte (1994b), which cover all Latin literature up to the Carolingian period. But the beginning of Christian Latin literature about AD 200 with Tertullian and Minucius Felix is a major watershed, and I resolved on this as a stopping point so as not to increase dramatically the size and diversity of the book. As a result the volume reflects the range of Latin literature commonly taught in universities, from the Early Republic to the High Empire, perhaps regrettably reinforcing the canonical status of this period.

Another element I consider important, which this volume (for reasons of space and convenience) alludes to only superficially, is that of the later reception of Latin literature. The burgeoning discipline of reception studies (see Machor and Goldstein 2001) is now having a greater impact on classical scholarship, and many interesting results are emerging (see in general Hardwick 2003, and for the reception of some individual Latin authors Martindale 1988 and 1993). Major poets in English such as Seamus Heaney (Heaney 2001) and Ted Hughes (Hughes 1997) have recently produced work which engages directly with the work of the major Latin poets. Even the history of Latin scholarship has served as the basis for a successful play by one of the leading dramatists in English (Stoppard 1997). This fascination with Latin literature continues a major strand in English Victorian writers (Vance 1997), and (of course) an influence that has been strongly felt in many earlier aspects of Western culture (cf. Jenkyns 1992).

This element of reception is to be found in this book, but in the 'General Resources and Author Bibliographies' section at the end of this introduction rather than in the main chapters. For each of the key authors treated there I have listed books where material on reception is to be found. One especially welcome recent development, recorded where relevant in my listings, is the inclusion in the series 'Penguin Poets in Translation' of volumes on Catullus, Horace, Martial, Ovid and Seneca, which give not only a range of translations from medieval to modern date, but also versions and poems substantially influenced by Latin poets. A recent anthology of such translations and versions for the whole of the period covered by this book is also available in Poole and Maule 1995.

A further feature of the 'General Resources and Author Bibliographies' section which reflects recent developments is the inclusion there of WWW resources. The use of the Internet is now a major feature in all humanities teaching and learning, and whether one needs to download a basic text of just about any Latin author or consult the most erudite e-journal, it is indispensable for students and scholars of the classics. I have included both general resources for texts and other materials, and particular resources for each of the listed authors.

In this section I have also paid close attention to including the most recent and easily available commentaries and translations in the standard series; this has sometimes meant the exclusion of classic older works still used by scholars, but this list is aimed at indicating the range of materials easily available for the student and teacher rather than the specialist expert, who will have his or her own much more extensive bibliography. In particular, the increasing availability of annotated translations by specialist scholars is of particular importance, not only in making available accurate and modern versions to those unable to read the Latin, but also in providing (through their introductions and bibliographies) excellent entry points for the study of the particular author or text.

2   General Resources and Author Bibliographies

There are a number of online banks of the works of Latin authors from which texts may be freely downloaded; for example: The Latin Library <http://www.thelatinlibrary.com>, the *Corpus Scriptorum Latinorum* <http://www.forumromanum.org/literature/authors_a.html> and the Perseus Digital Library <http://www.perseus.tufts.edu>, which also contains a good range of online English translations. A searchable CD-ROM of the Latin texts of the extensive *Bibliotheca Teubneriana* is available commercially from its publisher <http://www.saur.de>; likewise the Packard Humanities Institute CD-ROM of Latin literature for the period covered by this volume, the beginnings to AD 200 (see <http://www.packhum.org>, e-mail phi@packhum.org).

Modern general accounts of Latin literature in English with up-to-date bibliographies are available in Conte (1994b), Taplin (2000) and Braund (2002). Further secondary work on Latin literature, particularly on individual Latin authors, can be found via the annual journal *L'année philologique* (its WWW version is at <http://www.annee-philologique.com/aph [subscription needed]), and in the *Gnomon* data bank <http://www.gnomon.ku-eichstaett.de/Gnomon/en/ts.html>. Some classical journals are now online through JSTOR <http://www.jstor.org/> (subscription needed), and the contents of a large number of classical journals can be accessed online at the TOCS-IN site <http://www.chass.utoronto.ca/amphoras/tocs.html>. Reviews of most important books on Latin literature since 1990 can be found online in the *Bryn Mawr Classical Review* <http://ccat.sas.upenn.edu/bmcr/> (subscription free). Public gateways for classical resources are to be found at the British Academy's PORTAL site <http://www.britac.ac.uk/portal/h1/index.html> and the HUMBUL Humanities Hub <http://www.humbul.ac.uk/classics/>; the websites of classics departments at universities worldwide are also an important resource here.

The following list contains some key items in English on twenty of the more frequently studied Latin authors treated in this volume. It is not a complete listing in either breadth or depth; only books (not articles) are cited in the 'Studies' section, but these are usually the most recent scholarly works that give easy access to the broader secondary literature. The chapters in Parts II and III will often provide further bibliography in their 'Further Reading' sections.

The WWW resources cited for each author are often made publicly available by academic colleagues worldwide, to whom I should like to express my warm appreciation; all WWW URLs were successfully accessed in September 2003.

For further focused information and reading on the authors below, and for authors not mentioned here, see (e.g.) the relevant entries in the *Oxford Classical Dictionary* (1996), or those in Conte (1994b). Most dates of birth and death are necessarily approximate. All works cited are in English unless otherwise specified.

Full bibliographical details for each item cited below are found in the bibliography to this volume, except for those volumes in certain standard series. These series are referred to by the following abbreviations, and details of individual volumes can be found on the websites given below.

Latin texts only
'OCT' = Oxford Classical Texts (Oxford University Press)
<http://www.oup.co.uk/academic/humanities/classical_studies/series/>
'BT' = Bibliotheca Teubneriana (K. G. Saur) <http://www.saur.de>

Latin texts and commentaries only
'CGLC' = Cambridge Greek and Latin Classics (Cambridge University Press)
<http://publishing.cambridge.org/hss/classical/cglc/>
'BCP' = Bristol Classical Press (Duckworth) <http://www.duckw.com>

Latin texts and facing translations with commentary keyed to translation
'A&P' = Aris & Phillips Classical Texts (Aris & Phillips, Warminster)
<http://www.arisandphillips.com/cat98011.htm>

Texts and facing translations with limited notes
'B' = Collection des Universités de France/Association G. Budé (Les Belles Lettres; French translations) <http://www.lesbelleslettres.com>

'LCL' = Loeb Classical Library (Harvard University Press, Cambridge, Ma.)
<http://www.hup.harvard.edu/loeb>

Translations only
'WC' = The World's Classics (Oxford University Press)
<http://www.oup.co.uk/worldsclassics>
'PC' = The Penguin Classics (Penguin Books)
<http://www.penguinclassics.co.uk>

APULEIUS (*c.* AD 125–?180s): novelist, orator, philosophical writer
Works: (a) *Metamorphoses*, (b) *Apologia*, (c) *Florida*, (d) *De Deo Socratis*,
(e) *De Mundo*, (f) *De Platone*, (g) (?) *De Interpretatione*
Texts:
   (a) Robertson (3 vols) (1940–5); Helm (BT, 1931)
   (b) Vallette (B, 1924), Helm (BT, 2nd ed. 1912) and Hunink (1997)
   (c) Vallette (B, 1924), Helm (BT, 1910) and Hunink (2001)
   (d)–(f) Beaujeu (B, 1973); (d)–(g) Moreschini (BT, 1991)
Translations:
   (a) Walsh (WC, 1994) and Kenney (PC, 1998)
   (b)–(d) Harrison et al. (2001)
   (e), (f) (French) Beaujeu (B, 1973)
   (g) Londey and Johanson (1987)
Commentaries:
   (a) Groningen Commentaries on Apuleius series (see <http://www.forsten.
     nl>),
     Kenney (1990) and Gwyn Griffiths (1975)
   (b) Butler and Owen (1914/1983), Hunink (1997)
   (c) Hunink (2001)
Studies:
General: Sandy (1997) and Harrison (2000)
(a): Walsh (1970), Winkler (1985) and Finkelpearl (1998)
Reception: Haight (1927)
WWW resources: links at <http://www.ancientnarrative.com>

CATULLUS (80s BC–after 55): poet
Texts: Mynors (OCT, 1958) and Goold (1983)
Translations: Lee (WC, 1990) and Godwin (A&P, 1995 and 1999)
Commentaries: Fordyce (1961), Quinn (1970) and Godwin (A&P, 1995 and
1999)
Studies: Quinn (1972), Wiseman (1985), Fitzgerald (1995) and Wray (2001)
Reception: Gaisser (1993 and 2001)
WWW   resources: <http://www.petroniansociety.privat.t-online.de/catullbib.
html>

CICERO (106–43 BC): writer of speeches, rhetorical and philosophical treatises, letters and poems

Works: (a) speeches, (b) rhetorical treatises, (c) philosophical treatises, (d) letters, (e) poetic fragments

Texts: (a), (b), (c), (d) all in OCT, BT, B and LCL series, (e) Traglia (1950–2)

Translations: Complete in LCL series, 29 volumes (apart from '(e)' above)

(a) (e.g.) Shackleton Bailey (1986 and 1991), Berry (WC, 2000)

(b) May and Wisse (2001)

(c) Griffin and Atkins (1991), Rudd (WC, 1998), Walsh (WC, 1998) and Annas (2001)

(d) Shackleton Bailey (*Ad Att.*) (LCL, 1999), (*Ad Fam.*) (LCL, 2001), (selections) (PC, 1986)

Commentaries:

(a) (e.g.) Austin (1960), Nisbet (1961), Berry (1996) and Ramsey (CGLC, 2003)

(b) Douglas (1966), Leeman et al. (1981–96) (German)

(c) (*De Rep.*) Zetzel (CGLC, 1995), (*De Off.*) Dyck 1996, (*Nat. Deor.1*) Dyck (CGLC, 2003), (*De Am., Somn. Scip.*) Powell (A&P, 1990), (*De Sen.*) Powell (1988) and (*Tusc.*) Douglas (A&P, 1985 and 1990)

(d) Shackleton Bailey (1965–70, 1977 and 1980); (selections) (CGLC, 1980)

(e) Courtney (1993)

Studies:

General: May (2002)

(a) May (1988), Craig (1993), Vasaly (1993) and Steel (2001)

(b) Kennedy (1972)

(c) Powell (1995)

(d) Hutchinson (1998)

Reception: Narducci (2002) (Italian)

WWW resources: <http://www.utexas.edu/depts/classics/documents/Cic. html>

HORACE (*c.* 65–8 BC). Satiric, iambic, lyric and epistolary poet

Works: (a) *Satires*, (b) *Epodes*, (c) *Odes*, (d) *Epistles* and *Ars Poetica*

Texts: Shackleton Bailey (BT, 1984)

Translations: (a) and (d), Rudd (WC, 1979); (b) and (c), West (1997)

Commentaries:

(a) Brown (A&P, 1993) and Muecke (A&P, 1993)

(b) Mankin (CGLC, 1995) and Watson (2003)

(c) Nisbet and Hubbard (1970 and 1978); Nisbet and Rudd (2004) West (1995, 1998 and 2002); Putnam (1986)

(d) Book 1 in Mayer (CGLC, 1994); Book 2 and *Ars* in Rudd (CGLC, 1989), and Brink (1963–82)

Studies:
General: Fraenkel (1957), Oliensis (1998), Woodman and Feeney (2002)
  (a) Rudd (1966) and Freudenburg (1993)
  (c) Davis (1991), Edmunds (1992) and Lowrie (1997)
  (e) Kilpatrick (1986 and 1990)
Reception: Martindale (1993) and Carne-Ross (1996)
WWW resources: <http://www.lateinforum.de/pershor.htm>

JUVENAL (*c.* AD 70–?120s), satiric poet
Texts: Clausen (OCT, 1992), Willis (BT, 1997)
Translations: Rudd (WC, 1992)
Commentaries: Ferguson (1979), Courtney (1980) and Braund (Bk 1) (CGLC, 1996)
Studies: Anderson (1982) and Braund (1988)
Reception: Highet (1954) and Freudenburg (forthcoming)
WWW resources: <http://www.lateinforum.de/pershor.htm>

LIVY (*c.* 59 BC–AD 17), historian (*Ab Urbe Condita*)
Texts: complete in OCT, BT, B and LCL (only Bks 1–10 and 21–45 survive)
Translations: LCL (complete), 1–5 in Luce (WC, 1998), 6–10 in Radice (PB, 1982), 21–30 in De Sélincourt/Radice (PB, 1965) and 31–40 in Yardley (WC, 2000)
Commentaries: Bks 1–5 in Ogilvie 1965, Book 6 in Kraus (CGLC, 1994), Books 6–8 in Oakley (1997 and 1998), Book 21 in Walsh 1973 (repr. BCP, 1985), Books 31–7 in Briscoe (1973 and 1981), and Books 36–40 in Walsh (A&P, 1990–6)
Studies: Walsh (1961), Luce (1977), Miles (1995), Feldherr (1998) and Chaplin (2000)
Reception: Dorey (1971)
WWW resources: <http://ccwf.cc.utexas.edu/~tjmoore/livybib.html>

LUCAN (AD 39–65), epic poet (*De Bello Civili/Pharsalia*)
Texts: Housman (1926), Shackleton Bailey (BT, 1988)
Translations: Braund (WC, 1992)
Commentaries: Bk 1 in Getty (1940; BCP, 1992), Book 2 in Fantham (CGLC, 1992), Book 3 in Hunink (1992), Book 7 in Dilke (1960; BCP, 1990) and Book 8 in Mayer (A&P, 1981)
Studies: Ahl (1976), Johnson (1987), Masters (1992), Leigh (1997) and Bartsch (1997)
Reception: Brown and Martindale (1998)
WWW resources: <http://ancienthistory.about.com/cs/lucan/>, <http://uts.cc.utexas.edu/cgi-bin/cgiwrap/silver/frame.cgi?lucan, bibliography>

MARTIAL (AD 38/41–101/4), satirical epigrammatist
Texts: Shackleton Bailey (BT, 1990), (LCL 1993)

Translations: Shackleton Bailey (LCL, 1993)
Commentaries: Book 1 in Howell (1980), Book 5 in Howell (A&P, 1995), Book 11 in Kay (1985), selections in Watson and Watson (CGLC, 2003)
Studies: Sullivan (1991) and Nauta (2002)
Reception: Sullivan and Boyle (1996)
WWW resources: <http://www.petroniansociety.privat.t-online.de/martialbib.html>

OVID (43 BC–AD 17), erotic, didactic, epic and epistolary poet
Works: (a) *Amores*, (b) *Heroides*, (c) *Ars Amatoria, Medicamina Faciei Femineae, Remedia Amoris*, (d) *Fasti*, (e) *Metamorphoses*, (f) Exile poetry (*Tristia, Epistulae Ex Ponto, Ibis*)
Texts: Complete in LCL, OCT and BT series (except *Heroides* in the last two).
Translations: complete in LCL; (a) Lee (1968), (b) Isbell (PC, 1990), (c) Melville (WC, 1990), (d) Frazer/Goold (LCL, 1989) (e) Melville (WC, 1987) and Hill (A&P, 1985–2000) and (f) (*Tristia*) Melville (WC, 1992)
Commentaries:
  (a) McKeown (1987–), (*Am*.2) Booth (A&P, 1991)
  (b) (1, 2, 5, 6, 7, 10, 11, 15) Knox (GCLC, 1995) and (16–21) Kenney (CGLC, 1996)
  (c) (*Ars* 1) Hollis (1977), (*Ars* 3) Gibson 2003 and (*Rem*.) Henderson (1979)
  (d) Book 4 in Fantham (CGLC, 1998)
  (e) Hill (A&P, 1985–2000), Books 1–5 in Anderson (1997), Books 6–10 in Anderson (1972); (1) Lee (1953, BCP 1984), (8) Hollis (1970) and (13) Hopkinson (CGLC, 2000)
Studies:
General: Hinds (1987b), Hardie (2002) and Boyd (2002)
  (a) Boyd (1997)
  (b) Verducci (1985) and Jacobson (1974)
  (c) Myerowitz (1985) and Sharrock (1994)
  (d) Herbert-Brown (1994 and 2002), Newlands (1995), Barchiesi (1997b) and Gee (2000)
  (e) Galinsky (1975), Solodow (1988), Myers (1994), Tissol (1997) and Wheeler (1999)
  (f) Williams (1994 and 1996)
Reception: Martindale (1988) and Brown (1999)
WWW resources: <http://www.jiffycomp.com/smr/rob/ovidbib.php3>, http://www.kirke.hu-berlin.de/ovid/start.html, http://etext.virginia.edu/latin/ovid

PETRONIUS (*c.* AD 20–66), novelist
Text: Müller (BT, 1995)

Translations: Sullivan (PC, 1965), Walsh (WC, 1997), and Branham and Kinney (1996)

Commentaries: (*Cena Trimalchionis*) Smith (1975); (complete) Courtney (2001)

Studies: Sullivan (1968), Walsh (1970), Slater (1990) and Conte (1996)

Reception: Corbett (1970) and Hofmann (1999)

WWW resources: links at <http://www.ancientnarrative.com>

PLAUTUS (active 204–184 BC), comic dramatist

Texts: complete in OCT, BT, B and LCL

Translations: Slavitt and Bovie (1995)

Commentaries: (*Amphitryo*) Christensen (GCLC, 2001), (*Bacchides*) Barsby (A&P, 1986), (*Casina*) MacCary and Willcock (GCLC, 1976), (*Menaechmi*) Gratwick (CGLC, 1993) and (*Pseudolus*) Willcock (BCP, 1987)

Studies: Slater (1985), Anderson (1993), Moore (1998) and McCarthy (2000)

Reception: Duckworth (1952/1994)

WWW resources: <http://www.lateinforum.de/perspla.htm>

PLINY THE YOUNGER (*c.* AD 61–*c.* 112), orator and letter-writer

Works: (a) *Epistles*, (b) *Panegyric*

Texts: (a) in Mynors (OCT, 1963) and (b) in Mynors (OCT, 1964)

Translations: (a) in Radice (PC, 1963), (a) and (b) in Radice (LCL, 1969)

Commentaries: (a) Sherwin-White (1966), Book 10 in Williams (A&P, 1990)

Studies: Hoffer (1999), Morello and Gibson (2003)

WWW resources: <http://classics.uc.edu/johnson/pliny/plinybib.html>
<http://www.class.uidaho.edu/luschnig/Roman%20Letters/Index.htm>

PROPERTIUS (*c.* 50–after 16 BC), elegiac poet

Texts: Barber (OCT, 1953) and Goold (LCL, 1990)

Translations: Lee (WC, 1996) and Goold (LCL, 1990)

Commentaries: Camps (1961, 1965, 1966a and 1966b)

Studies: Hubbard (1974), Lyne (1980) and Stahl (1985)

Reception: Sullivan (1964) and Thomas (1983)

WWW resources: <http://www.let.kun.nl/~m.v.d.poel/bibliografie/propertius.htm>, <http://ancienthistory.about.com/cs/propertius/>

SALLUST (*c.* 86–35 BC), historian

Works: (a) *Bellum Catilinae*, (b) *Bellum Iugurthinum*, (c) *Historiae* (fragmentary)

Texts: Reynolds (OCT, 1991)

Translations: (a) and (b) Handford (PC, 1963) and (c) McGushin (1992)

Commentaries: (a) McGushin (1977), (b) Paul (1984) and (c) McGushin (1992)

Studies: Syme (1964) and Scanlon (1980)

Reception: Schmal (2001) (German)
WWW resources: <http://mitglied.lycos.de/TAllewelt/litsall.htm>

SENECA THE YOUNGER (4 BC/AD 1–AD 65), philosopher, tragic dramatist, letter-writer
Works: (a) philosophical treatises, (b) *Epistulae Morales*, (c) tragedies, (d) *Apocolocynctosis*
Texts: (a) Reynolds (OCT, 1977), (b) Reynolds (OCT, 1965), (c) Zwierlein (OCT, 1986) and (d) Eden (CGLC, 1984)
Translations: all in LCL; (a) (selections) Costa (PC, 1997) and Costa (A&P, 1994), (b) (all selections) Campbell (PC, 1974), Costa (A&P, 1988), (PC, 1997), (c) Slavitt (1992 and 1995), and (d) Eden (CGLC, 1984)
Commentaries: (a) (selection) Costa (A&P, 1994), Williams (CGLC, 2002), (b) Summers (1910, BCP 2000), Costa (A&P, 1988), (c) (*Agamemnon*) Tarrant (1976), (*Hercules Furens*) Fitch (1987), (*Medea*) Hine (A&P, 2001), (*Phoenissae*) Frank (1995), (*Phaedra*) Boyle (1987), Coffey and Mayer (CGLC, 1990), (*Thyestes*) Tarrant (1985), (*Troades*) Fantham (1982), Boyle (1994) and Keulen (2001)
Studies: Costa (1974), Griffin (1976) and Boyle (1997)
Reception: Share (1998)
WWW resources: <http://www.lateinforum.de/perssal.htm#Seneca>

SUETONIUS (AD 70–*c.* AD 130), biographer
Text: Ihm (BT, 1907), Rolfe et al. (LCL, 1998); (*Gramm.*) Kaster (1995)
Translation: Edwards (WC, 2000)
Commentaries: (*Caesar*) Butler/Cary/Townend (BCP, 1982), (*Augustus*) Carter (BCP, 1982), (*Tiberius*) Lindsay (BCP, 1995), (*Gaius*) Lindsay (BCP, 1993), (*Claudius*) Hurley (GCLC, 2001), (*Nero*) Warmington (BCP, 1977), Bradley (1978), (*Galba, Otho, Vitellius*) Murison (BCP, 1992), Shotter (A&P, 1993), (*Vespasian*), Jones (BCP, 1996), (*Domitian*) Jones (BCP, 1996) and (*Gramm.*) Kaster (1995)
Studies: Wallace-Hadrill (1983)
Reception: Dorey (1967)
WWW resources: <http://www.geometry.net/detail/authors/suetonius.html>

TACITUS (*c.* AD 56–after AD 118), historian
Works: (a) *Agricola*, (b) *Germania*, (c) *Dialogus*, (d) *Historiae*, (e) *Annales*
Texts: (a), (b), (c) Winterbottom and Ogilvie (OCT, 1975), (d) Fisher (OCT, 1911), Wellesley (BT, 1989), (e) Fisher (OCT, 1910) and Heubner (BT, 1983)
Translations: (a), (b), (c) Hutton et al. (LCL, 1970), (a) and (b) Birley (WC, 1999), (d) Fyfe/Levene (WC, 1997) and (e) Grant (PC, 1973)

Commentaries:
   (a) Ogilvie and Richmond (1967)
   (b) Benario (A&P, 1999) and Rives (keyed to translation) (1999)
   (c) Mayer (CGLC, 2001)
   (d) Book 1 in Damon (CGLC, 2003), Books 1–2 in Chilver (1979), Book 3 in
        Wellesley (1972) and Books 4–5 in Chilver and Townend (1985)
   (e) (complete) Furneaux et al. (1896 and 1907); Books 1–2 in Goodyear (1972
        and 1981), Book 3 in Woodman and Martin (1996), Book 4 in Martin and
        Woodman (CGLC, 1989) and Books 5 and 6 in Martin (A&P, 2001)
Studies: Syme (1958b), Martin (1981) and Woodman (1998)
Reception: Luce and Woodman (1993) and Rives (1999)
WWW resources: <http://www.lateinforum.de/persf.htm#Tacitus>

TERENCE (active from 166 BC; *d.c.* 159), comic dramatist
Texts: in OCT, LCL and B
Translations: Radice (PC, 1976)
Commentaries: (*Adelphoe*) Martin (CGLC, 1976), Gratwick (A&P, 1987),
(*Eun.*) Barsby (CGLC, 1999), (*Heaut.*) Brothers (A&P, 1988), (*Hecyra*) Ireland
(A&P, 1990)
Studies: Goldberg (1986)
Reception: Duckworth (1952/1994)
WWW resources: <http://spot.colorado.edu/~traill/Terence.html>

TIBULLUS (55/48 BC–*c.* 19 BC), elegiac poet
Text: Lee (1990), Luck (BT, 1988)
Translation: Lee (1990)
Commentaries: Lee (1990), Murgatroyd (1981 and 1994), Maltby (2002)
Studies: Cairns (1979) and Lee-Stecum (1998)
Reception: *Atti del convegno* (1986)
WWW resources: <http://www.unc.edu/~oharaj/Tibulluslinks.html>

VIRGIL (*c.* 70–*c.* 19 BC), pastoral, didactic and epic poet
Works: (a) *Eclogues,* (b) *Georgics* and (c) *Aeneid*
Text: Mynors (OCT), Fairclough/Goold (LCL, 1999 and 2000)
Translations: (a) and (b) Day Lewis (WC, 1983), (c) West (PC, 1990)
Commentaries:
   (a) Coleman (CGLC, 1979) and Clausen (1994)
   (b) Thomas (CGLC, 1988) and Mynors (1990)
   (c) (all) Williams (1972–3); Books 1, 2, 4 and 6 in Austin (1971, 1964, 1955
        and 1977); Books 3, 5 in Williams (1962 and 1960b); Book 7 in Horsfall
        (2000); Book 8 in Eden (1975) and Gransden (CGLC, 1976); Book 9 in

Stephen Harrison

Hardie (CGLC, 1994); Book 10 in Harrison (1991); Book 11 in Horsfall (2003)
Studies (general only): Martindale (1997); vast bibliography at Suerbaum (1980)
Reception: Ziolkowski (1993), Gransden (1996), Martindale (1997) and Thomas (2001)
WWW resources: <http://virgil.org>
<http://www.petroniansociety.privat.t-online.de/bibliographien.htm>

PART I

Periods

CHAPTER ONE

The Early Republic: the Beginnings to 90 BC

Sander M. Goldberg

1 The Beginnings

By the early first century BC the Romans had a literature. And they knew it. When Cicero (with some irony) taunts the freedman Erucius as a stranger 'not even to *litterae*' (*ne a litteris quidem*: *S. Rosc.* 46) or tells his friend Atticus that he is 'sustained and restored by *litterae*' (*litteris sustentor et recreor*: *Att.* 4.10.1) or argues for more serious attention to *Latinas litteras* (*Fin* 1.4), he means 'literature' in much the modern sense of verbal art that is prized as cultural capital, texts marked not simply by a quality of language but by a power manifest in their use. Literature thus provided a tool for the educated class to define and maintain its social position. How this idea of literature took hold among the Romans and how individual works acquired positions of privilege in an emerging canon are especially important questions for the study of early texts because they became 'literature' only in retrospect as readers preserved them, established their value and made them part of an emerging civic identity. The Republican literature we traditionally call 'early' is not just a product of the mid-Republic, when poetic texts began to circulate, but also of the *late* Republic, when those texts were first systematically collected, studied, canonized and put to new social and artistic uses.

The result of that process is clearly visible by 121, when Gaius Gracchus challenged a Roman mob with powerful words:

> quo me miser conferam? quo vortam? in Capitoliumne? at fratris sanguine redundat.
> an domum? matremne ut miseram lamentantem videam et abiectam?

> Where shall I go in my misery? Where shall I turn? To the Capitol? It reeks with my brother's blood. To my home? So that I see my mother wretched, in tears, and prostrate? (*ORF* 61)

Even here in the face of death, Gracchus reflects his reading. His words echo Medea in a famous tragedy by Ennius:

> quo nunc me vortam? quod iter incipiam ingredi?
> domum paternamne? anne ad Peliae filias?

> Where shall I turn now? What road shall I begin to travel?
> To my father's house? To the daughters of Pelias?
> (Ennius *Trag.* 217–18J)

In time, Gracchus' speech also became a benchmark text: he and his Ennian model can both be heard in the anguish of Accius' Thyestes (231–2R) and the despair of Catullus' Ariadne (64.177–81). How did the script of Ennius' *Medea exul* become a school text for Gracchus a generation later and his own speech survive to be quoted and imitated in turn (e.g. Cic. *de Or.* 3.124; *Mur.* 88; Sall. *Iurg.* 14.17)? What awakened Romans to the texts in their midst and the work they could do?

Traditional literary history does not offer much help with such questions. It has been too reluctant to shift its gaze from the work of authors to that of readers. Who was reading what, when and why are more difficult questions to address than who wrote what and when; traditional histories rarely ask why. Answers to questions about reading require a history more sensitive to the problems of reception and more willingness to problematize the very idea of 'literature' than those currently on the shelf. Such a history may well turn the traditional story we tell about early Roman literature on its head, but challenging old truths has the advantage of bringing some new ones into view.

The traditional story is at best inadequate. Though Romans of an antiquarian bent haggled over the details, they settled on some basic facts we can no longer accept at face value (see Cic. *Brut.* 72–3). Roman literature did not simply begin, as Romans apparently believed, in 240 BC when a Greek freedman named Livius Andronicus translated and produced Greek plays for the *ludi Romani* ('Roman Games'). The date is impossibly late. Early Latium had a rich and complex cultural history, with growing levels of literacy, a high level of social organization, and significant Greek influences discernible long before the third century. Much of the evidence for the cultural life of archaic Rome remains controversial, but the archaeological record certainly supports the philologists' long-standing suspicion that Andronicus' new constructions rested on significant native foundations. The fragments of his work, for example, show considerable skill in adapting the quantitative metres of Greek drama to Latin requirements. A line like *pulicesne an cimices an pedes? Responde mihi* ('Fleas or bugs or lice? Answer me', fr. 1) is not just a competent trochaic septenarius, the metre that became a favourite of Plautus, but employs the same parallelism, alliteration and homoioteleuton common to popular verse and to the emerging Roman comic style. A fragment from the tragedy *Equos Troianus* (20–22 Warmington)

> Da mihi
> hasce opes quas peto, quas precor! Porrige,
> opitula!
>
>   Grant me
> these powers which I request, for which I pray. Extend
> your aid!

preserves cretic dimeters, which suggests that Latin plays were lyric from the beginning. Since successful performance required actors sufficiently skilled to speak and sing complex Latin from the stage, the Roman theatre's first documented step cannot have been its first one. The notoriously obscure account of its origin in Livy (7.2), who says that Andronicus was the first to add plots to what he calls dramatic *saturae*, probably preserves a faint memory of the stage entertainments that gave Andronicus' Latin-speaking actors their start.

Nevertheless, the traditional date of 240 is also too *early* because what Andronicus and his successors created for the Roman festivals was not immediately 'literature' (on early Roman tragedy see Fantham, Chapter 8 below; on comedy see Panayotakis, Chapter 9 below). Their scripts were initially the jealously guarded possession of the companies that commissioned and performed them. Rome of the third century was unlike Athens of the fifth, where drama's role in civic and religious life bestowed official status and made it a cultural benchmark. The citizens who wrote, produced and performed Attic comedy and tragedy, who competed for its prizes at the great festivals, rehearsed its choruses, created its costumes and entertained its audiences had every reason to record and preserve the evidence of their success in monuments, inscriptions and, at least by the mid-fourth century, official copies of the plays performed. Rome was heir not to this Attic model of civic theatre but to the later, commercial model of the Hellenistic world, when plays were the property of self-contained, professional companies who performed for hire, bringing their own scripts, costumes, masks and music from city to city through the Greek, and eventually the Roman, world. Under this system, all a Roman magistrate did to provide plays for the festival in his charge was to contract with the head of such a company, a man like Plautus' Publilius Pellio or Terence's sponsor, Ambivius Turpio. He would then do the rest. Dramatists wrote for their companies, not for the state, and their scripts remained company property. The alternative scenes preserved in the manuscripts of Plautus' *Cistellaria* and *Poenulus* and Terence's *Andria* recall their origin as performance texts, produced and reproduced as the commerce of the stage required.

The production notes that accompany the plays of Terence (and, less completely, the *Pseudolus* and *Stichus* of Plautus) confirm this impression. Though their official look recalls the Athenian *didascaliae*, they are hardly as official or coherent as they appear. Here, for example, is the note for Terence's *Phormio* as printed in modern texts:

INCIPIT TERENTI PHORMIO: ACTA LUDIS ROMANIS L. POSTVMIO
ALBINO L. CORNELIO MERVLA AEDILIBVS CVRVLIBVS: EGERE L.
AMBIVIVS TVRPIO L. HATILIVS PRAENESTINVS: MODOS FECIT
FLACCVS CLAVDI TIBIIS INPARIBVS TOTA: GRAECA APOLLODORV EPI-
DICAZOMENOS: FACTA IIII C. FANIO M. VALERIO COS.

Here begins Terence's *Phormio*. Performed at the Roman Games when L. Postumius Albinus and L. Cornelius Merula were curule aediles. L. Ambivius Turpio and
L. Atilius from Praeneste starred. Claudius' slave Flaccus provided the music for
unequal pipes. The Greek original was Apollodorus' *Epidicazomenos*. Written
fourth. C. Fannius and M. Valerius were consuls.

Some of this may recall the first production. The year (161) is plausible, and a
story in the commentary of Donatus (on line 315) confirms that the actor-
manager Ambivius Turpio played the title role. Much more, however, is odd.
Why record the aediles, who did not preside over the *ludi Romani*? Who is Atilius
of Praeneste, and why preserve his name? Would any magistrate care about
Flaccus, the producer's hireling, or where the play fitted in the Terentian corpus?

The version of this note preserved in the late antique Bembine codex raises
further questions.

INCIPT TERENTI PHORMIO ACTA LVDIS MEGALENSIB(VS) Q. CAS-
PIONE GN SERVILIO COS GRAECA APOLLODORV EPIDICAZOMENOS
FACTA IIII

Here begins Terence's *Phormio* performed at the ludi Megalenses when Q. Caspio
and Gn. Servilius were consuls. The Greek was Apollodorus' *Epidicazomenos*. Written fourth.

As it happens, Donatus also assigns production of *Phormio* to the *Megalenses*,
which could explain the aediles' appearance in the record. Was the production of
Phormio, then, at the *ludi Megalenses* or *Romani*? In what year? The impossible
formula 'Q. Caspione Gn. Servilio cos' probably disguises the name Cn. Servilius
Caepio and the praenomen of his consular colleague, Q. Pompeius. Yet they were
consuls in 141, nearly a generation after Terence's death. What, then, are we
looking at, and where did it come from?

The simplest explanation is that the notes conflate performances on at least two
separate occasions (*ludi Megalenses* and *ludi Romani*) a generation apart (161 and
141) as presented by two impresarios (Ambivius and Atilius), and that likelihood
suggests further deductions of interest. First, the source of the *didascaliae* is not
official but professional: this is the kind of information that producers would
preserve, not magistrates. Second, the fact of multiple productions means that the
scripts, with scenes altered as required, remained with the companies that commissioned them until, presumably sometime after 141, someone outside the

professional world took an interest, secured (and thereby stabilized) the texts, sorted through the accumulated lore accompanying them, and turned them into the books that educated Romans like Cicero came to know. The process by which plays like *Phormio* became 'literature' therefore significantly postdates their creation, and this fact has serious consequence for the story we tell about how Romans acquired their literature.

The history of writing may have begun around 240, but serious reading began much later. There had long been teachers at Rome – Andronicus himself may have been one – but when Suetonius, in the second century AD, looked into the question, he could trace a disciplined interest in texts back only to the early 160s, when the Greek scholar Crates of Mallos came to Rome on a diplomatic mission from Pergamum. Crates, says Suetonius, took a false step near the Palatine, broke his leg, and spent his convalescence lecturing and discussing literary topics with an eager audience of Romans (Suet. *Rhet.* 1.2). His master classes were necessarily in and on Greek – a Roman competence in Greek is far easier to imagine than a learned Greek like Crates holding forth in Latin – but rather than intimidating his audiences, Crates stimulated them to apply his methods to their own texts, which they promptly did. But what texts? Not drama, since scripts remained with the acting companies. Epic was the genre that first caught their eye.

2   Roman Epic (see also Hardie, Chapter 6)

Epic too was, in a sense, Andronicus' invention. At some unknown time, and for some unknown reason, he translated the *Odyssey* into Latin verse. Unlike his plays, however, which adapted Greek metres to Latin requirements, Andronicus' epic poem used a native metre, the so-called Saturnian of oracles and hymns, and established a different relationship with its Greek predecessor. This is clear from its opening line:

> Virum mihi, Camena, insece versutum
> Tell me, Camena, of the clever man
>
> (fr. 1)

Ἄνδρα μοι ἔννεπε, Μοῦσα, πολύτροπον, ὃς μάλα πολλά ...
Tell me, Muse, of the clever man who many things ...

> (*Od.* 1.1)

Cognates and calques (*insece* ∼ ἔννεπε, *versutum* ∼ πολύτροπον) and a similar word order recall the original, while the new metre and the Italian Camena standing in for Homer's Muse put some distance between the Latin line and its original. This first line of the first Latin epic suggests a freshness well beyond the merely dutiful kind of translation Horace recalls in his *Ars poetica*: *dic mihi, Musa,*

virum...(141–2). Andronicus' innovations may not themselves have been sufficient to win a following – Horace knew the poem only as a school text (Hor. *Ep.*
2.1.69–71) and Suetonius ignored it completely – but Naevius clearly saw possibilities in Andronicus' approach to the challenge of writing epic in Latin. His
Bellum Punicum, the first original Roman epic and the first poem restored to
favour after Crates' visit, continued the Saturnian experiment. The result was a
highly innovative poem, blending myth and history in a powerful Roman idiom.
His technique of layering epithets with a delayed identification, for example, as in
the lines

> dein pollens sagittis inclutus arquitenens
> sanctus Iove prognatus Pythius Apollo

> Then mighty with arrows, the famous bow-holder,
> blessed son of Jupiter, Pythian Apollo[,]
>
> (fr. 20)

creates not only a larger unit than the short Saturnian cola might seem
to encourage, but anchors its novelty in a characteristic Roman fondness for
quasi-riddling effects. The sequence that culminates in identifying the bow-
holding son of Jupiter as Pythian Apollo is but a solemn variation on the short
cola followed by verbal payoff familiar from such unexceptional Plautine iambics
as these:

> Stultitia magna est, mea quidem sententia,
> hominem amatorem ullum ad forum procedere

> It's absolute folly, at least in my opinion,
> to follow any man in love to the forum
>
> (*Cas.* 563–4)

The success still discernible in the fragments of Naevius' poem suggests that
Saturnian narrative might have had a future and that Roman epic might then
have taken a different path had not the greatest poet of pre-Vergilian Rome,
Quintus Ennius, turned his back on Naevius' experiment and drawn closer to his
Greek predecessors.

Ennius' *Annales* not only created a Latin hexameter to replace the Saturnian
but capitalized on its epic associations to incorporate Homeric mannerisms and
Greek conventions: Ennius' Jupiter becomes *patrem divomque hominumque*,
'father of gods and men', closely imitating a Homeric phrase (592); a Roman
tribune at Ambracia fights like Ajax at the Achaean ships (391–8); A warrior
rushing to battle is likened to the high-spirited horse of a repeated Homeric
simile (535–9). The resulting change in epic style was profound, but it was not

inevitable. Nor does it represent a simple victory of Hellenism over native Italian impulses. Andronicus and Naevius were, like Ennius, products of Magna Graecia and scarcely innocent of Greek learning. Their choice of the Saturnian was as deliberate as Ennius' counter-choice. His greater willingness to exploit Greek forms is instead a mark of confidence in Roman culture, a recognition that Roman objectives could be enhanced rather than compromised by appropriating Greek devices and expanding the Latin idiom to embrace Greek examples. The fascination with Greek culture that comes to dominate second-century Rome brings with it a refusal to be intimidated by its example.

3   Historiography (cf. Kraus, Chapter 17)

Even Cato, who so famously resisted the more extravagant of Rome's Hellenizing tendencies, furthered this process of dominance through appropriation. Throughout his long life (234–149 BC), Cato exerted a profound influence on the cultural life of Rome. He was schooled in Greek and kept a Greek tutor in his household. He brought Ennius to Rome – they were said to have met in 204 while on campaign in Sardinia (Nep. *Cato* 1.4) – though Ennius went on to enjoy the friendship of many distinguished Romans. Cato was himself Rome's first significant orator, leaving a legacy of over 150 speeches (fragments of 80 survive) and figuring prominently in the major political and social controversies of his time. His manual on farming is our oldest intact example of Latin prose, but his greatest influence on Rome's literary development came through his history, the *Origines*.

This was not Rome's first historical narrative. By the end of the third century, the great deeds that were informing the Roman epic tradition were also being recorded in prose, and the first historians were not socially marginal figures like Naevius and Ennius. They were prominent Romans: Q. Fabius Pictor led the Senate's embassy to Delphi in the tense days after Cannae in 216, L. Cincius Alimentus was a praetor in 210 and held important commands in Sicily. Both wrote about the Punic Wars in Greek. That decision may have recommended their histories to Polybius and then to Dionysius of Halicarnassus, but it was the task rather than the intended audience that determined what language they used. For them, Greek was the natural choice since it offered stylistic precedents and historiographic conventions that were easier to adopt than to replace, even if it meant beginning a contemporary history with an excursus on the city's founding and dating Roman events by Olympiads. Fabius in particular must have taken well to this task. The great Polybius, never hesitant to criticize his predecessors, not only acknowledges Fabius' importance but treats his account with respect, even when refuting the logic of his analysis (Polyb. 1.14, 3.8.1–9.5). The works of Fabius and Cincius show how comfortable Romans could be in this ostensibly foreign idiom, and since Latin was widely described as a Greek dialect – Romulus was thought to have spoken Aeolic – we might find ourselves wondering not why there were so few efforts to make Greek do the Romans' work but why there were not more of them.

Cato's *Origines*, begun in 168 and still unfinished at his death in 149, established the Latin language as a medium capable of sustained prose narrative. There was still much Greek influence behind his work. He too, as the title suggests, owed a debt to Hellenistic foundation narratives. He drew examples from Greek history and dated Rome's founding from the Trojan War. When he claimed in his preface that 'what great men accomplished privately was as worthy of record as their official acts' (*clarorum hominum atque magnorum non minus otii quam negotii rationem exstare oportere*, fr. 2P), the elegance of his expression declares not just his mastery of Latin syntax but his ability to lift a sentence from Xenophon (*Symp.* 1.1) and make it his own. He also included in his history the texts of at least two of his own speeches, which automatically gave the language of political discourse new status and a new air of permanence. Cato thus set Roman history and Roman oratory on the road to becoming 'literature'.

4   Hellenism

Greek nevertheless remained a potent force in literature as in life: even Cicero would eventually write his consular memoir in Greek. Its use, however, came increasingly to suggest affectation rather than necessity. When A. Postumius Albinus, consul in 151, wrote a history in Greek and apologized in his preface for any stylistic inadequacies, Cato mocked the insincerity of this gesture (*ap.* Gell. 11.8) and Polybius, who had lodged no such complaint against Fabius Pictor, endorsed Cato's opinion (Polyb. 39.1). Postumius had had a choice of languages, and he chose the wrong one. Too much Greek in conversation also sounded affected, as the satirist Lucilius would declare:

> Porro 'clinopodas' 'lychnos' que ut diximus semnos
> anti 'pedes lecti' atque 'lucernas'
>
> Furthermore, we said 'clinopods' and 'lychnos' pompously
> instead of 'couch legs' and 'lamps'
>
> (15–16W)

Nevertheless, his choice of adverb (we should probably print *semnos* in Greek script), whether ironic or not, reflects the striking permeation of Greek ideas and tacit acceptance of Greek models increasingly characteristic of the second century. When the Scipios, early on, declared the moral qualities of their ancestor Barbatus to be the equal of his appearance (*quoius forma virtutei parisuma fuit*), the odd Latin phrase probably reflects the Greek idea of *kalokagathia*. A few generations later, Q. Lutatius Catulus, who became consul in 102, welcomed the poets Archias and Antipater of Sidon to his company and wrote Latin erotic epigrams in the Greek style. These instances are all well known and much discussed. Less fully acknowledged is how the Romans' way of thinking about texts was also shaped by the Greek example.

This should be no surprise. It took Crates to show Romans that they already possessed the elements of a national literature, and however impressive the epics of Naevius and Ennius were to their original audiences, it required editors working after Crates' example to edit and preserve their books for posterity. Porcius Licinus, the first historian of Roman literature, therefore traced its origin to epic, probably with Naevius' *Bellum Punicum* in mind:

> Poenico bello secundo Musa pinnato gradu
> intulit se bellicosam in Romuli gentem feram.
>
> At the time of the Second Punic War, the warlike Muse
> with winged step introduced herself to Romulus' savage race.
>
> (*ap.* Gell. 17.21.44)

The literary potential of drama was only acknowledged later, in the generation of Aelius Stilo and his son-in-law Servius Clodius (in the last part of the second century BC). In gathering texts, settling questions of authorship, and assembling the details of a theatre history, these first students of drama drew on the scholarly traditions of both Alexandria and Pergamum: the Terentian *didascaliae* suggest Callimachus' *Pinakes*, while Servius Clodius' use of sound to proclaim, 'This verse is not Plautine; this one is' (*ap.* Cic. *Fam.* 9.16.4) recalls the doctrine of poetic euphony for which Crates was famous. The process of reception that 'made' Roman literature was itself shaped by the Greek experience of texts, and the genres initially marked for canonical status all had Greek precedents: tragedy and comedy, epic, history and oratory. A negative example proves the point.

The *fabula praetexta* (see also Fantham, Chapter 8 below) was a genre that put the deeds of great Romans on the stage. It was said to be Naevius' invention: plays celebrating the founding of Rome (*Romulus* or *Lupus*) and a victory of Claudius Marcellus in 234 (*Clastidium*) are attributed to him. Ennius also wrote *praetextae*, as did the tragic poets Pacuvius and Accius. The plays were performed at festivals and triumphs and may have played a significant role in disseminating the facts of Roman history and developing a sense of Roman identity among the *populus*. Despite distinguished practitioners, however, and a well-defined role on the cultural scene, *praetextae* never became 'literature'. Accius' *Brutus*, a play about the last Tarquin that enjoyed a pointedly topical revival at the Floralia of 57, is cited once for content, but that exception only proves the rule (Cic. *Sest.* 123; cf. *Div.* 1.43–5). Fragments of *praetextae* are otherwise known only from the lexical oddities they supplied for ancient grammarians. Their lack of Greek origin denied them the cultural authority of tragedy and comedy. They were also too closely tied to the politics of praise, as some famous testimony of Cato confirms.

At the beginning of the *Tusculan Disputations*, Cicero supports his claim that Romans have equalled the achievements of Greek culture by pointing to the success of Latin poetry, which rivals the Greek despite its late start:

> Sero igitur a nostris poetae vel cogniti vel recepti. quamquam est in *Originibus* solitos esse in epulis canere convivas ad tibicinem de clarorum hominum virtutibus, honorem tamen huic generi non fuisse declarat oratio Catonis, in qua obiecit ut probrum M. Nobiliori, quod is in provinciam poetas duxisset; duxerat autem consul ille in Aetoliam, ut scimus, Ennium.

> Poets received late recognition or reception from our ancestors. Although he wrote in his *Origines* that guests around the table were accustomed to sing to the pipe about the deeds of famous men, Cato nevertheless declared in a speech that there was no honour in this sort of thing. That was the speech in which he criticized M. Nobilior for taking poets to his province; the consul had in fact, as we know, taken Ennius to Aetolia. (*Tusc* 1.3)

Cicero elsewhere treated these banquet songs, which modern scholars call *carmina convivalia*, as forerunners of epic (*Brut.* 75), and he may have assumed here that the object of Cato's displeasure was the description of Fulvius' Aetolian campaign in Book 15 of Ennius' *Annales*. This was not, however, the case. Cato's speech is dated to within a year of Fulvius' censorship in 179. What aroused Cato's scorn was therefore not *Annales* 15, a book not written until the late 170s, but Ennius' *praetexta* drama *Ambracia*, which was staged either at Fulvius' controversial triumph in 187 or at the votive games he held the following year. Cato was not attacking poetry in general or Ennius in particular but Fulvius' appropriation of poetry for political advantage in the highly charged atmosphere of the late 180s (cf. Liv. 38.44, 39.4–6).

The banquet songs also had a contemporary resonance for Cato, though Cicero's late Republican perspective again obscures the nature of Cato's concern a century or more earlier. The issue for him was the course of Roman Hellenization. Greek influences flooded Rome after the conquest of Macedonia in 168. The impact could be enlightening. Aemilius Paulus, the victor at Pydna, brought the royal Macedonian library to Rome, and Greek teachers and rhetoricians followed the books in such numbers that by 161 the Senate tried to curb their impact. Other developments were from the outset less benign. Drinking parties, for example, and musical entertainments in a Greek style grew increasingly lavish. Cato complained publicly about boys being sold for more than fields and preserved fish for more than plowmen. He railed at statues erected to honour Greek cooks and trumpeted the austerity of his own household (Polyb. 31.25.5; cf. *ORF* 96, 174). He figured prominently in the sumptuary debates of the late 160s, and this struggle over contemporary *mores* provides the likely context for a famous passage known to Aulus Gellius from an anthology of Cato's pronouncements under the title *Carmen de moribus* (Gell 11.2):

> Vestiri in foro honeste mos erat, domi quod satis erat. equos carius quam coquos emebant. poeticae artis honos non erat. siquis in ea re studebat aut sese ad convivia adplicabat, grassator vocabatur.

> It used to be the custom to dress becomingly in public, modestly at home. They paid more for horses than for cooks. Poetic art was not respected. Anyone who applied himself to that activity or devoted himself to parties was called a flatterer.

His target is the contemporary party scene, where people dress up, eat elaborate foods, and hear themselves praised by their hangers-on. Cato's complaint, not to mention the sumptuary legislation of the time, reminds us, however, that another element in Roman society was losing its taste for the poetry of praise, and their reaction may explain how even Ennius' *Annales* lost its appeal by mid-century and had to be rescued by that later generation of readers, who created Roman literature in the study (Suet. *Gram.* 2.2).

5   The Status of Poets: Lucilius

The recuperation of poetry's reputation in the late second century was thus also the legacy of Crates, though the phenomenon is best illustrated from the late Republic, when praise poetry again became respectable. The rationale for its acceptance is articulated especially well by Cicero in his defence of the poet Archias:

> At eis laudibus certe non solum ipse qui laudatur sed etiam populi Romani nomen ornatur. in caelum huius proavus Cato tollitur; magnus honos populi Romani rebus adiungitur. omnes denique illi Maximi, Marcelli, Fulvii non sine communi omnium nostrum laude decorantur.

> All that praise honours not just the individual who is praised but also the name of the Roman people. The ancestor of our Cato here was praised to the skies, adding a great honour to the affairs of the Roman people. Thus all those Maximi, Marcelli and Fulvii are not honoured without praising us all as a group. (*Arch.* 22)

Cicero may again be reading a contemporary attitude back into an earlier time, but the literary history of early Rome is inevitably the product of such back-projection and hindsight.

The growing acceptability of poetry in the later second century was further encouraged by a narrowing of the gap between poetry's writers and its readers. The first poets were outsiders to the society whose literature they created. Livius Andronicus and Terence came to Rome as slaves and were never more than freedmen. Plautus, Naevius and Ennius were Italian provincials who earned a living by teaching and writing. Caecilius, an Insubrian Gaul, was also a professional. They must all have been well connected. Andronicus received senatorial commissions. Naevius and Ennius served in the wars of expansion that their poetry glorified, and Ennius mixed with the highest levels of aristocracy. Yet they stood only as witnesses to the achievements of their social superiors. Gaius Lucilius was the first poet to observe Roman society from within. His brother was the senator Lucilius Hirrus, whose daughter became the mother of Pompey the Great. Lucilius himself served in the entourage of Scipio Aemilianus at Numantia in 134/3, but though a public career was open to him, he settled instead for the private life of an equestrian landowner, with estates in southern Italy and a house in Rome, where he observed the affectations, hypocrisies and foibles of his contemporaries.

Later generations would call the resulting poems 'satires' and make him the founder of a genre, but the fragments themselves refer only to 'playful chats' (*ludus ac sermones*, 1039W), 'jottings' (*chartae*, 1014W) and 'improvisations' (*schedia*, 1131, W). In an age of keen generic expectations – drama was particularly conservative in form and epic preserved its Ennian ring until the late Republic – Lucilius' poems were extremely varied, even experimental (see Morgan, Chapter 12). As an aristocrat himself, he had no need to cultivate access to an audience as, in their different ways, Plautus and Ennius had to do. He needed only to circulate his poems among his friends. Nor, as a pioneer in a new style of writing, did he have to concern himself with the expectations of that audience or with any particular complex of generic conventions: subjects, metres, tone, diction were all of his own choosing, as their variety makes clear. His social status thus vastly enhanced his creative licence. It also offered a measure of protection from the consequences of his wit. Defamation was actionable at Rome, and the evident impunity with which Lucilius attacked the excesses around him suggests the advantages of high social position.

That position was itself a feature of the poems, but the biographical details so easily culled from their fragments present a significant interpretive challenge for modern readers. We clearly hear the voice of a landowner – *mihi quidem non persuadetur publiceis mutem meos* (I at any rate won't be persuaded to swap my own realm for a public one, 647W) – and an equestrian, who bore the poet's own name:

> publicanus vero ut Asiae fiam, ut scripturarius
> pro Lucilio, id ego nolo, et uno hoc non muto omnia

> That I become a tax collector in Asia or an assessor
> instead of Lucilius, that I refuse and will not exchange for the world
>
>   (650–1W)

Horace would later say that the old satirist drew from his experience and put his life on view, as if on a painted tablet (*S.* 2.1.28–34). That may be so, but the alliance of poetry and biography, never an entirely comfortable arrangement for literary criticism, is especially problematic in the case of Lucilius: even a familiar face is not necessarily a good likeness. What, for example, are we to make of this fragment?

> at libertinus tricorius Syrus ipse ac mastigias
> quicum versipellis fio et quicum conmuto omnia
>
> but a triple-skinned freedman, a very Syrus, a whipping-post
> with whom I switch skins and with whom I trade everything
>
>   (652–3W)

The poet's voice has been heard here, too, taking on the role of gadfly, but the comic language (*libertinus, Syrus, mastigias, versipellis,* and probably *tricorius*) makes its sincerity problematic. Readers may even recall a notorious fragment from Naevius' comedy *Tarentilla*:

> quae ego in theatro hic meis probavi plausibus,
> ea non audere quemquam regem rumpere,
> quanto libertatem hanc hic superat servitus.
>
> What I in the theatre here approve with my plaudits
> those things no grandee dares to contravene:
> that's how much this servility surpasses that freedom.
>
>   (72–4R)

Once ascribed to the play's prologue, these lines became for biographically minded critics a bold declaration of free speech: the *rex* in question was even identified with Naevius' supposed 'enemy', Q. Caecilius Metellus. We now hear in them only the metatheatrical boast of a comic slave. The fragment has no programmatic significance, and the feisty Naevius, who mocked the Metelli from the stage and paid dearly for his independence, is increasingly recognized as a fiction of ancient biography.

A similar scepticism might be brought to the fragments of Lucilius, strengthened both by our experience with Naevius and by our recognition of voices and poses as a regular feature of later satire. Were Romans themselves equally wary of Lucilius? Probably not. When Cicero has a character remark that

'Lucilius, a very educated and sophisticated man, used to say that he did not wish to be read by either the uneducated nor the most educated', he suggests not just that programmatic statements were heard in Lucilius' poems but that they carried the authority of the author's own voice (Cic. *de Or.* 2.25; cf. *Fin.* 1.7). Cicero himself, hardly deaf to dialogic voices, did not doubt the reality of authorial intent. In referring his correspondent Volumnius, for example, to 'what I discussed about wit through the character of Antonius in the second book of *De oratore*' (*quae sunt a me in secundo libro 'de oratore' per Antoni personam disputata de ridiculis, Fam.* 7.32.2), his mouthpiece matters so little that he misidentifies him: the excursus in question belongs not to Antonius but to Caesar Strabo (*de Or.* 2.216b–290). Cicero did not doubt that the voice of Lucilius *was* Lucilius.

This matters because Lucilius' social status determined the nature of his poetic authority. Cicero's poetic quotations generally take their point from their content, not their source. In *De Officiis*, for example, he illustrates the nobility of wars for supremacy (*de imperio*) with an admiring quotation of Pyrrhus' words after the battle of Heraclea ('what a truly regal sentiment!') without noting that the verses in question belonged to Ennius, not Pyrrhus (*Off.* 1.38). Hecuba's dream in Ennius' tragedy *Alexander* is quoted *despite* its origin: 'although this is a poet's invention, it is not unlike the manner of dreams' (*Div.* 1.42). Contrast the beginning of *de Oratore*, where Crassus, speaking to Scaevola, introduces the central idea that good oratory requires wide learning:

> Sed, ut solebat C. Lucilius saepe dicere, homo tibi subiratus, mihi propter eam ipsam causam minus quam volebat familiaris, sed tamen et doctus et perurbanus, sic sentio neminem esse in oratorum numero habendum, qui non sit omnibus eis artibus, quae sunt libero dignae, perpolitus ...

> But I agree with C. Lucilius, a man rather hard on you and for that very reason less close to me than he wished, but nevertheless both learned and refined, who was often accustomed to say that nobody should be reckoned among the orators who is not accomplished in all those arts that befit a gentleman. (*de Or.* 1.72)

In citing Pyrrhus, Cicero offered the words without the poet. Here he cites the poet without the words, and for an opinion divorced from poetic context. Though Lucilius is introduced in terms of his poetry – *tibi subiratus*, 'a little angry with you', recalls the mockery of Scaevola in Lucilius' second book – his authority derives from personal qualities (*et doctus et perurbanus*, 'both learned and highly cultured') and commands the respect of a great orator and the pre-eminent voice of *De oratore*. The aristocrat Crassus acknowledges one of his own.

Cicero's studied invocation of Lucilius is far from the tumult of the early *ludi* or the respectful hush when Crates lectured on Greek poetry or even from Gracchus' unconscious echo of Ennian tragedy, and that is a measure of how far the Romans' literary sensibility travelled from its beginning to the last generation of the Republic. Rome's early literary history is of course a story of authors, but it is also a story of the readers who came to value their work. It took the joint effort of writers and men of letters to ensure that by the time of Sulla there was an ample stock of texts to read, to value, and to call by the name of literature.

FURTHER READING

The best author-centred histories of early Latin literature are the chapters by Gratwick in Kenney and Clausen (1982: 60–171) and, from the historian's perspective, Gruen (1990: 79–123). In recent years, significant challenges to the assumptions and results of this traditional approach have been posed by more theoretically aware critics; for example, Habinek (1998: 34–68), Rüpke (2000) and Schwindt (2001). Much of the impetus for these developments derives from archaeological discoveries, which have changed the nature of what was once a largely philological discussion. Contrast Momigliano (1957) with Zorzetti (1990), expanded by Zorzetti (1991), who is in turn challenged on key points by Cole (1991) and Philips (1991). Poucet (1989), Cornell (1991) and Horsfall (1994) review the problem. Holloway (1994) and Coulston and Dodge (2000) provide good introductions to the archaeological evidence. Rawson (1985) offers much useful information about the late Republican interests through which most knowledge of this earlier period has been filtered.

For the origins of Roman theatre and the *ludi scaenici*, see Schmidt (1989), Gruen (1993: 183–222) and Bernstein (1998: 234–51); for the impact of Crates on Roman letters, Pfeiffer (1968: 234–46) and the commentary on Suetonius by Kaster (1995). The teachings of Crates have themselves been the subject of much new work with important ramifications for Roman literary studies; for example, Asmis (1992) and Janko (2000: 120–34). Gruen (1990: 158–92) analyses the influence of Greek rhetoric and philosophy on the mid-Republic.

For the emerging epic aesthetic and its social position, see Barchiesi (1993a), Hinds (1998: 52–74) and Rüpke (2001a). Garbarino (1973) and Kaimio (1979) gather important source material for the influx of Greek culture in the mid-Republic. For Philhellenism as a cultural phenomenon in this period, see Gruen (1984: 250–72), and for Cato in particular, Gruen (1993: 52–83). Early Roman historiography is the subject of ongoing re-evaluation. Compare Badian (1966), Timpe (1973) and Dillery (2002).

The cultural significance of the *fabula praetexta* is examined by Zorzetti (1980), Flower (1995) and Wiseman (1994: 1–22; 1995: 129–41). The textual evidence is analysed in detail by Manuwald (2001).

Lucilius is not particularly well treated in modern scholarship. There is no authoritative edition of the fragments, and their interpretation is fraught with difficulties. In addition to Gratwick's spirited treatment in Kenney and Clausen (1982: 162–71), see Coffey (1976: 35–62), and for the satirist's political and social background, Gruen (1993: 272–317).

CHAPTER TWO

The Late Republican/Triumviral Period: 90–40 BC

D. S. Levene

1 Introduction

Latin literature in the period 90–40 BC presents one feature that is unique in Classical, and perhaps even in the whole of Western, literature. Although it is a period from which a substantial amount of literature in a wide variety of genres survives, more than 75 per cent of that literature was written by a single man: Marcus Tullius Cicero. Cicero wrote speeches, philosophical and rhetorical treatises, letters and poetry, which simply in terms of quantity outweigh all other extant writings of the period. This is not to suggest that other writers were unimportant: there survive relatively complete the lyric, hexameter and elegiac poetry of Catullus and the didactic epic of Lucretius, the war memoirs of Julius Caesar, of Aulus Hirtius and the other (anonymous) continuators of Caesar's works, as well as the two historical monographs of Sallust. We have significant portions of Varro's treatise on the Latin language, the anonymous rhetorical treatise addressed to Gaius Herennius, and the *Commentariolum Petitionis* (*Notebook on Political Campaigning*) by Cicero's brother Quintus (unless this is a forgery of a later period, as some have argued). More than a tenth of the letters in the Ciceronian collection comprise letters written by other people to or about Cicero, and finally a good number of other works of the period are known through brief fragments quoted or paraphrased by other writers. There are more than enough data to work with; yet the overwhelming dominance of Cicero creates a problem which any interpreter will struggle to overcome. Through Cicero's writings we obtain an invaluable and intimate insight into the time through the eyes of a leading political, intellectual and literary figure, something which no one could wish to sacrifice; yet for that very reason it seems almost unavoidable that scholars view that time largely through a Ciceronian lens, assessing the literature, often without seeming to realize that they are doing so, in terms of the associations, categories and explanations that Cicero all too conveniently supplies for us.

Take Catullus. Cicero never refers to Catullus, but Catullus knew Cicero (or knew of him) well enough to address an (apparently) complimentary poem to him (49). More importantly, many of Catullus' poems are addressed to a woman whom he calls 'Lesbia', who, on the basis of a passing reference in a much later writer (Apuleius, *Apology* 10), is commonly identified with a woman called Clodia whom Cicero mocked at length in a speech in defence of her lover Marcus Caelius Rufus. Cicero's Clodia is read into Catullus' Lesbia, and hints of Clodia-like behaviour attributed to Lesbia by Catullus are expanded on the basis of Cicero's slanders – all this despite the fact that the identification of 'Lesbia' with Cicero's Clodia is far from certain and has been challenged by a number of scholars (e.g. Wiseman 1969: 50–60). And, most significant of all, Cicero in one passage refers to a group of poets whom he calls *neoteroi* (*Att.* 7.2.1), in another to the 'new poets' (*Orator* 161), and in a third to the 'chanters of Euphorion' (*Tusc.* 3.45: Euphorion was a 3rd *c.* BC Greek poet). Out of this, combined with polemical passages in Catullus' own poetry (notably 95, but also e.g. 14, 36, 50), an entire literary movement – the 'neoterics' – has been deduced, of whom Catullus is, it seems, the only surviving representative. It is claimed that this was in some sense a coherent group of 'modernist' poets who based their technique on the third-century Greek writer Callimachus, and who were influenced by the Greek poet Parthenius of Nicaea who was brought to Rome in the late 70s or early 60s (e.g. Clausen 1964; Lyne 1978; for a more cautious view see Lightfoot 1999: 50–76). Almost every part of that story has been questioned, but it is widely accepted at least in outline, and it is Cicero's reading of his contemporaries that largely generates it.

So too every other surviving writer of the period has links with Cicero. Caesar and Sallust were his political contemporaries and rivals (and Cicero is a major character in Sallust's first monograph, the *Catiline*, describing the revolutionary conspiracy which Cicero foiled as consul in 63 BC). Varro dedicated part of his *De Lingua Latina* to Cicero, and Cicero was close enough to both him and Hirtius to make them characters in his philosophical dialogues. The only firm piece of data that we have about the life of Lucretius is that in 54 BC Cicero and his brother read and commented on his poetry (*Ad Q.F.* 2.9.3). Even the *Rhetorica ad Herennium* (which is transmitted to us as a work of Cicero, though it is clearly not by him) has close overlaps with Cicero's more or less contemporary work *De Inventione*, suggesting that at the very least they were drawing on a common source. And our judgements of those orators (in particular) contemporary to Cicero whose works no longer survive are strongly dependent on the accounts that he gives of them (especially in the *Brutus*, which is a polemical history of Roman oratory aimed at defending his own oratorical manner against the attacks of his younger contemporaries). With all of these, it is largely from the infor-mation that we glean from Cicero that we create the framework within which we read and understand the rest of the literature.

Our Ciceronian bias is obvious, but also perhaps inevitable. It would be easy merely to accept it and forget it; but it would be no more sound to try to compensate for it by automatic anti-Ciceronianism – and not only because any sort of reflex response is undesirable in scholarship. For the Ciceronian reading of this period is not just an unfortunate accident of modern ignorance, the result of deriving over three-quarters of our contemporary literary evidence from a single source. The Romans themselves of the following generations, who could read much that now is lost, when they looked back to the literature of the last years of the Republic, saw it above all as 'the age of Cicero'. The elder Seneca, Quintilian, and Tacitus in the *Dialogus* all treat Cicero as the consummate and unparalleled writer of his generation, and he is cited and alluded to far more than any other. It is true that all three are primarily concerned with oratory, the genre in which Cicero was the accepted Roman master, but Quintilian, at any rate, treats Cicero as the pinnacle of all Latin literature, not oratory alone (10.1.105–12). Velleius Paterculus, publishing in AD 30, twice singles out Cicero and places him at the centre of his generation of Latin writers (1.17.3; 2.36.2). And the Greek author of *On Sublimity*, who draws his examples from several literary genres, mentions only one Latin writer, Cicero, in order to provide a suitable comparison to Plato and Demosthenes that his Latin-speaking addressee will appreciate (12.4–5). This does not, of course, mean that these ancient readers were as closely dependent on Cicero for background material on his contemporaries as we are. Nor should one deduce from it that a Cicero-centred reading of the period is dispassionate and accurate, devoid of ideological or cultural bias: on the contrary, as we shall see shortly, Cicero mattered as a writer not least for what he was thought to represent politically. But it does show the difficulties we face if we are to attempt to make any assessment of the period that does not simply place Cicero's perspective at its centre: we are battling against not only the limitations of our evidence, but the whole tradition of literary history.

2 Political Literature

One obvious place where there is an almost overwhelming temptation to read in Ciceronian terms is in politics. The late Republic was a period of intense and brutal competition for political power between individuals and factions, culminating in a series of civil wars that led ultimately to the establishment of the Empire. That world is reflected vividly in Cicero's writing: he was both an observer of and passionate participant in the conflicts. His speeches include political orations to the Senate and to the popular assembly, most famously the four *Catilinarians* delivered in 63, when as consul he exposed and denounced the revolutionary Catiline and brought about the downfall of his conspiracy, and the fourteen *Philippics* of 44–43, in which he unsuccessfully attempted to prevent the domin-ance of Mark Antony after the assassination of Caesar. They include speeches in high-profile political trials, mainly for the defence, as when in 63 he defended the consul-elect L. Licinius Murena on a charge of electoral bribery, or in 52 he defended T. Annius Milo for killing in a brawl his (and Cicero's) political enemy P. Clodius Pulcher (brother of the Clodia who has been identified with Catullus' Lesbia – see above). There is also a single set of prosecution speeches dating from 70, prosecuting C. Verres for corruption while he was governor of Sicily (only the first speech was actually delivered: Verres gave up his defence and went into voluntary exile after the first session, but Cicero, then still on the rise, did not want to miss out on the political capital from the case, and so published five further speeches representing what he had intended to say in the rest of the trial). But even apart from the speeches, Cicero's letters, especially the 400 or so addressed to his intimate friend Atticus, provide a vivid picture of the daily political competition, which Cicero reports and seeks openly or covertly to manipulate.

Cicero died in 43, proscribed and assassinated on Antony's orders after Antony, Octavian and Lepidus formed the 'Second Triumvirate' and took control of the state. For later writers, his death thus represented both the culmination and the end of political freedom: he spoke out against Antony and paid with his life (cf. Seneca, *Suas.* 6–7). Read in such a way, the age of Cicero is easy to understand as the age of political writing par excellence: Maternus in Tacitus' *Dialogus* famously interprets it as such (*Dial.* 36–7), and contrasts it with the early Empire, in which petty private issues held sway in place of grand oratory (cf. *On Sublimity* 44 for the argument that political freedom is necessary for great literature). Scholars have often followed suit, and have sought to read, not only Cicero, but most other writings of the period in terms of the contemporary political competition.

In some cases such a reading is not difficult: it would be surprising, for example, if Caesar's memoirs were *not* published at least in part to gain a propaganda advantage over his rivals and enemies, given the intensity of the conflict in which he was engaged when he produced them. But with other authors it is less obviously desirable. Sallust shows up the problem. His monographs certainly engage with controversial characters and issues from the late Republic: the Gracchi, Marius and Sulla in the *Jugurtha*, Caesar, Cato and Cicero himself in the *Catiline*. Moreover, we have enough information about Sallust's career to know that he too was closely engaged in competitive politics: he opposed Cicero at the time of the Milo trial, and subsequently fought for Caesar in the civil wars, ending as governor of the province of Africa Nova before being indicted for corruption. Accordingly, many scholars have sought to tease out of Sallust's work a politically partisan interpretation: to show that he is writing in support of Caesar or against Cicero, or that he backed the 'populist' *populares* against the 'oligarchic' *optimates* (this itself a framework partly deriving from Cicero's writings – in particular *Sest.* 96–105). But such interpretations are hard to sustain against a close study of the texts, and the tendency in recent scholarship has been to move away from them, and instead to view the works in a less narrowly partisan way. This is not to suggest that they are apolitical: only that their politics are not best seen as the expressions of personal partisanship that Cicero's writings might lead one to expect.

But this, once recognized, takes us to a further question: is the literature of the late Republic in fact distinctively political at all? Certainly not if we think of 'politics' in its most common sense: on any normal definition of the 'political' it would be hard to conclude that Imperial writers like Virgil, Horace, Lucan or Tacitus were not writing 'political' works. But even if we focus on the type of competitive politics that found its expression in Cicero and Caesar, it is not clear that the distinction between this period and those that succeeded it is really to be drawn so sharply. Granted that it is hard to find precise parallels to the political immediacy of Cicero's speeches and letters at later periods, although this may be partly an accident of survival, since political participation (albeit on very different terms) did continue under the Empire, nevertheless it is also true that the changed political circumstances required considerably more circumspection on the part of the writer (Fairweather 1981: 138–42). But not all writers even of Cicero's day approached politics as did Cicero. Not only Sallust, who (it might be objected) was writing already after the Republican political system had died (the *Catiline* is almost certainly to be dated after 43), but also Lucretius (5.1105–60) and Catullus (64.394–408), who were writing as Cicero's contemporaries, approach politics in ways that align them with their Imperial successors: in place of the daily competitive struggle one finds quasi-mythical narratives presenting their own day as part of grand stages of historical development. And one might even observe that this style of political writing, detached from the particular conflicts of a particular month or year, is not always even alien to Cicero himself: his own works of political theory, *De Re Publica* and *De Legibus*, handle Roman politics in a broader manner reflecting less closely the day-to-day concerns of an engaged politician.

The natural conclusion of this might be that to represent the late Republic as a time of distinctively 'political' literature is a distortion: the result of allowing Cicero's speeches and letters to dominate our understanding of the period. But it would be equally wrong to ignore or downplay Cicero, since he unquestionably was an important and influential figure, and since his works do reflect a manner of political engagement which is very distinctive to the time: it is, after all, genuinely the case that the late Republic allowed forms of political engagement that the autocracy of the Empire did not. This is an area where one might say that there is no right answer: there are overlapping 'political' strands within the literature of the period, some of which link up with comparable strands at other periods, others of which are more individual. Which we highlight will depend on the reader's particular focus, and there is no reason, especially given how much of the literature has been lost, to regard one focus as intrinsically superior to another.

3   Intellectual Literature

A second area in which a Ciceronian bias is tempting comes with his books of philosophy and rhetorical theory. He published a good number of works in these areas: the volumes of rhetorical theory *De Inventione* in his youth; *De Oratore* on rhetoric and *De Re Publica* and *De Legibus* on political theory in the mid- to late 50s; and then a remarkable sequence of works written between 46 and 44, when he had temporarily retired from public life as a result of Caesar's dictatorship: works on rhetoric (*Brutus* and *Orator*), works on ethical theory (*De Finibus*) and practice (*Tusculan Disputations, De Officiis*), on epistemology (*Academica*) and theology and physics (*De Natura Deorum, De Divinatione, De Fato*), to mention only the most important. These works, apart from their intrinsic qualities, form our central record of the intellectual life of the period. The rhetorical works not only present the reflections on his art by the man accepted as the greatest orator of the day, but they also draw on the largely lost tradition of Greek rhetorical theory that had developed since Aristotle, and give a vivid picture of the controversies current in Cicero's time. The philosophical works are mainly written in dialogue form, purporting to record debates between the representatives of different schools, and as such are witnesses to the range of Hellenistic philosophical thinking that had been adopted at Rome, above all the Stoic, Epicurean and Academic. Here too the original writings of the thinkers on whom Cicero was drawing have mostly been lost, and Cicero in some areas provides the only major systematic expositions of their theories.

In Western Europe in the Middle Ages it was as a philosopher that Cicero was known above all: Greek philosophy was for the most part known only indirectly, and Cicero was one of the few ancient philosophical writers to whom there was unmediated access. His philosophical reputation then was high; it subsequently fell sharply, as the original works of Plato and Aristotle reached a wider readership, and Cicero was rejected as a mere purveyor of other men's ideas – and the reputation of the intellectual qualities of his age fell with him. Latin literature in the late Republic, despite its aesthetic qualities, tended to be seen as intellectually sterile and derivative, simply reproducing Greek ideas with no genuinely original thought to be found. Some recent scholarship has sought to rehabilitate Cicero somewhat, and to emphasize his own role in shaping the thoughts and arguments that he presents, and the reputation of the period is enhanced accordingly. But whether for praise or blame, it is hard to detach judgements on Cicero as a philosophical and theoretical writer from those of the period as a whole, precisely because Cicero's writings bulk so large in what we can read from the time.

And however we judge Cicero, the same judgement can readily be attached to other writers also. Lucretius is likewise reproducing Greek philosophical thought – in his case, the physical theories of Epicurus, an area in which, as it happens, Cicero has rather less to say. As with Cicero, Lucretius is demonstrably close to his Greek sources (see Sedley 1998): the overlap with the scanty surviving writing of Epicurus is striking. It is easy to treat the two in tandem, and to conclude that, for all their obvious differences, they are engaged in a very similar intellectual enterprise, whether that is in terms of their Latinizing of Greek vocabulary or in their introduction of specifically Roman illustrative material – or indeed to conclude that the primary intellectual interest of the day was focused in the philosophical fields, and to interpret other writers accordingly: hence, for example, the strenuous efforts that are made to identify philosophical sources for the (admittedly surprisingly abstract) prefaces of Sallust's monographs, or to determine the philosophical allegiance of Caesar.

Here too, however, other perspectives are possible. For many later Romans, and in particular those who were interested in antiquarian scholarship, Cicero was not as obviously the premier intellectual figure of the age as he sometimes appears to be today. The great counterbalance was Varro (see Powell, Chapter 16). Of his writings of the time, we now only have less than a quarter of his 25-volume work on the Latin language (his three-volume work on farming, *De Re Rustica*, which also survives, was written in the 30s and so falls outside the scope of this chapter). But we know of a vast quantity of writings in numerous other fields, which were repeatedly mined for information by later writers from Pliny the Elder to Augustine: his 41 volumes of antiquarian research entitled *Antiquitates Rerum Humanarum et Divinarum* (*Human and Divine Antiquities*) were especially prized, but he also wrote, for example, on geography and ethnography, on law (*De Iure Civili*), the *Disciplinae* on what might be called 'liberal arts' (it included volumes on architecture, music, medicine, rhetoric, astronomy and mathematics), and many other subjects.

It is an interesting, if inevitably inconclusive, exercise to imagine how we would be reading late-Republican Latin literature if it had been Varro who had supplied 75 per cent of our surviving texts, and if Cicero had been represented by no more than a couple of extant works combined with a large number of fragments and allusions in later writers. Certainly it seems unlikely that questions of philosophical background would be occupying us as closely as they do. While Varro is known to have written on philosophy (Tarver 1997), and indeed professed allegiance to the so-called Old Academy of Antiochus of Ascalon (with whom he had studied), the primary focus of his work, as far as we can judge, was elsewhere, and above all in deriving a scholarly understanding of Roman traditions. This is a major theme not only of his directly antiquarian works, but also works notionally on other subjects: *De Lingua Latina*, the work we are in the best position to judge, contains much scholarly material on aspects of Roman history and customs that (Varro claims) underlie the development of the language.

But, more importantly, reading from a Varronian rather than a Ciceronian perspective, we might be less ready to see the intellectual life of the period as so heavily parasitic on its Greek forebears. It is, of course, undeniably true that Rome at all periods was greatly indebted to Greece, and specifically that Latin literature took most of its forms and much of its subject matter from Greek predecessors. This was recognized by the Romans themselves, to the point that acknowledgement of one's Greek source became a literary trope in its own right, and it is no less true in this period than in any other. Lucretius not only reproduced Greek philosophical material, as said above, but also wrote in a genre, didactic epic, that derives from Greek antecedents. Catullus' poetry also uses Greek genres, and his collection includes poems that are close adaptations of works by Greek writers such as Sappho (51) or Callimachus (66); Sallust's monographs draw heavily on Thucydides for their themes and ideas (Scanlon 1980). Nor was Varro himself devoid of Greek influence. Among his lost works are 150 volumes of 'Menippean satires', satiric sketches in a mixture of prose and verse deriving from the writings of the Greek Cynic philosopher Menippus of Gadara. And of course Varro's scholarship, even on Roman topics, was not created in an intellectual vacuum: he was drawing on methods of systematic research and analysis that had been developed in Greece (see Rawson 1978). Nevertheless, the Romans themselves saw Varro as a scholar to match any in Greece (Lactantius, *Inst.* 1.6.7; cf. Quintilian 10.1.95), and the application of such scholarly methods to new topics at Rome inevitably involved an originality far beyond the image of the largely derivative Roman thinker: it suggests an intellectual dynamism that could easily be overlooked if we were to centre our focus on Cicero.

Forming our image of the intellectual aspects of Roman literature in the late Republic on Varro could lead to a significant rebalancing of the intellectual relationship that we perceive between Greece and Rome in the writers of the day: it might appear more as partnership than theft. For example, Varro's anti-quarian research on Rome often raised issues that were no less applicable to other countries (cf. *Ant. Div.* fr. 18 [Cardauns]): hence a 'Varronian' reading of Sallust might give a different perspective on the ethnographical sections of his work (notably *Jug.* 17–19), as indeed on the even longer ethnographic analyses in Caesar (esp. *BG* 6.11–28). For instance, Caesar had an interest in time-reckoning, that not only appears from his reform of the Roman calendar in 45 BC, but also informs his observation of and attempt to explain the style of reckoning used in Gaul (*BG* 6.18). It is not unreasonable to relate this to Varro's own substantial interest in time-reckoning, which he studied in specifically Roman terms via an analysis of the Roman religious calendar (*LL* 6.3–34: he also wrote on calendars in several other works). The Greeks naturally had a great deal of ethnographic writing of their own, which Varro and Caesar had certainly read, but the scholarly instinct to treat the Romans as purely derivative would surely have been lessened had original Roman research in these matters been better represented in surviving Latin literature. It is not, of course, that these aspects of these authors have ever gone unnoticed – far from it – but the weight and interpretation that one decides to give to them depends at least in part on the expectations that we derive from our general reading of the period, which in turn depends upon the selection of works that we choose (or are compelled) to treat as representative.

Here too, of course, we should not think that a 'Varronian' reading of late-Republican Latin literature is somehow 'truer' than a 'Ciceronian' one. Both writers have aspects that are genuinely reflected in other writers of the day – and indeed in each other. Varro, at least on the available evidence, often shows himself no less derivative of Greek thought than Cicero; conversely Cicero at times engages in distinctive and original thought of his own: one might, for example, note *De Oratore*, where Cicero takes existing rhetorical theory, but, through his characters' informal discussions, reworks it into something utterly distinctive. To assess the intellectual background to the literature requires us to consider each perspective at different times: and the appropriate balance between them will always be open to debate.

4   Literary Development

The accidents of survival have affected our judgement of late-Republican litera-ture in another way, one in which, this time, Cicero is not especially closely implicated. The genres in which Cicero's achievement was at its highest are also, as it happens, genres where he has relatively few surviving successors. We have no Latin oratory at all of the classical period outside Cicero's own work, apart from Pliny's *Panegyric* and the *Apologie* of Apuleius. We do have works of philosophy and rhetorical theory by writers such as Seneca, Tacitus and Quintil-ian, but for the most part Cicero's work is sufficiently distant from theirs in form and manner that there is little incentive to try to read them into a single pattern.

But in other genres the situation is different. In didactic epic and elegiac poetry, for example, the achievements of the surviving representatives are, while consider-able, assessed with at least half an eye on what was to come later. The point is not only that Lucretius and Catullus were immensely influential (though they cer-tainly were), but also that our readings of the genres do not tend to treat these Republican authors as central: rather our primary image of the genres is formed out of the works created in subsequent generations, and there is a strong tempta-tion to read teleologically, and to find significance in the Republican writers in their relation to their Imperial successors.

So, for example, Catullus' poetry (see also Harrison, Chapter 13 below) in various respects prefigures the Augustan elegists: above all Tibullus, Propertius and Ovid. Like them, he presents a sequence of poems in elegiac metre, many of them centring on a love affair. As with them, a woman – Lesbia – is named as his lover in those poems (although not every elegiac love poem refers to her by name, and it is worth remembering that there are also several poems addressed to a male lover called Iuventius). As with them, he presents a picture of an attractive but unfaithful mistress, and of the conflicting emotions of the poet faced with a lover whom he can neither live happily with nor break himself away from. And in particular poem 68b (assuming, as many scholars do, that poem 68 is actually two separate poems which have been conflated in the manuscript tradition) incorporates many of the features that are familiar from later writers. It is addressed to Allius, who apparently supplied a house where Catullus and Lesbia could meet: it then slips episodically from a brief account of his liaison into a long mythological comparison – in this case, the ill-starred marriage of Laodamia to

Protesilaus, the first man to be killed at Troy. From here he digresses into a reminder of another tragic death at Troy – namely his own brother, who had died and was buried in Asia Minor – before returning to Laodamia and Lesbia, and finally to Allius again. There is a richness and thematic complexity here that has long been admired, and that certainly influenced his successors the love elegists: with them likewise one finds an intimate love affair painted on a broad canvas with connections made to myth, and themes of death and love intertwined. To align Catullus with them is entirely natural and sensible.

And yet, if we imagine for a moment reading Catullus *without* the generic future of Tibullus, Propertius and the rest – in other words, reading him much as he might have been read in his own day – the balance of our reading might well be rather different. For the striking thing about poem 68b from the perspective of the Catullan corpus is precisely how anomalous it is in both its scale and its complexity, unsurprising though either may look from the perspective of poets who were writing on a similar scale and complexity. Catullus 68b is over 100 lines long. There is no other erotic elegy in the collection on even a remotely comparable scale; the closest is poem 76, an introspective analysis of the affair and his response to it, which is twenty-six lines long. But the remaining poems in elegiac metre are much shorter: a typical length is no more than six or eight lines, and one – the famous poem 85 – only two lines long. This sort of length recalls the numerous love epigrams found in Hellenistic poetry, which certainly influenced Catullus strongly. We thus have one massive love elegy standing at the head of a collection largely comprising brief epigrams.

Our appreciation of what this means is unfortunately hindered by the fact that we do not know in precisely what form Catullus assembled and published his poems. We are also hindered by a lack of knowledge of earlier Greek poetry: it is hotly contested among scholars whether the collections of extended elegiac poems certainly written in Greece ever included, in the Roman manner, sequences of first-person erotic poems exploring an affair with one lover. But, if Catullus' poems in elegiacs were indeed meant to be read together, we have something for which no parallel has ever been adduced: beginning by linking the love affair to myth at great length and in a highly personal way, and then collapsing the erotic theme into brief, pointed and sometimes scathing epigrams on (apparently) the same woman. From this perspective, poem 68b is the one that looks anomalous: the central linchpin in an abrupt, surprising and experimental sequence – even though from the perspective of the later elegy, which it so heavily influenced, it looks the most familiar of all. It is likely that the appeal of this poetry lay above all in its undermining of existing generic conventions: yet the fact that out of it new and familiar generic conventions emerged tends to hinder our reading it in those terms. This is of course the fate of revolutionary but influential artists across history (it takes a rare historical imagination to hear Beethoven or Wagner with the sense of shock and danger that their contemporaries did), but it is especially a problem with Republican Latin literature, where we have lost virtually all the earlier and contemporary poetry that might have allowed us to gain a sense of the context against which surviving authors were writing: the evidence allows us to conjecture that Catullus was innovative, but the nature of his innovation is hard to determine with any precision, which doubles the temptation to read from the perspective of his successors, whose works do at least survive in reasonable quantities.

The problems with Lucretius (on whom see further Gale, Chapter 7 below) manifest themself in a slightly different way. He also was highly influential on later writers, and in particular on Virgil in the *Georgics* and *Aeneid*. Here too, however, Lucretius is viewed from the perspective of the future: the fact that Virgil has regularly (and at Rome not least) been seen as the greatest Latin poet of all, along with the widespread use of his work in educational contexts, has, paradoxically, often led to his being viewed at least tacitly as the 'norm', and other writers assessed according to their deviations from him.

Take the issue of versification. Lucretius' hexameter verse employs various techniques that Virgil and his contemporaries and successors largely eschewed, but which were found to an even greater degree in earlier Republican writers such as Ennius: for example, the use of four- or five-syllable words at the end of the line, or heavy alliteration. It is temptingly easy to read Latin literature in terms of an inevitable progression from the 'crudity' of early Latin verse to the 'refinement' of Augustan verse, with Lucretius coming somewhere in the middle; and this is assisted by the fact that both Catullus and Cicero in his surviving poetry are in most of these respects closer to Virgil than Lucretius. A teleological narrative is readily constructed in which the progressive 'Callimachean' Catullus is moving towards Virgilian perfection, while his contemporary Lucretius is still, despite his acknowledged brilliance, rooted in some of the roughness of the unsophisticated past.

This picture *may* have some truth in it, in that it is not implausible to suggest that Lucretius in some ways may be self-consciously archaizing: certainly aspects of his vocabulary point to that. But that is a far cry from suggesting that he falls on a particular point on a road of linear development that extends beyond him. The claim that a 'Callimachean' approach is specifically associated with modernist 'neoteric' poets like Catullus (see above) is itself questionable (for all that it derives partly from Catullus' own polemic), since Callimachus' work had been known and imitated at Rome for at least a century, and Lucretius himself appears in at least some ways to share a similar aesthetic (see Kenney 1970). At times he draws on Callimachus directly (e.g. 6.749–55: cf. Callimachus, *Hecale* fr. 73 Hollis), and the very fact of writing a didactic poem on Epicurean physics indicates something of the Hellenistic delight in versifying intractable topics, since Epicurus was notoriously suspicious of verse. And, more generally, one is not entitled to assume that the development of literature is clearly directional: even if the measurable differences between Lucretius on the one hand, and Catullus and Cicero on the other, do point to some sort of artistic dispute, it does not mean that we should view that dispute in terms of movement or resistance of movement towards a later goal, since at the time the future was unpredictable: had Lucretius been the one whose metrical and stylistic patterns were adopted by later poets we would be more likely to view him as the upholder of a standard than as a sometimes clumsy archaizer.

The upshot is that a properly grounded appreciation of the literature of the late Republic is extremely hard to reach, partly because of our (understandable and inevitable) tendency to privilege surviving literature in giving contexts to our readings, even when that literature may post-date the period under consideration. This is not a problem unique to this period, but it is accentuated here because of the long tradition – a tradition beginning in antiquity itself – of thinking of the periods of Latin literature in terms of peaks and troughs, and of constructing a story of development to and from idealized goals. This is not to suggest that every part of that story is ill founded. Late-Republican writers, like writers of other times, certainly did define themselves in response to their own predecessors: Lucretius invokes Ennius at the start of his poem (1.112–26), and the succession of orators up to Cicero himself in the *Brutus* is especially revealing. There can be little doubt that at least some of the writers of the time saw themselves as both drawing on existing literature and as developing it in striking ways. But, while we should give this its proper place, we should resist the assumption that those features taken up by later generations are somehow more innovative or 'progressive' than those that were not. In literature, as in life, the fact that a particular road is taken does not show that it was the only one available to take.

FURTHER READING

The centrality of Cicero to the study of the period, as described in the chapter, makes it unfortunate that there is no modern book that attempts to capture all the facets of his achievement: Dorey (1964) is about as close as one comes, though it is an unsatisfactory work in many ways. Of the numerous biographies, Rawson (1975) is accessible and reasonably comprehensive. Stroh (1975) is central for modern scholarship on the speeches, on which there have been a number of excellent books more recently, notably Riggsby (1999) and Vasaly (1993).

On Cicero as philosopher, Powell (1995) provides a wide-ranging set of essays, and Wood (1988) gives a useful and intelligent account of Cicero as a specifically political thinker; Griffin and Barnes (1989) look at philosophy at Rome more broadly. On the wider intellectual background, the essential starting point is Rawson (1985), who does in detail a similar exercise to the one that the chapter sketches in outline, reading the intellectual life of the time from a largely non-Ciceronian perspective. Rawson (1972) shows Cicero's own debt to Varro-like antiquarianism.

There is a massive bibliography on 'neoteric' poetry; Lyne (1978) provides a solid discussion, Crowther (1970) is a fair representative of the sceptics, and Lightfoot (1999: 50–76) is the best study of the claims for Parthenius to be the driving force behind the movement. Wiseman (1974) discusses these issues, but also sets the poetry of the time more broadly against its historical background. Books on particular authors that do the same include Minyard (1985) on Lucretius, Wiseman (1985) on Catullus, La Penna (1968) on Sallust. Books on Caesar can hardly avoid the wider period: Rambaud (1953) is the classic study, Welch and Powell (1998) a good recent one.

On the problems of interpreting Catullus in the light of his generic successors see Ross (1969). Finally, I strongly recommend Hinds (1998: 52–98) which, although not only about this particular period, is an essential study of the problems inherent in discussing 'periods' of Latin literature, and whose approach has influenced this chapter throughout.

CHAPTER THREE

The Augustan Period: 40 BC–AD 14

Joseph Farrell

1 Introduction

The idea of an 'Augustan period' in Latin literature is firmly established among professional classicists and lay readers as well. Often one thinks less of a 'period' than of a moment at which gifted writers supported by enlightened patrons at a time of great historical importance, used these advantages to bring a number of genres to stylistic perfection; and this notion has become a touchstone for other moments in European cultural history. There is of course no doubt that some of the most important masterpieces of Latin literature were produced under Augustus and that these works share certain characteristics, including concern with the position of Augustus himself in Roman politics and society. Thus the idea of an 'Augustan period' is based on significant historical phenomena and will persist because of its convenience and because of Augustus' own influence on Roman culture throughout his principate and beyond.

We are speaking, however, not of a moment, but of almost sixty years. The sociopolitical climate that prevailed at the end was very different from that at the beginning, and this difference left its mark on literature as well. Just as historians conceive of Augustus' principate in dynamic and evolving terms (Salmon 1956; Lacey 1996), so should students of literature consider the Augustan period one of constant development. It would not be going too far to regard the period as one of transition from the open conditions of literary production that prevailed during the late Republic to the much more tightly controlled Imperial system. When all is said, our conception of the 'Age of Augustus' as a coherent whole derives very largely from two or three masterpieces that appeared during the middle years of the period. The importance of these works is so great that they tend to dictate our perception of the period as a whole. Nevertheless, our appreciation even of these defining works is enhanced if we adopt a more analytical approach to the sociopolitical forces that shaped literature during Augustus' lengthy career.

2   Three Distinct Phases

To understand how conditions changed during our period, it is useful to think of it as comprising three phases. The first begins in 44 BC with the death of Julius Caesar and ends in 29 when Caesar's successor returned to Rome in triumph after defeating all his rivals. The second extends to 2 BC, perhaps the height of Augustus' fortune, when he received the honorific title *pater patriae*. The third phase concludes our period with Augustus' death in AD 14, though we should perhaps stretch it to include the deaths of Ovid and Livy in 17. Each phase is marked by crucial changes in Augustus' political position and style of government, in the prevailing political and social climate, and in the patronage of literature.

Phase 1: The Triumviral years

The years following Caesar's death were troubled by nearly constant conflict as the future Augustus struggled against powerful opponents for military and political supremacy. These years are often considered the death-throes of the Republic, but to the historian of literature, they are an integral and formative phase of the Augustan period.

In 43 BC the government of Rome fell into the hands of three men who had ties to the assassinated dictator-for-life, Julius Caesar. These were Marcus Antonius, Caesar's consular colleague at the time of his death; Marcus Aemilius Lepidus, formally second-in-command to Caesar in his capacity as dictator; and Gaius Octavius, Caesar's great-nephew and posthumously adopted son (the name 'Octavian' is often used to denote the young Caesar during this phase of his career, before he received the name 'Augustus' on 30 January 27 BC; but, while the form 'Octavianus' follows Roman naming conventions in the case of adoptions, it is not in fact anciently attested; on Augustus' nomenclature in general see Syme 1958a: 172–88). The young Caesar was only 19 and a private citizen, and so risked being shunted aside by more experienced men, but he repeatedly proved himself more than a match for his elders. He began by raising his own army (*RG* 1). Twice he led soldiers into Rome in order to bend the senate to his will. He colluded with his Triumviral colleagues in the murder of political opponents and in the confiscation of property, and he countered the treachery of these same colleagues on several occasions. In addition, until 36 BC he faced serious opposition from Sextus Pompeius, son of Caesar's foe Pompeius the Great, in the western provinces that were nominally under the young Caesar's control. The future *princeps* (first man, the deliberately vague appellation he used after Actium) thus played a major role in at least four civil wars. In all these conflicts he emerged victorious, despite some very close calls and serious reversals along the way.

This is all far from the picture of peace and prosperity that one associates with the name of Augustus. Of course, during these troubled years the young Caesar was not yet 'Augustus' and his public image was very different from what it would become (Zanker 1988: 37–43, 97–100). In literature, too, conditions that we associate with the late Republic still prevailed. Important Republican writers such as Varro and Nepos remained active throughout the thirties, Sallust's literary career begins only after Caesar's assassination and lasts until Sallust's own death in 35. Such links with the past were rarer in poetry, where we tend to focus on poets like Vergil and Horace who were not finishing but launching careers that would peak during the second, post-Triumviral phase of our period. But the surviving poetry and prose of this initial phase clearly share specific concerns. Varro's *De re rustica*, for instance, published in 37, considers the Roman villa both as a working farm and as a centre of cultural production in the largest sense, and examines this institution against a contemporary background of political and social upheaval. This work, contemporary with Vergil's *Eclogues*, is a major source of inspiration for the *Georgics* (see e.g. Thomas 1987). It was then in such circumstances that those writers whom we regard as typically 'Augustan' made their reputations. What perspective on contemporary events do these works present?

In the preface to his history, Livy famously speaks of living in a time that has grown so corrupt that it can endure neither its illnesses nor their cure – neither of the Republic restored nor of a Golden Age. Vergil in the *Eclogues* does speak rather fantastically of the return of a Golden Age (4.9); but the abiding impression that these poems leave is one of regret for a lost world. In poem 1 (2–3, 70–2), a shepherd named Meliboeus must go into exile because a soldier has seized his lands – a reference to the aftermath of Philippi, when lands were seized and distributed among the veterans of the triumviral armies. Poem 9 returns to this theme, openly lamenting these events and their effect on Mantua and Cremona, Vergil's own *patria* (27–8). The young Caesar is never named in the *Eclogues*, in connection either with the Golden Age or with the land confiscations, though most interpreters associate both themes with him and identify him with the anonymous *iuvenis* of poem 1. But the young Triumvir remains a shadowy figure, while among those prominently addressed is Gaius Asinius Pollio, a supporter of Antonius (Appian 3.97, 399; Vell. Pat. 2.63.3), who refused to switch sides even on the eve of Actium (Vell. Pat. 2.86.3). Thus even if, by the time the collection received its final form, Vergil was moving exclusively in circles friendly to the eventual victors, the *Eclogues* definitely took shape before anyone could guess what history had in store either for Rome or for Caesar's youthful heir.

In Horace's Triumviral poetry as well the young Caesar is an *éminence grise* rather than a major theme. After Horace's misadventure at Philippi, where he fought on the side of Caesar's assassins, he managed somehow to return to Rome and organize his life in a manner that permitted him to concentrate on poetry (Armstrong 1986). In two books of *Sermones* he develops a picture, alternately idealized and ironical, of the quiet, disengaged life that he led during this time as a friend to powerful men, but one who harboured no illusions about playing a role in affairs of state (Oliensis 1998; Lyne 1995). In his *Epodes*, which were written in the same years, he adopts a similar persona, but speaks a bit more openly about the events of the day. The collection was published after Actium: poem 1 is set on the eve of the battle, and poem 9, the central poem of the collection (a position of great emphasis) celebrates Caesar's victory. But the penultimate poem of the book urges the Romans to abandon a lost cause, flee the city, and sail away to the Islands of the Blessed. The mood here clearly reflects the anxieties of the early thirties rather than the relief purchased at Actium – which to Horace and other war-weary Romans may at that moment have looked like little more than a temporary respite. Thus the shape of the book takes the reader back in time, from newborn hope to the earlier years, when there was no prospect of remedy or end to civil war.

In a sense, then, during these years even Vergil and Horace were not yet 'Augustan' poets. That they did become such is due to the most decisive literary development of the Triumviral years, which concerns not poetry, but patronage. Before the death of Caesar, relationships between writers and patrons were relatively open and decentralized. Early Triumviral poetry, such as Vergil's *Eclogues*, conforms to this model by addressing a variety of powerful friends. But all such figures were soon eclipsed by the most successful patron of letters the world has seen, who is arguably the person most responsible for creating our sense of a coherent 'Augustan period', Gaius Maecenas, a lifelong friend of the future Princeps. By the early thirties Maecenas began to assemble around him a group of literary men. The tragic and epic poet Varius Rufus and probably Pollio – himself a patron of letters, but also a tragic poet of some note – were among the first; Vergil joined them in 39 BC and was followed by Horace in 38 (Horace *Serm.* 1.6.54–5; 1.10.42–9), later by Propertius and no doubt others. The social, economic and discursive dynamics of patronage are a subject of ongoing research, and I offer no facile summary here of a highly complex topic. But Maecenas, by whatever means, was fantastically successful in cultivating relations with a group of remarkably talented writers and encouraging them to make Augustus a major theme in their work. The groundwork for this success was laid in the Triumviral years, before there was an 'Augustus', when Vergil and Horace were firmly tied to Maecenas by the bonds of *amicitia*; and in the very different political climate of years that followed, this fact proved decisive for fixing our notion of 'Augustan' literature.

Phase 2: The Augustan settlement

Victories at Actium in 31 and subsequently in Egypt left the entire empire in the young Caesar's hands. In 29 he returned to Rome and celebrated a triumph of unprecedented splendour. What is called 'the Augustan settlement' – the complex, evolving process of defining the role of the Princeps vis-à-vis the Senate and the people – occupied the next forty-five years, and none of the poets active at this time lived to see how far it would go. But they did react to the beginning of the Principate, and it is mainly to works produced during these years – the second of our three phases – that we owe our concept of an Augustan period.

Having overcome all challengers, Augustus (as I shall now call him) embarked on an effort to consolidate his victory and to move away from emergency measures towards stable government. Instead of civil strife, he promoted the idea of advancing the borders of the empire by making war on external enemies. In contrast to his earlier cold-blooded elimination of potential foes, he adopted a policy of cautious clemency towards former opponents (Sen. *Clem.* 9–11, Suet. *Aug.* 51). His constitutional position, reformulated in 27 (*RG* 34, Dio 53.12–13), 23 (Dio 53.32), and 19 BC (Dio 54.10), was unique. But Augustus was careful to respect at least the main forms of Republican government: as he himself says in his *Res gestae*, he excelled others not so much in actual power, but in *auctoritas* (34). This quality is difficult to define with precision (Galinsky 1996: 1–41), but in addition to formal powers, Augustus received a series of purely symbolic honours that contributed mightily to his charisma and to a general perception of his singular indispensability. Awards became more frequent with time – another indication that victory at Actium was not just the end of civil war, but the beginning of a long, gradual process of formulating a new government at Rome.

It would be absurd to suppose any leader who came to power amidst blood-shed to have no enemies at all, and we do hear of challenges to Augustus. These range from the rhetorical and symbolic to outright conspiracies and attempted coups (Raaflaub and Samons 1990). But Augustus' opponents faced an uphill battle. His most dangerous enemies had been killed off during the Triumviral years. Augustus also channelled the energies of ambitious men into an effective system of municipal and imperial government under his control that endured for generations. His public works, ubiquitous in Rome itself, were conspicuous in provincial centres as well. And with each passing year in which civil war failed to erupt anew, the Princeps' reputation as a saviour was consolidated.

Again, the literature of this phase reflects the mood of the times. Poems published soon after Actium strike a delicate balance between anxiety and hope. Over the next fifteen years, as peace was maintained, literature reflects a growing acknowledgement that hope was justified. One can chart Augustus' ever-greater importance by reading the poems of this middle phase in the order in which they appeared. In Vergil's *Georgics* – like Horace's *Epodes*, largely written under the Triumvirate but published after Actium – the young Caesar is, for the first time, a central theme of a major Roman poem. He is regarded as a kind of superman, divinely inspired and destined to ascend to Olympus upon his death (1.24–42, 503–4; 4.560–2). This is the conventional language of encomiastic poetry; and significantly, hyperbolic praise is complicated by questions about what kind of god the young Caesar will choose to become. But with the passage of years, Augustus looks like, if anything, a more impressive figure, with a solid record of peacetime achievement to match, and in some sense to replace, the military adventures of his youth. Propertius is particularly telling in this regard. The first book of elegies, published soon after Actium, wilfully ignores the Princeps' accomplishments, recalling instead as a kind of Parthian shot in two concluding epigrams (poems 21 and 22) his war against Antonius' forces at Perugia, in the poet's native region of Umbria, ten or more years in the past. But in the second, and even more so in the third, book, Propertius finds Augustus a theme worth his attention. Even if he often contrasts his life with that of the Princeps' ideal fellow citizen (e.g. in poems 2.1, 7, 16; 3.4, 9, 11, 18), both the specific terms of the contrast and the very fact that he draws it pays oblique tribute to Augustus' unique position in contemporary society. Less oblique tribute comes when Propertius writes about Augustus' building programme, and so advertises the civic munificence that was a central element of the Princeps' benign public image (2.31, 32). In his fourth and final book, Propertius stretches the genre of erotic elegy almost as far as it would go (only Ovid would take it farther) by writing on the origin of various Roman cults and institutions, an interest that formed yet another part of Augustus' cultural programme.

With each passing year, then, poetry becomes more involved with various aspects of Augustus' 'programme' – a word that I use for convenience and without implying that every detail of this programme had been planned or that it is best understood as a centrally directed 'propaganda' effort. These are matters of debate among specialists, and there may never be a consensus about them. But without question, poets and other intellectuals during the twenties and teens made Augustus a central theme in their work and credited him personally with improving Roman political and social life. These same writers also adopted a stance of at least ostensible independence from the regime, a stance supported by reminders of the past and of the price at which the peaceful conditions of the present were obtained. These brooding memories of the recent past are what give the best Augustan poetry its edge. We have contemporary panegyrics of a more ordinary kind, and it is no surprise that Vergil, Horace, Propertius and Tibullus – and not, for instance, the person who composed the *Panegyricus Messallae* – are the poets who are generally thought to epitomize the Augustan period. All of them frequently place themselves in the role of refusing to give Augustus something that he wants – usually an epic poem on his exploits, which they insist is a subject and a form to which they are simply unable to do justice (e.g. *Ecl.* 6; Prop. 2.1; Hor. *Carm.* 1.6). And the epic that Vergil ultimately did give Augustus defines the Augustan aesthetic so brilliantly, precisely because it does *not* give Augustus what the poets habitually claim he wants from them – namely a poem of unambiguous praise based on his own achievements – but rather a poem that addresses much more capacious and humanistic themes from a perspective that never loses sight of the fact that every victory has a cost, that the cost of great victories is proportionately large, and that this cost is borne by the losers as much or more than by the victors.

Vergil wrote the *Aeneid* during the early years of Augustus' principate. He died only ten years after the Princeps' triumphal return from Actium. Horace outlived Vergil by a decade or so, and thus witnessed more of Augustus' evolution. But even when Horace died, what we call the Augustan period was only half over. These accidents of history are of the utmost importance. The dominant impression left by works of the middle phase – Tibullus' elegies are particularly eloquent in this regard – is of catastrophe survived, a sense of loss, but also of relief that the worst may be over and of real hope for a brighter future. Equally important is the fact that, in the years following the imposition of order, these writers were at the height of their powers. All had established themselves as talented artists; but how different our image of them would be without the work of this middle phase: Horace without his *Odes*; Vergil without the *Aeneid*! And equally different, of course, would be our image of Augustus, whose reputation the poetry does so much to burnish. But one must not forget that the bright future, to which poets like Vergil and Tibullus looked forward, was something that they would never see. It is in many ways the experience of this first generation – the experience of living through the anxious initial phase and into the more hopeful second phase, *but no farther* – that gives the work of this first Augustan generation its character. It is tempting to regard such masterpieces as Vergil's *Aeneid* and Horace's *Odes* as defining the entire Augustan period. But to do so is to ignore another two decades of Augustan rule. To this sort of truncated history one might compare the still-too-common habit of reading the *Aeneid* through Book 6, and skipping the grimmer second half of the poem.

The *Aeneid* and the *Odes*, which appeared within just a few years of each other, defined anew the level of achievement to which Latin poetry could aspire. They also give evidence of a sea change in the relationship between poets and Princeps. Up until the publication of *Odes* 1–3, it is Maecenas who maintained close relationships with the poets and acted as a kind of buffer between them and Augustus. (Only one other patron of note was active at this time, M. Valerius Messalla, who is associated mainly with Tibullus; but where 'Augustanism' is concerned, Messalla and Tibullus can hardly be distinguished from Maecenas and his friends.) Maecenas' skills at mediation in the cultural sphere were as important in this post-Actian phase as his shrewdness in gathering this talent around him in the earlier, Triumviral phase. This is true because Augustus was a more demanding and less tactful patron of letters than Maecenas. A famously controversial story tells how Augustus forced Vergil to rewrite the end of the *Georgics* after 27–6 BC, because the original ending spoke favourably of Cornelius Gallus, Vergil's and Pollio's friend and Augustus' first equestrian prefect of Egypt. In this capacity Gallus indulged in some foolishly self-aggrandizing gestures that caused Augustus formally to renounce his friendship; whereupon Gallus committed suicide (Suet. *Aug.* 66). It is impossible to know whether this story about the

Georgics is substantially true, a garbled version that contains some grain of truth or merely wrong. What is clear is that, in Augustus, contemporaries were dealing with someone who had that kind of power. Augustus personally communicated to Livy the results of his own 'historical research' into the dedication of *spolia opima*, a kind of military honour (an investigation that the Princeps undertook for no reason other than personal political advantage), and Livy, while taking care to mention that all other authorities reach different conclusions, duly reports these results in his history (4.20). The ancient biographies speak of the pressure that Augustus brought to bear on Vergil to give him a report on work in progress, the *Aeneid* (*Vita Donati* 31). This interest only increased over time. In 20 or 19 BC (at least according to the ancient biographies) Vergil embarked on a journey to Greece and Asia intending to spend three years completing and polishing the epic. But shortly after his arrival in Athens, when the trip was just begun, he met Augustus, who was returning from business in the East and prevailed upon the poet to return with him to Rome. In Megara Vergil contracted a fever and, after making the crossing by sea to Brundisium, fell ill and died within a few days on September 20. Augustus ignored the poet's final wishes by publishing the unfinished *Aeneid* on his own volition, probably in 19 or early the next year.

After Vergil's death, Augustus trained his attention on Horace. In 17 BC the Princeps had resolved to celebrate Secular Games, an impressive ritual that had taken place only a few previous times in Roman history. For this occasion Horace was commissioned to compose a hymn (his *Carmen saeculare*), which conferred upon him the virtual status of poet laureate; and it is impossible to believe that anyone other than Augustus made this decision. We also have extracts from letters in which Augustus scolds Horace for his apparent reluctance to make him the addressee of any major work (Suet. *Vita Horati*). The extracts have a jocular tone; and Horace had once written that poets hate to sing on command, and typically refuse requests even from 'Caesar, who could use force' (*Caesar, qui cogere posset* [*Serm.* 1.3.4]). But when it comes from a man of such power, a joke is as good as a direct order. The extracts give some point, and some poignancy, to the publication of *Epistles* 1.1, where Horace promised Maecenas that he would be the addressee of his last poems as well as his first. It was a promise that he could not keep: in *Odes* 4 Maecenas is named only once and never actually addressed (in sharp contrast to the earlier three books of *Odes*), and in the so-called second book of *Epistles*, there is no Maecenas at all, his role as addressee being assumed by Augustus. Similarly, Maecenas is the addressee of Propertius' second and third books of elegies, but is not mentioned in Book 4, which is addressed to no one; but it is, as I have noted, heavy with Augustan themes, in particular, and Augustus' achievements are very much the subject of the central poem of the collection (number six out of eleven). It is very unclear exactly why or how Maecenas suddenly gave way to Augustus (Williams 1990; White 1991) but it seems clear that this is what happened. By the time of his death in 8 BC, Maecenas had already relinquished the role that he had played so successfully for so long. Augustan literature was, at last, in the hands of Augustus.

Even if Augustus assumes a new prominence as addressee, of course, the major poets of this middle phase are the same as those who define the Triumviral phase. There were starker changes in the sponsorship of prose. As we have seen, in the thirties it was still common for senators and other members of the elite to write history, biography or dialogues on technical and philosophical subjects. But as the older generation died out, this form of cultivated leisure largely disappeared as well. Pollio, it is true, sponsored recitations in the public library that he had founded (the first in Rome). But oratory in the old style died abruptly with the Republic, and these recitations, rather than perpetuating an old institution, inaugurated a new performance genre that was to be very characteristic of the Principate. History by the twenties had ceased to be written by retired generals and politicians, and became the province of gentlemen scholars, like Livy. The same is true of other genres, which passed out of the hands of aristocratic amateurs into those of professionals of lower rank – notably those with connections to Augustus' household. Verrius Flaccus, not a senator but a freedman and the well-paid tutor of Augustus' grandsons, wrote a work on lexicography that was equal in importance to Varro's. Just how this treatise may have served Augustus' purposes is a matter for conjecture; but another work by the same author on the Roman calendar certainly used the reforms in this area introduced by Julius Caesar and completed by his heir (Wallace-Hadrill 1986). Another intellectual freedman is C. Julius Hyginus, a prolific scholar who was the first head of Augustus' Palatine Library – Rome's second such establishment, after Pollio's, but not the last founded by the Princeps' family. And among the most important writers of the period is Vitruvius, whose ten books on architecture, published between 27 and 23 BC, enjoyed enormous influence during the Renaissance. Vitruvius' style suggests that he was no man of letters; in fact, he had been an officer in Caesar's engineering corps and wrote the work in his retirement, which was financed by Caesar's heir, to whom it is dedicated.

A partial exception to this general trend is jurisprudence, a profession that virtually entailed senatorial rank. Two opposed schools arose at this time, one headed by Ateius Capito, the other by M. Antistius Labeo, a prodigious writer who left behind almost 400 books. Like most other senators at this time, both men benefited from Augustus' patronage, which Capito seems to have accepted more gratefully: he was nominated as consul in AD 5 both as a reward for his loyalty and as a slap at the slightly older Labeo – who, when offered the consulate on a later occasion, refused it. Another honorary consulate of the same type went to Gaius Valgius Rufus in 12 BC, of whom it has been said that 'perhaps his chief claims to advancement were the fulsome dedication to Augustus of a work on medicinal herbs . . . and the translation of a *Rhetorica* by Augustus' old master Apollodorus . . .' (Horsfall 1974). Thus prose literature, even more clearly than poetry, fell now to retainers of the Princeps' household and to members of the upper orders who owed their advancement to Augustus' good will.

Phase 3: A lost generation

The middle phase was in many ways the high point of Augustan literature – and, by conventional reckoning, of Roman literature as a whole. It did not last long. Augustus lived on to grow in power and prestige. But, in spite of the honours that continued to accrue, Augustus too may have looked back on the twenties and teens as the best years of his long career.

No one expected Augustus, weak and sickly all his life, to live so long. Moreover, an earlier death might have done his posthumous reputation no harm. Augustus' later years mark a turn towards repression, suspicion and autocracy that contrast with the more open social and intellectual climate of the post-Actium years. It is true that Augustus' hypocritical moral legislation begins to be passed as early as 18, and thus appears in retrospect as an early indication of what was to come. Other events during the twenties and teens contribute towards the Princeps' darkening mood nearer the end. Most notably, his efforts to anoint a successor were repeatedly frustrated. His nephew Marcellus died in 23 BC at the age of 19. He was followed by Augustus' long-time aide Agrippa (12 BC) and then by his grandsons Lucius and Gaius (AD 2 and 4, respectively). When Augustus finally had to turn to his stepson, Tiberius, his attitude seems to have taken a turn for the worse (Syme 1974: 484; Fantham 1996: 126). Then there were the scandals involving his daughter (2 BC) and granddaughter (AD 8); the disgrace and exile of his grandson, Agrippa Postumus (AD 7); and more tangible setbacks, such as Quintilius Varus' spectacular military disaster in Germany (AD 9). Such were the tribulations of ruling Rome.

Only a few of these unhappy developments left a direct mark on literature, but literary culture during this autumn of the patriarch was very different from what it had been before. If the post-Actian phase of the Augustan period was still haunted by the ghosts of the Triumvirs, this third phase, when the *pax Augusta* was firmly established, should have been open to carefree celebration of everything that Augustus had achieved. Those writers who could remember the days before Actium were mostly dead or retired. Vergil and Tibullus died in 19 BC, and Horace followed Maecenas to the grave in 8. Livy of course outlived Augustus and continued writing until his own death; but we possess nothing that would have been written after about 15 BC or that deals with events later than 167 BC. Thus our access to Livy's perspective on the events of his own lifetime is practically non-existent. It is even thought that Livy waited for Augustus' death or his own to publish his account of more nearly contemporary events; and in any case there is good evidence that Augustus followed a source other than Livy in compiling the historical and biographical inscriptions that accompanied the statues of Roman heroes in the Forum Augustum (Luce 1990). Similarly, although we have no information on Propertius' death, nothing that he wrote can be dated after 14.

For various reasons, then, between 19 and 8 BC, the great voices of the first Augustan generation began to fall silent and few of the writers who took their places have left work that survives. This sheer dearth of surviving poetry from the last phase helps to explain why the poets who came up in the Triumviral years and lived to bask in the glow of Actium are the ones whom we now regard as definitively 'Augustan'. There are simply fewer candidates who wrote during the later period of Augustus' reign. It is almost as though Augustan literature came to an end about half-way through Augustus' reign.

There was, however, one poet in Rome during the third phase of Augustanism who bears comparison with the giants of the previous generation. This is Ovid, one of the most prolific, imaginative and diverse poetic talents of the ancient world. Born in the year that followed Caesar's assassination, Ovid began writing after Caesar's heir had prevailed at Actium, returned to Rome in triumph and accepted the title Augustus. Not surprisingly, his poetry betrays no anxiety about the possible renewal of conflict. His early work in particular flaunts a carefree attitude of enjoying the benefits of the peace without asking their price. Augustus, it is true, is a major presence in Ovid's poetry, but not as a saviour; rather he is the person who adorned Rome with theatres and porticoes, which Ovid mentions not just as marvellous works of civic munificence but also as great places to pick up girls. If we compare what Ovid has to say about Augustus with similar statements by his predecessors, it is very clear that he feels no sense of relief or personal gratitude towards the man who, by whatever means, has brought civil war to an end. Rather, the attitude that he projects is one of carefree irresponsibility – pleasure, perhaps, that he is free to pursue his chosen career, but no real sense that he owes this opportunity to anyone.

It was once common to regard Ovid as a precursor of Lucan, Martial and Statius rather than as a successor to Vergil, Horace, Tibullus and Propertius, and thus as a proto-imperial rather than an Augustan poet in the fullest sense; but this is obviously a tendentious position (and one called into question by Hinds 1988 and Galinsky 1989 in particular). Ovid was a creature of the Augustan age – the one writer who lived virtually his entire life under the ascendancy of the young Caesar and the Principate of Augustus (Millar 1993). It is highly ironic, then, that he somehow ran foul of the great man and met with a fate that cast a pall over the last years of his life – and one that stands as a very black mark on the Princeps' reputation. In AD 8, on one day's notice, Ovid was informed that he must – without trial, appeal or due process of any kind, but at Augustus' personal insistence – move from Rome to the city of Tomis on the shores of the Black Sea. It is impossible to be sure what caused Augustus' displeasure. Ovid is our only informant about the matter and here, if anywhere, he shows himself a potentially unreliable narrator. Two things undid him, he complains: a poem and a mistake (*carmen et error*, *Tristia* 2.207). The poem is supposed to be the *Ars amatoria*, which, he alleges, Augustus claimed to have found too lascivious (even though the sentence was passed an entire decade after the publication of the *Ars*, and Ovid expresses doubts whether the Princeps himself has even read the poem). The idea here is that those passages about picking up girls in Augustus' own monuments were simply too much for the Princeps, who was struggling unsuccessfully to raise the moral tone of Roman society by offering bounties for men who fathered three or more children, by making adultery a capital offence, and so on. About the mistake Ovid ostentatiously says nothing. What it may be is anybody's guess, and there have been many, but there is no certainty.

Ovid's relegation to Tomis was cruel punishment for the poet who celebrated the *pax Augusta* not just as relief from civil war, but as a thing in its own right. Few writers take such satisfaction in living in their times as Ovid does (*Ars* 3.122). This changes, of course, with relegation; but if the 'exile poetry' (as it is called) expresses anything but satisfaction with one's lot, relegation was far from a disaster in terms of Ovid's literary career. Longing and suffering are evident throughout – and, it may be said, add a note of poignancy and depth that might otherwise have been felt lacking from Ovid's tonal palate. Furthermore, Ovid enjoyed a posthumous reputation not only as classical antiquity's love poet par excellence and its greatest authority on mythology, but also as the prototype of a writer barely maintaining his ability to speak in the face of hardship, absurdity and the caprice of the powerful.

What Augustus did to Ovid was hardly characteristic. Later writers would contrast his record of tolerance with the repressive climate that prevailed under his successors. Emblematic are two Tacitean anecdotes. Cremutius Cordus was a senator who did write history, not only under Augustus but about him, covering the years from 43 to 18 and perhaps later. He was of a Republican temperament, and his work pointedly praised Caesar's assassins. We do not know exactly when this work was published, but we are told that Augustus was present at a reading – and made no protest. It was, however, under Tiberius in AD 25 that Cordus' work became the basis of an accusation of treason. In the speech that Tacitus gives him, Cordus draws a sharp contrast between the tolerance of Augustus' regime and the repression that followed under Tiberius (*Ann.* 4.34–8; cf. Sen. *Marc.* 1.3; Dio 57.24). But the case of Ovid is not the only harbinger of what was to come. The charge of treason, according to Tacitus, had never in the Republican period applied to words, but only to deeds. Augustus, he tells us, was the first to take action against libellous publication because he was disturbed by one Cassius Severus' defamation of some prominent men and women (*Ann.* 1.72). Tiberius later moved against Severus as well, first relegating him to Crete, and then ten years later formally sentencing him to exile on the island of Seriphus (*Ann.* 4.2). It is of course under Tiberius that imperial censorship becomes a major problem, and in the case of Cremutius Cordus, the contrast between the tolerant Augustan and repressive Tiberian policies appears to be great; but in the case of Cassius Severus, one finds differences not of kind, but only of degree.

3   Conclusion

The Augustan period ended very differently from the way it began. When Caesar's heir was thrust onto the stage of history, the literary culture of the free Republic was still largely in force; by the time of his exit, he had bequeathed to his successors a set of circumstances in which almost the only imaginative literature that could flourish would be court poetry or none at all. History and oratory, too, were in a bad way. Only technical, scholarly and scientific genres were really well served by the social developments that transformed literature during Augustus' long reign. Nevertheless, it is for poetry that this period is mainly known, and for Livy's monumental history, which is often commended for its epic or novelistic rather than its historical qualities. What I have described as the moment when our image of Augustanism crystallized should perhaps be thought of as the intersec- tion of two curves, the one, rising curve describing the ever-increasing powers of a handful of the most gifted writers that the world has yet seen, and the other describing the downward trajectory of free speech under an increasingly auto- cratic regime. The intersection of these curves, when literary talent was at its peak, and when the ability to speak truth to power had not yet disappeared, well deserves to be remembered as a crucial moment in literary history. The story of how that moment came to be, and the story of what happened then, are worth hearing as well.

FURTHER READING

On the political history, besides the relevant chapters of the *Cambridge Ancient History*, Syme (1939) remains well worth reading. It is usefully supplemented by two collections, Millar and Segal (1984) and Raaflaub and Toher (1990), which take advantage of more up-to-date research and provide a broader spectrum of opinion. Zanker (1988) is an excellent overview of the way in which political concerns were represented in the visual arts. The most recent comprehensive cultural overview is Galinsky (1996). As a general rule, all of these works give Augustus high marks (even if political historians in particular harbour few illu- sions about the methods that he sometimes employed to achieve the desired results) and tend to regard both art and literature as subservient to political forces.

Students of literature, on the other hand, whatever they may think about Augustus' political achievements, tend to be divided on the role that literature plays in commenting on that achievement. A (perhaps surprising) legacy of New Criticism in Latin studies was a tendency to find dissent, more or less veiled according to different critics, throughout Augustan poetry; the resulting division of literary scholarship into quite strongly divided two camps, pro-Augustan (or 'optimists') and anti-Augustan (or 'pessimists'), tended to correlate both with methodological preferences and, to a degree, with nationality, but these correlations were never perfect. A very strong strain of scepticism regarding intellectual support for Augustus remains; but the introduction of various post-structuralist approaches has tended to complicate the 'pessimist' position and to bring the two camps into more productive dialogue. Three important collections that document the movement of scholarly opinion over a crucial transitional period are Woodman and West (1984), Powell (1992a), and Habinek and Schiesaro (1997).

CHAPTER FOUR

The Early Empire: AD 14–68

Roland Mayer

1 Introduction: the Literary Landscape after Augustus

Epochs in literary history rarely coincide with a civil or political period. A change of ruler does not necessarily affect writers. But the time between the death of Augustus and the suicide of Nero is arguably just such a discrete epoch. Augustus died at about the same time as Livy and Ovid, whose deaths set a term to the great achievements of Augustan prose and verse. The immediately subsequent years were comparatively fallow. It is not that there were no writers, but none made any permanent mark on the historical record. We possess from this period, for instance, a didactic poem by Manilius on astrology, a sort of Stoic counterblast to Lucretius' Epicurean *De Rerum Natura* (for both see Gale, Chapter 7), but this accomplished work sank virtually without trace. It is good, but not quite good enough to have lodged in the literary memory.

After a while, however, new and powerful voices began to be heard, both in prose (the Younger Seneca) and poetry (the epic poet Lucan and the satirist Persius). They all flourished, and died, in the reign of Nero; Nero himself was not long in following them to the grave in AD 68. Thus it was that the two imperial deaths, coinciding more or less with those of the outstanding literary talents of the age, delimit this span of time as an epoch in Roman literary history. Our point of termination, the death of Nero, is, moreover, especially decisive. The greatest writers of the period – Persius, Petronius, Lucan and Seneca – lived and died in his reign, and his own death marked the end of a political and social epoch, the rule of Rome by a long-established aristocratic family. The new regime Vespasian established had quite a different outlook, since he was from the provinces and military in upbringing. So once again, unusually for literary history, a change of regime did herald a change of direction in literary activity. The quality of Flavian literature is less hectic and less brilliant in the main than what had just gone before it.

Why were the years just after the death of Augustus relatively barren? One factor may be that the issues, social, political, aesthetic, which the Augustans had wrestled with – chiefly the creation of an archaic Romanness as an ideal and blueprint for the future – no longer gripped the imagination when the conservative and enigmatic Tiberius uncontroversially succeeded Augustus. The grandeur of empire too, a theme that had provided an earlier generation with an escape from the anguish of recent civil conflict, was less compelling a topic for men who had grown to maturity with no experience of civil war; Tiberius, moreover, prolonged his predecessor's embargo on territorial expansion. So old themes, such as the renewal of Roman society and the triumphs of her arms, lapsed, with nothing of national significance to replace them. Peace had settled on Rome and the new imperial constitution held, especially among the equestrians, who still made up the main body of literary men. Senatorial discontent was reflected in history, but it is hardly seen elsewhere: the bucolics of Calpurnius Siculus, for instance, show none of the social anxieties of Virgil's; the only problem is satiety.

One of the other agendas of Augustan poetry, the continuing naturalization of Greek Callimachean poetics, was also now effected; the battle had been won. Of course this did not deter continuators, and if the *Culex* and *Ciris* (both epyllia; i.e. short epics) belong to our period we still have minor talents that found this form congenial. The sorts of poems dedicated to the mythical heroines Phyllis and Hypsipyle, ridiculed by Persius in his first satire, suggest too a certain aesthetic clinging to the neoteric past. But poetry had to move on, and successfully did so.

On the other hand, new features appear upon the literary scene, which must have had a deterrent effect: censorship and suppression. Augustus had as usual shown the way, by banning Ovid's *Ars Amatoria* from his library on the Palatine and by exiling its poet to a remote town on the Black Sea. The Senate followed suit, and ordered the burning of the outspoken history of Titus Labienus, a novel punishment that shocked the literary conscience. A similar attempt seems to have been made to obliterate the speeches of Cassius Severus. Tiberius suppressed the history of Cremutius Cordus (but his successor, the contrary Caligula, restored it), and he had Aemilius Scaurus killed for an ambiguous line in a tragedy (his published speeches were burned too). Tiberius' favourite, Sejanus, made trouble for Phaedrus, the fabulist (see Bk 3, Prologue 38–44). Nero tried to silence Lucan, not so much for his political views, but because he was the better poet. Literature had now become dangerous at Rome under absolutism.

In our survey of this period, it will be useful not just to draw attention to new features of the literary landscape, but also to point to the gaps, what has disappeared. Perhaps to us the most striking absence is elegy; a few attractive but short pieces by Petronius and the lost poems of Nerva are all we know of in a once-flourishing but now played-out genre. Ovid's humour probably killed its chances of recovering the erotic pathos of its earlier models. To the contemporary Roman, however, the striking change was the declining role of oratory (something Tacitus addressed himself to much later in his *Dialogus de Oratoribus*). The impulse for change was chiefly political: policy decisions were now taken by the emperor, advised by his council of friends, rather than by the Senate and People acting as free agents. The sort of civic oratory (*contio*) that had provided the orators of the Republic with one of their platforms simply ceased to exist. The oratory of the law courts too had now shifted ground, since political trials (especially those for high treason, *maiestas*) took place within the walls of the Senate House, not in the open Forum before crowds of interested citizens. Trials were still important matters, but careers tended to be made now in the Centumviral Court (roughly the equivalent of the British Chancery Division, concerned with property and wills, and about as exciting). It is significant that young men, after making a name as public speakers in the courts, tended to abandon oratory for the imperial administration; someone like Pliny the Younger, who kept up his pleading, was exceptional. All this explains the dearth of published speeches from our period (at any rate, none published has survived); the ablest orators did publish their speeches, but probably not on the scale of a Cicero (Scaurus for instance published only seven). To put it in our terms, oratory as a literary form declined in importance, and it was no longer felt to be an avenue to lasting fame. On the other hand, considered simply as a traditional elite activity, oratory of course remained a crucial accomplishment; persuasion never lost its place in Roman public life. But the record of that activity, the published speech, had a diminished role to play in a man's career. Literary aspiration therefore sought other outlets.

Another literary form that did not so much disappear as undergo radical transformation was drama, whose fate was sealed under Augustus. We hear of no regular comedies in this period. Contemporary tragedy by Pomponius Secundus, however, seems still to have been performed, but it certainly moved for the most part into the shelter of the recitation hall, where it was taken up by men of letters like the Younger Seneca (for the issue of the performance of his tragedies see Fantham, Chapter 8). The reformed stage proposed by Horace in his *Ars Poetica*, in a bid to produce a truly national drama, was never realized. Seneca's plays are an elite entertainment, too rarified for public consumption.

2   Recitation and Declamation

Two cultural activities of the age, which had a profound influence upon the shape taken by its literature, must be noticed here. One, recitation, has just been referred to as a mode of presenting tragedy. But the practice of recitation was extended to virtually all literary genres. It had a considerable effect upon the strategies of composition: appeal had to be instant, and the organic integration of a text was sacrificed to elaboration of the parts. We see this in the loose structure of Seneca's tragedies and philosophical treatises, and in the neatly episodic character of Lucan's epic. The most obvious result of reciting a text to a live audience was what we might call the spectacularization of the verbal style; this will be dealt with more fully below. The second contemporary practice of importance was related to oratory, which it was originally intended to subserve: declamation, the extemporaneous speaking upon a fictive (and often improbable) topic. Roman critics themselves recognized that declaimers lost sight both of the main goal of oratory (persuasion) and even of reality itself. They aimed rather to entertain and amaze, by wit and verbal ingenuity. The faults of their style were seen in the accumulation of rhetorical figures, excessive reliance upon epigrams, the wearisome refinement of a pointed style, and the exaggerated use of rhythm. Strictly speaking, declamation was not a literary form as such, since the declaimers rarely wrote up their efforts. But it was a very popular elite amusement, as we learn from the entertaining books of reminiscences of what he heard in the declamation halls by the elder Seneca, and declamation had a considerable influence beyond the sphere of public speaking. An obvious example of the declamatory mode in literature is the pair of speeches in Seneca's *Phaedra* in which the Nurse tries to convince Hippolytus that he should give up his chastity, and his reply, which turns into a denunciation of women. What really undermined the literature strongly influenced by declamation was the error of expecting such a rhetorical training to provide a skill transferable to all other literary endeavours.

3 Formal and Stylistic Developments

The sharpest break with the past, as has just been hinted, is seen in the development of new styles of writing (something noticed by the elder Seneca, and by Tacitus in his *Dialogus*). It may have been felt that Livy had developed the periodic style of prose which Cicero imposed upon Latin to a point of complexity that none could hope to match, let alone surpass; the tortured periods of Velleius Paterculus and of the emperor Claudius show how difficult the manner was to master. The literary language had therefore to take a fresh direction, and to do so it reverted to a more native and congenial manner, which was the opposite of periodic. Prose style, especially as exemplified in Seneca, becomes looser and simpler in structure. Vigour is the keynote, as Seneca's father noted (*Con.* 10 *praef.* 5). There is also a growing fondness, already noted, for verbal point, which owed much to the declamatory practices referred to above. The language of prose also now borrows freely from poetry, even adopting to an extent its sometimes unusual syntax.

It is during our period that Latin prose reaches the sort of maturity that can be identified in the existence of a 'model' style. Cicero and Livy were too singular to serve as models, and the oratorical or historical period had no real place in works of instruction or polite entertainment. This was a lesson Valerius Maximus failed to learn, but Celsus, Columella, Quintus Curtius and Petronius all write an easy, lucid, agreeable Latin perfectly suited to convey technical information or entertain with narrative. By way of comparison we have only to go back to Varro and

Vitruvius to see what strides had been made in overhauling prose style so that it would serve a wide variety of purposes more flexibly than of old. We can now speak of technical and of narrative literatures, in the strict sense of that word.

The style of poetry also moves away from the Augustan ideals of balance and measure. Virgil of course was unique and inimitable, but Ovid had shown the way forward, and poetry after him betrays its debt to his transformation of the language at every turn. This is most apparent in the didactic poem of Manilius, already referred to, and in the tragedies of Seneca, which recall Ovid's language and manner both in dialogue and in the choral interludes. The anonymous poets of the *Consolation to Livia* (written after 9 BC) and the *Laus Pisonis* (?late 50s / early 60s AD) reproduce Ovid's manner effortlessly. The more original talents had therefore to strike out on their own, and Persius and Lucan, despite their youth, rose to the challenge. Poetic style agrees with contemporary prose in its fondness for crispness and point.

Both forms of the literary language, prose and verse, adopt a sort of self-advertising artificiality. Writers strove to make their audiences at a recitation 'see' what they were hearing. Verbal style in performance needed to be showy, and language strove after ever more exaggerated effects. The audience's attention had to be grabbed and held somehow, and, along with hyperbole and paradox in expression, bizarre and far-fetched themes too are now welcomed. The grotesque, as seen especially in Lucan and Seneca, is on the rise; it is seen too in the sometimes drastic imagery of the satirist Persius. The roots of this taste lie in Ovid and in the often stark language of Stoicism (on which see further below), but they were nourished by contemporary declamation too. An older generation of critics detected strain in the style and condemned what it found tasteless in the subject matter. But fashion has changed, and we now more appreciate the verbal dazzle and exotic subject matter (e.g. Lucan's snakes, 9.700–838, and his Erictho, 6.507–69).

A reason for this taste for the extreme – the desire for novelty apart – may be that the literary language had now to compete with realistic public spectacles on the stage and in the amphitheatre, and writers asked themselves how language could be made as vivid and exciting as, say, the dance of the pantomime or a beast-fight. Language itself had to become spectacular, and convey not so much an idea as a picture. The theory that lay behind this was based upon the notion of 'phantasia', or visualization (Fantham 2000: 22 offers a helpful account). This is seen at its liveliest in the tragedies of Seneca: for instance the description of the death of Hippolytus in *Phaedra*.

But leaving the fireworks to one side, there was also a need, felt by Seneca and Persius, for a style appropriate to urgent moral discourse, simple, direct and down to earth. Seneca, in his *Epistle* 75, describes his epistolary style as *illaboratus et facilis* (easy and unadorned), and Persius, in his *Satire* 5.14 refers to his choice of *uerba togae* (words of everyday use). Fantham (1996: 137) has rightly noticed 'the emerging tradition of ethical prose writing on personal themes', but we should add that this new tradition required a new stylistic direction. It did not have to be entirely at odds with the refinements of the day, which tended to make language glib and glozing, because of the political need to conceal one's true thought. Sincerity is hard to convey. But Seneca in his letters (see further Edwards, Chapter 19 below) and Persius were at pains to establish the authenticity of their personal moral discourse. They managed to elude the style police – letters and satire are only marginally literary genres, and yet satisfy the aesthetic imperative of catching and holding interest. Hence they are both individual and in the best sense – paradoxically – artful.

Lucan too had to free himself from the smooth elegance of Ovid, a style unsuited to the tragic theme of his epos, the political suicide of Rome, from which arose for better, or, as he came to see it, for worse, the imperial settlement. Again, his achievement (see also Hardie, Chapter 6 below) is astonishing in one so young, who had to write against the background of the imitative tradition of literary production at Rome. His success in forging a personal style, weighty and impressive, was considerable; Bramble (1982a: 541–2) draws attention in detail to how Lucan broke with mainstream epic in matters of diction and metre. Indeed he is the only writer of this period who can be said to have achieved sublimity, a feature noted by Johnson (1987: 12). What other poet could have described the final conflagration of the universe (a Stoic notion) as the communal pyre that would mingle stars with bones (*communis rogus…ossibus astra mixturus*, 7.814–15)?

4   Literature and its Cultural Context

If we now turn from the formal aspects of literature, and consider its production as a more broadly social and cultural phenomenon, we first observe that patronage continues after a fashion. Sextus Pompeius (*cos.* 14), for instance, looked after the interests of Valerius Maximus. The dedications of literary works too indicate that the authors hoped for something more than merely favourable notice by members of the elite. Some dedicatees of the period are Marcus Vinicius (*cos.* 31; Velleius Paterculus), Calpurnius Piso (but it is uncertain which one of this famous family is intended; *Laus Pisonis*), the unidentified Meliboeus of Calpurnius Siculus *Ecl.* 4, and Eprius Marcellus (Columella Bk 11). The writer of verse fables, Phaedrus, broke with tradition and addressed some of his work to freedmen (probably quite prestigious ones); he perhaps chose socially humble figures to suit the unpretending genre. Calpurnius Siculus and the anonymous writer of the *Laus Pisonis* give a novel twist to the tradition in actually trying to secure patronage by virtue of their verse; they point out that their poetic activity should attract the notice of a potential supporter. This suggests the emergence of a new phenomenon, the professional poet, on the lookout for a protector. Persius, however, sought no patron (he was well-to-do), and in what is now called the

Prologue to his satires ridiculed those who set themselves up as poets in order to secure a handout. That glances at another new social aspect of the writing of this period: there were people prepared to reward flattery, and writers betray their own sycophancy. The invocation of Tiberius in the Preface to the first book of *Memorable Doings and Sayings* by Valerius Maximus exemplifies this trend, and the flattery of Nero at the beginning of his reign in a range of works in verse and prose is notorious.

Despite that invocation, Tiberius himself and the other emperors of our period seem not to have been nearly so interested as Augustus in fostering literary talent. Still, Tiberius (who liked Alexandrian poetry) probably 'inherited' Manilius from Augustus. Nero, we know, gave money to the Greek epigrammatist, Lucillius (*Anthologia Palatina* 9.572). He promoted Seneca to a consulship and advanced Lucan, by conferring upon him both a magistracy, the quaestorship, before the statutory age, and membership of one of the grander priesthoods, the augurs; but this is social rather than economic patronage, since both men were rich already. More spectacularly, Nero established literary competitions (e.g. the Neronia in 60) on Greek models, which gave a boost to talent (Lucan was prominent at the first quinquennial games).

But while patronage continued, there is a clear lack of long-standing support such as was found from Maecenas or Augustus' sister Octavia. This may be explained by the political changes in Rome. A general or consul under the Republic could expect that his personal achievements would be recorded in history or song, but in the principate no general triumphed (unless he was a member of the imperial family), and civil successes were bland. The writer of the *Laus Pisonis*, for instance, is hard put to it to find anything exciting to say about his honorand (an adept at draughts!). Little wonder then that individuals did not make an effort to secure for themselves the sort of literary commemoration that motivated a Pollio or a Messalla in the late Republic.

The upper-class author naturally required no support, and the increasing number of aristocratic writers shows the enhanced prestige of literary production. But that is also a symptom of their political marginality. What other outlet had they? Germanicus with his *Aratea*, Claudius (who published antiquarian writings), Piso, Nerva (an elegist in the Tibullian mode), the consular Petronius all tried their hands with varying success at literature. Writing was becoming an avenue to advancement; we have already noted that the equestrian Lucan and the senator Seneca were promoted for their literary talent.

5 Imperial Renewals

Earlier in this chapter we looked at the genres that had lapsed or been altered fundamentally in their scope. It is now time to review the revived or (apparently) brand new literary forms. Roman writers had a sort of standing challenge to annex to the empire of Latin letters any as yet undomesticated forms found in Greek. That challenge, obviously, diminished over time. Still, one man found terrain unannexed even by the Greeks: Phaedrus took the Aesopic fable in prose and turned it into verse, thus in effect creating a new genre (or a new mode within the genre of iambus). He deliberately presents himself as a marginal figure creating a marginal form, the verse fable for reading. In this he is a unique phenomenon in Latin literature, for Phaedrus gives the lower levels of Roman society a voice. But he is no bumpkin: his prologues show considerable literary self-consciousness. Not surprisingly he wins favourable notice from literary historians: Ogilvie (1980: 188–90) stresses his courage, and Conte (1994b: 433–5) notes the marginalized voice.

A far more striking innovation, to our taste, is the arrival of the novel at Rome (see Harrison, Chapter 15). Petronius, however, did not write a standard romance upon Greek lines. It is extraordinary that the first extant Roman novel should be entirely parodistic. To some degree this fits with the literary ethos of his time; as Johnson (1987: 43 n. 12) put it in reference to Lucan, '*quantum inane* [how empty it all is!] is the hallmark of the Neronians: it is the way they saw the world'. To put that another way, Petronius, who appeals so strongly to the modern taste, cannot accept the silly erotic conventions of the Greek novel, and has to send it all up. But behind the louche façade may lurk an old-fashioned literary conservative, missing the opportunities that his predecessors enjoyed in what he may have regarded as more favoured times (see for instance Conte 1996). That hidden Petronius is the devotee of the 'false sublime', a devotion we may detect in his contemporary Lucan too.

There was an older form of prose narrative than the novel, brought to Rome first by Varro, the Menippean satire; it is now brilliantly revived in the *Apocolocyntosis* of Seneca. The success of this scurrilous work depends on the personal animus that motivates it. Seneca, who had been injured by Claudius, takes the best revenge possible: cold humour.

The novel and Menippean satire are lowish narrative prose genres. The crown in that medium belonged to History. After Livy there were distinguished historians, for instance, Aufidius Bassus and Servilius Nonianus; the emperor Claudius too wrote history. But as even Claudius realized (according to Suetonius, *Life of Claudius* 41.2), the political climate was antithetical to free speech and truth, and as was noted above, history proved dangerous to the likes of Cremutius Cordus. In the early days of the principate it was a genre for the disaffected senatorial aristocrat, who maintained a republican coolness towards the imperial settlement. But the genre proved flexible in our period, and some unusual products result. Velleius Paterculus revived a tradition seen earlier in Nepos: he wrote an outline, specifically now of Roman history. It is openly tendentious, for it sees the imperial settlement as the crown of political development (Velleius was very much a 'new man'). Quintus Curtius too deserves special attention, for bringing the history of Alexander the Great closer to what we might call romance. Both writers deliberately part with the grand tradition of Roman historiography.

The last aspect of prose writing that deserves notice is also arguably the most interesting in our period, the development of a genuine literature of information (this was glanced at above in the general discussion of prose style); cf also Powell 1992a (chapter 16). A number of writers produced works of information or scholarship for a broadly cultured audience (the Romans were at last catching up with the Greeks). Pomponius Mela, writing perhaps under Claudius, produced a geographical treatise, describing the known world. His style owes much phraseology to the newly fashionable Sallust, but he sometimes relies on outdated Greek sources, which suggests the level of information expected by the undemanding gentleman at Rome, who wants to know something about the layout of his world. Equally urbane was the *Encyclopaedia* in six parts – Agriculture, Medicine (the only one extant, in eight books), Military Science, Rhetoric, Philosophy, Jurisprudence – by Celsus. He treated the branches of study of conventional liberal culture in a style clear and refined, but his books catered to a purely intellectual curiosity in the arts he covered (assuming his treatise on medicine is representative: he was not a doctor, but he might have felt himself called upon to exercise judgement in medical matters regarding his household). The last considerable technical writer of our period is Columella, who wrote twelve books on agriculture (the tenth book is in verse, ingeniously supplementing Virgil's *Georgics* with an omitted topic, gardens). He too writes neatly, but unlike Celsus his work is based upon experience and designed more for use than for entertainment.

We may also notice two further works of information as entertainment, the collection of notable 'sayings and doings' by Valerius Maximus, whose sycophancy – what Fantham (1996: 132) refers to as imperial 'newspeak' – has already been noted. The purpose of the work is debated, but the author himself seems to have a vaguely moral purpose; the reader is to be inspired or deterred as appropriate by the examples rehearsed. Lastly, Seneca as a technical writer here deserves a word. The range of his interests was considerable, and he was quick to exploit any trend. That he too should try his hand at technical treatises is not surprising. All that is now left of his considerable output in this field is the seven books of the *Problems of Nature*, in which he never quite drops the ethical mask.

Contemporary poetry too is imbued (some would say, 'infected') with an interest in technical lore, and didactic epos continues unabated from the previous generation. Germanicus, the nephew of Tiberius, composed an updated version of Aratus, and Manilius (already referred to) entered the lists with a substantial work on astrology with a strong Stoic bias (the Epicurean Lucretius is covertly put down). Perhaps to our era belongs the anonymous *Aetna*, a difficult but original account of volcanic activity. Columella's attempt to pick up Virgilian didactic on the subject of gardens has already been noted. Even non-didactic poets get in on the game, and now tend to show off a technical knowledge; for instance Lucan's Nile excursus (10.268–331), which is based upon the fourth book of the *Problems of Nature* of his uncle Seneca.

6 Neronian Renaissance

If we attempt a global picture of the poetry of this period, we are struck by what can only be called a revival under Nero. This revival moreover seems to take a strongly Augustan tone, following indeed the emperor's own lead: he had for instance adopted Apollo as his patron divinity. During his reign bucolic reappears by Calpurnius Siculus and the anonymous author of the Einsiedeln eclogues. Caesius Bassus revived Horatian lyric, and wrote a treatise on his metres (see Harrison, Chapter 13 below), while Persius (see Morgan, Chapter 12 below) picked up the threads of satire and verse epistle. We may again recall Columella's nod towards Virgilian georgic. This is a surprising revival, and the emperor's own artistic enthusiasm, and latterly his interest in composition, must go some way to explaining it.

One feature of contemporary writing that generates discussion is the political posture of the writers. As we have seen already, a senatorial historian (Cremutius Cordus) might court displeasure on the one hand, while on the other hand sycophancy or at any rate eulogy of the regimes is commonplace. In this regard the social origin of a writer is important. Senators are a race apart, with a tradition of command and a political prestige that the principate diminished; hence their disenchantment. But most of our writers are equestrians or perhaps lower in standing, and they traditionally had little interest in political life. Indeed as a class the equestrians flourished under the principate, so had little to complain of. We have only one writer from a yet lower social level, Phaedrus, and his attitude to society is clear from the fables in which the strong terrorize the weak; according to Holzberg (2001: 54), his is an ideology of accommodation (*Anpassungsideologie*), according to which the inferior would do well to adjust himself to humour his superior. Others from among our writers were 'new men' (Velleius Paterculus, Seneca, Lucan) who owed their advance to the emperor. Radical opposition could hardly be expected from such careerists. But some of them can and do criticize the character of the individual ruler. Calpurnius Siculus for instance deplored the reign of Claudius in praising the accession of Nero, and Seneca satirized him cruelly, but safely, after his death. Lucan gives the impression of having been driven into outright opposition to the imperial settlement (though it must be stressed that the conspiracy he joined merely sought to replace Nero, not the principate). The issues are never very clear, and much care is needed in the assessment of each case.

The common most distinguishing feature of the literature of the age is the widespread commitment to Stoicism. Manilius, Seneca, Lucan and above all Persius are strong adherents of this philosophy and, with the exception of Lucan, may all be regarded as activists: they aim to win us over to a serious engagement with its moral influence. This aspect of the literature of the early principate, its moral earnestness, is often underrated, and the rhetorical dazzle of the contemporary style has sometimes blinded historians to the serious undertone of much of the writing of this age. These authors in particular want to make us better people.

FURTHER READING

The *Oxford Classical Dictionary* (Hornblower and Spawforth 1996) has crisp articles on all of the authors mentioned in this chapter; it also provides help with the literary institutions of 'declamation' and the *recitatio*. Bonner (1949: 149–67) remains the most useful account of the influence of declamation upon literature. Detailed bibliography on the authors dealt with here is given in the reference section at the start of this book. But work on some issues and minor figures may be mentioned here. Goodyear (1982) dealt magisterially with most of our lesser writers and works. Summers (1910) wrote an indispensable account of the pointed style in Latin. Jocelyn (1985) is important for a just appreciation of Celsus. Kroll (1924) is still important on Curtius. The most up-to-date discussion of the problem of dating Calpurnius Siculus is Horsfall (1997). Mayer (1983) discusses the Augustan revival under Nero. Since this chapter is cast in the form of a survey, it may be usefully compared and contrasted with the larger-scale literary histories that cover the same (or roughly the same) period. These histories may be organized chronologically, generically or by topic. Rose (1966), Summers (1920) and Hutchinson (1993) exemplify these three approaches, each of which has strengths and weaknesses. For instance, it is really only Fantham (1996) and Kraus (2000) who stress the anxieties of the period in their surveys. Hutchinson (1993) is an enthusiast, but aims to put his authors in a most favourable light; thus while he deals ably with their 'extravagance', he downplays the 'grotesque', for which we still rely upon less squeamish critics: Lefèvre (1970), Burck (1971), Serban (1973) and Johnson (1987). The political issues of this period are discussed in Ogilvie (1980) and Sullivan (1985).

CHAPTER FIVE

The High Empire: AD 69–200

Bruce Gibson

1 Background

After the last Julio-Claudian emperor, Nero, committed suicide in AD 68, there was a rapid succession of emperors and civil war, before the establishment of the Flavian dynasty under the emperor Vespasian (reigned AD 69–79), and his two sons Titus (79–81) and Domitian (81–96). Though Domitian, who had no heir, died as a result of a palace revolution in September 96, there was no repetition of the civil wars that had followed the collapse of the previous dynasty in 68–9. Domitian's immediate successor, Nerva (96–8) staved off the threat of internal turmoil by adopting the military man Trajan (98–117), and adoptions of the next three emperors, Hadrian (117–38), Antoninus Pius (138–61) and Marcus Aurelius (161–80), the 'Antonines', allowed a prolonged period of domestic calm. Even though Marcus Aurelius did not continue the policy of adoption and permitted his son to succeed him, which led to abuses in Rome, the condition of the provinces may not have been substantially different under Commodus (180–92). Commodus' death, however, led to a repetition of instability and civil war, with provincial commanders fighting it out before the eventual victory of Septimius Severus (193–211).

As the designation 'The High Empire' suggests, it is tempting to view this period as a long and splendid unity. Gibbon's verdict on the period between AD 96 and 180, offered in the third chapter of his *Decline and Fall of the Roman Empire*, has had a powerful influence on subsequent historiography:

> If a man were called to fix the period in the history of the world, during which the condition of the human race was most happy and prosperous, he would without hesitation, name that which elapsed from the death of Domitian to the accession of Commodus.

The literary picture may however be more complex. Though this chapter's concern is with writings in Latin, it is worth noting at the outset that this was above all a period where 'Roman literature' should be seen to include the extensive literature produced in Greek by figures such as Plutarch, Dio Chrysostom, Lucian and Aelius Aristides, authors who all responded to the Roman world in which they lived while at the same time drawing on the classical Greek literature that had preceded them.

Even if the focus is restricted to Latin literature, it is more difficult to see the years 69–200 as a single unity, though the temptation to break this period into smaller unities can also be problematic. Thus Coleman (2000) has usefully pointed to the dangers of regarding Domitian's death and the end of the Flavian emperors as a decisive turning point in the history of Latin literature, one that would interestingly mirror Gibbon's starting point for the golden age of the second-century emperors. Indeed one can argue that the nature of the evidence might push us towards different kinds of periodization. Thus Flavian authors such as Valerius Flaccus, Statius and Silius are naturally connected through figures such as Martial (whose writing career begun under Titus and ended under Trajan) and Pliny (who knew Martial and Silius) with authors from the reigns of Trajan such as Tacitus and Suetonius, both correspondents of Pliny, and Juvenal (addressed by Martial in his poetry). Though this game of 'connections' might allow us to bridge the gap between Flavian writers and their immediate successors, it is much harder to do this for the later part of the second century, which in this chapter is treated in a separate section.

It is a curious irony that some of the literary historiography of the 'High Empire' has tended to characterize it as an era of decline, with only marginal relevance to the overall history of Latin literature. In part the spur for the rhetoric of decline comes from the texts themselves. Thus Tacitus' *Dialogus de oratoribus*, a work now considered to date from the period after Domitian's death (see Mayer 2001: 22–7 for a convenient summary of the debate), takes for its larger premise the idea that the orators of the present cannot hope to match the achievements of the orators of the past such as the great Cicero. Though Marcus Aper is given the opportunity to put the opposing case in the dialogue, the work's overall effect is to offer a pessimistic answer to Fabius Iustus' opening questions, as to why previous ages were so outstanding in oratory, and why the present is so bereft of talent. In poetry, one may compare fleeting hints such as Statius' praise of his friend Manilius Vopiscus as a man *qui praecipue uindicat a situ litteras iam paene fugientes* (who especially protects from decay literature that has now virtually disappeared) (*Silv.* 1 *pr.* 24–5), or Pliny's treatment of the epic poet Silius Italicus and the latter's devotion for his poetic forebear Virgil (*Epist.* 3.7.1–9). Even epic poetry itself, traditionally the highest of genres, acknowledges and pays homage to what has gone before. Thus Statius' closing address to the *Thebaid* not to attempt to follow too closely behind Virgil (*Theb.* 12.816–17), is on the surface part of the same tendency, even if scholars have produced more nuanced readings of this gesture in recent years (see e.g. Hardie 1993: 110–11; Henderson 1998a: 217; Hinds 1998: 91–6).

Perceptions of decline and comparisons with earlier texts do also, however, contribute to continuity. Even if Statius' own response to the *Aeneid* at the end of the *Thebaid* is couched in a rhetoric of homage, other texts offer less explicitly deferential accounts of literary history and succession. Thus Juvenal in his first satire presents himself as the successor of the satirists Lucilius and Horace, a move that superficially appears to be a simple acceptance of literary predecessors, comparable to the Augustan poet Ovid's account of his own role in the tradition of love elegy as a successor to Gallus, Propertius and Tibullus (*Trist.* 4.10.53–4). However, Juvenal's particular interest in Lucilius has the effect of destablilizing the position that Horace had claimed for himself in his own *Satires* as a superior poet to Lucilius (see e.g. Hor. *Sat.* 1.4.1–13; 1.10); the return to the earlier poet represents a challenge to the central, canonical position occupied by Horace. Less confrontational is Silius' decision to acknowledge Ennius' earlier poetry about the Punic Wars by including him as a character in the course of his poem (Sil. 12.390–419), which suggests the plurality of epic inspirations available, as is confirmed by the inclusion of Homer as a character whom Scipio Africanus encounters among the shades of the underworld (Sil. 13.778–97; cf. Hardie 1993: 113–16).

In historiography (see Kraus, Chapter 17), Tacitus' *Annals*, which recount the reigns of the Julio-Claudian emperors from Tiberius to Nero, exhibit a complex attitude to the past. On the one hand Tacitus concedes that his work cannot please the reader in the way that republican history would have done (*Ann.* 4.32), yet at the same time he suggests that the changed world of the principate means that the methods and interests of previous writers cannot be of use to an audience in the same way (*Ann.* 4.33). Both these passages can also be set alongside *Annals* 3.55, where, as part of a digression on luxury, which had declined in the Flavian period, Tacitus also countenances the possibility of other challenges to the past, implicitly including his own historiography. Similar too is *Annals* 16.16, where Tacitus, echoing *Annals* 4.32, laments that he has to write of deaths under Nero, but then remarks that it is for posterity to provide a proper record of the deaths of illustrious men. We shall also see later in this chapter how the reinvestigation of past (sometimes dead and buried) *literary* history is manifested in the taste for pre-Augustan writers and archaism that is characteristic of much second-century writing.

2   Literature and Politics

Patronage continued to have an important role in Latin literature. Thus the epigrammatist Martial and Statius both reveal clear patronage relationships in their poems, with private individuals and with the emperor. However, this period is also notable for the number of writers who were men of rank and station. Silius

Italicus had been a consul under Nero, before retiring to a life of letters (Plin. *Epist.* 3.7), while Pliny, orator and writer of letters (for the latter see Edwards, Chapter 19), was a consul in AD 100 under Trajan, before governing the province of Bithynia. Tacitus' career was even more distinguished, since he was governor of Asia, one of the two plum senatorial postings available to ex-consuls. Frontinus, author of works on stratagems and on aqueducts, was also a consul, while later in the century Fronto, whose letters survive, would also hold this rank. And Suetonius, author not only of biographies of emperors and other figures such as poets and grammarians, but also of a range of learned works reflecting an interest in antiquarianism and the Latin language (see further Wallace-Hadrill 1983: 43–9), held the post of *ab epistulis*, with responsibility for imperial correspondence, under Hadrian. Emperors too participated in literature: there is some evidence of literary interests on the part of Titus, while Domitian was praised in his day as a noted poet, at least before he assumed the purple. His two immediate successors, Nerva and Trajan, pursued contrasting literary ambitions, Nerva writing poetry that Martial compared to that of Tibullus (Mart. 8.70.7–8), while Trajan left behind a work on his Dacian wars (Coleman 2000: 19 n. 3). Hadrian encouraged letters, especially in the Greek world, and also wrote Latin poetry, while Marcus Aurelius is noted for his *Meditations*, a philosophic memoir written in Greek.

By this time, Latin culture now includes figures from an even wider geographical spectrum than before. True enough, the contribution made to Roman letters by Spain in preceding generations by figures such as the Senecas and Lucan is continued with such figures as Martial and the rhetor Quintilian. Our period also sees for the first time authors from Roman provinces in Africa such as Fronto and Apuleius; this tradition would continue with the flowering of Christian writings such as Tertullian at the end of the second century AD, who represented the beginnings of Christian literature in Latin as opposed to Greek. Tacitus too may have hailed from Narbonnese Gaul, on the far side of the Alps from Italy, though it is also possible that his home town of Forum Iulii lay in what is now northern Italy, in Cisalpine Gaul (see Syme 1958b: 614–24).

Even if men of high rank are involved in literature, it is striking how little direct engagement there is with the politics of the day. Even Pliny's *Panegyricus*, a speech in praise of the emperor Trajan given on the occasion of his consulship in September AD 100, offers its critique of rulership indirectly, through the strategy of assailing the principate of Domitian. And Juvenal in his first satire, writing perhaps at the end of Trajan's reign, even expresses caution about attacking figures even from the reign of Nero, some sixty years prior to his own time (Juv. 1.153–71). Tacitus had of course contrasted the reign of Domitian, which he categorized as a time of literary intolerance, with succeeding reigns, where one could enjoy the freedom to write as one pleased (Tac. *Agr.* 3, *Hist.* 1.1), but even in the light of this it is possible to discern silences in the literature of the succeeding reigns as well. Thus Tacitus in his *Annals*, most probably completed in the reign of Hadrian, comments on how even writing about the reign of Tiberius could be dangerous, as one could offend descendants of those one was writing about, and even offend by the representation of virtue (*Ann.* 4.33). Similarly, there is case for arguing that one learns more from Pliny's letters, written under Trajan, about figures from the pre-Trajanic era than about politics under Trajan himself.

Tacitus' *Dialogus* explicitly adumbrates the difficulties of political activity, and therefore implicitly hints at the difficulties involved in writing about political activity. One of the reasons advanced for the failure of orators in the imperial period to live up to their forebears such as Cicero is the fact that under the imperial system, it is no longer possible for truly great oratory to flourish without a political context of real significance (Tac. *Dial.* 36, 40). This is strikingly similar to a Greek text, Longinus' *On the Sublime* 44, though the latter's authorship and dating are uncertain. The *Dialogus* also hints at the difficulties of working in other genres as well: one of the participants in the dialogue, Curiatius Maternus, is represented as the author of dramas that have the power to offend the *potentes* (the powerful), presumably a reference to the imperial court (Tac. *Dial.* 2.1).

Oddly enough, it is perhaps the *Silvae* of Statius, traditionally dismissed as containing honeyed flatteries of the emperor Domitian and other patrons of the poet, which have most to offer in terms of engagement with contemporary political figures. It is, for instance, from Statius that we learn of the role of imperial freedmen, such as Flavius Abascantus, Domitian's *ab epistulis*, in charge of imperial correspondence (*Silv.* 5.1). Even more striking is *Silv.* 3.3, which deals with the figure of Claudius Etruscus, another imperial freedman whose career had included a period when he had been out of favour and exiled from Rome.

A separate question is the interpretation of literature whose very subject matter appears to represent withdrawal from engagement with the politics of the day. Can literature that takes refuge either in mythology or in remoter history at the same time engage with the political realities of its own time, as perhaps Tacitus implies with his discussion of Maternus' dramas? It is significant that the titles of the two dramas mentioned in the *Dialogus*, the *Cato* and the *Thyestes*, engage with the history of the late republic and with mythology, yet are both potential loci for offending the emperor and his court indirectly. Frederick Ahl in particular has suggested (Ahl 1984) that one feature of much imperial Latin literature is a tendency to confront imperial autocracy indirectly, through the device of figured speech, where praise can conceal criticism. It is striking that even under Domitian, the emperor with the worst reputation in this period, Quintilian in his manual on oratory mentions the possibility of how one might use ambiguity in dealing with a tyrant (*Inst.* 9.2.65–8). Though Quintilian's concern is with the training of an orator in rhetorical exercises (and one may note here Tacitus' censure of declamatory training as being irrelevantly concerned with unreal situations such as tyrannicide, *Dial.* 35.5), the example of Maternus' dramas from Tacitus, as well as references in Suetonius' imperial biographies for double interpretations of even single lines of dramas performed on the Roman stage, perhaps open up even epic poetry to interpretations of this type.

The example of Statius is an interesting case in point. It is now fashionable to see Statius' *Thebaid* as a work that confronts autocracy and power in its representation of the Theban tyrant, Eteocles, who is sometimes seen as a parallel to Domitian (see e.g. Dominik 1994: 148–56). The problem is more complex, however, since the work opens with praise of the emperor, so that the text on the surface does not appear to invite any such comparison at all. The incomplete *Achilleid* also opens with similar material on the emperor. However, since Statius promises that he will raise his song to Domitianic heights when he is able to live up to the subject, there have inevitably been those who have argued that panegyric deferred is equivalent to panegyric refused. Although Ahl and others have suggested that the *Silvae* can be read with an eye to ambiguities and tensions, the case for seeing these directly encomiastic poems as ironic is a much harder one to make. It is difficult to see how Statius could have made a career writing for patrons if at the same time he was attempting to subvert them. But while Statius presents a complex picture to interpreters, perhaps following in tradition of the Neronian epic poet Lucan whose own epic proem is a famous battleground for interpreters (see also Statius' memorial poem dedicated to the poet's widow on the occasion of Lucan's birthday, *Silv.* 2.7), it is much harder to find such ambiguous material in either Valerius Flaccus' mythological epic on the Argonauts or in Silius Italicus' *Punica*, on the Second Punic War.

3   The Later Second Century AD

The epics by Statius and Silius discussed above date, however, from the first thirty years of the period, and we are left with very little material from the second century with which to compare them, something of a problem with other genres of Latin literature as well, as we shall see. If Juvenal's impatience with epic in his first satire (probably datable to the end of Trajan's reign) is to be taken seriously (Juv. *Sat.* 1.1–2, 52–4), then epic continued to be written quite extensively in the immediately succeeding period. Beyond this point, however, one can only have resort to speculation: thus the only later second century Latin epic poet securely recorded is Clemens (Apuleius *Flor.* 7; see also Courtney 1993: 401), as the author of a poem on Alexander the Great. A similar picture emerges for elegiac poetry as well: there is evidence for its composition by the emperor Nerva (Mart. 8.70.7–8) and Arruntius Stella, the friend of Statius (Stat. *Silv.* 1.2.7–10, 247–55), but again little evidence for the second century, while for Latin satire there is virtually no evidence either before or after Juvenal. We have two fragments of Turnus, who wrote satires in the Flavian period that appear to have looked back to Neronian times (see Courtney 1993: 362–3), while Apuleius lists *satiras* (satires) in an exhaustive list of genres he has worked in at *Florida* 9.27–8.

However, the evidence offered by the fragments of Apuleius' lost *Ludicra* would suggest that the term is not being used in a strict generic sense, but may instead refer to the bantering and ironic tone of Apuleius' writings, which, like the poems of Pliny and his circle, may have had more in common with figures like Catullus than with satirists such as Juvenal and his forebears.

What does emerge, if we consider the remains of the poetry of the second century, is an emphasis on small, carefully crafted compositions, with an interest on minor and obscure metres, which may account for the paucity of either elegiacs or hexameters. One may wonder whether the non-hexameter poems of the *Silvae* of Statius represent an early foray in this direction; there is also some evidence that Sulpicia's love poetry addressed to her husband, mentioned first by Martial (Mart. 10.35; 10.38), employed such metres as iambic trimeters, hendecasyllables and scazons (Courtney 1993: 361; Citroni 1996). This tendency is also reflected in the poetic compositions of the younger Pliny, who wrote lighter verses of various kinds, only a few lines of which survive (see e.g. Plin. *Epist.* 4.14; 5.3; 7.4; 7.9; Hershkowitz 1995), yet invariably with the thought that verse-composition is merely an adjunct to one's career as an orator; hence his praise of the orator Pompeius Saturninus for writing poetry in the style of Catullus or Licinius Calvus, *Epistulae* 1.16, a view in keeping with Quintilian's beliefs that a knowledge of the poets was essential for the training of the orator (*Inst.* 10.1). Such Latin poetry as we know of from later in the second century does not seem far removed in its ambitions from the types of poetry that Pliny praises, even if the previous tendency to consider poets such as Florus, Annianus and others as part of a school of *poetae nouelli* (analogous to the only marginally less controversial *poetae noui* of the late Republic) has rightly been called into question (Courtney 1993: 372–4). Thus Florus and Hadrian exchange elegant verses playfully mocking each other (Flor. fr. 1 Courtney; Hadrian fr. 1 Courtney), while revivals of old metres are also not uncommon (see e.g. Flor. fr. 3 Courtney, written in septenarii) as well as metrical experiments (see e.g. Annianus frs 1–4 Courtney). The avoidance of grander subjects is also reflected in the poetical fragments of Apuleius, such as fragment 2 Courtney, on cleaning of the teeth, while the erotic heritage of poets such as Catullus is reflected in compositions such as Hadrian fragment 2 Courtney and in Apuleius fragment 7 Courtney.

The evidence for poetry in this period is slight, when set alongside the works that have survived in prose. However, even in prose, the situation is not parallel to that of Flavian literature and the period under Nerva and Trajan that immediately followed it, since we are essentially left with only three substantial figures. Whereas the student of the Flavian era is able, for example, to compare the contributions in epic of Valerius Flaccus, Statius and Silius, the three major literary figures in Latin literature of the later second century, Fronto, Aulus Gellius and Apuleius, share features in common but cannot be so directly compared.

The eldest of the three, Fronto, consul in AD 143, is thought to have been born perhaps in the last decade of the first century and to have died around 167

(Champlin 1980: 137–42); Fronto was, moreover, a tutor to Marcus Aurelius. Fronto's works survive in an unfortunate and haphazard fashion since they survive imperfectly in a palimpsest. Fronto's writings are of particular interest for his views on matters of style and literary history. He is especially striking for his affirmation of archaism as a key concern. Thus in a letter to Marcus, Fronto notes that in his youth the taste for archaic words had not yet come to be in fashion (*ad M. Caes.* 2.2.4). This is in keeping with our knowledge of the emperor Hadrian, who, despite his taste for things Greek, was also interested in Latin letters as well, but preferred the poetry of Ennius over that of Virgil and the prose of Cato to that of Cicero (*SHA Hadrianus* 16.6). Thus Fronto affirms the use of the best possible vocabulary in his writings (see e.g. *ad M. Antonin. Imp.* 1.2.7), and is keen to affirm the value of pre-classical authors such as Lucilius, Lucretius, Sallust, Ennius and Gracchus in the search for stylistic models (e.g. *De eloquentia* 1.2). Thus his genuine admiration for Cicero is tempered with the thought that Cicero did not trouble to search out enough *insperata atque inopina uerba* (unexpected and unthought-of words) (*ad M. Caes.* 4.3.3). Although the taste for archaic vocabulary itself should not be seen as a second-century innovation, since Latin historiography from the time of Sallust had looked to the past for its stylistic inspiration, a tradition continued by Tacitus, the widening scope for archaisms outside the confines of historiography should be seen as a distinctively second-century feature, a feature as appropriate for oratory as it is for Apuleius' Milesian 'novel', the *Metamorphoses* (for which see Harrison, Chapter 15 below).

This reaction in favour of pre-classical authors can also be observed in the writings of Aulus Gellius, who was born between AD 125 and 128 (Holford-Strevens 1988: 12), and who may have outlived Marcus Aurelius (1988: 15). His *Noctes Atticae* (*Attic Nights*), survives in twenty books and is a commonplace book, which deals with a whole range of subjects, both literary and linguistic, culled from numerous authors. Gellius offers various purposes for the work, including the desire to spur others to *ad honestae eruditionis cupidinem* (the desire for honourable erudition), and the desire to protect men of affairs from *turpi certe agrestique rerum atque uerborum imperitia* (shameful and certainly rustic ignorance of things and words, *NA praef.* 12). The mention of 'words' here reflects in no uncertain terms a major interest Gellius shares with Fronto, a concern for vocabulary as an end in itself. Thus it is no surprise, for instance, to find sections such as an explanation of the archaic language used in a senatorial decree from republican times (*NA* 4.6), and those on archaic reduplicated forms of the perfect tense used in republican writers (*NA* 6.9). The temptation to dismiss Gellius as nothing more than a nostalgic follower of republican letters should however be resisted. It has for instance been shown that Gellius' own literary style includes not only pre-classical elements, which could have come straight from the republican writers he admired, but also many innovations in vocabulary and syntax (Holford-Strevens 1988: 35–46).

Gellius' importance in the period is for his striving to combine erudition with stylistic flair, reflecting at the same time a deep antiquarian interest in Roman history and in the history of Roman letters. At the same time, the *Noctes Atticae* are also of value for reflecting the manner in which Greek and Latin literary culture could overlap. It was possible even for a man like Gellius, with his enthusiasm for the Latin language and its history, to be an associate of such diverse figures as Fronto, the philosopher Favorinus from Gaul who wrote in Greek, and Herodes Atticus, the profoundly wealthy Athenian and patron of letters.

It is in the final figure of this second-century triad, Apuleius, that we see even closer connexions with the contemporary Greek letters. Before saying more about Apuleius, however, it is worth introducing developments in Greek literature in this period, so that the parallel between Apuleius and figures writing in Greek can be all the clearer.

A phenomenon that develops in Greek literature in this period is the rise of the so-called 'Second Sophistic', a title that reflects a possible parallel with the sophists prominent in Athens in the fifth century BC, though its complexities have been well explored by Anderson (1990). A working definition of the term might be that one is speaking primarily of rhetors with a wide reputation in large part obtained through making public speeches on such occasions as imperial visits. This should not however obscure the fact that the literary productions of such figures were not solely speeches; declamation, and indeed compositions in a whole host of other genres such as fiction, historiography and encyclopaedic writing as well, all could contribute to the reputation of a sophist. Thus, Anderson (1990: 101) has noted that figures with such prominent profiles as Favorinus or Scopelian are also credited with much less public works such as the former's work on Pyrrhonic tropes or the latter's *Gigantomachy*.

We can also see the culture of public literary achievement as also being evinced in the poetic and oratorical contests that were available for near-professional poets such as Statius' father, who had competed in Greek games at Naples (which traced their foundation to Augustus), as well as the more famous contests such as the traditional Greek contests at Nemea, Delphi and the Isthmus (Stat. *Silv.* 5.3.112–15, 141–5); professional poets were also noted for travelling from one city to another in search of public patronage (see Hardie 1983: 15–36, 74–102), in a manner that has clear parallels with the activities associated with the 'Second Sophistic'. In the case of Statius' father, the parallels are even more striking, since the elder Statius was also a teacher of Greek poetry and Roman religion, a combination that recalls the wide-ranging interests of a figure such as Plutarch. The fact that the Greek contests of Magna Graecia and of Greece itself are imitated in the time of Domitian, who established an Alban contest in honour of Minerva and one in honour of Capitoline Jupiter, points to the cross-currents between Latin and Greek culture even before the second century AD had begun. In a different way, these trends are reflected in the friendships of figures such as

Fronto and Gellius, exemplified in Fronto's Greek correspondence with Appian, a Greek historian from Alexandria, and in Aulus Gellius' associations with figures such as Herodes Atticus and Favorinus. This was also an age when it was possible for men from the Greek East to rise to the high office in Rome, including the consulate. Among practitioners of Greek literature in this category, one can note such figures as Arrian, famous for his *Anabasis* on the expedition of Alexander against the Persians, as well as the medical writer Galen, who worked at court as a doctor for Marcus Aurelius.

All this points in fact to continuity and points of contact between Greek and Roman culture, and which can therefore serve usefully to bring us to the figure of Apuleius, who like Fronto came from north Africa, being born in Madaura, in what is now Algeria in the AD 120s, and subsequently being educated in Carthage and in Athens before a career in public speaking. He is also perhaps the person in Latin letters to whom the label of 'sophist' can most usefully be applied, as by Harrison (2000). When one considers the whole *oeuvre* of Apuleius, what is most striking is the range of this writer's interests. He is most famous nowadays for his novel the *Metamorphoses*, which along with Petronius' *Satyrica* has often been considered to be representative of that elusive genre, the Latin novel (see Harrison, Chapter 15; we also have scant testimonies of a lost Apuleian novel called the *Hermagoras*), but was at the same time the author of display pieces of oratory such as the *Apologia*, a speech in his own defence against charges of having corrupted his wife through magic, and the *Florida*, extracts from other speeches, as well as philosophical writings dealing especially with Plato, and also works of scientific interest dealing with such subjects as medicine, arboriculture and arithmetic. This diverse range of interests and works by Apuleius offers another point of contact with the practice of Greek writers of the period, one that is perhaps sometimes overlooked under the influence of the term 'Second Sophistic': the combination of public works of self-projection and display with private writings reflecting erudition and, sometimes, the desire to collect and accumulate knowledge for its own sake.

4   Conclusion

The literature of the 'High Empire' offers a diversity that belies the notions of this as a historical period where little of note happened. Some Latin writers continue to draw inspiration from the classic genres and authors of previous Roman literature; the epics that survive from the time of the Flavian emperors are a good example of this. However, the Latin literature of the period is much more part of a continuum with works being written in Greek as well than at any previous time. A figure such as Apuleius, author of two novels (one lost and one surviving), is perhaps the best instance of this tendency, but at the same time even those most passionately associated with the taste for archaic Latin, such as

Fronto and Aulus Gellius, can still be seen in terms of their connections with intellectual life and letters in Greece. Lastly, it is worth remembering how this period ends with the first stirrings of Christian writings in Latin, another area of cross-fertilization between Greek and Latin culture, with the writings of the African Tertullian representing the Latin beginning of Christian apologetics, a genre that had been pursued in Greek throughout the second century.

FURTHER READING

For an overview of the historical period, in terms of political and social background, the new second edition of volume 11 of the *Cambridge Ancient History* (Bowman, Garnsey and Rathbone 2000) offers a comprehensive and authoritative treatment, including a useful discussion in Bowie (2000) of literary culture. The pessimistic assessments of imperial literature of this era that have dominated in the scholarship are perhaps most conveniently enshrined in Williams (1978), but there have been a range of more modern responses that have suggested a more fluid dynamic in literary succession, such as Hardie (1993) and Hinds (1998), both of whom have explored the implications of Roman epic under the empire. Hardie (1983) and Nauta (2002) are two invaluable studies for the context of personal poetry such as Statius' *Silvae* and Martial's epigrams and the role of patronage. For subversive metholodogies for reading imperial literature, see Ahl (1984) and Bartsch (1994), and contrast Dewar (1994), who argues against such approaches to panegyrical texts; Newlands (2002), writing on the *Silvae* of Statius, exemplifies a less polarized and more fluid approach to such questions.

For the second century, Steinmetz (1982) provides a useful overview of the whole period in German. Coleman (2000) offers a valuable study of developments in Latin literature under Nerva and Trajan, while Courtney (1993) collects the poetic remains from this period. For the Latin intellectual culture of the post-Trajanic age, much can be gained from the studies of Champlin (1980), Holford-Strevens (1988) and Harrison (2000) on Fronto, Aulus Gellius and Apuleius. The Greek background to this period can be usefully considered in such works as Russell (1990), an edited collection of essays on Antonine literature, while the interplay of Rome and Greek culture is explored in Swain (1996), Goldhill (2001) and Whitmarsh (2001).

PART II

Genres

CHAPTER SIX

Narrative Epic

Philip Hardie

1 Introduction

Homer stands at the beginning and at the centre of Greek literary culture, constituting epic as the original and originary genre for the Greeks. In Latin the genre of epic was to achieve a similar status with Virgil's *Aeneid*, but only through a heroic act on Virgil's part of constructing the fiction of an original epic authority out of a tradition of Latin epic already two centuries old, and which had begun as a self-conscious importation of the Greek epic tradition, whose early Latin practitioners saw in epic just one of a number of Greek genres from which to choose. Note in particular that the three major pre-Virgilian writers of Latin epic, Livius Andronicus, Naevius and Ennius, were also the major mid-Republican dramatists, authors of both tragedies and comedies based on classical and Hellenistic Greek models. For later generations 'father' Ennius became *the* great pre-Virgilian Roman epic poet, but for his contemporaries Ennius' dramatic output was probably as significant as his epic *Annals*.

2 Pre-Virgilian Epic: Livius Andronicus, Naevius, Ennius (see also Goldberg, Chapter 1)

According to Cicero (*Brut.* 75) the elder Cato wrote in the *Origines*, his history of Italy, that at banquets in the old days feasters used to sing songs on the praises of famous men. Praise is often viewed as a defining feature of the genre of epic, and this was perhaps an attempt on the part of the man who more than any other 'invented' Roman tradition to identify something like a native tradition of praise poetry. But for us, and probably for Cato, Latin epic begins with the words *uirum mihi, Camena, insece uersutum* (Tell me, Muse, of the cunning man), the opening of Livius Andronicus' translation of the *Odyssey*. As Goldberg (Chapter 1) has noted, this is a close rendering of the first five words of the Homeric poem, but with significant divergences, suggesting both Italianization and a degree of scholarly sophistication.

We should not forget that what from a later viewpoint seems the primitive beginnings of Latin literature is in fact the product of a meeting between an already advanced society and the sophisticated and self-conscious culture of the Hellenistic Greek world, although the exact level of Livius' scholarly pretensions is debated (Goldberg 1995: 47–50; Hinds 1998: 58–63). As for the audience for the epic narratives of Livius and other Republican writers, it is generally assumed that these are texts for reading, as opposed to the performance texts of Livius' stage plays or his liturgical hymn to Juno composed for a critical moment in the Hannibalic war, although it has been argued that these narratives were to be performed at aristocratic banquets (Rüpke 2001a).

Homer is a panHellenic poet, and his supreme god Zeus is not tied to any one Greek state. Zeus' Latin equivalent, Jupiter, is the state god of Rome, and the Latin epic tradition became a national epic in a way impossible in Greece, where the multiplicity of later historical epics on individual cities and rulers never smothered the authority of Homer as the epic poet par excellence (Feeney 1991: 113–15). Latin national epic was inaugurated by Naevius' *Bellum Punicum*, in the Saturnian metre, on the First Punic War (264–241 BC). Naevius, who had fought in the war himself, linked Roman history to the legendary past of Homer through flashbacks, introduced by means of which we cannot be sure, telling of Aeneas' flight to Troy, his visit to Carthage (possibly including the story of a love affair with Dido), and the foundation of Rome

Within a few decades Naevius' epic was overtaken by Ennius' *Annals*, which established itself as the national epic of Rome until successfully being challenged by Virgil's *Aeneid*. A historical epic, it adopted a simple 'annalistic' structure, based on the year-by-year chronicle of the *pontifex maximus*, which also became the standard structure of Latin prose historiography. The narrative started with Aeneas' flight from Troy, and was brought down in fifteen books to the triumph in 187 BC of Ennius' patron M. Fulvius Nobilior over the Aetolians, to which was later added a further three books on more recent wars. Ennius became the yardstick for historical Roman epic celebrating the military victories of Rome and the triumphs of its generals, confirming the core values and virtues of the Republican system. One of its best-known lines, from the speech of Manlius Torquatus delivering his son to execution for disobeying orders, despite having killed an enemy commander, is *moribus antiquis res stat Romana uirisque* (the Roman state is founded on the customs and men of old) (fr. 156 Skutsch). Ennius himself had fought as a soldier in the war against Hannibal, and was close to leading men in Rome, including Cato the Elder and Fulvius Nobilior; Goldberg argues however that his relationship to Fulvius was not that of a dependent client writing to commission, like the Greek poet Archias who celebrated the victories of Marius and Lucullus in the early first century BC (Goldberg 1995: ch. 5).

For the Augustans Ennius became a figure of hoary antiquity, endowed with more *ingenium* 'native talent' than *ars* (art) (Ov. *Tr.* 2.424). Yet Ennius presented himself as a revolutionary: in the prologue to Book 7 of the *Annals* (fr.206–9 Skutsch) he contrasted earlier poets like Naevius who used the primitive verses (Saturnian) of *Faunei uatesque* (Fauns and bards), with one like himself, *dicti studiosus*, a translation of Greek *philologos* (scholar). Ennius was the first Latin poet to use the Homeric hexameter. Not only does he start his narrative with a Homeric hero, Aeneas, but the prologue to the *Annales* told of a dream-vision, possibly alluding to the dream at the beginning of Callimachus' *Aitia* (the touchstone of Alexandrian literary sophistication), in which, in accordance with Pythagorean doctrine, a phantom of Homer appeared to announce that the true soul of Homer had been reincarnated in the body of Ennius: Ennius is the Roman Homer. This wholesale appropriation of the Greek poetic tradition to celebrate Roman success may have been reflected in an account, at the end of the first edition of the *Annals*, of Fulvius Nobilior's physical removal from Aetolia of statues of the Muses to be set up in the temple of 'Hercules of Muses'.

In the century and a half after Ennius Latin hexameter epic made itself at home in the various subgenres available in the Greek tradition (see e.g. Goldberg 1995: 135): historical epic, often with a strong panegyrical thrust, including epics on the campaigns of Julius Caesar by Varro of Atax and a Furius, and Cicero's exercises in self-laudation in poems 'On his own Consulship' and 'On his Times'; mytho-logical epics, notably the lost but influential *Argonautica* by Varro of Atax, modelled on the poem with that title by the Hellenistic poet Apollonius of Rhodes. The story of the journey on the Argo of heroes from the generation before the Trojan War, a tale of wandering and adventure that offers an alternative to the model of the *Odyssey*, is second in importance only to the Homeric epics for the Latin epic tradition; the extent of Virgil's debt to Apollonius in the *Aeneid* has only recently been fully assessed (Nelis 2001). There were also further Latin translations of the *Iliad* and the *Odyssey*, including excerpts translated in high epic manner by Cicero as illustrations in his prose philosophical works (Goldberg 1995: ch. 6).

3 Virgil's *Aeneid*

Latin epic receives definitive shape in the *Aeneid*, the poem that, in T. S. Eliot's phrase, was to become 'the classic of all Europe'. Begun shortly after Octavian's final victory at the Battle of Actium in 31 BC, it is the product of, but also a crucial text in the production of, the 'Augustan moment', when Augustus (as Octavian named himself in 27 BC) constructed the enduring form of the principate out of the tattered and mutating fragments of the political traditions of the Republic, and when the Augustan poets established a lasting canon of Latin texts building both on the Greek classics and on the earlier Latin experiments in Greek forms.

The *Aeneid* both constructs the classical shape of Latin epic, through an intensive engagement with the previous Graeco-Roman tradition, and at the same time constructs a historical fiction to explain and legitimate the Roman, and specifically Augustan, order of things. Like the Augustan principate, the *Aeneid* is a revolutionary work that insists on its traditional nature. Yet the capacity of the *Aeneid* to engage successive generations of readers even after the demise in the political sphere of the (remarkably long-lived) 'Augustan idea' is a sign of the poem's openness to an interrogation of its own political and poetic messages. Readers in the second half of the twentieth century increasingly alienated from the idea of empire found no difficulty in locating within the poem a second, 'private', voice alongside the 'public' Augustan voice (the 'two voices' approach was formulated by Parry 1963; the voices proliferate still further in Lyne 1987).

Something of Virgil's thinking about how to position his epic within the previous traditions is found in the prologue to the third *Georgic*. Looking to the next stage of his career after completing his didactic poem on farming, the poet fantasizes that he will bring back the Muses in triumph from Greece, and build a temple in Italy dedicated to Caesar (Octavian). On the doors of the temple the poet will put scenes of Caesar's military victories; the temple will also contain marble statues of Octavian's Trojan ancestors. Virgil imagines himself in the role of Ennius' patron Fulvius Nobilior, returning in triumph from Greece with the Muses and building a temple associated with the Muses. The scenes on the doors are an artistic equivalent of the historical subject matter of the *Annals*, which also reached back to the Trojan ancestors.

In the event Virgil's 'conquest' of the Greek Muses was a far more daring raid on Greece than merely following in the footsteps of Ennius' re-embodiment of the Homeric tradition in a Roman historical epic. The *Aeneid* pays homage to Ennius at two important points: the parade of the souls of future Roman heroes viewed by Aeneas in the Underworld at the end of Book 6, and the scenes of Roman history from Romulus to Augustus portrayed by Vulcan on the Shield of Aeneas at the end of Book 8. Both sequences rework the *Annals* in general outline and allusive detail, but they are supplementary, if climactic, episodes framed within the main narrative of the poem, and that tells a story about a legendary, not a historical, hero, Aeneas. Instead of being a predominantly historical epic that glances back to the legendary origins of the Roman race, the *Aeneid* is a legendary epic that looks forward to the history of Rome.

Aeneas, the supposed Trojan ancestor of the Julian family of Julius Caesar and Augustus, is a secondary character in the *Iliad*; Virgil elevates him to a major character by the device of modelling his roles on those of the main characters of the two Homeric epics. Virgil's boldness lies in his condensation within the twelve books of the *Aeneid* of both the *Iliad* and the *Odyssey*, thus staking a far stronger claim to be the Roman Homer than Ennius (the major study of Virgil's use of Homer is Knauer 1964a; see also Gransden 1984 on Virgil's 'Iliad'). The sequence of the Homeric poems is reversed: crudely, the first six books of the

Aeneid are Aeneas' 'Odyssey', as the hero travels from Troy via a series of adventures modelled more or less closely on those of Odysseus to a new home in Italy, and the last six books are Aeneas' 'Iliad', as he is compelled to fight a second Trojan War in Italy, in which the tables are finally turned when Aeneas, acting the part of the greatest Greek hero, Achilles, strikes down the Italian leader Turnus, doomed to die the death of Achilles' victim Hector.

Virgil's Homeric imitation is far more complex than this simple outline would suggest, intricately interweaving episodes and motifs from both epics. For example the killing of Turnus replays both the death of Hector at the climax of the *Iliad and* the killing of the suitors at the end of the *Odyssey,* when Odysseus reclaims his rightful wife and home. An important reason for this particular combination of the Iliadic and Odyssean lies in the more satisfactory closure offered by the Odyssean than by the Iliadic model to Virgil's strongly teleological plot. The 'happy ever after' ending of the *Odyssey* is a pattern for the end of the Augustan story, the lasting social, familial and political stability of the *pax Augusta* after the storms of civil war, whereas the end of the *Iliad*, the death of Hector followed by the return of his body for burial by Achilles to his father Priam, chronicles the destruction of family continuity. The reconciliation of Achilles and Priam is only a temporary pause in the story of the war at Troy that will continue after the end of the *Iliad* to the sack of the city of Troy. Similarly, the conclusion to Aeneas' war in Italy at the end of the *Aeneid* will be followed by many more wars, but, in contrast to the story of Troy, leading to the final triumph of the city of Rome unified under the leadership of Augustus. But the fact remains that the last line of the *Aeneid*, *uitaque cum gemitu fugit indignata sub umbras* (with a groan his life fled indignant down into the shadows), does narrate the violent and unappeased death of Turnus, for whom many readers have a measure of sympathy. Rather than being a sign of the unfinished nature of the poem, this brutally abrupt ending marks Virgil's awareness of the complexities of closure and of the dangers of a simplistic teleology (on the end of the *Aeneid* see e.g. many of the essays in Putnam 1995).

The Homeric 'fundamentalism' of the *Aeneid* aims at creating an epic as foundational within Roman culture as the Homeric epics are within Greek. But Virgil does not try to conceal the fact that this is a thoroughly belated attempt to create an originary text. The poet of the *Eclogues* and *Georgics*, works that flaunt their debts to the Alexandrian poets Theocritus and Callimachus, does not cease to be an Alexandrian scholar-poet working in Rome when he turns to the *Aeneid*. Imitation of Homer bears the traces of Hellenistic criticism and interpretation of the Homeric poems under such rubrics as decorum theory (Schlunk 1974) and allegory (Hardie 1986: index s.v. 'allegory'). The *Aeneid* is burdened with a heavy awareness of the past, and of the relationship of past to present, of a kind barely present in Homer, but which is as central an obsession of the epic *Argonautica* of Apollonius of Rhodes as it is of the *Aitia* of his contemporary Callimachus. The researcher's nostalgia for an almost irrecoverable past is sensed in the invocation to the Muses before the Catalogue of Italians:

> Pandite nunc Helicona, deae, cantusque mouete,
> qui bello exciti reges, quae quemque secutae
> complerint campos acies, quibus Itala iam tum
> floruerit terra alma uiris, quibus arserit armis;
> et meministis enim, diuae, et memorare potestis;
> ad nos uix tenuis famae perlabitur aura.
>
> (*Aeneid* 7.641–6)

Now open up Helicon, goddesses, and move my song, to tell which kings were stirred to war, what troops followed each to fill the battlefield, what men already in those times flourished on Italy's nurturing soil, what weapons blazed there. For you both remember, goddesses, and you can remind; to us there barely wafts down fame's faint breeze.

The Homeric model, the invocation before the Catalogue of Ships (*Iliad* 2.484–93) is now freighted with an awareness of Roman annalistic and antiquarian traditions; Virgil's Catalogue of Italians proceeds to overlay antiquarian and ethnographic research on the epic model.

The decision to write an epic about the remote Homeric past that explains and comments on more recent Roman history sets up a relation between past and present of a thoroughly Alexandrian cast. Genealogy and aetiology are constitutive principles of an epic that tells families and cities where they come from. In the most general terms the *Aeneid* is not so much an epic about the hero Aeneas, as about the 'origins' or 'causes' (*aitia*) of a city and its institutions, as programmatically laid out in the prologue in a *dum*-clause the final goals of Aeneas' Homeric labours:

> dum conderet urbem
> inferretque deos Latio; genus unde Latinum
> Albanique patres atque altae moenia Romae.

> Until he might found a city and introduce gods to Latium; whence would spring the Latin race, the senators of Alba Longa, and the walls of lofty Rome.
>
> (*Aeneid* 1.5–7)

The *Aeneid* may be categorized as a Hellenistic 'ktistic' epic, an aetiological narrative of the 'foundation' (*ktisis*) of a city. Aetiological antiquarianism is most densely concentrated in Book 8, where on the site of what will one day be Rome Aeneas is provided with verbal and visual displays of origins by the wise Arcadian king Evander, to whom Aeneas stands in a relationship similar to that between Callimachus and his fictional interlocutors in the *Aitia* (George 1974).

An Arcadian whose 'city' consists of a few huts in a wooded landscape, and whose own epic narrative, the story of Cacus' theft of Hercules' cattle, turns the greatest of Greek heroes into a herdsman, suggests the presence of pastoral, that most quintessentially Hellenistic of genres, at the heart of the future Rome and of Virgil's epic. As an epic the *Aeneid* is surprisingly hospitable to a wide range of other genres, which may either pull against or work with the poem's overriding epic drive. Pastoral elements in Books 7 and 8 reflect Roman fantasies about the simple rustic origins of their great city, but they must be destroyed or left behind for the poem to move into its militaristic, Iliadic, gear, a shift also figured through the forging of swords out of the ploughshares of Italian farmers who have hitherto been faithful students of the *Georgics* (*Aen.* 7.635–6). Aeneas' diversion from his epic track at Carthage in Book 4 is an errancy into the world of elegiac lovers that defines itself as not-epic, not-Roman. The impossible dilemma in which Dido finds herself traps her in the roles of a tragic heroine, a Phaedra, a Medea, an Antigone – even an Ajax; Aeneas cuts the tragic knot by severing the mooring-rope that keeps him in Carthage with one 'lightning' (*fulmineus*) blow from his epic sword (4.579–80); the 'thunderbolt' (*fulmen*) is the weapon of the supreme god Jupiter who ensures that Fate follows its epic path. But the violence of the tragic world converges with the epic plot when Juno summons the Fury Allecto to motivate, in very un-Homeric fashion, the Iliadic war of the second half of the poem. Philosophical didactic is pressed into the service of the longer-term epic story of Rome in Book 6 when Anchises prefaces his Ennian review of Roman heroes with an account, highly Lucretian in style if not in philosophical content, of the nature of the universe and the nature of the soul. But this plurality of other genres jostling within the epic frame ceases to surprise given the ancient belief that Homer, as well as being the first and greatest epic poet, was also the fountainhead of all other kinds of literature and discourse. From one perspective the intertextual richness of the *Aeneid* makes it a kind of Alexandrian encyclo-paedia of the history of Graeco-Roman literary culture; from the perspective of its 'Homeric fundamentalism' the *Aeneid* makes an audacious bid to assert itself as the wellhead.

The *Aeneid* is faithful to its Homeric models at all levels. At each the challenge to the reader is to understand how the old is made relevant to the concerns of the new age. What do the heroes of the remote world of Homer have to offer the cosmopolitan reader of Augustus' Rome? Aeneas, himself a character from the *Iliad*, enters the poem with a speech of despair in the storm (1.94–101) that mimics a speech made by Odysseus at a similar moment in the *Odyssey* (5.299–312), and as he exits he repeats Achilles' killing of Hector in *Iliad* 22 (*Aen.* 12.919–52). In between, his responses and actions track those of a number of Homeric characters, but are framed within behavioural and psychological models from other contexts and later centuries. Hellenistic theor-ies of the good king, philosophical ideals of the wise man, Roman paradigms of generalship, and not least the evolving mirror of the good *princeps* to be held up to Augustus himself, all contribute to the reader's evaluation of how Aeneas behaves. The dynamics of characterization involve a continual testing and readjustment of what is expected of a Homeric hero, although it is wrong to see Aeneas' career as a simple evolution from an old-fashioned and self-defeating Homeric heroism to a new, Roman model of political and philosophical rectitude. Even the famous *pietas*, which emerges as Aeneas' centrally Roman virtue, can be read as an intensification and refinement of the attachments to family, city and gods that variously motivate a number of Homeric heroes. And we should remember that the testing and adjustment of the 'heroic code' is a defining feature of Homeric epic from the start: in the *Iliad* the behaviour of the 'greatest of the Achaeans', Achilles, strains the accepted model for the hero almost to breaking point, and once Odysseus leaves Troy in the *Odyssey* he must largely unlearn the role of city-sacker to practise a heroism of intelligence and endurance.

Other characters can be similarly assessed in terms of their closeness or distance from their Homeric models. This is true of the female, as well as the male, characters, but there is a shift from Homeric society to a more sharply gendered world, in which a 'poetics of manhood' is threatened by an enervating and maddening femininity. Although the *Aeneid* is a crucial model for later dynastic epic, the 'good woman', and future bride of Aeneas, Lavinia, is curiously faceless; perhaps the greatest absence, in Homeric terms, from the *Aeneid* is a strong female counterpart to Penelope, reunion with whom in a stable and prosperous marriage is the ultimate goal of Odysseus. The two most striking females in the *Aeneid*, Dido and the Italian 'Amazon' Camilla, are both destroyed as a result of their inability to sustain an 'unnatural' male role (on gender in the *Aeneid* see Keith 2000).

A polarized gendering also characterizes Virgil's reworking of the traditional divine machinery of epic. The Homeric husband and wife pair Zeus and Hera become a Jupiter and Juno whose opposition over the destiny of Aeneas' descendants motivates the entire plot. Their division is expressed as one between a masculine providence and a feminine madness, between the bright spaces of heaven and the darkness of the Underworld: Juno's agent in stirring up the fury of war in Italy is the female Allecto, a Fury from Hell (on theological dualism in the *Aeneid* and later Latin epic see Hardie 1993: ch. 3). But the tendency to theological abstraction is counterbalanced by a largely faithful reproduction of the anthropomorphic society of the Homeric Olympus, with examples of the 'sublime frivolity' of Homer's divine comedy in scenes such as Venus' seduction of Vulcan in Book 8, or the reconciliation of Jupiter and Juno in Book 12. There are times when Virgil's gods start to turn into allegories of philosophical principles, betraying the influence of post-Homeric rationalization, and other times when the poetic theology is tilted to foreshadow the state religion of Rome. But Jupiter never becomes *just* a personification of a Stoic Fate, and the imaginative fictional world of Virgil's gods resists any attempt to explain it all away as merely a colourful illustration of philosophical or psychological systems.

4 Post-Virgilian Epic

Ovid's Metamorphoses

The *Aeneid* instantly became the central classic of Latin literature, and all surviving post-Virgilian epics relate to the *Aeneid* in the way that the *Aeneid* relates to Homer, as the intertext by which they define their own aesthetic and ideological ambitions. This self-conscious dependence should not be taken as the mark of an exhausted and servile tradition, but as the precondition for a vigorous and creative allusivity.

One sign of this is the variety epics produced in response to the *Aeneid*, both historical and mythological. The first major epic to take up the challenge, Ovid's *Metamorphoses*, is so strange and original a poem that its status as epic has often been denied and the centrality of the Virgilian model misrecognized. Fifteen books of stories involving fantastic transformations are strung out on a chronological line from the creation of the world down to Ovid's own day, ending with the metamorphosis of the murdered Julius Caesar into a god and the prospective deification of Augustus himself. The chronological sequence is often tenuous, and complicated by inset narratives; ingenious transitional devices lend superficial continuity to what some have seen as less an epic and more a collection of brief narratives in the manner of the Hellenistic 'epyllion' practised by the neoteric poets like Catullus (Knox 1986). Metamorphosis is itself a theme particularly favoured by Hellenistic poets such as Nicander.

The *Metamorphoses* displays a generic polyphony, shifting up and down the hierarchy of literary kinds, from tragedy and epic to elegy and pastoral. A seismic shift occurs in the first book when, after narratives in philosophico-didactic and epic modes on the origins of the universe and the early struggles of the gods against monstrous enemies, Apollo, who has just killed the Python in a hyper-epic dragon-slaying episode, is diverted into the world of elegy:

> primus amor Phoebi Daphne Peneia: quem non
> fors ignara dedit, sed saeua Cupidinis ira.
> Delius hunc nuper, uicto serpente superbus,
> uiderat adducto flectentem cornua neruo
> 'quid'que 'tibi, lasciue puer, cum fortibus armis?'
> dixerat, 'ista decent umeros gestamina nostros . . .'

The first love of Apollo was for Daphne, daughter of Peneus. This was the result not of blind chance, but of Cupid's savage anger. Recently the Delian god, proud of his victory over the serpent, had seen him bending his bow with tightened string, and 'What', he said, 'do you, playful boy, have to do with a hero's weapons? That is proper equipment for my shoulders.'

(*Metamorphoses* 1.452–7)

In answer Cupid shoots Apollo so that he falls in love with Daphne, forgetting his epic exploits. The encounter between the two gods rewrites the first poem in Ovid's elegiac *Amores* (*primus Amor...*), in which the poet setting out to write military epic is confronted by Cupid, who steals one of Ovid's metrical 'feet', forcing him to limp in elegiac couplets, and then shoots him with his bow and arrow: Amor rules (Nicoll 1980). The metaliterary quality of the meeting in the *Metamorphoses* emerges through allusion to the first words of the *Aeneid*, *arma uirumque* (arms and the man), in Apollo's indignant question as to what a *boy* has to do with arms; *decent* (befits) suggests the infringement of a literary decorum.

This is not a simple swerve from (Virgilian) epic into elegy, for what motivates Cupid is a very epic emotion, the 'savage anger' that drives Juno at *Aeneid* 1.25. Ovid delights in pointing out that the most frequently read part of the *Aeneid* is the *love* story of Dido and Aeneas, engineered by Venus and Cupid in a scene at the end of Book 1, and which is imitated by Ovid in Venus' plot to extend the empire of love to the kingdom of Pluto through the rape of Proserpina (*Met.* 5.362–84). Daphne is the first of the many visions in the poem of a female beauty that provokes rape or seduction, and behind many of these apparitions glimmers the image of Dido on her first appearance to Aeneas at *Aeneid* 1.494–504. Ovid provocatively combines the martial and erotic in rewritings of the final duel between Aeneas and Turnus in the hyperbolically violent fight between Perseus and the suitors of Andromeda at the beginning of *Metamorphoses* 5, and in the wrestling-match of Hercules and the river-god Achelous for possession of Deianira at the beginning of *Metamorphoses* 9; but it should be recalled that marriage to the princess Lavinia *was* the cause of the quarrel between Aeneas and Turnus. The generic encyclopaedism of the *Metamorphoses* tends to dissolve the epic character of this long hexameter poem, but it also represents an engagement with the generic inclusiveness of the *Aeneid* itself, which we saw to be an aspect of Virgil's claim to a Homeric universality. By shifting the balance between the epic and non-epic elements of the *Aeneid*, as well as by highlighting the Alexandrianism accommodated within Virgil's Homeric framework, Ovid distorts and metamorphoses the Virgilian model, but the traces are always there for the discerning reader, just as an animal, plant or rock preserves a memory of the human being from which it was transformed.

The typical Ovidian metamorphosis tells of a single, irreversible change from one state to another (a 'terminal metamorphosis'). Its structure is that of an aetiology, a tale that explains the existence of something in the present as the result of something that happened in the past (Myers 1994). Here the influence of Callimachus' *Aitia* is seen, as also in the *Fasti*, Ovid's elegiac poem on the Roman calendar telling the causes of the rituals and institutions of Roman religion, month by month. The *Fasti* overlaps with the Roman and Augustan aetiology of the *Aeneid*; the *Metamorphoses*, as aetiology, offers a pointedly different version of how the world we live in came to be through its welter of strange Greek myths, converging with a Romanocentric and Augustan order of things only at the beginning, in the story of a very Roman Jupiter punishing the sins of the wicked Arcadian tyrant Lycaon, and in the last two books, in which the narrative moves in space from the Greek East to Italy, and in time down to the history of Rome, culminating in the transformation into gods of Aeneas, Romulus, Julius Caesar and Augustus, stories of the heavenly legitimation of Roman power. Elsewhere Virgilian aetiology undergoes displacement and distortion. In Book 8 we hear the story of the pious couple Philemon and Baucis. As reward for entertaining the gods when they came to earth in disguise, their humble thatched cottage is metamorphosed into a marble and gold temple:

> dominis etiam casa parua duobus
> uertitur in templum: furcas subiere columnae,
> stramina flauescunt, adopertaque marmore tellus
> caelataeque fores aurataque tecta uidentur.

The two householders see their little cottage changed into a temple: columns propped up the gables, the thatch turned golden, the floor was covered with marble, and they behold engraved doors and gilded roofs.

(Metamorphoses 8.699–702)

This metamorphosis encapsulates the historical transformation of Rome foreseen in *Aeneid* 8, from the rustic huts of the pious king Evander, who entertains divine men like Hercules and Aeneas, to the gilded temples of Augustus' Rome. But the story of Philemon and Baucis is told simply to make a point about the metamorphic power of the gods, at the dinner-table of the Greek river-god Achelous, and the scene is set not in Rome, but in Phrygia.

The *Metamorphoses* is also a universal poem in the more obvious sense that it narrates the whole history of the universe, an eccentric version of the prose universal histories fashionable in Ovid's time. In terms of the management of an epic plot this is diametrically opposed to the *Aeneid*, which famously launches *in medias res*, and which is constructed as a tightly unified plot, of the kind for which Aristotle praised the *Iliad* and *Odyssey*, covering just a short section of the life of its hero, Aeneas. But through devices of allusion and prophecy, looking back, for example, to the great struggles between gods and Titans or giants at the beginning of mythological time, and forward to the history of Rome and Augustus, the *Aeneid* also places its main narrative within a universal frame, to suggest that Rome's world-rule is the preordained conclusion to a cosmic history. In an exercise of literal-mindedness Ovid unpacks the *Aeneid*'s allusive universal history, but the way in which the Roman and Augustan Books 14 and 15 are made to perch on top of a 'world history' that seems to bear little relevance to Roman interests questions Virgil's Roman teleology. And by positing change, often of a violent and unpredictable kind, as the central principle of his narrative, Ovid draws attention to the fact that the *Aeneid* too is centrally about change, as Trojans turn into Romans, a Homeric hero turns into an Augustan *princeps*, thatched huts turn into the marble cityscape of Rome, and raises a doubt whether these processes of historical change can be tidily controlled and contained by the goals of Augustan ideology.

Lucan's Bellum Civile

The *Aeneid* is a legendary epic directly related to Roman history; its surviving successors of a more conventional brand than the *Metamorphoses* include two Roman historical epics and two epics on legendary matter having no direct Roman connection.

   The ten books of Lucan's *Bellum Civile*, left unfinished at his forced suicide in AD 65, narrate the convulsive civil war between Julius Caesar and his son-in-law Pompey the Great, beginning with Caesar's crossing of the Rubicon in 49 BC, and reaching climaxes in Books 7 and 8 with the battle of Pharsalus and the murder of Pompey. Drawing on prose histories by Caesar, Livy and others, Lucan uses a sombre register of language that largely avoids poeticism, and eliminates the machinery of Olympian gods that forms half of epic action, traditionally defined as 'narrative of the deeds of gods and men'. This is not, however, straightforwardly in the service of a historiographical realism: Lucan's world is instinct with scarcely intelligible and malign supernatural forces, embodied for example in the tremendous witch Erictho in Book 6, that may partly be understood as a negative version of the immanent Providence of the Stoic philosophy in which Lucan, like his uncle the younger Seneca, was immersed. Of Stoic colouring too is the sympathy between the human action and a natural world that reacts to the horrors on the historical stage. This cosmic sympathy is flagged in the simile at the opening of the poem that compares the collapse of Rome to the final destruction of the universe:

> sic, cum compage soluta
> saecula tot mundi suprema coegerit hora
> antiquum repetens chaos, ignea pontum
> astra petent, tellus extendere litora nolet
> excutietque fretum, fratri contraria Phoebe
> ibit et obliquum bigas agitare per orbem
> indignata diem poscet sibi, totaque discors
> machina diuolsi turbabit foedera mundi.

So, when the last hour closes all the ages of the world, breaking up its fabric in a return to the primeval chaos, the fiery stars will rush into the ocean, the land will refuse to stretch out its level shores and will shake off the sea, and the moon will confront her brother and, not content to drive her chariot on its slanting course, will claim the day for herself. The whole structure of the world will tear itself apart in civil war and overturn the laws of nature.

(*Bellum Civile* 1.72–80)

The *Aeneid* tells of Trojan and Roman heroes working with a providential divinity to build the universal empire of Rome. The *Bellum Civile* is an 'anti-*Aeneid*', in which Aeneas' descendant Julius Caesar presides over the death, not birth, of a nation. Engagement with the *Aeneid* is continuous and profound, from the moment at the Rubicon when a nocturnal vision of the grief-stricken goddess Roma tries vainly to dissuade Caesar from bearing arms against her, echoing Aeneas' dream-vision of the lacerated Hector on the night of the sack of Troy. The emotionality of this encounter is programmatic for the poem's constant working on the reader's pity and indignation, screwing up the Virgilian pathos to unbearable levels of what should be an 'unspeakable' horror. At the same time as readers we find it hard to divert our fascinated gaze from the spectacles of pain and dismemberment; the amphitheatrical analogy is frequently explicit (Leigh 1997). It is often difficult to know whether we should feel shock and sympathy, or laugh at the cartoon-like caricatures. This ambivalence of response is not made easier by the fact that the prologue contains a fulsome panegyric of Nero, the present ruler in the system made possible by Caesar's destruction of the Roman Republic; critics differ sharply on whether to read this as sincere praise, savage irony, or the flattery exacted by an absolute ruler.

Extremity of subject matter is matched by a studied use of hyperbole and paradox. In a parody of the conventional episode of the deeds of prowess of a great hero, Scaeva, a centurion of Caesar, single-handedly fights off a whole army, although so many spears are lodged in his body that there is no room for any others to hit him; this great display of military virtue is simultaneously an example of utter criminality (6.138–262). The paradox makes a serious point: in civil war traditional Roman virtues turn into their opposites, when the masculine strength and purpose of general and soldier are aimed to self-destruction. The Roman people's suicidal turning of their swords against their own entrails (1.2–3) is the ultimate disempowerment (on paradox see Bartsch 1997: ch. 2). The hyperbole is appropriate in an epic that tells of the greatest conceivable conflict, if we accept the premiss that this is a war in which the city that rules the world uses all of its strength against itself.

In such an epic the (anti-)hero in a sense is the whole people of Rome, not this or that individual actor. But the *Bellum Civile* has three characters, each of whom has some claim to be the 'hero'. Julius Caesar is the demonic embodiment of an unstoppable drive for power, a Turnus who succeeds in playing the role of Achilles, a Hannibal who finds no Scipio to defeat him. Pompey is the last great Republican statesman, but now a shadow of his former self, doomed to die the death of Priam rather than follow Aeneas in a path of flight that will lead to ultimate victory. In his death Pompey comes close to achieving the private perfection of a Stoic wise man impassive in the face of humiliation and suffering. The banner of the lost Republican cause is then taken up by the younger Cato, a doctrinaire Stoic whose rigid endurance amidst the grotesquely venomous serpents encountered in a march across the Libyan desert in Book 9 has been variously read as a model of Stoic sainthood or as an alienating portrait of a zealot who has passed beyond the limits of the humane.

Silius Italicus' Punica

Very different in feel, although richly indebted at points to Lucan, is the *Punica* of Silius Italicus, a seventeen-book epic on the Second Punic War against Hannibal, and like the poems of Statius and Valerius (see below) written in the Flavian period (AD 69–96). The poem is an act of literary devotion to the memory of Virgil, a textual equivalent to Silius' reverence for the tomb of Virgil, which he actually owned (Martial 11.48); but what might appear as slavish veneration need not exclude an allusive independence and skill. Silius writes a kind of sequel to the *Aeneid*, motivating the war as the fulfilment of Dido's dying curse in *Aeneid* 4. As the agent of her continuing anger against the descendants of Aeneas, Juno uses Hannibal, a figure modelled on both Virgil's Turnus and Lucan's Caesar. At the shrine of Dido in Carthage Hannibal swears by the shade of Dido to pursue the Romans, 'unrolling again the fate of Troy' (1.115). Metapoetically Silius evokes the shade of Virgil in order to rewrite the *Aeneid*.

For his historical subject Silius chooses the critical war in which Romans and Carthaginians contended for mastery over the world of the Mediterranean, consciously locating his epic between Virgil's legendary narrative of foundations and Lucan's historical narrative of the destruction of the Republic (Tipping forthcoming). The chief source is Livy's history of the Hannibalic war, but Silius restores to epic the Olympian machinery and the full range of poetic devices that Lucan had denied himself. Like the *Aeneid*, the *Punica* tells of a mortal danger to Rome, whose overcoming paves the way to future glories. The central three books (8–10) narrate the disastrous defeat of the Romans at Cannae. The epic – and Roman history – is in danger of coming to a sudden end in the twelfth book, as Hannibal comes up to the walls of Rome, only to be turned away by Jupiter and Juno, acting on Jupiter's orders. The story can thus continue beyond the numerical limit of the *Aeneid*'s twelve books, and in the last five books Scipio emerges as the central hero, re-enacting the career of Aeneas and supplying a model for the triumphs of future Roman emperors. But all is not a simple Roman jingoism: at the moment of military defeat Roman moral fibre is at its greatest:

> haec tum Roma fuit; post te cui uertere mores
> si stabat fatis, potius, Carthago, maneres.

Such was Rome then; if her character was fated to change after you, Carthage, would that you were still standing!

(Punica 10.657–8)

Thereafter luxury and ambition will weaken the nation. Through its moral strength Rome recovered from the dissension between the two consuls that led to disaster at Cannae, but there will come a time when such discord will tear the state to pieces. It was a historiographical cliché that Roman success leads inevitably to decline, but this nuanced version of a nationalist epic can also be read as Silius' response to the moral complexities of the *Aeneid*.

Statius' Thebaid *and* Achilleid

The full resources of the epic tradition are poured into Statius' mythological *Thebaid*, a twelve-book narrative of the Seven against Thebes that begins with Eteocles' refusal to share the throne of Thebes with his brother Polynices, and reaches a climax with the death of the brothers by each other's hand on the battlefield, before the arrival of the Athenian king Theseus, in the last book, to defeat the new Theban king Creon after the latter's inhumane ban on the burial of the dead of the Argive army which had supported Polynices' claim to Thebes. In the Epilogue Statius proclaims his poem's humble veneration of the *Aeneid*. This self-effacement does scant justice to the exuberant ambition of the *Thebaid*: Statius goes beyond the *Aeneid* to a renewed and intensive engagement with the Homeric epics and with Attic tragedy, Greek texts that Virgil had naturalized within Latin epic. For example the night expedition of the young heroes Hopleus and Dymas to recover the bodies of their captains in Book 10 reworks *both* the night expedition of Nisus and Euryalus in *Aeneid* 9, *and* Virgil's own model, the Doloneia in *Iliad* 10. The influence of tragedy is seen both in the use of specific models, in particular Euripides' *Phoenissae*, and in a recurrent interest in the transgression of the boundaries of personal and social identity, and of the theological boundary between Olympus and the Underworld. The baleful influence of the brothers' father Oedipus pervades the poem.

The extreme emotions driving the transgressive actions are personified in the Fury, at once tragic and Virgilian, whom Oedipus calls upon to unleash discord between his sons at the beginning, and who before the fratricidal duel sends a personified Pietas packing from the earth. Statius' use of personifications as epic characters fully integrated within the plot alongside the traditional Olympians is an important step towards the personification allegories of late antiquity and the Middle Ages, and they are handled in full awareness of the linguistic and conceptual slipperiness of the device (Feeney 1991: 364–91). At the climax the withdrawal of the Furies both marks an extreme of hyperbole, and registers an awareness that ultimate reality lies within the human psyche:

> nec iam opus est Furiis; tantum mirantur et adstant
> laudantes, hominumque dolent plus posse furores.
> fratris uterque furens cupit adfectatque cruorem
> et nescit manare suum; tandem inruit exsul,
> hortatusque manum, cui fortior ira nefasque
> iustius, alte ensem germani in corpore pressit.

There is no longer any use for the Furies; they can only marvel and applaud as spectators, and grieve that man's fury is more powerful than themselves. In his fury each lusts after his brother's blood, oblivious to the shedding of his own; at last the exile charged and urging on his right arm, its anger the stronger and its crime the juster, thrust his sword deep in his brother's body.

(*Thebaid* 11.537–42)

Statius delights in the imaginative freedom of the world of Greek myth and culture. He was born in the Greek city of Naples and his father had had a successful career in poetic contests in the Greek festivals. He himself enjoyed the patronage of the Roman court and aristocracy, and his occasional poems, the *Silvae*, are energized by the tension between the politics and society of Rome, and the cultured leisure of his Hellenized place of origin. The *Thebaid* is highly alert to the Roman meanings of its Greek mythology: the war between the Theban brothers is an image of Roman civil war; the paradox in the above passage of *nefas iustius* (a juster crime) is a direct allusion to Lucan's *Bellum Civile*, an important presence within the *Thebaid*, as also are the tragedies of the younger Seneca with their inescapable Roman resonances. The use of Greek myth to comment on Roman reality is however itself an aspect of Statius' Virgilianism.

Another tragic dimension of the *Thebaid* is the space afforded to female characters, often to provide an alternative perspective to the hyper-masculine world of epic. Statius also explores the uncertain border between the masculine and the feminine, notably in a number of adolescent characters poised between boyhood and adulthood, leaving the feminine space of the mother for the masculine world of war, for example the doomed Arcadian youth Parthenopaeus. A similar fascination with the epicene is found in the unfinished *Achilleid*, whose one-and-a-bit-book fragment narrates the boyhood of its hero Achilles and his mother Thetis' attempt to spare him from the Trojan War by dressing him up as a girl on Scyros. The completed poem would have run a wide gamut of situations and moods: the proem declares that its subject will be the *whole* story of Achilles (1.4–5), a choice of plot deliberately at odds with the Homeric and Virgilian models of a concentrated and unified segment of a larger story.

Valerius Flaccus' Argonautica

A comparable interweaving of Greek myth with the concerns of Roman history and culture is found in Valerius Flaccus' *Argonautica*, whose narrative breaks off before the return of the Argonauts to Greece in what probably would have been its last, eighth, book. Like the *Thebaid* this is a thoroughly Virgilian epic, but one that looks beyond the *Aeneid* to intensive reworking of one of Virgil's own central models, the *Argonautica* of Apollonius of Rhodes. For example, Virgil's Dido is rewritten in the figures of two of the major ancestors of Dido herself, the Apollonian Hypsipyle and Medea. The Roman slant appears most forcibly in a major Valerian addition to the traditional story: when Jason arrives at Colchis he finds that king Aeetes is at war with his brother Perses, and Aeetes demands that Jason help in this civil war before he can take the Golden Fleece. In this way Valerius also allows himself to incorporate a major episode (Bks 6 and 7) of full-scale warfare in the manner of the *Iliad* and the second half of the *Aeneid* within the traditional plot of epic quest and erotic intrigue.

Inverting the usual idea that the voyage of the Argo, the first ship, brings the end of the Golden Age and man's decline into criminality, Valerius presents the journey as the heroic advance of technology and the opening up of the world to civilization. In a Virgilian opening prophecy Jupiter foretells the heavenly destiny after their labours of the Argonauts Hercules and Castor and Pollux, and looks forward to the chain-reaction set off by the Argo's voyage that will result in the translation of empire from Asia to Greece, and from Greece to Rome. In the dedication of the epic to Vespasian and his sons, references to Roman voyages to the 'Caledonian sea' and to Titus' capture of the eastern city of Jerusalem carry obvious implications for the contemporary reader's response to Argonautic themes. But Valerius is Virgilian too in his acceptance of the moral complexities of his subject; if Jason is at the mercy of dissimulating tyrants, he himself must practise dissimulation to succeed (Hershkowitz 1998), and the poem is fully receptive to the darker sides of Medea's career, and to the forces of the irrational in general.

5   Conclusion

From its beginnings Roman epic combines a reverence for the authority of the past with an ability to absorb and comment on changing political and cultural conditions. The early twentieth century rolled back the previous century's preju-dice of a slavishly imitative Virgil, the later twentieth century saw a similar rehabilitation of the post-Virgilian epics. Ennius' *Annals* ceased to be read by the end of antiquity, and survive only in fragments; Silius Italicus and Valerius

Flaccus went underground until the Renaissance. The epics of Virgil, Ovid, Lucan and Statius all enjoyed a wide readership through the Middle Ages and Renaissance, and were imitated in numerous new poems both in Latin and the vernaculars, evidence of the capacity of epic in the Homeric and Virgilian tradition to renew itself as a mainstream vehicle for political, ideological, and religious reflection until well into the early modern period.

FURTHER READING

Boyle (1993) contains essays on the whole Roman epic tradition. There is much of value and interest on all of the epics discussed in Feeney (1991). The best general coverage of pre-Virgilian epic is Goldberg (1995); for Ennius, use the monumental edition by Skutsch (1985). **Virgil *Aeneid*.** General books: Heinze (1993) started off modern criticism; important literary approaches were developed by Pöschl (1962), Otis (1964) and Putnam (1965); of more recent works Hardie (1986) and Cairns (1989) explore the politics and ideology of the poem; Johnson (1976) and Lyne (1987) develop pessimistic, 'Harvard school' readings. On Virgil's imitation of Homer see Knauer (1964a and 1964b); of Hellenistic poets, Clausen (1987). Collections of articles: Harrison (1990), with useful Introduction on the history of Virgilian criticism; Hardie (1999). Martindale (1997) contains a wide range of essays, many with a theoretical angle. The response of post-Virgilian epic to the *Aeneid* is discussed in Hardie (1993). **Ovid *Metamorphoses*.** General books: Fränkel (1945), Otis (1970), Due (1974), Galinsky (1975) and Solodow (1988); Hinds (1987b) has been determinative for the recent study of generic play in the *Metamorphoses*; Knox (1986) explores the poem's Alexandrianism, Myers (1994) the poem's aetiological quality. Tissol (1997) rehabilitates Ovidian wit; aspects of narratology are studied by Wheeler (1999 and 2000). A range of modern approaches are represented in Hardie (2002). **Lucan *Bellum Civile*.** Ahl (1976) is still the best general introduction; Masters (1992) studies the metapoetics of the poem; Leigh (1997) and Bartsch (1997) offer different approaches to Lucan's engagement with his readers. **Statius *Thebaid*.** Vessey (1973) is a solid introduction, but predates the new wave of criticism largely kick-started by Henderson (1991; revised version in Henderson 1998a). Dominik (1994) explores the poem's relevance for contemporary Roman politics. **Valerius Flaccus *Argonautica*.** Hershkowitz (1998). **Silius Italicus *Punica*.** Ahl et al. (1986), von Albrecht (1964).

CHAPTER SEVEN

Didactic Epic

Monica Gale

1 Epic and Didactic

Didactic poetry is poetry that teaches: the name is derived from the Greek verb *didaskein* (teach), and the genre – or subgenre – is defined primarily by its subject matter. This is usually technical or philosophical in nature: the subjects of surviving didactic poems range from agriculture and hunting to astronomy and Epicurean physics. Though, as we shall see, most didactic poems have a more or less explicit moral subtext, the ostensible aim of such works is traditionally the systematic teaching of a skill or a philosophical system, rather than ethical exhortation as such.

With one significant exception (Ovid's *Ars Amatoria* and *Remedia Amoris*, discussed below), didactic poets composed their works in dactylic hexameters, the 'epic' metre of Homer, Virgil and their successors. Hence, the Greek and Roman critics – who employed this rather blunt instrument as their main criterion in distinguishing between different genres of poetry – did not in general regard didactic as a separate genre or subgenre in its own right. This fact may seem rather surprising to the modern reader, for whom subject matter is perhaps the most obvious factor to be taken into consideration when grouping works of literature into different categories. Yet the idea that narrative or heroic epic and didactic epic belong closely together is not wholly misguided: didactic poetry is intensely concerned from an early date about its own status in relation to that of heroic epic, and employs a number of techniques and stylistic features that might be regarded as characteristic of epic in general.

On the other hand, it is clear that the didactic poets did regard themselves as forming a distinctively different tradition, parallel to and slightly lower in the hierarchy of genres than that established by the *Iliad* and *Odyssey*. Both Greek and Roman didactic poets allude frequently to their predecessors, particularly to Hesiod – universally regarded as the founder of the (sub)genre – in such a way as to suggest a kind of family resemblance or line of succession from poet to poet. We can also point to passages in the poetry of Propertius, Virgil and others which imply that the subject matter and style of didactic are distinctively different from that of heroic epic. Propertius, for example, foresees a time when he will write on philosophical themes, but rejects martial poetry (3.5.23–48); this opposition between natural science and warfare corresponds precisely to the distinction between the two kinds of poetry under discussion. Virgil, similarly, opens the third book of his *Georgics* by anticipating the composition of a poem – evidently a kind of prototype of the *Aeneid* – in honour of Augustus, and contrasts this ambitious enterprise with the more lowly, agricultural subject matter of the *Georgics* itself.

It seems legitimate, then, to treat didactic as a subgenre of epic, distinct from but closely related to the main, Homeric, tradition, discussed in Chapter 6 above. Further similarities and differences that can be identified at the formal level tend to confirm this identification. In addition to their common use of the hexameter, both heroic epic and didactic tend to employ relatively elevated language; in the case of didactic, this often entails an avoidance of prosaic and/or technical terminology, notwithstanding the difficulties this may create for the poet. On the other hand, didactic poems are usually considerably smaller in scale than their narrative counterparts (Lucretius' six-book *De Rerum Natura* is a partial exception to this rule, though – at a total of 7,415 lines – it remains significantly shorter than, say, Virgil's *Aeneid* [9,896 lines]). A further important distinguishing feature is the addressee: whereas epic poems are conventionally addressed to a non-specific general audience, the didactic poets address their technical instruction or philosophical theory to a usually named individual. The resulting triangular relationship between the 'didactic speaker' (*praeceptor*), the pupil addressed within the work, and the actual or implied reader is exploited in different – often quite subtle and sophisticated – ways by different poets.

Further formal features common to the two branches of the epic tradition are the extended simile and the inclusion of conventional scenes or digressions. The latter become increasingly fixed by tradition over the course of the genre's development. In heroic epic, such scenes as the arming of the hero, the divine council or the arrival and entertainment of a guest, can be traced back to the Homeric 'type-scene' (a feature of oral narrative, which becomes fossilized with the transition from oral to written epic); in didactic, on the other hand, such set-pieces tend to evolve, as each poet responds to the work of his predecessors. The oldest and most firmly established among such conventional episodes is the Myth of Ages or history of civilization; the Hesiodic myth of decline and fall from a primitive golden age of peace and plenty to the horrors of the present iron age (*Works and Days* 106–201) is imitated more or less closely by many subsequent didactic poets (e.g. Aratus *Phaen.* 108--36, Lucretius 5.925–1457; Virgil, *Georgics* 1.125–59; Ovid, *Ars Amatoria* 2.467–80; Manilius 1.25–112), and becomes a virtual *sine qua non* of the genre. Lucretius' concluding account of the Athenian plague (*De Rerum Natura* 6.1138–286) and Virgil's catalogue of portents following the death of Julius Caesar (*Georgics* 1.466–88) set further precedents for their successors, while the brief mythological excursuses which punctuate Lucretius' poem (e.g. the sacrifice of Iphigenia, 1.84–101; Phaethon and the Flood, 5.394–415) are developed by his successors into much more elaborate inset narratives. Such set-piece digressions are an important locus for the creation of meaning, evoking as they do the succession of earlier works to which each didactic poet can be seen in his turn to respond: I shall return briefly at the end of this chapter to the issue of intertextuality, poetic succession and poetic rivalry and consider some of the ways in which the handling of recurrent themes varies from poem to poem.

2   Greek Antecedents: Hesiod to Aratus

Hesiod's *Works and Days* (*c.* 700 BC) sets the pattern in various ways for all later didactic poetry, Roman as well as Greek. As Martin West (1978: 3–30; cf. West 1997: 306–32) has eloquently argued, Hesiod is himself indebted to the wisdom literature of the near East (exemplified, for instance, by the biblical book of Proverbs), and the *Works and Days* combines advice on the practical aspects of agriculture with a strong moralizing and reflective undercurrent. The first part of the poem consists of a series of myths and parables, linked by the common themes of justice, piety and the hardship of human life; these interconnected ideas recur in the more overtly practical sections of the work. Hesiod's recipe for success rests on a combination of practical and ethical wisdom: diligence, piety and fair dealing are as important in ensuring a good harvest as is technical agricultural know-how.

Several fragmentary didactic poems (notably the philosophical works of Parmenides and Empedocles) survive from the two centuries after the probable date of composition of the *Works and Days*; but, by the later fifth century BC, didactic seems to have been effectively superseded by the development of the prose treatise, the usual vehicle by this date for the dissemination of ideas. Like other archaic forms, however, the genre underwent something of a resurgence in the hands of the scholar-poets of Hellenistic Greece. Unsurprisingly, the 'neo-didactic' poems (as we might call them) of the third and second centuries BC are rather different in character from the poetry of Hesiod. The poets of this era – Callimachus and his contemporaries – no longer regarded themselves as educators of their fellow-citizens, but wrote rather for the select few who could appreciate the rarefied elegance of their verse. Such writers evidently relished an artistic challenge, and these attitudes are reflected in the highly technical, even prosaic subjects with which they chose to deal: Aratus' *Phaenomena* (mid-3rd c. BC) concerns the stars and constellations, with a kind of appendix on weather-forecasting; while the *Theriaca* and *Alexipharmaca* of the slightly later Nicander focus on the still less promising themes of poisonous animals and plants and their antidotes. Hellenistic didactic also differs from that of Hesiod, Parmenides and Empedocles in that the poet no longer adopts the manner of the inspired sage, communicating wisdom imparted by the Muses or the gods; the 'science' of Aratus and Nicander is learning acquired in the library, and reworked in verse-form (thus, the *Phaenomena* seems to have been based directly on the prose-writings of the astronomer Eudoxus).

Nevertheless, the Hesiodic combination of the technical with the ethical still, arguably, exerts its influence; though Aratus' poem has often been characterized by scholars as 'art for art's sake', there has been a tendency in recent criticism to detect the influence of early Stoicism on the poem, and to identify a philosophical subtext underlying the account of constellations and weather signs. The relationship between addressee and implied reader is also of some importance here. It has been pointed out (Bing 1993) that the (anonymous) addressee of the poem is characterized as one who will find the information addressed to him *practically* useful, for agricultural or navigational purposes; but that, at the same time, Aratus speaks, as it were, over the head of the nominal addressee, to an implied reader for whom the subject matter of the poem is of interest for other reasons (whether literary or philosophical). The triangular relationship between *praeceptor*, addressee and reader can already be found in Hesiod (whose nominal addressee, the poet's good-for-nothing brother Perses, is something of an Aunt Sally: the actual reader is scarcely expected to identify with him, given the very negative way in which he is presented throughout). The highly sophisticated and self-conscious manner in which the relationship is exploited by Aratus is taken up in various ways by his Roman successors.

3   The Development of Latin Didactic

The first didactic poems composed in Latin seem – like many of the earliest works of Latin literature – to have been loose translations or paraphrases of works in Greek. The didactic poets of the Republic thus have a kind of a priori affinity with the Hellenistic 'metaphrasts' ('versifiers' of prose works, such as Aratus). The founding figure here – as in so many genres of Roman poetry – is Ennius, whose very fragmentary *Epicharmus* and *Hedyphagetica* almost certainly fell into this category (the latter appears to have been a translation of a kind of mock-didactic poem on gastronomy, composed by Archestratus of Gela in the mid-4th c. BC). A third work, the *Euhemerus*, was also based on a Greek source-text, the *Hiera Anagraphe* or *Sacred Scripture* (a kind of philosophical 'novel') of Euhemerus of Messene (fl. *c*. 300 BC), though it is not clear from the surviving fragments whether Ennius' version was in verse or prose. We also have more extensive fragments of Cicero's translation of the *Phaenomena*, under the title *Aratea*. Titles and odd fragments of other poems from this period are also suggestive of translations: the *Empedoclea* of Sallustius, unfavourably compared to Lucretius'

De Rerum Natura in a letter from Cicero to his brother Quintus (*ad Q.F.* 2.9.3), is likely to have borne a similar relation to Empedocles' *On Nature* to that of Cicero's own *Aratea* to the *Phaenomena*; we have a few fragments of a *Theriaca* and perhaps an *Alexipharmaca*, based on the works of Nicander, by Aemilius Macer (d. 16 BC); and the *Phaenomena* was translated no fewer than three more times, by Varro of Atax (1st c. BC), by Germanicus Caesar (15 BC–AD 19) and by Avienus (4th c. AD). Two tiny fragments assigned by the fourth-/fifth-century writer Macrobius to the *De Rerum Natura* of an otherwise unknown Egnatius (perhaps the hapless Spaniard of Catullus 37 and 39?) may also belong in this category, but are too exiguous to allow any certainty.

A decisive step away from the rarefied style of Hellenistic poetry was taken by Lucretius, whose *De Rerum Natura* (*On the Nature of the Universe, c.* 55 BC) is not a direct translation, but a work inspired and thoroughly informed by the extensive writings of the philosopher Epicurus (341–270 BC). Lucretius, moreover, adopts an impassioned manner more closely resembling the direct ethical engagement of Hesiod than the detached and playful intellectualism of Aratus. This aspect of the poem is most obviously represented in the proems (or introductions) of the six books, passages of sublime poetry that celebrate the achievements of Epicurus, represented as a quasi-divine saviour of mankind, and warn the reader against the false values and futile fears (especially of the gods and of death) that hinder the attainment of true happiness. Also important from this point of view are the concluding sections of the two central books, 3 and 4, which deal in turn with death and with romantic love: the former is depicted as simply the end of existence, and therefore literally 'nothing to us' (3.830); the latter as an intensely disturbing but easily avoidable delusion. Both finales are characterized by their powerful and stinging satire. Lucretius' treatment of love seems to respond directly to the themes and language of Hellenistic and contemporary Roman love poetry, de-romanticizing such clichés as Cupid's arrow or the flames of passion by applying them with rigorous 'scientific' accuracy to physiological processes (the 'wound' of love, e.g., is reinterpreted as the physical effect of arousal caused by the impact of beautiful images on the adolescent mind, which results in an ejection of seed analogous to the blood pouring from a wound, 4.1041–57). The finale to Book 3 includes a series of mocking sketches in which the poet mercilessly unmasks the inconsistency and illogicality of sentiments commonly associated with death and the funeral (3.870–930), as well as the justly famous personification of Nature, represented in 931–62 as delivering a scathing harangue against those who are reluctant to accept their own mortality.

Ethical engagement is not confined, however, to these so-called 'purple passages'. While the bulk of the poem deals overtly with the – often highly technical – minutiae of Epicurean physics, Lucretius arguably has one eye always on the ultimate aim of his project: to dispel the anxieties and false values which make it impossible for us to enjoy true happiness. In Epicurus' own words, 'if we had never been troubled by anxieties about natural phenomena or about death . . . we would have no need to study science' (*Principal Doctrines* 11). The ultimate goal of life, according to Epicurean doctrine, is peace of mind rather than knowledge for its own sake: the object of scientific and philosophical study is to assure ourselves that the universe can be explained in purely mechanistic terms, and that we are not – therefore – at the mercy of arbitrary gods, nor do we have to fear that our souls might be in any way afflicted after the death of our bodies. On a more positive note, happiness – which consists in the satisfaction of very simple and limited bodily needs and desires – is easy to attain, so long as we do not delude ourselves into thinking that we need something more (be it fame, political success, wealth and luxuries, or union with an idealized beloved). Lucretius' scientific subject matter (the poem deals in turn with the basic constituents of the universe – atoms and empty space; with human and animal biology; and with the origins and workings of the cosmos) is structured in such a way that these key ethical doctrines are never far below the surface.

Two themes of the poem that might be regarded as particularly important in this connection are the cycle of growth and decay and the susceptibility of all natural phenomena to rational, mechanistic explanation. The latter is particularly prominent in the second half of the poem, where Lucretius is concerned above all to exclude the idea that the gods had anything to do with the creation of the world or the rise of civilization, and to demonstrate that such 'portentous' phenomena as earthquakes and plagues are not in fact manifestations of divine anger. The cyclical pattern of atomic combination and dissolution, on the other hand, is evident in the structure of the poem as a whole, which begins, for instance, with the complementary propositions that 'nothing comes into being out of nothing' (1.150), and that 'Nature does not destroy things into nothing' (1.215–16), and is framed by images of birth – the opening address to the goddess Venus as a kind of personification of natural creativity – and death – the account of the Athenian Plague, which concludes Book 6. The cycle receives particular emphasis, however, in the first two books, and might be regarded as preparing the reader for the discussion of the mortality of the soul in Book 3: there is, Lucretius suggests, a kind of consolation in the thought that 'one thing never ceases to arise from another, and life is given to no one as a freehold, but to all on lease' (3.970–1). A similar thought underlies one of the most appealing passages in the poem, 1.250–64, where the poet memorably portrays new life arising as a result of the 'death' of raindrops when they fall to earth.

A further striking feature of Lucretius' poem that seems significant from the ideological perspective is his use of military imagery. Epicurus is represented in 1.62–79 as a conquering hero, triumphing over the monstrous personification of religion; the atoms are repeatedly described in terms that suggest warriors battling each other or forming alliances and holding assemblies; and Nature – with her 'laws' or 'treaties' (*foedera naturae*) – acts as their general (Mayer 1990; Gale 1994: 117–27). Military and political activity on the literal level are correspondingly downgraded as futile and ultimately damaging to society (notably in the proems to Books 2 and 3 and the history of civilization at the end of Book 5). The ramifications of this strategy are at once literary and ideological: Lucretius implicitly stakes a claim for the superiority of didactic (or at least of *this* didactic poem) over heroic epic, whose traditional subjects are, in Epicurean terms, negligible; at the same time, Roman values – specifically, the supreme importance traditionally accorded to military achievement – are provocatively overturned. (It is worth noting, in this context, that Lucretius' dedicatee, Memmius, was probably the Gaius Memmius mentioned in other sources as a prominent figure on the political scene of the 50s BC: the addressee acts, especially in the opening books, as a model for the *non*-Epicurean reader, a subject ripe for conversion.) Lucretius' use of personification and other kinds of imagery thus serves not only to enliven and diversify his technical subject matter, but has a significant contribution to make to the poem's ethical subtext. At the formal level, too, epic convention is appropriated and subordinated to the poet's didactic purpose. The extended epic simile, notably, becomes in Lucretius' hands a heuristic and explanatory device: scientific explanations for natural processes not readily subject to empirical observation are derived by a process of analogy from those that are (the action of the wind, for instance, is compared at length to that of a flooding river, both being in fact manifestations of similar processes at the atomic level, 1.271–97). Similarly, the repetitive, formulaic style of Homeric epic is adapted – following the model already established by Empedocles – as a means of impressing important ideas upon the reader's mind (e.g. $1.670-1 = 1.792-3 = 2.753-4 = 3.519-20$; $3.806-18 = 5.351-63$).

4   Didactic Poetry after Lucretius

Both the style of Lucretius' poem and the Epicurean world view expounded in it provide the major stimulus for the didactic poets of the next two generations. Virgil's *Georgics*, Ovid's *Ars Amatoria* and *Remedia Amoris* and the *Astronomica* of Manilius can each be seen to respond in different ways to the challenges presented by the *De Rerum Natura*. The *Georgics* (29 BC), a four-book poem on the theme of agriculture, emulates the Hellenistic didactic poets in its pursuit of stylistic elegance and refinement; like Aratus, too, Virgil draws much of his material from a series of readily identifiable source-texts (including the *Phaenomena* itself, which provides the model for the catalogue of weather-signs in *Geo.* 1.351–464). Virgil's interest in aetiology (i.e. the mythical/historical origins of various customs and practices), apparent throughout the poem, is similarly suggestive of an affiliation with Hellenistic poetry (Schechter 1975). At the same time, the emphasis laid by Virgil on the value of hard work and piety, as well as his agricultural subject matter, forge a strong link with Hesiod's *Works and Days*; and the whole poem is permeated by verbal echoes of and structural resemblances to the *De Rerum Natura* (cf. e.g. Gale 2001). The *Georgics* might be said, thus, to subsume the entire didactic tradition, with all its divergent world views and ideologies; in consequence, perhaps, of this all-embracing character, it is an exceptionally complex and multifaceted work, filled with internal tensions and even contradictions, and with striking variations in tone and mood, and has evoked a range of widely differing reactions from critics and readers in general.

It is sometimes argued that the plants and animals which constitute the overt subject matter of Virgil's poem act as metaphors (or even allegories) for relationships between human beings in society. It might, however, be more accurate to say that the farmer's relationship with his crops and livestock is *exemplary of* relationships between human beings and the natural world in general. Like Hesiod's agricultural precepts and Lucretius' exposition of Epicurean physics, Virgil's superficially practical advice serves as a vehicle for the exploration of broader concerns. Particularly important from this perspective are the emphasis laid on the need to impose order and control on unruly plant-growth and animal instinct (a theme whose ramifications on the political level become most obvious in Book 4, where Virgil deals with the 'society' of the beehive: Dahlmann 1954; Griffin 1979); on the relationship between humans and the gods; and on the farmer's vulnerability to natural disasters such as the violent storm of 1.316–34 or the animal plague of 3.478–566. Connections between different levels of meaning are suggested by the highly anthropomorphic treatment of animals and plants throughout the poem, and also by Virgil's exploitation of the didactic speaker–addressee–reader constellation (the poem is directly addressed to the statesman and literary patron Maecenas, but the advice embodied in the majority of second-person verbs and pronouns is notionally directed at a quite separate addressee, the small farmer working his own land; the didactic addressee is thus a much less straightforward model for the reader in general than is Lucretius' Memmius: Schiesaro 1993; Rutherford 1995).

The two dominant tendencies in scholarship on the poem over the last half-century are often loosely referred to as the 'optimist' and 'pessimist' schools of thought. The former reading tends to emphasize such passages as the 'praise of Italy' (2.136–76) and the idealized images of rural life in the finale to Book 2, interpreting the poem as, essentially, a celebration of the iconic figure of the tough, morally upright countryman (frequently opposed in Roman moral discourse to the decadent city-dweller). On the political level, the control exerted by the farmer over his crops and animals is analogous to Octavian's restoration of order to Rome after the chaos of the Civil Wars (the ill effects of which are lamented in the finale to Book 1). 'Pessimist' critics, on the other hand, have given greater weight to such gloomy episodes as the plague at the end of Book 3, and drawn attention to the violent treatment to which the farmer is depicted as subjecting the natural world in such passages as 2.23–5, 2.207–11 and 4.106–7. It has been suggested that Virgil seeks in this way to question or protest against the newly established Augustan autocracy (Boyle 1979). One way out of this dilemma is to argue that Virgil – unlike Hesiod or Lucretius – does not present a univocal or consistent moral 'line', but seeks rather to explore and reflect on the problems of his society without necessarily offering a decisive solution to those problems. In his treatment – particularly – of the relationship between human beings and the gods, and of 'passions' such as love and anxiety, Virgil can be seen specifically to question the assurance with which Lucretius represents these problems as easily soluble. Digressing on the destructive power of *amor* (love/sexual attraction) in 3.209–83, for example, Virgil recalls both the beginning of *De Rerum Natura* 1 (where animal sexuality is presented as unproblematic) and the end of Book 4 (where human love is condemned as a painful but easily avoided delusion). These two passages are, however, conflated in such a way that sexual attraction itself is shown to arouse violent, destructive instincts, and yet to be both natural and necessary for the creation of new life: Lucretius' easy assurance that the pitfalls of *amor* can be bypassed by anyone willing to see sense is thus opened up to searching scrutiny.

Virgil's poem ends with a lengthy mythological narrative, often described as an *epyllion* or miniature epic, which combines the stories of the bee-keeper Aristaeus and the singer and lover Orpheus. The significance of the two stories, and of the connections between them, has been much discussed by critics: though it would be misleading to suggest that any kind of consensus has been reached, most would agree that the meaning of the epyllion hinges on the contrast between the practical, active Aristaeus, who assiduously obeys the instructions of his divine mother Cyrene and succeeds in replacing the swarm of bees he has lost through disease, and the artistic, passionate Orpheus, who loses his beloved Eurydice because he fails to obey the injunction of the goddess Proserpina (Segal 1966; Conte 1986: 130–40). The fact that Orpheus is both a musician and a victim of passion sets up suggestive links with Virgil's reflections elsewhere in the poem (notably at the end of Book 2 and the opening of Book 3) on his own calling as a poet: like other writers of didactic, Virgil adopts in the *Georgics* a highly self-conscious manner, and digresses on several occasions to reflect explicitly on the nature of his didactic enterprise.

A similar concern with didactic authority is apparent in Ovid's *Ars Amatoria* and *Remedia Amoris* (*c.* AD 2), though Ovid amusingly reverses the traditional assertion that the work is divinely inspired, claiming instead to rely exclusively on personal experience (*A.A.* 1.25–30). It rapidly becomes apparent that the 'experience' in question is that of the poet's earlier persona as elegiac lover in the *Amores*: both verbal echoes of the earlier collection and references to stock situations of elegy occur frequently throughout the two poems; and Ovid's fusion of two distinct genres is further underlined by the anomalous use (noted above) of the elegiac couplet, rather than the traditional hexameter. It is the conflation of two apparently incompatible kinds of poetic discourse that is the source of much of the humour in the *Ars* and *Remedia*: love – traditionally regarded by the Romans as a relatively trivial and non-serious subject – is an amusingly incongruous theme when expounded in the elevated and sententious manner proper to the didactic *praeceptor*. Love elegy, furthermore, conventionally depicts the lover as frustrated, betrayed and ill-matched with an unworthy mistress: given that elegiac love is almost by definition unhappy and unfulfilled, the *praeceptor's* boast that he will ensure his pupil's success is a highly paradoxical one. Indeed, it might be argued that love (as an irrational passion) is something inherently unteachable; and, while the subject matter of the *Ars* consists essentially of techniques for courtship or seduction rather than love and its attendant emotions, a degree of equivocation as to whether the pupil is actually to be regarded as 'in love' with the object of his pursuit is apparent throughout, while the reader of the *Remedia* is more explicitly portrayed as attempting to 'fall out of love'.

A further source of humour – derived, in this instance, from both the elegiac and the didactic tradition – lies in the mythological excursuses that punctuate the two poems. The exemplary or illustrative myths briefly alluded to by earlier didactic poets (e.g. the myths of Phaethon and the Flood in Lucretius 5.394–415, or of Io and the gadfly in *Georgics* 3.152–3) provide the main model for such inset narratives, but there are also connections with the lists of mythological *exempla* characteristic of elegy. Ovid handles the mythical characters with engaging wit and irreverence, focusing on mundane or incongruous details (Pasiphae's jealousy of the cows who are her rivals in her perverse love for the bull of Minos; Ulysses drawing maps of the Trojan War in the sand to entertain Calypso), or tracing risqué aetiologies (the Rape of the Sabine Women as the original instance of seduction at the theatre).

It is perhaps simplistic, however, to categorize the *Ars Amatoria* and *Remedia Amoris* as parodies (either of didactic or of elegy). Not only does Ovid's highly sophisticated manipulation of generic convention rely on the *combination* of the two genres, but it is arguable that his playful manner conceals a serious (or semi-serious) 'message' (Solodow 1977a; Myerowitz 1985). It might even be argued that, *mutatis mutandis*, the two poems conform to the Hesiodic model, combining 'technical' subject matter with an 'ethical' subtext. A recurring theme in both poems is the importance of *cultus* (cultivation), artistry and moderation or self-control. Ovid boasts at the beginning of the *Ars* that he will be a teacher of love – in the obvious sense that love is the subject matter of the poem, but also in the metaphorical sense that he will be a schoolmaster set over Love, personified in the character of the notoriously flighty god Cupid. Cupid, that is, will be tamed and disciplined by the *praeceptor*: what was for Lucretius and Virgil an overwhelming and destructive passion will be treated by Ovid as a sophisticated game, with rules and predictable outcomes. Though this initial claim is to some extent undermined as the poem proceeds, we may be justified in reading this inversion of Lucretian and Virgilian themes as more than just a joke: whereas passion is for Lucretius an encumbrance of which we must strive to divest ourselves, and for Virgil a problem that threatens any attempt to impose order and control on nature or human society, Ovid implies that our emotions can and should be controlled and civilized. The ideal proclaimed by the two poems would, on this reading, be one of sophisticated artistry, in the realm of social behaviour and relations between the sexes as in the realm of poetic composition.

If the *Ars Amatoria* and *Remedia Amoris* resist straightforward categorization along generic lines, the same is true a fortiori of the *Fasti*, an apparently unfinished poem on the religious festivals of the Roman year (six books, one devoted to each month from January to June, were completed). The calendrical form of the work may remind the reader of the concluding section of Hesiod's *Works and Days*, a catalogue of days of the month regarded as propitious or unlucky for the undertaking of various activities; more overtly, Ovid looks to Aratus for the astronomical intermezzi that he employs to mark the passage of time (Gee 2000). The bulk of the poem, however, differs markedly in form and content from the norms of didactic poetry, and can be connected more closely with a specific model, the *Aetia* of Callimachus (an elegiac poem in four books, now fragmentary, which explained the origins of various rites and customs). Like Callimachus, Ovid once again employs the elegiac metre, and frequently represents himself in the role of pupil rather than teacher (the 'narrator' engages in conversation with a succession of deities, who respond to his questions about the origins of their festivals); the tone of both poets, too, is more playful than that conventionally adopted by the didactic *praeceptor*. But perhaps the most striking formal feature common to the two poems is their discontinuity: one story follows another, with no overt connection beyond (in Ovid's case) the contingencies of the calendar. Recent critics, notably Barchiesi (1997b) and Newlands (1995), have argued that this lack of continuity is highly significant: Ovid, in their view, exploits apparently fortuitous juxtapositions and mutually contradictory stories as a means of undermining the very notion of authority, which is normally so crucial to the didactic project.

The pattern of engagement with and inversion of Lucretius that we have traced both in Virgil's *Georgics* and in Ovid continues with the last major didactic poem to survive from antiquity, the *Astronomica* of Manilius. Composed probably during the early years of the first century AD, this five-book poem on astrology rivals the *De Rerum Natura* in scale, and frequently echoes Lucretian (and, to a lesser extent, Virgilian) language and imagery.

On the face of it, the *Astronomica* may appear to represent a return to the rarefied style of Hellenistic didactic. Like Aratus and Nicander, Manilius seems to relish the challenge presented by his highly technical subject matter: Books 2 and 3, in particular, display considerable ingenuity in the rendering of arithmetical calculations into verse, though the modern reader may feel some sympathy at this point with A. E. Housman's scathing dismissal of this 'facile and frivolous poet, the brightest facet of whose genius was an eminent aptitude for doing sums in verse' (quoted by Volk 2002: 196). Taken in the context of the work as a whole, however, these abstruse calculations can be seen to carry considerable ideological weight. Manilius' cosmos (like that of the similarly Stoic-influenced Aratus) is characterized, above all, by its orderly and – so to speak – legible character: it is like a hierarchically organized society, or a book open to the informed reader (5.734–45, 2.755–71). This latter image – based as it is on a recurring analogy in Lucretius' poem between the atoms and the letters of the alphabet – is a particularly striking one, which at once establishes a connection with and at the same time polemically overturns the world view presented by the earlier poet. Whereas, for Lucretius, the movements of the atoms are essentially *random*, Manilius regards the universe as the product of rational design. Human intelligence, moreover, is able to 'conquer' the secrets of the heavens and even to look into the future, precisely because the stars – which, for Manilius, control our destinies – are informed by the same divine spirit which endows us with *ratio* (rationality). This notion is embodied above all in Manilius' frequent self-representation as rising up to or journeying among the stars (Volk 2001): once again, this image is indebted to Lucretius, who depicts Epicurus in 1.62–79 as 'conquering' the heavens.

Manilius further diversifies his somewhat repetitive subject matter by means of personification and mythological allusion: the constellations are frequently referred to in terms appropriate either to the human or animal forms they are supposed to represent, or to the associated myths. The apologetic excursus in 4.430–43 (where Manilius disclaims poetic elegance in favour of unadorned Truth) can thus be regarded as highly disingenuous, and even as drawing attention to his artistry in transforming such intractable subject matter into poetry.

Closer in spirit to the scientific rationalism of Lucretius is the *Aetna*, a poem of some 650 lines traditionally attributed to (but almost certainly of later date than) Virgil. Two lengthy programmatic passages (29–93, 219–82; cf. 569–603) contrast erroneous mythological aetiologies for the volcanic activity of Mount Etna with the scientific explanation offered by the poet: both the scornful tone in which 'superstition' is rejected here and the mechanics of the account itself are reminiscent of Lucretius (who deals with volcanic activity in 6.639–702). The *Aetna*-poet seems eager to assert the importance of his own subject matter in contrast to that of earlier writers: the long digression on the pleasures of scientific enquiry and the poet's task at 219–82 condemns those (Manilius?) who 'wish to explore and wander through the kingdom of Jove' rather than investigate what lies at their feet, and the greed of farmers who strive to derive maximum profit from their land (recalling the advice of Virgil? Cf. especially 266–70 with *Georgics* 1.50–6 and 2.109–13). The condemnation of greed in this passage is picked up in the concluding 'myth' (604–46), a story of two brothers who dutifully rescued their parents from an eruption (while others rushed to save their worldly goods). Like his predecessors, then, the *Aetna*-poet seeks to combine his technical subject matter with a moral subtext, though the two levels seem less successfully meshed here than is the case in the other poems discussed.

A more subtle combination of practical and ethical elements is achieved by Grattius, a contemporary of Ovid, whose *Cynegetica* (*Hunting with Dogs*) perhaps takes its impetus from the very brief observations on the rearing of dogs in *Georgics* 3.404–13, together with Lucretius' parenthetical comments on the development of hunting by early man (5.1250–1). The *Cynegetica*, like the *Aetna*, is relatively short in compass (the text as we have it, however, is apparently incomplete), and centres on the breeding and care of hunting dogs, with briefer discussions of horses and the equipment required by the hunter. Grattius is particularly concerned with aetiology, emphasizing the role of Diana and her heroic pupil Dercylos; his insistence on the divine origin of the art may suggest self-conscious rejection of Lucretian rationalism (cf. also the ecphrasis of Vulcan's grotto in 430–66). A further striking feature of the poem is its repeated application of military imagery to the hunt (especially in 13–15, 152–8, 334–5 and 344–6; but the hunter's equipment is referred to as *arma*, 'weaponry', and the hunter's prey as *hostis*, 'the enemy', throughout). In combination with the digression on the evils of luxury in 310–25, which culminates in praise of the farmer-soldiers Camillus and Serranus (both exemplary heroes of the Republic, frequently celebrated for their austere and simple lifestyle), this recurrent system of metaphors suggests that Grattius views hunting as a morally improving pursuit, specifically because – like military service – it toughens the body and promotes disciplined self-control.

In addition to the works already discussed, a number of fragmentary poems have survived. These include the remains of a poem by Ovid on women's cosmetics (*Medicamina Faciei Femineae*), and another on fishing (*Halieutica*) attributed to the same author. More difficult to classify in generic terms are Horace's *Ars Poetica* or *Epistle to the Pisones*, and the tenth book of Columella's *De Re Rustica*. Both share many features with the didactic poems considered, but (like Ovid's *Fasti*) are in other ways anomalous. Columella's excursion into verse forms part of a much longer agricultural treatise: the remaining eleven books are all in prose. Horace's poem takes the form of a verse-essay concerned (self-reflexively) with poetic composition itself, especially the writing of drama: like Aratus and his successors, Horace seems to have drawn extensively on a prose model or models (his main source being probably the 3rd c. literary theorist Neoptolemus of Parium). On the other hand, the informal and somewhat rambling style of the *Ars Poetica* seems to align it more closely with the *Satires* and *Epistles* (particularly the 'literary' *Epistles* of Book 2) than with the clearly articulated structures characteristic of Lucretius and his successors.

5   Intertextuality and Recurrent Themes of Didactic Poetry

The preceding discussion has touched at several points on the issues of intertextuality and poetic succession. We have seen that didactic is a highly self-conscious genre (Volk 2002: 6–24), with a marked tendency to include passages of more or less explicit reflection on the poem's relationship with its predecessors and with other genres (notably narrative/heroic epic). The inclusion of set-piece digressions or conventional scenes plays an important role here, as noted above:

such scenes not only offer the poets an opportunity for literary one-upmanship, but can also be exploited as a means of orientating the poet's world view and the ideological significance of his subject matter with respect to those of his prede-cessors. From Lucretius onwards, for example, the detailed description of plagues and diseases becomes de rigueur: but whereas Lucretius' finale (whatever other functions it may have) is clearly designed to demonstrate the randomness and non-purposive nature of such natural disasters, successive accounts often reverse this emphasis while echoing Lucretian language and phrasing. The causation of the animal plague at the end of *Georgics* 3 is typically ambiguous: Virgil leaves it unclear whether this is to be seen as a divine punishment or a random event. Manilius conflates echoes of both passages with allusion to the catalogue of portents at the end of *Georgics* 1 (and the prophecy of Jupiter in the first book of the *Aeneid*); but makes it explicit that these portents *are* sent by a merciful god, as warnings of impending disaster (1.874–5). Grattius, finally, includes a lengthy discussion of canine diseases and their remedies (366–496), culminating in the strikingly un-Lucretian excursus on the healing powers of Vulcan's grotto, men-tioned above. All these passages gain in meaning if read as successive members of a series: each author can be seen to respond to (or, in many cases, react against) the work of his predecessors. Other recurrent themes such as the origins of civilization, the relationship between the poet's chosen subject matter and the military themes of epic, or theodicy and the relationship between gods and mortals could be analysed in a similar light.

FURTHER READING

For a comprehensive survey of both Greek and Roman didactic poetry, see Toohey (1996); Effe (1977) attempts to establish a typology based on differing relationships between form and content. Both are somewhat over-schematic in their methods, but remain useful if treated with due caution. The generic status of didactic poetry is discussed by Conte (1994a: 119–20), Gale (1994: 99–104), Dalzell (1996: 8–34) (whose introductory chapter is followed by studies of Lucretius, the *Georgics* and the *Ars Amatoria* and *Remedia Amoris*) and Volk (2002: 25–68); for a more theoretical treatment, see Riffaterre (1972). On the didactic speaker and addressee, see especially Schiesaro et al. (1993), which includes essays on Aratus, Lucretius, Virgil, Ovid and Manilius; see also Conte (1994a) and Sharrock (1994: 5–17). This and other characteristics of the genre are also examined by Cox (1969), Pöhlmann (1973) and Volk (2002).

On intertextual relationships between didactic poets, see especially Gale (1994: 161–74) (Lucretius and Hesiod); Hardie (1986: 158–66) (Virgil and Lucretius), Farrell (1991) and Gale (2000) (*Georgics*, Hesiod, Aratus and Lucretius); Leach

(1964) and Shulmann (1981) (Ovid and Virgil/Lucretius); Volk (2001) (Manilius and Lucretius).

Several of the points touched on above in relation to Lucretius are developed in greater detail in Gale (2001). On the cycle of growth and decay, see also Minadeo (1965) and Liebeschuetz (1968). On Lucretius' use of imagery, see especially West's lively study (1969), and – in Italian – Schiesaro (1990).

The 'optimist' and 'pessimist' readings of Virgil's *Georgics* are perhaps best represented by Otis (1964) and Ross (1987) respectively. Putnam (1979), Miles (1980) and Perkell (1989) come down somewhere between the two; see also the introduction to Thomas (1988). For a history of the debate, see now Thomas (2001). An excellent introduction to this and other aspects of the poem is provided by Hardie (1998: 28–52) (with further bibliography).

On Ovid's *Ars Amatoria* and *Remedia Amoris*, see especially the monographs by Myerowitz (1985) and Sharrock (1994); also helpful are Mack (1988: 83–98) and Holzberg (2002: 92–113). Manilius' *Astronomica* has been little studied by scholars writing in English; in addition to the relevant chapters in Toohey (1996) and especially Volk (2002), there is a useful introduction in the Loeb edition by Goold (1977).

CHAPTER EIGHT

Roman Tragedy

Elaine Fantham

1 Introduction: from Greek to Roman Tragedy

It is a misfortune and irony of the history of tragic drama at Rome that complete texts have only survived from its final phase. These comprise the eight plays of Seneca himself (to be discussed in section 4, 'Tragedy under the Empire: Seneca', below) and two Senecan imitations (*Hercules on Oeta* and the historical drama *Octavia*), none of which was, as far as we know, performed on the public stage or intended for public staging. Little is left of Roman tragedy during the first centuries (on the general background see Goldberg, Chapter 1); a few fragments of the pioneer translator-poets Livius and Naevius; some rather richer and more informative fragments of about seventy tragedies and historical dramas written between 200 and 85 BC by Ennius, Pacuvius and Accius, and virtually nothing of the highly praised Augustan tragedies of Varius and Ovid.

The history of tragedy at Rome is not a story of gradual development like that of Attic tragedy, precisely because it came after Attic tragedy had reached and passed beyond its maturity. Because Roman merchants and soldiers had seen tragic performances in the Greek theatres of Tarentum and Syracuse during the campaigns against Pyrrhus and the Carthaginians, they wanted to introduce this kind of drama at Rome, and in 240 BC Livius Andronicus, a Tarentine Greek who bore the name of his Roman patron, was commissioned to translate – or rather adapt – a tragedy and a comedy for the victory games. Andronicus must have won the interest of the magistrates who supervised the games through the earlier success of his Latin *Odyssia*, but with the change of genre to drama, he also changed from writing narrative epic in an old Italic metre (the accentual Saturnian) to copying both the dramatic form of Greek tragedy, with its alternating actors' dialogue and choral odes, and the Greek quantitative metres. These iambic and lyric metres could only be applied to the much heavier word-forms of Latin by adopting a series of adjustments and substitutions for the abundant short syllables of Greek. The Roman theatre came to develop its own metrical variety, but the basic challenge of transferring Greek versification into Latin should not be underestimated.

Besides the polished structure and versification of their texts, Greek tragedies could rely on circumstances of performance for which Rome had no equivalent. Greek cities like Syracuse and Tarentum had monumental stone theatres, but at Rome there was no permanent auditorium for some generations after Livius' first play. Instead audiences used portable seating for the *ludi scaenici* (theatrical games) of each festival, or sat on the steps leading up to a god's temple, facing a temporary wooden stage. South Italian vases show examples of this kind of stage, set up for performances in smaller communities. But we should not assume the same staging for tragedy and comedy. Comedy was traditionally set in a street in front of two or three houses, each with its entrance-doorway. Tragedy required a single more imposing façade, representing a palace, and if gods appeared *ex machina* they would speak from the roof of the stage building. Again the art of South Italy suggests that the actors used a two-storey structure, with a balcony at roof level: this is shown on a famous vase by Assteas depicting the Madness of Herakles, and in a small terracotta relief of a theatre façade from Naples (Bieber 1961: 479a, 480). In the absence of any single complete script from early Roman tragedy, Plautus' self-styled tragicomedy *Amphitryo* confirms this model, when Jupiter describes himself speaking from 'upstairs' above the stage (1131–43).

The third way in which Rome fell short of Greek standards was in the availability of trained actors. Athenian actors were citizens, performing with citizen choruses: the Greeks of southern Italy could watch skilled professionals, members of the guilds of *Dionysotechnitae*, but at Rome there was no theatrical tradition, nor were there enough theatrical performances at the games during the third and second centuries BC to provide a living. There might be twenty to forty days of theatre each year, but unless there was a formal demand for repetition, each play had only one performance. It was probably the limitations of the actors, usually slaves owned by the *dominus gregis* (master of the company), that led Roman comedy to dispense with choral interludes (these had become incidental in Greek New Comedy). However, choral odes were more integral to tragedy, and Roman producers had not only to provide a competent chorus, but to consider how to handle its presence on stage since there was no separate orchestra. In Greek tragedy choral odes and occasional monodies were accompanied by the *aulos* (an oboe-like instrument). Roman drama used varieties of *aulos* (*tibia*) to accompany both choral lyric and actors' solos, whether lyric arias or arioso speeches in long iambo-trochaic rhythms. Republican tragic poets converted much of the regular dialogue into these longer, more exuberant verses, and composed anapaestic sequences for both actors and chorus.

2   The Beginnings: Livius, Naevius and Ennius
(see also Goldberg, Chapter 1 above)

We do not know what plays Livius offered for his debut in 240 BC, mentioned above, but isolated lines are quoted by later writers from the following tragedies: *Achilles, Aegisthus, Ajax, Andromeda, Hermione, Tereus,* and perhaps *Danae* and *Equus Troianus.* There seems to have been a tradition favoured by the magistrates who paid for both scripts and performances, that dramatists did not adapt plays previously adapted, so when the same sources attribute the last two titles to Livius' younger contemporary, the Campanian Naevius, it is more likely only one of these poets adapted each tragedy. But to speak of adapting tragedies raises another question. There were plays entitled *Aegisthus, Ajax* and *Andromeda* by the great Greek dramatists, but not a *Trojan Horse.* Was this necessarily adapted from a Greek tragedy, rather than from the cyclic epics? Aristotle mentions a number of fourth-century tragedies based on the action of the *Iliad*: could not these early Roman poets, each of whom also wrote epic, have created dramas out of the action of the *Iliad* or *Odyssey* instead of unknown Greek dramas derived from Homer? The issue will return more significantly with Ennius.

Naevius was probably born a Latin speaker, and was apparently old enough to fight in the First Punic War before presenting his first play in 235 BC; he may have died as early as 204. Apart from *Danae* and perhaps *Equus Troianus* he is cited for an *Andromache, Hector Proficiscens, Hesione, Iphigenia* and *Lycurgus.* The fragments are too few to enable reconstruction of the plots. The *Andromache* is represented by two lines addressed by Andromache to her child – perhaps her son Molossus by Pyrrhus, as in Euripides' *Andromache,* since she does not address Astyanax in the *Troades.* The 'Departure of Hector' may be drawn straight from the *Iliad,* and includes the famous words to his father Priam 'I am proud to be praised by you, father, a man much praised' (Naevius fr.17 Warmington [1936–8]). Fragments of *Iphigenia* show that Naevius was adapting Euripides' *Iphigenia among the Taurians*: the *Iphigenia at Aulis* was adapted later by Ennius. Most interesting are the twenty-six lines attested from the *Lycurgus,* a play describing the opposition of the Thracian king to Dionysus and his punishment. Like Euripides' *Bacchai,* Naevius' play has a chorus of Bacchants: in an early scene the King sends his bodyguard into the wilderness to seize them: 'you who keep guard over the royal body, go instantly into the leafy places where shrubs grow naturally, not by plantation' (24–6W; cf. 27–32W). The Bacchants sing anapaests as they begin to dance, brandishing their thyrsi. As in the *Bacchai,* a messenger narrative describes their joyous and innocent play (41–2W); the decadent oriental clothing of their leader is described (39W; cf. 43): there is a confrontation between the disguised god and monarch (48–53), and a climax in which the king's palace burns down, and the god reveals himself, ordering the king to be brought before him for punishment (54–6W). Although Aeschylus wrote a tetralogy on Lycurgus, given the many structural echoes of *Bacchai*, Euripides' last play, Naevius' Greek model may well have been post-Euripidean.

Quintus Ennius, born at Rudiae in Calabria in 239 BC, spoke Greek, Latin and his native Oscan. He associated with the Roman elite from the age of 34 when he won the favour of his contemporary Cato, who brought him to Rome, and soon after of Scipio Africanus and his clan. He probably did not start to write epic or drama until after the Second Punic War (218–201), but he continued the narrative of his national chronicle *Annales* up to the events of the 170s and presented *Thyestes*, his last tragedy, shortly before his death in 169. Ennius is really the first tragedian to retain the interest of Cicero's generation, although a century later Seneca will apparently condemn Cicero for his love of the 'primitive' poet. Titles survive of twenty tragedies, mostly based on Euripides, with enough excerpts to compare some of them with the Greek models that survive. There is little evidence for *Achilles*, *Ajax*, *Alcumeo*, *Andromeda*, *Athamas* (another play with a Bacchic chorus), *Cresphontes*, *Erechtheus*, *Eumenides* (from Aeschylus), *Melanippe*, *Nemea*, *Phoenix*, *Telamo* and *Telephus* (from the notorious Euripidean play in which the King of Mysia came to Argos disguised as a beggar, and took baby Orestes hostage). Ennius obviously valued Euripides and chose plays for their pathos and melodrama. There is a basis for discussion of *Hectoris lutra* (*Hector's Ransom*), and five of the plays from Euripides – *Alexander*, *Andromache*, *Hecuba*, *Iphigenia* and *Medea* (for the last three, scholars can establish some line for line parallels) – and *Thyestes*, of unknown origin but pointing to future Roman tragedies.

Like his predecessors, Ennius favours plays with Trojan subjects, or Iliadic material. Hyginus, apparently using Roman tragedies (see Boriaud 1997) gives the title 'Hector's Ransom' (CVI) to a plot covering the second half of the *Iliad*. Whether it comes from Aeschylus or directly from Homer, it is full of fighting, even if, like Jocelyn (1967), we exclude the dialogue of Patroclus and Eurypylus (169–81W): the messenger-speech reporting the final combat achieves epic effects in dramatic metre – 'savagely they establish with steel the fortune of victory', 'see now a mist arises: it has taken away his sight: suddenly he has taken to his heels', 'brass resounds, spears are smashed, the soil sweats with blood' (193–6W).

Euripides' *Alexander* was the first play of the trilogy ending in 'Trojan Women' (*Troiades*). Recent study of evidence for the Greek play confirms that Ennius' theme is the recognition of the exposed Paris (Varro *LL* 7.82 quotes the line 'for this reason the shepherds now call Paris Alexander' as copying Euripides). Cicero quotes extensively from the prologue where Cassandra reports Hecuba's prophetic dream that she was giving birth to a firebrand that would inflame all Troy (38–40W), and from an episode in which Hecuba comments on Cassandra's raving visions, represented by excited cries in mixed lyric verse systems (68–79W). Ennius' depiction of madness in Cassandra's prophecy and Alcmeon's hallucinations (25–37W) enthused spectators and even readers. Cicero saw at least two performances of Ennius' *Andromache* and loved to quote her great solo, opening with cries of despair in the peculiarly Roman cretic (long–short–long) rhythm, and followed by anapaestic lament for the past glory of Priam's palace, its firing and his sacrilegious murder at the altar (94–100W, 101–8W) This is really opera, not drama, and these lines also inspired Virgil's memorable account of the sack of Priam's palace and his death in *Aeneid* 2 (505–59).

Where Ennius' tragedies can be compared with their Euripidean model we find some variation in the degree of freedom he allows himself. For the *Hecuba*, with its pathos and violent vengeance, each surviving fragment stays close to its equivalent, justifying Gellius' praise in *NA* 11.4 (comparing 206–8W with its original, Eur. 293–5). In one striking innovation, Hecuba bitterly perverts the formula of thanksgiving: 'Jupiter almighty, at last I give thee thanks that all has ended ill' (219W). The *Iphigenia* differs radically from Euripides in introducing a soldiers' chorus, either instead of the Greek chorus of local women, or (if the soldiers arrived with Achilles) to supplement them. Several Senecan tragedies have double choruses. If the soldiers' theme of impatience with idle waiting was in fact taken from an ode in Sophocles' lost *Iphigenia*, as some have suggested, it illustrates for tragedy the contamination of different plays (even by different playwrights) practised by Terence in comedy.

I have left *Medea* and *Thyestes* to last, because these two studies of vengeance would continue to be favorites until Roman tragedy fades from sight. Ennius seems to follow Euripides' *Medea* closely, so that we can trace small changes; such as the insertion of an etymological account of the name Argo in the nurse's opening lament, and the reversal of Euripides' order, following the building of the ship from Pelion to its launching and voyage. When Medea addresses the chorus, Ennius not only elaborates 'women of Corinth' into 'you who dwell in Corinth's lofty citadel, rich and noble ladies' but changes her apology for leaving her home to speak in public to a defence of her immigration as a foreigner – perhaps because he felt it was needed by a Roman audience. Again he gives the chorus sonorous long trochaic verses (291–3) and it seems that Ennius not only brought Aegeus from Athens (as in Euripides) to promise Medea asylum, but continued the action into her arrival there: 'Stand there and gaze upon the ancient powerful city of Athens, and see the temple of Ceres on your left' (294–5W). Aeschylus had moved Orestes from Delphi to Athens in the *Eumenides*, and Ennius may have wanted to foreshadow Medea's next crimes. It is characteristic of Roman comedy to absorb extra action or additional characters so as to make the action livelier: we shall see the same weakness in at least one Senecan tragedy.

Since the murderous anger of Medea remained a popular theme of Roman drama and poetry, it will be useful to anticipate. Little remains of Accius' *Medea* or *Argonautae*, but Medea's love for Jason was the theme of Varro of Atax's lost translation of the *Argonautica* and Ovid *Metamorphoses* 7, while his desertion and her vengeance at Corinth seems to have provided the plot of Ovid's lost tragedy as well as the context of her dramatic letter *Heroides* 12. Medea was still the symbol of wicked female vengeance two hundred years after Ennius in Seneca's

Agamemnon (119–20) and *Phaedra* (565–6), plays probably composed before his *Medea*, and finally a strange work by the amateur Hosidius Geta from the second century AD presents the tragic action in a patchwork of hexameters and half-lines from the *Aeneid*.

Thyestes, with its miracle of the sun's reversed direction, was performed at the games of the sun-god Apollo in 169 BC. The complex mythical feud of the grandsons of Tantalus, Thyestes and Atreus, was subject of many Roman traged- ies. Tantalus had tried to pollute the gods by feeding them the flesh of his child Pelops at a feast, but although this was forestalled and Pelops survived to father Thyestes and Atreus, Tantalus was punished by eternal hunger and thirst in Hades, and left the curse of his wickedness on his descendants. Thyestes stole the talismanic lamb that guaranteed royal power at Argos and seduced Atreus' wife: he was exiled but recalled by Atreus, who in a pretence of reconciliation slaughtered Thyestes' sons and fed them to their father. When Thyestes fled, he incurred further guilt in the incestuous begetting of his last child, Aegisthus, as his ghost reports in the prologue of Seneca's *Agamemnon*:

> I, Thyestes, will outdo all men in my crimes. Am I to be outdone by my brother, filled with my three sons interred within me? I have consumed the fruit of my own loins. Nor did fortune only pollute the father to this extent, but dared a greater crime than had been committed: she orders me to seek the abominable embrace of my daughter. I did not fear to swallow her words, but seized this evil. So that I as parent might run through all my children, my daughter, compelled by the fates, carries a pregnant womb worthy of her father. (*Ag.* 25–35)

Ennius seems to have included the fatal feast within his play as well as the aftermath, for someone invokes the sun (which reversed its direction in horror at the feast) and Thyestes himself speaks of the great evil that has befallen him 'this day' (351–2W). But the scene best represented is Thyestes' arrival in The- sprotia, where he identifies himself to a chorus of local citizens and urges them to shun his contagion (355–63). He has already received the oracle from Delphi foretelling the birth of an avenger from incest with his daughter, so she may give birth during the action (cf. Hyginus LXXXVIII, *Atreus*). Normally wrongs done to a father were avenged by his son(s), but since they are dead he must now beget a (grand)son by his daughter. According to Hyginus, Atreus pursued Thyestes to Thesprotia; but again we have no context for Thyestes' dreadful curse (366–70W) that Atreus should be shipwrecked and die unburied.

Although the title *Thyestes* is attributed to many Greek dramatists, there is no clue to indicate where Ennius found all or part of his dramatic action. Over two generations later Accius took up this saga in his *Atreus*, focused on the dreadful meal: Varius Rufus composed a *Thyestes* (whose action cannot be reconstructed) to celebrate Octavian's triumph in 29 BC and was richly rewarded. Seneca would be next to take up the saga.

3   Later Republican Tragedy

Ennius' nephew Pacuvius does not seem to have produced tragedies until late in life, after a career as a religious painter. Two stories link him to the last serious republican tragedian, Accius: we hear that Accius read his *Atreus* to the older playwright, who found it a bit harsh and unripe, while Accius himself reports that they both presented plays in 140 BC when Accius was 30 and Pacuvius 80. Only thirteen titles are known: *Antiope, Atalanta, Armorum iudicium, Chryses, Dou-lorestes, Hermiona, Iliona, Medus, Niptra, Pentheus, Periboea, Protesilaus,* and *Teucer.* Pacuvius favoured plays of concealed (or confused) identity, such as the *Medus,* in which Medea and her son by Aegeus each come separately to Colchis to take revenge on the tyrant Perses who has imprisoned her father Aeetes. Because he has falsely claimed to be the son of her enemy Creon, Medea plots the young man's death, and he is about to kill her when they are saved by a last-minute recognition and together overthrow Perses and release Aeetes. This kind of action, where recognition narrowly averts kin-murder was preferred by Aristotle (*Poetics* 16).

Pacuvius was relished for his rich vocabulary and scenes of pathos. In his adaptation of Euripides' *Antiope* the musician Amphion teases his brother the hunter Zethus with a riddle about the tortoiseshell from which his lyre was made (2–10W); a chorus of Bacchantes threatens to lacerate Antiope on the rocks in alliterative anapaests (18–20W), and she recognizes her rescuers as her twin sons (22W). Pacuvius wrote three plays about Orestes, but the moving scene in which Orestes and Pylades competed to die for each other (163–6W) almost certainly comes from their defiance of Thoas in *Chryses,* described by Cicero as one of Pacuvius' last and most popular plays. His *Niptra* (*The Washing,* based on Sophocles) is another play of mistaken identity: Ulysses is misled by an oracle to expect a murderous attack by his son Telemachus, but is instead attacked by his unknown son by Circe, Telegonus: in a strange scene his lyric cries of pain are reproached by the chorus (280–91W). One more play had an important influence: in the *Teucer* the hero is banished by his angry father Telamon for failing to save his half-brother Ajax. The famous messenger narrative of the storm that destroyed the Greek fleet, echoed through the storms of Roman epic (from *Aeneid* 1 to *Met.* 11 to Lucan 5) and that in Seneca's *Agamemnon.* It opens, like Seneca (*Ag.* 449–51) and the earlier *Aegisthus* of Livius (5–6W), with a calm voyage surrounded by frolicking dolphins (353–7W); then suddenly the storm breaks, piling on lightning, winds, downpours of rain and surging seas to wreck the ships, as their masts and rigging shriek and groan (358–65W).

Last of the republican professional poets, Accius enjoyed the patronage of Decimus Brutus Callaicus (Cos. 138); he also set himself up as a literary critic and was prominent in the guild of poets, dying as late as the 80s. Accius' many plays (some duplicating previous titles) impressed by their rhetoric, conveying the fiercer passions in angry retorts and alliterative abuse. Several tragedies are based on the *Iliad* (*Epinausimache* [*The Battle by the Ships*], and *Nuktegresia* [*The Night Expedition*]) or Trojan themes; for the first time there are plays on the house of Oedipus (*Antigone, Phoenissae, Epigoni* and perhaps *Thebais*) and several (*Pelopidae, Atreus, Aegisthus, Clytemnestra* and *Agamemnonidae*) on the house of Atreus. Like Pacuvius (and Ovid after him) Accius composed an *Armorum Iudicium*, with fiery rhetoric from Ajax (103–8, 109–17) while from *Philoctetes* (adapted not from the familiar Sophoclean play but from the lost play of Aeschylus) lines survive of lyric address to Ulysses (522–6W) followed by a description of the volcanic landscape of Lemnos (527–41W): Philoctetes gives a pathetic account of his wound and hardship (549–60W) and as in Pacuvius' *Niptra* Accius represents the onset of his pain (564–7W). But his chief legacy is the portrayal of the tyrant Atreus, proclaiming *oderint dum metuant* (let them hate me, so long as they fear me), complaining of Thyestes' adultery and, worse, his theft of the golden lamb (169–73W). With a self-consciousness that will be paramount in Seneca, Atreus speaks of himself in the third person: 'again Thyestes comes to provoke Atreus, again he attacks and rouses me when I am calm. I must mould a mightier mass, mixing a mightier menace, so as to crush and quench his harsh heart' (163–6). Other lines show Thyestes' futile caution, the chorus's alarm at the celestial disturbance (183–5W), preparation for the feast (187–9) and Atreus' gloating revelation to his brother: 'the father is himself his children's tomb' (190W).

The second-century tragedies were revived throughout the late republic, and it seems there were no new productions of merit until Varius' specially commissioned *Thyestes* (29 BC) and Ovid's *Medea*, which may not have been written for the stage; the tragedies of Pollio are mentioned by his Augustan contemporaries and by Tacitus, but we know of no titles or citations. Seneca's older contemporary Pomponius did write for the stage, and Quintilian (who reports their disagreement on diction and once cites Sen. *Med.* 453) includes Pomponius, but not Seneca, in his account of Roman tragedy at 10.1.97–8.

4 Tragedy under the Empire: Seneca

We do not know precisely when Seneca wrote his tragedies, or whether he intended any of them for the stage. The freedom of modern convention makes it easy to stage these dramas, but their text shows 'a lack of concern for theatrical realities' (Tarrant 1985: 14) and would challenge the conventions of ancient production. Echoes of *Hercules Furens* in Seneca's own *Pumpkinification of Claudius* written in 55, suggest this play was recent, and Fitch (1987) has argued convincingly on technical grounds that *Agamemnon, Oedipus* and *Phaedra* were early plays (between 41 and 54?), *Medea* and *Troades* close in time to *Hercules*, and *Thyestes* and the unfinished *Phoenissae* later, perhaps as late as 62. (*Hercules*

Oetaeus is usually but not universally regarded as an imitation of Seneca: on *Octavia* see the separate discussion of historical drama below.)

Seneca's tragedies are composed independent of specific Greek models, and reflect a far greater sophistication than republican drama in several respects. Firstly, in their more refined observance of Greek versification: dialogue is now limited to (regular) Greek iambic trimeters, and apart from some lyric experimentation in *Agamemnon* and *Oedipus*, lyrics too are mostly set in Greek anapaestic systems or the sapphic and asclepiadean metres of Horace's *Odes*. Secondly, Senecan tragedies are constructed with the five-act form first recommended in Horace's *Ars Poetica*, although they often flout his taboo on stage violence. A third feature is more erratic; as Tarrant (1978) has established, Seneca knows and uses dramaturgical techniques of entrance and identification, exit and asides that can be traced from late Euripides through the librettos of Roman comedy. But his use is more sporadic than would be expected if he were writing for the stage. Awkward transitions are not confined to the earlier plays but will be exemplified from them.

The unique impact of Senecan tragedy comes from the solipsism of its leading figures, who may exchange verbal retorts with their interlocutors but mostly talk only to (and about) themselves: the 'struggle' (*agon*) is not with other persons but with their own passions. (Tarrant rightly describes Medea and Atreus as 'fully under the control of the madness of *Ira*...perverted mirror images of the *Sapiens*' [1985: 24].) Their decision is always for evil, and the evil is described in process of infecting and destroying the world over and beyond humanity. Whether or not these supernatural effects were shown on stage, the words are there to represent them.

The action of the *Agamemnon* (possibly reusing the action of Livius' *Aegisthus* and Accius' *Clytemnestra*: see Tarrant 1976) was not related to Aeschylus' tragedy and should not be measured against it. The prologue of Thyestes' ghost prepares the intrigue of Aegisthus with Clytemnestra (act 2, framed by a warning ode of the Argive chorus to Fortune and a hymn to the gods of Argos), but she is dominant. Like other passionate Senecan evil-doers she confronts a subordinate (the nurse) who attempts to reason her out of wrongdoing: she seems unconvinced but starts to repudiate Aegisthus, before succumbing and without making explicit any plan of murder. The third 'act', a prolonged messenger account of the destructive storm, has poetic rather than dramatic value, and leads to the entry of the second chorus, captive Trojan women who exchange dialogue and lyric lament for Troy with Cassandra: she increases in prophetic frenzy, ending in visions of Hades. Only then does Agamemnon appear in a brief dialogue with Cassandra (781–807) whose warnings he ignores. The drama accelerates, and after the Argive chorus, unaware, sing praises of Hercules, Cassandra in an ecstatic vision reports the king's (offstage) murder as an act of vengeance committed by 'Thyestes' son and Helen's sister' (907); now the sun may again reverse its course. In this last 'act' the action disintegrates. First Strophius rides in (!) with his son

Pylades in a chariot and is persuaded by Electra to rescue the child Orestes (910–43), then Electra confronts Clytemnestra: Seneca innovates in keeping Cassandra (traditionally killed with the king) alive and on his virtual stage (cf. 951–2, 1001), while Electra defies first Clytemnestra, then Aegisthus, and he orders her dragged to a remote prison (953–1000). In a parallel movement Clytemnestra orders Cassandra dragged away, and then apparently kills her ('die, crazy woman!'), as she rejoices in their future downfall and the ruin of Argos that matches the fate of Troy (1001–12).

The *Thyestes*, probably Seneca's latest tragedy, but in mythical terms a preliminary to *Agamemnon*, shows how much the poet had gained in the power to unify his drama. Again an ancestral ghost introduces the play, as Tantalus struggles vainly to resist the Fury who is sending him to pollute Atreus' palace. This pollution is felt by the Argive chorus in the withering of nature, but by Atreus as a new passionate urge for vengeance on his brother. Browbeating his impotent courtier, he hints elaborately at his trap. The victim Thyestes enters in the third act, and despite warning his sons, is easily convinced by Atreus' offer of shared kingship to take part in the feast marking their reconciliation. In this tragedy the long messenger narrative is central and necessary, describing Atreus' vicious sacrifice and cooking of the children. In the description given by the final chorus the cosmos is already disturbed and they dread imminent annihilation (789–883). Atreus returns triumphant to describe Thyestes' solitary feast inside: then suddenly (as if revealed by an eccyclema) Thyestes is with us, singing a hideous monody, half-drunk and beset by increasing horror, whose reality is confirmed in the painfully prolonged finale. When Atreus follows dreadful hints by displaying the severed heads (1004–5), Thyestes, only partly recognizing his brother's vicious nature (*agnosco fratrem* 1007 – 'I recognize my brother'), thinks of simple murder. Once he finally understands (1034), he calls on Jupiter to annihilate the world, and strike himself as the entombment of his children. Tarrant (1985) brings out Seneca's skilful use of Augustan epic, perverting the account of Latinus' palace in *Aeneid* 7, and enhancing Tereus' violence in *Metamorphoses* 6. The undoubted dominance of Augustan epic may explain Seneca's excess of description (see Tietze-Larson 1994: 31–44, 53–62), but he also reuses epic motifs effectively in their traditional context: *Troades*, presenting the fate of Priam's family after the fall of Troy, owes as much to Virgil and Ovid as to Euripides' *Hecuba* and *Troiades* (see Fantham 1982).

Matching the return of Thyestes and Agamemnon, the returns of Theseus and of Hercules are the pivots on which *Phaedra* and *Hercules furens* turn to disaster. First is *Phaedra*, using the same myth as Sophocles' lost *Phaidra* and Euripides' two *Hippolytus* plays, but probably independent of them all. Three features distinguish it from the extant *Hippolytus*: neither Aphrodite nor Artemis appears, though each goddess is hymned in choral odes: Phaedra in person tells Hippolytus of her love, and she lives on to confirm the nurse's slander to Theseus. Instead of the moving reconciliation of father and dying son, Theseus and a distraught

Phaedra exchange reproaches over Hippolytus' mangled body before she kills herself. Scholars differ on this play: its 'hero' lacks spirituality and undermines his proper horror of incest by an excessive hatred of all women, but Phaedra's unstable condition is well motivated, her shameless behaviour triggered first by recovering consciousness in Hippolytus' arms, then by fear of his denunciation to Theseus. Hippolytus' opening song and the main choral odes are vivid evocations of love and death in the world of nature. Its failures are the overwrought messenger-speech with its polychrome monster (1035–49), Theseus' grotesque speech as he pieces the corpse together, and the careless switch of Phaedra's location from roof (1154) to ground level (1181–2).

The cult of Hercules was so important at Rome that it is strange that no Roman tragedy celebrates his deeds before *Hercules furens*. Were earlier poets deterred by the strong Italian comic tradition? Despite Ovid's treatment of Hercules' apotheosis (*Metamorphoses* 9), Seneca chose in the *Hercules furens* to show the hero as human and vulnerable: far from playing a heroic role, Hercules, like Ajax, is humiliated by his own uncontrolled heroism. But unlike the Euripidean tragedy, which sends personified Madness (Lyssa) on stage in mid-action to enrage the hero, Seneca has Juno herself pronounce the prologue denouncing Hercules' aspirations to godhead, and foreshadowing his ruin. Megara and Amphitryo have resisted the tyrant Lycus because they trust in Hercules' return, but once returned in Act 3 the hero promptly leaves them to take vengeance on Lycus, while Theseus occupies the third act with a diversionary account of Hades. I follow Fitch (1987) in seeing Hercules as driven by obsessive violence to self-destruction; disregarding his father he even prays to the gods with blood on his hands, seeking new monsters (918–40) and finding them in his own wife and children. The chorus can only mourn and pray for his return to grief and sanity. In the Athenian tragedy Theseus took on the role of saviour, but it is more Roman that the (human) father should shame his son into taking up the burden of living (1302–19), leaving only the external mechanism of purification to Theseus and his Attica.

In *Medea* Seneca achieves a terrifying unity. Not only is the whole tragedy in Medea's control, but her prologue displays that control by foreshadowing all that she intends to do (18–19, 24–5). She invokes the hellish gods of night, but only in her last act of infanticide do they take control of her. As in other Senecan tragedies the identity of the chorus is undefined, but they are clearly Corinthians hostile to Medea. Medea overwhelms first her nurse, more prudential than moral, then the mistrustful Creon, then even Jason who relaxes his hostility when she asks first to take her children with her into exile, then for at least a final interview, and his forgiveness (540–56). This is the turning point, as she prepares the poisoned robe and crown for her children to present them to the bride. At the close of a powerful ode stressing the destructive power of a wife betrayed (579–94), and the retribution incurred by other Argonauts for their transgressive journey, the chorus begs for divine vengeance to spare Jason and go no further

(596–668). In the fourth act, as in *Thyestes*, a descriptive speech (by the nurse, listing Medea's magic ingredients) prepares for the appearance of the transformed Medea, and her dazzling parade of hexameter, dialogue and lyric sequences as Hecate answers her imprecation. The children are summoned, the pace accelerates in a swift ode in short trochaic rhythms, until the nurse breathlessly announces the deaths of bride and father.

Far from fleeing, Medea voices the battle between her anger and her mother's love, clutches them in a last embrace, and surrenders to anger as the furies incurred by her brother's murder now possess her and she kills one son (958–71). According to the text she mounts to the roof dragging the other son, to display her valour to the city; Jason rushes on with armed men and must watch her second murder helpless: now he knows his wife for what she is (*coniugem agnoscis tuam?* 1019–21 – 'do you recognize your wife?') More brutally than *Thyestes*, Seneca's other play of vengeance ends in the survival of evil and denial of the gods.

If this survey gives *Oedipus* less attention, it is not because the tragedy lacks poetry or effective drama. The Senecan action differs most conspicuously from Sophocles in adding two descriptive episodes: Manto's report of the sacrifice for the blind Teiresias (represented as happening 'Here' but impossible to stage [Fitch 2000: 9–11]) and Creon's gruesome account of the necromancy of Laius (530–625) ending in Laius' denunciation of Oedipus (626–58). This substitutes for the standard third-act messenger narrative, but there is also an additional messenger who comes from the palace to describe Oedipus' self-blinding (915–79). In the final (apparently sixth) act Jocasta returns to condemn her blind son and stab her guilty womb. Defiantly Oedipus mocks Apollo because he has outdone even his fated impieties. The two extant episodes of *Phoenissae* keep the same characterization, but as Antigone struggles to keep Oedipus from suicide on Cithaeron, Jocasta still lives in the city, and tries in vain to dissuade Polynices from attack.

5   Historical Dramas

We have left aside the long but scanty tradition of *praetextae*, historical plays (so-called from the actors' wearing the *toga praetexta*, the striped toga of elite Romans), from Naevius' *Romulus* (also called *Lupus*) and *Clastidium*, to Ennius' *Sabinae*, the *Paulus* of Pacuvius, and Accius' *Decius* (also called *Aeneadae*) and *Brutus*. There are virtually no fragments or testimonia to help determine whether these plays without Greek originals were composed imitating the generic model of Greek tragedy, with alternating dialogue and choral odes, or were more pageant-like in form. *Romulus* and *Sabinae* are mythical, *Decius* and *Brutus* set in the historical past, while *Clastidium* and *Paulus* honour contemporary commanders and their victories, and were probably performed at votive or funeral games (Flower 1995). It is difficult to imagine how a play about the single combat of Marcellus or *devotio* of Decius could take a tragic form; only the excerpts from *Brutus* (Accius, *Praetextae* 17–41W) covering a scene between the last Tarquin and dream interpreters, Lucretia's 'confession' and the establishment of the consuls, show the potential for a drama of several episodes, spread across different times and even places.

The only complete historical drama is *Octavia*, a play that includes Seneca among its dramatis personae, and yet is preserved in one manuscript family with Seneca's tragedies. The action matches (and may have influenced; see Ferri, 2003) the compressed narrative of Tacitus *Annals* 14.60–5 covering Nero's divorce of Claudius' daughter Octavia to marry Poppaea, and Octavia's exile and murder. It borrows many of the conventions of tragedy, a prophetic ghost (Agrippina, in mid-action), confidential scenes between woman and nurse (first Octavia, and then Poppaea) prophetic dreams, and two separate choruses. This time around, the ineffectual subordinate who cannot dissuade the tyrant from evil action is Seneca himself, but the play's prophetic allusions include events that occurred after the deaths of both Seneca (in 65) and Nero. I do not believe the author intended to pass the play off as by Seneca, but its diction and verse technique, though more limited, more closely resembles Seneca than any other surviving text (such as Petronius' *Iliou Persis*, the 65-line 'tragic fragment' presented at *Satyrica* 89). If the play's fast-moving melodrama leaves the reader breathless, it still has fine operatic qualities: I would argue that it had an operatic afterlife in Monteverdi's celebrated *Incoronazione di Poppaea*.

Seneca was not the last Roman to compose tragedy: Tacitus introduces readers of the *Dialogus de Oratoribus* to Curiatius Maternus, a dramatic poet writing under Vespasian. Maternus' historical drama *Cato* had supposedly offended the powerful, but he is preparing a *Thyestes*, which he sees as no less suited to political implications than the *Cato* (3). A friend asks him why he neglects public oratory for plays like *Thyestes* and *Medea* (!), or worse, incurs hostility with Roman historical material like *Cato* and *Domitius*. In his reply (11) Maternus argues that his dramas were politically effective against Neronian sycophants like Vatinius, but his proclaimed tragic models (12) are not Seneca, whose dramatic works may have been unknown to Tacitus, but Ovid and Varius. A 'sophist' called Maternus was executed under Domitian; it may perhaps have been our man. Was it fear, then, that stifled tragedy? Or was the cause literary? As Seneca himself had filled his tragedies with narrative and description under the influence of Augustan epic (see Tietze-Larson 1994), did later poets choose instead to follow his nephew in composing epic? Historical epic was dangerous if it dealt with Caesar's civil war: but it was safe to write about the Hannibalic war, or Jason and Medea, or even a civil war if it was Theban. So Rome's serious poets wrote *Punica*, *Argonautica* and *Thebaid*. If as I believe, even tragedy was recited or read, not staged, why prefer it to narrative epic? The genre had lost its *raison d'être*.

FURTHER READING

On the circumstances of the early Roman theatre see Bieber (1961), Beacham (1991) and Wiseman (1994: 68–85); on the Roman scenic games see Taylor (1937) and Goldberg (1998). For ease of consultation the tragic poets are cited from Warmington (1936–8), still the most convenient edition; for more scholarly editions and modern scholarship see for Ennius, Jocelyn (1967), for Pacuvius, the edition of D'Anna (1967) and Fantham (2003), for Accius, the edition of Dangel (1995) and the essays in Faller and Manuwald (2002). On Hyginus' evidence for Roman tragedies see Boriaud (1997). On the literary aspects of Senecan tragedy, see Herington (1966 and 1982), and on its models see Tarrant (1978); for the first part of a new text and translation of all the plays see Fitch (2002 and 2004), and for commentaries see Tarrant (1976) (*Agamemnon*), Tarrant (1985) (*Thyestes*), Fitch (1987) (*Hercules furens*), Fantham (1982) (*Troades*) and Hine (2000) (*Medea*). On undramatic description in Seneca, see Tietze-Larson (1994); for the staging of Seneca, see Sutton (1986), Fitch (2000) and Fantham (2000). For general criticism and discussions of each play see Boyle (1983 and 1997). On the *fabula praetexta* see Flower (1995) and Manuwald (2001); on the *Octavia* see Herington (1961 and 1982) and Ferri (2003).

CHAPTER NINE

Comedy, Atellane Farce and Mime

Costas Panayotakis

1 Introduction

Roman comedy occupies a distinctive position in the history of Latin literature. It enables the student of Latin language and Roman civilization to glimpse how Latin (in its pre-classical stage) may have been spoken outside the educated elite, and how the victorious Romans, influenced (at the beginning of their history as a nation) by the culture of their defeated opponents, forged their literary and national identity (see Goldberg, Chapter 1 above). The inferiority complex created by Rome's contact with foreign civilizations, especially Greek culture, turned out to be extremely fruitful from a literary point of view.

The twenty-seven (more or less) complete comedies of the playwrights traditionally representing this genre, T. Maccius Plautus (whose plays span the period 206–183 BC) and P. Terentius Afer (whose comedies were performed from 166 to 160 BC), along with the works – now extant only in fragments – of numerous other equally important comic dramatists of the third and second centuries BC (e.g. Livius Andronicus, Naevius, and Caecilius Statius), were initially called *comoediae*, but by the first century BC (Varro *gramm*. 36) acquired the generic title *fabulae palliatae* (plays dressed in a Greek cloak). This conventional name both indicated that such plays had been adapted from Greek originals, and distinguished the repertory of comedies with Greek characters, costumes, and subject matter not only from the *fabulae togatae* (plays dressed in a toga), comedies normally set in Rome or Italy and composed mainly in the second century BC by Titinius and Afranius, but also from the *fabulae Atellanae*, native Italian farces named after the town Atella in Campania and given a literary form in the early first century BC by Pomponius and Novius. 'Toga-clad' comedies in general were not as popular as 'Greek-cloaked' plays, which dominated the Roman stage for at least two centuries; even these, however, were eventually upstaged by the low theatre of the 'mime' (*mimus*), a form of entertainment given literary qualities by Decimus Laberius and Publilius Syrus (mimographers of the first century BC), and associated with everyday-life scenes of an intensely sexual and satirical content with occasional outspoken comments on political issues.

The Romans, a warlike nation without a strong tradition of theatrical performances focusing on its state, were keen to point out that drama – a potential source of moral corruption – was a foreign institution, and its introduction into and gradual establishment within their society was closely related to religious needs and to the influence of foreign nations. That theatre was an imported product is the common element in the differing accounts of the origins of Roman drama offered by Vergil (*Georg.* 2.380–96), Horace (*Ep.* 2.1.139–55), Tibullus (2.1.51–8) and Livy (7.2) – all writing in the Augustan era, centuries after the events they were describing. Their theories are not reliable and were most likely formulated on the basis of the now lost treatise *De Scaenicis Originibus* of the polymath Varro (116–27 BC), which itself probably imported into Rome the views of Hellenistic scholars on the genesis of theatre in general. But Livy's complicated reconstruction of this event in seven stages deserves a closer look, not because of its detailed nature but because of the facts it omits.

The important dates in Livy's chronological scheme are 364 BC, the year in which the Romans had their first theatrical experience through a troupe of professional Etruscan dancers accompanied by a pipe-player, and 240 BC – the date at which a Greek from Tarentum in southern Italy named Livius Andronicus, having allegedly invented the element of dramatic plot, put on a tragedy and a comedy at a festival (see Goldberg, Chapter 1 above). But the events leading to this important occasion are far from clear in the exposition of Livy, who offers an imaginative hotch-potch of Etruscan dancing, pipe-playing, native Italian improvised verses, mime, pantomime and (most peculiarly) an obscure dramatic species called *satura*. It may well be the case that this 'musical medley', which apparently lacked a coherent plot but seems to have had songs with fixed lyrics and musical accompaniment, was invented by Livy as a pristine phase of Roman theatrical entertainment, out of which drama proper eventually emerged. Even more odd is the fact that, for entirely unclear reasons, Livy fails to mention the various forms of Greek drama that contributed to the shaping of Roman theatre: the Doric mythological mimes of the Sicilian Epicharmus (fifth century BC), the burlesque tragedies of the Tarentine Rhinthon (third century BC) and (most importantly) the plays of Menander, Philemon, Diphilus and other playwrights, whose works belonged to the period of Greek drama conventionally known as New Comedy, and were performed in the Greek-speaking world (including Sicily and south Italy) by wandering troupes of actors, musicians, and playwrights – the so-called 'Artists of Dionysus' – after 290 BC.

Greek New Comedy was a type of five-act drama cultivated mainly after the death of Alexander the Great (323 BC); although it shared structural and thematic motifs with earlier periods of Greek comedy, it differed from them in its chorus, which was apparently used for musical interludes only, the stock characters who were presented as members of a family rather than of the *polis*, the subject matter which was drawn usually from the lives of fictional prosperous Athenians, the rarity of long musically accompanied songs, the apparent lack of obscene jokes and explicit political comments, and the greater tendency toward realism, which was exemplified through language, costumes, masks and theatrical conventions such as the unity of time and space – itself associated with a major change in the architectural space in which these plays were performed. The audience's superior knowledge, acquired through the expository prologues uttered by omniscient deities, the emphasis on character-portrayal by means of lengthy soliloquies, and the multiple levels on which a character's words operated indicate that New Comedy was a sophisticated means of entertainment, required an attentive audience and had a moral agenda in the guise of troubled human relationships ending happily.

The successful adoption and original adaptation of Greek New Comedy by Roman theatrical culture was not an isolated artistic phenomenon, but should be seen in the wider context of the cultural influence Greece – through military conquests and merchants' travels to Greek-speaking lands – exerted on Roman civilization in terms of literature, morals and material culture, and also in relation to the current political circumstances: it was safer to deride fictional characters and social institutions rather than real individuals, and it was even more conveni-ent if these were associated with a foreign nation. On the other hand, the amusingly chaotic world of Roman adaptations of Greek New Comedy, and the subversion of the social hierarchy witnessed in them, served both as a pleasant break from the routine of everyday life and as a case of 'negative exemplarity': the plays with their happy endings featuring the punishment of the bad and the reward of the good functioned as a salutary re-enforcement of the values, order and discipline that traditional Romans so strongly advocated for their families and themselves.

We do not know the criteria according to which Roman playwrights adapted their Greek originals; this is partly due to the fact that of all the extant Latin comedies only a small part from Plautus' *Bacchides* (494–562) can be compared with its (fragmentary) original, a mere hundred lines from Menander's *Dis exapatōn*. Before this discovery (as recently as 1968), we relied on more or less plausible speculations about Plautine originality and Terentian craftsmanship and on the comparison the erudite Aulus Gellius (2.23) made in the second century AD between three passages of Caecilius' *Plocium* and the corresponding thirty-two lines of its Greek original, Menander's *Plokion*.

No doubt, each Roman playwright had his own views on adaptation, and these may have been dictated by both personal taste and the literary trends of his time, but judging from the (admittedly scanty) evidence it seems clear that the play-wrights' ideas about 'translating' a foreign text into their language (a process referred to by the verb *vertere*, 'to turn') were more akin to our concept of loose adaptation than to faithful rendering. The process of reconstructing the plot of the Greek original and signalling the intellectual originality of the Roman play-wright on the basis of pointing out Roman allusions, inconsistencies in character-portrayal and in narrative events, and other such dramatic infelicities occupied scholars for nearly a century – mainly under the influence of Eduard Fraenkel, whose strong views on Plautine innovation appeared in 1922 and dominated approaches to the study of Plautus until the 1980s, when there was a shift in Plautine scholarship to issues of performance-criticism and the evaluation of Plautus and Terence as playwrights on their own merit (see e.g. Slater 1985).

Although it is difficult to disentangle the question of the comic value of Plautine and Terentian plays from the quest for their lost Greek originals, it is equally important to remember that the original Roman audience, about whose exact social and gender identity we can only speculate, very likely went to the theatre without having studied or knowing anything about the Greek original of the play they were about to watch (they may not even have known its title). If Suetonius' testimony (cited by Donatus, *Commentum Terenti*, 3 Wessner) on the outstanding success of Terence's *Eunuchus* is reliable, the prize awarded to that play and the fact that, because of popular demand, it was performed twice on the day of its first performance, are surely not due to the admiration the Roman audience felt for the complex way in which Terence had combined in his Latin adaptation Menander's *Eunoukhos* and *Kolax*. It is, therefore, more instructive, when examining the theatricality of Roman playwrights, to do so not in its Hellenistic but in its Roman context by looking, as far as possible, at how the visual, verbal and metrical techniques of a playwright compare with the corres-ponding techniques of his (near) contemporary (comic and tragic) fellow play-wrights, rather than with the techniques of his Greek predecessors.

Perhaps the most striking change from the Greek originals concerns the disap-pearance of choral interludes from the structure of a Roman comedy (the refer-ence in Plautus' *Bacchides* 107 to a crowd of people approaching the stage, and in Plautus' *Pseudolus* 573 ff. to a pipe-player, who is invited to entertain the audience until the triumphant return of the wily slave, are isolated cases that are best viewed within the context of the particular scenes in which they are found). This alteration, which suggests that performances of Roman comedies were not interrupted by breaks, did not mean that the musical element vanished; in fact, it was in Aristophanic fashion skilfully incorporated into the heart of the play itself. Expressed in the form of long iambic and trochaic lines, anapaestic rhythms, bacchiac and cretic metres (musically accompanied rhythmical patterns known as *cantica*, 'songs', favoured by Plautus but avoided by Terence perhaps because of the unrealistic picture they created), it presented a contrast with the spoken parts of the plot, which Livy (7.2) described with the term *diverbia*. These modes of delivery, which can be usefully compared to the corresponding modes of opera (spoken lines, recitative, and arias) are – at least in Plautus and Terence – functional, not merely decorative. Their position in the play and the combinations they are allowed to form are deliberate, and they serve to stress the emotional atmosphere of a scene, delineate a character, introduce a person on stage and divide long episodes into smaller thematic units.

The comedies themselves were performed only by male actors who very likely wore masks and probably belonged to lower social classes (they were probably freedmen and slaves who belonged to the *dominus gregis*, the owner, director, producer and perhaps leading actor of the theatrical troupe). The resistance of (traditionalist) Romans to the construction of a permanent stone theatre in Rome (Pompey's theatre is dated as late as 55 BC) was surely due to both moral and political reasons. Consequently, at the time of Plautus and Terence performances were given on temporary wooden stages, perhaps resembling the buildings of Hellenistic theatres, and set on various locations in a city (the steps of a temple would have provided the ideal location for the audience to sit and watch a play). Although the context in which Roman comedies were performed may, as with Athenian drama, have been religious, there were also celebrations that included dramatic performances but were not associated with the cult of a god (Terence's *Adelphoe* was first performed at the funeral games in honour of the philhellene general L. Aemilius Paullus). Already at the end of the third century BC the Romans had the opportunity to watch plays as part of religious festivals that formed a season from spring to early winter (the *ludi Megalenses* were celebrated in April, the *ludi Apollinares* in July, the *ludi Romani* in September, and the *ludi Plebei* in November). Such occasions multiplied quickly.

Playwrights seem not to have dealt directly with the organizers of the festivals, junior officials (*aediles*) interested in securing the people's and their superiors' approval and votes by means of having only potentially successful plays staged in their sponsored celebrations, but through influential impresarios who – in spite of their social status and profession – probably moved in high circles and could pull many strings in the careers of both these officials and the young playwrights. In this respect the contribution of T. Publilius Pellio and L. Ambivius Turpio to the success of Plautus and Terence, respectively, should not be underestimated. But were the plays performed within a festival competing against each other? How many plays were performed on a single day of a festival? What were the financial arrangements between playwright, officials and impresarios? Such problems about the Roman stage have only recently come to the forefront of scholarship on Latin drama, and cannot yet be given definite answers.

2   Plautus

The life and works of Plautus – particularly the question of authorship of the (at least) 130 plays circulating in antiquity under his name – were scrutinized by the tragic playwright Accius (in his lost treatise *Didascalica*), the scholar Varro (in his non-extant works *De poetis* and *De comoediis Plautinis*), and the polymath Gellius

(3.3). Twenty-one of those plays were selected as Plautus' own compositions only because there was 'general agreement' (*consensu omnium*, Gellius 3.3.3) on this matter, and in spite of the fact that Varro himself had also selected a further group of nineteen, whose style and humour were strikingly similar to the style and humour of the chosen twenty-one. It is nowadays assumed that the twenty-one plays selected through Varro's research are identical with the Plautine comedies transmitted to us in the manuscript tradition. Some indicate explicitly that they were based on works by Diphilus, Philemon and Menander; for most of them there is no indication of the date of the first performance, and no mention of a Greek playwright or a title of the Greek original; perhaps there was none in some cases. On the whole, however, the homogeneity in language, style, metre and comic spirit has been taken as proof that these texts were composed by the same person. These are *Amphitruo, Asinaria, Aulularia, Bacchides, Captivi, Casina* (dated 186–184 BC), *Cistellaria* (after 201 BC), *Curculio, Epidicus* (before the *Bacchides*), *Menaechmi, Mercator, Miles Gloriosus* (206–204/3 BC), *Mostellaria, Persa, Poenulus, Pseudolus* (191 BC), *Rudens, Stichus* (200 BC), *Trinummus, Truculentus* and *Vidularia*.

Uncertainty also surrounds Plautus' identity. The ancient reconstructions of his life as the trials and tribulations of a slave who worked as a stage-hand, invested and lost his earnings in merchandise, and ended up writing comedies in his spare time from his occupation in a baker's mill, are unreliable and based on information deduced from the plays themselves. Moreover, Gratwick (1973: 2–3) has demonstrated that Plautus' name – transmitted in the manuscripts as *Plautus, Plauti* ('of Plautus' but also 'of Plautius'), *Macci Titi* ('of Maccus Titus' but also 'of Maccius Titus'), *Maccus,* and *T. Macci Plauti* – could be a brilliantly conceived theatrical pseudonym with aristocratic pretensions associated with native Roman low theatre and rendered as 'Dickie Clownson Tumbler, Esq.'. Whether Plautus was a member of a noble family or a freedman is now beside the point. His popularity is exemplified by the revivals of his plays even in the third century AD (if Arnobius, *Adv. Nat.* 7.33, is to be trusted) – long after the days of Cicero, who refers to Roscius' famous stage-portrayals of the Plautine pimp Ballio (*Phil.* 2.6.15; *Rosc. Com.* 7.20). His linguistic talent earned him the praise of scholars and orators such as Aelius Stilo, Varro, Cicero, and Fronto (Varro *Sat.* 399B; Cic. *Off.* 1.104; Quint. 10.1.99; Fronto *Ep. ad M. Caes. et invicem* 4.3.3), but his loosely composed plots and his exaggerated humour were censured by Horace, whose metrical, linguistic and artistic preferences were squarely placed within the tastes of the Augustan elite (*Ep.* 2.1.58; 2.1.170–6; *Ars Poet.* 270–4; cf. Jocelyn 1995).

Horace's criticisms are not entirely unfounded. Plautus neither translates faithfully nor adapts loosely his Greek originals: he transforms them into extravagant musical shows, and essentially alters both the substance of Greek New Comedy and the social hierarchy of his time. For he lowers the tone of Hellenistic comedy, uses an entirely original and exaggerated style of language (abounding in rhetorical devices, neologisms, elevated vocabulary, and colloquialisms), prefers musical 'numbers' to sections of spoken verse, has as many as six speaking actors on stage at the same time, prolongs the exchange of jokes in scenes that do not advance the plot, makes his Greek characters allude to Roman customs, stresses the motif of treachery and deceit, sacrifices subtlety of character-portrayal to amusingly violent images of verbal and visual humour, and (most importantly) gives a new dimension to the character of the cunning slave, who dominates the action and becomes not only the hero of the play but also the poet's *alter ego*. 'Plautopolis' (as Gratwick 1982 happily called it) is a topsy-turvy world, in which everything is possible, but the Saturnalian anarchy that reigns supreme in the toings and froings of the familiar characters in these plays is almost always followed by a return to social and moral order.

A discussion (even a brief one) of all the Plautine comedies is not within the scope of this chapter. It will be useful, however, to view Plautus' overwhelming comic spirit in action by looking at one passage from the *Rudens* (*The Rope*), whose main theme is the reinstatement of moral order that has been violated twice at the expense of the virtuous maiden Palaestra (having been abducted by pirates, she has lost both her parents and her freedom at the hands of a pimp). The motif of the restoration of justice appears firstly in the opening speech of the constellation Arcturus, who observes people's actions and reports their immoral deeds to Jupiter. The current victim of his tempestuous wrath is the impious pimp Labrax ('Mr Dirty-Fish'), a wonderfully evil and greedy perjurer pursued at sea by Palaestra's beloved, Plesidippus. Having survived the shipwreck caused by Arcturus, Labrax is keen to retrieve his lost property, the tragically portrayed Palaestra ('Miss Wrestling-Ground'), who seeks refuge in the temple of Venus and asks for the assistance of the priestess Ptolemocratia ('Ms Warpower'), a dreadfully old-fashioned lady representing divine solace on earth. Subsequently Palaestra is aided by another unfairly treated but eventually rewarded person, the honest old Daemones ('Mr Divine Spirits'), Palaestra's father; he represents divine justice on earth, since he punishes Labrax and enables Palaestra to identify himself as her long-lost father. Plautus, however, an expert in comic timing, knows when to change 'comic gear', as it were. Slapstick sequences follow serious scenes and create a variety of tone that attracts attention and advances the storyline. Picture the scene. Labrax is attacking both the priestess and the girl. There is a lot of noise off-stage. An actor, whose mask and costume indicate that he plays the role of a slave (his name is Trachalio, 'Trustful Neck'), runs out of the temple door and delivers the following monologue:

> Good people of Cyrene, I beseech you, place your trust in me.
> You farmer fellows, country dwellers now residing in these parts,
> Dear neighbours, help the helpless and repel a most repulsive deed!
> Be instruments of vengeance! Don't let wicked people wield more weight
> Than innocents who do not wish a notoriety from crime.

Make shameless conduct stand condemned, grant decency its just reward;
Allow our lives to be controlled by law, not low brutality.
Come running here to Venus' temple (I implore you once again),
All of you present with me now and all who hear my urgent cry.
Assist these suppliants who have placed themselves, by custom old as time,
In Venus' care and in the hands of Venus' lady overseer.
Seize injustice: wring its neck before it can affect your lives.
                                              (*Rudens* 615–26, trans. Smith 1991: 255)

The humour in this rhetorically constructed plea for help (notice the repetition of similar sounds in lines 618 *inpiorum potior sit pollentia*, 621 *vi victo vivere*, 625 *in custodelam suom commiserunt caput*; the pun *exemplum pessumum pessum date* in line 617; and the personification of injustice in line 626) is based not only on the incongruity of the situation (urgent action is needed, not lengthy speeches) but also on the legal inconsistency of the incident (a Greek character, and a slave at that, is appealing for help according to the Roman custom of *quiritatio*, public request for aid). Plautus wants to get the maximum comic effect from such a scene, and prolongs the state of the slave's alarm and his entertaining panic in his ensuing discussion with Daemones.

3   Terence

Such scenes are much rarer in the plays of Terence (d. 159 BC), whose view of drama is, on the whole, incompatible with the verbal fireworks and the slapstick visual humour of his predecessor. Allegedly a slave of Carthaginian origin and of such wit and good looks that he was manumitted, Terence was patronized by powerful philhellenes (prominent among them was P. Cornelius Scipio Aemilianus), whose aesthetic preferences he followed only partly. Six plays are attributed to him: *Andria* (performed 166 BC), *Heauton Timorumenos* (163 BC), *Eunuchus* (161 BC), *Phormio* (161 BC), *Hecyra* (having failed to impress the audience in 165 BC, it was successfully performed in 160 BC), *Adelphoe* (160 BC). *Phormio* and *Hecyra* are based on plays by Apollodorus of Carystos, the others on Menandrean comedies (with a small contribution in *Adelphoe* from Diphilus). None of his originals survives complete.

The theatrical self-awareness that forms such an indispensable part of Plautine humour is barely felt in some of Terence's plays (*Andria*, *Hecyra*), and is wholly absent in others. Terence both 'translates' his Greek originals more faithfully than Plautus and 'adapts' them in ways that may have been unacceptable to a more conservative dramatist. Using the prologue not in its traditional expository function but as a means of defending himself (an echo of the Aristophanic *parabasis*) against the charges of a theatrical nature levelled at him by a 'ma icious old poet' he never names (how accurately reported these charges are is questionable), Terence holds his audience's attention with surprise as well as irony and suspense, since he withholds information that is only gradually revealed to the audience and to the stage-characters at the same time. His characters are superbly drawn; the courageous courtesan Thais in *The Eunuch*, for instance, is a fully rounded individual with her virtues and faults: she combines feelings of genuine affection toward the young man Phaedria (feelings normally displayed by chaste maidens) with cruelty and manipulative tenderness toward the soldier Thraso (qualities usually associated with greedy and mercenary courtesans).

Terence's language, which contributes to the impression of watching individuals rather than stock characters and realistic plays rather than Saturnalian farces, earned him a place in ancient school curricula, while his sparing use of musical scenes ensured that his comedies were not endowed with Plautine artificiality. But despite the apparent seriousness of his themes (the maltreatment of women in *The Mother-in-Law*, the proper bringing up of boys in *The Brothers*, the relation between love and profit in *The Eunuch*), Terence also injects his storylines with generous doses of visual humour but does not allow it to take priority over character-portrayal. Consider the celebrated opening lines of *The Eunuch* (46–9), admired by Cicero, Horace, Persius and Quintilian: the rhetorical figures in Phaedria's speech not only function as cues for visually entertaining gestures but also reveal the agitation of the unhappy young-man-in-love. Comedy for Terence is intellectual amusement of a Menandrean quality.

4   *Fabula Togata* and *Fabula Atellana*

Side by side with the *fabula palliata* were performances of 'toga-clad' farcical plays with Italian characters enacting (probably with masks) fictional events set in Italian settings. The fragmentary remains of this *fabula togata* (about 65 titles and 600 lines) give the impression that – at least as far as repertory and dramaturgical techniques were concerned – the second-century BC playwrights Titinius, Afranius, and the first-century Atta (praised by Varro for his character-portrayal) derived their inspiration (possibly more than that) from Greek New Comedy: the cast comprises slaves, prostitutes and parasites, and the affairs of problematic families seem to have been vital to the plots; there is also evidence for the use of lyric metres. Some would like to draw a sharper line between *palliata* and *togata*: Quintilian (10.1.100) rebukes Afranius for the pederastic affairs of his plays (a motif unattested in the extant *palliata*), while Donatus (on Ter. *Eun.* 57) implies that the master–slave relationship was not subverted in the *togata*. Surely, however, there was cross-fertilization between these genres. 'Toga-clad plays' were revived in the first century AD (Afranius' *Incendium*: Suet. *Nero* 11.2) and new ones composed, though for recitation rather than for full-scale performance, in the second (Juv. 1.3).

A different impression is given by the 115 titles and the (approximately) 320 lines of the extant *fabula Atellana* in its literary form, which seems to have evolved from largely improvised Italian farces delivered originally in Oscan dialect and associated with amateur actors (Livy 7.2; Val. Max. 2.4.4). Though composed in the metres of the *palliata* and the *togata*, the plays of Pomponius, Novius, Aprissius and Mummius (largely from the early first century BC) seem to have dealt with low-life situations (many of the plays are entitled after disreputable professions) couched in equally low language. Five stock characters (Bucco, Dossennus, Maccus, Manducus and Pappus) – played by masked actors – starred in various comic situations (some indication of the plot is given by the titles *The Adopted Bucco, Pappus' Jug, The Maccus Twins, Maccus the Soldier, Maccus the Trustee, Maccus the Maiden, Pappus the Farmer, Pappus Past and Gone, Pappus' Spouse, The Two Dosenni, Maccus the Innkeeper* and *Maccus in Exile*), while parody of mythological scenes (known from tragedy) seem to have featured frequently in the repertory (*The False Agamemnon, Ariadne, The Dispute over the Armour, Atalanta, Sisyphus, Andromache* and *The Phoenician Women*). Suetonius (*Nero* 39.3) and Juvenal (3.173–6) testify to the continuation of such performances until at least the second century AD. In a letter to L. Papirius Paetus, dated July 46 BC, Cicero (*Ad fam.* 9.16.7) implies that Atellane farces were traditionally performed after tragedies (this might explain the mythological content of some of them) but also that the current trend was to have low mimes rather than *Atellanae* as 'after-pieces' (*exodia*). Even if Cicero's testimony does not reflect general theatrical practice, it clearly demonstrates how mime gradually ousted other types of comedy from the Roman stage.

5 Mime

The word *mimus* in both its meanings of an imitator, actor and a form of drama, covering any kind of theatrical spectacle that did not belong to masked tragic and comic drama, was taken over from the Greek into Latin, and a great number of mimic performers came to Italy from Greek-speaking lands. Mime, however, was not a purely Greek phenomenon transplanted to Rome. Greek mime and farcical comedy had flourished in Greek-speaking southern Italy and Sicily for centuries in the comedies of Epicharmus, the prose mimes of Sophron and the burlesque plays of Rhinthon. With this native Italian mimic tradition the mime from the East was blended, and formed what should be more correctly defined as the Graeco-Roman mime.

Surviving from the Roman mime today are 734 moral apophthegms lacking a theatrical context, some 55 titles of literary plays, and a number of fragments that amount to a total of 241 lines (of which 201 are generally considered to be genuine). These fragments, whose length varies from one word to twenty-seven lines, were composed in iambic and trochaic rhythm, and cited by polymaths

(Pliny the Elder, Fronto, Gellius and Macrobius), grammarians (Bede, Charisius, Diomedes and Priscian), and lexicographers (Nonius) not for their theatrical merits but on account of their linguistic peculiarities or literary virtues. The publication in 1912 of a Pompeian inscription added one more line to our meagre corpus. The improvisational character of the mime as a theatrical genre, its non-educational character and the low reputation mime had acquired already in antiquity are more plausible explanations for the almost complete disappearance of these scripts rather than a hypothesis that the quality of the playwrights' skills was so poor, or that the content of their plays was so obscene that it condemned the scripts to oblivion.

The literary mime, composed in verse and performed in theatres, featured political satire, literary parody, philosophical burlesque and mythological traves-ties. Nowadays it is usually contrasted with the so-called 'popular' mime (what Elaine Fantham aptly called 'the missing link in Latin literature' [1989, 153]), which may have been enacted in streets, squares, theatres and private houses, and which included in its repertory adulteries, mock-weddings, staged trials, staged shipwrecks, and false deaths presented in a grotesque fashion. These 'popular' mimes had words, but possibly not a fixed script that could have been copied by later scribes and assessed on literary grounds. But this distinction between the two strands of mimic drama was not made by ancient authors, whose testimonies betray an obvious contempt for all of these shows.

Although mime influenced, and was influenced by, widely divergent literary genres, such as love elegy, the novel and satire, it was regarded as inferior in comparison not only to other types of Roman theatre (usually tragedy, the highest type of drama) but also to the rest of Latin literature, and pejorative adjectives such as *turpis* (shameful), *vilis* (cheap) and *levis* (insignificant) often accompany the word *mimus* in our testimonies on the mime throughout the centuries. Even in the treatises of grammarians and antiquarians of late antiquity (Diomedes, *Art. Gramm. Lib. III*, p. 491 Kiel, and Evanthius, *exc. de com.* 4.1, p. 21 Wessner; 6.2, p. 26 Wessner) mime almost always comes last in the list of theatrical genres examined and defined by them. This is hardly surprising. Mime with its imitation of base things and worthless characters was pre-eminently the genre of crude realism in antiquity: a maskless actor or actress, usually a slave or freedman/freedwoman, would expose himself/herself to the public gaze, and satirize people and contemporary events with inelegant and uncouth words that belonged to the vocabulary of the lower classes. Such performances did not seem to have any moral message to convey to their audience. As far as we know, a mime aimed only at making its audience burst out laughing (J. Lydus, *Magistr.* 1.40; Choricius, *Apol. Mim.* 30). This laughter (*mimicus risus*) was characterized by Quintilian (6.3.8) as 'a light thing, aroused generally by buffoons, mimes and brainless characters'.

The head of a mimic troupe was called *archimimus* (or *archimima*, when a woman was in charge) or *magister mimariorum*. He would own the company, direct the plays, and take a part. There also seems to have been a hierarchy in the division of parts: the *archimimus* (or *archimima*) would dominate the scene. Then there are the *actores secundarum, tertiarum* and *quartarum partium*. The reference to 'secondary parts' does not necessarily imply that this role was of a lesser or inferior importance. The *actor secundarum* may have played the part of the *stupidus*, mimic fool or the parasite (see Hor. *Ep.* 1.18.10–4). There are also the characters of the flatterer, the slave, the adulterer, the jealous husband, the jealous woman, the mother-in-law and the foolish scholar. In his sixth-century description of mimic characters Choricius (*Apol. Mim.* 110) listed 'the master, the household slaves, the inn-keepers, the sausage-sellers, the cook, the host and his guests, the notaries, the lisping child, the young lover, the angry rival, and the man who attempts to soothe another man's anger'. Evidence for more mimic characters may be found in the surviving titles of mimic plays: *Augur* (*The Soothsayer*), *Piscator* (*The Fisherman*), *Hetaera* (*The Courtesan*), *Restio* (*The Rope-dealer*).

According to Cicero (*De Orat.* 2.251–2) the characteristics of mimic wit were ridicule of human figures who exhibit particular vices, emphasis on mimicry, exaggerated facial expressions (an indication that mimic actors and actresses did not wear masks) and obscenity. Cicero (*De Orat.* 2.242) too urges future orators to avoid excessive mimicry, 'for, if the imitation is exaggerated, it becomes a characteristic of mimic actors who portrayed characters, as also does obscenity'. Quintilian, faithfully following Cicero's doctrine, corroborates this notion (6.3.29).

A feature peculiar to the mimic stage, and surely linked with its low reputation, was the employment of women for female roles. Although it may be argued that the voice of a female character portrayed by an actress is 'a real woman's voice' (i.e. the expression of – and an insight into – what a woman of that time would have felt about certain issues, such as adultery, presented on the stage), such a view is seriously undermined by the surviving evidence of the mimes of Laberius and Publilius, and the non-dramatic references to lost mimic plays, according to which the female characters of Roman mime are as artificial and conventional in their behaviour as their female counterparts in the other genres of popular theatrical shows. Moreover, the reliability of the majority of our evidence on historical women who acted in mimes is affected by the image of the 'starlet' that was deliberately created and projected on to these women, who functioned as attractive, even seductive, social scapegoats to preserve the chastity of decent wives, whose role was to be faithful to their husbands and produce legitimate children. In fact, the body of the mime-actress seems to have been exploited to such an extent that it became a stereotypical source of entertainment; this was the case especially in the obscene festival traditionally associated with the mimes, the Floralia, instituted in or after 173 BC (Val. Max. 2.10.8; Ovid *F.* 5.347–50; Lact. *Div. Inst.* 1.20.10).

Perhaps the most important feature of mimic performances was their very heterogeneity. The great variety of performances called mimes in antiquity makes an exact definition of mime particularly difficult. Mimic performers are often named alongside jugglers and magicians, and mime itself seems to have derived from this circus milieu. Its opportunistic nature sought amusement in any topic, but social mores, religion, philosophy and politics were targeted in a most extraordinary style, which comprised instances of vulgar obscenity happily coexisting with sophisticated apophthegms of highly moral standards.

Most of these features may be exemplified in the extant fragments of Laberius, which are much more numerous than the sum of the other mimic fragments written in Latin. Thirty-three titles and 178 lines are currently acknowledged to be by Laberius. It is not surprising, therefore, that his plays have formed the basis for much generalization about the mimic theatre. Macrobius's account (*Sat.* 2.6.6) of Laberius's refusal to write a mime for Clodius Pulcher indicates that he had probably already gained recognition for his works by 56 BC. His outspokenness is more clearly shown in his bold attacks on Caesar. Although, in accordance with his status as a Roman knight, he had not previously acted publicly the mimes he had written, in 46 BC (allegedly at the age of 60) he was said to have been forced by Caesar to compete with Publilius as a mimic actor. Macrobius informs us that Laberius obtained his revenge by a veiled threat to the dictator; he appeared dressed as a Syrian slave (without doubt, a disparaging comment on the servile origin of his theatrical opponent), who had allegedly been flogged because he was a thief, and started shouting at the top of his voice:

> 'furthermore, Roman citizens, we lose our liberty' and after a while he [Laberius] added: 'He whom many fear should inevitably fear many.' At the sound of these words everyone in the audience turned their eyes and faces towards Caesar alone, observing that his immoderate behaviour had received a fatal blow with this caustic jibe. (*Sat.* 2.7.4–5)

In the *Necyomantia* Laberius is thought to have made another attack upon Caesar. The first fragment of this mime refers to two wives and six aediles; editors of the mimes have interpreted this as a reference to Caesar's action in early 44 BC of raising the number of aediles from four to six, and to the rumour prevalent at that time that he was also thinking of legalizing polygamy (cf. Suet. *Iul.* 52). Moreover, Laberius did not spare philosophical trends; in the *Cancer* he referred to the Pythagorean doctrine of transfiguration of souls, while in the *Compitalia* he attacked the philosophy of the Cynics. He also targeted mythology, the gods and religious ceremonies: the titles *Anna Peranna*, *Lacus Avernus* and *Necyomantia* have been taken to represent travestied mythology, which may have also been presented in the five mimes attributed to him, named after signs of the Zodiac, *Aries*, *Cancer*, *Gemelli*, *Taurus* and *Virgo*; mimes named after festivals were *Parilicii*, *Compitalia* and *Saturnalia*.

As a poet, Laberius was admired by Horace (*Sat.* 1.10.1–10) for his satirical power but also criticized by him for his crude and unpolished diction. It is true that Laberius sometimes used colloquial Latin, and perhaps neologisms, which attracted the attention of grammarians and antiquarians (Gellius devotes a whole chapter (10.17) to Laberius' literary archaisms). But the colloquial Latin that appears in Laberius preserved many old words that the literary language of the Augustan age usually rejected as coarse; moreover, Laberius was also capable of effective diction. This is evident from a fragment from *Restio* (*The Rope-dealer*):

> Democritus, the natural scientist of Abdera,
> positioned a shield to face the rising of Hyperion,
> so that, by the splendid sheen of brass, he could poke his eyes out.
> Thus by the sun's rays he destroyed his vision,
> not wishing to see the good fortune of bad citizens.
> Likewise, I want the sheen of my gleaming gold
> to deprive of light my last days,
> so that I may not see my worthless son's good fortune.

A good critique of this fragment is to be found in Gellius. Having recounted the self-blinding of Democritus, he remarks:

> It is that deed and the very manner in which he readily inflicted blindness on himself by the cleverest of tricks that the playwright Laberius, in a mime entitled *The Rope-dealer*, described in very elegant and vivid verses (*versibus quidem satis munde atque graphice factis descripsit*); however, Laberius came up with a different reason for the self-blinding and transferred it, quite neatly (*non inconcinniter*), to the story which he was then presenting on stage. (10.17.2)

Gellius praises the elegance of Laberius' writing, his power of description, and his inventiveness. Laberius was not the first or, indeed, the last to exploit the spectacular incident of Democritus' self-blinding; but the motive of the philosopher's action is different in the various accounts of his self-blinding: Lucretius (3.1039–41) attributes this decision to the onset of old age, which weakened his mental powers; Cicero (*Tusc. Disp.* 5.114 and *Fin.* 5.87) states that Democritus' eyesight was a distraction and an obstacle to the piercing vision of his soul (*aciem animi*), while Tertullian (*Apol.* 46.11), predictably enough, exploits the story to convey a message of Christian morality. Laberius' Democritus blinds himself *malis bene esse ne videret civibus* (not wishing to see the good fortune of bad citizens).

The speaker, a *dives avarus et parcus* (a rich and stingy miser) (according to Gellius), presents the blinding process in a mock-epic style, emphasized by the reference to Hyperion, and the humour of the passage is derived from bathos: contrast the elevated tone established by the reference to Democritus and the reason for the miser's introduction of it – namely, his exaggerated desire not to see the good fortune of his worthless son. Laberius' joke can thus be summarized as follows: 'A did x; his intention was y; I want to be like A in order to do x, because my intention is z'. The logic of this joke is not uncommon in earlier comedy, both Menandrean (e.g. *Dysk.* 153–9) and Plautine (e.g. *Men.* 77–95), and demonstrates that Laberius was working along the lines of a well-established comic tradition. The humour of the passage was surely emphasized by the actor's gestures, tone of voice or other comic business, which are now irretrievably lost to us. Care has also been taken, however, by the playwright not only to amuse his audience visually but also to satisfy its literary expectations. Consider, for example, the repetition of *ph* in the first line (*physicus philosophus*), and of *c* and *t* in the second (*clipeum constituit contra exortum*), or the symmetrical arrangement of the two parts of the comparison (so, *splendore aereo* in line 3 corresponds to *fulgentis splendorem pecuniae* in line 6, *bene esse* in line 5 to *in re bona esse* in line 8, and *malis civibus* in line 5 to *nequam filium* in line 8).

Attention to linguistic detail is a common feature of Laberius' works. His fragments contain 32 neologisms that can be divided into three categories: compound words composed by two or more nouns (e.g. *testitrahus*, 'bollocks-dragging'); compound words composed by a preposition and an otherwise un-attested verbal form derived from a noun (e.g. *collabellare* ,'to purse one's lips for a kiss'); and compound words composed with the aid of suffixes: these could be nouns (e.g. *adulterio* instead of *adulter*, 'adulterer'), adjectives (e.g. *bibosus*, 'boozy'), and verbs (e.g. *adulescenturire*, 'to behave like a youth'). Parallelisms with comic neologisms in Plautine drama are especially revealing here, and it is reasonable to assume that Laberius may have been deliberately attempting to revive the Plautine tradition of entertaining the audience by means of extravagant imagery and amusingly coined words.

Publilius was the great contemporary and rival of Laberius. He was born probably at Antioch and came to Italy, together with the astronomer Manilius and the grammarian Staberius Eros, as a young slave (Pliny *Nat. Hist.* 35.199). From Macrobius (*Sat.* 2.7.6–7) we hear that Publilius gained his manumission by his wit and beauty and received a careful education. According to Suetonius (*Vita Terenti* 1), Terence had exactly the same qualifications and, likewise, was educated with the support of a rich patron. The similarity of these romantic accounts undermines their reliability, and suggests that Pliny the Elder, Suetonius and Macrobius – who do not specify their sources – were drawing from a stock tradition of biographies of poor and unknown foreigners who became famous and influential public figures once they arrived in Italy, and specifically in Rome. Although it is unknown at what time he made his professional debut as writer and actor of mimes, Macrobius' words seem to imply that this occurred not long before his contest with Laberius in 46 BC. Of Publilius' mimes we have merely two titles (*Murmurco, The Mutterer* [Ribbeck's emendation for various unintelligible manuscript readings], and *Putatores, The Pruners*, a manuscript reading that has been emended to *Portatores* or, more plausibly, *Potatores, The Drinkers*) and approximately four lines. In addition, there have come down to us 734 *sententiae* (iambic aphorisms) bearing Publilius' name, although opinions vary as to how many of these are genuine.

The brilliance of Publilius' style was greatly admired in antiquity. Seneca the Elder declares that this writer excelled in this respect all the tragedians and comedians (*Contr.* 7.3.8), while Seneca the Younger explicitly compares the *dicta* of Publilius with those of tragedy (*Ep.* 8.8; *Tranqu. An.* 11.8). That Publilius, like Laberius, was not averse to commenting on current events or to parodying Roman manners can be inferred from a letter of Cicero, written on 8 April 44, a few weeks after the assassination of Caesar (*Ad Att.* 14.2.1), and from Petronius' (or, better, Trimalchio's) imitation of Publilius' style (55.6).

The contempt felt toward the mimes in antiquity may militate against a generous assessment of their literary value and artistic worth. I would like to suggest, however, that this contempt may often be explained not only as intellectual snobbery but also as a reaction to the potential (and often actual) threat mime posed to the social and political status quo. Mime was attacked on stylistic, linguistic and moral grounds, but its satirical spirit against authority remained unchallenged. The exclusion of even literary mimes from 'serious literature' was both convenient and safe, because mime with its huge popularity could become an important political weapon that might manipulate and influence people's feelings concerning public figures, social norms and prestigious institutions. Its inferior status and its 'subliterary' label meant that it could be controlled and that its subject matter was not meant to be taken very seriously. Sulla was really the first to diagnose the usefulness of mime as a strategic tool for political propaganda, and so not only maintained close (sometimes quite intimate) relationships with actors and actresses, but also is thought to have composed mimes himself. In fact, Sulla is also the first clear example of the long-standing tension that may be detected in the feelings of the Romans toward mime. For although mimes were very poorly regarded in terms of both social prestige and artistic worth, there is evidence that throughout most of the period from Sulla to Domitian educated people enjoyed watching unrefined mimic shows, and sometimes engaged in writing mimes designed for scenic performance.

A good case study of this tension is none other than Cicero. He often saw mimic plays, and even more often expressed contempt for them. This scorn frequently appears both in his speeches, in some of which references to mime are used as terms of abuse against Cicero's political opponents, and in his correspondence. Yet it is not easy to decide what weight should be attributed to Cicero's opinion as an accurate barometer of the general public's feelings toward mime, nor should his dismissive remarks be interpreted as indicative of the low literary value of the *poemata* of Laberius and Publilius. For occasionally Cicero's attitude toward mime is less unfriendly. In the *De Oratore*, especially, he acknowledges the wit of mimic actors, and in fact cites several fragments of Roman mimes older than those of Laberius. The topical nature of mimic satire seems to frighten and attract him at the same time. In 61 BC he fears that his glorious consulship may come to resemble a ridiculous mime entitled *The Bean* (*Ad Att.* 1.16.13), while in January 53 BC he jokingly expresses his anxiety for the subject matter of a new mime of Valerius (*Ad fam.* 7.11.2). In two other letters, written shortly after the assassination of Caesar, Cicero implies that the mimes reflect popular sentiments about this event, and is highly interested in them (*Ad Att.* 14.2.1; 14.3.2).

The uncouth language of the mime, its vulgar subject matter, and some of its stage-conventions (acting without masks, women playing female roles) are usually brought forth as the main reasons for the generic inferiority attached to mime within the literary hierarchy of Roman theatrical entertainment. These reasons conveniently obscured the fact that mime could cause considerable damage and exert strong influence in Roman politics, and should not be taken to mean that mimic texts did not observe high literary standards. After all, Laberius is mentioned – along with Plautus, Ennius, Accius, Caecilius, Naevius and Lucretius – in Fronto's correspondence as a poet Marcus Aurelius is urged to study in order to polish his literary style (*Ad M. Caes. et invicem* 4.3.3).

FURTHER READING

Fabula palliata. The fragments of this genre are in Ribbeck (1898) and (with a facing English translation) in Warmington (1936–8). In the absence of a commentary on them Wright (1974) remains invaluable. The best edition of Plautus is still Leo's (1895–6), although it is not as easily accessible as Lindsay's in the OCT series (1903–10). Terence's text is well presented in the Kauer et al. edition, also in the OCT series (1958). There are numerous scholarly editions and commentaries in English, German, Italian and Latin for individual Plautine and Terentian plays. Especially valuable for English readers are the editions by Gratwick (1993 and 1999), Barsby (1986 and 1999), Christenson (2000), MacCary and Willcock (1976), and Martin (1976). Complete sets of English translations of Plautus and Terence are in the Loeb Classical Library (there is now a new version of Terence by Barsby 2001) and in the series edited by Slavitt and Bovie (1974 and 1995). Terence has also been translated by Radice (1976), while select plays of Plautus were rendered by Watling (1964 and 1965), Stace (1981), Tatum (1983), Smith (1991) and Segal (1996). All the Roman comedies edited in the Aris & Phillips series (Barsby 1986; Brothers 1988 and 2000; Gratwick (1999); and Ireland 1990) include an English translation.

The most reliable general works in English on Roman drama are Duckworth (1952/1994), Beare (1964), Sandbach (1977), Hunter (1985), Beacham (1991) and Conte (1994b). Bieber (1961) is invaluable for her illustrations of all aspects of Greek and Roman theatre, while the recent collection of articles on Graeco-Roman acting in Easterling and Hall (2002) superbly illuminates neglected aspects of ancient drama. The bibliography on Plautus and Terence is vast. Comprehensive lists of secondary sources (more than 5,000 items thematically classified) have been compiled by Hughes (1975), Bubel (1992), Cupaiolo (1984 and 1992) and Hunter (1994). The best accounts in English of Plautus and Terence are Norwood (1923), Arnott (1975), Gratwick (1982 – especially recommended), Slater (1985 – a ground-breaking book on Plautine performance-criticism), Goldberg (1986), Segal (1987) and Anderson (1993). Jocelyn (1995) on Horace and Plautus is well worth reading. However, no scholar has contributed to our understanding of the Plautine comic spirit at work more than Fraenkel (1922, rev. Ital. transl. 1960). His views still dominate Plautine criticism, and should be consulted along with Handley (1968) and Bain (1979). Helpful concordances of Plautine and Terentian vocabulary have been compiled by Lodge (1904–33) and McGlynn (1963–7), while Gratwick (in all of his works) and Soubiran (1988) have cleared up many misconceptions about the function of Roman comic (especially Plautine) metre.

Fabula Atellana and *fabula togata*. Frassinetti (1967), Daviault (1981) and Guardì (1985) remain the only modern editions (with translations) of the fragments of the *Atellana* and the *togata*. Short introductions to these two literary genres in English may be found in most of the histories of Roman drama mentioned above.

Mime. The most recent edition of the fragments (with a brief commentary, an Italian translation, and a list of chronologically arranged *testimonia* on mime and pantomime) is Bonaria (1965). Ribbeck (1898) remains invaluable in presenting a stimulating text and a concise *apparatus criticus*. The most influential edition of Publilius' *sententiae* is Meyer's (1880). The few Greek mimes that survived from Roman antiquity are gathered in Page (1962) and Wiemken (1972), but the most detailed discussion of the lengthiest of these pieces is now Andreassi (2001).

English histories of Roman drama are not generous in allocating space to the study of the mimographers. Bieber (1961 – with excellent illustrations), Beare (1964), Horsfall (1982) and Beacham (1991) provide brief accounts of the Roman mime, which are more accurate and critical of the evidence than Nicoll's book on the subject (1931). But the most comprehensive treatments of this genre are in German (Gryzar 1854, Wüst 1932 and Rieks 1978 are the best; Reich 1903 is less helpful) or in Italian (Bernini 1915, Cicu 1988 and Giancotti 1967 is less reliable). Special scholarly attention has been given to the study of the mimic repertory that includes adultery, parody of philosophical doctrines and Christian rituals, and mythological travesties (Reynolds 1946; Eden 1964; Kehoe 1984; Herrmann 1985; Coleman 1990; Panayotakis 1997). Fantham (1988) rightly argues for the influence mimic subjects exerted on Rome's formal literature (elegy, lyric, the novel, Ovid's poetry) – a topic that still generates scholarly contributions: Stemplinger (1918), Wiemken (1972), McKeown (1979), Panayotakis (1995), Andreassi (1997) and Wiseman (2002). The language of the mimographers (and of the *fabula Atellana*) is discussed by Bonfante (1967) and Traglia (1972).

CHAPTER TEN

Pastoral

Stephen Heyworth

1   Vergil's *Eclogues* and the Theocritean Tradition

It is a truth now commonly accepted that Vergil was the inventor of pastoral as a genre. As with so many genres the seeds can be found in Homer (Griffin 1992), and many of the characteristic elements are found in the artfully rustic poems of the Hellenistic poet Theocritus: shepherds, while in the hills pasturing their sheep, compose songs and exchange these (and sometimes abuse) when their herding brings them into contact with one another; the beauties of the country-side are described with loving detail, and there is regular reflection on love and death. However, the Theocritean corpus includes a high proportion of poems that are urban, mythological or panegyrical, while containing no material that is distinctively bucolic; and unlike Vergil, he seems not clearly to have marked any distinction between the different parts of his oeuvre. For the other Greek poets known as *Bucolici* (Moschus, Bion and their anonymous associates) the most significant pastoral feature is when the poet takes on the guise of a cowherd. It took the genius of Vergil, perhaps under the influence of a collection of Greek Bucolic poems, to refine what had been a partial mode into a genre that has had an impact on the history of poetry quite out of proportion to the space it occupies on the library shelf (see Martindale 1997: 107–9, for a more theoretical discussion).

Vergil takes the varied constituents of Theocritus' poetry, and strains them and moulds them into a persistently pastoral form. He begins the *Eclogues* with Tityrus lying under the shade of the spreading beech tree, and ends it rising from the spot where he has woven a basket while singing and pasturing his goats until evening has come and they are full. But in between he has much comment on Roman politics and many references to mythology, including some narratives; and the two poems that have the least pastoral material (4, 6) both start with strong assertions of their generic affiliation:

> *Sicelides* Musae, paulo maiora canamus.
> non omnis *arbusta* iuuant *humilesque myricae*;
> si canimus *siluas*, *siluae* sint consule dignae.

> *Sicilian* Muses, let us sing something a little grander. Not everyone is delighted by
> *shrubs* and *humble tamarisks*; if we sing *woods*, let them be *woods* worthy of a consul.
>
> > (*Eclogues* 4.1–3)

The pastoral Muses are 'Sicilian' because Theocritus was from Syracuse. 'Woods'
(*siluae*), along with 'shade' (*umbra*; e.g.1.4, 10.75–6), is Vergil's favoured meto-
nym for the genre. These lines open a sequence that is indeed *paulo maiora*, with
4 saluting Pollio as consul at the start of a new golden era, and 5 setting a lament
for Daphnis against a celebration of his apotheosis. Poem 6 then marks the start
of the second half of the book and the supposed return to a more typically
pastoral mode of discourse:

> Prima *Syracosio* dignata est ludere uersu
> nostra neque erubuit *siluas* habitare Thalea.
> cum canerem reges et proelia, Cynthius aurem
> uellit et admonuit: '*pastorem*, *Tityre*, pinguis
> *pascere* oportet *ouis*, deductum dicere carmen.'

> My Muse first deigned to play in *Syracusan* verse, and was not ashamed to inhabit
> the *woods*. When I began to sing kings and battles, Cynthian Apollo tweaked my ear
> and advised: 'A *shepherd*, *Tityrus*, ought to *pasture his sheep* so they get fat, but utter a
> refined song.'
>
> > (*Eclogues* 6.1–5)

This functions as a commentary on the progress of the book so far: in this
account, poems 1–3 (evoked by *Tityre* at 6.4, and by the citation of the opening
verses of 2 and 3 in 5.85–6) have been playful, and set firmly in the woods.
Apollo, designated by his Callimachean name *Cynthius* at this moment where (as
in the prologue to Callimachus' *Aetia*) he guides the poet away from epic
grandeur, responds to the higher material he observes in 4–5, and urges Vergil
to complete the pastoral book in a minor key. This articulation of the ten-poem
book is reinforced by the strong closure at the end of poem 3:

> claudite iam riuos, pueri; sat prata biberunt.

> Shut off the streams now, boys; the meadows have drunk enough.
>
> > (*Eclogues* 3.111)

Also by the way poem 10 marks its final position in its first word, *Extremum*,
matching the *Prima* with which the second half of the book has begun.

The artful complexity of the book's organization is one of its great delights. As was observed already by the ancient commentator Servius, mimetic and non-mimetic poems alternate. Modern editions obscure this by adding the names *Damon* and *Alphesiboeus* in the margins at 8.17 and 64; in 7 similarly the repeated *Corydon* and *Thyrsis* are rendered unnecessary by verse 20 – but the whole poem is in the mouth of the herdsman Meliboeus. Odd-numbered poems exploit the form to present exchanges, polemical and competitive in 3 and 7, collaborative in 5. However, in poems 1 and 9, the effect of the land-confiscations is such that one of the herdsmen no longer has the heart to sing (*carmina nulla canam* ('I shall sing no songs'), says Meliboeus at 1.77; *nunc oblita mihi tot carmina* ('now I have forgotten so many songs) says Moeris at 9.53). Here we see one clear manifestation of Vergil's genius, as he uses structure and form to enhance his meaning, and exploits two different ways of using pastoral to comment on contemporary politics: on the margins the shepherds' world and the pastoral genre are upset by the intrusion of disruptive reality, of soldiers and the city; at the book's idyllic heart, in poem 5, the allegorical mode reflects on the death and deification of Julius Caesar.

Though the allegorical reading of the Fifth Eclogue has been disputed by some, it seems hard to avoid in a poem written less than a decade after 44, especially when one notices the emphasis on *astra* in the account of Daphnis' apotheosis. These stars recall the comet that appeared during Caesar's funeral games (Ramsey and Licht 1997), and was taken as a sign of the heavenly ascent of *Diuus Iulius*: cf. the snippet of song cited by Lycidas:

> Daphni, quid antiquos signorum suspicis ortus?
> ecce Dionaei processit Caesaris astrum.

> Daphnis, why do you look up at the risings of ancient constellations? Look, the star of Caesar, son of Venus, has come out.

(Eclogues 9.46–7)

Reference to Daphnis destabilizes the identification of pastoral hero with the Roman dynast at the same time as drawing attention to it. *Dionaei* helps clarify the allegorical reading of Daphnis' mother, who laments his death in the first of the pair of songs in poem 5. In the Theocritean model for the dying Daphnis (*Idyll* 1), it is Aphrodite who brings about the death; Vergil creates a delightful effect by conjuring up the same goddess as a mourner for his allegorized Daphnis.

Political panegyric is an appropriate constituent of a book that recreates the Theocritean mode; so is the prophecy that we find in 4, which uses the imminent birth of a child to look ahead to the future Golden Age he will enjoy, and thus caps *Idyll* 16, which merely foresees a victory for Hieron of Syracuse over the Carthaginians. Though we may find poetic allegory in *Idyll* 7 and read as Ptolemy the Zeus to whose attention Simichidas' poems have come, yet Theocritus never seems to use the figure of the herdsman as an image of the ruler: that is a Vergilian development, and one he maintains into the epic *Aeneid*, where Aeneas is repeat-edly figured as *pastor* (2.308; 4.71; 12.587). Another distinctive feature is the way he increases the solemn force of his prophecy (and simultaneously hedges his bets) by leaving open the identity of the child in 4. The dating of the poem to the consulship of Pollio associates it with the Treaty of Brundisium and the marriage between Antony and Octavia that sealed the agreement between the dynasts. The Herculean language of 4.17 (*pacatumque reget patriis uirtutibus orbem* [he will rule the world tamed by his father's *or* ancestors' *or* country's valour]: see Clausen 1994: 122), and the reference to the place of Jove in the child's ancestry (49) confirm the reading of the baby as the expected offspring of Antony, descendant of Anton, son of Hercules. But nothing is said that prevents the identification of the boy with any male Roman citizen born in the consulship of Pollio. The *iuuenis deus* in 1 and the tragedy-writing general of 8.6–13 are likewise unnamed. Indeed nowhere in the whole book do we meet the names either of Antony or of Octavian (the *deus* in 1; and the patron addressed in 8 [see Clausen 1994; others think Pollio]).

Emulation of Theocritus at points turns to competition, especially (and appro-priately) in the amoebaean (i.e. responsive and competitive) pair 3 and 7. Poem 3 responds to the wonderful cup offered as a reward for Thyrsis' song in *Idyll* 1, which has pictures of a woman and two men courting her, an old man fishing, and a boy constructing a cricket-cage while two foxes find food in the vineyard he is supposed to be watching (this vignette famously symbolizes the whole genre). Theocritus' passage has rightly been seen as a masterpiece of realism (Zanker 1987: 79–81), the vividness of the description delightfully at odds with the verbal interpretation and the implausibility of such detailed artistry on a herdsman's wooden cup. Rather than describe pictures at similar length, Vergil moves the realism to the context, in imitation of the non-Theocritean Eighth Idyll, and he keeps capping his models. In *Idyll* 8, Menalcas is unwilling to stake one of the flock, because his parents count them every evening; Vergil's Menalcas has a father, and a stepmother, a far more threatening figure, at least in literature, and they *both* count the flock *twice* a day, and one of them the kids too. He offers not a cup, but cups (*pocula . . . fagina*, the beechwood echoing the *fagus* of 1.1, and thus making the cups symbolic of the *Eclogues*). The realism lies not in the carvings, for the cups improbably contain images of the Alexandrian astronomer Conon – and another whose name realistically escapes the speaker's memory (though Vergil encourages us to remember Aratus, the Hellenistic poet of the heavens, whose name is found anagramatized in *curuus arator* [bending plough-man] in the lines that describe his work: Fisher 1982; Springer 1983–4). And then Damoetas caps Menalcas by claiming to own two more cups by the same artist. Damoetas and Menalcas are declared equal at the end of 3; *Eclogue* 7 has a victor, Corydon, the lovesick singer of Vergil's Second *Eclogue*, who overcomes Thyrsis, in Theocritus the mastersinger, whose tale of Daphnis in *Idyll* 1 has earned him the cup without any contest.

Imitation of Theocritus starts in the first five lines (*Eclogue* 1, with Meliboeus speaking, and echoing the repetitions of sounds and words that we find opening *Idyll* 1):

> Tityre, tu patulae recubans sub tegmine fagi
> siluestrem tenui Musam meditaris auena;
> nos patriae finis et dulcia linquimus arua.
> nos patriam fugimus; tu, Tityre, lentus in umbra
> formosam resonare doces Amaryllida siluas.

Tityrus, you lie under the cover of the spreading beech-tree and practise the woodland Muse on your slender pipe; we are leaving the borders of our homeland and the sweet fields, we are going in exile from our homeland; you, Tityrus, at ease in the shade teach the woods to echo the beauties of Amaryllis (*or, perhaps,* teach the beautiful Amaryllis to make the woods resound).

(*Eclogues* 1.1–5)

The book begins with a profound contrast between the restful ease of Tityrus and the grim departure of Meliboeus. Even at the book's opening, pastoral is revealed as existing already when the woods echo the lovely name of Amaryllis, but also as abandoned, through the exile of Meliboeus. The shepherd remains for ever in the shade of the trees, but 'we' (*nos*) – the speaker, the author, the reader – know even as we catch sight of the idyllic scene that this is somewhere we cannot stay. As the poem progresses, it is Meliboeus, speaking in a spirit of nostalgia, who gives us most of the vivid description of the countryside; Tityrus, who has seemed an embodiment of pastoral ease, tells us about the city, and not the local market town, but Rome itself, where he has found the political favour that enables him to retain his land and his place in the pastoral world. For Vergil, such bliss does not come through primitive innocence; it is created by a man imitating a lost past, and depends upon his exploiting Italy's system of patronage, under which all roads lead to Rome.

This first poem is masterly in evoking the delights of the *locus amoenus* and setting up the contrast between country and town, but it brings out specific issues too: the confiscations of land to provide for the veterans of Caesar (67–72), the extraordinary extent to which Rome dominates Italy (19–25), and the way that its empire has given a reality to geographical fantasy (61–6): as a prospective Roman legionary Meliboeus can expect to see unimaginably distant places (so too Gallus at 10.64–8). There is realism also in the loss of Meliboeus' kids (12–15), and in the qualifications he admits to his celebration of Tityrus' farm (46–8; the following lines are far more lyrical):

> fortunate senex, ergo tua rura manebunt
> et tibi magna satis, quamuis lapis omnia nudus
> limosoque palus obducat pascua iunco.

Lucky old man, your land will remain yours then, and it is big enough for you too, though bare stone covers all the pasture, and marsh with mud-loving reed.

If poems 1, 4, 5 and 9 display pastoral's capacity for reflection on political issues, 2, 8 and 10 explore love, and 6 crystallizes the interest in mythology, with a summary of Silenus' wonderful song that begins with creation out of chaos (an imitation of Orpheus' enchanting song at *Argonautica* 1.496ff., done with several Lucretian touches) and passes through a miscellany of myths. Some are touched on in a brief phrase: *lapides Pyrrhae iactos* [the stones thrown by Pyrrha, 6.41] quickly evokes the whole myth of Deucalion's flood and mankind's rebirth. Others are lingered over with emotional intensity, in particular the love of Pasiphae for the bull (6.45–60). The singer consoles her in her misfortune, quotes her summoning of the nymphs to help her find the animal in the woods, and contrasts her infatuation with the madness of the Proetides. The inset adumbration of their tale imitates the kind of structure we find in Catullus 64, where the marriage of Peleus and Thetis embraces the ecphrastic narrative of Ariadne, and this evocation of neoteric style is confirmed when the commentator Servius reveals a double echo of Calvus' *Io* (*a uirgo infelix* [ah, unfortunate girl], 47, 52). The queen who wishes to play the part of a cow is contrasted explicitly with the maidens who are made to think they have become cows, and allusively with the nymph who was really changed into a heifer. Then we move to the poet's own time, with the investiture of his fellow poet Gallus by Linus and the Muses. The fragments that survive of Gallus' work (6 whole and 5 part lines) are in elegiac couplets, and Ovid treats him as the first of the sequence of four love elegists (followed by Tibullus, Propertius and Ovid himself: *Tristia* 4.10.51–4), but Vergil's narrative in verses 64–73 implies that he also worked on more elevated topics, in particular an aetiological account of the grove of Apollo at Gryneum in Asia Minor, presumably in hexameters. In poem 4 we should be struck by the boldness that allows a poet living amid civil strife to have a vision of an imminent Golden Age. So here Vergil's elevation of his friend to mythical status is an extraordinary assertion of poetic confidence; and he covertly includes himself in the scene, with the epithet *aMARO* (see Carter 2002). The song as a whole functions as a genealogy of Vergil's poetry, in which Theocritus for once plays a lesser role, and Apollonius and Lucretius, Calvus and the neoterics come to the fore.

Even love is used to reflect on the power and uses of song. The *persona* in Damon's song (8.17–60) produces a suicide note, a gift for Nysa, the girl who has betrayed him; in Alphesiboeus' response, the female voice uses her *carmina* as charms to draw Daphnis back from the city. This is the first time the city has appeared since poem 1, and it is a shocking indication that we are nearing the margins of pastoral, especially as the figure who has abandoned the countryside (even if temporarily) is Daphnis, the model herdsman of Theocritean *Idyll* 1. Movement to the city dominates 9, before Gallus returns in 10, this time in the role of the lovesick Daphnis of *Idyll* 1. The comments of Servius and elements shared with passages in the elegists confirm that the soliloquy Vergil gives him exploits Gallus' own writing: as often in elegy, we find the despair of love set against travel and war, and interest in poetic genre. Pastoral song seems to offer Gallus an alternative to elegy, but in the end he finds no truer medicine here, and admits that neither woods nor songs please amid the bitterness of love. What has seemed to announce a change of genre for Gallus comes to mark a change for Vergil himself, and he says farewell to bucolic with eight verses packed with closural images and pointers to the *Georgics* (Kennedy 1983) culminating in the final line in the concepts of home, satiety, arrival, evening and departure:

> ite domum saturae, uenit Hesperus, ite capellae.

> Go home, she-goats, now you are full, evening comes, go home.
> (*Eclogues* 10.77)

2 After the *Eclogues*

As we have seen, Vergil evokes the world of the *Eclogues* with references to the *pastor* in his later works, but the most substantial use of pastoral within another genre in the Augustan age comes in Ovid's *Metamorphoses*. In Book 1 of that poem Jupiter turns Io into a cow to evade Juno's suspicions, but is then forced to hand her over as a gift. When Juno sets the thousand-eyed Argus to watch over Io, Jupiter, acting with epic authority, sends Mercury to kill him. As the messenger god discards his cap and wings, steals some goats (a momentary appearance for the god of thieves), and turns his sleep-inducing staff into a herdsman's crook, the scene changes from epic to pastoral. Argus welcomes the piping passer-by with words that stress the generic markers (*Met.* 1.681) *aptam . . . uides pastoribus umbram* [You see the shade that suits herdsmen]. However, after Mercury's singing and piping and the tale of Pan and Syrinx have induced sleep, the idyllic locale is spattered with the cowherd's blood, and we return to epic. The Cyclops episode in Book 13 develops another monstrous figure of pastoral, in this case one already naturalized within the genre by Theocritus, *Idylls* 6 and 13 (see Farrell 1992). Ovid increases the comedy: the giant uses a rake for a comb (765), and has a pipe with a hundred reeds (784). Polyphemus' love-lorn soliloquy opens by describing Galatea with typically pastoral comparisons (*Met.* 13.789–807; cf. Theoc. 11.20–1; Verg. *Ecl.* 7.37–8, 41–2): she is brighter than ice, sweeter than a ripe grape, softer than swan's down, but also more savage than unbroken steers, harder than an ancient oak, less trustworthy than the waves, and so on for thirteen positive and thirteen pejorative comparatives. The giant is as uncontrolled in his use of pastoral language as he is in his epic anger: when at

13.874 he spots Galatea listening, with his rival Acis in her arms, the episode is again brought to a swift end by a sudden shift from pastoral song to murderous violence.

The formal genre surfaces again in the Neronian age, with seven artful, but neglected, poems attributed to Calpurnius Siculus, of whom we know nothing else. The poet shows himself to be an alert reader of Vergil, imitating detailed passages, structural patterns, and the use of rustic figures to reflect on political events. He also follows Vergil in his delight in exploring the boundaries of the genre. Poems 1, 4 and 7 are political in substance, retailing Faunus' prophecy of the peaceful reign of a new emperor (1), celebrating Caesar through an amoebaean sung before the patron Meliboeus (4), and bringing back to the countryside news of a spectacle in Rome (7). These enclose between them two pairs concerned with rural material. The first pair is erotic in theme: Idas and Astacus are matched as singers and as aspiring lovers of Crocale in 2; in 3 Lycidas sings for Iollas the verses that he hopes will reconcile Phyllis to him. Both 2 and 5 follow Vergil's lead in expanding the boundaries of the genre into the territory of the *Georgics*, the former by introducing a gardener (Astacus) as one of the competitors in an amoebaean, the latter through a long didactic speech in which Micon hands over flocks to his *alumnus* Canthus, and instructs him how to look after them through the course of the year. *Uere nouo* (at the beginning of spring, Calp. 5.16) echoes the opening of Vergil's instruction in the *Georgics* (1.43), but also the closural foreshadowing of this at *Ecl.* 10.74.

Poem 6 follows 2 and 4 in being a formal amoebaean; or at least it would if the agreed umpire did not give up in despair when Astylus and Lycidas refuse to finish their wrangling so that they can get on with singing the praises of Petale and Phyllis. This daring evocation of fatuity, oddly reminiscent of the endless disputation of the brothers Thyestes and Atreus in the final lines of Seneca's *Thyestes*, builds on the opening admission of late arrival, *serus ades* (you come too late) addressed to the Theocritean epitome of a goatherd, Lycidas. In the middle of the central poem we find a more positive evocation of the bucolic tradition. The shepherd Corydon reports the words with which Iollas has passed on a pipe:

> Tityrus hanc habuit, cecinit qui primus in istis
> montibus Hyblaea modulabile carmen auena.

Tityrus owned this pipe, he who was the first in these hills to sing a melodious song to the Hyblaean reed.

(Calpurnius, Eclogues 4.62–3)

Calpurnius acknowledges Vergil (Tityrus) as the first Italian singer of pastoral and imitator of the Sicilian Theocritus. The phrase *in istis montibus* implies Italy, but in this political context it also evokes the hills of Rome, and equates them with the mountains of pastoral.

The *Einsiedeln Eclogues*, so-called from the place where the unique manuscript resides, are two incomplete and corrupt poems. Though they have aroused much controversy about date (possibly Neronian, but later than Calpurnius) and the identity of the author (or authors), the most striking feature is incompetence: the abstract dominates the realistic and particular (e.g. 1.3–4 *secreta uoluptas / inuitat calamos*; 1.14 *iudicis e gremio uictoris gloria surgat*); the plotting is incoherent (Ladas is the only one of the two competitors to pledge a prize in 1; Mystes' *curae* [cares] are forgotten in 2); the panegyrical intrudes with clumsy suddenness in each (1.15; 2.15ff.) and the pastoral world gets left behind.

After the period of this volume, it is worth drawing attention to some interesting developments in the third-century poet, Nemesianus, which comment on the earlier pastoral tradition. The first of his four poems emphasizes belatedness: it features a lament for the dead patron Meliboeus and it stresses the age of Meliboeus himself and of Tityrus, one of the speakers (they are both of course prominent figures in the *Eclogues*, the *dramatis personae* of *Ecl.* 1). Timetas does not sing a fresh lament, or even one he remembers, but *carmina* (poems) he has inscribed on a cherry tree for safe-keeping. The second poem sets against each other two songs of love for Donace: there is obvious, and elegant, imitation of *Eclogues* 7 and 8, and of Calpurnius 3, but Nemesianus leads into the amoebaean not through pastoral invective or poetic rivalry, but with a disturbingly casual description of a double rape (Donace attacked in classic fashion, while gathering flowers) and the subsequent locking up of the girl once she starts to show symptoms of having lost her maidenhead. Again the figure of Tityrus is used to evoke Vergil:

> nec sumus indocti calamis: cantamus auena,
> qua diui cantauere prius, qua dulce locutus
> Tityrus e siluis dominam peruenit in urbem.

Nor are we unskilled on the reeds: we sing to the pipe, on which gods sang in the past, on which Tityrus spoke sweetly, and advanced from the woods to the imperial city.

(Nemesianus, *Eclogues* 2.82–4)

This neatly recalls both Tityrus' journey to Rome, described in *Eclogue* 1, and Vergil's poetic movement from pastoral to the imperial aetiology of the *Aeneid*, foreseen in just such terms by Vergil himself in the Ninth Eclogue.

The third poem reprises the Sixth Eclogue, with boys gaining a divine song not by capturing a drunken Silenus, but by stealing pipes from a sleeping Pan, who sings not a cosmogonical catalogue poem, but a hymn to Bacchus of a markedly didactic nature (note e.g. the georgic imperatives of 39–40, *maturos carpite fetus, calcate racemos* [pluck the ripe produce; tread the bunches]; the Lucretian echo at 63: *deus ille, deus* [he is a god, a god]; and the closing emphasis on teaching in *haec Pan ... docebat*, 66 [this is what Pan taught]). Like his predecessor, Nemesianus will go on to produce rural didactic (a *Cynegetica*) as well as pastoral. Unfortunately the pastoral collection is either unfinished or fragmentary; poem 4 ends with nothing more closural than the end of the fifth pair of exchanges between two lovesick shepherds.

The tradition continues into medieval Latin and modern languages (and into other art forms as well, such as music and landscape design). The culmination of this progress comes in Milton's *Lycidas*, which shows its understanding of Vergil's genre in many ways, including a discursive interest in the art of poetry and the author's own poetic progress, and some other aspects that have been neglected here, such as the use of the traditional name, and of the setting of the sun to mark the end of shepherd's day, and song, and poem:

> And now the sun had stretched out all the hills,
> And now was dropped into the western bay;
> At last he rose and twitched his mantle blue:
> Tomorrow to fresh woods and pastures new.
>
> (*Lycidas* 190–3)

FURTHER READING

Theocritus' main bucolic poems are *Idylls* 1, 3–7, 11, all (bar 5) collected in Hunter (1999), an excellent commentary. *Idylls* 8 and 9, though not by Theocritus, display many of the key elements; and 10 fascinatingly explores the differences between the bucolic and agricultural worlds, with one, inefficient, reaper singing a lovesong to which his more serious colleague replies with didactic instruction for the farmer: a model for the early Vergil, as it were *Eclogues* plus *Georgics*. For one reconstruction of the transmission of the Theocritean *bucolica* (and references to earlier efforts) see Gutzwiller (1996); the paper also has interesting things to say on the evolution of the genre. On pastoral elements in Homer, see Griffin (1992). On the development of the tradition into Latin and then beyond, see Hubbard 1998; Jenkyns 1992.

Much of the pleasure in reading the *Eclogues* comes from an awareness of literary ancestry, and good commentaries provide this most helpfully: in English we have Coleman (1977) and Clausen (1994); the latter provides much bibliographical assistance. There is also a fine annotated translation by Lee (1984). Basic on the reworking of Theocritus is Posch (1969), but most writing on the *Eclogues* engages in part with this issue. The following are items that consider the Eclogues as a whole: Alpers (1979), Boyle (1986), Flintoff (1974; 1975–6), Jenkyns (1999), Lee (1989), Martindale (1997), Putnam (1970) and van Sickle (1978). Some especially worthwhile discussions of individual poems: 1: Wright (1983); 2: DuQuesnay (1979); 3: Henderson (1998b); 4: Nisbet (1978); 5: Lee

(1977); 6: Ross (1975: 18–38); 10: Conte (1986: 100–29) and Kennedy (1983). On sequences of poems within the book, see Hubbard (1995) and Solodow (1977a). Rudd (1976) is a helpfully sceptical review of earlier theories about the structure of the *Eclogues* book. On the place of the *Eclogues* within the corpus as a whole, see Theodorakopoulos (1997). The notion that Arcadia (rather than Sicily or northern Italy) is the home of Vergilian pastoral was exploded in different ways by Kennedy (1987) and Jenkyns (1989).

Little has been written on Calpurnius and Nemesianus in recent decades, and most of that consists of sections in survey books and technical pieces, especially on the dating of Calpurnius. Many (e.g. Horsfall 1997) have doubted that he can be writing in the Neronian period in which the poems are apparently set; for the conventional dating, see Townend (1980) and Mayer (1980). Modern editions and commentaries are urgently needed (despite Williams 1986: see Green 1988), as well as literary investigation (but see Hubbard 1996). Texts and translations are most conveniently found in the Loeb *Minor Latin Poets* volumes (Duff and Duff 1934).

CHAPTER ELEVEN

Love Elegy

Roy Gibson

1   Introduction

The great first-century educator Quintilian, while reviewing Roman works worthy of comparison with the Greek classics, declares:

> We also challenge the supremacy of the Greeks in elegy. Of our elegiac poets Tibullus seems to me to be the most terse and elegant. There are, however, some who prefer Propertius. Ovid is more unrestrained than either, while Gallus is more austere. Satire, on the other hand, is all our own . . . (*Inst.* 10.1.93)

In grouping these four authors together, Quintilian appears to be referring to what is known loosely today as 'Roman love elegy'; that is, book-length collections of poems in the elegiac metre, written for the most part in the first person, recounting the poet's experiences with a named lover. 'Love elegy' in this sense, however, was not considered a separate genre in antiquity in the same way as (for example) epic. Greek elegy never produced anything very comparable to 'Roman love elegy', yet Quintilian places the two side by side: a clear indication that his four elegists form not a separate genre but a premier class (or canon) of Roman authors writing in the elegiac metre. While the focus of this chapter will inevitably be on these 'canonical' elegists, an understanding of their achievement can only be enriched by an awareness of the authors who did not make it into Quintilian's canon, particularly Catullus, Lygdamus and Sulpicia, and the numerous other elegiac works of Ovid, particularly his didactic-elegiac *Ars Amatoria*.

2 The Elegists and the Shape of Elegy

'Canonical' elegy flourished within a relatively short period of time, beginning with the four books of Cornelius Gallus (probably known as *Amores*), perhaps all published by the early 30s BC, and ending with the second edition of Ovid's three books of *Amores*, perhaps published in c. 7 BC (although the poet had been writing *Amores* poems since c. 26–25 BC). Between these approximate dates were published the four books of Propertius' elegies (although his second book was probably two separate works in antiquity), beginning in c. 30/29 BC and ending c. 16 BC, and the two books of Tibullus' elegies, the first appearing in c. 27/26 BC and the second (unfinished) book perhaps in 19 BC.

Of the first canonical elegist, only ten lines survive, nine of which were published for the first time only in 1979 (see Anderson et al. 1979; Courtney 1993: 259–70). The poems of the other canonical elegists are mostly between 20 and 100 lines in length and, with the exception of Propertius' fourth book, in general offer a variety of scenes from the poet's love affair with a woman (although a boy named Marathus appears in Tibullus' first book). In each case the woman is given a (pseudonymous) name: Lycoris (Gallus), Cynthia (Propertius), Delia and Nemesis (in Bks 1 and 2 respectively of Tibullus), and Corinna (Ovid). The poems themselves take a variety of forms including soliloquy, direct address (of the beloved or another, particularly friends and rivals), narrative (including mythological narrative) and dramatic monologue (where, in a series of shifting scenes, one or more persons may be addressed). Speaking formally or expressly to oneself or another – rather than (e.g.) private meditation or disembodied narration – is in fact the characteristic mode of the genre.

Before looking more closely at the content of elegy, it seems necessary to ask what we expect to find in poetry about love. Transcendence? A communion between souls? A romantic partnership of equals? Roman love elegy offers none of these things. Instead of communion between equals in love, love elegy typically offers confrontation – and one at that between a speaker who claims he is dominated by Love or the beloved. As illustration take the striking opening of the first elegy of Propertius:

> Cynthia prima suis miserum me cepit ocellis,
>   contactum nullis ante cupidinibus.
> tum mihi constantis deiecit lumina fastus
>   et caput impositis pressit Amor pedibus,
> donec me docuit castas odisse puellas
>   improbus, et nullo vivere consilio.
> ei mihi, iam toto furor hic non deficit anno,
>   cum tamen adversos cogor habere deos.
> Milanion nullos fugiendo, Tulle, labores
>   saevitiam durae contudit Iasidos.

Cynthia first, with her eyes, caught wretched me | Smitten before by no desires; | Then, lowering my stare of steady arrogance. | With feet imposed Love pressed my head, | Until he taught me hatred of chaste girls – | The villain – and living aimlessly. | And now for a whole year this mania has not left me, | Though I am forced to suffer adverse Gods. | Milanion by facing every hardship, Tullus, | Conquered the cruelty of Atalanta.

(Propertius 1.1.1–10, trans. Lee 1994)

This passage offers a good introduction to the character of Roman love elegy: a man is dominated by one woman, love for whom he experiences as a deeply unwanted crisis – invasion, madness, a kind of servitude like that suffered by a hero of Greek myth (Milanion) in service to a heroine (Atalanta). (Note also that these lines are not the private meditation of Propertius, but part of a speech addressed to his friend Tullus.) Instead of transcendence, Propertius, and Roman love elegy in general, offer a poet's tormented love affair with a mercurial and unfaithful beloved, which is denied any sort of closure other than that of abandonment of the affair (Prop. 3.24). The elegists talk – in addition to slavery and mania – of love as a disease (Prop. 1.5.21ff.), a fire (Ov. *Am.* 1.2.9ff.), or even of love as like a war (Tib. 1.10.53ff.), where he is a soldier (Tib. 1.1.75–6; Ov. *Am.* 1.9), and the enemy is love (Prop. 4.1.137–8) or the beloved herself (Prop. 3.8.33–4); see Kennedy (1993: 53–63). The keynote of elegy is one of alienation rather than exaltation.

Many of elegy's metaphors for love, such as slavery and war, although strikingly expressed, are in fact highly conventional, attested already in Greek poetry written centuries before; see Murgatroyd (1975 and 1981). Similarly conventional is the basic situation underlying many elegies, namely the triangle of lover, beloved and rival and the tensions that arise from the clashes between the three (Prop. 1.5; 1.8; Tib. 1.5; 1.6; Ov. *Am.* 2.5; 2.19). Stock characters likewise appear, including various slaves such as the doorkeeper (Tib. 1.2.5–6; Ov. *Am.* 1.6), the chaperon (Prop. 2.23.9ff.; Tib. 1.8.55; Ov. *Am.* 2.2; 2.3), and the go-between (Prop. 3.6; Tib. 1.2.95–6; Ov. *Am.* 1.11; 1.12), and others such as the *lena*-procuress (Prop. 4.5; Tib. 1.5.48; Ov. *Am.* 1.8). The lover also finds himself in standard situations, such as accusing his beloved of infidelity (Prop. 1.15; Tib. 1.5; Ov. *Am.* 3.8; 3.14), being separated from his mistress by a locked door (Prop. 1.16; Tib. 2.6.11ff.; Ov. *Am.* 1.6; 3.11.9ff.) or by distance (Prop. 1.17; 1.18; 3.16; Ov. *Am.* 3.6), or giving or receiving advice on love (Prop. 1.10.21ff.; Tib. 1.4; Ov. *Am.* 1.4). Conventionality can alienate today's readers, associated as it is with banal or unambitious entertainment. But two points must be stressed. First, this conventionality represents a deliberate artistic choice on the part of the elegists. Propertius, Tibullus and Ovid could easily have added – as Ovid would begin to do later in the *Ars Amatoria* – strong local colour to their poems in order to distinguish more strongly from previous centuries the backgrounds against which they play out their love affairs. Instead they chose to turn their backs, for the most part, on contemporary society and to inhabit a space which, while still Roman, is in evident continuity with the stock characters and milieu of Greek New Comedy. The complex circumstances surrounding this choice will emerge later.

Secondly, the conventionality of elegy should not blind readers to what is new in the genre (either in itself or in combination with other features) or expressed with special vividness – especially as ancient aesthetic standards tended to equate 'originality' with a gift for finding new ways to express the conventional. Particularly striking here are the elegists' obsession with the value and standing of their poetry and accompanying emphasis on its role as a way of winning the affection of the beloved (Prop. 1.7; 2.1; 2.34; 3.1; 3.3; 4.1; Tib. 1.4.57ff.; 2.4.13ff.; Ov. *Am.* 1.3; 1.15; 2.1; 2.18; 3.1; 3.8; 3.15; Stroh (1971)); a fixation with death (Prop. 1.19; 2.13b; 2.26; 4.7; 4.11; Tib. 1.1.59ff., 1.3; 1.10; Ov. *Am.* 2.10.29ff.; Griffin (1985: 142–62); and a fondness for appealing to the world of Greek myth (particularly in the case of Propertius and Ovid: Prop. 1.1.9ff.; 1.3.1ff.; 1.20; 2.9; 3.15; Tib. 2.3.11ff.; Ov. *Am.* 1.1.7ff.; 1.10.1ff.; 3.6.25ff.; Lyne (1980: 82–102, 252–7).

3   Key Features of Elegy: the 'Alienation' of the Elegist

The elegists have various ways of communicating a sense of alienation from the norms of behaviour observed by contemporary society. As will become clear, the poets make a simultaneous, and paradoxical, attempt to enforce some of those norms on the women of elegy – a feature of elegy that is only beginning to receive its proper focus.

Roman love elegists declare themselves to be slaves to their mistresses. Such willing acceptance by a freeborn Roman male of the degraded status of slavery (and slavery at that to a woman) is – and is designed to be – shocking to traditional Roman sensibilities. The idea of love as slavery in fact pervades the writing of the elegists: *domina* (mistress – including mistress of slaves) is a standard term for the woman in love elegy; love is equated with a loss of liberty (Prop. 1.9.1ff.; 2.23.23–4; Tib. 2.4.1–4); the lover may speak of himself as being in chains (Tib. 1.1.55) or as undergoing the physical punishments typically inflicted on slaves (Tib. 1.9.21–2); and he may plead for his freedom (Prop. 3.17.41). In a society where slaves formed a large and omnipresent minority it was thought to be of the utmost importance for free citizens to distance themselves from this most humiliating and oppressive of conditions. Yet the elegists may be found doing the opposite, openly declaring that they are slaves to their mistresses. If the elegists are slaves, then the women to whom they are enslaved logically have power over them.

Some modern critics have seen in this inversion of the usual gender relations in Roman society a potentially liberating transfer of social responsibility to women and a corresponding removal of it from men. But, as Maria Wyke persuasively argues:

> It is not the concern of elegiac poetry to upgrade the position of women, only to portray the male narrator as alienated from positions of power and to differentiate him from other, socially responsible male types ... generally elegiac metaphors are concerned with male servitude not female mastery. (2002: 42–3)

In this sense the metaphor of slavery coheres with a range of other devices used by the elegists to express their alienation from conventional society, most obviously their adoption of qualities associated with women's 'place' in society. The elegists declare themselves to be sexually faithful (Prop. 1.11), submissive (Prop. 3.11), obedient to the commands of their mistress (Prop. 4.8.71ff.), and – worst of all – effeminate or 'soft' (mollis), both in themselves (Prop. 2.22a.13) and in terms of the kind of poetry they write (Prop. 1.7.19). To traditional Roman eyes each of these qualities would be proper to women rather than to men.

Coherent with this expression of alienation from society is an aloofness that the elegists maintain from contemporary affairs. This aloofness expresses itself either through refusals to join in with public society and affairs, or (more commonly) a simple lack of reference to them. One might read through the first book of Propertius and never guess until the final two short (and uncharacteristic) poems that Italy had just begun to emerge from decades of devastating civil war. By contrast the *Georgics* of Vergil, published around the same time (29 BC), are unmistakably written in a post-war context. From the first book of Tibullus a little more is to be learnt, thanks mainly to a poem (1.7) written in honour of the triumph of the poet's patron Messalla in 27 BC. Elsewhere in this first collection Tibullus lives in a relatively timeless world, stripping important personal events – such as his probable trip to the east with Messalla in 30–29 BC – of most of their contextual detail (1.3; 1.7.13ff.). In the first book of Ovid's *Amores*, one learns almost nothing of the historical context in which these poems were written (McKeown 1987: 78ff.). As for the refusal to engage with contemporary public society, Propertius, for example, declines the opportunity to accompany his friend Tullus on his uncle's proconsulship in Asia (1.6); professes himself poetically unfit to celebrate the achievements of Octavian in song (2.1; 3.9); states (in 3.4) that the limits of his involvement in Octavian's triumphs will be to applaud from the side of the Sacra Via (and in the sequel, 3.5, that Love is a god of a peace). Tibullus' refusal to engage in similar aspects of contemporary society is a little more complex. He too expresses an unwillingness to serve Rome abroad (1.3; 1.10), but in 1.7.9ff. teases readers with the possibility he had actually served in some capacity with Messalla in Gaul. This is in fact a reminder that a strong sense of irony should be allowed for in Roman love elegy (Morgan 2000a: 94–7; cf. Veyne 1988: 93).

Perhaps most revealing of the attitude of the elegists to contemporary society is the role played by the physical city of Rome in their poetry. Both before and during the period in which the elegists wrote, Rome had been undergoing a profound change, as Octavian, his family and lieutenants began to mould the city in Octavian's image (Favro 1996: 79–142). But Tibullus and Ovid in his *Amores* evince little interest in the urban setting of their elegies, and Tibullus on a number of occasions expresses a 'moral' preference for the countryside (2.3.1ff.; cf. also 1.1; 1.5; 1.10). This same pastoral vein is also found occasionally in Propertius (e.g. 2.19; 3.13; esp. 25ff.), and, while the poet does include poems in praise of the beauty of contemporary Rome (2.31), his thoughts soon turn to Cynthia's infidelity and avarice when she is imagined in this environment (2.32, esp. 41ff.). In general Propertius, particularly in Book 4, focuses on Rome's grottoes and waters rather than on its marble edifices; see Fantham (1997). This tendency to turn the back on the city of Rome would be reversed only in Ovid's *Ars Amatoria*, where the poet strongly encourages readers to participate in the public life of the city – albeit with a personal erotic agenda. Propertius' declaration that he will only applaud a triumph from the sidelines contrasts strongly with Ovid's encourage-ment of his pupils at *Ars* 1.213ff. to make use of the events of a triumph to open conversation with a girl; see further Gibson (2003: 134–5, 257–9).

Despite this declared alienation, the elegists preserve a paradoxical adherence to some of the strictest standards of conventional society. Propertius may depict Cynthia as the kind of woman a man of his class does not marry (2.7), and who can hold her drink and play dice into the small hours (2.33b). But elsewhere he is perfectly at home demanding high standards of personal probity (3.13) or an-tique standards of sexual fidelity (2.6.15ff.), or even envisaging Cynthia in the morally bracing environment of the countryside (2.19). The elegists' conservative attitudes are seen best in their attitude to cosmetics and personal adornment. Paradigmatic here is the second poem in the first book of Propertius:

> quid iuvat ornato procedere, vita, capillo
>   et tenuis Coa veste movere sinus,
> aut quid Orontea crines perfundere murra,
>   teque peregrinis vendere muneribus,
> naturaeque decus mercato perdere cultu,
>   nec sinere in propriis membra nitere bonis?
> crede mihi, non ulla tuae est medicina figurae:
>   nudus Amor formae non amat artificem.

Why choose, my life, to step out with styled hair | And move sheer curves in Coan costume? | Or why to drench your tresses in Orontes' myrrh | And sell yourself with foreign gifts | And lose the charm of Nature for bought elegance, | Not letting your limbs shine with their own attractions? | This doctoring of your looks is pointless, believe me; | Love, being naked, does not love beauticians.

(Propertius 1.2.1–8, trans. Lee 1994)

In this poem Propertius takes on the role of a husband instructing his wife on the hairstyles, dress and appearance appropriate to her, a scenario played out three hundred years before in Xenophon's *Oeconomicus* (10.2ff.). Similar attitudes preferring natural to artificial beauty may be found dotted all over the whole corpus of elegy. Propertius objects to Cynthia's use of make-up and jewellery (1.15.5ff.), to her hair dyes (2.18b.27–8), her wearing of expensive clothing and perfume (3.14.27–8); Tibullus complains of the wearing of Coan silks (2.4.27ff.), of the constant changing of hairstyles and the artful trimming of nails (1.8.9ff.); and Ovid, with characteristic comedy, laments that a hair dye has caused his beloved's hair to fall out (*Am.* 1.14). Such complaints are commonly found in the mouths of conservative Greek moralists from the sixth century BC on, and were enthusiastically echoed by Roman traditionalists both before and after the elegists' time; see Gibson (2003: 21–5, 174–6). Clearly, so far as the elegists are concerned, unconventionality is proper to men, and not to the women for whom men declare their (improper) devotion. This characteristic, but paradoxical, combination of alienation from society and a preservation of its most conservative values where women are concerned is finally abandoned by Ovid in the *Ars Amatoria* (and accompanying *Medicamina Faciei Femineae, Cosmetics for Ladies*), where lovers are not only encouraged to participate in the life of the city, but, for the first and last time in Roman literature, women are encouraged to wear make-up and give serious attention to hairdressing; see Gibson (2003: 149–50, 174–6).

4   The Elegiac Woman

The emphasis of Roman love elegy is then the opposite of what might have been expected: the lover's primary concern is for himself and not for his beloved. This may be seen in other ways too. To approach elegy with the expectation of finding powerful character portraits of beautiful and tempestuous women is to invite disappointment. The focus is instead on how the woman affects the male lover. Relatively few authenticating details are revealed of the women of love elegy; rather, a highly conventional beauty and temperament are ascribed to them. Some details, for example, of Cynthia's looks are concentrated in the second and third poems of Book 2, enough at least to build a picture of a tall woman with blond hair, long thin hands, a snow-white complexion and striking eyes (2.2.5–6; 2.3.9ff.). But these are the generic looks proper to goddesses and heroines (such as Dido in the *Aeneid*), and elsewhere in his poetry Propertius, like the other elegiac poets, is mostly content with general and unspecific references to hair, eyes, clothes and looks (see further Wyke 2002: 19ff.). In addition, while elegy does offer the alluring appearance of a beginning-to-end narrative of the elegists' relationships with their women, a closer look reveals that it is impossible to construct a chronology for the affair of (e.g.) Propertius and Cynthia from the former's variously conflicting statements about its length and episodes (Allen 1962: 112–18); few recent scholars have even tried to do the same for the various affairs of Tibullus and Ovid. One ancient writer, Apuleius, some two centuries after the elegists, it is true, claims in his *Apologia* (10) to provide the names behind the pseudonyms of Cynthia and Delia (although not, interestingly, the Nemesis of Tibullus' second book, or the Corinna of Ovid). But suspicions that Cynthia and her ilk may be (mainly) a fiction must be raised further when it is observed that such characteristics as are given to the women of elegy are often said equally to be characteristics of the elegist's poetry. This may be seen most clearly in Ovid *Amores* 3.1.7–10, where Elegy herself is given a female form whose details replicate features attributed elsewhere to Cynthia and Corinna; see Wyke (2002: 122–4). In other words, readers of elegy must live with the constant suspicion that when elegists talk of their mistresses they are talking also about their poetry. One other indication of the strong implicit connection between the women of love elegy and elegiac poetics is that each of Lycoris, Cynthia and Delia bear a name also known to be a cult title of Apollo, god of poetry, while Corinna's name recalls that of a famous Greek poetess (McKeown 1987: 19–24: Wyke 2002: 27–8).

5 Origins and Development

The question of the origins and development of elegy has intrigued critics for the simple reason that, unlike most other genres taken up by the Romans, love elegy lacks an obvious predecessor in Greek literature. This is striking because Roman authors usually rely on an audience's knowledge of Greek predecessors in a genre to create meaning in and for their own works. However, a number of traditions that possess elements similar to those of Roman love elegy can be identified; they provide a context for the Roman genre as well as helping to establish what is unique and distinctive in it.

Of two traditions often cited in this connection – archaic Greek elegy and Hellenistic elegy – we can dispose quickly. About the first and its authors, such as Mimnermus (mentioned at Prop. 1.9.11), we know too little to be confident of its relation to Roman love elegy. More interesting is the case of Hellenistic elegy. The elegists mention some of its authors by name in prominent positions, particularly Callimachus (e.g. Prop. 2.1.40; 2.34.32; 3.1.1; 3.9.43; 4.1.64; Ov. *Am.* 1.15.13; 2.4.19; *Ars* 3.329; *Rem.* 381, 759, 760) and Philetas (e.g. Prop. 2.34.31; 3.1.1; 3.9.44; 4.6.3; Ov. *Ars* 3.329; *Rem.* 760). Yet what survives of these poets reveals very little in the way of possible direct influence on the elegists (with the exception of Propertius Book 4; see below). Resembling Roman love elegy little in terms of content, at most these Hellenistic elegists offered the Roman elegists a style, manner and poetics to imitate; see Knox (1993). Apparently more promising – in terms of content – are a number of Hellenistic elegies that survive only on papyrus and combine erotic mythological narratives with 'personal' frames (the latter conspicuously absent in the elegiac poetry of Callimachus). These poems (e.g. P. Oxy. 2885 fr. 1.1–20, 21–45) are, crucially, 'in some sense subjective, in that the mythological content could be exploited for some purpose that is, within the fiction of the poem, of vital interest to the author's persona' (Butrica 1996: 315). Roman love elegy offers a number of poems similar in construction to these papyrus verses (e.g. Prop. 1.19; 3.11; 3.15; 3.19; Tib. 2.3; Ov. *Am.* 3.6; 3.10), and the earlier oeuvre of Catullus offers one conspicuous example – the remarkable poem 68 in which the doomed marriage of the mythical Protesilaus and Laodamia is placed in parallel to Catullus' own erotic experiences (on which see Lyne 1980: 52–60; Feeney 1992). But erotic mythological narratives with personal introductions and conclusions do not dominate the elegists' collections, and it is hard to imagine most of their poems growing directly out of such Hellenistic predecessors (see Butrica 1996; Lightfoot 1999: 71–5).

Nevertheless, in one sense critics have been right to pursue the Hellenistic elegy question: they have followed where the elegists themselves pointed and have so remained true to the poetic pretensions of Roman love elegy. I say 'pretensions' because love elegy is clearly more influenced by a genre which the elegists all but neglect to mention – Roman New Comedy. New Comedy – as represented in Greek by Menander (4th–3rd c. BC) and in Latin by Plautus (3rd–2nd c. BC) and Terence (2nd c. BC) – displays numerous features shared with love-elegy. Its heroes are frequently young lovers who typically operate in an urban context whose features are not made especially distinctive, and where the focus is on the private world of individuals rather than the contemporary world of politics. The lovers encounter stock characters (e.g. slaves, courtesans, soldiers) in stock situations (e.g. frustrations in love). Roman comedy, particularly that of Plautus, places greater emphasis than its Greek counterpart on two features that are prominent also in love elegy: the alienation of the obsessed young lover from society (as represented by the older generation), and his rejection of war and the soldier. (For the influence of these features on elegy, see Griffin 1985: 198–210; Yardley 1973.) Yet, for all the obviousness (to us) of the influence of Roman comedy on love elegy, there is not one explicit reference in love elegy to a Roman comic poet. The elegists were happy to give prominence instead to more prestigious Hellenistic elegists, as well as to the Greek predecessor of Plautus and Terence, Menander (named at Prop. 2.6.3; 3.21.28; 4.5.43; Ov. *Am.* 1.15.18). Here the literary ambition of love elegy can be most keenly sensed. For the influence of even 'lower' genre on elegy, namely mime – also without explicit acknowledgement – see McKeown (1979).

Perhaps the closest surviving Greek precursor to Roman love elegy is erotic epigram. The influence of this genre is one the Roman elegists are happy to acknowledge implicitly: the opening lines of Propertius' first elegy (quoted above) carry a strong (and potentially programmatic) reference to a classic of Greek epigram, namely Meleager, *Greek Anthology* 12.101. In both poems a speaker, previously untouched by love, is smitten by the eyes of a named beloved, experiences love as a personal humiliation and appeals to an episode from Greek

mythology to frame his experience. Elegiac epigram had developed by the 3rd
century BC into a separate literary form, in which a wide range of themes was
handled, including women, boys, wine and song. The hallmarks of the genre were
concision and wit, and successful epigrammatists sometimes collected their poems
into books – as recently revealed, for example, in the case of Poseidippus (see
Austin and Bastianini 2002). Propertius signals his allegiance to this genre with
his opening reference to Meleager, but in some ways this declaration of allegiance
is misleading. For all the similarities to Greek epigram, canonical Roman love
elegy is characterized by a greater poetic ambition, evident not only in its
references to Hellenistic elegists, but exemplified by its collection of poems
often four times the length of epigram into unified collections devoted to one
mistress.

Romans had been writing their versions of erotic epigram since at least the
second century BC, but Roman achievement in this arena was taken to a new level
by Catullus. Catullus' elegiac corpus comprises four or five 'long' pieces of
between 24 and over 100 lines (poems 65–8 in his collected works) and forty-
eight shorter pieces of between 2 and 26 lines, most in the region of 6–12 lines
(poems 69–116). Catullus anticipates love elegy in two respects: he writes a series
of poems, more extensive than anything found in Greek epigram, devoted to one
mistress, identified only by a pseudonym (Lesbia); and these poems offer the
appearance of a narrative (no matter how superficial), with an identifiable beginning, middle and end to the relationship. As in love elegy, this narrative was
evidently judged not artistically important enough to be made the central thread
of the poet's collection – indeed Catullus, or whoever put the collection together,
flouts narrative expectations by placing the 'first' poem for Lesbia (51) well after
the poet's 'farewell' to her (11). Furthermore Lesbia does not dominate Catullus'
collection, as in love elegy the mistresses do not always dominate. But, for all
these similarities and precedents, Catullus differs markedly from the love elegists:
many of his most famous and resonant love poems are not written in the elegiac
metre (51 and 11, e.g., are in sapphics); and as a collection the poems, for all their
artistic arrangement on the principle of variation in theme and tone and mutually
deepening effect on one another, were probably not gathered into a book or
series of books designed to form part of their meaning. (For this as a feature,
however, particularly of Propertius' work, see below.)

Nevertheless, critics have consistently picked out one of Catullus' elegies as a
forerunner of elegy: poem 76. In this 26-line poem the speaker is riven with
ambivalence about an oppressive relationship that he prays to the gods to help
him break. The similarities with, for example, the first poem of Propertius
(quoted above) are obvious, yet the poem has at least as much to tell us about
the distinctiveness of Roman love elegy. As Paul Veyne has pointed out (1988:
34–7; cf. Wyke 2002: 19, 48), Catullus adheres to an aesthetics of 'sincerity',
working hard to 'present the reader with an impression of simplicity, spontaneity,
lack of artifice'. These 'rules' for achieving the effect of sincerity are conspicuously

– in fact pointedly – eschewed by the elegists, who prefer a more mannered style, full of conventional conceits, literary games and Greek myth (often obscure). Furthermore, in poem 76 Catullus with great deliberateness employs the language of aristocratic obligation, to create the impression that the unfaithful beloved has broken the Roman social code in her relationship with the poet (Fitzgerald 1995: 120). The elegists are keen to create the same impression, but appear to have found the moralistic vocabulary of obligation poetically unappealing (Gibson 1995), and prefer to turn to the more mannered poetic resources of Greek myth or erotic slavery.

6   Individual Characteristics and Contributions of the Elegists

The necessarily general nature of the discussion of the elegists' work so far obscures the contributions of the individual elegists to their 'genre'. Nearly every statement made above could be qualified with some such statements as '(but not in Tibullus)', or 'somewhat less seriously in Ovid'. So I want to end this survey of the elegists with some brief remarks on some of the characteristics of the individual elegists.

   Propertius produced collections which, more so than the other two surviving elegists, are individually memorable for their artistic achievements as books. His first collection, apparently known in antiquity as the monobyblos (Martial 14.189; Leary 1996: 253–4), contains 22 poems, most of which are about the poet's affair with Cynthia in some way, but less than half of which have her as addressee – a role that is filled in 11 of the poems by Propertius' four friends, Tullus, Bassus, Gallus and Ponticus; for their importance, see Sharrock (2000). With its deliberately artistic interweaving of theme and addressee the book formally resembles nothing so much – oddly it may seem – as one of Pliny the Younger's book of letters. Book 2 is still largely devoted to love poems, although sometimes the beloved clearly cannot be Cynthia (e.g. 2.22a; 2.23). It has a distinctive style, with increased discursiveness, parentheses and abrupt transitions; detectable here is a response to the style of the recently published first book of Tibullus, and in one poem in particular (2.19) an engagement with the distinctively rural subject matter of that book (Wyke 2002: 24–5). At 2.5.21ff. Propertius also refers unmistakably to Tibullus 1.10.61ff., branding his elegiac rival a 'peasant'; see Gibson (2003: 320–1). Book 3 shows more variety of subject matter; many of the poems are not about Cynthia or even about love (e.g. 3.7 and 3.18 on the deaths of Paetus and Marcellus respectively; 3.22 urging the Tullus of 1.6 to return home to Italy). The book also sees an engagement now with Horace's recently published *Odes* (Wyke 2002: 25–6), and introduction of the claim to be the Roman Callimachus (3.1; 3.3). It is Book 4, however, that really substantiates this claim, for here Propertius, in imitation of the Hellenistic elegist's *Aetia*, provides specifically Roman aetiologies for places and customs (1, 2, 4, 6, 9, 10). Only two poems include Cynthia, each designed to recall episodes from the Iliad (4.7) and Odyssey (4.8) respectively.

Tibullus, in the eyes of Quintilian, was the greatest of the Roman elegists – a judgement that, not surprisingly for one concerned with the education of the young Roman elite in public speaking, he based on the elegance of the elegist's style. (For a modern evaluation of Tibullus' style, see Maltby 1999.) In recent studies of elegy Tibullus has been comparatively neglected (see Wyke 2002: 2 n. 1). One reason for this neglect is that his restrained and cultivated tone can appear (to modern tastes) anaemic when placed alongside the vigour of Propertius or the wit of Ovid. Another is that his poems are initially difficult to follow, with unexpected or (at first) baffling transitions between scenes and subjects. (For an intriguing attempt to deal creatively with this feature of his work, see Lee-Stecum 1998.) More worryingly, Tibullus is often neglected because he is quite unlike the other two elegists in some respects. Like Propertius, Tibullus insists that love must take precedence over all else (1.1), and make sustained use of the metaphors of war and slavery (although in this last he introduces a masochism both comic and disturbing; cf. e.g. 1.5.5–6; 1.9.21–2). But Tibullus professes love for a boy (1.8; 1.9; cf. 1.4) as well as two women, and, unlike both Propertius and Ovid, makes almost no use of mythology; his romantic dream is rather that he should live in the country with Delia (1.5.21ff.). This rural focus (cf. 1.1; 1.10; 2.1) marks him off from the other elegists, as well as from Catullus.

Modern editions of Tibullus end with a third book of elegies from the circle of Messalla, Tibullus' patron. These elegies provide a fascinating insight into 'non-canonical' elegy as it must have existed at Rome. The first six are the work of an author who calls himself Lygdamus and are addressed to a girl named Neaera. The seventh poem in the collection is a long hexameter piece in honour of Messalla, while poems 8–18 focus on the love of Sulpicia, a relative of Messalla, for a young man named Cerinthus. The five elegies in the sequence 8–12, often referred to as 'Sulpicia's Garland', alternate between those written in the voice of an unnamed poet, and those placed in the mouth of Sulpicia. There follow six elegies of between four and ten lines apparently written by Sulpicia herself – the only poetry to be written by a pagan Roman woman to survive (see also Keith, Chapter 23 below). Aside from their evident artistry, the poems astonish with an open assertion of sexual independence remarkable for its era and the high social class of their author; see Hinds (1987a), Lowe (1988), and on the fascinating history of the poems' reception since the Renaissance, Skoie (2002).

Not all of Tibullus' elegies are about love (1.7; 1.10; 2.1; 2.5), and Propertius increasingly moved away from an exclusive focus on Cynthia. One might have expected Ovid to follow in their footsteps and continue to expand the genre's range of subject matter in his *Amores*. In fact he did quite the opposite, for the *Amores* are almost exclusively concerned with Ovid's own supposed experiences as lover and as love-poet (McKeown 1987: 13). Nevertheless, the *Amores* have a strong claim to be the greatest of the elegiac collections, above all for the verve, wit and zest with which they are written. The appreciation of the strength of this claim, however, demands close knowledge of the work of his two predecessors. For Ovid the lover acts according to – just as Ovid the poet manipulates – the conventions of earlier elegy in a highly knowing manner. Or, to put it more strongly, it is Ovid himself who turns earlier elegy into a series of conventions to be observed or flouted; the work of Propertius and Tibullus becomes in Ovid's hands a literary code. The earlier elegists, for example, display a fixation with death. Propertius imagines Cynthia at his funeral (2.13b), while Tibullus expresses his wish to hold Delia's hand in his last moments (1.1.59ff.). Ovid, however, after turning Propertius' wish (2.22a) for two love affairs (where the second one would act as insurance for the first) into a celebration of the sexual possibilities of two girls at the same time, expresses this final erotic ambition (*Am.* 2.10.29ff.):

> felix, quem Veneris certamina mutua perdunt!
> di faciant, leti causa sit ista mei!
> induat adversis contraria pectora telis
> miles et aeternum sanguine nomen emat.
> quaerat avarus opes et, quae lassarit arando,
> aequora periuro naufragus ore bibat.
> at mihi contingat Veneris languescere motu,
> cum moriar, medium solvar et inter opus;
> atque aliquis nostro lacrimans in funere dicat:
> 'conveniens vitae mors fuit ista tuae!'

To die in love's duel – what final bliss! | It's the death I should choose. | Let soldiers impale their hearts on a pike | And pay down blood for glory. | Let seafaring merchants make their millions | Till they and their lies are shipwrecked at last. | But when I die let me faint in the to and fro of love | And fade out at its climax. | I can just imagine the mourners' comment: | 'Death was the consummation of his life'.

(Trans. G. Lee)

The other elegists had talked of dying of love (Prop. 1.6.25ff.; 2.1.43ff.); that is, dying of the hardships endured in loving their mistresses; but Ovid literally imagines dying of sexual overindulgence and brings his poem to a climax with a humorous version of the earlier elegists' imagined final moments or funeral; see McKeown (1998: 215–21). Similarly brilliant, for example, in its conception and execution is Ovid's witty exposal in *Amores* 1.3 and 2.17 of the contradiction between the elegiac poet's offer to immortalize his beloved in poetry and the fact of her immortalization under a pseudonym; see McKeown (1987: 24).

7   Ovid and after

After the *Amores* Ovid continued to write elegiac poetry, but extended its themes far beyond the confines of love elegy to include an extraordinarily wide range of poetic topics. In fact, as for example Harrison (2002a) demonstrates at greater length than is possible here, Ovid's career after the *Amores* demonstrates both 'a clear strategy of diversification in erotic elegy' and a concern for 'generic ascent'. His letters from fictional heroines to their absent lovers – the *Heroides* – allow a voice to (powerless) women, where earlier elegy offered in the main a male speaker. This innovation had already been made in the fourth book of Propertius (4.3; 4.4; 4.5; 4.7; 4.11), but is sustained by Ovid over fifteen poems equivalent in length to three Augustan poetry books. The fourth book of Propertius – in the letter of the pseudonymous Arethusa to Lycotas, absent abroad on Roman military service (4.3) – also provided a model for the epistolary framework of the *Heroides*. In generic terms these letters represent an elevation in subject matter, as they derive their material not from the (alleged) experience of the lover, but from Greek epic, Attic tragedy and Hellenistic poetry. Further generic ascent is evident in the three books of the *Ars Amatoria*, where Ovid takes elegy's strain of offering informal advice on love (e.g. Prop. 1.7; 4.5; Tib. 1.4; Ov. *Am.* 1.4; 1.8) and transforms it into a system designed formally to recall the traditions of didactic poetry (see Gale, Chapter 7 above, and Volk 2002: 157–95; Gibson 2003: 7–13). The *Remedia Amoris*, a one-book companion to the *Ars*, is self-consciously presented as Ovid's final contribution to love elegy, not only in terms of its subject matter – cures for love – but also through some sustained reflection by the poet on his career thus far (*Rem.* 357–96). However, love is not entirely absent from Ovid's next elegiac work, the *Fasti* (see also Gale, Chapter 7 above). A work in six books on the Roman calendar and its festivals from January to June, this work of religious antiquarian research (and associated erotic tales) is designed to recall the most prestigious of all Hellenistic elegiac works, the *Aetia* (Causes) of Callimachus. Also evident is a desire, once more, to better the achievements of the Propertius of Book 4, who prefaces the numerous aetiological elegies of that book with a claim to be the Roman Callimachus (4.1.64). In the *Fasti* Ovid stresses the generic grandeur of his project (e.g. 2.3–4), but it is with the *Metamorphoses* that the poet finally ascends the generic summit, in a fifteen-book poem that takes on virtually every species of literature within a formally epic framework. Nevertheless, it is in elegiac mode that Ovid, perforce, ends his career, with the nine books of elegiac poetry written from exile (*Tristia, Epistulae ex Ponto*). The poems of these books represent a return to the epistolary format of the *Heroides*, but frequently strive both to distance themselves from 'unrespectable' earlier elegy, and to extend the range of subject matter admitted to Roman elegy.

Although its range was much expanded, elegy never lost its generic identity, and remained a place where, in contradistinction to epic, the private, the 'soft' and the peaceful might find expression or emphasis. But after Ovid, and until Ausonius and Claudian, no major (surviving) poems were written in elegiacs, and work in this metre is confined to the witty epigrams of Martial and the occasional poems found in the *Anthologia Latina*. As for love elegy 'proper', after Ovid we hear of minor practitioners writing in the style of (e.g.) Propertius, such as Passenus Paulus, acquaintance of Pliny the Younger (*Epist.* 6.15; 9.22). But of him, and perhaps many others like him, nothing survives. After the outstanding achievements of Ovid with elegy in all its forms, talented young poets will surely have recognized that to achieve fame and fulfil their ambitions they would have to look elsewhere – to epic, drama and satire.

FURTHER READING

Love elegy is well served by secondary literature in English. I give below some information about general books on elegy, followed by a critical list of important works and commentaries on individual authors. Three very different general works on elegy have been influential. Lyne (1980) provides an accessible guide to the poems, but more recent work on elegy has taken issue at length with a number of his critical assumptions. More demanding is Veyne (1988), but this is probably still the best general introduction to the full range of the elegists' achievements. Rather narrower in its focus is Kennedy (1993), which subjects selected aspects of elegy and its scholarship to rigorous theoretical scrutiny. The standard introductory work on Propertius is Hubbard (1974); but the articles of Maria Wyke – now revised and collected in Wyke (2002) – are essential to understanding how debate on this author has moved on. The best modern commentaries on Propertius are in Italian (Fedeli 1980 on Bk 1; 1985 on Bk 3). There are only two general works on Tibullus available in English at present, and each approaches this author from quite different angles. Cairns (1979) attempts to understand the poet through relating his work to Hellenistic poetic traditions; while Lee-Stecum (1998) provides a sustained close reading of each of the elegies of the first book. There are a number of good commentaries on Tibullus: Murgatroyd (1980 on Bk 1; 1994 on Bk 2); and Maltby (2002) on both books. Ovid's *Amores* are particularly well served by a number of introductory studies: DuQuesnay (1973), McKeown (1987), Davis (1989) and Boyd (1997). McKeown has also written excellent commentaries on the first two books of the *Amores* (1989 on Bk 1; 1998 on Bk 2); a commentary on the third is expected. For the other elegiac works of Ovid, consult the two *Companions to Ovid*, edited by Boyd (2002) and Hardie (ed. 2002). On Catullus, two recently published works will provide a good introduction to the vast scholarship on this poet: Fitzgerald (1995) and Wray (2001). For Sulpicia, see Hinds (1987a), Lowe (1988), Skoie (2002) and Keith, Chapter 23 below.

CHAPTER TWELVE

Satire

Llewelyn Morgan

1 Introduction: Definition and Beginnings

In satire we have the most developed surviving specimen of an ancient literary genre – as it was invented, by Quintus Ennius; achieved its seminal shape, in the works of Gaius Lucilius; and then developed in a classic pattern of imitation and reaction from one exponent of the form to the next (Horace to Persius to Juvenal) over a period (all told) of four centuries. Ironically, though, this near-perfect literary genre consistently disputed the suggestion that it was in any proper sense literary at all, and made a rich career out of doing precisely what literature should not.

It is appropriately as an alternative to (proper) literature that 'satire' makes its first appearance in Latin letters. The word *satura* as a description of a type of writing (for its use in Livy's description of dramatic performances, see Goldberg, Chapter 1 above, and Panayotakis, Chapter 9 above) originates in connection with Quintus Ennius, author of the great national epic *Annales*. Alongside this more serious, public poetry, Ennius seems to have composed occasional pieces that were diverse in topic and (especially metrical) form, but consistently of a less elevated nature than the *Annales*. Only 'seems', because our knowledge of Ennius' *Satires* is extremely limited, only a few fragments surviving. But we can tell that he wrote about his own everyday experiences in these poems, moralized a little and delivered some homespun philosophy. The later satirist Persius has Ennius writing his satire (specifically, in this case, exhorting his readers to visit a particular seaside resort) after he had 'snored off being Quintus Homer', that is, laid off pretending to be the awkward Roman version of Homer, which (Persius thought) Ennius could not help but be in his epic poetry. In Persius' account, at least, Ennius' satire is associated with a disdain for higher art (and for the pretence that was part and parcel of it) that is very familiar from the later history of the genre: Ennius' satire is a case of 'waking up' to reality, from the dream that corresponds to literary production. But as far as the future of the genre was concerned, Ennius' greatest contribution was the name itself, *satura*, a word whose rich associations would continue to be felt in the genre, and to shape it (or misshape it, as we shall see), throughout its history. The source of the word is discussed in what is for us a precious passage in a grammarian called Diomedes:

'Satire' (*satira*) is the name for a type of Roman poetry which is now abusive and designed to attack human failings on the model of Old Comedy, such as was written by Lucilius, Horace and Persius. At one time also poetry which was composed out of diverse small poems, such as was written by Pacuvius and Ennius, was called 'satire'... The word 'satire' (*satura*) comes from the dish (*lanx*) which in ancient times was crammed with a large number of diverse first fruits during religious rites and offered to the gods and which was called 'full to bursting' (*satura*) from the abundance and plenitude (*saturitas*) of the material... or else from a particular type of sausage which was crammed with many things and according to Varro was referred to as 'stuffed' (*satura*) ... Others think that the name came from the 'catch-all law' (*lex satura*), which encompasses in one bill many provisions at the same time, the argument being that in the poetry known as 'satire' (*satura*) many small poems are combined together... (Diomedes *Grammatici Latini* ed. Keil, 1.485).

We can, following Gowers (1993a: 109–26), take from this passage at least four associations that the term *satura* will have possessed for authors and readers of a genre bearing the name. *Satura* describes things that are disorderly agglomerations, mixtures of subordinate objects – laws, fruits or poems – made without much concern for organization. *Satura* also implies a characteristically exuberant excess: the dish of first fruits, the catch-all law, and the sausage all comprise materials that are in constant danger of breaking out of their confines. *Satura* is thus poetry that is 'full to bursting' in this respect as well as in its internal disorder, always threatening that quality of order and system that is an intrinsic feature of conventional literature. But *satura* is also a low, subliterary word, a term properly applied to things as alien to literature, as generally understood, as food, or messy foodlike phenomena such as the 'catch-all law', more literally 'mishmash law', a pejorative description not unlike our 'dog's breakfast'. Finally, though, *satura* is a word with clear nationalistic associations. The Greek epigrammatist Meleager, apparently referring to the *lanx satura* mentioned by Diomedes, talks of the 'Roman dish', suggesting it was a dish with the same kind of associations as roast beef or apple pie, capable of representing the Roman race itself. In short, then, by virtue of writing a style of literature going by the name of *satura*, satirists were committing themselves to literature that had no internal consistency, no external shape, and low to non-existent artistic aspirations, but Roman to the core. Each one of those characteristics could amount to a denial of literary status *tout court*. It was a recipe rich in contradictions, which would provide fuel for creativity for a long time to come.

2   Lucilius (see also Goldberg, Chapter 1 above)

There is more of Lucilius' satire surviving than Ennius', but then again there was much more to lose, thirty books in total. Even the fragments fill a whole volume, Warmington (vol. 4, 1938). This is a deplorable loss, since Lucilius set the terms of the genre for his successors in an unusually authoritative way. But we have some extended fragments from his works that allow us to see how the characteristics hinted at by Diomedes may have played themselves out. A fragment survives from Book 17 in which somebody, probably Lucilius' satirical persona, attacks and debunks, in terms instantly recognizable from later satire, complimentary descriptions of women, specifically those found in Homeric epic:

> num censes calliplocamon callisphyron ullam
> non licitum esse uterum atque etiam inguina tangere mammis,
> conpernem aut uaram fuisse Amphitryonis acoetin
> Alcmenam atque alias, Ledam ipsam denique – nolo
> dicere; tute uide atque disyllabon elige quoduis –
> couren eupatereiam aliquam rem insignem habuisse,
> uerrucam naeuum punctum dentem eminulum unum.

You don't think, do you that any 'fair-tressed', 'fair-ankled' woman could not have touched belly and even groin with her breasts, or that Alcmena 'spouse of Amphitryon' could not have been knock-kneed or bandy-legged, and that others, even Leda herself, could not have been – I don't want to say it: see to it yourself and choose any disyllable you want – that 'a girl of good parentage' could not have had some outstanding mark, a wart, a mole, a spot, one little protruding tooth?
>   (frs 567–73, Warmington 1938)

This passage very obviously rejoices in demeaning its subjects. It takes glamorizing descriptions of women and exposes them for their dishonesty. The flattering descriptions are, not coincidentally, all in Greek: the collision between misleading fantasy and brute reality is at the same time one between glib Greek and honest-to-goodness Latin. They are all from Homer, too, so the passage is also, among other things, a critique of specifically epic ways of speaking. But the antagonistic stance it adopts towards high literature is perceptible in other ways too. One of Lucilius' most telling contributions to satirical practice is his decision early on in his career to abandon the motley collection of mainly dramatic metres Ennius had used in his satire, and to compose exclusively in the hexameter, the form associated with the epic poetry of Homer and Ennius. But Lucilius' hexameter is a standing affront to the principles of order and beauty for which the epic hexameter was meant to be the vehicle. In this passage the fragments of Homeric verse are a reminder of how hexameters should flow, the splendid cadence of 'Amphitryonis acoetin', 'spouse of Amphitryon', for example, from the *Odyssey*. The line before it is an equally splendid piece of metrical vandalism on Lucilius' part. It is huge, at first sight far too big for the metrical scheme, but crammed in by means of elision between vowels of a staggering order: the central part of the line (*licitum esse uterum atque etiam inguina*) has to be pronounced something like 'licitwessu- terwatquetiaenguina', a gobstopper worthy of James Joyce, another exuberant abuser of Homer's *Odyssey*. Lucilius is deliberately misusing the glorious met- rical vehicle of epic, in other words, even to the extent (in the fourth and fifth lines) of resigning control of his composition to another party: asking an interlocutor to complete the fourth line however he wants is a marvellous way of demeaning the hitherto mystical process of composing in the measure of heroes. But bound up with this abuse of the metrical form is a commitment to the satirical anti-principles of shapelessness and disorder. Like Diomedes' sausage, the second line is barely contained by its formal structure, and in its bloatedness obviously reflects the bloated female body it describes. The passage as a whole represents the unstructured drift of an ordinary conversation, as far from the artificial linguistic forms of conventional hexameter poetry as it is possible to imagine. In all these respects, then, this fragment from the middle of Lucilius' collection exemplifies satire's hatred of artificial order, which it identified with deceit, its impulse towards the ugly, its glorious shapelessness, but above all perhaps its Romanness. Satire was the only genre that Romans could with any confidence claim as their own, as opposed to borrowed from the Greeks. In its exposure of Greek modes of expression, its corruption of a Greek metrical form and most of all its adoption of such a brutally misogynistic standpoint (Romanness and virility were concepts thoroughly interlinked), this piece of satire is a potent exercise in racial, cultural and national self-definition.

This being so, it is little wonder that Lucilius' satire occupied a very special place not only on Romans' bookshelves but also in their very sense of themselves. Lucilius was outspoken, politically opinionated and in ways we have investigated self-consciously Roman. Later Romans, consequently, were in the habit of reach- ing for the satire of Lucilius when they wanted to express something essential about their culture. Cicero, for example, describing to Atticus how surprisingly pleasant a visit to his villa had been by the dictator Caesar, lets his sense of the normality of an event which could so easily have driven home the massive gulf which separated these former political equals express itself through quotation of Lucilius' prescription for a perfect dinner party:

> Strange that so onerous a guest should leave a memory not disagreeable! It was really very pleasant . . . . After anointing he took his place at dinner. He was following a course of emetics, and so both ate and drank with uninhibited enjoyment. It was a really fine, well-appointed meal, and not only that but 'well cooked and garnished, good talking too – in fact a very pleasant meal'. (*Att.* 13.52.1)

Adoption of the Lucilian mode conveys that all is right with the Roman world, is one way of putting it. And as DuQuesnay (1984: 27–32) has suggested, this is not the least important reason for Horace's adoption of that mode under circumstances not dissimilar to those obtaining at the time of Cicero's letter to Atticus.

3   Horace

In 35 BC, amid the troubled conditions of the Second Triumvirate (see Farrell, Chapter 3 above), Horace composed the first of two books of satires, one of the aims of which was to exploit the nostalgic associations of the form to improve the standing of the warlord to whom Horace had tied his colours, the future emperor Augustus. Here was Lucilius' style of literature being deployed to represent the circle of Augustus and Maecenas in the way Lucilius had depicted the lives of his contemporaries and friends Scipio Aemilianus and C. Laelius, Roman heroes of a bygone age. But if readers of Horace's satires were expecting the blunt frankness and explicit politics, the *libertas*, of his predecessor, the quality that endeared Lucilius more than anything else to Romans, they were disappointed. The dramatic changes in Roman public life since Lucilius' time, the movement from the rough and tumble of oligarchic politics to the restrictions of autocracy, show up clearly in the satirical genre. Horace's satire has its fascinations, but they are of a quite different kind from Lucilius'. Targets of abuse have become anonymous, or generalized into stock characters; the aggressive tone of Lucilian satire has been moderated; and the key virtue of *libertas* is in a process (continued later by Persius) of becoming more and more a quality of the individual soul, less and less of interactions between members of an active political elite. Satire is being privatized, in other words, and Horace adopts an oblique, ironic style fundamentally true to the restrictive political circumstances of his time.

Much of the energy that Lucilius expended on political tirades Horace diverts into dwelling almost obsessively on his relation to his dominating predecessor. Poem 1.5, for example, brilliantly analysed in Gowers (1993b), describes a rather aimless (from Horace's viewpoint) journey in the direction of Brundisium, carefully avoiding letting us in on the precise nature and purpose of the mission (though we are told enough to appreciate it is important and *worth* knowing) and engaging at the same time in a complex and elusive contest with a poem of Lucilius that had described a similar journey away from Rome. The grounds for competition are largely provided by the Callimacheanism that Horace consistently professes in this collection. Lucilius' undisciplined prolixity in his journey poem is countered by brevity and polish in Horace's – except that so unequivocal a correction would be far too straightforward for Horace. What makes his satire so demanding and compelling, so much more difficult, ultimately, than the superficially more obscure satire of Persius, are the layers of irony and evasion in which he wreathes his material. Poem 1.5 is very short by his own standards, let alone by Lucilius' (whose journey poem is still sizeable even in fragments). And yet Horace insists on how long his poem is: 'Brundisium is the end of a long text and journey,' is how it concludes. Elsewhere Horace draws attention to his extremely sluggish progress as compared with Lucilius:

> inde Forum Appi,
> differtum nautis cauponibus atque malignis.
> hoc iter ignaui diuisimus, altius ac nos
> praecinctis unum: minus est grauis Appia tardis.

> From Aricia we went to Forum Appi,
> stuffed with sailors and unfriendly innkeepers.
> We lazily broke this journey into two, which to travellers more energetic than us
> is one: but the Appian Way is less wearing when you take your time.
> (Horace *Satires* 1.5.3–6)

One of the 'more energetic' travellers is apparently Lucilius himself, who seems to have covered the same stretch of the Appian Way at a much brisker pace. Horace is playing with us, then: he describes a slower journey than Lucilius' in tighter, brisker verse, encouraging us to discern a consistent programme in his satire, but ultimately denying us anything so clear and categorical: it would not be satire if he did not.

At another level Horace develops the tendency we have already seen in Lucilius of foregrounding the issue of satire's literary, or subliterary, status. Lucilius' grotesques occupied the heroic space of the hexameter. In a similar way here there is a tension between poetic form and the formless substance it encompasses. Horace's satire expresses itself with superb economy. In this passage the delay in the supply of the connective *atque* (and) in the second line allows the (characteristically satirical) cramming together of 'sailors innkeepers' (*nautis cauponibus*), which expresses the sense of *differtus* (stuffed) perfectly; similarly the sloth of Horace's journey in the third line is communicated by the falling of *ignaui* (lazily) and *diuisimus* (we broke) on either side of the caesura, or breath break, in the hexameter: 'lazily' – pause – 'we broke'. The speed and energy of other travellers, on the other hand, is communicated by the brevity of the expression in the following line: *praecinctis unum* (one to the energetic). Yet what is described in this poetry is definitively mean: laziness, roadtrips, dodgy innkeepers. There is an exquisite counterpoint between Horace's beautifully expressive versification and the grubby scene it depicts; and the irresolvable doubts this raises about satire's relation to real literature are closely akin to those provoked by Lucilius' brilliantly dreadful hexameters. Horace's introduction of Callimachean standards of composition to satire has been interpreted as an attempt to mitigate the excesses of his predecessor: that bloated hexameter of Lucilius did not even *have* a caesura. But what appears at first sight a toning down of satire's provocative stance regarding respectable literature is in fact a tightening of the screw. The scandal of Lucilius' disfigured hexameters becomes the paradox of Horace's Callimachean satire, a wonderful contradiction in terms.

The obsession of Horatian satire with its predecessor is a dominant feature of the first book. But it is characteristic of the workings of a genre that, as Oliensis (1998: 17–63) shows, Horace's second book, published five years later in 30 BC, takes not Lucilius but his own first book as the main target of its generic self-positioning. The big difference is a shift from mainly first-person narrative in the first book to the proliferation of other voices that take up the story in the second. The result is that whereas Book 1 offered a fairly complacent narrative of Horace's effortless entry into the charmed social circle of Maecenas, Book 2 questions and subverts that comfortable account. Perhaps the most striking example of this self-exposure is in the move from satires 2.6 to 2.7. Satire 2.6 is a brilliant, but morally unchallenging, assertion of the superiority of rural over urban life, starting from Horace's villa in the Sabine country, gifted to him by a grateful Maecenas, encompassing generous references to his proximity to the great man and ending with the famous parable of the town mouse and the country mouse, according to which a country mouse, tempted by the rich pickings of a city life, learns also to appreciate its cost in stress and anxiety, expressing himself at the close like a pint-sized Epicurean:

> ille cubans gaudet mutata sorte bonisque
> rebus agit laetum conuiuam; cum subito ingens
> ualuarum strepitus lectis excussit utrumque.
> currere per totum pauidi conclaue, magisque
> exanimes trepidare simul domus alta Molossis
> personuit canibus. tum rusticus, 'haud mihi uita
> est opus hac,' ait et, 'ualeas. me silua cauusque
> tutus ab insidiis tenui solabitur eruo.'

The country mouse, reclining, rejoices in his change of fortune
and since things were going well, plays the happy guest – when suddenly a huge
crash of doors startled them both from their couches.
They ran startled all over the dining room, and were the more
terrified and panicked when the high house
resounded with Molossian dogs. Then the countryman said, 'I don't need
this kind of life,' and 'Farewell. My woodland burrow,
safe from ambush will keep me content with simple vetch.'

(Horace *Satires* 2.6.110–17)

A mouse spouting philosophy is not without its irony, but we emerge from 2.6, nevertheless, with a warm feeling about the countryside, the good life, and Horace himself – which Horace goes on directly to complicate. Satire 2.7 features

Dauus, one of Horace's slaves, who takes the opportunity of the Saturnalia, a time of the year when societal structures were relaxed, to expatiate on a favourite theme of satire, *libertas* (freedom), and expose his master's moral failings, *his* enslavement to conflicting and destructive impulses. Far from the consistent devotee of the good life presented in 2.6, then, Horace is all at sea:

> Romae rus optas, absentem rusticus urbem
> tollis ad astra leuis.

> At Rome you long for the country, in the country the far-off city
> is praised by you to the stars, inconsistent man!
>
> (Horace *Satires* 2.7.28–9)

It would be quite unlike satire to offer a clear and comfortable direction, whether literary or moral, and Horace's second book is happy not to oblige on either count. In terms of the history of the genre, though, the most striking feature of Horace's satire, as compared with Lucilius', is its self-obsession. We learn a lot about Horace in this collection, but that public dimension so crucial to Lucilius' production and reputation has atrophied correspondingly. Reading Lucilius had once inspired the assassins of Julius Caesar; now, according to Dauus, *libertas* is strictly a matter of an individual's relation to himself.

4   Persius and Menippean Satire

This tendency towards solipsism is one of the many respects in which Persius accepts a Horatian precedent, and then pushes it to extremes. Some way into his first poem Persius lets on that the individual he has been arguing with about contemporary literary and ethical values (for Persius they are two sides of the same coin) is his own invention. This is obviously true of any satirical interlocutor, on a moment's reflection, but Persius' explicit confession of the fact is part of a bigger tendency to emphasise his own solitariness. 'Who will read this?' he has his interlocutor ask him, to which his reply is, 'No one, By Hercules.' Elsewhere he plans to confide his satirical assault on Rome not to an audience but to a hole in the ground. The atmosphere of his satires is consequently a very claustrophobic one. Even when a poem like his sixth opens with an address to a friend, Caesius Bassus, this hint of a social dimension to his satire does not last, the clearly delineated interlocutor soon forgotten. Horace's satire had retreated indoors; Persius for most of the time is entirely on his own. He is extreme in other ways, too. Horace's satires were short and polished (with all the contradictions that entails); Persius' are the densest, most intense works in Latin literature. At the same time they display a comparably intense engagement with physical and subpoetical subject matter. So our Horatian paradox of artistic descriptions of the indescribably ghastly is raised to yet another degree. In the first poem, for example, Persius criticizes contemporary tastes in literature, citing an (invented) example and then exclaiming:

> haec fierent si testiculi uena ulla paterni
> uiueret in nobis? summa delumbe saliua
> hoc natat in labris et in udo est Maenas et Attis
> nec pluteum cadit nec demorsos sapit ungues.

> Would these things happen, if a single vein of the ancestral testicle
> lived in us? This stuff floats emasculated at the surface of the saliva
> on the lips, and the Maenad and Attis grow where it's wet
> and never bangs the chair back or tastes of chewed nails.
> (Persius *Satires* 1.103–6)

Image is piled on vivid image, and the meticulousness of the composition is clear, but Persius takes us places not visited by the respectable literature that he is attacking. And this of course is the point. Here enormous care has gone into reflecting the superficiality of the literature he is criticizing in the *sound*, as well as the sense, of the passage: *summa delumbe saliua* (emasculated at the surface of the saliva) acts out *in our mouths* what it describes, an achievement of great poetic skill that is at the same time quite disgusting. More blatantly, the passage begins with a blunt statement of the connection between masculinity and Romanity (contemporary literature 'has no balls'), and satire's role as the self-appointed guardian of both. Gross physicality and rank chauvinism are part and parcel of this most offensive form of art.

Persian satire continues to wrestle with the principle of *libertas*, with which Lucilius and his works had practically been synonymous, but in Persius' case there is a fascinating comparison to be made with a near-contemporary work by the philosopher Seneca, the *Apocolocyntosis* (*Pumpkinification*), our best surviving example of 'Menippean Satire', an alternative tradition of satire consisting of verse and prose intermingled (and thus appropriately 'satirical'), which had originated with the Greek-Syrian author Menippus of Gadara and had been introduced to Rome by the great polymath Varro (116–27 BC): this subgenre is well discussed by Coffey (1976: 149–203) and Eden (1984: 13–16). Varro's output eclipsed even Lucilius', but regrettably is just as fragmentary. Seneca's satire is a brilliant (and merciless) attack on the emperor Claudius after his death in AD 54, and by the same token a celebration of the restoration of Roman order, *libertas* in particular, which Claudius' successor Nero claimed to be undertaking. Most of the action of the *Apocolocyntosis* (the name is a parody of the apotheosis Claudius had received soon after he died) takes place in a council of the gods closely modelled on a similar gathering in Lucilius' first book. In particular Seneca's divine council follows Lucilius' in taking the form of a meeting of the Roman senate, a powerful symbol (in the context of the start of Nero's reign) of the restoration of the liberty and power that the Roman elite had progressively forfeited since the end of the Republic. The *Apocolocyntosis* is thus another attempt to assert the restoration of Rome, and its quintessential virtue of *libertas*, through satire, here, for example, brutally caricaturing the tradition of a great man's 'famous last words' and exploiting Claudius' physical disability:

> ultima uox eius haec inter hominess audita est, cum maiorem sonitum emisisset illa parte, qua facilius loquebatur: 'uae me, puto, concacaui me.' quod an fecerit, nescio; omnia certe concacauit.

> This was the last utterance of his to be heard on earth, after he had let out a louder sound from that part with which he found it easier to communicate: 'Oh dear, I think I've shit myself.' And I'm inclined to think he had. He certainly shat on everything else. (*Apocolocyntosis* 4.3)

We look in vain for similar, risky contemporary material in Persius, though commentators from ancient times on have tried very hard to find it. Many ancients, for example, and quite a few moderns, have been convinced that the dreadful poetry attacked in Persius' first satire was written by Nero. It certainly was not, but the mistake is understandable: it was just impossible to believe that a satirist could be at work in the reign of Nero and not satirize *Nero*, a gift to caricature if ever there was one. For of course Seneca's high hopes of his former pupil proved utterly misplaced, as he was to discover long before the suicide that Nero insisted he commit in AD 65. In Persius, in stark contrast with the *Apocolocyntosis*, *libertas* has become the strictly philosophical principle it was threatening to become in Horace's satire. In his fifth satire Persius attacks the notion that a slave can achieve true freedom by the elaborate Roman rituals of emancipation:

> libertate opus est. non hac, ut quisque Velina
> Publius emeruit, scabiosum tesserula far
> possidet. heu steriles ueri, quibus una Quiritem
> uertigo facit! hic Dama est non tresis agaso,
> uappa lippus et in tenui farragine mendax.
> uerterit hunc dominus, momento turbinis exit
> Marcus Dama. papae!

> We need freedom – not the kind every Johnny of the Veline tribe
> has earned, entitling him by ticket to mouldy groats.
> Alas, barren of truth are they who suppose one dizzy turn
> makes a Roman. Dama here's a two-bob stable-boy,
> red-eyed with plonk, a liar, waters down the animal feed.
> His master gives him a spin, from one short whirl emerges
> *Citizen* Dama. Wowee!
> (Persius *Satires* 5.73–9)

Freedom really consists, Persius goes on to argue in his characteristically mordant and vivid style, in controlling our self-destructive impulses, which exert much more immediate control over our lives than any slave master does:

> an dominum ignoras nisi quem uindicta relaxat?
> 'i, puer, et strigiles Crispini ad balnea defer'
> si increpuit, 'cessas nugator?', seruitium acre
> te nihil inpellit nec quicquam extrinsecus intrat
> quod neruos agitet; sed si intus et in iecore aegro
> nascuntur domini, qui tu inpunitior exis
> atque hic quem ad strigiles scutica et metus egit erilis?

> Do you recognize no master but the one the official baton removes?
> Suppose the master yells, 'Off, boy, and take Crispinus' strigils
> down to the baths. Get on with it, idiot!', harsh slavery
> has no power to compel you, nothing enters from outside
> to operate your muscles. But if you've got masters growing
> inside you and in your decrepit liver, how do *you* come off better
> than the man sent off after strigils by the lash and fear of his master?
>
> (Persius *Satires* 5.125–31)

5 Juvenal

When Juvenal surveyed the genre of satire, he clearly felt the Horatian-Persian reaction against Lucilius' verbosity had run its course. His response to the miniaturism of Persian satire is to break out and cut loose, not least from the physical confines of Horatian and Persian satire back into the mean streets of the city of Rome, though significantly it is the city of a generation before Juvenal's time: that original Lucilian immediacy was never to be recovered fully. Juvenal is expansive, in every respect, but particularly in his elevated style of expression. Where Lucilius had stolen epic's metre to tell his decidedly unepic tales of corruption and debauchery, Juvenal steals its language too. But his topics are still as lowbrow. Where epic talks of achievement and success, satire dwells on failure and downfall, here the downfall of Tiberius' minister Sejanus, as reflected in the demolition of his statue:

> iam strident ignes, iam follibus atque caminis
> ardet adoratum populo caput et crepat ingens
> Seianus, deinde ex facie toto orbe secunda
> fiunt urceoli, pelues, sartago, matellae.

> Now the fires roar, now with the bellows and furnace
> the head beloved by the people glows and great Sejanus is crackling,

and then from the face which was second in the whole world
are made pitchers, basins, frying pans and piss-pots.

(Juvenal *Satires* 10.61–4)

The violence done to elevated modes of speech here precisely reflects the violence being done to a former symbol of authority. Sejanus *was* great, and the epic language of *toto orbe secunda* (second in the whole world) expresses this at a stylistic as well as semantic level. What he, or rather his statue, becomes, on the other hand, is both base – kitchenware and toiletries – and basely expressed in a plain, unembellished list of words which themselves have no possible place in respectable literature. Comparable in its dynamic exploitation of registers of speech is the superb contrast drawn in Juvenal's fifth satire between the magnificent food eaten by the rich patron at a dinner he throws and the scrapings he serves up to his impoverished hangers-on. The fruit that wealthy Virro feasts upon 'had a scent that was a meal in itself', were such as King Alcinous grew in his magical garden in the *Odyssey*, or like the golden apples that Heracles stole from the Garden of the Hesperides. 'You, on the other hand, enjoy a rotten apple such as is gnawed / by that performing monkey on the Embankment who wears a shield and helmet and from fear of the whip / learns to throw a spear sitting on a hairy she-goat' (5.153–5).

But if Juvenal had restored to satire something approaching Lucilius' amplitude and vehemence, what is still missing is the sense of a literary form engaging directly and dangerously with real politics. Sejanus was a safe target, dead not far short of a century before Juvenal wrote against him. Most of Juvenal's satirical targets date to the regime of Domitian, which preceded the dynasty of the 'Spanish Emperors' under which he was writing. There is thus an odd feeling of displacement in Juvenal's satire, which has all the force of Lucilius but is directed at villains who have been off the scene for a generation. The dislocation speaks volumes about the condition of that *libertas* so central to the Romans' sense of themselves, not to mention the genre of satire, even under the relatively benign rule of Trajan and Hadrian: Freudenberg (2001) discusses the issue at length. But against Domitian, at any rate, Juvenal can vent an authentic satirical fury. In his fourth satire Juvenal, like Lucilius and Seneca before him, convenes a council, but this time it is a meeting of Domitian with his circle of advisers, apparently to discuss some matter of great moment to the Roman Empire – in fact to decide how to cook a particularly large fish which has been presented to the emperor:

> sed derat pisci patinae mensura. uocantur
> ergo in consilium proceres, quos oderat ille,
> in quorum facie miserae magnaeque sedebat
> pallor amicitiae.
>
> But a dimension of dish to match the fish was lacking, and therefore
> the elite were summoned to council. He hated them,

and in their faces there sat the pallor that goes with a sickening and great
friendship.

(Juvenal *Satires* 4.72–5)

We have the same collision of elevated and low registers of language and material
that we saw in the Sejanus passage; 'there was no dish big enough' is elevated into
'a dimension of dish was lacking', but the elevation is undermined by the mean
associations of the serving dish, *patina*, which is the object of the exercise. But
what is also on show here is Juvenal's absolute control of poetic form. Juvenal
possessed to a sublime degree what might inadequately be described as comic
timing. Here the word for 'friendship', *amicitiae*, is separated from the adjectives
defining it, 'sickening and great' (*miserae magnaeque*) in such a way as to provide
a perfect impact for the paradox which the word 'friendship' introduces. A
friendship that *harms* should be a blatant contradiction in terms, of course, but
expresses the utter corruption of moral values which as a satirist Juvenal had to
find, and as a satirist of the imperial period had to find in the past.

It is not a promising formula, and it should not really work, but it does. For
most readers Juvenal is by far the most compelling of ancient satirists. His wit,
rhetorical skill and mastery of form are such that satirical assaults on the tamest
and tritest of targets, for his contemporary readers let alone for us, retain an
unparalleled power to engage, amuse and not infrequently disturb. Here, for
example, Juvenal illustrates his contention that it is a man's character, not his
ancestry, which bestows true nobility with an account of Nero, now dead about
half a century, and specifically with an unfavourable comparison of the emperor
with Orestes, the desperate protagonist of Aeschylus' dramatic trilogy *Oresteia*
who like Nero killed his own mother, but *unlike* Nero did not also butcher his
wives, his adoptive father (Claudius, in Nero's case), sister and brother:

> libera si dentur populo suffragia, quis tam
> perditus ut dubitet Senecam praeferre Neroni?
> cuius supplicio non debuit una parari
> simia nec serpens unus nec culleus unus.
> par Agamemnonidae crimen, sed causa facit rem
> dissimilem. quippe ille deis auctoribus ultor
> patris erat caesi media inter pocula, sed nec
> Electrae iugulo se polluit aut Spartani
> sanguine coniugii, nullis aconita propinquis
> miscuit, in scena numquam cantauit Oresten,
> Troica non scripsit.

> If the people were given a free vote, who would be
> so depraved as not to prefer Seneca to Nero without hesitation?
> To punish Nero properly a single ape, a single snake
> and a single bag would not have sufficed.

His crime was the same as Orestes', but motivation makes the cases
different. Orestes at the behest of the gods themselves avenged
a father slaughtered as he celebrated, but he never
defiled himself by strangling Electra or shedding the blood
of his Spartan wife; he never mixed poisons
for his own relatives; he never acted the part of Orestes,
or wrote a Trojan epic.

(Juvenal *Satires* 8.211–21)

The idea of condemning Nero by absolving Orestes of Nero's crimes, one by one,
is brilliantly inventive in itself, as is the notion that Nero was so bad that the
already appalling punishment for *parricida*, the murder of close relations – to be
sewn up in a bag with a dog, a cock, a snake and a monkey and thrown into the sea
– was inadequate to his misdeeds. The last two lines puncture the grandeur of
what precedes in a manner typical of Juvenal, and of the satirical instinct, implying
that Nero's undignified devotion to the stage and his bad poetry were crimes of
comparable magnitude to the murder of his own family. *Troica non scripsit* is
another case of perfect timing, but to express the difference between a figure from
the theatre and a devotee of the theatre as 'Orestes was never so depraved as to act
the part of Orestes' is genius pure and simple.

Juvenal was the most influential of the satirists, in the sense that we now
consider the kinds of strategies which we find in his work to be defining features
of satire. Most important of these is the pointedly dubious status of the satirist
himself. Juvenal's verse is clever, funny, but morally repellent at the same time:
nothing is exempt from his satire, and he offers no secure moral standpoint from
which to view the world he caricatures: Bramble (1982b: 600) writes how
'Juvenal mockingly entertains us with the vice we all demand, but takes it much
too far, disturbing us with half-voiced questions about the basis of our values.'
Consequently the readers' typical experience is to respond powerfully to its
rhetorical brilliance, but to feel tarnished by their involvement. An extreme
example, but a telling one, is the epigrammatic wit with which Juvenal satirizes
the act of anal sex. 'Do you think it's easy,' asks a male prostitute, 'to shove a
decent-sized penis into someone's guts, and there encounter yesterday's dinner?'
(9.43–4):

an facile et pronum est agere intra uiscera penem
legitimum atque illic hesternae occurrere cenae?

A truly repellent image, exquisitely expressed, at once amusing and disgusting.
It is much more than our sense of literary proprieties which satire sets out to
offend.

FURTHER READING

An accessible introduction to Roman verse satire is provided by Braund (1992), and in greater detail by Coffey (1976) and Rudd (1986). The third chapter of Gowers (1993a) is good on the ways in which the terms of Diomedes' etymologies of *satura* are reflected in the satirists' own accounts of their poetry. Warmington (vol. 4, 1938) offers a text, translation and interpretation of the surviving fragments of Lucilius, and there are good translations of Horace, Persius and Juvenal in Rudd (1979 and 1991). The translation and commentary of Persius in Lee and Barr (1987) is excellent, and Brown (1993) and Muecke (1993) are commentaries on Horace's first and second books of satires, respectively. The pick of the commentaries on Juvenal is Ferguson (1979); see also Courtney (1980) and Braund (1996).

To appreciate the elusive character of Horace's satire, Gowers (1993b) on 1.5 is an excellent place to start, while Harrison (1987) shows the layers of irony which complicate even so superficially straightforward a piece of self-justification as Horace 2.1. Zetzel (1980), similarly, displays how Horace's paradox of 'Callimachean satire' works itself out at the level of the overall organization (or, ultimately, lack of it) of his first book. An exemplary close reading of Horace's parable of the town and country mouse is offered in West (1974).

Bramble (1974) is a seminal, book-length rehabilitation of Persius' satires (paying particular attention to the first), and the most important recent contribution to scholarship of the poet. The 'alternative tradition' of Menippean satire is best approached through Coffey (1976) and (more succinctly) Eden (1984). Anderson (1982) is a collection of essays on the whole genre of satire by a leading recent scholar of satire, who pays particular attention to the artificiality of the persona projected by Juvenal, thereby seeking to distance the objectionably ranting and prurient narrator of Juvenal's satire from Juvenal himself. More recent critics have emphasized the 'self-diagnostic' power – a term from Freudenburg (2001) – of Juvenal's satire: the reader is disgusted by its amorality, but also compelled by its wit and rhetorical power, and hence alerted to her/his own *nostalgie de la boue*: Bramble (1982a) is eloquent on this aspect of Juvenal's perverse appeal.

CHAPTER THIRTEEN

Lyric and Iambic

Stephen Harrison

1 Introduction

These two genres, neither of which survives in profusion, have been placed together here largely because they are both practised by the major Roman poets Catullus and Horace; the two are consequently similarly juxtaposed in Quintilian's syllabus of Latin literature (10.1.96).

Lyric poetry, notoriously fluid in modern literary categorization, was not much easier to pin down in the Graeco-Roman world (see Johnson 1982: 76–95). Even the idea originally fundamental to the genre that lyric poetry was to be sung by its performer(s) to the lyre was not a unique generic marker, even in archaic and classical Greece when such performances were frequent, since the rhapsodes who recited Homeric epic poetry also used the lyre as accompaniment (e.g. Homer *Odyssey* 8.66). Indeed, the label 'lyric' was only invented in the course of the categorizing of earlier Greek poetry that took place in Hellenistic Alexandria (Pfeiffer 1968: 181–8). This work classified kinds of poetry by metre, and it is largely by metrical criteria that lyric poetry is generally defined in the ancient world, as well as by the nine-poet lyric canon established by the Alexandrian classification (Alcaeus, Alcman Anacreon, Bacchylides, Ibycus, Pindar, Sappho, Simonides and Stesichorus). There was a difference in principle between choral lyric, intended for choruses of particular kinds in particular circumstances (e.g. the *Partheneion* of Alcman, written for an all-girl ritual group), and monodic lyric, performed by a single singer in the first person (e.g. the poems of Sappho and Alcaeus); but even in the classical period, this distinction seems to have been unclear at times, for example in the extant victory odes of Pindar from the fifth century BC (see Lefkowitz 1991: 191–201).

Greek lyric metres varied considerably. Choral lyric generally followed patterns of triadic response (strophe, antistrophe, epode, replicated by a further triad with matching metrical patterns), linked with the chorus's dance movements, as we find in the victory odes of Pindar and the lyric choruses of Greek tragedy, while monodic lyric often used repeating four-line stanzas; for example in Sappho and Alcaeus. Lyric measures generally provided more rhythmical variety than the more familiar iambic trimeter used in the spoken parts of tragedy and the epic hexameter, often based on a unit with a choriambic element (long, short, short, long). By the time we reach the Roman period, the few choral lyrics we find (e.g. Horace's *Carmen Saeculare* – see section 3, 'Horace's *Epodes* and *Odes*', below) make no real attempt to imitate the triadic structure (strophe/antistrophe/ epode), and in general the history of post-Hellenistic lyric tells a story of gradual metrical simplification.

Iambic poetry, written in simple verse-forms using the basic unit of the iambus (short, long), is associated primarily with the early Greek poet Archilochus (7th c. BC) and Hipponax (6th c. BC), who used poetry in iambic metres to mount attacks on others, thus giving iambic verse an aggressive character fundamental to the genre (cf. Aristotle, *Poetics* 4.1448b), though iambic themes were by no means restricted to abuse. Iambic poetry was considered lower and more colloquial than lyric poetry, partly because of the traditional view that iambic metre was the simplest of verse-forms and close to normal human speech (Aristotle, *Poetics* 4.1449a), partly because of the often undignified content: quite apart from the violent invective of both writers, Archilochus' iambic fragments are highly explicit about sex (frs 40–6, 188–91, 196 West), while Hipponax includes scenes where the poet and a prostitute drink wine from a bucket (frs 13–14 West). This relatively lower level is retained in the Latin iambic poetry of Catullus, Horace and Phaedrus. In the Hellenistic age, Callimachus' *Iambi* claimed to follow the model of Hipponax, and in their flexible content, more literary and more elevated concerns, and many points of contact with other genres provide an important predecessor for some elements in Horace's *Epodes*.

2   The Beginnings to Catullus

The earliest Latin lyric poetry we have consists of the lyric parts of the twenty-one plays of Plautus (2nd c. BC), and fragments of choral song from the remains of Latin tragedy. Neither shows triadic structure or responsion; Plautus' lyric songs, performed by actors rather than a chorus (choruses had by then disappeared from comedy; see Chapter 9 above), show great exuberance and variety (e.g. Anderson 1993: 118–32), while the few tragic fragments we can identify as choral are metrically relatively unexciting (e.g. the 'Soldiers' Chorus' from Ennius' *Iphige-nia*: Skutsch 1968: 157–65). But lyric poetry in the conventional sense, poems in the first person outside a dramatic framework, begins to be found in Laevius in the early first century BC, who experimented with a range of lyric metres in his *Erotopaegnia*, something of a miscellaneous collection (Courtney 1993: 118–22). Cicero is famously cited as saying that life was too short to read all the Greek lyric poets (Seneca *Epist.* 49.5), and it was really after Cicero that Latin lyric, with its new interest in Greek poetry (see Chapter 2) through Callimachus, who had written in lyric metres himself, begins to imitate the riches of the Greek tradition.

The prime figure here was Catullus in the 50s BC (for Catullus see also Levene, Chapter 2 above; Watson, Chapter 14 below; Keith, Chapter 23 below; and Konstan, Chapter 24 below). The collection of 116 poems that has come down to us in his name contains more than sixty poems in lyric metres. Most of these are written in the Phalaecian hendecasyllable, a simple lyric metre of one repeated eleven-syllable line associated with the 'book-lyric' of the Hellenistic period; by the time of Catullus there seems to be no necessity to imagine lyric poetry as sung. The hendecasyllabic poems of Catullus do not confine themselves to traditional topics of monodic lyric such as love and the symposium; though they include the famous love poems to Lesbia, such as the poems about kisses (5, 7) and her pet sparrow (2, 3), they also include scabrous invectives (16, 23, 33, 42, 43, 46), comic invitations (13, 32, 35) and amusing anecdotes (10, 12, 50), and versions of epigrammatic topics such as spring poems (46). In the invectives we can see close contact between this lyric metre and traditional iambic content (see above and Heyworth 2001).

There are also examples of more complex stanza-forms consciously imitating the archaic Greek lyric poetry of Sappho and Alcaeus. Especially striking is Catullus 51, a virtual translation of one of the few extant poems of Sappho, in the four-line Sapphic stanza (fr. 31 L/P), which presents the poet as feeling jealous of his rival who has time to gaze on the beloved Lesbia:

> Ille mi par esse deo uidetur,
> ille, si fas est, superare diuos,
> qui sedens aduersus identidem te
>   spectat et audit
> dulce ridentem . . . .

He seems to me to be the equal of a god, he seems (if that is right) to surpass the gods, who can sit opposite you continually, watch you and hear your sweet laughter . . .

(Catullus 51.1–5)

The only other Sapphic poem in the collection (11), in which the poet rejects Lesbia, invites juxtaposition with 51; scholars have often argued that the rejection-poem 11 deliberately echoes the ecstatic 51 in winding up the affair; their relative order in the collection may well belong to a hand other than Catullus, since it is far from clear that the Catullan collection we have was put together by its author. Catullus also has examples of stanzaic choral lyric in the hymn to Diana (34) and the marriage-hymn for Torquatus (61), both in established Greek lyric metres.

Catullus is also an important channel for the iambic tradition at Rome. Though other iambic verses in a non-dramatic context can be found before Catullus, in Ennius (see Russo 2001) and in the earlier books of Lucilian satires known to us as Books 26–30 (see Morgan, Chapter 12 above), it is in the Catullan collection that we first find traditional iambic invectives in the manner of Archilochus and Hipponax (22, 25, 29, 37, 39), though iambic metres can also be used for different types of poems such as versions of epigrammatic dedications (4). The obscene and rumbustious spirit of Archilochean iambic is well expressed in Catullus 59:

> Bononiensis Rufa Rufulum fellat,
> uxor Meneni, saepe quam in sepulcretis
> uidistis ipso rapere de rogo cenam,
> cum deuolutum ex igne prosequens panem
> ab semiraso tunderetur ustore.

Rufa from Bologna gives head to Rufulus – she, the wife of Menenius, she whom you have often seen in burial-grounds stealing the funeral meal from the very pyre, when (chasing after some bread which had rolled down from the fire) she was being given a good pounding by the half-shaven corpse-burner.

It has also been plausibly argued that the iambic spirit suffuses much of Catullus' non-iambic poetry, especially some of the hendecasyllabic invectives (see above).

3   Horace's *Epodes* and *Odes*

Looking back on the *Epodes* (published *c.* 30 BC) more than a decade later, Horace claimed to have been the first to imitate in Latin the iambic metre and spirit of Archilochus, but that he did not follow his subject matter in the hounding of his victims (*Epistles* 1.19.23–5). Modern scholars are largely agreed that much of the invective in Horace's seventeen-poem collection, probably named after a similar collection of Archilochus that likewise used 'epodic' iambic metres in which a longer line is paired with a shorter one as the unit of composition, is contrived or comic (e.g. the satirizing of Alfius in 2, the mock-curse in 3, the ex-slave who is like the poet himself in 4, the repulsive women of 8 and 12), and that the poet deliberatedly presents a weak and impotent persona contrasting with that of the vigorous Archilochus, especially in his contacts with the witch Canidia (5, 17; cf. Watson 1995; Oliensis 1998: 68–76). One aspect of this impotence is political: *Epodes* 7 and 16, probably among the earliest in the collection, show helpless pessimism about the civil wars (see further Harrison, Chapter 20 below).

One example of this modification of Greek iambus is *Epode* 10, a poem clearly related to the Cologne fragment usually attributed to Hipponax (fr. 115, West 1997); the raw invective of the Greek poem, wishing in very realistic terms that the enemy be shipwrecked and enslaved amongst barbarians, is turned by Horace into a comically overblown picture of the man's cowardice in shipwreck and the celebrations on his (unlikely) death:

> o quantus instat navitis sudor tuis
>   tibique pallor luteus
> et illa non virilis heiulatio
>   preces et aversum ad Iovem,
> Ionius udo cum remugiens sinus
>   Noto carinam ruperit
> opima quodsi praeda curvo litore
>   porrecta mergos iuverit,
> libidinosus immolabitur caper
>   et agna Tempestatibus.

> The crew will sweat, how they will sweat,
>   and your own face go green,
> and there will be such womanly wailing then
>   and prayers to an overbearing Jupiter
> while shrieks the Ionic Gulf and streaming Notus
>   shatters the keel.

> If then rich pickings lie upon the curving shore
>   and feed the gulls,
> the gods of tempest will receive a sacrifice –
>   a randy billy-goat and lamb.
>   (*Epode* 10.15–24, trans. West 1997)

Another element of transformation of the iambic tradition in the *Epodes* consists in those poems that have a nationalistic element. Published soon after the victory of the future Augustus at Actium (31 BC), the first and central poems of the book (1 and 9) are concerned with that battle: in *Epode* 1 Horace promises to accompany his patron Maecenas to the battle to support Augustus, while in *Epode* 9 he presents a celebratory account of Augustus' victory in apparent reportage, suggesting to many that he was at the battle himself (as *Epode* 1 would naturally imply). Both these poems exploit iambic scenarios from Archilochus, who tells of sailing with friends, battles at sea, and shipboard symposia, but the encomiastic and panegyrical element is new, fitting the different circumstances of leadership and patronage in triumviral Rome (see Harrison 2001b: 167–74). The private feuds of Greek iambic have now become the hatred of a public enemy, to be celebrated in the same medium of the symposium, as in the depiction of the loser Antony at the end of *Epode* 9:

aut ille centum nobilem Cretam urbibus
    ventis iturus non suis
exercitatas aut petit Syrtis noto
    aut fertur incerto mari.
capaciores adfer huc, puer, Scyphos
    et Chia vina aut Lesbia
vel quod fluentem nauseam coerceat
    metire nobis Caecubum.
curam metumque Caesaris rerum iuvat
    dulci Lyaeo solvere.

Either he flies to glorious hundred-citied Crete
    carried by winds he did not choose,
or steers towards the Syrtes where the southerlies hold sway,
    or sails the sea he knows not where.

Bring more capacious goblets, boy,
    and Chian wine and Lesbian,
or dose us with the Caecuban
    – seasickness must be checked.
what joy to end anxiety and fear
    for Caesar's fate with sweet Lyaeus!
                              (*Epode* 9.29–38, trans. West 1997)

A further mode of transformation of archaic Greek iambic poetry in Horace is owed directly to the *Iambi* of Callimachus and their concern with other types of poetry; several of the fragmentary pieces from that book appear to exploit other genres within the iambic form (e.g. descriptive epigram in *Iambus* 6, lyric victory ode in *Iambus* 8). This tendency is continued in Horace, especially in *Epodes* 11–14, which seem to represent a change of gear in the collection after 1–10, all in the same especially Archilochean epodic iambics, followed by 11–17 in further varieties of iambics. *Epodes* 11 and 14 seem especially close to contemporary love poetry, the elegy that was being written by Gallus and others at this time (see Gibson, Chapter 11 above), and seem to use many of its topics – lovesickness, the rejected lover, the torture of infidelity (see Harrison 2001b). *Epode* 13 is especially interesting: its sympotic setting, observations on the weather, and use of a mythological story including sententious character-speech all look irresistibly to features of Horace's *Odes* (see. esp. *Odes* 1.7 and 1.9), which must have been in the process of composition at the time.

The first collection of Horace's *Odes* (Books 1–3), probably published together in 23 BC (for discussion of the date see Hutchinson 2002), clearly presents itself as a revival of the Greek lyric tradition; in its opening poem the poet impossibly requests inclusion in the Hellenistic canon of lyric poets (1.1.35). Horace's claim a few years later (*Epistles* 1.19.32–3) was that he had been the first to present Alcaeus in Latin, and it is Alcaeus who provides the primary model for Horatian lyric, as combining the symposium, love and politics, the three major themes of his collection. This is made explicit in *Odes* 1.32:

> age, dic Latinum, barbite, carmen,
> Lesbio primum modulate ciui,
> qui, ferox bello, tamen inter arma,
> siue iactatam religarat udo
> > litore nauem,
> Liberum et Musas Veneremque et illi
> semper haerentem puerum canebat
> et Lycum nigris oculis nigroque
> > crine decorum

> come, my Greek lyre, and sound a Latin song.

> You were first tuned by a citizen of Lesbos,
> Fierce in war, who, whether he was where the steel
> Was flying or had tied up his battered ship
> > On the spray-soaked shore,

> Would still sing of Bacchus and the Muses,
> Of Venus and the boy who is always by her side,
> And of Lycus with his jet-black eyes
> > And jet-black hair.
> > > (*Odes* 1.32.3–12, trans. West, 1997)

Horace was disinclined to claim to be the Roman Sappho: quite apart from Catullus' two Sapphic poems (which Horace knew and quotes together in the same poem, *Odes* 1.22.5–8, 23), which prevented such a claim, he presents Sappho as inferior to Alcaeus because of her concentration on erotic complaint (2.13.24–5), and her gender made her unsuitable for close identification. Alcaeus, on the other hand, was very convenient, not just for his range of content but also for his career as a warrior in civil wars, a neat parallel for Horace's adventures at Actium seen in *Epode* 9 (above).

The virtuosity and variety of Horace's imitation of the Greek lyric poets (on which see in general Feeney 1993 and Barchiesi 2000) is clear from the first half of the first book of *Odes*. The first nine poems are all in different lyric metres (echoing the canonical nine lyric poets?), and there is a clear sequence of six poems imitating particular Greek lyric poets in 1.12–1.18 (cf. Lowrie 1995). But at a more detailed level, the almost complete lack of whole poems in the surviving remains of Greek lyric (outside the victory odes of Pindar) means that direct comparison of Horatian odes with Greek poems is mostly impossible; the two occasions on which Horace can be seen to rework an extant Greek lyric poem (Pindar *Olympian* 2 in 1.12; Pindar *Pythian* 1 in 3.4) show an imaginative imitation of the original Greek frameworks rather than pedestrian reproduction of detail. It has been widely claimed that Horace generally began by close citation of a Greek poem and then moved away, the so-called 'motto' technique; but in just about every case we know only the beginning of the Greek poem and have little idea how it developed.

The three categories listed as Alcaean in *Odes* 1.32 (symposium, love and politics) are amply represented in Horatian lyric, though Alcaeus' homosexual love poems are not really imitated in Book 1 (perhaps owing to Roman disapproval: cf. Cicero *Tusc.* 4.71). A classic example of the symposiastic ode is found in 1.7, addressed to Plancus, in which analogies from nature are adduced to urge the relief of pleasure:

> albus ut obscuro deterget nubila caelo
> > saepe Notus neque parturit imbris
> perpetuo, sic tu sapiens finire memento
> > tristitiam uitaeque labores
> molli, Plance, mero, seu te fulgentia signis
> > castra tenent seu densa tenebit
> Tiburis umbra tui.

> The bright south wind will often wipe the clouds from the
> > dark sky.
> It is not always pregnant with rain.

> So you too, Plancus, would be wise to remember to put a stop
> > to sadness and the labors of life
> with mellow, undiluted wine, whether you are in camp among
> > the gleaming standards or whether you will be
> in the deep shade of your beloved Tibur.
> > > > (*Odes* 1.7.15–21, trans. West 1997)

This poem also shows typical Horatian concern with the addressee: Plancus' military command and villa at Tibur (a location also favoured by Horace himself: *Odes* 2.6) are carefully mentioned in complimentary mode.

Love is a common subject in Horace's *Odes*, usually presented as an appropriate and transient entertainment for youth, though longer-term relations can also be envisaged (e.g. 3.9.24). The poet himself commonly takes the role of an experienced observer, a sharp difference from the participating lover-poet of Latin elegy, the main love poetry of the time (see Chapter 11 above and Lyne 1980). Horace's lovers usually have Greek names, but these are at least sometimes adopted for their symbolic value and apply to characters who are plainly Roman. See for example *Odes* 1.8:

> Lydia, dic, per omnis
> te deos oro, Sybarin cur properes amando
>   perdere, cur apricum
> oderit Campum, patiens pulueris atque solis,
>   cur neque militaris
> inter aequalis equitet, Gallica nec lupatis
>   temperet ora frenis.
> Cur timet flauum Tiberim tangere?

> Tell me, Lydia, by all the gods I beg you,
> why you are in such a hurry to destroy Sybaris with your love.
>   And why is he deserting the sunny Campus?
> He never used to complain about dust or heat.
>   Why is he not on horseback and training
> for war with his young friends? Why is he not disciplining
>   Gallic mouths with jagged bits?
> Why is he afraid to put his toe in the yellow Tiber?
>   (*Odes* 1.8.1–8, trans. West 1997)

Here Lydia bears a servile ethnic name, but Sybaris has the name of the ultimately luxurious ancient city, fittingly for an ex-athlete who is being effeminized by love; his elite exercises on the Campus Martius also suggest that he is Roman, another reason for seeing the name as amusingly symbolic rather than socially realistic.

Contemporary politics are also an important theme. The second poem of the collection, though not technically addressed to Augustus, greets him as a new Mercury and 'avenger of Caesar' (1.2.44 *Caesaris ultor*), a clear renunciation of Horace's youthful military service for Caesar's assassins (cf. also 2.7). The penultimate poem of the first book, perhaps a ring compositional echo, is 1.37, the ode celebrating the defeat and death of Cleopatra. This clearly owes at least something to a poem of Alcaeus on the defeat and death of the tyrant Myrsilus, of which it translates the first line, and neatly turns Cleopatra's final courage to Augustus' account by emphasizing the stature of his defeated enemy, with no mention at all of the hated Antony. *Odes* 3.14 greets Augustus on his return from Spain, comparing him to Hercules returning from the Underworld, and the so-called Roman Odes of Book 3 (3.1–6) take on big issues of political power and leadership in an indirect, oracular mode which allows Horace to make impressive poetry. Maecenas, channel of Augustan patronage and perhaps requirements as well as a personal friend, is the recipient of seven odes, including the first dedicatory poem.

Ethics and moralizing (prominent in the Roman Odes and in Book 2) are characteristically Horatian elements that owe little to the tradition of Greek lyric: Horace's generally Epicurean views are not forced on the reader with the passionate conviction of a Lucretius (see Chapter 7 above), but fit neatly into his sympotic ideology of pleasure summed up in *carpe diem*, 'pluck the day' (1.11.8); Stoic views can be expressed when talking about high moral courage (*Odes* 3.3.1–4), and in addressing someone with Stoic interests (*Odes* 2.2), and later in his *Epistles*, though referring comically to himself as *Epicuri de grege porcum* (a pig from Epicurus' herd:*Epist.* 1.4.16), Horace can also proclaim that he is an eclectic and an adherent of no particular school (*Epist.* 1.1.13–15). In general Horace draws a great deal on the philosophical prose of the Hellenistic period, reflecting the importance of Greek philosophy in contemporary Roman culture.

Horace's *Odes* contain at least one poem that plays with the concept of choral lyric within a monodic framework (1.21, where the poet addressed the kind of mixed chorus found in Catullus 34). In 17 BC he was commissioned to write a real-life choral lyric for performance by a chorus of twenty-seven boys and twenty-seven girls at the great propaganda festival of Augustus, the *Ludi Saecu- lares* or Secular Games, the poem preserved as the *Carmen Saeculare*, or Secular Hymn. This is a true choric lyric piece, spoken not in the individual voice of the poet but in the collective voice of the chorus, and has clear affinities with the Greek lyric paean (see Barchiesi 2002). This renewal of lyric (whether or not stimulated by further commissions from Augustus) led to the fourth book of *Odes*, published about 13 BC. Though this book begins by representing itself as an unwilling return to erotic topics in 4.1, that poem also honours a young noble about to marry into the imperial family, and Book 4 is much concerned with praising and promoting such rising stars (Syme 1986: 396–402), and with panegyric of Augustus (4.5, 4.15) and of the military achievements of his stepsons (4.4; 4.14). Sympotic and erotic lyrics reappear, but in limited amount and in darker tones suiting the older poet (4.7; 4.10; 4.11), and there is much talk of Horace's status as poet (4.3; 4.6) and the function of poetry as commemoration (4.8; 4.9), both likely consequences of the *Carmen Saeculare* commission. Horace, though he warns of Pindarizing in 4.2, has like Pindar in his victory odes become the memorializer of achievements, both those of his addressees in politics and war and his own as the acknowledged doyen of Roman poets after the death of Vergil.

4 Lyric and Iambic after Horace

We have very little lyric poetry between Horace and 200 AD. Under Nero, Caesius Bassus, addressed by Persius (*Sat.* 6) and later praised by Quintilian as lyric poet (10.1.96), wrote at least two books of lyric poems, but we have only a single line certainly preserved, though the metrical treatise attributed to him makes clear his knowledge of Horatian metres (cf. Courtney 1993: 351 and Mayer, Chapter 4 above). The younger Pliny seems to have written some lyric poems, including some hendecasyllables, which remained unpublished (Hershkowitz 1995).

Statius' *Silvae*, as well as hendecasyllables (4.9), include an Alcaic ode (4.5) to Septimius, himself a lyric poet (4.5.59–60), and a Sapphic ode to Vibius Maximus (4.7), perhaps showing mastery of the two most famous Horatian forms, but this is clearly a token use of these metres in a largely hexameter collection. Martial used hendecasyllables extensively in his collection (about 20% of his poems), largely a homage to Catullus, as does the *Carmina Priapea*, probably from the first century AD, a collection of poems to and about the phallic god, no doubt again recalling Catullan usage. In the second century we find a few lyric metres used in scattered fragments, but these are clearly limited experiments (see Courtney 1993: 372–4; Steinmetz 1982) and there is no evidence of sophisticated lyric enterprises until the advent of major Christian hymnography in the fourth century (see Raby 1927: 1–101).

Little more remains of iambic poetry. Nothing survives of Ovid's contemporary Bassus, said to be *clarus iambis*, 'famed for iambics' (*Tr.* 4.10.47). Phaedrus (*c.* 15 BC–*c.* AD 50), the only Latin poet whose entire output consists of iambic verse, wrote five books of iambic senarii in which Aesopic animal fables were narrated. These were the first separate books of verse fables, which had previously been part of satire (cf. Horace *Sat.* 2.6 and Chapter 12 above), and the ancestor of modern collections such as that of La Fontaine. The iambic metre marked these poems as humble rather than abusive, appropriate for Phaedrus' supposed social status as an imperial slave of Greek origin (cf. 3 prol. 55–9; and see Habinek, Chapter 27 below), freed by Augustus (something attested only by the manuscripts of his work, though cf. 3 prol. 33–40, where the status is perhaps implied). Phaedrus himself claims that though he suffered personally at the hands of Tiberius' minister Sejanus he wants not to attack individuals but to show 'life itself and the ways of men' (3 prol. 49–50), and his fables with their bestial casts present general morals without specific invective edge, though an interesting case has recently been made for more political subversion (Henderson 2001).

Otherwise, the iambics that remain are scarce and generally look back to earlier texts. Persius' seven-line preface to his hexameter satires is in choliambics, a possible echo of the early iambic satires of Ennius and Lucilius (see above). Some of Martial's books of epigrams (see Chapter 14 below), like his hendecasyllables (see above) look back to Catullus; the same is true of the eight choliambic poems in the *Carmina Priapea* (see above). The fragments of the archaizing poets of the second century AD contain a number of pieces in various iambic metres.

FURTHER READING

On the genre of lyric in antiquity in general see Johnson (1982), on ancient iambic in general see the essays in Cavarzere et al. (2001). On the tradition of

Greek lyric and iambic poetry (both treated, despite the title) see Gerber (1997). For the texts of Greek iambic poetry with translation and some useful notes see Gerber (1999), and for those of Greek lyric, Campbell (1982–93). On Callimachus' *Iambi* see Kerkhecker (1999) and Acosta-Hughes (2002). On Greek lyric and iambic metres and their Latin adaptations see West (1982).

On Catullan lyric, Fitzgerald (1995) provides some stimulating ideas on Catullus' lyric stance, while Wray (2001) provides an interesting anthropological perspective on Catullan iambic invective; older, though still useful, are Quinn (1972) and Wheeler (1934). The commentaries of Quinn (1970), lively and literary, and Fordyce (1961), dry and technical, are the most convenient in English.

On Horace's *Odes* and *Epodes*, Fraenkel (1957), despite its biographical approach, is still fundamental, Oliensis (1998) more modern and challenging; for a good idea of recent work on Horace see Woodman and Feeney (2002). Recent stimulating work on the *Epodes* can be found via Cavarzere et al. (2001) and the commentaries of Mankin (1995) and Watson (2003). For commentaries on *Odes* 1–3, the volumes of Nisbet and Hubbard (1970 and 1978) and Nisbet and Rudd (2004) are utterly indispensable, and the briefer commentaries of West (1995, 1998 and 2002) are highly stimulating; for *Odes* 4 see Putnam (1986). Useful modern work on the *Odes* includes Davis (1991) and Lowrie (1997); worth trying too are the multiple interpretations of *Odes* 1.9 in Edmunds (1992).

For Phaedrus see Bloomer (1997) and Henderson (2001), and for the fragmentary remains of post-first-century lyric and iambic poetry see Steinmetz (1982) and Courtney (1993).

CHAPTER FOURTEEN

Epigram

Lindsay C. Watson

1 General Characteristics

The question 'what is an epigram?' is famously difficult to answer. A standard formulation such as 'a short witty poem culminating in a striking thought or expression' is less than satisfactory in the context of a survey of Latin epigram. In the first place, it leaves out of account the vast (and for the Romans vastly influential) corpus of Greek, especially Hellenistic, epigram, which does not (broadly speaking) conform to the above definition. More important, it is predicated on the canonical form imposed upon epigram by its most famous exponent, the first century AD writer Martial, whose work represents the culmination of a long process of development in the course of which the genre's polymorphous diversity was amply displayed. A more representative definition might run 'a brief tightly structured poem, written for preference in the elegiac distich, tied to an object or a particular circumstance, the interpretation of which is shaped by a powerful controlling intellect' (Laurens 1989: 25).

In what follows I look briefly at the major surviving representatives of Roman epigram. These are, in rough chronological order, the so-called 'circle' of Lutatius Catulus, Catullus and the Neoterics, the pseudo-Vergilian *Catalepton*, Martial and the *Priapea*. Space does not permit consideration of works of marginal importance such as the seventy epigrams attributed to the younger Seneca or late flowerings beyond the period of this volume such as the *Epigrams* of Ausonius, the *Epigrammata Bobiensia* (*c.* AD 400) and the derivative epigrams of the Carthaginian Luxorius (early 6th c. AD). Before proceeding to a diachronic survey, it will be helpful, in view of epigram's receptivity to a wide range of styles and subject matter, to catalogue various characteristics which are common to all or most of its main exponents and serve to erect a profile of this most hospitable of genres. Of course, even to speak of the 'genre' of epigram is problematical. The term 'epigram' did not come into currency as the designation for a recognizable literary form until the 1st century AD (Puelma 1996). Moreover, Catullus, the major Roman epigrammatist prior to Martial, was in Antiquity and continues to be variously designated an iambist, a lyric poet or an elegist, as well as an epigrammatist: compare Quintil. *Inst. Or.* 10. 1. 96, Newman (1990: 43–74), Wray (2001), Heyworth (2001), Havelock (1939), Johnson (1982: 108–23), Fitzgerald (1995), Wheeler (1934: 153–82) and Day (1938: 106–11). Finally, the terminology applied by the ancients to what is now categorized by the portmanteau term 'epigram' was distinctly labile; Pliny the Younger famously spoke of such productions in the following terms (*Ep.* 4.14.9): 'whether you prefer "epigrams" or "idylls" or "eclogues" or, as many do, "short poems", you may so call them: but I stick to "hendecasyllables"'.

It has been thought paradoxical that Statius in the preface to *Silvae* 2 assimilated these sometimes extremely lengthy pieces to epigram. Yet Statius had a rationale for so characterizing the *Silvae*, their occasionality. For there is no doubt that this was a defining characteristic of Latin epigram. Countless pieces have their origin in a particular set of circumstances (whether real or fictitious); for example Martial 12.77, on a hunter of dinner invitations who farted in the temple of Jupiter Capitolinus and was punished with dining at home for three nights; 7.37, a quaestor who arranged that, when he wiped his nose, this should serve as a signal for an execution, but found himself unable to remove a frozen icicle which hung from his nostrils lest the gesture be fatally misinterpreted; or a brief anecdote of Catullus:

> Risi nescio quem modo e corona,
> qui, cum mirifice Vatiniana
> meus crimina Calvos explicasset,
> admirans ait haec manusque tollens,
> 'di magni, salaputium disertum!'

I laughed just now at someone from the crowd who, when my mate Calvus had brilliantly expounded the crimes of Vatinius, said in admiration and lifting up his arms 'ye gods, what an an eloquent phallicle!'

(Catullus 53)

All three poems just mentioned are relatively short (of twelve, eight and five verses respectively). This too is a characteristic feature. Brevity was a watchword of epigram, at times insisted upon by its practitioners with a doctrinalism that borders on hyperbole (Lausberg 1982: 20–76): it is most conspicuously realized in numerous pieces that comprise only a single elegiac couplet. In the debate over the appropriate length for an epigram Martial had his say: while generally embracing the principle of brevity, he intersperses poems such as 1.49 (forty-two lines) or 6.64 (thirty-two lines), which in compass far exceed the norms observed in the near-contemporaneous *Garland of Philip* (mostly eight lines maximum) and offers a spirited defence of the practice by appealing to the precedent of his Latin models (2.77).

Epigram, which already by the fourth century BC enjoyed a *de facto* existence as an independent literary form (Reitzenstein 1907: 81) was traditionally located at the base of the generic ladder (cf. Mart. 12.94; Tac. *Dial.* 10.4), labelled a *lusus* or *paignion*, 'triviality': a verdict which Martial, in a conscious inversion of literary hierarchies, counters by pointing out that it is mythological epic or tragedy which, with their fantastical divagations on tralatician or recondite themes, are in fact trivial, whereas epigram, firmly anchored in the everyday and empowered by sociocritical zeal, has a moral earnestness lacking in the more elevated genres (Citroni 1968). But Martial speaks in a spirit of deliberate paradox, and epigram's low generic ranking is confirmed above all by its language, which, in conformity with the principle of stylistic decorum, is everyday and colloquial in flavour (Watson and Watson 2003: 21–6). Of particular note here is the free admixture of primary obscenities that would not be countenanced in more repectable genres, a feature towards which Latin epigram adopts a disingenuously ambiguous stance. On the one hand it excuses its linguistic crudity by invoking the *lex operis* (law prescribing what is appropriate to a genre): in the prefatory epistle to Book 1 Martial states, 'I should apologize for the bawdy explicitness of my vocabulary, that is to say the language of epigram, were the example of my making; but this is how Catullus writes, and Marsus, Pedo and Gaetulicus and anyone else who is read right through' (see Sullivan 1991: 64–74), while Pliny the Younger, apropos of his forays into epigram, issues a similar apologia (*Ep.* 4.14.4). On the other hand, the epigrammatists unabashedly avow that the purpose of including erotic material and language is to gratify readers by provoking sexual arousal, a line of argument spawned by Catullus:

> qui [versiculi] tum denique habent salem et leporem,
> si sunt molliculi ac parum pudici,
> et quod pruriat incitare possunt,
> non dico pueris, sed his pilosis
> qui duros nequeunt movere lumbos,

'which [trifling verses] then and only then have wit and charm if they are rather suggestive and a bit naughty and can provoke a sexual itch – I don't mean in young lads, but in those hairy types who are unable to bestir their unresponsive groins' (Catullus 16. 7–11; cf. Mart. 1.35, Hallett 1996).

Explicit verbal obscenity, it is vital to note, was a distinguishing feature of Roman, as opposed to Greek, epigram: Martial styles it *latine loqui*, 'to speak Latin' (Book 1, *praef.*). Greek epigram, while by no means eschewing sexual themes, largely avoids what we term four-letter words. The difference in approach may be illustrated by comparing *Priapea* 29 (three primary obscenities, 'balls', 'cunt' and 'prick' in five verses) with a twelve-line piece, *AP* 11.328, by the (?) Neronian epigrammatist Nicharchus. Here, although the subject matter is expressly pornographic (the triple penetration of a woman), the several entry positions adopted in this extemporized *ménage à quatre* are recounted in figurative terms compounded parodically from a farrago of Homeric allusions; for example:

> but Hermogenes got a loathsome dank dwelling, the farthest spot, passing down into an unseen place, where are the shores of the dead, and breeze-stirred wild figs are tossed by the blast of ill-sounding winds
>
> (Nicharchus *AP* 11.325–8).

A constant in mainstream Latin epigram – with the notable exception of the *Priapea* – is the foregrounding of the authorial *persona*. There is an insistence on the importance of the speaker's likes and dislikes, opinions and prejudices, one of a number of features that epigram shares with iambus. This characteristic, omnipresent in Catullus' shorter poems, duly reappears in the *Catalepton*, with its markedly Catullan flavour, and is one of the most important strands in Martial's Catullan legacy. Anchored as it is in the everyday life of Rome, much of Martial's poetry is devoted to articulating sardonic or mocking responses to the ingrained norms, *bêtises* and idiosyncrasies of metropolitan society: indeed he complains in the preface to Book 12 that his retirement to Biblilis has deprived him of the inspiration for his themes.

Next, a few words on metre. By the fifth century BC or possibly earlier (Holzberg 2002: 21) the elegiac couplet is established as the metre of choice for Greek epigram. In Latin epigram elegiacs likewise predominate. Also important are Catullus' or, rather, the Neoterics' favourite hendecasyllabics, as well as iambics, particularly the *scazon* or 'limping' iambic. The reasons that determined a personal poet's choice of metre in a given piece are in need of investigation (Morgan 2000) and can be difficult to fathom. Nonetheless certain factors were identifiably at work in Roman epigrammatists' privileging of these particular systems. The scazon had long been associated with abuse (Loomis 1972: 102–18; Kay 1985: 203–4) and as such was appropriate to the invective and satire that bulk so large in Latin epigram. As for the hendecasyllable, it seems to have been considered a suitable vehicle (Quintil. *Inst. Or.* 1.8.6; Plin. *Ep.* 4.14; Morgan 2000b: 115) for the obscenity that was a distinguishing feature of the genre: in the case of Martial, its use also serves as an act of homage to Catullus and on occasion adverts to the existence of a specific Catullan model. Lastly, the elegiac couplet, with its inbuilt rise and fall, is well accommodated to the balance and antithesis, point and counterpoint that are a feature of Latin epigram, particularly Martial, and admirably subserves its tight and self-contained logical structure. At the broader level, all three systems are notably simple and thus suited to the directness and incisiveness of epigram. Martial surely has such considerations in mind when he rails against the preciosity of abstruse metrical systems (2. 86).

One last general point is the genre's enormous thematic receptivity. Most visible in the conventional division of the *Palatine Anthology*, our major surviving collection of Greek literary epigram, into sixteen books according to subject categories, great breadth of thematic range is equally characteristic of its Roman sibling. As regards Catullus, the sheer diversity of topic and tone encountered in his shorter poems has been one factor in sparking the debate over how to classify him generically, while the individual pieces in the *Catalepton* exhibit a remarkable heterogeneity that embraces *inter alia* an *envoi* to poetry in favour of Epicurean quietism, a sophisticated take-off of Catullus' *phaselus ille* and several examples of excoriating invective. Martial enriches still further the thematic ambit of Latin epigram, availing himself liberally of the satiric and courtly strains that were a late arrival on the epigrammatic scene (Laurens 1965) and elevating to poetic status the hitherto largely unexplored minutiae of Roman society. The sole exception to this pattern is the *Priapea*, where the monomanic phallocentrism of the divine protagonist inevitably circumscribes both thematically and physiologically the collection's focus.

2 The Beginnings

Historians of Latin epigram cite as its earliest beginnings, in the third to second centuries BC, the Scipionic *elogia*, mostly in Saturnians, from the family tomb on the Via Appia (see Courtney 1995: nos. 9–13). Latin epigram, like Greek, thus begins its career by faithfully reflecting its etymology (Gk *epigramma*, 'inscription'). But in contrast to its Greek congener, Roman epigram rapidly became divorced from its original inscriptional context. Another clutch of early epigrams, of dubious authenticity but seemingly datable to the second century BC, the verse epitaphs for Naevius, Plautus and Pacuvius preserved by Gellius *NA* 1.24, are parasitic on the fictitious and highly literary epitaphs for dead poets that are common in *Anthologia Palatina* Book 7. Equally marked is the literary character of the next works to call for mention, the four- or six-line epigrams by Valerius Aedituus, Porcius Licinus and Lutatius Catulus quoted by Gellius 19.9 and supplemented in Catulus' case by Cic. *ND* 1.79: they are sometimes taken as evidence for a poetic grouping that formed itself around Catulus, who, born in the 150s BC, was consul in 102 and committed autothanasia in 87. All five poems are amatory, showing profoundly the influence of Meleager's *Garland* (*c.* 100 BC), the first artistically arranged anthology of pre-Hellenistic and Hellenistic epigram. They are characterized by alliteration, preciosity of expression, mannered striving after verbal conceit and rigorously ordered balance and antitheses. All in all, they represent an early blossoming of Roman Alexandrianism

(Laurens 1989: 163–77; Morelli 2000: 109–223). Such indebtedness is most marked in the epigram of Catulus preserved by Gellius,

> Aufugit mi animus; credo, ut solet, ad Theotimum
>   devenit. sic est; perfugium illud habet.
> quid si non interdixem ne illunc fugitivum
>   mitteret ad se intro, sed magis eiceret?
> ibimus quaesitum. verum, ne ipsi teneamur,
>   formido. quid ago? da, Venus, consilium,

My soul has fled. I believe that, as usual, it has gone to Theotimus. Yes, that's it: it has taken refuge there. Just as well that I forbade him to take the runaway into his house, but [told him] rather to toss it out. We shall go to look for it. But I'm afraid, lest I myself be captured. What am I to do? Advise me, Venus.

(Catulus fr.1 Courtney)

This is a refashioning of Callimachus *Epigr.* 4 Pf:

Half my soul is still breathing, but as for the other half, I know not whether Eros or Hades has stolen it, except that it not to be found. Has it gone off again to one of the boys? And yet I often forbade them 'do not receive the runaway, young men'. For it is somewhere there, I'm sure, that the miscreant, the disastrously in love, is hanging about.

The most notable feature of the adaptation (leaving aside its skewed logic) is its explicit Greekness, advertised not merely in the overt evocation of its model but also in the recasting of the original as a miniaturized drama, a recognized technique of Hellenistic epigram. This stands in stark contrast to the later tradition as represented in Martial, who insists on the essential Romanness of his oeuvre, self-consciously invoking his Latin predecessors and making no more than passing mention of Greek epigram (4.23.3–4).

3   Catullus and the Catalepton

The discussion now turns to Catullus, whose status however as an epigrammatist is, as noted, moot (for other discussions of Catullus' diverse output, see Levene, Chapter 2 above, and Harrison, Chapter 13 above). He himself never speaks of his 'epigrams', only of *nugae*, *iambi* and *hendecasyllabi*, the last of which might with some justification be regarded as melic (Laurens 1989: 197; Cameron 1995: 165). The final third of the collection (69–116) could qualify as epigram on account of the metre, elegiac couplet, the preferred medium of the genre, yet it is the first third of the corpus (1–60), the so-called *polymetra*, which exhibits far closer resemblances to earlier epigram: poems 3 (on the death of Lesbia's *passer*) and 4 (*phaselus ille*) are two examples among many (Laurens 1989: 184–7). It is, then, not entirely a paradox that Laurens in his major study of the form devotes twenty pages to questioning the applicability of the term epigrammatist to Catullus (Laurens 1989: 183–203). Among other things, he notes that the *polymetra* exhibit a complexity of structure and sentiment which is alien to epigram, that the length and elaboration of many of these pieces exceed the canons of epigram and that single poems (as in the Lesbia-and-Gellius-cycles of the elegiac segment) often represent a fragment of a larger experience, which distinguishes them from Hellenistic epigram, where the individual compositions are typically self-contained.

Against these qualifications must be set the undeniable fact that Martial considers Catullus the greatest of Roman epigrammatists (Swann 1994; Citroni 1991: 181). There are several reasons why Martial so regarded him. It was Catullus above all who was responsible for determining the future shape of Roman epigram. First, many of his poems are fashioned as intense and outrageously one-sided outbursts of personal opinion; and vigorously trumpeted prejudices and feelings – be they of love, hate, sorrow, derision or contempt – lie at the very bedrock of Latin epigram, Greek epigram being an emotionally altogether more jejune affair. A good instance of such intensity, complete with epigrammatic *fulmen in clausula* (concluding thunderbolt), is the famous lines accusing Lesbia of behaving like the cheapest of prostitutes:

> Caeli, Lesbia nostra, Lesbia illa,
> illa Lesbia, quam Catullus unam
> plus quam se atque suos amavit omnes,
> nunc in quadriviis et angiportis
> glubit magnamimi Remi nepotes.

Caelius, our Lesbia, that Lesbia, that Lesbia whom Catullus loved above all, more than himself and all his own people, now at the crossroads and in back alleys peels back the descendants of great-hearted Remus.

(Catullus 58)

Second, Catullus provocatively affirms the pre-eminence of private life, using his verse to articulate personal values and to mirror his experience of social and literary intercourse. This development too proves profoundly influential. At the very core of Martial's epigrams is the poet's depiction of himself as a poor client and struggling *artiste* orbiting the *atria* of the great, while successful prosecution of the lead character's ithyphallically determined lifestyle also gives to the *Priapea* its thematic locus. Greek epigram is not on the whole characterized by humour: Catullus on the other hand is replete with it, particularly humour of a sardonic or self-mocking vein. This feature is one of Catullus' most important bequests to Martial, and the *Priapea* too are a beneficiary, the emphasis on the god's intrinsic

ridiculousness and obsessive pursuit of sexual gratification being a radical departure from the Greek tradition of Priapea. Most important, Catullus' savage invectives, particularly against sexual malfeasance, find countless echoes in the *Priapea*,
the *Catalepton* and above all Martial. Of course such invective represents the
confluence of several influences, Greek and Roman, literary and popular, but in
the case of epigram Catullan precedent will have been the primary determinant: a
notable example is poem 97, a scabrous attack on one Aemilius, where the density
of imagery, grotesquerie of language and extreme obscenity all have their correlate in Martial. Here are lines 1–8:

> I did not think (so help me Gods) that it made any difference whether it was
> Aemilius' mouth or bum that I smelled. The one is no cleaner, the other not a jot
> dirtier, but (in fact) his bum is cleaner and preferable. For it is without teeth. The
> other has teeth a foot and a half long, and gums resembling an old waggon-box,
> besides, a gaping maw like the split cunt of a she-mule pissing in a heatwave.

It is important here to note that vicious personal attacks, particularly politically
coloured attacks like those of Catullus on Caesar and Mamurra, were a preoccupation, not just of Catullus, but of Neoteric epigram as a whole. Tacitus *Ann.*
4.34 remarks 'one can read poems of [Furius] Bibaculus and Catullus packed with
abuse of the Caesars' and two samples of political lampoons by Calvus survive; the
second reads:

> Magnus, quem metuunt omnes, digito caput uno
> scalpit; quid credas hunc sibi velle? virum.

> Magnus, of whom all are afraid, scratches his head with a single finger. What is one
> to believe he is after? A man.
>
> (frs 17–18, Courtney)

There is, however, an important difference between the pasquinades of the first
century BC and those of the later tradition: the former attacked individuals by
name, a procedure that Martial, in the altered circumstances of the next century,
explicitly decried:

> I hope that I have struck a balance in my little books such that whoever has a good
> opinion of himself cannot complain of them, in that their jests respect the dignity
> of even the humblest of persons, something which was so far lacking in
> writers of old that they used without respect not only real names but also great
> ones. (*praef. Epigr.* 1)

Only cursory notice can be taken of the fifteen mostly brief poems comprising the
pseudo-Vergilian *Catalepton*. Thought to have been issued between the end of

the first century BC and the beginning of the next, the collection contains internal references to events of the 40s and 30s: a few of the pieces may be authentically Vergilian. Varied in content and metre (distichs, pure iambics, scazons and one epodic piece), with a pseudo(?)-autobiographical flavour, they show markedly the influence of Catullus and Horace's *Epodes*. Their title (*kata lepton*, namely in the small-scale, refined style of Callimachus or Aratus) suggests a possible way of categorizing poems, such as certain of Catullus' and a number in the *Catalepton* itself, which earn only dubiously the label 'epigram': that all such pieces belong to a broader category of *paignia*, *ludicra*, brief occasional pieces (cf. Catull. 50) characterized by unpretentiousness of style and content, of which epigram represents only the most identifiable subset. The *Catalepton* proffers far more of interest than has been realized, and stands in need of serious interpretative attention.

4 Martial

For many, the name Martial is synonymous with epigram. He stands at the apex of a tradition upon which he imposed definitive form. Above all, epigram becomes in his hands a vehicle for witty satire: he combines the pugnacity of Catullus with the scoptic vein that enters Greek epigram of the first century AD, most notably in the person of the Neronian writer Loukillios, whose technique anticipates Martial's in important ways (taste for hyperbole, paradox, attacks on stock figures, series on set themes [e.g. athletic incompetence], a modicum of cheeky irreverence in addressing the emperor [Nisbet 2004], and to whom the parentage of some seventeen of Martial's epigrams may be traced [Burnikel 1980]). Debate has raged over whether Martial's satire is powered by social criticism (Holzberg 1986; Laurens (1989: 244–51), a despairing moral nihilism (Seel 1961) or simply the desire to amuse: a powerful case has been made for the last position by Holzberg (2002) who, in an engagingly frank recantation of his earlier view, treats Martial as a classic of wit – even in the touchy area of imperial panegyric, a well-developed side of the *Epigrams* which has drawn upon the poet, unfairly (see Lorenz 2002: 247–50), the reputation of a hypocritical and oleaginous sycophant.

No discussion of Martial would be complete without mention of the profoundly influential theory of Lessing, who argued that epigram (in Lessing's mind effectively equated with Martialian epigram) typically exhibits a bipartite structure, consisting of a 'set up' (*Erwartung*), in which the reader's curiosity is aroused regarding a specific subject and a 'conclusion' (*Aufschluss*), which offers personal, generally witty, brief comment thereon:

> de nullo loqueris, nulli maledicis, Apicii.
> rumor ait linguae te tamen esse malae.

You talk about no one, you badmouth no one, Apicius. Yet rumour says that you have an evil tongue.

(Martial 3.80)

gives a good idea of what Lessing had in mind. In the hexameter Apicius is held up to view as an exemplary instance of freedom from malice in a society notorious for its corrosive wit. The pentameter explodes the initially positive impression by radically recontextualizing the meaning of *mala lingua*. Apicius may not have a 'poisonous' tongue (cf. *nulli maledicis* 1), but his tongue is *mala* in another, and, in Roman eyes, worse sense: he practises oral sex.

Lessing's formulation, valuable as it is, has come in for criticism. It is objected *inter alia* that *Erwartung* and *Aufschluss* are misleading terms, and that it is more productive to speak of an 'objective' (1st) and a 'subjective' (2nd) part of an epigram (Barwick 1959: 5); that insistence on a bipartite structure underplays the unity of a Martialian epigram and ignores the dynamic movement which sustains it (Citroni 1969: 225, 238, 242; Kay 1985: 7–9); that the schema is predicated on Martial's scoptic pieces while ignoring his numerous epigrams of other types, epideictic, declamatory, laudatory (Citroni 1969: 220; Howell 1980: 11; Sullivan 1991: 223–4); and that Lessing placed excessive emphasis on the structure of the epigram, at the expense of other aspects, such as literary technique, sharpness and wit (Laurens 1989: 12). Yet Lessing was incontestably right in one essential, his insistence on the centrality of the conclusion to the working of Martial's epigrams, which are typically rounded off with some incisive thought, surprise or striking expression (*sententia*), in a word, by what is known as 'point'. For example:

Omnes quas habuit, Fabiane, Lycoris amicas
extulit; uxori fiat amica meae.

Fabianus, Lycoris has buried all the female friends she had. May she make friends with my wife.

(Martial 4.24)

As the technical term *sententia* implies, Martial's epigrams, above all his conclusions, are deeply informed by rhetoric, especially rhetorical theories of wit (Barwick 1959). The influence of Domitius Marsus' treatise *De Urbanitate* is often posited, not only because Marsus is named by Martial as his predecessor in epigram, but also because his definition of wit, preserved by Quintilian, conforms so closely to Martial's conception of it:

wit is a certain power compressed into a brief expression and appropriate for delighting and moving people to every kind of emotion: it is especially suited to objections or personal attacks, according as each circumstance or personage calls for it. (Quintilian *Inst. Or.* 6.3.104)

For Marsus, wit depends on a genius for pithy and ingenious verbal formulation, a constant in Martial; an example is his grotesque neologism debunking the vanity of a follicularly challenged individual, *calvam triflem semitatus unguento* (with [streaks of] unguent cutting a swathe across his bald pate with its three strands) (*Inst. Or.* 6.74.2).

5   The *Priapea*

By way of conclusion, the *Priapea* call for mention. Clear overlaps between Martial and this eighty-poem corpus, particularly the opening *apologiae* for obscenity, establish an interrelationship, but the relative chronology is contested: the *Priapea* have been dated to the Augustan period, to *circa* AD 100, and to various points in between: a case has recently been made for composition prior to Martial (Kissel 1994; O'Connor in Grewing 1998: 189). For the most part spoken in the *persona* of the anally fixated fertility god and scarecrow Priapus, the collection is notable for genuine wit, sophisticated use of parody, the drastic and exuberant quality of its language – all in all, a notable hybrid in which gross obscenity is successfully twinned with an unexpected literariness: 68, a scatological re-etymologizing of Homer, is a nice example. The subject of recent attention, the *Priapea* have been seriously undervalued as a literary artefact.

FURTHER READING

There is no comprehensive work on Latin epigram. The fullest treatment is by Laurens (1989). Lausberg (1982) offers much more of interest on Greek and Roman epigram as a whole than his title promises. Gutzwiller (1998) provides a detailed if somewhat repetitious account of Hellenistic epigram. For the text of most pre-Catullan epigram see Courtney (1993): this is discussed by Morelli (2000), more briefly and casuistically by Ross (1969). Recent work on Catullus pays little attention to his epigrammatic side. The best translation of C., with facing text, is by Lee (1990). Of commentaries Quinn (1970) is adequate, Fordyce (1961) superior but disfigured by Calvinistic prudery, Kroll (1929) the best. On Martial's debt to Catullus compare Paukstadt (1876), Ferguson (1963) and Swann (1994). The approach of all is mechanical: detailed intertextual work is a desideratum. The relationship of Martial to Loukillios is sensitively analysed by Burnikel (1980): also excellent is Holzberg (2002: 100–9), whose brief but comprehensive introduction to Martial is much superior to the standard study in English by Sullivan (1991). The preface to Watson and Watson (2003) examines different aspects of Martial's *Epigrams*. On the rhetorical dimension of Martial's oeuvre Burnikel (1980) is fundamental. Of commentaries Citroni

(1975) and Howell (1980) on 1, Grewing (1997) on 6 and Kay (1985) on 11 stand out. The three-volume Loeb translation by Shackleton Bailey (1993) is lively but not always reliable, compromised by inadequate investigation of *Realien*. On the *Catalepton* the commentary of Westendorp Boerma (1949 and 1963) in Latin, with English translation of the poems, is detailed and helpful; interpretatively almost nothing has been done since the 60s (for a recent Italian edition with some notes see Iodice 2002). The *Priapea* have fared better, with one general study (O'Connor 1989) and three commentaries, a full one by Goldberg (1992) in German and shorter ones in English by Parker (1988; the accompanying verse translation has overtones of William McGonagall, but the lengthy introduction is valuable), and in Italian by Bianchini (2001). A good bibliography of epigrammatic works of lesser importance is given by Citroni (1991: 203–7. To it add the excellent new commentary on Ausonius' *Epigrammata* by Kay (2002).

CHAPTER FIFTEEN

The Novel

Stephen Harrison

1 Introduction

The prose fiction of Rome for the period before AD 200 consists of two extant texts: the *Satyrica* of Petronius, generally agreed to belong to the 60s AD and the reign of Nero (on the date and title see conveniently Harrison 1999: xiii, xvi–xvii), and the *Metamorphoses* or *Golden Ass* of Apuleius (on the date and title see conveniently S. J. Harrison 2000: 9–10, 210 n. 1), from the second half of the second century AD: Apuleius was also author of a lost *Hermagoras*, which seems very likely to have been another low-life novel (S. J. Harrison 2000: 21–2). Given that both are extensive prose fictions with characters and narrative plots, we can conveniently refer to these texts as 'novels', though that label has no ancient status.

The plots of these two works are largely comic, bawdy and sensational; Petronius' novel tells of a double homosexual *ménage à trois* of educated scroungers (Encolpius, the narrator, his beloved Giton and his successive erotic rivals Ascyltus and Eumolpus), who between them experience a highly colourful series of low-life and erotic adventures in the area of the Bay of Naples: in various combinations, they cadge an invitation to a stupendously gross dinner-party at the house of the *nouveau riche* freedman Trimalchio, the description of which forms the major coherent episode in the novel (*Sat.* 26.7–78.8), quarrel about who enjoys Giton's sexual favours (79–98), try to escape from trouble by boarding a ship bound for Croton only to find that it carries other passengers with whom they have an unpleasant history, suffer shipwreck in a storm (100–15) and reach Croton where we leave them carrying on their usual life of ineffectively libidinous confidence tricksters (116–41). Encolpius presents this story all the while with melodramatic and overblown allusions drawn from his student reading of mythology and literature.

Apuleius' novel narrates in the first person the story of the young Corinthian Lucius, curious about sex and magic, who travels to the black-magic country of

Thessaly and is there accidentally metamorphosed into an ass as a result of over-curious probing into the household affairs of a local witch. As an ass he undergoes a series of low-life adventures, including contact with robbers and religious confidence tricksters, hears many comic and erotic stories that he reports regularly to the reader, and is about to be exhibited performing the sexual act in the amphitheatre at his home town of Corinth with a condemned woman, when he is retransformed owing to the intervention of the goddess Isis, and then turns to the religious service of that goddess and her consort Osiris, first in Greece and then at Rome.

Both these texts are thus extensive fictional narratives in settings of low-life realism, interested in sensational themes such as sex, fraud, theft, magic and ghosts; this makes it unsurprising that the elements that Apuleius seems to take directly from Petronius, whom he clearly knew (cf. Walsh 1978), are comic/satiric episodes: the 'attempted suicide' in the inn (*Sat.* 94.8 ~ *Met.*1.16), the humble hospitality motif, with a comparison with Callimachus' Hecale (*Sat.* 135.15 ~ *Met.* 1.23.4), and the ghost-story at the feast told at the host's insistence (*Sat.* 61.1 ~ *Met.* 2.20.5). The two texts also show similar narrative techniques, combining first-person main narration with inserted tales that tell stories apparently tangential to the main plot; both also use similar literary textures, including extensive irreverent allusion to other genres (see below). In what follows I shall look briefly at the key defining features of each novel, and then consider the common elements of literary texture that can be claimed to hold them together. Many elements are inevitably shared with my other work (S. J. Harrison 1996, 1999 and 2000), where I present my views at greater length.

2   Petronius' *Satyrica*

The two immediately striking features of Petronius' novel are formal: it is transmitted to us by various textual channels in a form that is clearly incomplete and fragmentary, and it uses a prosimetric technique in which verse passages apparently expressing the views or literary aspirations of its characters are interspersed within a general prose framework. Most modern scholars (for theories see Harrison 1999: xvii–xviii) think that the original *Satyrica* contained at least twenty books, while the fragments that remain probably contain material equivalent to fewer than six of these books. This radical loss of the majority of the original inevitably constrains criticism of the work, and all that follows should be judged in the light of this deficiency.

The prosimetric form of the *Satyrica*, along with the overt etymology of its title from *satira*, '[literary] satire' (as well as perhaps from *satyr*, suggesting its evident emphasis on satyric sensual excess), points to a connection with Varronian/Menippean prosimetric satire, evidenced in Seneca's *Apocolocynctosis* which belongs to the previous decade; the *Satyrica* also shows a clear link to the themes of the hexameter satire of Horace and Lucilius such as food, corruption and hypocrisy (see for all these texts Chapter 12 above). But prosimetric form can now be shown through the *Iolaus*-papyrus (published in 1970) to have belonged to the tradition of Greek prose fiction and not to have been unique to Varronian/Menippean satire, and Petronian *prosimetrum* may be drawn from low-life Greek prose fiction as well as the Roman Varronian/Menippean tradition (cf. Astbury 1977/1999; Barchiesi 1986/1999; Conte 1996: 140–70). There is certainly no sign of the philosophical moralizing of the Varronian/Menippean satire in Petronius' amoral tale of low doings as we have it; the most that one can argue is that it is a nihilist 'bonfire of the vanities' in which the emptiness of material self-indulgence is repeatedly demonstrated (see Arrowsmith 1966), or an analysis of a world falling apart (Zeitlin 1971), but the evident relish and detail with which such self-indulgence is so frequently described does not suggest an edifying purpose to the work.

The celebrated argument of Heinze (1899) that the *Satyrica* is a parody of the ideal Greek novel, inverting its faithful heterosexual couple by presenting a promiscuous homosexual couple, and representing on the low-life level its themes of travel and adventure, swiftly became established doctrine, and is fundamental for many modern discussions of the *Satyrica*. Equally important is the argument of Klebs (1889), reprised by Sullivan (1968) and Walsh (1970), that the Greek and Roman epic poems of Homer and Vergil form a structural model for the work and many of its episodes; the wandering Encolpius, afflicted and wrecked by Priapus, in general strongly resembles the wandering Odysseus, afflicted and wrecked by Poseidon, and there are particular moments such as the Circe episode (*Sat.* 126–33), where Encolpius attempts an erotic relationship with a lady who has the same name as Odysseus' magical hostess, at which the novel's Odyssean role-playing is especially self-conscious.

Such literary self-consciousness in the *Satyrica* is a key technique in the work. To give two prominent examples, Cameron (1969) neatly suggests that the speeches of the freedmen in the *Cena* and the late entry of the stonemason Habinnas parody the speeches in Plato's *Symposium* and the late entry of Alcibiades, while the two longer poetic inserts presented as the work of the hack poet Eumolpus, the 'Capture of Troy' (65 iambic lines at *Sat.* 89) and the 'Civil War' (295 hexameters at *Sat.* 119–24) plainly look to the contemporary Neronian literary scene, hitting at the tragedies of Seneca and the epic of Lucan in particular – see e.g. Sullivan (1985), and the sophisticated treatments by Connors (1998). Here as elsewhere the *Satyrica* is firmly rooted in its Neronian cultural context: we may compare the way in which the imperious Trimalchio of the *Cena Trimalchionis* has more than a touch of Nero about him (see Walsh 1970: 137–9). A further literary strand in the *Satyrica* that has rightly become more prominent is that of drama and the mime. The importance of popular drama in Petronius not only stresses its low-life and contemporary realism, but also allows the interpretation of particular episodes in theatrical mode: this has been done excellently by Rosati (1983/1999) and Panayotakis (1995).

The fact that such a wide range of texts is drawn on through parody and other forms of allusion intersects neatly with Bakhtin's influential theory of the novel as an 'open' literary form, a generic and polyphonic mixture, which he himself applied with success to Petronius and Apuleius (Bakhtin 1981: 111–29; cf. Fusillo 1996: 279–80). Recent study of Petronius, with its increased interest in narrative analysis and narratology, has naturally become more interested in narrative technique and structure, though this is naturally an area where the incompleteness of the text of the *Satyrica* is especially problematic. The main issue has been recently well stated by Fusillo, arguing that the *Satyrica*

> shows a very complex dialectic among author, I-narrator and I-character; in every part of the work we perceive the destructive irony of the first and the constant tension between the second and the third, that is the various attempts of Encolpius to interpret his experience as the main actor of adventures. (1996:286)

Beck (1973/1999) has argued that the whole of the *Satyrica* is narrated by an older and wiser Encolpius looking back on his youthful errors, producing the double perspective of young Encolpius-*actor* and older Encolpius-*auctor*, to use the terms popularized for Apuleius by Winkler (1985). Conte (1996) attractively sees Encolpius as a 'mythomaniac narrator', a naive young intellectual reading the low-life events of a sordid story in terms of elevated literary models such as epic and tragedy, while placed by the 'hidden author' (the Petronius of the text) in low-life melodramatic situations from novelistic and pantomimic contexts, with irony resulting from the evident gap between the two.

Some of the above features are well brought out through citation of the *Satyrica* itself, for example from the dinner at Trimalchio's house, where the self-made millionaire repeatedly demonstrates his poor taste, disgusting extravagance and profound cultural ignorance. At 50.5 Trimalchio gives a wonderfully garbled version of the origin of 'Corinthian bronze', the alloy of bronze and a precious metal:

> when Troy was captured, Hannibal, a shrewd guy and a major rat [literally 'lizard', *stelio*], piled up all the bronze, gold and silver statues on to one bonfire and set fire to them: the different metals turned into one.

Trimalchio shows simultaneously his earthy and uncultured style of speech, and his desire to present himself as a cultural connoisseur despite a complete lack of grasp of metallurgy, history and mythology.

Another typically witty scene is at *Sat.* 94, where the narrator Encolpius has been shut in his low-class hotel room by the hack poet Eumolpus, who has gone off with Encolpius' lover, Giton. Encolpius in despair prepares to commit suicide by hanging himself from his bed-frame, but is interrupted by the return of Eumolpus and Giton, and the latter's melodramatic speech:

'you've got it wrong, Encolpius', said Giton, 'if you think you can manage to die first. I started earlier: I went to look for the sword in Ascyltus' lodgings. If I hadn't found you, I would have died by throwing myself off something. And just so you know that death is never far off for those who seek it, see yourself the sight you wanted me to see.' Having said this he snatched a razor from Eumolpus' servant, and slashing his neck not once but twice he collapsed before our feet. I shouted out in shock, and following him as he fell I sought the road to death by means of the same implement. But Giton was not harmed by even the suspicion of a wound, and I could not feel any pain either. For the razor was unused and blunted so as to give a barber's confidence to boys learning the trade, and equipped with a sheath. Accordingly the servant had not panicked about the snatching of the implement, nor had Eumolpus interrupted this mime-stage death. (*Sat.* 94.11–15)

The high camp humour of this passage is evident: both characters use grandiloquent, quasi-philosophizing language in a deeply farcical context (note Giton's sententious 'death is never far off for those who seek it ' and Encolpius' pretentious narratorial phrase 'I sought the road to death'). Giton's melodramatic 'suicide' comes to nothing, and the reader is left with the strong suspicion that he too (like Eumolpus and the latter's servant, in whose company he has just been) was aware that the razor was a blunt one. Encolpius' own analysis that Giton did not know this may be an element of naive self-deception and a typical lack of realization that Giton is highly manipulative; the reader may suspect more than the narrator here. The suicide-attempt is presented in something of a tragic parody: Giton envisages different modes of suicide before choosing one, a trope from Greek tragedy (Fraenkel 1932), and the whole scene is characterized as belonging to the farcical register of theatrical mime.

This is typical of the world of the *Satyrica*, a narrative of surreal farce and wit with a complex literary and narrative texture.

3 Apuleius' *Metamorphoses*

Apuleius' novel owes a not inconsiderable debt to Ovid's homonymous epic poem: in both the witty approach to the theme of metamorphosis, dense literary texture and overt narratorial play produce a work that is both frivolous in content and highly ambitious in artistic terms. Scholars are sharply divided on the issue of whether the narrative of Lucius' religious conversion in the eleventh and last book of the novel confers religious or philosophical seriousness on the work as a whole. The apparent inconsistency between Books 1–10 and Book 11 (how can an apparently religious book be the conclusion to a collection of low-life and sensational tales and adventures ?) used to be thought evidence of the author's poor literary capacity, and one major critic suggested that the final Book 11 was simply 'bolted on' to ensure intellectual respectability for an otherwise light work (Perry 1967: 244–5). Winkler (1985), the most influential of recent interpreters, has suggested that Book 11 allows both a satirical and a religious interpretation and is deliberately indeterminate between them, Merkelbach (1962) provides the strongest version of the religious interpretation, while S. J. Harrison (1996 and 2000) argues that the last book is firmly satirical and that the prime purpose of the *Met.* is to entertain and demonstrate the author's literary, philosophical and religious learning in the intellectual age of the Second Sophistic (for the background see Gibson, Chapter 5 above), not to convert its readers to Egyptian cultic religion or Platonic philosophy. The reader must make his or her own choice.

Literary texture is a key issue for Apuleius as for Petronius. Scholars have now largely agreed (see Mason 1978/1999) on interpreting the evidence of Photius *Bibl.* Cod. 129 as suggesting the *Met.* is directly derived from a lost Greek *Metamorphoses* attributed by Photius to Lucius of Patrae, of which the extant *Onos* attributed to Lucian is an epitome; Apuleius' two fundamental changes to the plot of the two Greek ass-tales were the introduction of the Isiac conclusion in Book 11 (replacing a comic ending in the Greek tradition), and the addition of many inserted tales (not least the famous central episode of Cupid and Psyche, 4.28–6.24). Modern scholarship has in general tended to stress the wide range of literary sources of the *Met.*, partly (as for Petronius; see above) under the influence of Bakhtin's theory of the novel. Here links with epic have been much explored, a natural line of enquiry given that in antiquity epic provided the only major predecessor of the novel as a long fictional narrative, and had many episodes and structures that could be suitably reworked, usually parodically – for example in Psyche's descent to the Underworld (6.17–21), clearly a lower version of that of Aeneas (see Finkelpearl 1990/1999). Intertexts recently studied in addition to the *Aeneid* (see Harrison 1997) have included the *Odyssey*, Ovid's *Metamorphoses*, Latin historiography and Greek tragedy – see the material collected in Harrison (1999: xxxiv–xxxv) and in the important treatment of Finkelpearl (1998).

The recognition of complex narrative technique in Apuleius has been a favourite topic of modern scholarship: apart from the *tour de force* of Winkler (1985), who treats the novel as a kind of detective story in which previous readerly opinions have to be revised after reading the ending. Tatum (1969/1999) has systematically linked all the inserted tales to their narrative contexts; the central and substantial Cupid and Psyche tale, for example, can be plausibly seen as a *mise en abyme* replicating and miniaturizing the main story of the novel, with the figure of Psyche matching Lucius in her foolish *curiositas*, consequent sufferings and final divine rescue.

Two passages of the *Met.* crucial for its narrative technique have been particularly debated. The first is the prologue (*Met.* 1.1), where the unnamed speaker has been variously interpreted as Apuleius the author, Lucius the narrator, a combination of the two, an anonymous *prologus* in the manner of Roman comedy, or even the book itself; for a wide-ranging discussion involving many scholars see

Kahane and Laird (2001). The second is the celebrated passage near the end of the last book (11.27), where the priest Asinius Marcellus reports to the narrator Lucius that he (Asinius) has been told in a dream that a man from Madauros (*Madaurensem*) would come to him for initiation and achieve great glory in literature, implicitly identifying Lucius with the man from Madauros, the birthplace of Apuleius himself, an identification that Lucius fails to deny. Many have seen *Madaurensem* as a signal of Apuleian autobiography in some sense, and thus of the seriousness of the last book as a religious testimony. Narratological considerations, however, offer a third solution that says nothing about the book's 'sincerity', and suggest that this is a playful gesture akin to the determinedly anonymous speaker of the prologue, providing a deliberately balanced complication of the first-person voice at the beginning and the end of the text: thus narrative considerations can add a further approach to the old problem of unity in the *Met.*, of coherence between Books 1–10 and 11.

These concerns can be well illustrated by some citations from the text itself. At 6.25 Lucius-ass as narrator comments on the story of Cupid and Psyche which he has just heard from an old woman:

> this was the story told to the captive girl by the raving and drunken old woman; but I standing close by was mightily sorry that I did not have tablets and a stylus to note down such a pretty story.

This passage contains multiple wit and irony. The ass-narrator laments that he did not have writing materials (which he could not anyway have used in his bestial state) to note down this story (which he is nevertheless relating to the reader in a written text), and suggests that the episode is simply a pretty old wives' tale of no great import, whereas it is in some sense his own impending story, since (as already noted) the tale of Cupid and Psyche provides a clear parallel for Lucius' own future career in the novel. The text also highlights the role of the primary narrator (the old woman) and the primary narratee (the captive girl, later named as Charite): the tale is relevant to the narratee as another young girl seeking a similar happy conclusion to tribulations (a happy conclusion that seems to happen in her marriage in the next book, but which is then subverted by her tragic widowhood and suicide in Book 8), and even the narrating old woman, too insignificant to be named, may have left her imprint on the shape of the story (see Van Mal-Maeder and Zimmermann 1998).

A further key feature of Apuleius' novel is its often exuberant and baroque style (for an excellent brief analysis see Kenney 1990: 28–38). At its most heightened moments the effect is almost incantatory, with dense use of archaic poetic vocabulary, assonance, rhyme, asyndeton (omission of connecting words) and isocolon (balancing groups of words of equal length). I cite some lines from one of the grandest scenes of the novel, where the goddess Isis appears to Lucius in answer to his prayers:

en adsum tuis commota, Luci, precibus, rerum naturae parens, elementorum omnium domina, saeculorum progenies initialis, summa numinum, regina manium, prima caelitum, deorum dearumque facies uniformis, quae caeli luminosa culmina, maris salubria flamina, inferum deplorata silentia nutibus meis dispenso: cuius numen unicum multiformi specie, ritu vario, nomine multiiugo totus veneratur orbis.

Here I am, Lucius, moved by your prayers, the mother of creation, lady of all the elements, the original issue of the ages, the greatest of divine powers, the queen of the shades, first amongst the heaven-dwellers, the uniform appearance of all gods and goddesses, who rule with my nod the luminous heights of the sky, the healthy breezes of the sea, and the lamented silence of those below, whose single power the whole world reveres through manifold form, diverse ritual, and many a name. (*Metamorphoses* 11.5)

Apuleius is indubitably one of the most striking stylists of Latin prose as well as a subtle and learned writer.

Like the *Sat.*, the *Met.* must be seen firmly within its own intellectual context. It was written by a highly prolific professional intellectual with evident interest in Platonic philosophy and religion, and it is no surprise to see these themes emerging in the novel, though I would argue that they are there to show off knowledge rather than to show ideological commitment (see S. J. Harrison 2000: 238–59). Like the *Sat.* again, the *Met.* engages closely with the concerns of contemporary intellectual life, and with a learned readership in the age of the Second Sophistic which can appreciate a wide range of literary allusion in both Latin and Greek. Apuleius, a competitive professional intellectual, eloquent speaker, prolific writer and local educator, surely earns the title of 'sophist' given to many of his similar Greek contemporaries.

4   The Roman Novel: Common Features

As we have seen, the novels of Petronius and Apuleius have many common features that enable us to talk meaningfully of 'the Roman novel', though they are also two texts written in two different intellectual and cultural climates. Both are written at a high literary level with many allusions to Greek and Latin classics and parody of higher genres, especially epic and the Greek romantic novel; Apuleius' sexually curious traveller Lucius, like Petronius' homosexual *ménage à trois*, clearly provides a further variation on the chastity and conjugality of the Greek novels as well as on the wanderings of Odysseus.

Both texts are also interested in complex narrative technique. We have seen above the problems that arise with the narrative voices of both Petronius' Encolpius, perhaps narrating his youthful errors from a more mature perspective, and Apuleius' Lucius, whose identity as narrator is wilfully obscured at both the beginning and the end of the novel. Their shared frame of first-person narrative (found only in Achilles Tatius in the Greek novels), and common architecture in which a lively main story contains further subnarratives of a similar witty, obscene and sensationalist nature, may also derive from a common source, the notorious *Milesian Tales* of Aristides from the late Hellenistic period, translated into Latin by Sisenna in the first century BC. Petronian scholars generally agree that Eumolpus' highly entertaining inserted tales of the Boy of Pergamum (*Sat.* 85–9) and the Widow of Ephesus (*Sat.* 111–12) derive from this tradition of racy short stories, which is explicitly mentioned in programmatic passages by Apuleius as a tradition in which he is writing (*Met.* 1.1; 4.32). The *Milesian Tales* may thus have influenced both the low-life content and the narrative framework of both the Roman novels (see Harrison 1998b).

In the Roman novels we see Latin literature at its most relaxed and entertaining; the combination of quasi-pornography with dense literary texture and narrative complexity seems to cater both to basic Roman instincts and to the strong intertextual element in Latin literature, and with satire, epigram, comedy and mime form part of a network of 'lower' genres that were especially popular, if not entirely respectable in the eyes of the high-minded (on the low prestige of the Roman novels in antiquity cf. e.g. Macrobius *Somn.* 1.2.8, SHA *Clod.Alb.* 12.12; and on their mixed reception until recently see Harrison 2002b).

FURTHER READING

An important milestone in the history of the criticism of the Roman novels is Walsh (1970), showing through demonstration of their complex literary texture that these works deserve higher estimation than given them by previous scholars; for example Perry (1967). Important too was the stimulating work of J. P. Sullivan on Petronius, especially Sullivan (1968). These two scholars have also produced important translations of the two novels, Sullivan (1965) for Petronius, and Walsh for both novels (1994 and 1996); for Apuleius see also the version by Kenney (1998). Harrison (1999) collects some classic articles and provides a commented bibliography in the introduction, which covers work on both novels since 1900, and Hofmann (1999) contains many useful short essays and a good guide to the field.

Work on Petronius is still hampered by the lack of a complete commentary on the *Sat.*, but Courtney (2001) now provides a useful if austere guide to the whole work, and on the central 'Dinner of Trimalchio' M. S. Smith (1975) remains useful. Of more recent critical work, Slater (1990) provides much of interest, especially on the aspect of role-playing in the *Sat.*, while Conte (1996) is very helpful on the literary form and narrative voice of the work. Panayotakis (1995) is excellent on the theatrical elements, while Boyce (1991) is a handy guide to the thorny issue of how far the low characters of the work reflect spoken Latin; on Petronian style in general the best guide in English is Petersmann (1999), summarizing his work in German.

The major Groningen series of commentaries on Apuleius in English is now almost complete (see <http://www.forsten.nl> for details); in smaller compass Kenney (1990) is very useful on the key Cupid and Psyche episode. Among recent critical work, Hijmans and van der Paardt (1978) is an important collection, Tatum (1979) and Schlam (1992) are useful works, but the outstanding book is Winkler (1985), which in many ways redrew the boundaries of studying the *Met.*, with its radical scepticism, brilliant use of narratology and mildly deconstructive turn. More recent work has looked more specifically at techniques of literary allusion in the *Met.* (Finkelpearl 1998), and at its intellectual context and place in Apuleius' works (S. J. Harrison 2000), and a good index of the range of work on the *Met.* is given in Kahane and Laird (2001), with twenty-four widely differing pieces on the work's controversial first paragraph.

CHAPTER SIXTEEN

Dialogues and Treatises

J. G. F. Powell

1   Introduction

This chapter deals broadly with that class of prose literature in Latin that is
devoted to the exposition of some branch of theoretical or practical knowledge.
The field is vast and diverse, and it is impossible to do full justice to it in a short
essay such as this one; only some of the main lines can be indicated. The genre of
the expository treatise (what in Greek would be called a *technē*) in Latin is as old
as Roman literature itself. It is convenient in a historical survey to treat this as the
basic form, on which later developments (from a Latin point of view) such as
the reflective dialogue (e.g. Cicero's *De Oratore*) or the encyclopaedic compilation (e.g. Pliny's *Natural History*) may be regarded as elaborations. Writing of
this kind continued throughout antiquity, and survived vigorously into the post-
classical world. Indeed, it outlived many other kinds of Latin literature as a
productive genre: the convention that scientific or philological dissertations
should be written in Latin still applied, in places at least, until the beginning of
the twentieth century AD.

The general notion of 'expository prose' presupposes at least an author who is
sufficiently competent in the subject to be a credible expositor, and a readership in
search of information or understanding rather than entertainment. Within that
wide definition, various distinctions can be made, some of which are more useful
than others in a Roman context. Von Albrecht (1992: 452) distinguishes between
a technical treatise (*Fachbuch*) for specialists or aspiring specialists, and a work of
non-fiction meant for the general reader (*Sachbuch*); though the distinction in
that form is a modern one, it can help at least to define the problems of
classification. A genuine specialist literature in the modern sense is an ever-
growing corpus, constantly added to by specialists who write on specific topics
or offer new syntheses: it could well be argued that the Romans developed
something like this in only two areas, which also happen to be the two most

enduring legacies of Roman non-material culture to the modern world: Latin grammar and Roman law (see e.g. Kaster 1988 for the former, Schulz 1953 for the latter). A related distinction can be made between works that aim to impart skills or to prescribe procedures, for example in architecture or medicine, and those that merely offer systematized information, for example in natural history; but that difference seems determined more by the nature of the subject matter than by the literary genre. Technical books themselves (see Fuhrmann 1960) can be divided into categories: one may mention the systematic textbook, the elementary primer for use in a teaching context, the 'Teach Yourself' manual for use without a teacher, or the *aide-mémoire* for those who already have some competence in the subject. Notoriously, the cookbook of 'Apicius' comes into the last category: it is difficult to use for anyone who does not already have some knowledge of cookery, as it rarely makes mention of precise quantities or basic cooking methods (for attempts to supply these see e.g. Edwards 1984). Furthermore, writings with any of these purposes may be presented with greater or less attention to literary form, ranging from a highly elaborated literary artefact such as Cicero's *De Oratore* at one end of the scale to a largely unadorned set of notes like 'Apicius' at the other. This scale is a continuous one without well-defined divisions; to use German terminology again, in a Roman context there is no sharp generic distinction between *Kunstliteratur* (art-literature or *belles-lettres*) and *Fachliteratur* (subject-literature or technical literature); works like the *De Oratore*, Varro's *Res Rusticae* and, much later, Martianus Capella's *De Nuptiis Mercurii et Philologiae* do not belong neatly in either category. It is, however, less misleading to make use of this terminology than to deny the title of 'literature' altogether to those writings that lack the necessary artistic pretensions; for, as Cicero observed, 'exposition is itself an art' (*Leg.* 2.47, *est quaedam ars etiam docendi*) and even the most mundane technical treatise can deploy its linguistic resources effectively or not, depending on the competence of the author.

Perhaps more misleading than any of these distinctions, because it also has social and historical implications, is that between 'amateur' and 'professional'. The institutionalization and professionalization of most branches of human knowledge since the nineteenth century has made this distinction a fundamental one for us; but it depends on the presence of complex social institutions for which no exact equivalents existed in the classical Roman world (though it can be argued that a process of professionalization was under way in certain areas: see e.g. Frier 1985 and Crook 1995 on jurists and advocates respectively). Roman writers on specialized subjects have been labelled as 'amateur' for various reasons, and in particular because they are not always practitioners of the art they claim to expound. An exception has usually been made for Vitruvius, who claimed the status of *architectus* (*Arch.* 1.1.18) and who had at least one major building to his credit (*Arch.* 5.1.6); yet his official position under Augustus was as an inspector of artillery, and the latter parts of his treatise cover that topic as well as other kinds of engineering, the management of water supplies, and the mathematics and astronomy needed to construct sundials – topics that in modern times would usually be regarded as tangential from an architect's point of view. Julius Frontinus, a man with a highly distinguished military and administrative career, engagingly tells us in his treatise on aqueducts (AD 97) that he wrote the book after being put in charge of the Roman water supply, in order to find out about the subject. We know Cornelius Celsus (early 1st c. AD) for his work on medicine, but he was an encyclopaedist, not a doctor. Certainly, his knowledge derived from books is extensive, he is fully at home with medical terminology and phraseology (see Langslow 2000) and he sometimes apparently appeals to his own medical experience (e.g. 7.7.6 C; 7.12.4), but he always refers to the practitioners, *medici*, in the third person. Celsus wrote also on agriculture, warfare, philosophy, rhetoric and law – a range of interests that would nowadays tend to disqualify him from being taken seriously as a specialist in any of those topics.

To understand this aspect of Roman technical writing, we must lay aside modern notions of professionalism and think instead of the different branches of knowledge as the Romans thought of them, that is as *disciplinae* or forms of learning, any of which a member of the Roman governing and administrative class might be called upon to master in the course of his public duties, at least to the extent that he could direct the work of others in an effective and knowledgeable fashion, and, in the absence of a system of professional qualifications, distinguish between competent and incompetent subordinates. A man with good natural gifts and proper education, so it was held, could understand the essentials of any subject without long professional training, because all the branches of learning were, after all, interrelated; a rhetorically and philosophically educated person with a grasp of first principles would be better able to expound the theory of a subject than a practitioner who relied merely on experience and therefore might not be able to see the wood for the trees; and, conversely, a knowledge of a wide range of subjects was desirable for anyone with a claim to intellectual distinction (*sapientia*) and learning (*doctrina*). This attitude finds perhaps its most striking expression at the beginning of Vitruvius' work (*Arch.* 1.1), where he claims to write *non modo aedificantibus sed etiam omnibus sapientibus* (not only for those engaged in building, but for all intelligent readers), and explains how an architect needs to be not only literate and numerate, but also to have some acquaintance with the whole range of scientific knowledge that might become relevant at some point, not to mention the law (so that he could avoid boundary disputes and the like) and mythology (so that he could explain the sculptured motifs on his buildings): see further André (1987).

This question of the relation between general education and technical expertise (whose earlier and later history is of the greatest interest, but too complex to trace now) surfaces many times. Cicero, for example, in the *De Legibus* (2.46–53) protests at the involved definitions of legal experts, who make heavy weather of a simple issue of classification: his intellectual training enables him to see to the heart of an issue where the experts allegedly cannot. In his *De Oratore* he makes

Crassus (generally taken to represent at least one aspect of the author's own view) argue that an advocate or politician needed the kind of education that would enable him to master at short notice any issue that might arise (1.48–73, esp. 59). The principle extended to practical subjects as well. With the increasing demands of urban life, which took landowners away from their farms for a large part of the year, a need arose for quick and easy instruction in the principles of agriculture; in spite of Cicero's insistence (again in *De Oratore*, 1.249) that these principles are common knowledge, a landlord needed enough detailed expertise to see that things were being done properly, and to deal if necessary with a contumacious bailiff. A medical compendium such as that of Celsus would not be of negligible value for a Roman *paterfamilias*, who had an interest in preserving the health of a large number of family members, clients and slaves, and who might well prefer to make use of such knowledge as he could gain in this way rather than trust a medical practitioner. Pliny's *Natural History* was not merely a collection of scientific curiosities, but a guide to the natural resources available for exploitation in the Roman world, including some very *engagé* discussion of the rights and wrongs of such exploitation: see further Beagon (1992).

The Roman aristocratic ethos, especially in Republican times, was against making a living from most of these technical skills; but this did not prevent Romans from aspiring to the same expertise as those who did so. Indeed, the Roman writers liked to present themselves as going one better than the mere practitioners, by claiming mastery of Greek theory and of the history of the subject – things that were acquired primarily through literary study – as well as of practical techniques. Cicero himself disparaged technical rhetoric and the 'philosophy factories' of the Hellenistic schools, despite the large debt he owed them. Furthermore, many technical writers included an element of protreptic, claiming that their chosen subject was an honourable art and part of universal education (and not just a way of making money). In subjects where the Greek tradition offered several rival schools of thought, the Romans liked to appear to be above such disputes, and to be critical evaluators, not merely passive inheritors of Greek doctrine. Cicero's adoption of the Neo-Academic refusal of philosophical dogma provided a useful precedent here; Celsus arbitrates between Dogmatics, Empirics and Methodists in medicine much as Cicero does between the philosophical schools.

As regards the literary form, there were obvious models in the Greek technical literature on medicine (the Hippocratic corpus), mathematics (Euclid), astronomy (Eudoxus), military matters (Xenophon, Aeneas Tacticus), rhetoric (the *Rhetorica ad Alexandrum*), and so on. Most of these were plain in style and businesslike in approach, avoiding any literary complexities that did not serve the purposes of exposition and often plunging straight into the subject without preliminaries. On the other hand, there were also precedents for more elaborate literary treatment (such as Xenophon's treatment of farming and household management in the guise of a Socratic dialogue in the *Oeconomicus*) or for establishing the author's credentials in a preface (like the historians). Roman technical writers might disclaim rhetorical expertise (as did Vitruvius), or protest that their subject was not suitable for eloquent treatment (Pomponius Mela on geography); but this is itself a standard topic in the conventional dedicatory or self-justificatory prologue, which, whether extensive or perfunctory, is generally composed with studied rhetorical urbanity: see Janson (1964). The self-presentation of the writer, in other words, was often important as a means of establishing authority. Furthermore, Roman expository literature can easily accommodate philosophical, historical and moralizing flourishes, as well as the Greek-inspired use of the literary dialogue as a medium of exposition. These conventions remained familiar throughout Western European literary history, at least until the eighteenth century AD; and although they may be decidedly unfamiliar now, we should not be misled by them into thinking that the works that employ them are mere literary exercises. The subjects on which these Romans wrote were serious business, as they had been for the Greeks before them; and their writings reflect not only a drive towards technical mastery, but also at least sometimes a sense of moral and political responsibility and personal involvement, which the rhetorical style served to enhance.

2 Beginnings: Cato and Others

Of the standard topics of Roman expository literature, the first to appear, and doubtless always among the first in importance for the Roman reading public, was agriculture: see White (1973). The treatise on agriculture by M. Porcius Cato the Elder (234–149 BC: see Herzog and Schmidt 2002: 400–9) is the earliest work of Latin prose that survives into modern times. It is easily regarded as quaint and old fashioned (but hardly more so than Mrs Beeton's *Cookery and Household Management* now seems after a twentieth part of the time). Later Romans chuckled at Cato's cake recipes and his prophylactic against drunkenness (cabbage leaves in vinegar). Yet the bulk of it consists of precise and practical instructions for the acquisition and maintenance of an estate in the wine and olive country of central Italy, with a view not only to maximizing profit but also to minimizing expense (hence the directions for making the farm as self-sufficient as possible). Little attention is paid to pasturage, which was regarded as a different subject altogether from *agri cultura* (strictly 'the cultivation of the land'). Slightly more surprising is the virtual absence of advice on grain farming, but the region of Italy to which Cato chiefly refers is not a grain-growing area, and by his time much of Rome's grain supply already came from abroad. Cato includes instructions on religious rites, cookery and home remedies, which were essential activities in any ancient agricultural concern.

The style of exposition is economical, indeed laconic, but clear enough except where corruption of the text has interfered. The characteristic mindset of the author shows through particularly in the occasional aphorisms, some of which became famous; 'A farmer should be a seller, not a buyer' (*Agr.* 2.7); *ne villa fundum quaerat neve fundus villam* (very roughly: 'a farmhouse without a farm is as bad as a farm without a farmhouse', 3.1); 'if no work is being done, expenses run on nonetheless' (39.2). The preface expresses Cato's conviction that agricul-ture is a better occupation than either trade (which is too risky) or finance (which is regarded as dishonourable), but his moralistic alignment with the supposed ideals of the *maiores* is, as far as can be seen, merely self-justification; Cato's instructions are as clearly directed towards profit as those in any modern business manual.

The structure of the *De Agri Cultura* is, notoriously, somewhat disorganized; whether that is the fault of Cato or of the transmission remains an open question; but it does raise the problem of how such a work was to be used by its first readers. Received scholarly opinion has it that continuous oral performance was the most common, if not the only practicable method of realising a text written on a papyrus roll; but with the best will in the world, it is not easy to imagine Cato inviting his friends to a recital of the complete *De Agri Cultura*, and the same could be said of most other technical literature from the ancient world. It seems on general grounds far more likely that users of these works would have searched through them for instructions on the particular point they were interested in. This task would have been assisted by the fact that the topic of each section is often visible from the first few words; the structure of the Latin language is itself a help here, as it lends itself more than many modern languages to the feature called 'topicalization' whereby the topic of a sentence can be placed first regardless of its grammatical function. The typical method of using such a treatise may well have been more like what we see in Cicero's casual note to his lawyer friend Trebatius (*Fam.* 7.22): when a controversial point of law had arisen over dinner, Cicero was able to locate the relevant chapter the same night and have a copy made to send to his friend. In short, the active use of these works relied on the skill of excerpting, whose role in ancient literary culture may have tended to be underestimated (though it is familiar to every medievalist). On the later development of logical organization in Roman technical literature, see Rawson (1978).

Cato is also said to have written a book of general advice to his son, together with treatises on medicine, military matters and civil law (Herzog and Schmidt 2002: 409–13). The last mentioned was an area of great importance to all upper-class Romans and at the same time potentially a difficult and controversial one, where both application and acumen were needed in order to attain expertise. In the Republic there was no official codification of the corpus of civil law, but the treatises of famous jurisconsults were regarded as having varying degrees of authority. Of these perhaps the first was the *Tripertita* of Sextus Aelius Paetus Catus (consul 198 BC): it contained a text of the Twelve Tables, a commentary on them, and an account of the *legis actiones* (forms of pleading). Later, Manius Manilius, the leading jurist of his generation (who appears as one of the speakers in Cicero's *De Republica*), wrote on civil law in the second half of the second century BC; and towards the end of that century the Scaevola family became pre-eminent in this field. Publius Mucius Scaevola, the consul of 133, wrote ten books on civil law, and Quintus Mucius Scaevola 'the Pontifex' (consul 95 BC) wrote eighteen. The form of these lost but influential works can only be guessed at; it may have been as severely technical as that of later juristic writings, although probably less systematic in places (it is the Scaevolae who are the objects of Cicero's criticism in the *De Legibus* for their lack of system). It was here, perhaps, that the need was least pressing to make the exposition attractive in a literary sense or to persuade readers of the advantages of studying this obviously important subject. Even so, we learn (again from Cicero) that a second-century treatise on civil law, that of one M. Junius Brutus (perhaps praetor in 140 BC), was cast in the form of a dialogue between father and son – apparently the first prose dialogue to be written in Latin.

No less serious was the interest of the Roman upper classes in their own political constitution, religion, language and culture (for these and other intellectual interests see Rawson 1985). The label 'antiquarian' often applied to writers on these subjects, is surely misleading: it gives the impression that these writers confined their efforts to digging up, or perhaps concocting, obsolete details from the distant past, whereas they were in fact writing about important and sometimes controversial topics in their own contemporary world. To take an example from the late Republic, one Cincius (mentioned by Macrobius, *Sat.* 1.12.12 and perhaps identical with the 2nd-c. BC historian Cincius Alimentus: see Herzog and Schmidt 2002: 370–2) is known to have written on the calendar, the constitutional powers of the consuls, electoral procedure, and the function of legal experts. To label him an 'antiquarian' on the basis of these interests would be as unfair as it would be to use that word to characterize a modern constitutional historian. Though nothing of these works survives beyond their titles, the titles themselves are enough to show that Cincius was in fact writing on matters of live interest to any upper-class Roman of the Republic.

Linguistic and literary scholarship was introduced to Rome during the second century BC; Lucius Aelius Stilo, born in 150 BC and working around the end of the century, produced among other things a commentary on the Salian hymn (a religious text of extreme archaism and obscurity), and a work on the theory of propositions, a topic belonging to the grey area between syntax and logic and presumably the first ever attempt to apply Greek linguistic or logical theory to Latin. Again, this interest both in the relics of archaic Latin and in the workings of language in general is not to be taken as a frivolous academic or antiquarian pursuit, but rather as an attempt to understand the Roman cultural tradition from within, and to establish Latin as a major linguistic medium on a par with Greek. Concern of this kind for the native language is more easily understood almost anywhere else than in England, where it is generally regarded as the preserve of pedants; in Rome, linguistics was not thought beneath the notice of public men, and – to anticipate a little – even Julius Caesar, apparently while campaigning in Gaul, wrote a treatise on grammatical analogy (the principle that dictates e.g. that the plural of 'mouse' should be 'mouses'; attempts to apply it to Latin would have had equally risible consequences).

One further topic should be mentioned as an interest of Roman aristocrats in the second century BC: astronomy. C. Sulpicius Galus (consul 166 BC; his name should be spelt thus, not as 'Gallus') had achieved a considerable reputation for expertise in this field: at the battle of Pydna in 168 BC he assuaged the fears of the Roman troops by explaining the cause of an eclipse of the sun, and according to Pliny, *Nat. Hist.* 2.53 he wrote a treatise on the topic (Herzog and Schmidt 2002: 533–4). Roman interest in astronomy should not be underestimated or, again, relegated to the realm of the 'amateur': it was of vital importance not only for counteracting popular superstition in the interests of morale, as in the case of the eclipse, but also for direction-finding and for the adjustment of the calendar.

3   Philosophy and Rhetoric at Rome: the Works of Cicero

By the beginning of the first century BC, then, there was in existence a considerable body of expository literature in Latin on a wide range of subjects. The first century brought two important new arrivals to the list of subjects thought fit for exposition in literary form: rhetoric and philosophy. The two were intimately connected in the work of Cicero, who cited Aristotle and Isocrates as precedents for his interest in combining them. He was influenced in that direction by his Academic master Philo of Larissa, who taught rhetorical techniques of argument as part of philosophy, and by the practice in the rhetorical schools of debating philosophical questions (an example of this is found in Cicero's own *Paradoxa Stoicorum*). Cicero's espousal of the rhetorical conception of philosophy had a strong influence on the directions taken by philosophical writing in the Roman world, where the persuasive and exhortatory element is usually no less prominent than the purely expository or didactic.

Both rhetoric and philosophy had been introduced gradually into Rome as part of Hellenistic culture during the second century BC, and had finally been accepted in the first century as unavoidable, if still not always entirely suitable, studies for a Roman of good standing. Not only did the task of explaining these two subjects to a Roman readership call for considerable expertise and application: it also required that they should be provided with a justification and purged of any morally or politically dubious associations. Rhetoric had a particularly sticky start at Rome: the teaching of this subject was several times forbidden, and in Cicero's youth formal training in rhetoric at a high level was available only in Greece; it was not until the early Principate that rhetorical teaching through the medium of Latin became, in practice, the mainstay of Roman elite education. Philosophy was not naturalized in quite the same way; throughout the classical Roman period it was accepted that most serious philosophical study would still take place in Greek, either in a centre of Greek culture or else with a philosopher resident in a Roman household, despite the well-regarded efforts of Cicero, Lucretius, Seneca and others to 'teach Philosophy to speak Latin' (the phrase is from Cic. *Fin.* 3.40), and the attempt of the Sextii to set up a Roman philosophical school in the early first century AD; on Roman philosophy see in general Clarke (1956) and Morford (2002).

The first Latin rhetorical treatise, the so-called *Rhetorica ad Herennium*, is attributed in the manuscript tradition to Cicero and shares some material with Cicero's own youthful *De Inventione*, but it is clearly enough not by him: the balance of scholarly opinion is in favour of attribution to an unknown author of the Sullan period, possibly belonging to the school of Latin rhetors that L. Plotius Gallus attempted to establish and that in 92 BC attracted censorial disapproval. It is a valuable source for the technical rhetoric of the period, and includes some interesting examples of good and bad style. The *De Inventione* itself (88 BC) is a manual of forensic strategy, which one may suppose to have been written chiefly as an *aide-mémoire* by the 18-year-old future leader of the Roman bar; it reflects the methods of the Hellenistic teachers of rhetoric and in particular the division of issues (*staseis*) recommended by Hermagoras.

The rhetorical and philosophical works of Cicero's maturity begin with *De Oratore* (55 BC), Cicero's first essay in the dialogue form. The choice of dialogue as a medium distances it from the ordinary rhetorical *technē* such as the *De Inventione*: it is not only an exposition but also a critical evaluation of the science of rhetoric, demonstrating (in a manner that owes much to Aristotelian doctrine) that a successful orator cannot simply be manufactured by means of a course of technical training: see May and Wisse (2001). After the *De Oratore* Cicero turned to political theory and to the composition of what was doubtless his most ambitious literary work of all, the six-book *De Republica* (of which about a quarter is now extant), together with its sequel *De Legibus* (probably never published by the author); the pair of dialogues was loosely inspired by Plato's *Republic* and *Laws*. At least in one way, it is misleading to pigeonhole the *De Oratore* as a work on rhetoric and the *De Republica* as a work on philosophy, although that is a correct description of the subject matter on which they draw. Designed to some extent as literary companion-pieces, they are both reflective dialogues, both formally modelled on Plato, and both dealing above all with the character of the ideal Roman – in the former case specifically as an orator, in the latter as a politician (*rector rei publicae*: for the meaning of this phrase see Powell 1994). In both, the didactic element is rhetorically subordinated; the foreground is occupied by the problems, as in an aporetic dialogue of Plato – what makes an effective orator and politician? What education does he need? What is the best form of political organization? Is that what matters, or can different kinds of constitution work provided their principles are applied justly? Is there in fact such a thing as political justice? What laws and customs does a state need in order to be durable and successful?

During Caesar's dictatorship (46–44 BC), Cicero sought an alternative to political activity, and embarked on an extensive programme of expository writing for the education, so he claimed, of his fellow-citizens. First came two further rhetorical books as sequels to *De Oratore*: the *Brutus*, a history of Roman oratory and especially of forensic advocacy, and the *Orator*, a treatise on style. Then Cicero composed an extensive and, as he claims, reasonably comprehensive series of works, mostly in dialogue form, on various aspects of philosophy (see Powell 1995): *Hortensius* on the value of philosophical study (lost), *Academica* on theory of knowledge, *De Finibus Bonorum et Malorum* on moral philosophy, *De Natura Deorum* on the nature of the gods, *De Divinatione* on divination, *De Fato* on freedom versus determinism, *Tusculan Disputations* on what may loosely be called moral psychology, *Cato Maior* a consolation on old age, *Laelius* a celebration of friendship, *De Gloria* on the pursuit of fame (lost), *De Officiis* on right conduct, a translation of part of Plato's *Timaeus*, *Topica* on logical argument (usually classified among the rhetorical works; logic has a foot in both camps).

There had been philosophical writing in Latin before Cicero; he refers fairly contemptuously to some Epicureans – Amafinius and Catius – who had written expositions of the doctrines of their school in Latin and who had made some attempts to solve the problems of translating technical terminology (Cic. *Fam.* 15.16.1–2; 15.19.1), and there may also have been some who attempted the same for Stoicism, though we cannot identify them. But as far as surviving texts are concerned, philosophical writing in Latin prose begins with Cicero; and at this point we should not forget the almost simultaneous appearance of didactic poetry on philosophical themes, obviously by Lucretius but also by others (according to Cicero, *Q. Fr.* 2.9.3, the *Empedoclea* of Sallustius – not the historian – was hard going). As a medium for the presentation of philosophical or reflective material, Plato was not the only precedent for the use of dialogue, and Plato's dialogues themselves offered several different models to choose from. Xenophon's works had been familiar to Romans for some generations, Aristotle's lost dialogues were praised for their style, and a number of Hellenistic philosophers had also written in the form. Cicero himself varied his technique from one dialogue to another. In *De Oratore* and *De Republica* and then again in the minor essays *Laelius* and *Cato Maior* the dialogue is presented in a full-scale fictional setting with characters from the past. *De Republica* is set in 129 BC, more than seventy years before the time of writing; we learn from Cicero's letters that he settled on the final form only after several drafts, one of which involved a more contemporary setting (see P. L. Schmidt 2001). In some of his later philosophical works he made use of contemporary or recently deceased Romans as characters, introducing himself as a minor interlocutor (*De Natura Deorum*) or as a major participant (*Brutus, De Finibus, De Divinatione*). In the *Academica*, Cicero changed his plan more than once; we now have the second book of the first edition, in which a youthful Cicero (representing the scepticism of the New Academy) is presented in a rather formal disputation with Lucullus (representing the views of his protégé Antiochus of Ascalon); but Cicero thought better of this on the ground that the attribution of philosophical arguments to Lucullus and his contemporaries was too historically implausible, and soon published a second version in four books (of which we have only part of the first book) in which the task of expounding Antiochus' theories was given to Varro (see Griffin 1997).

There have been useful studies of particular aspects of Cicero's dialogue technique (Kiaulehn 1914; Becker 1938; Jones 1939; Süß 1952; Zoll 1962) but there may still be a tendency to underestimate the success of his treatment of the genre. His dialogues contain some attractive scene-setting (e.g. *De Legibus* 1 and 2; *De Finibus* 3 and 5) and one striking excursion into mythography in the Platonic manner (the 'Dream of Scipio' at the end of *De Republica*); granted that these passages are largely imitative of Plato, Cicero imports a distinctive Roman flavour (see Becker 1938) and, in general, comes off by no means badly as a composer of imaginary narrative. He has occasional amusing touches of self-consciousness about the conventions of dialogue writing: in the *De Legibus* (3.26) Cicero reminds his brother Quintus that in a dialogue of this sort, the speakers are supposed to agree, so that they can get on to the next point. Quintus retorts, 'Well, I don't agree; but I'd like you to get on to the next point anyway.' There are many literary allusions to famous passages of Plato: the 'Dream of Scipio' recalls the Myth of Er and contains a verbatim translation from a passage of the *Phaedrus*, the opening of the *De Legibus* recalls the *Phaedrus* as well as the *Laws*, the departure of Scaevola at the beginning of the *De Oratore* is explicitly stated (in a letter) to recall that of Cephalus at the beginning of the *Republic*, and the dialogue proper in the *Laelius* is introduced with an imitation of a passage from the *Theaetetus* (see De Graff 1940). Cicero takes care with the characterization of his main speakers. It is conventional to refer to Scipio in the *De Republica* as Cicero's mouthpiece, but I have argued elsewhere (Powell 1996) that there is more to him than that: Scipio and Laelius within the context of the dialogue have complementary points of view, both of which are in some sense Ciceronian, and Laelius is consistently shown as pouring a certain amount of cold water on Scipio's Platonic idealism. Other characters also have personal features delineated by a few strokes of the pen: Manilius is the venerable lawyer, while Spurius Mummius is an inveterate oligarch who cannot be brought to admit that the democratic constitution of Rhodes has any merit. In the third book, we find an Academic-style disputation *pro* and *contra* on the subject of justice in government; this method was also cultivated in the rhetorical schools, and forms the basis for several of Cicero's later dialogues, where it becomes a convenient method for presenting and criticising the views of rival sects (on this see Leonhardt 1999). Despite its origins in the sceptical Academy, Cicero's use of this form in philosophical writing was evidently not primarily designed to further scepticism: even when both sides of an issue are presented with reasonable fairness, it is usually clear which one we are supposed to believe; in *Rep.* 3, the spokesman for cynical relativism and pragmatism, L. Furius Philus, makes it very clear that he does not believe in the position he is about to argue. Even so, there is an oddity at the end of *De Natura Deorum*, when Cicero in his own person (despite his Academic affiliation, which is reflected clearly in his language) comments that he finds the Stoic exposition of Balbus more plausible than the sceptical Academic one of Cotta. Discussion continues on the precise significance of this parting shot (see e.g. Glucker 1995: 137).

The full-scale dialogue form did not always suit Cicero's purposes. In the *Tusculan Disputations* it is reduced to an exposition by a character more or less clearly identified as Cicero himself, posing rather self-consciously as a philosophical teacher, with occasional responses or comments by an anonymous pupil (the speaking parts are marked in the manuscripts simply by 'M' for *magister* and 'A' for *auditor*: see Andrieu 1954: 297–8). A similar form is used in the minor rhetorical work *Partitiones Oratoriae*, with the role of the pupil played by Cicero's son (another example of the father–son dialogue, which, as Hirzel 1895: 429 pointed out, appealed so much to Roman taste). In the *De Officiis* the dialogue form is abandoned entirely, though the treatise is addressed to Cicero's son Marcus and acknowledges his presence from time to time; of a similar kind is the *Orator* addressed to Brutus and the *Topica* addressed to Trebatius. It was presumably the *De Officiis* that provided a model for Seneca's so-called 'dialogues', which are no more than extended essays written to a particular addressee (since *dialogus* in its origin simply meant 'conversation', a one-sided *dialogus* is not a theoretical impossibility, even though at variance with the normal usage of the word). Seneca's *Epistulae Morales*, a series of over 100 brief philosophical essays addressed in epistolary form to a single recipient, may be seen as a continuation of the same tendency.

4   After Cicero: Varro and Others

Cicero's contemporary M. Terentius Varro (116–27 BC), though his elder by ten years, outlived him by a considerable time, and was most productive in his later years, so it is reasonable to count him among Cicero's literary successors. Early in life Varro came under the influence of L. Aelius Stilo and was his successor as the leading Roman researcher in philological matters. He had an active military and political career in the mid-first century; he supported Pompey until he found himself on the losing side in the civil war; he was pardoned and honoured by Caesar, proscribed by Antony, rescued by Octavian, and (just) lived to see the last-mentioned proclaimed as Augustus. His earlier literary output belonged chiefly to the genre of satire (the *Menippeae*); there is also very fragmentary evidence for a series of writings called *Logistorici* which may possibly have been dialogues on general topics, rather along the lines of Cicero's *Cato* and *Laelius*. Varro also wrote biographies (the *Imagines*), works on history, geography, law, literary criticism and philosophy, and a work entitled *Disciplinae* which dealt with at least some of what were later referred to as the 'liberal arts', along with medicine and architecture, and which seems to have set the pattern for later encyclopaedic works such as that of Celsus. In terms of his contemporary and later influence, Varro's most significant works were his scholarly treatises on various aspects of Roman culture: on the origins of the Roman race, on the Latin language, on the Roman way of life, on Roman religion, and on Roman institutions. Cicero in his *Academicus Primus* (§9) compliments Varro on the value of his work from a patriotic perspective: Varro had finally taught the Romans who they were and where they lived. For Hellenized Romans anxious to avoid the label of barbarian and to justify their dominance over the Greek world, it was precisely the right time to be reassured that their language was actually a form of Greek (the identification was of course based on real similarities, due either to lexical borrowing or to common Indo-European descent). There could also be a con-temporary political context for this kind of writing; the *Divine Antiquities* were dedicated to the victorious Caesar at a time when he was reforming the civil and religious calendar: see Tarver (1994).

Two works of Varro survive from his vast output: six books of the *De Lingua Latina*, and the more or less complete *Res Rusticae*, a treatise on agriculture in dialogue form dating from 37 BC when Varro was in his eightieth year, dedicated (at least as far as the first book is concerned) to his wife Fundania, ostensibly with a practical purpose. Xenophon's *Oeconomicus* doubtless provided the main prece-dent for a dialogue on farming, and the recent example of Cicero may have stimulated Varro to write in this form, but Varro gives it a peculiar flavour of his own, not least in the choice of characters, all of whom in the first book have names etymologically related to agriculture: Fundanius (Varro's father-in-law) and Fundilius from *fundus*, 'farm', Agrius and Agrasius from *ager*, 'field', and the two farming experts Licinius Stolo (*stolo*, a 'sucker' growing round the roots of a tree) and Tremellius Scrofa (*scrofa*, 'pig'), not to mention the dedicatee; in the second book, Scrofa discourses at length on pigs, whereas one Vaccius deals with cows; the third book, which begins on the subject of aviaries, is dedicated to a man named Pinnius (cf. *pinna*, 'feather') and involves characters called Merula 'Blackbird', Pavo 'Peacock', Pica 'Magpie' and Passer 'Sparrow'. Varro's expos-ition is characteristically learned, urbane and in places whimsical, reflecting wide reading in the existing literature on farming (his extensive sources are listed at the beginning) as well as the predictable interests in etymology, antiquities, and out-of-the-way information. The characters exchange witticisms, proverbs and anecdotes with much local Roman and Italian colouring. One of Varro's most important themes, in contrast to Cato's earlier treatise, is the variety of agricul-tural practice in different parts of Italy: the dialogue begins, indeed, with the participants examining a painting of Italy on the wall of the temple of Tellus (whether a map, as scholars tend to assume, or a symbolic depiction, is not clear). The philosophical dialogue tradition is exploited: the character Agrius is introduced as a 'Socratic', and there is a recurrent if sometimes playful concern with definitions and systematic subdivisions of the subject. Moreover, the wider world does not go unnoticed; the first book ends quite startlingly with a murder, the third with an election victory. The virtually complete lack of integration between these 'noises off' and the rest of the work may be taken as a sign of lack of attention on the author's part, or it may be taken as a deliberately abrupt reminder that life was not altogether a rural idyll. The literary qualities of Varro's extant works have been disparaged, in particular his tendency to pedantic digressions; but if read in the right spirit, the three books of *Res Rusticae* have considerable charm as well as interest. On his Latin style see Laughton (1960).

Among the technical literature of the Augustan age, one work in particular stands out as a classic of its kind: the *De Architectura* of Vitruvius. This work is clearly written (at least on the whole), knowledgeable and precise, it is of considerable interest for the information it provides not only on architecture but also on ancient science and engineering, and its practical influence on later European building can hardly be overestimated. Even so, few scholarly accounts of Augustan literature accord it much recognition – a reflection of the narrowly aesthetic conception of 'literature' that still prevails among Latinists. The works on astronomy, mythology and land-surveying attributed to Julius Hyginus, freedman of Augustus and friend of Ovid, are of doubtful authorship (cf. von Albrecht 1997: i.877; Duret 1982: 1540–2). The study of philology and antiquities continued in the work of Verrius Flaccus, tutor to Augustus' grandsons: he was known particularly as a grammarian and for his researches on the calendar, which were embodied in the *Fasti Praenestini* displayed in his home town of Praeneste (Palestrina).

Moving later into the first century AD we find Celsus on medicine and much else, Pomponius Mela on geography, Pliny the Elder on all aspects of the natural (and human) world, Columella on agriculture (who represents an improvement on Varro at least as regards economy of exposition). In literary studies, we have parts of Asconius' commentary on Cicero's speeches. In the field of rhetoric, Seneca the Elder's work (see Fairweather 1981) entitled *Sententiae, Divisiones, Colores* should be mentioned, though it is not a systematic treatise: it is a collection of reminiscences of the ways in which the rhetoricians of Seneca's lifetime treated various standard debating topics (*suasoriae* and *controversiae*). In modern terms a *sententia* is a soundbite and a *divisio* is a set of bullet points; a *color* is a line of argument (the usage survives in phrases such as 'a colourable excuse'). This compilation contains numerous points of interest, such as the extracts from historical accounts of the death of Cicero and a glimpse of Ovid's performance in school rhetoric (*Suas.* 6.14–27; *Contr.* 2.2.9–12); yet one cannot avoid the impression that it is a bad guide to what actually went on in Roman rhetorical education, since it concentrates so heavily on declamation as display rather than as pedagogy or as practice for real oratory in the courts. Far more informative is

Quintilian's magisterial treatise on the orator's education (*Institutio Oratoria*) in twelve books, which presents a notably humane ideal of education, an A to Z of rhetorical composition and performance, and a mine of information on Roman forensic practice (see Russell 2001). In philosophy the main extant figure is the younger Seneca (see Griffin 1976), whose moral 'dialogues' and letters have already been mentioned, and who also expounded Stoic accounts of physical phenomena in the *Natural Questions*. Here, as elsewhere, the understanding of natural phenomena in scientific and philosophical terms appears not only as a legitimate aim of intellectual curiosity, but also as a step towards the development of correct moral and psychological attitudes.

The dialogue properly so called was revived towards the end of the first century AD by Cornelius Tacitus, if (as is generally though not universally accepted: see Mayer 2001: 18–22) Tacitus is indeed the author of the *Dialogus de Oratoribus*. Stylistic differences between this and Tacitus' other works are easily explained by the difference of genre; in the *Dialogus* he was writing the natural conversational Latin of his time (possibly with some Ciceronian colouring) rather than the grandiose historian's idiolect that became his trademark in the later works. The dialogue form was a logical choice for the presentation of contrasting viewpoints: that of Messalla who thought that oratory had declined since the Republic, versus that of Aper who thought it had improved. The third speaker, the poet Curiatius Maternus, arbitrates between them with a historical view: the decline of both political and forensic oratory is inevitable in an age of order and consensus under a wise and all-powerful ruler, and is really a sign of health in the community. The conclusion is thought-provoking, especially if, as some have argued, the speaker in the dialogue is the same as the Maternus who according to Dio Cassius was put to death by the supposedly wise and all-powerful Domitian in AD 91 (see Mayer 2001: 44 n. 102 for references).

The production of expository treatises of various kinds continued in the middle and late empire. At the more literary end of the scale, Apuleius wrote on Platonic philosophy (see S. J. Harrison 2000); Aulus Gellius collected scholarly miscellanea in the *Noctes Atticae* (*c.* AD 180), a compilation of perennial interest (see Holford-Strevens 1988); later, in a similar vein, Censorinus wrote (among other scholarly works) a treatise *De Die Natali* (*On Birthdays*, AD 238), a source of much information on the calendar and related matters. From the second century comes the legal treatise of Gaius (*c.* AD 161), fundamental for the modern study of Roman law; this was the beginning of the great age of the Roman jurists, which lasted from the reign of Hadrian until Justinian's codification of Roman law (AD 529). Frontinus, already mentioned as the author of *On Aqueducts*, wrote also on military matters, following the Greek tradition of collections of 'stratagems' (*Strategemata*); for a more systematic military manual we must wait until Vegetius in the late fourth century. Geographical literature was continued by C. Julius Solinus (early 3rd c. AD); the science of astrology received its fullest Latin prose treatment from Firmicus Maternus (AD 334–7). In the later empire, agricultural literature is represented by Palladius (date uncertain, perhaps as late as the 5th c. AD). Veterinary medicine now reappears as a separate topic, as does land-surveying (the *gromatici*), for which see Dilke (1971) and Campbell (2000). At this stage there is more sign than before of a divorce between the literary and the subliterary: the language of medical and veterinary texts in particular differ in many respects from standard classical Latin. This is not because their language derives from a lower social stratum, as the often-used term 'Vulgar Latin' mis-leadingly suggests, but merely because they reflect changes that had occurred in the contemporary spoken language, for the reconstruction of which they are a valuable source (see Adams 1995), while more self-consciously literary and rhet-orical works still observed the classical norms prescribed by the grammarians. Compendia of literary learning in the old style took various forms: Macrobius' *Saturnalia* (late 4th c., dramatic date AD 383) is a dialogue in the symposiastic tradition (see Flamant 1969), and in style rather reminiscent of Varro; Martianus Capella's encyclopedia of the liberal arts (*De Nuptiis Mercurii et Philologiae*, late 5th c.) owes its literary framework to the tradition of Menippean satire. Under Gothic rule in the West, the tradition of pagan philosophical learning was strikingly upheld by Boethius (*c.* AD 480–524), who in the intervals of a public career wrote treatises on logic, mathematics and music (highly influential in transmitting these ancient skills to the Middle Ages), together with commen-taries on Aristotle, Cicero and Porphyry; while he reserved the dialogue form for a literary meditation written in prison, the famous *De Consolatione Philoso-phiae* (see Chadwick 1981; Lerer 1985). Another significant figure for the transmission of pagan learning, this time philological, was Isidore, Bishop of Seville, whose *Etymologies* (*c.* AD 630) takes the form of a straightforward encyclo-paedic compilation.

A further and very important development of the classical expository treatise, often with an admixture of political or forensic rhetoric, is to be seen in Christian apologetic writing, of which the first notable practitioner was Tertullian (*c.* AD 160–240; see Sider 1972). The dialogue form reappears with renewed creativity as a vehicle for Christian controversy. Contemporary with Tertullian in the first half of the third century, the *Octavius* of Minucius Felix (see O'Connor 1976) sets out a debate between paganism and Christianity in a straightforward fashion, reflecting Cicero's arguments *in utramque partem* in which the supposedly stronger side is given the last word: there is a pleasant piece of scene-setting at the beginning, followed by a speech on behalf of the pagans, and a speech on behalf of Christianity which succeeds in converting the pagan interlocutor. Philosophically, the development of the argument is fairly superficial; the representative of Christianity does not effectively meet all the points made by the pagan, and some of the more difficult parts of Christian doctrine are kept discreetly in the background. The style is doubtless what Minucius thought was Ciceronian (i.e. the highly ornate rhetorical style of his own age), with occasional authentic Ciceronian rhythms and other stylistic touches. Further examples of dialogue used for apologetic purposes are found later in the works of St Jerome (*c.* AD 347–420) and in the early works of St Augustine (AD 354–430). In his *Soliloquia*, Augustine adapted the dialogue form as a conversation with himself, and his famous *Confessions*, which have something of the nature of a one-sided conversation with God, may be seen as giving a further creative twist to the familiar dialogue tradition. Other familiar forms of literary or philosophical exposition and exhortation – speeches, letters, and commentaries on texts – have their Christian counterparts in the sermon, the pastoral letter and the biblical commentary, all of which have survived vigorously as constituents of Christian literary culture through the Middle Ages to the present day. Thus the classical dialogue and treatise continued in use as vehicles for exposition, disputation and reflection in both Christian and secular traditions, while a number of classical and late-antique treatises (Cicero's *De Inventione* on rhetoric, Boethius on logic, arithmetic and music, Martianus Capella on everything) became the basis of education in the medieval curriculum of 'liberal arts'.

FURTHER READING

The genre of the technical handbook is surveyed by Fuhrmann (1960); Rawson (1978) deals with the important question of logical organization in Roman expository prose. In the last decade, considerable attention has been paid to Roman technical writing in its literary and social context: see Nicolet et al. (1995), Colace and Zumbo (2000), Meissner (1999) reviewed by Reeve (2003) with additional references, and now the collection of essays edited by Horster and Reitz (2003). Convenient and comprehensive overviews of the expository literature of each period may be found in the histories of Latin literature by von Albrecht (1997), Conte (1994b), and Herzog and Schmidt (1997 and 2002). On prefaces, in addition to Janson (1964), see the collection edited by Santini and Scivoletto (1990). On the language of technical writing, see Callebat (1982) for Vitruvius, Langslow (2000) on medical Latin, Horster and Reitz (2003) esp. the chapters by Krenkel and Fögen, Mayer (forthcoming). On the dialogue as a literary form, Hirzel (1895) remains a classic treatment; on some more formal aspects of dialogue composition and presentation in Latin see, with caution, Andrieu (1954), chapters 16–18; on dialogue in the Christian writers see Voss (1970). Selected further reading on particular subjects: on agricultural writing, including esp. Cato and Varro, see White (1973); science and natural history, Stahl (1962) and Beagon (1992); military matters, Campbell (1987); legal writing, Schulz (1953); philology and antiquarianism in the Republican period, Rawson (1985); grammar, Kaster (1988); rhetoric, Kennedy (1972) and Clarke (1996); philosophy, Morford (2002). Further information on individual authors is to be found in OCD^3, in the introductions to editions of their works (especially conveniently in the Loeb series), and in the relevant sections of the general histories of Latin literature already mentioned. For those wishing to pursue the subject at a more specialized level, a useful bibliographical survey to 1990 is provided by Mazzoli (1991).

CHAPTER SEVENTEEN

Historiography and Biography

Christina Shuttleworth Kraus

1 Some Formal Considerations

It is striking that the narrative history of Rome by Romans was for decades written in Greek. The earliest known native historian, who crystallized in written form the traditions and self-image of the Roman aristocracy, also established some of this history's most salient characteristics. Q. Fabius Pictor (see also Goldberg, Chapter 1 above) had a military career and participated in an official embassy to Delphi during the Second Punic War (218–202 BCE). Though literary Latin existed in Fabius' day, one can easily see why an experienced diplomat would choose to write Rome's history in the lingua franca of the Mediterranean; the language of the histories of Alexander the Great, whose conquests and pre-eminence were already being self-consciously challenged by the Romans; and the prestige language, above all, of the great works of Greek literature, not least of Herodotus, Thucydides and Xenophon, and of the Hellenistic historians of the west, especially Timaeus.

Fabius' was, as far as we can tell, a truly Graeco-Roman text (Dillery 2002). It was probably annalistic in structure – that is, organized chronologically by the annually elected consuls: a distinctly Roman dating system. Following Fabius' lead, history at Rome was written by men who had held public office, almost always by senators, for audiences of their own kind. Even when historians of less exalted status began writing, their texts were not markedly different from those of their precursors: Roman *historia* concentrated on the collective deeds, both political and military, of great Roman individuals who worked together – albeit in competition for public recognition and glory – for the good of the *res publica*. It was by definition *patri*otic, concerned with the *patria*, or fatherland. More-over, like its Greek precursors it was narrative history, using what we may call novelistic devices to create lifelike characters, bring distant places and past events in front of the mind's eye, and inspire emotions in its audience.

Authors might start, as Fabius did, *ab urbe condita* (from the founding of the city; i.e. from the beginning; cf. the works of Cassius Hemina and Cn. Calpurnius Piso Frugi); or they might write the history of a smaller segment, often a war (cf. Coelius Antipater on the second Punic war, Sallust on the Jugurthine war, or Asinius Pollio on the civil wars); or universal history, of the whole inhabited world (first essayed in Latin 1st c. BCE by Cornelius Nepos). Some, like M. Porcius Cato 'the Elder' (234–149 BCE), chose a hybrid form. His seven-book *Origines* was initially organized by topic, the founding of Italian cities (perhaps following a tradition of Hellenistic *ktisis*, 'founding', literature), but shifted midway to a chronological record of Rome extending up to Cato's own day, and naturally including the politician-turned-historian's own deeds (Astin 1978: ch. 10). This work, the first history written in Latin, is also the first to have been preserved in any quantity: though still fragmentary, enough of Cato's prose remains to give a tentative idea of the style and technique that Latin historical narrative would henceforth imitate.

2   History's Purpose, History's Rhetoric

From the beginning, Roman history focused on the life, character and deeds of exemplary men and women, both good and bad. Synchronic history (e.g. genealogical, religious or anthropological history) was written in a different stylistic register and a primarily non-narrative form now often referred to as antiquarianism; still, historical narratives could and did engage with economic, social and anthropological issues, though they tended to analyse them through the lens of personal interaction among human actors. History's purpose, again from the beginning, seems to have combined commemoration with education: re-citing the 'great deeds' (*res gestae*) of the past in order to build a collective memory that would in turn serve as predictor and guide to the future (Gowing, forthcoming). This blend of entertainment with didactic *utilitas* was designed to make 'men less willing to do harm, and more eager to serve the commonwealth' (Sempronius Asellio, 2nd c. BCE, F 2). So too Sallust (86–35 BCE), for whom writing history 'is as useful to the commonwealth as are the occupations of others', and who sees historical narrative as the written equivalent of the inspiring physical representations of dead Roman notables (*BJ* 4.3–6); Livy (59 BCE–17 CE), who describes his history as 'health-giving and fruitful' for his reader's commonwealth (*Preface* 10); and Tacitus (56–120 CE), for whom history is designed at least partly to provide practical lessons for those who cannot themselves distinguish good and bad (*A.* 4.33.2).

Ancient notions of historical accuracy were very different from modern expectations that history should be 'scientific' or 'objective'. Though programmatically claiming to write the 'truth', all historians presented that truth in artistically persuasive ways, availing themselves of the 'paint box' of rhetoric (Cic. *Att.* 2.1 [21].1–2). That paint box contained a professional rhetorician's full range of stylistic and argumentative devices, including those suited to the high or ornamental style, in keeping with the ancient descriptions of *historia* as both a 'job for the orator' (Cic. *De Orat.* 2.62) and as 'the closest thing to [epic] poetry' (Quint. 10.1.31).

Aristotle distinguished between history and poetry: 'poetry tends to express the universal, history the particular. By the universal, I mean how a person of a certain type on occasion speaks or acts, according to probability or necessity .... The particular is – for example – what Alcibiades did or suffered' (*Poet.* 1451b). But no historian has room for every detail. More importantly, since unique past experiences can be comprehended only by assimilation to the familiar and the stylized, any literary rendition of past events will inevitably move into the realm of the figurative, indeed, of the poetic. That is doubly true for ancient artistic prose, with its overriding sense of literary history and rhetorical conventions. In Rome, the links between history and epic were particularly close, given that Roman history was the subject of some of the earliest Latin epic poems. And while oratory and epic are far apart in many ways, they share a primary aim of telling a persuasively realistic, emotionally compelling story: one can compare Odysseus' weeping at the song of the fall of Troy (Homer, *Od.* 8.499–531) with Quintilian's advice to the young orator on how to describe things vividly, using precisely the theme of the capture of a city (Quint. 8.3.67–71).

This literary climate, in which poetry, oratory, and history shared important fundamental qualities, had significant consequences for ancient historiography. Since audiences, like authors, were used to the elaborate, traditional system within which ancient rhetoric operated, historical narrative tended to describe not 'real life' but a world made recognizable by other literature, including oratory (Oakley 1997: 10). Within that literary and rhetorical framework, departures from or manipulation of convention could both establish originality and engage the reader more actively in the process of communication (Rigney 1992: 220). Moreover, the close relationship felt to subsist between history and epic meant that the vocabulary and the poetics of *historia* were nearer those of elevated verse than those of more 'practical' prose such as philosophy or the scholarly treatise. Even Caesar, who consciously downplays the high artistic qualities of his prose, repeatedly uses the epic paradigm of the besieged city (e.g. *BG* 7.47–51), and relies on the '*topos*-code' of the decadent Asiatic east to 'build a network of correspondences' with past texts and events (Rossi 2000). At the same time, his deliberate use of the same single word for a given thing (e.g. always using *flumen* for 'river') renders Caesar's superficially precise text useless for pragmatic recon-struction of topography, battlefields, even events as a whole.

3 History's Language

The style of Roman historiography ranges from Caesar's super-efficient plain style to Florus' ornate, emotive prose. Yet within that diversity there is a universal tendency to aim for *variatio*. On a basic level, this is achieved by alternating narrative with digressions, or by interspersing it with historiographical variants or discussions of method. Both formal digressions and narrative may borrow from the language and style of other, related literature, such as ethnography, paradox-ography or the antiquarian treatise. So Sallust's *Bellum Jugurthinum* includes a full-scale ethnography of North Africa (cf. also Livy 5.33–5 on the Gauls, Tacitus *H.* 5.2–10 on the Jews); Livy has antiquarian passages on Roman drama (7.2) and Samnite armour (9.40), while Velleius Paterculus analyses literary hotspots (1.16–18; 2.9; 2.36) and catalogues colonies (1.14–15); Caesar and Curtius Rufus have expansive technical descriptions (*BG* 4.17; Curt. 4.2–3); Tacitus includes a short, analytical history of Roman law (*A.* 3.25–8), an interlude on the marvellous phoenix (*A.* 6.28; cf. Cato F 39 and 52 on amazing beasts), and creatively reworks paradoxographical travellers' tales to describe Neronian Rome (*A.* 15.36–7: see Woodman 1998: 168–89).

Non-digressive sections as well vary in tone and style. The criteria for choice of style at any given point are effectiveness and appropriateness: consideration of what kind of language will best achieve the persuasive and artistic aims of the author, with careful attention to the linguistic *decorum* (degree of poetic diction, elaboration of syntax, use of tropes etc.) dictated by the passage's content and pur-pose. Historiographical narrative includes scenes constructed from tragic and comic conventions (e.g. the story of Lucretia at Livy 1.57–9; see Wiseman 1998; passages imitative of military communiqués [Fraenkel 1956] or of ancient epic [e.g. Livy 1.29, the fall of Alba Longa] or of epigraphic language; and especially of speeches, deliberative, judicial and epideictic, presented in reported, free indirect and direct speech.

This alternation of descriptive narration and speeches is perhaps the most characteristic feature of ancient historical narrative, one probably borrowed from epic. Beyond using them for simple characterization and argumentation, in their speeches historians from the time of Herodotus on articulate the terms in which they perceive a given debate to have been conducted, often using speeches as extra-narrative analyses of historical trends, ideologies and causality. Inserted orations can even, through intertextual reference, afford an opportunity for comparative historical analysis: so, when Tacitus' senators debate the propriety of sending governors' wives to the provinces with their husbands (*A.* 3.33–4), their language and arguments evoke a famous mid-republican debate on luxury (Livy 34.1–8), offering Tacitus' readers a chance to compare his text with Livy's as well as using the earlier historical situation as a lens through which to refract the later (Ginsburg 1993).

Finally, from its Herodotean beginnings ancient history used speeches to enhance the sense of vivid presence. For to fulfil their pragmatic, didactic and ethical aims, historians had to hook, and keep, their audience. The attraction of literary artistry cannot be underestimated: scenes such as the battle of the Horatii and the Curiatii at Livy 1.24–5, or the Pisonian conspiracy at Tacitus

A. 15.48–74, grip us by their deployment of spectacular effects, suspense, and appeal to extra-literary experiences such as theatre-going or gladiatorial combat. But persuasion works best when the emotions are deeply engaged, and ancient rhetoric makes a special study of how to trigger, and use, a jury's emotions. So the technique of vivid description centred on the inspiration of emotion: 'Thucydides is always striving for this vividness in his writing, desiring eagerly to make the listener a spectator, as it were, and to produce in those reading the events the astounding and disturbing emotions experienced by those who saw them' (Plut. *De glor. Athen.* = *Moralia* 347A). What Plutarch says of Thucydides is true right through the tradition of ancient historiography, particularly so in Rome, where as we have seen, there was a perceived relationship between history and oratory, especially political oratory. Speeches and other verbal utterances (shouts, *bons mots* etc.), which by their evocation of living human voices create an immediate sense of presence, are an essential part of the process of making a reader or audience *see* an event. The stylistic and rhetorical qualities of historiographical prose, then, are not incidental, but fundamental: like the honey on the cup of medicine in Lucretius' famous simile (1.933–50) the pleasure afforded by *historia*'s poetics blends with its didactic content, resulting in the pedagogical seduction of the reader.

4 Reading History

Most Roman historiography from Fabius Pictor to Caesar is preserved in relatively short fragments. The few longer fragments that survive, quoted apparently verbatim from the narratives of Cato the Elder, Calpurnius Piso (2nd c. BCE), Claudius Quadrigarius (1st c. BCE), and a contemporary, but anonymous, writer (Claudius F 12), have been exhaustively analysed, especially in comparison with their later adaptations by Livy. The style of these writers was described tendentiously by Cicero as lean, uncouth, childish and full of lassitude (*De Leg.* 1.6–7) – tendentiously, because he was himself putting forth a 'superior' style for *historia*, one more in keeping with his own theories. Modern scholars tend to take up Cicero's criticisms, but to grant these early historians a 'vigour' and 'vitality' of style that compensates for their repetitiveness and paratactic (i.e. unsubordinated) syntax. Rather than rehearsing the arguments here, I shall focus on another aspect of these early histories: that is, their apparent concentration on human actors and their habits, or *mores*.

All the surviving verbatim narrative extracts are vignettes: a tribune leading a diversionary action while the main army escapes a trap (Cato F 83); a plebeian *scriba* asserting his authority to patrician mockers (Piso F 27); Roman soldiers fighting Gauls in single combat (Claudius F 10b and F 12). The end of Cato's tribune is quoted directly:

The immortal gods granted the military tribune a fate in keeping with his courage. It happened thus. Though he had been wounded in the battle in many places, yet there was no wound to his head and they identified him among the dead, unconscious because of his wound and from loss of blood. They carried him off and he recovered; often thereafter he performed brave and active service for the state and because he led that march to distract the Carthaginians saved the rest of the army. But it makes a great deal of difference where you perform one and the same service. Leonides the Spartan [who] did something similar at Thermopylae and on account of his virtues all Greece conferred on him exceptional thanks and honors, and decorated him with tributes to his most outstanding renown: with pictures, statues, inscriptions, histories, and in other ways they treated his deed as most welcome, but the tribune of the soldiers was left little praise for his deeds, though he did the same thing and saved the day. (Aulus Gellius 3.7, trans. Horsfall 1989)

Like the other narrative fragments, this one highlights an individual's actions in a politico-military (rather than a domestic) context; shows a striking concern for visual detail and for drawing an audience in through the use of direct speech or spectacular language; and is simultaneously interested in commemoration and in exemplarity – that is, in preserving and celebrating Roman actions, while providing models for future behaviour, both within the text and without. Despite his closing complaint about the lack of commemoration available in Roman history, Cato's text is clearly meant to provide just that. Such self-consciousness, too, about the nature and purpose of history is frequent throughout the Roman historians.

By Ciceronian standards, Cato's prose is underdeveloped; yet its (self-conscious) simplicity and ruggedness provided a model for subsequent historians, much as Cato's contemporary Ennius forged an archaizing style for Latin epic. Cato was closely imitated by Sallust, both in style – Sallust employed a research assistant to find unusual Catonian words – and in mindset (Levene 2000). Even before Sallust, the functional prose style of Caesar's narratives has a distinctly Catonian feel, as does their concentration on the virtuous, often unnamed soldiers of Caesar's army (cf. Cato F 88). By choosing to call his works 'Commentaries' (Kelsey 1905) – a word with many uses, but invariably associated with outlines, summaries, technical treatises or lists – Caesar proclaims his text's affiliation with the plain style and the military communiqué. Yet (and again like Cato) he is throughout experimental, raising the stylistic level – and consequently the literary capital – of the *commentarius*, which thereby becomes one form of proper *historia*. (It is especially interesting that Caesar's challenging stance evoked pointed criticism from a rival contemporary historian, Pollio: Suet. *DJ* 56.4.)

All novelty requires familiar ground from which to stand out, and Caesar frequently advertises his affiliation with the mainstream of Roman historiography, as in his account of two rivalrous centurions:

in this legion there were two men (*viri*) of great courage . . . Titus Pullo and Lucius Vorenus. There were constant disputes (*controversias*) between them as to which had precedence . . . . While the fighting at the defences was at its fiercest, Pullo said, 'Why are you hesitating, Vorenus? What chance are you waiting for of proving your valor (*virtutis*)? Today will decide the dispute (*controversiis*) between us.' With these words he made his way outside the defences and launched an attack where the enemy ranks were densest. Nor indeed did Vorenus remain within the defences, but followed on, fearing (*veritus*) what men would think of him . . . . Pullo's shield was pierced and a dart (*verutum*) stuck in his swordbelt; this knocked (*avertit*) his sheath aside and hindered his attempt to draw his sword. While he was in difficulties the enemy surrounded him. To the rescue came his rival Vorenus . . . . Straightaway the Gauls turned their attention (*convertit*) to him . . . now he was surrounded, and Pullo came to his aid. They both . . . returned safely within the defences, to great acclaim. Thus fortune played with them (*versavit*) . . . so that . . . it was impossible to decide which should be preferred in valor (*virtute*). (*BG* 5.44, trans. Hammond 1996, modified)

The scene has clear affinities with Cato's tribune and with scenes of single combat, including the spectacular focus on visual details – heightened here by the direct speech, rare in the *Bellum Gallicum* – and the evaluation of the courage and talent of the soldiers, whose loyalty to each other as citizens ultimately surpasses thoughts of personal safety or even of glory. Caesar has added the slightly gladiatorial frisson of the contest between evenly matched individuals, and the nationalistic thrill of seeing the familiar competition for excellence between Romans redirected against a barbarian enemy. In his emphasis on *virtus* (the word itself is used twice, at beginning and end of the chapter, the whole of which resounds – as indicated above – with the subliminal verbal patterning of *vir*, *ver* and *vor*) Caesar shows a typically Roman preoccupation with that defining quality of excellence, a preoccupation that will continue to manifest itself in Sallust, Livy, Velleius and Tacitus.

Caesar's rivalrous centurions show *mores* in action, a dramatic procedure in which words and deeds reveal character, as in a theatrical performance. But *historia* also described character, and was particularly interested in the *mores* of foreigners, especially foreign enemies, as in Livy's description of the Carthaginian Hannibal:

never was the same nature more adaptable to the most contradictory things, obedience and command. And so you could not easily have told whether he was dearer to the general or to the army . . . . He had excessive recklessness in incurring dangers, but excessive good judgment when in the midst of them. Neither could his body be exhausted nor his mind conquered by any toil. He could endure hot and cold equally; his level of eating and drinking was regulated by natural desire, not pleasure; his times of waking and sleeping were not determined by daylight or night: what was left after his work was done, he allotted to sleep, which he took neither on a soft bed nor at a quiet time: many often spied him wrapped in a soldier's cloak lying on the ground among the sentinels and guards. His dress was no better than his fellows, but his weapons and his horses were conspicuous. He was by far the first among horsemen and infantry; he went into battle first, and returned last once the fighting was engaged. These admirable virtues of the man were equalled by enormous vices: inhuman cruelty, perfidy worse than Punic, no regard for truth, none for sanctity, no fear of the gods, no reverence for an oath, no religious scruple. (Livy 21.4.3–9, trans. Foster et al. 1919–59, modified)

The structure of the passage leaves no doubt about its emphasis: the heady mix of exceptional qualities displayed by the prodigious Hannibal comes down, in the end, to a list of anti-Roman traits hammered home by the anaphoric *nihil… nihil… nullus… nullum… nulla*, a virtual declension of Hannibal's faults. The preceding detailed portrait, which effectively describes an ideal (Roman) general, is nullified – and yet not so, as it both establishes Hannibal as a formidable enemy and lives on (extra-narratively) in Latin historiography after Livy. Modelled on Sallust's descriptions of Catiline (*BC* 5) and Jugurtha (*BJ* 6, 8), this passage would be echoed in turn by Tacitus on Sejanus (*Ann.* 4.1, see §5, 'The Shift to Biography: Praise, Blame and Historical Narrative', below). The voice of the outsider, of the doomed barbarian, resonates through Roman history, from Caesar (*BG* 1.44) to Sallust (*H.* 4.69) to Livy (9.1) to Tacitus (*A.* 14.31). It is perhaps most moving in Tacitus' *Agricola*, where the Celtic leader Calgacus delivers a devastating criticism of Roman foreign policy (*Ag.* 30–2). History uses the enemy not only to show off Roman excellence, but also to mirror, refract and analyse Roman faults: hence the frequent intersection between foreign and domestic enemies such as Catiline and Sejanus, where perverted *virtus* is the most dangerous type of vice.

Roman history monumentalizes, creating larger-than-life, often stylized figures whose *mores* become a point of reference for the Roman character itself. Yet it also particularizes, focusing our attention on small details. These are sometimes of appearance – the flash of a crimson cloak (Caes. *BG* 7.88); a sky 'stiff' with gloom (Sisenna [1st c. BCE] F 130); the shame of a socially inexperienced young woman (Livy 6.34) – or sometimes of procedure, either religious (e.g. lists of prodigies, aetiologies or ritual formulae) or curial: for example a senatorial debate on the legitimacy of a claim to triumph (Livy 36.39–40), an embassy of eastern cities vying for precedence based on their mythological lineage (Tac. *A.* 4.55–6). This specificity forms part of the rhetorical procedure of *enargeia*, vivid depiction. Yet it can also provide the historian with a means of establishing his superior knowledge and thus his authority (Marincola 1997: 261–2). In such cases, where the specificity often takes the form of little-known variants on a name or event, methodological points arise. These, in good didactic fashion, offer an opportunity of further instructing and involving the reader in the process of collection, selection, presentation and evaluation of historical material, as in this Livian passage on the taking of the Etruscan city Veii:

at this point a tale is inserted: when the Veian king was sacrificing, Roman soldiers in the mine heard the voice of the haruspex declaring that victory would be given to the man who severed the victim's entrails, and this moved them to open the mine, seize the entrails, and carry them to the dictator. But in such ancient matters I would be content if things like the truth are accepted as true: it is not worth while either to affirm or to refute these matters, which are fit more for display on the stage which delights in miracles. (Livy 5.21.8–9; trans. Foster et al. 1919–59, modified)

This authorial intervention forms a ring with Livy's clear prefatory statement that he will 'neither affirm nor refute' things that happened 'before the city was founded or its foundation planned' (*Preface* 6). That *Preface*, in which Livy repeatedly challenges his readers to evaluate and use the historical text in front of them, also sets up certain boundaries between the legendary and the historical, the plausible and the true (Moles 1993). At 5.21 the debate is reprised, in ways characteristically Livian: (1) the reader is expected to notice the strong verbal allusion to the earlier passage, which constructs important links both thematically and structurally (Book 5 concludes the first large published unit of the *History*); (2) that engagement of the reader produces a contradiction – the fall of Veii, in 396 BCE, is well outside the time scale proposed in *Preface* 6 for the limits of the legendary – which in turn requires readers to re-evaluate what they think they know about history and about the nature of historical evidence; (3) a tension is created by the surrounding narrative, which is highly 'dramatic', and the authorial aside, in which 'things more fitting to the stage which delights in miracles' are dismissed from serious history: that tension is not fully resolved, but instead invites a creative reassessment of how we learn from, and how we use, historical narrative.

5 The Shift to Biography: Praise, Blame and Historical Narrative

Livy's carefully balanced, intellectually open voice was not much imitated by subsequent historians. Tacitus divides imperial history into flattery and malice (*A.* 1.1.2; *H.* 1.1.1): though the categories are not as clear-cut as he polemically maintains (Marincola 1999b), from Tiberius onward we can separate the surviving Latin historical narratives into those that praise and those that blame the institution of the Principate, and life under it. The division of *historia* into blame (*uituperatio*) and praise (*laudatio*) – or, if we like, into history that essentially approves of its topic and that which is essentially critical – is as old as historiography itself, and there is no reason to think that pre-Livian history was fundamentally different (Woodman 1988: 40–4, 74, 95). Aside from the improved quality of our surviving evidence, however, what changes with the Principate is that, as the person of the emperor arrogates to himself the gaze of reader and writer alike, as history essentially shifts from the *res gestae populi Romani* to the *res gestae diui Augusti* (etc.), historiography begins to shade into (usually imperial) biography. Of course, imperial *historia* continues its republican precursor's emphasis on character and action. The difference is partly one of quantity rather than quality: as the many political and military leaders of the republic are reduced to the single person of the emperor and those around him, especially the 'royal' family, so the new concentration on an individual subject intensifies *historia*'s concentration on the multiple great leaders of the Roman past.

This account is oversimplified, yet its overall validity is suggested by Jerome's labelling of what we know as Tacitus' *Historiae* and *Annales* as 'The *Lives* of the Caesars in 30 Books' (*in Zach.* B iii.14) and its very overschematization is helpful for understanding generic developments in broad terms. On the side of history-as-praise fall, for example Velleius Paterculus (?20 BCE–after 30 CE, author of a summary history covering events from before the Trojan War to his own time), Pliny the Elder (23–79 CE; on his lost *Bella Germaniae* see his *Naturalis Historia, Preface* 20), the Claudian Curtius Rufus (his *Historia de Rebus Alexandri Magni* is often taken to reflect the Principate; as such it is praise but not unmixed), and Florus (2nd c. CE, author of an outline history of Rome). On the critical side the sole surviving example is Tacitus – but even he writes encomium of his own day (e.g. *Ag.* 3; *H.* 1.1.4) while excoriating dead emperors, a relatively uncontroversial procedure, and indeed one that is recommended in handbooks on how to praise an emperor. Tacitus, then, despite his notoriously grumpy authorial *persona*, can be seen as accentuating the positive at least for the time of writing.

The different spins that can be put on an event or a description emerge clearly from comparing two brief narratives of the rise of Sejanus, Tiberius' notorious partner in power. The first is by Velleius, a contemporary who knew Tiberius personally:

> rarely have eminent men not employed great men as helpers in directing their fortune, as the two Scipiones employed the two Laelii, whom they treated as equals in all things, as the deified Augustus used Marcus Agrippa and after him Statilius Taurus .... For great tasks require great helpers .... Following these examples, Tiberius Caesar had and has still as his remarkable associate in all the burdens of the Principate Aelius Sejanus, son of a leading equestrian, but connected on his mother's side to old and illustrious families distinguished by public honors, with a brother, cousins, and an uncle who had been consuls; he himself has a great capacity for labor and loyalty, with vigor of mind that matches his well-knit body – a man of traditional gravity and merry gaiety, in action like men of leisure, claiming no honors for himself and so acquiring all honors, whose self-estimation is always below the estimate of others, calm in expression and lifestyle, sleeplessly alert. (Velleius 2.127, trans. Shipley 1924, modified)

Nearly a century later, Tacitus described the same situation:

When Gaius Asinius and Gaius Antistius were consuls Tiberius enjoyed his ninth year of public order and domestic felicity…when suddenly fortune threw things into confusion, and he began to be savage himself and to empower the savage. The starting point and the cause were in Aelius Sejanus ….Born at Vulsinii to the Roman equestrian Seius Strabo, he became in early youth a follower of Gaius Caesar, grandson of the deified Augustus, not without a rumor that he had prostituted himself to the wealthy and prodigal Apicius. Then, by various arts, he bound Tiberius so tightly that a man inscrutable to others was to Sejanus alone incautious and uncovered ….His body was tolerant of labour, his spirit daring; he concealed himself and incriminated others; he was at once flattering and insolent; orderly and modest to outward view, but within a towering lust for acquisition, and on this account at times lavish and prone to luxuriousness, more often to industry and vigilance – qualities no less harmful when assumed for winning a kingdom. (*Annals* 4.1, trans. Jackson 1937, modified)

Several crucial differences – none to do with the hard core of facts reported – leap out. First, both historians give roughly the same information about Sejanus, and use roughly the same terms of description: each highlights his family, his energy and his mental and physical virtues. Velleius elaborates on the status of Sejanus' relatives, information which Tacitus omits, giving instead a rumour (an ideal source, being untraceable) about his youthful self-prostitution; in describing Sejanus' characteristics, Velleius shows Tiberius and his *adiutor* as partners, while Tacitus emphasizes the capture of the one by the other. Velleius prefaces the passage with comparative information about famous past leaders whose example Tiberius the example-setter himself follows; the whole comes after a description of Tiberius' own good management of the state, including praise for his ability to be a model for his people (2.126). Tiberius was famous for his traditionalism, grounding his acts in Augustan and republican precedent; Velleius, who probably did not approve of Sejanus (Woodman 1977: 248 calls chapter 127 'an awkwardly inserted digression'), nevertheless introduces him in an exemplary context which anchors his position firmly. Tacitus, on the other hand, uses Sejanus as the *archē kakōn*, the 'start of evils', under whose influence the government of the passive, unreadable Tiberius deteriorates rapidly; a survey of the state of the common-wealth follows that introduction (*Annals* 4.5–6), punctuated with the informa-tion that 'this year saw the beginning in Tiberius' Principate of a change for the worse' (4.6.1). For *his* chief exemplary text Tacitus takes the character sketch of Catiline from Sallust's *Catiline's War*, altering Velleius' comparatively positive portrait of Sejanus into a picture of a monster. The use of intertextuality fits with Tacitus' pervasive tendency to make even more demands on his audience than most Roman historians: his language, like his subject, is often opaque and unex-pected, and his narrative poetics reward readers with experience both of Roman literature (Sallust, Virgil, Livy, Velleius and Lucan are just a few of the texts to which Tacitus alludes) and of the workings of Roman politics.

Secondly, the style of the two historians strongly reinforces their message. Velleius (like Tacitus' florid contemporary Florus) is expansive, employing emotive rhetorical questions and exclamations that invite readers to share his interpretation as well as his excitement. Tacitus also uses emotive language, rhetorical point and violent metaphor to make his version convincing; like Velleius and Florus, he makes his own presence felt through use of the first person. Nevertheless, the overall impression of his *persona* is less that of an excited observer unable to restrain his emotion, whether of praise or blame, than that of one whose emotions are subordinate to his judgement. (Both impressions, be it noted, are deliberate, and both help construct the kind of audience they imply.) His measuredly critical tones go a considerable way to producing that effect, as malice – particularly controlled malice – tends to inspire belief (Tac. *H.* 1.1.2). In neither of these extracts, finally, is anything like objectivity – if by that we mean the invisible third-person narrator, presenting 'facts' without 'description' – visible. Indeed, both authors have been felt, in their various ways, to be 'mendacious' (Syme 1978) or 'distorting' (Walker 1960): and yet both create an artistic, rhetorically informed narrative that fully conforms to the canons of literary historiography, and that projects a picture, if not of the literal truth, then of an interpreted model of the past which they – and their Roman audience – found most credible and most useful to remember.

6 Biography

> For it is not *Histories* we are writing, but *Lives*. Nor is it always the most illustrious actions which reveal virtue or vice: a small matter, a remark or a jest, often gives better insight into a man's character than do battles where thousands die, or the greatest pitched battles, or sieges of cities. (Plut. *Alex.* 1.2, trans. Perrin 1914–26, modified)

As Plutarch implies, biography is like history – so like it, in fact, that a biographer might feel it necessary to preface a work with an explanation of why some salient characteristics of *historia* will *not* be found therein. The shift (outlined above) to a historiography focused on single actors helped to feed the popularity of a relatively new subgenre of Roman history, biography (*vita*, or *bios*, in Greek). First fully recognizable as a literary form in the last decades BCE, Latin biography was produced by men who, like historians, were acutely and creatively conscious of their Greek precursors and co-practitioners, and who wrote in a carefully crafted, literary and rhetorical style. Unlike history, however, which was almost exclusively political or military, biography took as its subject a range of men and (occasionally) women, ranging from philosophers to poets to grammarians to political and military leaders.

The latter category – the one that comes closest to history – is also the one best represented by the surviving evidence. Like history, it has its founding father, one Cornelius Nepos (110–24 BCE), the dedicatee of Catullus' *libellus* (Catullus 1). Whatever the polymath Nepos may or may not have started with his *De Viris Illustribus*, however, he was not in fact alone in the field of biography. His contemporary M. Terentius Varro's illustrated *Imagines* (which do not survive) were biographical in nature, while both men were preceded by a series of auto-biographical works – all now fragmentary – by political figures. These memoirs, which included works in Greek by the dictator Sulla and by Cicero, formed part of the mechanism of competition and display engaged in by the Roman political elite, which incorporated honorific inscriptions and buildings, family histories, funeral *laudationes* (an influential form in Roman literary culture), and literary texts. That intimate link between *bios* and the habit of self-aggrandizement among Roman aristocrats engendered a close connection between biography and encomium.

The two genres were closely related in Greek as well, but the connection becomes especially relevant as the focus of biography – like that of history – narrowed to the person of the emperor and the imperial court. To take a single example, in his *De Vita Caesarum* Suetonius (70 CE–after 130) reports no super-natural signs (prodigies, omens etc.) except those relating to the rise or fall of an emperor (Wallace-Hadrill 1983: 191): far different from the pervasive reporting of such signs by Livy, for whom they are relevant to the proper functioning of the *res publica* as a whole. It became gradually impossible to write biography of a living emperor, as such a text would inevitably become panegyric (Nicolaos of Damascus, Augustus' Greek biographer, whose work survives in a few fragments only, provides a rare example of a *Life* of a living ruler). Indeed, though Augustus wrote an autobiography and left an epigraphic record of his reign in his *Res Gestae*, all the surviving biographies of emperors, in Latin (by Suetonius and the 4th-c. composer of the *Historia Augusta*), or in Greek (primarily by Plutarch, a contem-porary of Tacitus), were published after their subject's death.

A pull away from encomium was, perhaps paradoxically, generated by the very concentration on character and personality that makes biography look hard at emperors. Given its wider subject matter, biography enjoyed a correspondingly wider scope than historiography for including anecdotal and documentary material, and 'a predilection for odd and scandalous detail' (Syme 1958b: 501). Suetonius on Caligula is particularly infamous, here on the tyrant's lust for abnormal sex and cruelty:

> he habitually indulged in incest with all his sisters... Of his sisters it was Drusilla whose virginity he is believed to have violated while still a boy. Indeed, it is believed that their grandmother Antonia... once actually caught them in bed together .... The manager of the games and beast fights he had beaten with chains for days on end while he himself looked on, and only had him killed when the smell of the

man's rotting brains made him ill .... When a Roman knight who had been thrown
to the wild beasts shouted out that he was innocent, he had him taken out, his
tongue cut out, and then thrown back into the arena. (*Cal.* 24, 27, trans. Edwards
2000)

This specificity is unlike the circumstantiality of much historical narrative (see
above), as it admits of details no 'high' genre such as history or epic would allow,
and hence violates the rhetorical decorum of *historia*. Also unlike history, biography was not primarily narrative; instead, in its fully developed form it deployed a
combination of synchronic and diachronic exposition; so, for example, the extracts above come from the section *ut de monstro*, 'as it were about the monster'
(Suet. *Cal.* 22.1).

History, biography and autobiography are, then, *genera proxima* – closely
related genres. They were not clearly distinguished in antiquity and are hard to
distinguish even now, though critics offer some useful criteria, such as density of
first/third person verbs, the structure and sequence of literary organization
(biography tends more toward organization by topic, or rubric, than does history), length, setting and the quality/density of characterization. Even a usefully
simple definition like that of Momigliano, that biography is an 'account of the
life of a man from birth to death' (Momigliano 1971:11) is blurred by
works such as Tacitus' *Agricola*. This begins by advertising its similarities to the
Stoic martyrologies of the early empire (*Ag.* 2.1), includes a formal account
of the birth and youth of its subject and ends with his death and eulogy (43–6);
yet it also comprises a substantial historiographical section on Agricola's campaigns in Britain – including paired speeches before battle, a characteristically
historical scene (30–4) – and an ethnography of Britain (10–12), followed by a
brief history of the island under Roman rule (13–16). Title, framework and
authorial pronouncements point us toward biography; but the monograph's
content and many of its narrative conventions pull us toward *historia* (Marincola
1999a).

Generic fluidity allowed Roman biography to emphasize particularly Roman
themes, especially the place of a political or military leader in the commonwealth;
so Suetonius' imperial biographies highlight the emperors' family and their place
within the succession of monarchs, their public works and the manner of their
deaths – all preoccupations both of *historia* and of Roman commemorative
inscriptions. Suetonius' long lives show a development from Nepos' far briefer
De Viris Illustribus, though the latter did produce at least three longer lives, of
Cato the Elder, Cicero (both lost) and T. Pomponius Atticus. But Nepos,
pioneering in content as well as in form, introduced most of the elements that
would become standard in Suetonian biography: the interest in both public and
private details; the mix of chronological and topical organization; the stress on
character; the deployment of themes drawn from *encomium* (and its opposite,
invective: on all this see Horsfall 1989: 7–14). Nepos pioneered as well in writing

lives of foreign figures; in this he was not followed by Suetonius, who however produced an encyclopedic range of antiquarian treatises, including works on Greek games, Roman customs and lexicography. Finally, Nepos – along with Varro and more shadowy contemporaries – followed Greek precursors in developing literary biography (his extant *Vita Attici* comes from the lives of the historians), again providing a model for the later Suetonius in his *De Grammaticis et Rhetoribus* and *De Poetis.*

FURTHER READING

This note does not, as a general rule, include works cited in the chapter above. There is much recent interest in the early Roman historians; for consistency I have cited their texts from Peter (1914), though new collected editions are appearing (Beck and Walter 2001 and Chassignet 1996). On the three types of ancient history see Wiseman (1987: 246–8), with Clarke (1999) on the particular case of universal history; on the question of *historia* forming a genre Marincola (1997) has important things to say, while detailing the characteristic authorial gestures that inform historical narrative. Wiseman (1979) and Woodman (1988) lay the groundwork for the contemporary discussion of the relationship between ancient history and rhetoric, while Roberts (2001) is a valuable source for the modern debate on history and narrative. For history and poetry, see Foucher (2000) and the broad-ranging collection of articles in Levene and Nelis (2002); for the place and effect of speech in historical narrative see the discussion of Laird (1999: ch. 10). Finally, for analyses of the lost historiographers see the Introduction to Oakley (1997) and Wilkes (1972); for commentary on the early narrative fragments see Courtney (1999: 74–8, 141–52); and for the change from republican to imperial historiography see Woodman (1977: 28–56), Gabba (1984) and Kraus (forthcoming).

On spectacle and its place both in creating *enargeia* and in the didacticism proper to history see Walker (1993, on Greek), Solodow (1979), Keitel (1992), Feldherr (1998) and Woodman (1998: chs 10 and 11). Bartsch (1994) is an important treatment of the relationship among author, reader and text, while Miles (1995: ch. 1), Kraus (2000) and Pelling (2000) discuss, from different viewpoints, the methodology and issues involved in 'reconstructing' ancient audiences' reactions.

Material on antiquarians and antiquarian research is treated *passim* by Rawson (1985); for an overview of the issues with special emphasis on Arnaldo Momigliano, one of the greatest modern scholars of the subject, see Crawford and Ligota (1995). Burridge (1992) is particularly useful on biography as a genre; other good treatments include Pelling (1997) – primarily on Dio Cassius but with much of general relevance – and (2002); on Nepos see Geiger (1975), though his thesis has been modified, most recently by Tuplin (2000). For Suetonius and literary biography see especially Kaster (1995).

Barbarians and their place in Roman historiographical thought are discussed by Dauge (1981), O'Gorman (1993) – primarily on Tacitus' *Germania* – and Williams (2001). Finally, on Alexander the Great and his uses for historians, see Spencer (2002) and Morello (2002).

CHAPTER EIGHTEEN

Oratory

D. H. Berry

1 Introduction

This chapter will offer a brief survey of the history of Roman oratory (speeches, delivered and/or published by orators), and will also take some account of the parallel history of rhetoric (the theoretical rules underlying oratory, expounded by rhetoricians in treatises). Scholars take care not to confuse the terms 'oratory' and 'rhetoric', since the term 'rhetoric' is commonly and inappropriately used by non-specialists as a derogatory substitute for 'oratory' (as in 'No one was taken in by the politician's rhetoric').

At Rome, as in Greece, oratory came before rhetoric. Homer included specimens of oratory in his epics, several centuries before the principles of oratory were first theorized by rhetoricians. Likewise, the Romans had a republic in which speeches influenced decision-making long before rhetorical theory arrived at Rome in the second century BC. The speeches in Homer, incidentally, remind us that, although the term 'oratory' generally denotes speeches that stand on their own, speeches, and hence oratory, could also be incorporated in other genres such as epic (Virgil's *Aeneid* or Lucan's *De Bello Civili*) or historiography (the works of Sallust, Livy or Tacitus).

The earliest Latin speech we know of was delivered in 280 BC when App. Claudius Caecus persuaded the senate not to make peace with King Pyrrhus of Epirus. The speech is entirely lost, however, as are the six other speeches (three political and three funeral speeches) that we know of from the third century. When we come to the second century, we do at least have some fragments of speeches. This is the period when Rome, as a consequence of her defeat of Macedon and resulting involvement in the affairs of the liberated Greek states, was starting to fall heavily under the influence of Greek culture. Greek embassies visited Rome and 'after hearing the Greek orators . . . our people burned with an incredible desire to speak' (Cic. *De or.* 1.14). To meet this demand, Greek rhetoricians began to provide instruction. Romans of a conservative nature viewed them with suspicion (there was an attempt by the Senate to expel them in 161 BC); but on the other hand their discipline was one of considerable practical usefulness in an age that saw increasing inequality of wealth, and increasing competition, within the governing class. The best-known orator of the first half of the century was the elder M. Porcius Cato (234–149 BC), the Censor (see also Goldberg, Chapter 1 above). It is unclear to what extent his speeches (he published more than 150) were indebted to the new Greek theory. His guiding principle *rem tene, verba sequentur* (hold to the subject, the words will follow, *ap.* Jul. Vict. 374 Halm) seems to imply a rejection of rhetorical teaching; but on the other hand he is said to have written on rhetoric (Quint. *Inst.* 3.1.19). The evidence of the fragments themselves is inconclusive. Anaphora, *praeteritio* and rhetorical questions are found (Aulus Gellius speaks of Cato's employment of 'all the arms and assistance of rhetorical teaching', 6.3.52); but use of such devices need not necessarily imply Greek influence. It would not be surprising, however, if he did make use of the new teaching while publicly maintaining a conservative stance. In any case, he is the best example of Roman ambivalence to the arrival of Greek culture, and of the transition to a fully Hellenized Roman oratory.

The most celebrated orator of the second half of the century was C. Sempronius Gracchus (154–121 BC). He and his elder brother Tiberius both had Greek teachers: Gaius, Menelaus of Marathus (Cic. *Brut.* 100) and Tiberius, Diophanes of Mytilene (*Brut.* 104). Gaius' Greek training is evident in his most famous fragment:

> quo me miser conferam? quo vortam? in Capitoliumne? at fratris sanguine redundat. an domum? matremne ut miseram lamentantem videam et abiectam?

> Where can I take myself in my wretchedness? Where can I turn? To the Capitol? But it is steeped in my brother's blood. To my home? To see my poor mother weeping and prostrate? (fr. 61 Malcovati 1967)

We may note here the use of the figure *dubitatio* (rhetorical doubt), the dilemma structure; and the resemblance to Euripides:

> Where now can I turn? To my father's house, and the land which I betrayed to come with you? Or to Pelias' wretched daughters? A fine welcome they would give me, who murdered their father! (*Medea* 502–5)

(The parallel with Ennius *Medea* fr. 104 Jocelyn 1967 is less close.) Greek rhetoricians used quotations from the poets to illustrate their precepts, and Gaius' fragment therefore has a textbook quality to it. But the fragment has a further quality that those of Cato do not: the ends of the clauses (except the shortest) have the same rhythmical patterns that are commonly found in the speeches of M. Tullius Cicero (106–43 BC) in the next century (there is even one of Cicero's favourite *esse videatur* ['seem to be'] rhythms, *sanguine redundat* [flows with blood]). This 'prose rhythm', by which the ends of clauses ('cola') and sentences conform to certain preferred metrical patterns (known as 'clausulae'), was one of the most significant changes that Hellenistic rhetoric introduced into Roman oratory; for an excellent brief guide to its use see Nisbet (1961: xvii–xx). When a tribune of the plebs, C. Papirius Carbo Arvina, used it before the people in 90 BC, they responded with loud applause (Cic. *Orat.* 213–14; cf. 168).

2   Rhetoric at Rome in the First Century BC

At the beginning of the first century we find that there were Latin rhetoricians at Rome as well as Greek: in 92 the censors issued an edict saying that it had come to their notice that the young were studying under Latin rhetoricians, and since this had not happened in their ancestors' time, they disapproved (Suet. *Rhet.* 25.2). We know the name of one such rhetorician, L. Plotius Gallus, because the young Cicero wanted to study under him; his mentors, however, decided that he would do better to study in Greek.

Soon afterwards (some time in the 80s) Cicero wrote his first rhetorical treatise, *De inventione*, covering one branch of the system of rhetoric as it then existed, and from the same period we also have the *Rhetorica ad Herennium* (the author's name is lost), covering the complete system; these works, which are closely related, show us Hellenistic rhetoric as taught by the Latin rhetoricians. Oratory was divided into three types, 'forensic' or 'judicial' (*genus iudiciale*), 'deliberative' (*genus deliberativum*) and 'epideictic' (*genus demonstrativum*). Forensic was the oratory of the law courts (which at Rome were located in the forum: hence the description 'forensic'), deliberative that of the political assemblies, and epideictic that of other public occasions (where typically persuasion would be a less important aim: 'epideictic' means 'involving display'). Next, there were the five functions of the orator or 'parts of rhetoric', invention (*inventio*, formulation of the arguments – the area treated in detail by Cicero), arrangement (*dispositio*), style (*elocutio*), memory (*memoria*: orators normally spoke without notes) and delivery (*actio*, including the use of physical gestures). Then there were the six parts of a speech (opening, statement of facts, partition or division, proof, refutation and conclusion or peroration), the four issues (conjecture, definition, quality and objection), the three styles (grand, middle and plain) and so on. Roman orators learned this system, and drew on it when composing their speeches. In practice, however, the greatest influence on a speech would generally be the real-life context, and so speeches do not normally read as if they were written to a formula (epideictic speeches are perhaps the exception in this regard). Any skilled orator would know to select from the great body of theory only those parts that would be useful to him in any given case, and to break the rules where necessary.

The first century BC was the period in which, in a protracted and painful process, a 500-year-old republic, governed by annual magistrates, was transformed into an absolute monarchy, under the control of an emperor, who held power for life (see Levene, Chapter 2 above). During this period of upheaval and intermittent civil war, oratory – specifically forensic and deliberative oratory – assumed an importance which it had at no other time in Roman history, before or afterwards. The uncertain times made for great oratory – a point the historian Tacitus was later to make in his *Dialogus de oratoribus*, written in the more settled era of the early second century AD. As the republic disintegrated, political opponents prosecuted each other for crimes real or imaginary (electoral malpractice, murder, violence, extortion and treason were the main ones); conviction would entail exile and hence political extinction. It was traditional at Rome for a defendant in a trial to seek out an advocate (*patronus*) to speak on his behalf (Roman practice differed from Greek in this respect: in Greece speakers had pleaded their own cases, although their speeches might have been written for them by a speech-writer). Successful advocates were therefore in a position to influence the course of events, determining who would or would not be removed from political life; in addition, they earned political favours that could be called in at a later date, and amassed great wealth. Cicero is the best example of this: because of his ability in the courts, he won the support necessary to rise to the consulship in 63 BC, despite being of Italian, not Roman birth, and from a family that had never even produced a Roman senator. Deliberative oratory, on the other hand, was just as important as forensic, and could also bring substantial rewards: the *popularis* (popular) politician P. Clodius Pulcher harangued the people in the 50s, and built up a large popular following with which he was able to challenge the power of both the triumvirs and the senate.

The speeches of any prominent person of this period could not fail to be of exceptional interest, and we are lucky indeed to have those of Cicero (which, together with his letters, constitute the most important historical source for this period, and make it the best-attested period in ancient history; cf. Levene, Chapter 2 above). Cicero was viewed by his contemporaries as an outstanding orator, and posterity has generally regarded him as the greatest that Rome ever produced, and, in addition, the writer of the best Latin prose. ' "Cicero" ', wrote the first-century AD rhetorician Quintilian, 'has come to be regarded as the name not of a person, but of eloquence itself' (*Inst.* 10.1.112). Cicero's pre-eminence, particularly his role as a model for Latin prose, has had both fortunate and unfortunate consequences. The fortunate one is that a vast amount of his writings have been preserved, including fifty-eight speeches surviving in whole or part (out of a total of at least 162 that he is known to have made). The unfortunate consequence is that very few other Latin speeches have survived at all. Cicero's brilliance has eclipsed all his predecessors and contemporaries, and almost all his successors. So, for example, although we have twenty-eight forensic (mostly defence) speeches by Cicero, in no case do we have a speech from the other side, and this severely limits our knowledge of such matters as the extent of Cicero's deception of the jury, the innocence or guilt of his clients, and even whether his cases were really about the issues that he claims they were – not to mention the loss to our understanding of the procedure and of the political and social context of the trials themselves.

We would willingly trade in (without any disrespect implied) large parts of Cicero's massive oeuvre in return for a speech by his great rival Q. Hortensius Hortalus (114–50 BC), a florid 'Asianist' orator and ready advocate of aristocrats in trouble; or one by the stern and self-righteous Stoic moralist M. Porcius Cato (95–46 BC), great-grandson of the Censor; or by the aggressive and urbane M. Caelius Rufus (*c.* 88–48 BC); or by C. Julius Caesar (100–44 BC), an orator admired for the purity of his language and the author (in 55 or 54) of a treatise on this subject, *De analogia*, which he dedicated to Cicero; or by Catullus' friend C. Licinius Calvus (born 82, dead by 47 BC), whose plain, unadorned 'Atticism' brought him into literary conflict with Cicero (Cicero's *Orator*, of 46 BC, contains a note of self-justification absent in his earlier mature rhetorical treatise, *De oratore*, of 55 BC); or by M. Junius Brutus (*c.* 85–42 BC), another famous orator who criticized Cicero's style, which he described as 'mincing and dislocated' (Tac. *Dial.* 18.5 *fractum atque elumbem*). We do have a pair of opposing speeches by Caesar and Cato in Sallust's *Catiline* (§§51–2), from the senatorial debate on the captured Catilinarian conspirators held on 5 December 63, the same debate at which Cicero's extant *Fourth Catilinarian* was delivered. But those speeches are Sallust's creations, and can offer at best only a general impression of what Caesar's and Cato's oratory might have been like. We know something of these and more than 200 other orators from Cicero's *Brutus* (46 BC), a history of Roman oratory down to and including Cicero himself. But if we had the actual speeches, we might then be in a position to judge what is otherwise unknowable – whether Cicero really was far and away Rome's greatest orator, in a class of his own, or whether he was merely the best out of a group of men of similar talent (the view of Messalla at Tacitus, *Dialogus* 25).

The rest of this chapter, then, will of necessity focus in large part on the speeches of Cicero. Other surveys of this type (e.g. Nisbet 1964; Berry and Heath 1997) have discussed Ciceronian oratory by reviewing selected speeches. Instead, therefore, I shall pick out and briefly discuss some of the characteristic features of Cicero's speeches. Many of these features would also of course be applicable to some of the oratory that is lost as well as to Cicero's.

3 The Speeches of Cicero

Of Cicero's fifty-eight extant speeches, about half (twenty-eight) are forensic, twenty-seven are deliberative and three (*Post reditum in senatu*, *Post reditum ad populum* (both 57 BC), *Pro Marcello* (46 BC)) are epideictic. His first speech, *Pro*

Quinctio, dates from 81 BC and his last, the *Fourteenth Philippic*, from 43 (eight months before his murder). All, however, are written in 'periodic style'. The essence of periodic style is suspense: once the sentence or 'period' has begun, the listener has to wait some time before the various subordinate clauses have been delivered and the sense is complete. While the period is evolving, the listener has certain expectations about how it is going to continue and end (grammatically, and in sense), and when it is finally completed these expectations are either fulfilled (giving the listener a sense of satisfaction) or, more rarely, cheated (startling the listener). The clauses that make up the period can sometimes be mere padding, but this is unusual; often they make the argument more impressive or powerful, and in addition they serve to delay the completion of the period, providing a greater feeling of satisfaction when the grammar and sense are finally completed. The clauses themselves and the words or groups of words within them are often arranged in carefully balanced pairs, sometimes to form a contrast, or sometimes in a symmetrical pattern ('chiasmus'); or they can be arranged in threes ('tricolon'), with increasing weight placed on each item, or greater weight placed on the final or second and final item ('rising tricolon'). The opening sentence of *Pro Archia* (62 BC), a speech from the middle of Cicero's career, may serve as an example:

> si quid est in me īngĕnī, iūdĭcēs, quod sentio quām sĭt ēxĭgŭŭm, aut si qua exercitatio dicendi, in qua me non infitior mediocriter ēssĕ vērsātŭm, aut si huiusce rei ratio aliqua ab optimarum artium studiis ac dīscĭplīnā prŏfēctă, a qua ego nullum confiteor aetatis meāē tēmpŭs ăbhōrrŭīssĕ, earum rerum omnium vel in primis hic A. Licinius fructum a me repetere prŏpĕ sŭō iūrĕ dēbĕt.

> If I have any natural talent, members of the jury – and I am aware how limited it is; or if I have any experience in public speaking – in which I do not deny that I am moderately well practised; or if there is any technical skill in my oratory which has been derived from application and training in the liberal arts – and I admit that I have never at any period of my life been averse to such training: if I do have any of these capabilities, then Aulus Licinius here is entitled almost as of right to be among the very first to claim from me the benefits which they may bring. (*Pro Archia* §1, trans. Berry 2000)

In this period, there is a lengthy delay before the sense is completed: the subject *A. Licinius* is held back almost until the end, and the main verb *debet* occupies the final place. This emphasizes both words, increasing the dignity inherent in Archias' formal Roman name A. Licinius (which Cicero wishes to emphasize, since it is Archias' right to such a name, and to Roman citizenship, that is in question in this trial) and underlining the sense of obligation inherent in the word *debet*. The delay is achieved by the use of three parallel conditional clauses, each of which is concluded with a relative clause followed by a complementary clause (tricolon); and the second and third units are each more extended than the previous one (rising tricolon).

A further feature of periodic style is prose rhythm: the ends of each of the major clauses or cola are marked by metrical patterns, clausulae, which experience had shown to be suitable to prose (largely because they were distinct from the most common metrical patterns of verse). Clausulae which are most characteristic of Cicero (and – since his practice was not unique – of other orators, particularly those of the florid, Asianist variety) have been indicated in the extract quoted above (on Roman Asianism, see Leeman 1963: 91–111; Clarke/Berry 1996: 80–3). It will be noticed that they occur not just at the end of the period, as is commonly supposed, but at virtually every point where there is a natural pause. Only *exercitatio dicendi* lacks one the most common clausulae, having instead one of a rarer type, although still attested in Cicero (*exercitātĭŏ dīcēndī* – the clausula is less favoured because the spondees are suggestive of verse). In fact, one could go further than I have done and break down the text into even smaller units: further clausulae would materialize (Nisbet 1961: xvii–xx; Berry 1996: 49–54).

Other stylistic features of Ciceronian prose include rhetorical questions (questions that do not expect an answer), anaphora (repetition of a word or phrase in successive clauses), asyndeton (omission of connectives), apostrophe (turning away to address an absent person or thing), exclamation, alliteration and assonance, wordplay, and metaphor. There is anaphora of *si* (if) in the extract quoted above.

Let us now turn to other features of Cicero's speeches. Some of these features are related to his own personality, which of course we know of independently of his speeches, from the letters. Cicero is an author who tells us a great deal about himself, and except in invectives, such as *In Pisonem* (55 BC) or the *Second Philippic* (44 BC), he comes across as a most attractive character. The exploitation of one's own character was an important element in Roman oratory. The point of giving speeches, at least forensic and deliberative ones, was to persuade people, and an audience would be more likely to be persuaded if the speaker came across as honest, responsible, patriotic, not overly intellectual, a believer in traditional values, a person of importance in the state, and a supporter of the audience's interests. In most of his speeches, this is how Cicero presents himself. He was concerned above all to project his own *auctoritas*, the personal standing and prestige a senior senator or magistrate would possess, and that would incline audiences to take on trust whatever he said (the Romans looked up to their great men much more than we do). His attainment of the consulship in 63 added considerably to the *auctoritas* he was able to deploy: his consular *auctoritas* enabled him, for example, to persuade the people in his four speeches *De lege agraria* (63 BC; the fourth speech is lost) to vote down a proposal to divide up the public land in Italy among the poor. The next year, he was able in *Pro Sulla* to use his *auctoritas* as the consul who had suppressed the conspirator Catiline to secure the acquittal of a decidedly unsavoury aristocrat who had been accused of supporting Catiline: the argument was essentially 'My client must be innocent, because I of all people would hardly be defending him if he were not.' At the beginning of his career, of course, he lacked the requisite *auctoritas*; but in *Pro Roscio Amerino* (80 BC), a defence on a charge of parricide, he succeeds in turning this to his advantage by presenting himself as the underdog and claiming that his insignificance gives him greater opportunity to speak the truth.

As well as seeking to establish his own *auctoritas*, an orator would naturally seek also to undermine his opponent's. In *Pro Murena* (63 BC), for example, a defence on a charge of electoral malpractice, Cicero faces the difficult challenge of defending his client against Cato, a man of considerable moral stature who – the jury might assume – would not have undertaken his prosecution had he not known for a fact that his victim was guilty (the argument of *Pro Sulla* in reverse). Cicero successfully undermines Cato's *auctoritas* by treating the jury to a highly unflattering and devastatingly funny account of the Stoic philosophy that Cato professes, persuading them that a man with such an other-worldly interest is incapable of arriving at common-sense judgements on anything, let alone discerning where the interest of the state lies. 'Gentlemen, what an amusing consul we have!' was Cato's impotent and disapproving response (Plut. *Cat. Min.* 21.5).

Cicero's humour is in fact his most attractive characteristic, and one that explains the enduring popularity of *Pro Caelio* (56 BC), a defence of one of his most violent and disreputable clients. In this speech humour is used, as in *Pro Murena*, to distract the jury from the actual charges. Caelius was accused of the murder of an important ambassador from Alexandria, the philosopher Dio, who had come to Rome to ask the senate not to reinstate the deposed Ptolemy as king of Egypt; there were also various other charges of rioting, assault and criminal damage. One would scarcely know this from the speech, however. For the most part paying little attention to the charges, Cicero concentrates instead on the private life of Clodia Metelli, Caelius' ex-lover, claiming that Caelius' rejection of her was the chief reason why the prosecution had brought the case. Much of the speech is devoted to exposing and attacking Clodia's promiscuity. Gentle mockery of her life of wealth and luxury is interwoven with attacks of a more bitter kind: she is described as a prostitute (*meretrix*), and accused of incest with her brother, Cicero's enemy Clodius. The result makes for compelling reading. By the device of prosopopoeia (putting a speech into the mouth of a person who is absent), Cicero invokes Clodia's ancestor App. Claudius Caecus (mentioned at the start of this chapter) and makes him thunder against his wayward descendant:

ideone ego pacem Pyrrhi diremi ut tu amorum turpissimorum cotidie foedera ferires, ideo aquam adduxi ut ea tu inceste uterere, ideo viam munivi ut eam tu alienis viris comitata celebrares?

Did I destroy the peace treaty with Pyrrhus so that you could strike the most disgraceful sexual bargains on a daily basis? Did I bring water to the city for you to foul with your incestuous practices? Did I build a road so that you could parade up and down it in the company of other women's husbands? (*Pro Caelio* §34, trans. Berry 2000)

The references are to Appius' commissioning, in 312 BC, of the Aqua Appia, Rome's first aqueduct, and the Appian Way, a road from Rome to Capua. In this speech, put into the mouth of Appius, the reader is reminded not just of the difference between the harsh, almost primitive (§36 *durum ac paene agrestem*) third-century Roman and his decadent descendant, but of that between the blunt and forceful nature of archaic Roman oratory and the playful sophistication of Cicero.

The humorous approach was not appropriate to every speech. In the case of *Pro Caelio*, it was suitable because Cicero's speech, the final one of the trial, was taking place on a public holiday, when the rest of Rome was watching the Megalesian games (violence trials were potentially so important that they were an exception to the normal rule that the courts did not sit on public holidays). Cicero therefore set out to give the jurors a speech that would be at least as entertaining as what they would otherwise be seeing. In his speech he makes a number of allusions to the theatre: the comic poets Caecilius and Terence are quoted (§§37–8) to give the proceedings a relaxed feel, and Caelius' alleged attempt to poison Clodia is narrated as if it were a farce, and is explicitly likened to a mime (§64 *fabella*; §65 *mimi*). At Rome, orators were in a sense actors, and speeches theatrical performances (Cic. *Brut.* 290); this idea is repeatedly invoked in *Pro Caelio* in order to play down the seriousness of the accusation.

There is great variety in the tactics Cicero uses in different speeches. Some speeches depend on rallying the audience to a particular political standpoint: Cicero's position is identified as the patriotic one, so that all dissenters are automatically classified as enemies of the state. Thus, whether the enemy is Catiline (in the *Catilinarians*, 63 BC), Clodius (in the *Post reditum* speeches, particularly *Pro Sestio* of 56 BC) or Mark Antony (in the *Philippics*, 44–43 BC), humanity is divided into the loyal, patriotic 'good men' (*boni*) on the one hand and, on the other, the 'wicked' traitors and would-be destroyers of their country (*improbi*) who support his opponent: there is no neutral position. Other speeches, such as the *Verrines* (70 BC), a prosecution of a corrupt governor of Sicily, depend on narrative skill – the ability to give a coherent and convincing account of the facts under dispute in such as way as to bring over the audience unavoidably to one's own way of thinking. Others, such as *Pro Milone* (52 BC), a defence of Clodius' murderer, depend on forceful argument combined with wholesale distortion of the truth; as in *Pro Cluentio* (66 BC), a complex murder case, an important function of argument can be to confuse as well as to clarify. Many other speeches depend on lengthy digressions that seek to remove prejudices the audience may feel against the speaker or client while also distracting attention from the main point at issue; and all speeches depend on Cicero's devastating powers of characterization.

But Cicero was particularly a master of emotional manipulation: it was because of his acknowledged effectiveness in this area that his fellow advocates always let him give the closing speech (Cic. *Orat.* 130). His defences often conclude with an appeal to pity (*miseratio* or *conquestio*), during which he himself – and, if he was successful, his audience – would weep profusely. These appeals tend to follow a standard pattern: if the defendant is convicted, his aged father's life will be crushed by the calamity and/or his young son's future prospects blighted (e.g. in *Pro Murena*, *Pro Sulla*, *Pro Flacco* [59 BC] and *Pro Caelio*). Cicero attributed his success in these appeals not to technical skill but to his own genuine sympathy (*Orat.* 130, 132; cf. *De orat.* 189–90), and his letters (e.g. those written from exile) do indeed reveal him to have been of a highly emotional disposition. Emotion of a different kind, however, is displayed when he speaks from the heart in support of a cause to which he is deeply committed. At the end of the *Second Philippic*, his address to Antony gains force from his own personal commitment to a free republic:

> defendi rem publicam adulescens: non deseram senex. contempsi Catilinae gladios: non pertimescam tuos. quin etiam corpus libenter obtulerim, si repraesentari morte mea libertas civitatis potest, ut aliquando dolor populi Romani pariat quod iam diu parturit! etenim si abhinc annos prope viginti hoc ipso in templo negavi posse mortem immaturam esse consulari, quanto verius nunc negabo seni? mihi vero, patres conscripti, iam etiam optanda mors est, perfuncto rebus eis quas adeptus sum quasque gessi. duo modo haec opto, unum ut moriens populum Romanum liberum relinquam – hoc mihi maius ab dis immortalibus dari nihil potest – alterum ut ita cuique eveniat ut de re publica quisque mereatur.

> I defended this country when I was a young man: I shall not desert it now that I am old. I faced down the swords of Catiline: I shall not flinch before yours. Yes, and I would willingly offer my body, if the freedom of the country could at once be secured by my death, and the suffering of the Roman people at last give birth to that with which it has long been pregnant. If nearly twenty years ago in this very temple I declared that death could not be untimely for a man who had reached the consulship, with how much more truth could I now say 'for an old man'? In fact, for me, senators, death is actually desirable now that I have discharged the responsibilities of the offices that I attained and undertook. Two things alone I long for: first, that when I die I may leave the Roman people free – the immortal gods could bestow on me no greater blessing; and second, that each person's fate may reflect the way he has behaved towards his country. (*Second Philippic* §§118–19, trans. Berry)

A year or so after writing these words, Cicero faced Antony's swords without flinching; but his death was followed by the end of the republic.

4   Oratory under the Empire

Under the empire, there was no longer any scope for great forensic or deliberative oratory: the emperor made all the decisions (see Mayer, Chapter 4 above). Since magistrates now had a superior watching everything they did, major criminal trials (now held before the senate or the emperor himself) became rare events. Advocates therefore had to content themselves with civil cases in the centumviral court, where restrictions had been placed on the length of speeches and the number of pleaders. The only criminal trials which were political were those for treason (*maiestas*), a charge which was now taken to mean conspiracy against the emperor: the law of *maiestas* provided opportunities, particularly under Tiberius and Domitian, for unscrupulous informers (*delatores*) to further their careers and enrich themselves at the expense of their eminent and often blameless victims. The outcome of such trials was unfortunately seldom in doubt.

Enthusiasm for oratory nevertheless remained as great as ever. The result was the emergence of declamation (speech-making as a rhetorical exercise) as a major cultural institution (Bonner 1949; Clarke/Berry 1996: 85–99). The crowds that under the republic had flocked to the forum now packed the declamation halls, where popular rhetoricians demonstrated their mastery of their art. If speeches had been like theatrical performances, this was even more the case with declamation: its subject matter, which was made up of tyrants, pirates, stepmothers and other stock characters, could have been taken straight from the comic poets. M. Fabius Quintilianus, the great first-century AD teacher of rhetoric and author of the extant *Institutio oratoria*, criticized the remoteness of declamation from real life, but still considered it a useful training. The *Minor Declamations ascribed to Quintilian* consist of the last 145 out of an original 388 mini-declamations or extracts, and appear to show the influence of his school. The nineteen *Major Declamations ascribed to Quintilian*, on the other hand, date from a later period, but consist of full-length declamations. There also survive various other speeches which show the influence of declamation and presumably emanate from the rhetorical schools of the empire, the *Invectiva in Ciceronem* (spoken as if by Sallust), the *Invectiva in Sallustium* (spoken as if by Cicero), the *Pridie quam in exsilium iret* (spoken as if by Cicero on his departure into exile) and the *Declamatio in Catilinam* (spoken as if by Cicero in an imaginary prosecution of Catiline; this speech, sometimes referred to as the *Fifth Catilinarian*, is not to be confused with the extant medieval *Fifth Catilinarian*). These four speeches (the last two of which have scarcely been noticed by scholars) point to an interest in Cicero both as a model for oratory and as a character from a period in history – a period that, in contrast to the writers' own time, had been rich in possibilities for great oratory.

But if the empire was not conducive to great forensic or deliberative oratory, epideictic on the other hand now came into its own. There had certainly been a role for the oratory of formal public occasions under the republic: the Roman funeral *laudatio* (eulogy), for example, had a long history. But with the arrival of one-man rule, opportunities arose for prominent orators to offer formal addresses to their ruler. Panegyrics could aim simply to flatter the ruler, or, more ambitiously, to warn him of the consequences of ruling badly or encourage him to rule well (the advice would also be applicable to his successors). A collection of twelve such panegyrics survives, the first one addressed by the younger Pliny (*c.* AD 61–*c.*112) to the emperor Trajan in AD 100 (but afterwards revised), and the rest, clearly modelled on Pliny's, addressed to Roman emperors of the third and fourth centuries (various other, even later, panegyrics survive in whole or part). Pliny was a pupil of Quintilian and friend of Tacitus, and was famed as an orator of the first order, with long experience in the civil courts. However, the seemingly unending flattery of the *Panegyricus* (the speech takes up 81 pages in the Oxford Classical Texts edition) does not appeal to modern taste. Even though it aims (unnecessarily, in Trajan's case) to influence the emperor by encouraging him to continue his good government, Pliny's eloquent servility quickly becomes tiresome. But this is surely more the fault of the genre than of the orator: a more independent critique of government (such as is found, for instance, in Tacitus' *Dialogus*) could hardly be expected in a speech addressed to the emperor.

But oratory under the empire was not exclusively concerned with the emperor and events at Rome. At the local level, oratory flourished throughout the classical period. Arriving and departing provincial governors would be addressed with epideictic speeches (sections of such are preserved in the *Florida* of Apuleius); and courts continued to be places where fortunes and reputations were won and lost through oratory. The only surviving forensic speech not by Cicero is the *Pro se de magia*, better known as the *Apologia*, of Apuleius (b. *c.* AD 125); this is also the only complete Roman speech from the second century besides the *Panegyricus* (see also Gibson, Chapter 5 above). Apuleius was an epideictic orator and sophist from North Africa, and the *Apologia* is a defence of himself on a charge of sorcery, given in a court at Sabratha in Tripolitania in late 158 or early 159. The speech has important differences from the majority of Cicero's speeches, being a self-defence, not a defence of a client, delivered in Africa, not at Rome, and concerned with magic, not politics. A further difference is that, whereas Cicero usually tries to conceal the extent of his erudition from his audience, not wishing to alienate it, Apuleius goes out of his way to parade his learning on every page with extensive quotation from Greek and Roman literature and displays of philosophical and scientific knowledge. Indeed, he betrays a greater knowledge of magic than helps his case (and thereby earned a reputation as a magician that was to endure for centuries). Cicero and Apuleius both make considerable use of logical argument; but whereas Cicero supplements this with emotional appeals, Apuleius prefers to impress and dazzle his audience into submission. This is a different kind of oratory – oratory in the tradition of the declaimers, but belonging intellectually to the Second Sophistic. The aim is not merely to secure an acquittal (as seems in this case to have been achieved), but to advertise his sophistic talents to an audience of potential clients. In this respect the speech has an epideictic dimension, which threatens to eclipse the forensic. Apuleius' epideictic talents are also evident in the *Florida*, an anthology of extracts from his speeches, centring around Carthage in the 160s AD, and the *De Deo Socratis*, a lively philosophical lecture from the same milieu.

Here our survey must end, for lack of surviving material. But Apuleius' *Apologia* serves nevertheless to give us a valuable indication of the diversity, complexity and vitality of oratory at the high point of the Roman Empire.

FURTHER READING

Cicero's speeches are quoted from Berry (2000); reliable translations of other Cicero speeches are in Shackleton Bailey (1986 and 1991). Apuleius' *Apologia* is translated by Hunink in Harrison et al. (2001). The fragments of the lost republican orators are to be found in Malcovati (1967), but without translation. The most convenient survey of Roman rhetoric is Clarke/Berry (1996); Kennedy (1972) covers the same ground but gives more attention to the speeches, while Dominik (1997) explores the role of rhetoric in Roman society and literature. Leeman (1963) provides a history of Roman oratory, historiography and philosophy. Short surveys of Ciceronian oratory are offered by Nisbet (1964), and of oratory and declamation by Berry and Heath (1997). Sumner (1973) gives prosopographical information on 221 republican orators. Von Albrecht (1989) analyses specimens of prose from a variety of writers, including fragmentary orators. On Cicero, May (2002) is a fine general handbook, with a useful survey of recent scholarship and extensive bibliography. Stroh (1975) and Classen (1985) examine the rhetorical strategy of particular Cicero speeches, while May (1988) discusses Cicero's manipulation of ethos (character), Craig (1993) his use of dilemma, and Vasaly (1993) his exploitation of place or ambience. Bonner (1949) is the standard work on Roman declamation. Winterbottom (1975) and MacCormack (1975) are helpful starting points on Quintilian and on the Latin panegyrics respectively. S. J. Harrison (2000) has detailed chapters on all Apuleius' rhetorical works, which are to be found in annotated translation in Harrison et al. (2001).

CHAPTER NINETEEN

Epistolography

Catharine Edwards

1 Introduction

In the *Envois* section of *La Carte postale* (a text presented in epistolary form as a series of postcards addressed to an unnamed lover), Derrida asserts that 'the letter, the epistle . . . . is not a genre but all genres, literature itself' (1980:48). If the letter is to be seen as a genre, it is one of particular fluidity (Rosenmeyer 1997:31). Nevertheless, to be classed as a letter, a text does perhaps require a specific addressee (or addressees). The place of the reader is more insistently foregrounded in a letter than in any other kind of writing (Altman 1982: 87–8). But the most crucial element is the separation of writer and addressee. As Altman has persuasively put it, a letter serves both to bridge the distance between writer and addressee and, at the same time, to remind us of that distance, while the author can choose whether to emphasize the bridge or the gap (Altman 1982: ch. 1).

Letters involve writing for a specific occasion; they are the product of particular circumstances. Hence the frequent association of letters, as opposed to other kinds of text, with spontaneity, sincerity. A distinction is often invoked between literary and non-literary letters, such as those found scribbled on pieces of bark from Vindolanda or on papyri from Egypt. Yet as de Pretis argues, we should not overemphasize the artlessness of letters written even by the relatively uneducated, as if this were a guarantee of sincerity (2002: 5–16). It makes more sense to stress the distinctive nature of the letter as a written document, in contrast to the spoken word. A written document always has the potential to be read by a third party. The 'external' reader, as we may term the reader who is not the addressee, is thus always an implicit presence.

The conventions of letter-writing, the issue of what style might be appropriate to the composition of a letter, are by and large marginal to the concerns of ancient treatises on rhetorical style (see Malherbe 1988:3). The first extended discussion of the subject occurs in a work entitled *On Style* attributed to the otherwise unknown Demetrius and usually dated to the first century BC. Demetrius and other writers on style suggest an equivalence between letters on the one hand and conversation on the other. Similar comments on the relationship between letters and conversation are also to be found in specific letters from, for instance, Cicero *Ad Att.* 8.14.1; 9.10.1. Seneca compares the style of his letters with that of a conversation between friends: 'My letters should be just what my conversation would be, if you and I were sitting in one another's company or going for a walk together – spontaneous and easy (*inlaboratus et facilis*)' (75.1). Linked to this is the perception that, in Demetrius' words: 'A letter should be very largely an expression of character .... Perhaps everyone reflects his own soul in writing a letter. It is possible to discern a writer's character in every other form of literature but in none so fully as in the letter' (§227 trans. D. Innes in Russell and Winterbottom 1972:211). Later readers have often looked to the collections of letters that have survived from ancient Rome to offer privileged access to the people who wrote them. Thus have Cicero, the Younger Seneca and the Younger Pliny been seen as individuals whom the modern reader may come to know intimately.

Yet alongside these prose letters, which are often regarded as 'genuine' correspondence, we need to consider a number of poems composed in epistolary form. Scholars have generally been less ready to see these as written essentially for the addressee. Indeed some, most obviously Ovid's *Heroides*, verse letters attributed to mythological heroines and heroes and addressed to their loved ones, are plainly fictional. Nevertheless it does, I think, make sense to consider all these varieties of letter together. In particular, looking at prose letters alongside verse ones can serve to highlight some of the more literary and self-conscious features of the former.

2 Cicero

Cicero's letters have generally been seen as offering revealing insights both into the eventful period in which Cicero wrote and into the personality of their author (see Levene, Chapter 2 above). The letters were published in two main collections, *To his Friends* (*Ad familiares*) and *To Atticus*, as well as the smaller collections *Ad Quintum fratrem* and *Ad Brutum* (others may also have circulated in antiquity). *To his Friends* (in sixteen books) also includes nearly 100 letters addressed to Cicero. This collection was assembled and published after Cicero's death by his freedman M. Tullius Tiro (who seems to have kept copies of letters that were dictated to him, *Fam.* 7.25.1). Tiro also collected most of the letters to Atticus (which Cicero seems mainly to have written in his own hand), though there is no firm evidence that the latter were in circulation until the time of Nero.

Cicero's correspondence includes examples of a wide variety of different forms and registers of letter. Among the most distinct types are letters of recommendation and consolation; Book 13 of *Ad familiares* is entirely devoted to the former. Cicero himself offers a basic classification of kinds and registers of letter in a letter to his friend Curio (*Fam.* 2.4). The first kind is that which conveys important information to those who are far away. But when there is no such information to be sent, letters may be classed as 'intimate and humorous' (*familiare et iocosum*) or else as 'austere and serious' (*severum et grave*). Cicero's addressees include those with whom Cicero was evidently on close terms, such as Curio and Caelius, but also others, such as the powerful aristocrats Lentulus Spinther and Appius Pulcher, whom he knew much less well. Letters to those in the second category tend to be couched in an elaborate and formal style that differs little from that of Cicero's published works of other kinds. Letters to close friends, above all those to Atticus, are by contrast full of the vulgar terms, neologisms and diminutives that have come to be seen as the distinctive features of Cicero's informal letter-writing. This latter style is of course no less self-conscious and carefully worked. The literary qualities of Cicero's letters received much admiration in antiquity (Quintilian 10.1.107; Pliny *Ep.* 9.2.2; Fronto *Ant.* 3.8.2; *Caes.* 3.15 van den Hout[2]). Some literary aspects of the letters have recently been explored by Hutchinson (1998).

In some ways, the letters as a whole may be seen as a complement to Cicero's oratory. These two modes of expression are explicitly compared by Cicero himself (*Fam.* 9.21.1). The letters to Atticus in particular serve to parade their author's *urbanitas*. In his public speeches, Cicero might present himself as indifferent to the charms of Greek art; he affects ignorance of the names of the most notable Greek artists in his speeches prosecuting Gaius Verres. His letters to Atticus, by contrast, show Cicero as an avid (if not especially discerning) collector, constantly urging his friend to locate antiquities to lend an appropriate air of refinement to Cicero's villa (*Att.* 1.4; 1.8). While it was considered inappropriate to use Greek in the context of more formal writings, Greek words and phrases frequently appear in Cicero's letters, above all, those addressed to Atticus. Their particular frequency here serves not only to reflect and reinforce the degree to which both Cicero and Atticus were at home with Greek literary culture but also functions as an index of their intimacy.

Absence is a frequent concern in Cicero's letters to Atticus. His separation from Atticus allows Cicero to formulate and reformulate the nature of their friendship, a friendship that takes part of its significance precisely from these prolonged periods of separation. 'Whether working or resting, in business or in leisure, in professional or domestic affairs, in public life or in private, I cannot for any length of time do without your affectionate advice and the delight of your conversation' (*Att.* 1.17, 61 BC, trans. Shackleton Bailey 1965–70 vol.1 p.167). Later letters too proclaim Cicero's dependence on Atticus and specifically on writing to Atticus, for instance 8.14.1 (49 BC): 'I do, believe me, find a modicum of relaxation in these miseries when I am, as it were, talking to you, much more still when I am reading your letters.' Elsewhere he writes, 'I have nothing to write about. . . . But since my distress of mind is such that it is not only impossible to sleep but torment to be awake, I have started this scrawl without any subject in view, just in order as it were to talk to you, which is my only relief' (*Att.* 9.10, 49 BC).

Such proclamations might seem spontaneous, artless even. Yet we can also read these letters as carefully wrought instruments of self-representation – or perhaps rather self-fashioning. Cicero and Atticus are repeatedly contrasted, the better to delineate Cicero as an engaged public figure (see particularly *Att.* 9.10). And it is in the context of a letter to Atticus (written after Cicero had been sent into exile in 58) that Cicero feels able to lament the dissolution of his carefully constructed public self: 'I mourn the loss not only of the things and persons that were mine, but of my very self. What am I now?' (*Att.* 3.15). The letters chart shifts in Cicero's self-perception, at the same time working to present a more fluid, intimate picture of their author to external readers, a picture that many have found significantly more attractive than those discernible from Cicero's public speeches or philosophical writings.

Cicero's letters were apparently composed without the anticipation that they would be published. They are full of allusions and references that need explication if they are to be understood by later readers. Indeed the letters to Atticus occasionally seem to assume that no one besides the addressee will read them; Cicero comments, for instance, in 1.16, 'I don't feel that I am bragging when I talk about myself in your hearing, especially in a letter that I don't wish to be read to other people' (61 BC). The letters of Cicero are often contrasted, in this – and other – respects with Pliny's letters, which, as we shall see below, were, it seems, written specifically with a view to publication. Yet towards the end of his life, Cicero did explicitly consider publishing a selection of his correspondence (*Att.* 16.5.5; *Fam.* 16.17.1). Even at the time they were written we should not suppose Cicero imagined that their addressees would be the letters' only readers. There is perhaps something rather disingenuous in Cicero's comments on the privacy of the letters, which could be seen as making his boasting, for instance, much more forgivable. From his explicit injunction not to read letter 1.16 to others, we should perhaps infer that it was more usual for a letter to be passed around friends and family.

It is important, too, to distinguish between the letter as actually sent and the preserved or copied letter. In writing to Atticus, Cicero specifically talks of 'examining and correcting' his letters prior to publication, *eas ego oportet perspiciam, corrigam* (16.5.5). He chose to preserve certain letters – and must have edited at least some of them. It is clear he did not keep all the letters he himself was sent. That problematic or damaging letters were suppressed is a strong possibility. Many of the later letters to Atticus in particular have self-exculpation as their theme; letter 9.10 for instance (dated to March 49) quotes numerous passages from Atticus' earlier letters endorsing Cicero's political choices.

There was perhaps a sense in which 'private' correspondence offered a medium for the expression of political views at times when more public expressions of opinion – in the senate house, for instance, or the law courts – might be inhibited by a concern not to offend Rome's dominant politicians. It may be no coincidence that most of Cicero's surviving speeches date from the years leading up to his consulship in 63, while most of his surviving correspondence dates from the years that followed, thus serving to document Cicero's time in exile, his re-establishment in Rome, his period as governor of Cilicia and the increasingly troubled years from 50 until his death in 43.

3   Philosophical Letters: Horace's *Epistles*

Well before the 'publication' of Cicero's letters, there were collections of letters circulating as literary texts, most notably the philosophical letters attributed to Plato and to Epicurus (some of which are still extant) and to Aristotle (now lost). While most scholars agree that the letters attributed to Plato are not authentic, they were well known and influential in antiquity. Indeed Cicero himself alludes to the letters ascribed to Plato (e.g. *Att.* 9.10). The letters of Epicurus, addressed to individual pupils, served to clarify his philosophical doctrines and offer encouragement to his followers. These, too, were known to Cicero (cf. *Tusc.* 2.45), though he did not choose an epistolary form for his own philosophical writings. The *Epistles* of Horace, however, written towards the end of the poet's career, can to some degree be seen as drawing on this tradition of philosophical letter-writing.

The poetic epistle in Latin is first attested in the second century BC; the satirist Lucilius is known to have composed a letter to a friend, reproving him for not coming to visit when Lucilius was ill (frs 181–3, 341 Marx). Some of Catullus' poems take the form of letters (e.g. 13, 35, 65, 68a). However, Horace's *Epistles* constitute the first collection of such writings, even if Horace disclaims their status as poetry (1.1.10; 2.1.111). The two books of *Epistles* frequently play on the conventions of everyday letter-writing (de Pretis 2002: 21–3). Each poem is addressed to a specific individual, such as Maecenas. They invite their addressees to visit the poet or come to a party (1.4; 1.5), recommend one friend to another (1.12) and offer support for a friend seeking a position (1.9). Some of the poems create an epistolary effect through profusion of detail, while others, such as 1.6, are much more sparing in their use of formulae associated with letter-writing. Nevertheless, Horace's use of epistolary form is central to the effect of the poems. In particular, the identity of the individual addressees, who include the slave in charge of Horace's country estate, as well as Maecenas, and indeed Augustus himself, plays a crucial role (see de Pretis 2002: ch. 3). Thus two epistles treating very similar subjects – the relationship between patron and client – can adopt quite distinct tones, apparently in response to the differing characters of their addressees, Scaeva and Lollius (*Ep.* 1.17; 1.18).

Ethics are insistently presented as a concern in the *Epistles*. The epistolary form, which foregrounds the author, allows Horace to pay particular attention to his own role as a fallible philosophical exemplar (Harrison 1995: 57–60). In *Ep*.1.1.1–12, Horace describes himself as analogous to a retired gladiator, withdrawing from the competitive engagements of public life. Yet as Oliensis comments, 'This portrait of studious retirement effectively keeps its author in the world's eye' (1998:154). And while some of the poems in the collection seem to emphasize Horace's 'philosophical distance', the *Epistles* also seem to present Horace as a figure of some public standing, a man whose relationship with some of Rome's leading figures, including of course Augustus, may offer a model for others. In Mayer's view, 'Horace now defends and advises upon the life of the dependant in Roman society. The *Epistles* thus become his most essentially Roman production' (1994: 5). *Epistle* 1.9 is presented as a letter to Augustus' stepson Tiberius, asking a favour on behalf of Horace's friend Septimius. Central to the poem is Horace's apparent self-deprecation; Septimius has overestimated the closeness of the poet's friendship with Tiberius (Oliensis 1998: 184–5). Thus this letter simultaneously parades Horace's modesty and asserts his status as someone who can lay claim to the friendship of the imperial family.

In the *Epistles*, Horace may be seen as exploiting a new form in which to pursue the 'self-revelation' characteristic of his earlier work (Oliensis 1998: 13–14). Indeed the project of self-construction is pursued here more persistently than in any of Horace's other works (de Pretis 2002: 70). At last the real Horace is within the reader's grasp, perhaps? But numerous features of these poems, in particular, the plurality of addressees serve to make the 'self' that emerges slippery and shifting.

4 Ovid's Epistolary Poetry

Probably published in some form shortly after Horace's *Epistles* 1, Ovid's single *Heroides* mark another new departure; these poems are explicitly fictional. Ovid's self-characterization in the *Art of Love* (3.345–6) lists among his modes of poetic expression the recitation of 'letters in an assumed voice' (*composita ... epistula voce*), and comments of himself, 'this type of work, unknown to others, he pioneered' (there is dispute, however, as to whether Propertius' fourth book of elegies may not have preceeded Ovid here; the book's third poem is in the form of a love letter written by a Roman woman to her absent soldier husband). The collection of *Heroides* as we have it now comprises fifteen single epistles, beginning with the epistle of Penelope to Ulysses (which may well have been placed first in the collection by Ovid himself), and three pairs of double epistles (possibly written much later, in Ovid's exile, and some of disputed authenticity) in which heroes and heroines exchange letters. Ovid's *Heroides* offer variations on the lament voiced by a heroine abandoned by or separated from her lover, which was already an established theme in Greek and Latin literature. The *Heroides* have often been criticized for their repetitiveness but their similarities are perhaps rather a function of their sophistication. Their fictive authors model themselves on each other; their role-playing is at certain points quite self-conscious (see, for instance, Hypsipyle's anticipation of Medea's future at 6.149–51, discussed by Kauffman, 1986: 41).

Their status as letters, though often overlooked by scholars, is, as Kennedy (2002) has recently emphasized, crucial to their functioning. While the 'external reader' familiar with a version of the story from Homer or some other source sees the sequence of events as already determined, the fictive writers experience their circumstances as 'open and contingent' (Kennedy 2002: 225). The time-specific nature of the letter for its fictive writer is a crucial part of its meaning, as Kennedy (1984) argues in relation to Ovid's Penelope as depicted in *Her.* 1. Penelope's anxiety for Ulysses, when her husband has already returned but in disguise, is poignantly conveyed. Each of the *Heroides* offers its assumed author's perceptions of the addressee and often of the addressee's response – and the concern given to the time when the letter will actually be received. Hope is often expressed that there will not be an unhappy discrepancy between the time when the letter is read and the time when the letter was written (Kennedy 2002: 223). Such expressions of hope can generate a strong sense of irony for the reader already familiar with the story's canonical ending. Yet Kennedy also draws attention to the subversive sense in which a letter written by a legendary author positions itself as prior to the canonical version of the story (Kennedy 2002: 226).

Two collections of Ovid's poems written during his years in exile by the Black Sea (AD 8–13), the *Tristia* in five books and *Ex Ponto* in four, should also be read as letters. While only the poems of the *Ex Ponto* are explicitly referred to as letters, the *Tristia*, too, are characterized by several distinguishing features of the epistolary form (Rosenmeyer 1997: 30–2, 44). A number of specific addressees are identified and even when the addressee is indeterminate the reader may be invited to guess his or her identity (e.g. *Tristia* 1.5). Ovid's choice of the letter form for his exile poems is seen by Rosenmeyer (1997) as 'not only an allusion to, but also an authorial statement of identification – on some level – with his earlier epistolary work, the *Heroides*' (29).

In exile in 58 BC (following political repercussions from his role in the suppression of the Catilinarian conspiracy of 63 BC), Cicero complains at length about being separated from his friends and family. The letters he has received are, he writes, blotted with his own tears (*Fam.* 9.1). In an interesting echo of Cicero's letters from exile, Ovid's too are stained with tears (e.g. *Tristia* 3.1.15; cf. Nagle 1980: 33–5). At the same time, however, tear-stains can be seen as a trademark of Ovid's own *Heroides*; for example 3.3 (Hinds 1985: 14–15). There is perhaps something disconcerting, though, in this evocation of a parallel with fictive correspondence, which may be seen as subtly undermining the reality effect of the tear-stains described by both Cicero and the exiled Ovid.

In the poems from exile Ovid 'in letters to loved ones, writes from the position of a kind of abandoned hero' (Rosenmeyer 1997:29), explicitly comparing him- self to Ulysses (*Trist.* 1.5.57–70). At the same time, his wife, left behind in Rome, takes on the role of Penelope (most explicitly in *Trist.* 1.6), thus evoking the programmatic first poem of the *Heroides*. The predominant theme of the exile poems is separation. Relegated to the margins of the Empire as punishment for *carmen et error* 'a poem and a misdemeanour' (*Trist.* 2.207), Ovid has been separated from wife, family, friends, readers – and from the city of Rome (*Trist.* 1.5.69–70). The exile poems – like the *Heroides* – are characterized by 'desper- ation, longing, self-deception and resistance to fate' (Rosenmeyer 1997:31).

In the *Heroides*, Ovid's Briseis is made to lament, eloquently, her own deficien- cies in writing Greek in her 'barbarian hand'(*Her.* 3.1–3). We might see an echo of this in the poet's own complaints that, isolated in his remote place of exile, he is forgetting Latin and losing his literary powers (*Ex Pont.* 4.13). As Rosenmeyer (1997) has argued, Ovid's invocation of mythological comparisons can some- times seem to problematize his own status as a 'real' exile. Recent scholarship has also emphasized other artful features of the exile poetry; the literary pedigree of Ovid's account of savage Tomis has been teased out by Williams (1994: 7–49). Ovid's exile poetry is characterized by some slippery role-playing. At times he ventriloquizes the role of the abandoned heroine, at times that of the epic hero. But his choice of the letter form, as Rosenmeyer emphasizes, allows him 'the freedom to write himself into being over and over again' (1997:31).

5   Seneca

Seneca's *Letters to Lucilius* (of which the first 124 survive) certainly need to be seen in the context of the Greek tradition of philosophical letter-writing. Indeed this tradition is specifically evoked by Seneca's frequent quotations from Epi- curus, particularly in the earlier letters in the collection. While some scholars have wanted to see the letters as genuine correspondence (sent to Lucilius and re- sponding to letters received from Lucilius), most now agree that the letters make more sense viewed as a philosophical project, addressed to a specific recipient but written with an 'external reader' in mind. Seneca explicitly envisages himself as writing for posterity (8.2; 21.4). While Seneca's *Letters* are often presented as responses to letters from Lucilius, or else as sparked by specific incidents, it is rarely possible to locate them in time. There are almost no references in the letters to matters that require explanation to be intelligible to the external reader.

Yet this is not to say that their epistolary status does not matter. Wilson (2001) has recently argued against the tendency of some scholars to treat the letters as essays in disguise, though he concedes that their form was to have an influence on the subsequent development of the philosophical essay. Rather the epistolary mode allows Seneca an important degree of fluidity. As Wilson comments,

'Each new epistle resituates the author differently in a new time, a new mood, sometimes in a new place' (2001:167).

The letters as a sequence allow Seneca to chart the philosophical progress of his pupil (though the 'pupil' Lucilius is not much younger than Seneca himself and has served as an equestrian procurator). This is a particular focus of the earlier letters in the collection. Letter 5, for instance, praises Lucilius for his commitment to self-improvement, while Letter 34 begins, 'I grow in spirit, jump for joy and, throwing off old age, grow warm again, when I get a sense from what you do and what you write of how far you have outdone yourself – for you surpassed the common herd long ago.' A degree of eclecticism in the earlier letters (which, as has been noted, often draw on Epicurus) is succeeded in the later ones by a more sustained engagement with increasingly complex aspects of Stoic thought. A number of philosophical themes run through the letters. These include the brevity of human life, the nature of Stoic *ratio*, the irrelevance of worldly goods, the advisability of suicide, the endurance of pain. Topics are raised in one letter, to be revisited, perhaps from a different angle, later in the collection. Seneca includes letters on what might appear to be more conventional epistolary themes, such as consolation to the bereaved, though with a distinctive twist (*Ep.* 63, 99).

While Seneca draws on the Greek tradition of the philosophical letter, he also plays with the Roman literary tradition, most particularly Cicero, with whose correspondence he compares – and contrasts – his own. Indeed Wilson surmises that it may well have been the 'publication' of Cicero's letters to Atticus that offered Seneca immediate inspiration for a collection of letters addressed to a single correspondent (Wilson 2001: 186). Letter 21.4 boasts that Seneca's *Letters to Lucilius* will bring Lucilius as much fame as Cicero's letters brought Atticus (it is tempting to see a certain irony here, as Seneca elsewhere deprecates the desirability of worldly fame). Letter 118 offers a more explicitly critical response to Cicero's legacy, suggesting a contrast between the political news and gossip exchanged by Cicero and Atticus and the more significant concerns of his own correspondence:

> it is better to deal with one's own troubles rather than those of other people – to scrutinize oneself, see for how many pointless things one is a candidate and not vote for any of them. This, my dear Lucilius, is a noble thing – to canvass for nothing, and to pass by all fortune's elections.

Thus Roman public life, the primary concern of Cicero's letters, the context in which and from which the Ciceronian persona takes its meaning, is transformed into a vocabulary of image and metaphor through which the would-be philosopher's inner life can be articulated.

Other letters, too, evoke an intimacy between author and addressee, which seems to echo that between Cicero and Atticus. Letter 40 begins by thanking

Lucilius for his frequent letters: *numquam epistulam tuam accipio, ut non proti-nus una simus* (I never receive a letter from you without at once being in your company). Letter 46 praises a work written by Lucilius in the warmest terms. Letter 49 begins by describing how a visit to Campania, and particularly Naples and Puteoli, reminded him of his absent friend:

> they struck me with an amazingly fresh sense of longing for you (*desiderium tui*). You stand right in front of my eyes. I am just about to leave you. I see you choking back your tears and failing to resist the emotions that well up inside you, as you try to control them.

But this vividly personal picture is swiftly subsumed to a more philosophical purpose, a reminder of the shortness of life and the consequent need to dispense with dialectical trivia in order to concentrate on coming to terms with the fear of death.

Seneca's letters tell the reader remarkably little about Seneca's life. Details that may appear autobiographical invariably serve a philosophical purpose and should hardly be relied on for their accuracy. At the same time, the letter's capacity to disclose the inner self of its author is something Seneca exploits, indeed subverts. Here he perhaps comes closer to Horace's *Epistles* than to those of Cicero (see Wilson 2001: 187). Seneca writes of himself as undergoing constant transform-ation; Letter 6 begins, *Intellego, Lucili, non emendari me tantum sed transfigur-ari* (I sense, my dear Lucilius, that I am being not just reformed but transformed). Seneca in his letters slips incessantly from one persona to another. Certainly Cicero to some degree switches between personae in his correspond-ence. But Seneca's mobility, his self-conscious exploration of the disjunctions between different possible selves, perhaps comes closer to that of the epistolary Ovid (Edwards 1997).

6 Pliny the Younger

The Younger Pliny's letters, written a few decades after those of Seneca, show little obvious engagement with Seneca's treatment of the epistolary form (though for a suggestive comparison between the two authors see Henderson 2002: 24–30). Cicero, however, rapidly emerges as a significant model. The first nine books of the Younger Pliny's correspondence are generally agreed to have been assem-bled by Pliny himself, while Book 10, dating from his time as governor of Bithynia, seems to have been published posthumously. Pliny's decision to collect his own correspondence for publication was most likely influenced by the prece-dent of Cicero. In Pliny's case, the actual composition of the letters themselves (as we have them, at least) seems to have been conditioned by the prospect of publication.

The artistry with which the letters are arranged has recently been highlighted. The first letter, evidently written well after the rest of the letters in Book 1, serves as a programmatic introduction: 'You have frequently encouraged me to make a selection of my letters and publish them (if there are any written with a greater degree of polish)' (1.1). While the order of the letters tends to be roughly chronological, it sometimes appears that the sequence has been altered to ensure that a good range of topics is covered in different books (Murgia 1985: 195–6). The opening letters of Book 1, in particular, can be seen as offering a thematic showcase of the topics to be covered by the collection (Hoffer 1999: 4). The first letter of Book 9 intended as the final book by Pliny, Murgia argues (1985: 198–9), offers a mirror image of the wording of Book 1's opening letter.

Literary allusion characterizes numerous letters. Septicius Clarus, to whom the programmatic first letter in the collection was addressed, is also the addressee of letter 1.15, which chastises him for failing to come to dinner at Pliny's house. This letter, which contrasts the refined but frugal entertainment to be had at Pliny's with the debauched evening Septicius allegedly enjoyed elsewhere engages with a complex literary tradition of invitation poems (Gowers 1993a: 267–79).

A telling indication that the letters as we have them were written for publication is the fact that, as in the case of Seneca's letters, so little of their content requires any additional explanation. Phrases seem to have been added to letters to make clear for the general reader something that would have been known to the addressee (Murgia 1985: 196). At the same time, individual letters acquire greater significance when they are read in conjunction with others in the collection. Letter 4.2, which records the death of Regulus' son (and Regulus' inappropriately extravagant gestures of mourning), adds a bitter irony to the earlier letter (2.20.5), which documented Regulus' false oaths on his son's life. Pliny never explicitly claims his letters are unrevised but the epistolary framework of greeting, message apparently generated at a particular point in time and farewell works to imply their authenticity (Hoffer 1999:9).

Pliny's career had flourished under Domitian (though his letters make no reference to the treasury position, known only from inscriptions, which he held in Domitian's last years). His 'private' correspondence, published later in less troubled times, was perhaps especially useful to underline the propriety of Pliny's behaviour – and views – in the problematic years of Domitian's reign (as Hoffer emphasizes, 1999:8, 90–1). A number of letters (e.g. 1.4; 9.13.4–5) serve to emphasize Pliny's links with those, such as Helvidius Priscus, who had opposed Domitian.

Pliny's letters can be read as offering a systematic self-portrait of their author. The emphasis is not, however, on Pliny's inner life but rather on the exemplary manner in which he fulfils a range of social and political roles. Through his letters he appears as leading orator, the friend of other leading senators, patron of the deserving, a philanthropist (note, for instance, his donations to Comum, 1.8), a landowner, man of refinement – and husband. As Veyne comments, 'the letters are and are meant to be a handbook for the perfect Roman senator' (1980: 9). The glowing endorsements offered by his peers (and others, including, of course, the emperor) serve as the prime index of his achievements.

Cicero is cited as Pliny's model both as a letter-writer and, in a number of other respects too, particularly as a leading orator (1.2; 1.5.12; 9.26). Both Pliny himself and, it seems, his correspondents, frequently draw comparisons between the two men (4.8.4–5; 9.2.2–3). Even the views Pliny expresses on oratorical style closely resemble those expressed by Cicero (Riggsby 1995: 128–9). Pliny also presents himself as an author of poetry. He recounts a number of occasions on which he has read examples of his compositions to friends, soliciting their advice on how his work might be improved (4.14, 5.3). Pliny and his friends exchange their writings asking for criticism – but receiving praise (Hoffer 1999:108). Pliny's verse is apparently erotic in content and lyric and elegiac in form. His engagement with the poetry of Catullus has been the subject of several recent studies (Gunderson 1997; Riggsby 1998; and Roller 1998). Ultimately, it is still Cicero who serves as his authority (Pliny cites the erotic epigram he addressed to his freedman Tiro, 7.4), guaranteeing that here as elsewhere Pliny has succeeded in balancing the competing demands made on the 'perfect senator'.

Pliny's portraits of others, most particularly the elderly senator Vestricius Spurinna and the emperor Trajan himself, can also be seen as reflections of Pliny's self-image, as Henderson has recently argued (2002). Vestricius Spurinna, now retired after a high-flying career of public service, seems to offer us a vision of the future Pliny (*Ep.* 3.1; Henderson 2002: 58–66). Pliny's *Panegyric* of Trajan is a subject returned to repeatedly in the *Letters* (e.g. 3.13; 3.18). Who but the perfect senator can compose appropriate words to praise the perfect emperor? And only under such an emperor can letters such as Pliny's, preserving an image of public life at its best, be written (3.20.12; Henderson 2002:141–5).

As in the case of Cicero's correspondence, Pliny's letters are addressed to a large number of different individuals. As Riggsby comments, 'The rhetorical force of many of the letters depends on the reader's assumption ... that they are directed at the addressee' (1995:131). This is perhaps particularly clear in the case of the historian Tacitus, the most distinguished of Pliny's addressees (bar the emperor), and the recipient of eleven letters – more than anyone else in Books 1–9. Tacitus' *Dialogus* is echoed in 1.6 and 9.10 (Murgia 1985). The nature of friendship is explored in Pliny's letters but rarely seems to be a source of pain or anxiety. Indeed, despite the fact that the letter is predicated on the separation of author and addressee, separation itself is rarely an issue in Pliny's letters (though it is a source of complaint in his letters to his wife; e.g. 6.4). Rather through their correspondence he and his friends serve to reflect and reinforce one another's public images. Pliny's main concern, for instance, in discussing the nature of his relationship with Tacitus is the way other people bracket them together and compare them (7.20). The self presented by Pliny in his letters is clearly constructed for public consumption; the analogy with a public monument, explored by Henderson (2002), is especially apt. In contrast to the other authors discussed here, Pliny alone, it seems, is never reduced to the extremity of questioning his identity.

7 Conclusion

Composed a few years before those of Pliny, verse letters are to be found among the poems of Martial and Statius. The form is especially favoured for dedicatory opening poems (e.g. Statius *Silvae* 4.1). Prose letters dating from the middle years of the second century written by Marcus Cornelius Fronto, tutor to Marcus Aurelius, were rediscovered in the nineteenth century. These letters, full of expressions of affection and references to the family life of the Antonines, seem not to have been intended for publication and have met with a cool critical reception (Champlin 1974). Letter-writing of all kinds appears to have been popular among Christian writers (the letter form is used extensively in the New Testament). Some important collections have survived, including from later centuries, those of Ambrose, Jerome and Augustine.

Poets, statesmen and proselytizers exploited the letter form in Roman antiquity to generate a host of authorial personae ranging from the slickly homogeneous Pliny to the self-consciously fragmented Seneca. No matter how artfully composed, letters tend to give their readers the sense of having direct access to the author's real feelings. The circulation in antiquity of letters that were evidently fictional suggests some ancient readers, at least, may have been alert to the fictive nature even of such a plausible epistolary self as that of Cicero.

FURTHER READING

Recent decades have seen some important theoretical work on epistolarity, largely focusing on epistolary novels of the eighteenth century but with a bearing on and some discussion of the epistolary form more generally (Altman 1982; Kauffman 1986 and 1992). While Cicero's correspondence has been exhaustively mined by historians of late republican politics, little helpful work has appeared on Cicero's strategies of self-fashioning in these texts (a possible model here from another historical period could be the influential study of Sir Thomas More's self-construction by Greenblatt 1980). Horace's exploitation of the epistolary form is effectively explored by Oliensis (1998) and, in more detail, de Pretis (2002). Ovid's *Heroides* have been the subject of some insightful recent studies by Kennedy (1984 and 2002), Barchiesi (1993b), Hinds (1993) and Farrell (1998). Rosenmeyer (1997) suggestively compares the *Heroides* and the exile poetry in terms of their use of epistolary form, while the literary strategies deployed in the exile poetry have also been effectively discussed by Nagle (1980), Hinds (1985) and Williams (1994 and 2002). The literary dynamics of Seneca's letters have recently been the focus of renewed critical attention (see particularly the work of Wilson, e.g. 2001, and Edwards 1997). Much excellent work has appeared in the last few years on the construction of the authorial self in Pliny's letters. See Gunderson (1997), Riggsby (1995 and 1998), Roller (1998) and, above all, Henderson (2002).

PART III

Themes

CHAPTER TWENTY

Decline and Nostalgia

Stephen Harrison

1 Introduction

From the late Republic onwards, Roman writers often spoke of the present as corrupt, and of Rome's past as a prelapsarian golden age; at least in their high literature, the inhabitants of the imperial metropolis looked back with some nostalgia to the supposedly pristine morals and lifestyle of the early Republic, and Rome's imagined beginnings as a primitively virtuous rustic community. Decline was often thought to have started when in the second century BC Rome came into closer contact through conquest and cultural exchange with the larger and more 'corrupt' world of the Mediterranean. Paradoxically, this was often accompanied by a recognition of vast material progress, of extraordinary cultural advances through contact with the Greeks, and of a remarkable ascent to international hegemony. But even in its most triumphalist moments, post-Republican Roman culture could still think of itself as morally inferior to the values of its ancestors, the conservative *mos maiorum* (ancestral custom). The purpose of this chapter is to explore in a little detail the representations of this complex of ideas in literary texts.

2 Decline, Expansion and Civil War

Ideas of national decline seem to emerge after the end of the Republic in the civil wars of the first century BC (for the period see Levene, Chapter 2 above, and Farrell, Chapter 3 above). The historians of the late Republican and triumviral periods suggested several crucial dates for the onset of decline, all in the second century BC when Rome conquered large areas of the Mediterranean. Livy (39.6.7) reports the version that Rome was first corrupted by the luxurious booty brought back from Asia by the victorious army of Manlius Vulso in 187 BC, and represents the elder Cato as stressing as early as 195 BC that increased prosperity and luxury through expansion into Greece and Asia is weakening the moral strength of the Republic (34.2.1–2); even the embassy to Rome of the two Greek philosophers Carneades and Diogenes the Stoic in 155 BC, a landmark in Roman Hellenism, was seen by Cato at the end of his life as a symptom of the corruption of old Roman values through contact with Greek culture (Plutarch *Cato* 49–50). The Greek historian Polybius, writing in second century BC Rome with extensive contact with the Roman elite, makes an explicit link between Roman world domination after the defeat of Greece in 168 BC and moral decline (31.25.3ff.), while his younger contemporary the Roman annalist Piso identified 154 BC as the beginning of the rot, pointing to the portent of the destruction by a storm of a fig-tree in the national temple of Jupiter Capitolinus (Pliny *NH* 17.244).

The most notable expression of these ideas in literature is perhaps in Sallust's *Catiline* 10–13, where (writing in the 40s BC) he lays out the decline of Rome as a background for Catiline's depravity in the 60s, constructing a two-stage process, the beginnings of ambition for power and the beginnings of material greed. The first stage is the final defeat and destruction of Carthage by Rome at the end of the Third Punic War in 146 BC: as Sallust puts it:

> but after the state had grown through hard work and just behaviour, great kings had been conquered in war, fierce tribes and mightly peoples had been overcome by force, Carthage, Rome's rival for overall power, had perished root and all, and all the seas and lands lay open to Rome, Fortune began to be cruel and to throw everything into confusion. Those who had easily endured tribulations, dangers, unstable and difficult circumstances found leisure and riches, desirable in another context, a burden and a misery. And so desire for power grew, and then desire for money; that was the raw material of all Rome's misfortunes. For greed overturns loyalty, honesty and all the other good qualities, and teaches instead pride, cruelty, neglect of the gods, and to think that everything has its price. (*Catiline* 10.1–2)

This was very influential; 146 BC was the date most favoured by subsequent historians as the beginning of Roman decline (e.g. Velleius 2.11; Florus 1.33.1; cf. Augustine *Civ.* 1.30), and the defeat of Rome's last great rival for international hegemony at a time of rapid and luxurious Hellenization is a natural candidate. But Sallust's second stage is much later, the return of Sulla from the East in 84 BC, which he sees as the origin of modern avarice. The corruption of Sulla's army in the fleshpots of the East through the un-Roman indulgence of their commander is linked with their close personal loyalty to him that allowed him to use them in his invasion of Italy, thus suggesting a direct causal connection not just with the decline of Roman morals but also with the downfall of the Republic:

> Lucius Sulla had treated the army which he had commanded in Asia with an extravagant indulgence and excessive laxity which contravened the practice of our ancestors, in order to render it loyal to himself. Beautiful locations and places of

pleasure had easily softened the fierce spirit of the soldiers in time of peace. There it was that the army of the Roman state first learnt to whore, drink and admire statues, paintings and engraved vessels, to appropriate the latter on an individual and collective scale, to despoil shrines and pollute all areas both sacred and profane. (*Catiline* 11.5–6)

Note how the fine arts of Greek culture are on the same level as other more physical temptations, all portrayed as turning the manly Roman from his proper warlike activities, and corrupting his natural tendency to ascetic virtue.

In the last decades of the Republic, ethical decline is also a common theme in poetry. Catullus' long epyllion, poem 64, presents a vigorous indictment of morals towards its end:

> sed postquam tellus scelere est imbuta nefando
> iustitiamque omnes cupida de mente fugarunt,
> perfudere manus fraterno sanguine fratres,
> destitit extinctos gnatus lugere parentes,
> optauit genitor primaeui funera nati,
> liber ut innuptae poteretur flore nouercae,
> ignaro mater substernens se impia nato
> impia non uerita est diuos scelerare penates.
> omnia fanda nefanda malo permixta furore
> iustificam nobis mentem auertere deorum.

> But after Earth was stained with crime unspeakable
> And all evicted Justice from their greedy thoughts,
> Brothers poured the blood of brothers on their hands,
> Sons no longer grieved when parents passed away,
> Father prayed for death of son in his first youth
> So as freely to possess the bloom of a new bride,
> Mother, lying impiously with ignorant son,
> Dared impiously to sin against divine Penates,
> Our evil madness by confounding fair with foul,
> Has turned away from us the Gods' forgiving thoughts.
> (Catullus 64.397–408, trans. Lee 1990)

Though many of the more spectacular vices here (fratricide, incest) echo the world of heroic myth in which the poem is set rather than contemporary society, it is not surprising that this passage is written in the dying decades of the Roman Republic, perhaps even as late as the 40s BC. Though Catullus' datable poems belong to the 50s, there is no reason why he should not have lived into the 40s, since the only ancient evidence on his life (Jerome) suggests that he died in 58 BC, before datable allusions in the poems (see Wiseman 1985: 189–91); the main location of the poem is in fact Pharsalus, scene of the decisive battle between Caesar and Pompey in 48 BC.

A more philosophical view of Roman ethical anxiety in this period is to be found in Catullus' contemporary Lucretius. He strikingly describes a modern Roman, unable to escape from the material concerns of life, travelling between his multiple homes in the ancient equivalent of a sports car:

> ut nunc plerumque videmus
> quid sibi quisque velit nescire et quaerere semper,
> commutare locum, quasi onus deponere possit.
> exit saepe foras magnis ex aedibus ille,
> esse domi quem pertaesumst, subitoque revertit,
> quippe foris nihilo melius qui sentiat esse.
> currit agens mannos ad villam praecipitanter
> auxilium tectis quasi ferre ardentibus instans;
> oscitat extemplo, tetigit cum limina villae,
> aut abit in somnum gravis atque oblivia quaerit,
> aut etiam properans urbem petit atque revisit.

Just as now we generally see them do, each ignorant what he wants, each seeking always to change his place as if he could drop his burden. The man who has been bored to death at home often goes forth from his great mansion, and then suddenly returns because he feels himself no better abroad. Off he courses, driving his Gallic ponies to his country house in headlong haste, as if he were bringing urgent help to a house on fire. The moment he has reached the threshold of the house, he yawns, or falls into heavy sleep and seeks oblivion, or even makes haste to get back and see the city again.

(Lucretius 3.1057–67, trans. M. F. Smith 1975)

This is an eerily modern view of an affluent society without an ethical direction, presenting material wealth and mental poverty.

In the 30s BC we find poetry responding directly to the moral crisis of the civil wars, now in their last phase. Horace's *Epodes*, published about 30, contain two poems, 7 and 16, that can be plausibly seen as belonging to the early 30s and the renewal of civil war against Sextus Pompey (Nisbet 1984). *Epode* 16, after claiming that degenerate modern Romans are destroying their own country, undefeated by a whole host of past enemies from Porsenna to Spartacus, presents an ironic solution in a proposal of mass emigration to the mythical and paradisiacal Islands of the Blest, while *Epode* 7, similarly framed as an address to all Romans, interestingly reverses the normal idea of decline from initial virtue in claiming that Rome's internecine struggles derive from the foundational fratricide of Romulus:

> sic est: acerba fata Romanos agunt
>   scelusque fraternae necis,
> ut inmerentis fluxit in terram Remi
>   sacer nepotibus cruor.

> The case is made. It is harsh fate that drives
>   the Romans, and the crime of fratricide
> since Remus' blameless lifeblood poured upon the ground –
>   a curse to generations yet unborn.
>
>   (*Epode* 16.17–20, trans. D. West 1997)

The finale of the first book of Vergil's *Georgics*, reflecting the atmosphere of the mid-30s rather than of the poem's date of publication *circa* 29, ends with an apocalyptic vision of the civil wars, and sees the young Caesar (the future Augustus) as a potential solution, but ends with a vivid picture of an anarchic world at war, with no guarantee that control will be re-restablished:

> hinc mouet Euphrates, illinc Germania bellum;
> uicinae ruptis inter se legibus urbes
> arma ferunt; saeuit toto Mars impius orbe,
> ut cum carceribus sese effudere quadrigae,
> addunt in spatia, et frustra retinacula tendens
> fertur equis auriga neque audit currus habenas.
>
> There the East is in arms, here Germany marches:
> Neighbour cities, breaking their treaties, attack each other:
> The wicked War-god runs amok through all the world.
> So, when racing chariots have rushed from the starting-gate,
> They gather speed on the course, and the driver tugs at the curb-rein
> – his horses runaway, car out of control, quite helpless.
>
>   (*Georgics* 509–14, trans. Day Lewis, 1940/1983)

The civil war has moved to total conflict at global level, with accompanying further fear and anxiety about the future of Rome.

3   The Golden Age, Decadence and Nostalgic Primitivism

After Actium in 31 BC it could of course be claimed that control had been re-established by Augustus as 'charioteer', and even that the Golden Age had returned. In a post-Actium passage in the *Georgics*, praising Italy, Vergil describes Italy as a modern paradise (2.136–76), flowing with gold (2.166), and the idea that the Golden Age has now returned is a key feature of Augustan art and literature, no doubt stimulated from the top (Galinsky 1996: 90–120). This idea of the Golden Age is associated with the figure of Augustus, his bringing of domestic peace and morality, and his pacification through conquest of the larger world, and can be seen in two typical passages. The first is from Vergil's *Aeneid*, where Aeneas' father Anchises waxes lyrical on seeing the future Augustus in the Underworld, ready to enter life:

> hic uir, hic est, tibi quem promitti saepius audis,
> Augustus Caesar, diui genus, aurea condet
> saecula qui rursus Latio regnata per arua
> Saturno quondam, super et Garamantas et Indos
> proferet imperium.

This is the man, this is he, whom you hear so often promised to you, Augustus Caesar, stock of the gods; he will again found a Golden Age through the fields long ago ruled by Saturn, and will carry his power beyond the Garamantes and Indians.

(*Aeneid* 6.791–5)

The last of Horace's *Odes*, though not using the idea of gold, makes much the same points, responding to the particular propaganda context after the *Ludi Saeculares* of 17 BC, technically proclaiming the coming of a new age:

> tua, Caesar, aetas
> fruges et agris rettulit uberes
> et signa nostro restituit Ioui
> derepta Parthorum superbis
> postibus et uacuum duellis
> Ianum Quirini clausit et ordinem
> rectum euaganti frena licentiae
> iniecit emouitque culpas
> et ueteres reuocauit artes
> per quas Latinum nomen et Italae
> creuere uires famaque et imperi
> porrecta maiestas ad ortus
> solis ab Hesperio cubili.

Your age, Caesar, has brought lush crops back to the fields and restored to our Jupiter the standards ripped from the proud doorposts of the Parthians, and has closed the temple of Janus Quirinus, free from war, has imposed right order as a curb on wandering self-indulgence, has removed our guilt, and revived the character of old through which the Latin peoples and the power of Italy grew, and the majesty of our dominion was stretched out from the western bed of the sun to his eastern rising.

(*Odes* 4.15.4–16)

Peace and plenty at home, suppression of enemies abroad, and the ethical renewal of Rome through Augustan moral legislation and the propaganda festival of the *Ludi Saeculares* suggest that Rome is re-achieving the political and moral status it has lost through decades of civil war.

But peace has its anxieties no less than war, and Republican Roman worries about the corrupting effects of world conquest, material luxury and self-indulgence on its citizens continue well into the Augustan age. Livy, for example, in the preface to the first pentad of his history, which is likely to date from the 20s BC (for the dating and a full discussion see Moles 1993), suggests that Rome, having expanded so much over the years, is struggling under its own size (*praef.* 4), picking up a point made by Horace in the 30s (*Epodes* 16.2), and in particular that the reader can see that the moral decline of Romans since the virtuous early Republic has hastened in his own time:

> labente deinde paulatim disciplina velut desidentes primo mores sequatur animo, deinde ut magis magisque lapsi sint, tum ire coeperint praecipites, donec ad haec tempora quibus nec uitia nostra nec remedia pati possumus perventum est.

> Then let him follow in his mind how (as it were) morals at first subsided as self-discipline began to slip, and then how they fell further and further, and then began to rush headlong down, until we have arrived at this time of ours in which we can endure neither our own vices nor their remedies. (*praef.* 9)

The vices are then defined as *avaritia* and *luxuria* (*praef.* 11), brought on by acquisition of wealth and territorial possessions: in the old days, Livy pithily states (*praef.* 12), *quanto rerum minus, tanto minus cupiditatis erat* (fewer possessions meant less greed).

Similar concerns with the negative aspects of affluence and success are to be found in some of the most 'Augustan' writing of the same period, the Roman Odes (*Odes* 3.1–6) of Horace, published *circa* 23 BC. The first of these poems, which use a prophetic persona and an often obscure oracular style to comment on the major issues of contemporary Rome, climaxes by condemning the vanity of luxurious building (3.1.33–48), and the third presents Rome as ideally leaving gold in the ground rather than mining it to its own moral loss (3.3.49–52), but full moral weight is reserved for the sixth poem. Here the poet castigates contemporary citizens in a dark and detailed vision of contemporary vices, a vision surely connected with Augustan religious and moral reforms, looking back to pre-Actium civil wars as the cause of modern degeneracy:

> Fecunda culpae saecula nuptias
> primum inquinauere et genus et domos:
>   hoc fonte deriuata clades
>   in patriam populumque fluxit.

> These ages, fertile in crime, first stained marriage, family and households; from this spring flowed the disaster which poured upon our country and people.
>   (*Odes* 3.6.17–20)

After cataloguing modes of adultery, the poem concludes with an unrelievedly negative climax:

Non his iuuentus orta parentibus
infecit aequor sanguine Punico
    Pyrrhumque et ingentem cecidit
      Antiochum Hannibalemque dirum;

sed rusticorum mascula militum
proles, Sabellis docta ligonibus
    uersare glaebas et seuerae
      matris ad arbitrium recisos

portare fustis, sol ubi montium
mutaret umbras et iuga demeret
    bobus fatigatis, amicum
      tempus agens abeunte curru.

Damnosa quid non inminuit dies?
aetas parentum, peior auis, tulit
    nos nequiores, mox daturos
      progeniem uitiosiorem.

Not such were the parents of the army which stained the sea with Punic blood, and
laid low Pyrrhus, great Antiochus and the accursed Hannibal; but they were the
manly issue of peasant soldiers, well versed in turning the soil with Sabine mattocks
and carrying sticks cut to the will of a severe mother, when the sun changed the
shadows cast by the mountains and unharnessed the yokes from tired oxen, bringing
on the kindly time of rest with its departing chariot. What has time which brings only
loss not diminished? The age of our parents, worse than our grandparents, brought
forth us, more wicked, set in due course to spawn an even more vicious stock.

(*Odes* 3.6.32–48)

Decadent, cosmopolitan contemporary Romans are morally inferior to their
virtuous peasant ancestors, who lived a pure, bucolic life, and are doomed to go
on getting worse – unless, the poet implies, they mend their ways by avoiding the
kind of behaviour castigated in this poem.

These lines gather together many of the images concerned with Roman decline
and nostalgia. The material corruption and moral decadence of Rome since the
glory days of the Punic Wars, the idealizing picture of their simple Italian
ancestors, and a warning that Rome will continue to get worse without correction
all seem to be elements that appeal at a fundamental level to the anxieties of
Roman self-perception.

As just evidenced, the Latin literature of the Augustan age is often concerned
with the contrast between primitive and modern Rome. This contrast is often
articulated through the presentation of the city itself, above all in the eighth book
of Vergil's *Aeneid*, where Aeneas visits Pallanteum, a primitive village built on what
will become the site of Rome, and is guided by its king Evander around the
locations of future city landmarks, identified in the omniscient voice of the narrator; the Capitol, the ideological heart of the city, is merely a hill covered with scrub:

> hinc ad Tarpeiam sedem et Capitolia ducit,
> aurea nunc, olim silvestribus horrida dumis.

From here he leads him to the Tarpeian seat and the Capitol, now golden, but once bristling with woody thorn-bushes.

(*Aeneid* 8.348–9)

This interest in the primitive landscape of Rome, providing a firm contrast between then and now, naturally lent itself to the Callimachean framework of aetiology, concerned to seek the distant and preferable primitive origins of contemporary institutions. It is in this spirit that it is deployed by Propertius, who begins his fourth book with a tourist-type monologue on the past of Rome, which obviously owes much to Evander's guided tour for Aeneas:

> Hoc quodcumque vides, hospes, qua maxima Romast,
>   ante Phrygem Aenean collis et herba fuit;
> atque ubi Navali stant sacra Palatia Phoebo,
>   Euandri profugae procubuere boves.

All the region you see, guest, where mighty Rome now is, was hills and grass before Trojan Aeneas; and where the Palatine stands, sacred to naval Apollo, the refugee cattle of Evander lay down.

(Propertius 4.1.1–4)

The moral simplicity of those early times is also stressed in the poem (4.1.37–8): Romans then had no wealth apart from their names, and could not be pretentious about their ancestry when 'descended' from a she-wolf (the famous wet-nurse of Romulus and Remus). The book as a whole goes on to give explanations dating from early Rome or the legendary period for a range of features of modern Rome – the statue of Vertumnus (4.2), the Tarpeian rock (4.4), the Ara Maxima (4.9) and the temple of Jupiter Feretrius.

This Augustan romantic cult of the primitive, simple and virtuous past of the city of Rome is turned on its head with typical irreverence in a passage of Ovid, who rejoices in Rome's growth from a primitive village into a cosmopolis (*Ars* 3.113–34); he rejects the types of decadent affluence lamented by Horace, but only because these are subordinate to urban civilzation in general, which far surpasses old-fashioned peasant culture:

> Prisca iuvent alios: ego me nunc denique natum
>   Gratulor: haec aetas moribus apta meis.
> Non quia nunc terrae lentum subducitur aurum,
>   Lectaque diverso litore concha venit:
> Nec quia decrescunt effosso marmore montes,
>   Nec quia caeruleae mole fugantur aquae:

> Sed quia cultus adest, nec nostros mansit in annos
> Rusticitas, priscis illa superstes avis.

Let others take pleasure in the old; I congratulate myself for being born in this late time, and this age is suitable for my ways. This is not because now pliant gold is mined from the earth, or because the conch-shell comes gathered from a far-off shore, or because mountains are shrinking with the digging-out of marble, or because blue waters are displaced by building piles, but because civilization is now here, and peasant ways have not lasted up to our times, surviving from our ancestors of old.

(*Ars* 3.121–8)

But even Ovid felt the need to subscribe to this cult in his elegiac *Fasti*, a later poem partly aimed (like the elegiac Propertius 4) at learned Callimachean exegesis of Roman phenomena, in this case the festivals of the newly revised religious calendar, and obligingly provides a range of explanatory stories from primitive and heroic times (see Gale Chapter 7 above, and Gibson Chapter 11 above).

4   Imperial Decline

For authors writing under the empire, especially authors who had experienced tyrannical emperors, there was a strong temptation to idealize the Republican past by contrast with the Imperial present. This is certainly a key element in Lucan's *Bellum Civile*, written under Nero, on the civil war between Caesar and Pompey (see further Hardie, Chapter 6), which laments the passing of Republican freedom and its replacement by slavery to the Caesars: Lucan talks strikingly of the perpetual gladiatorial contest between freedom and Caesar (7.695–6 *sed par quod semper habemus, / libertas et Caesar* (the gladiatorial pair we always have, freedom and Caesar). In the poem Pompey is the most sympathetic character, though he in some sense represents in his own role the decline of Republican virtue; Cato, though proclaimed as the exemplar of ancestral and Stoic values (cf. 2.380–91), seems at times surreally and obsessively severe, but is still more attractive than the daemonically evil Caesar (cf. e.g. 7.786–99). Naturally enough in a poem on this topic, the Roman talent for self-destruction and propensity to decline is stressed: in a stretch of the poem that describes the causes of the war, the poet virtually versifies the kinds of concerns found in Livy and Sallust about Rome's incapacity to deal with its own growth (1.71–2 *nimioque graves sub pondere lapsus, / nec se Roma ferens*, 'and terrible falls under an excessive weight, and Rome unable to support herself').

Similar concerns are found in the works of Tacitus, who in his *Annals* and *Histories* set out the foibles and tyrannies of Roman emperors from the death of Augustus to that of Domitian. A famous passage of the *Histories*, stimulated by the civil war for imperial power between Otho and Vitellius, connects wealth, world dominance and autocracy as the causes of Roman decline and internecine strife, bringing together a number of the themes we have already considered:

> the old ingrained human passion for power has matured and burst into prominence with the growth of the empire. With straiter resources equality was easily preserved. But when once we had brought the world to our feet and exterminated every rival state or king, we were left free to covet wealth without fear. It was then that strife first flared up between patricians and plebeians: at one time arose seditious tribunes, at another over-mighty consuls: in the Forum at Rome they had trial runs for civil war. Before long, Gaius Marius, rising from the lowest ranks of the people, and Lucius Sulla, the most cruel of all the nobles, crushed our liberty by force of arms and substituted a despotism. Then came Gnaeus Pompey, whose aims, though less patent, were no better. From that time on the one end sought was autocracy. (*Histories* 2.38, trans. Fyfe/Levene 1997)

Another connected aspect of perceived decline under the Empire was that of oratory: the advent of the emperor as supreme political and judicial arbiter naturally downgraded the function of senatorial and court-room oratory from its central importance in the late Republic (see Mayer, Chapter 4 above, and Berry, Chapter 18 above). This is the central topic of Tacitus' Ciceronian-style dialogue *Dialogus de Oratoribus*, probably published soon after the death of Domitian (96 AD), and of a number of other imperial texts (see conveniently Mayer 2001: 12–16). The character Maternus in the *Dialogus* seems to envisage a limited but effective role for oratory despite its agreed decline in importance under imperial rule, and although Quintilian wrote a (lost) work on corrupt features in contemporary oratory, his extant work on the training of the orator takes a positive view. The triteness and artificiality of declamation, the school-room practice oratory that grew massively in popularity and importance under the Empire, is an easy target in satirical writers such as Petronius and Juvenal (1.15–17); in Petronius the mediocre poet Eumolpus claims that declamation has led to the decline of poetry (*Sat.* 118), a view that has found strong echoes in modern criticism (though for objections see Williams (1978: 267–71)).

The dilution of Roman values through an increasingly diverse and fluid society is also a concern in imperial Latin literature; Petronius' vulgar millionaire Syrian freedman Trimalchio is a case in point (see Harrison, Chapter 15). The great bard of Roman xenophobia (see further Syed, Chapter 25 below) is Juvenal (see further Morgan, Chapter 12), whose satires (he claims) are partly motivated by the prosperity of socially mobile foreign freedmen at the expense of 'genuine' Romans:

> patricios omnis opibus cum prouocet unus
> quo tondente grauis iuueni mihi barba sonabat,
> cum pars Niliacae plebis, cum uerna Canopi

> Crispinus Tyrias umero reuocante lacernas
> uentilet aestiuum digitis sudantibus aurum
> nec sufferre queat maioris pondera gemmae,
> difficile est saturam non scribere.

> When a fellow who made my stiff young beard crunch with his clippers,
> can challenge the whole upper class with his millions, single-handed;
> when Crispinus, a blob of Nilotic scum, bred in Canopus,
> hitches a cloak of Tyrian purple onto his shoulder
> and flutters a simple ring of gold on his sweaty finger
> (in summer he cannot bear the weight of a heavy stone),
> it's hard *not* to write satire.
>   (Juvenal 1.24–30, trans. Rudd 1991)

In his third satire Juvenal's mouthpiece Umbricius attacks Greeks and (Greek-speaking) Syrians for ethnically 'polluting' Rome:

> non possum ferre, Quirites,
> Graecam urbem. quamuis quota portio faecis Achaei?
> iam pridem Syrus in Tiberim defluxit Orontes . . .

> My fellow Romans, I cannot put up with
> a city of Greeks; yet how much of the dregs is truly Achaean?
> The Syrian Orontes has long been discharging into the Tiber . . .
>   (Juvenal 3.60–2, trans. Rudd 1991)

All these ideas share the view that Rome is not what it was. In literary terms, the consciousness on the part of Latin authors of 'belatedness', that Roman imperial writing comes in a decadent period after the great literature of the Augustan period, is not uncommon (see especially Hardie 1993). Where Augustan writers claimed parity with or superiority to the Greek writers in their genres, writers of the Roman imperial period often looked back in deference to their established Latin predecessors from the Augustan age, and in one famous case actually proclaimed the inferiority of a work to its Augustan predecessor (see Gibson, Chapter 5, on the end of Statius' *Thebaid*). In the later second century, such ideas of belatedness and decadence led to a search for the past that went back before the Augustan period. Roman literary culture was to be renewed by returning to its roots; hence the archaizing movement, which sought to imitate the early Latin writers such as Plautus, Ennius and Cato (see also Chapter 5).

5 Conclusion

Roman anxieties about decline and decadence are a major theme in Latin literature from the late Republic on, stimulated especially by the decades of civil war that created some national psychological trauma, and by the contrast between the supposedly 'free' Republic and the monarchic control exercised under the empire after Augustus. The sense of ancestral values enshrined in the *mos maiorum*, and a general opposition to change (it is not for nothing that the Latin for 'revolution' is simply *res novae*; literally 'new things') tended to create an environment in which the past was viewed nostalgically as a golden age, and in which present decline and decadence was consequently inevitable. Attempts to invoke a new Golden Age (e.g. in the Augustan period) cut across this deep cultural value, and Romans were very aware of their success as an imperial, conquering culture; but often we find a sense of the moral values and simple life lost in becoming a rich, successful and diverse world-state. Such discomfort with material success and longing for a better past strikes interesting chords with the world of the twenty-first century, where globalization and prosperity can cause similar anxiety, and where similar longings for a simpler and less luxurious lifestyle can be found.

FURTHER READING

This chapter touches on some fundamental issues of Roman cultural values. There are many helpful books in this general area. Of older works Earl (1961) and Wilkinson (1975; more literary) both chart the history of Roman values from the beginning of Roman literature to the fall of the Western Empire (410). Hopkins (1978 and 1983) provides stimulating examinations of Roman attitudes to death and slavery, grounded in sociological models and telling detail; in the same tradition but more literary and nuanced is Edwards (1993), looking at Roman ideas of (im)morality in their cultural contexts. The two books of Carlin Barton provide striking and often fascinating perspectives on the anxieties of Roman elite psychology (1993) and the Roman sense of honour (2001). Some key areas are also well treated in Braund (2002).

For more particular topics, Gruen (1993) is especially helpful on the complexities of Roman Hellenism; on the Golden Age and other Augustan ideas see Wallace-Hadrill (1982) and Galinsky (1996), and for Roman ideas on primitivism see still Lovejoy and Boas (1935). On ideas of decline in imperial Roman literature see Williams (1978), and on the 'anxiety of influence' felt by post-Augustan poets see Hardie (1993). On the description of and attitudes to civil war in Latin literature the standard work and collection of material is still Jal (1963, French), though some of the essays in Henderson (1998a) are provocative and stimulating (see also the material on civil war in Barton 1993). On Roman attitudes to non-Romans see Balsdon (1979) and Veyne (1993), Syed in Chapter 25 below and Syed (forthcoming).

CHAPTER TWENTY-ONE

Art and Text

Jaś Elsner

1 Writing on Art: the Epigraphic Habit

The inclusion of an essay on art and text in this *Companion to Latin Literature* implies (on the editor's part, at least!) the proposition that the visual element is important for the writing of literary Latin. I should like to open, however, by briefly raising the reverse proposition, namely the importance of the written for visual culture. Most works of sculpture in the Roman world – whether portraits or dedications or funerary memorials – were accompanied by some kind of writing. So funerary altars had inscriptions, usually incised in a specially designated panel, while the lids of sarcophagi had an epitaph inscribed or sometimes painted in a framed section (perhaps flanked by erotes or other figures) at the centre (e.g. Koch and Sichtermann 1982: 25–77). Normally we think of the lower part of a sarcophagus as its most important element, with its large visual field, but arguably the inscription that defines the deceased's identity should make us give at least equal weight to the lid. Often the inscribed texts that survive on Roman monuments are simple, recording the dedicatee or donor or an artist's signature. Although art history has not given full recognition to the phenomenon, it is almost impossible to imagine Roman art without the epigraphic habit that accompanied it – helping to define objects for their patrons or viewers with something perhaps a little like a museum label today (figure 21.1). The text, including the style of the inscription's incised lettering and its language (whether Greek or Latin), functioned as a visual sign as well as a literary one – giving an enhanced dignity and an inscriptional monumentality even to relatively humble objects, as well as helping to determine their meanings.

This widespread inscriptional culture – in which the text functions *as* monument and as a visual supplement to artistic monuments – has deep roots in Greece, looking back for instance to the wonderfully vivid epigrams that accompanied archaic free-standing figure-sculpture, to the tribute and treasury lists

Figure 21.1 Funerary altar of Aulus Servilius Paulianus and Aulus Servilius Paulinus with portrait busts and inscription. Provenance unknown but certainly Italy. Marble. *c.* AD 165. The epigraph tells us that this altar was erected by their parents, Aulus Servilius Aesopus and Servilia Verecunda, for two brothers who died at different times but both at the age of 30. Now in the Vatican. Photograph: DAI, Rome. Inst. Neg. 30.633

erected in temples, to the great variety of inscribed votives and dedications in such Panhellenic sanctuaries as Olympia (e.g. Robert 1989; Millar 1983). Just as some inscriptions were simple and in prose, others were more complex – poems brief and lengthy, of all kinds and of all literary levels. Just as art history has failed to do justice to the textuality of Roman monumental culture, so literary studies have systematically ignored (or at best underestimated) the monumental nature of inscribed texts as fundamentally different in genre from their brethren on pa-pyrus-rolls or writing-tablets. For they are designed to be read in very different kinds of contexts, with significantly different experiential frames envisaged for the reader (e.g. on response, Woolf 1996: 25–34). Rarely are collections of such texts published with photographs of the whole monument or of the images that accompanied the writing in its original form (e.g. Courtney 1995; for an explicit call to consider the visual, see Sanders 1991: 87–110).

Yet clearly the challenge to produce elegant verses for monumental contexts exercised the finest Roman poets from the beginnings of Latin literature (Massaro 1992: 3–61). We find epigrams (among the first elegiac couplets composed in Latin) ascribed to Ennius in the early second century BC – which, even if they may be impugned as spurious by some modern authorities, were certainly thought authentic by Cicero and Seneca. For example, Ennius' epigram on himself was clearly designed to go alongside an image – perhaps a painting, statue or bust:

> Aspicite, o cives, senis Enni imaginis formam.
>   Hic vestrum panxit maxima facta patrum.

> Look, citizens, on the portrait of Ennius in old age.
> It was he that composed the great deeds of your fathers.
>   (Courtney 1993: 42–3, no. 45)

Like the best verse in this necessarily terse (indeed ultimately lapidary) genre, this poem overturns the assumptions it initially sets up. The old age of the poet turns out to be not a sign of decrepitude, but rather of his grandeur since he is the one who sang of the still older ancestors, in a Republican culture deeply embedded in the values of the *maiores*. Ennius the image and the object of the gaze becomes Ennius the artist and composer of images of ancestral deeds in the second line. A second Ennian epigram, on Scipio Africanus (who died in 183 BC) – restored from two citations in Cicero – may well not have been carved on the great man's tomb but was written as though it were. It indicates the way that the monumental quality implicit in carved inscriptions could be appropriated into non-epigraphic poetry:

> Hic est ille situs cui nemo civis neque hostis
>   quivit pro factis reddere opis pretium

> Here lies the man to whom no one, fellow countryman or foe,
> can make due return for his services.
>   (Courtney 1993: 39–40, no. 43)

The Ennian move from inscriptional culture as such to a self-consciously playful, literary and in this case panegyrical mode, such as that practised above all by Martial in later Latin (Sullivan 1991: 78–114) and also Statius (Newlands 2002: 38–43, 49–50, 74), is paralleled by (indeed modelled on) the development of the literary epigram in the Hellenistic Greek tradition (Bing 1988: 17–18; Cameron 1993: 1–6; Gutzwiller 1998: 47–114). Collections of compilations like the third-century BC Posidippus papyrus in Milan (which is thought to be an early anthology of the epigrams of a single poet: see Austin and Bastianini 2002, nos. 1–112) or the Hellenistic *Garland of Meleager*, or in the later Roman period the *Garland of Philip* and in Byzantium the *Greek Anthology* are testimony to the continued vibrancy of the genre in Greek throughout antiquity and the Middle Ages (Cameron 1993; Gutzwiller 1998: 227–322). While later examples of this elegantly literary form of what was once a monumental statement may relatively rarely have been inscribed, the frequency with which works of art are addressed within epigram indicates that the genre never wholly forgot its roots in material culture and its relations to the viewing of art (Goldhill 1994; Gutzwiller 2001). Indeed isolated examples could of course always be composed for inscription, as in the Christian poems of Paulinus of Nola inscribed alongside the mosaics of his basilica of St Felix at the end of the fourth century AD (especially the *tituli* recorded in Paulinus' letter 32 of about AD 403, with Goldschmidt 1940: 35–47, 97–8; also Conybeare 2000: 94–9).

When the inscription is of a complex literary kind, the textuality of art works in several ways. An inscription may serve to play alongside the visual depiction – extending its meanings through puns or allusions. Take the cinerary grave altar of Titus Statilius Aper and his wife Orcivia Anthis, dating to about AD 120 (Figure 21.2). The image has a bust of Anthis in a shell flanked by dolphins in the pediment and a frontal togate image of Aper with a dead boar at his feet, a closed box to his right and a boy (once, but no longer, winged) who may represent death. This altar boasts two inscriptions, the first in prose at the base recording the names of the deceased, Aper's profession and the donors, Aper's parents, Titus Statilius Proculus and Argentaria Eutychia. The second, a verse epigram in four hexameters inscribed in three lines above the prose as a sort of second textual base for the image, is more personal:

> Innocuus Aper ecce iaces non virginis ira,
> nec Meleager atrox perfodit viscera ferro:
> mors tacita obrepsit subito fectique ruinam
> quae tibi crescenti rapuit iuvenilem figuram.

> Lo, you lie here harmless Aper [= boar]! Your flesh pierced neither
> by the wrath of the maiden goddess [Diana] nor fierce Meleager's spear.
> Silent death crept up suddenly and wrought destruction,
> seizing your youthful flourishing form.
>
> (Courtney 1995: 164–5, 374, no. 176)

Figure 21.2 Cinerary grave altar of T. Statilius Aper and Orchivia Anthis, with two cavities in the rear for cinerary urns, a portrait statue of the former in the front, a bust of the latter above, and two inscriptions below. From Rome. Marble *c.* AD 120. The upper inscription is in verse, the lower gives the names of the donors, Aper's parents Titus Statilius Proculus and Argentaria Eutychia, and Aper's age at the time of his death (22 years, 8 months and 15 days). Capitoline Museum, Rome. Photograph: Alinari/Art Resource, New York

The text puns on Aper's name – shared with the dead boar depicted beside him – while at the same time making explicit verbal reference to Aper as Meleager, standing over the dead boar in a pose familiar from funerary sarcophagi of the second century. The poem however denies the pun even as it makes it – claiming that Aper was not slain, as Meleager was, as a consequence of the wrath of Diana, nor, as the boar was, by Meleager's spear. The epigram works side by side with the image – both of them alluding in different ways to the myth and together raising

Aper's status to a mythological level. The epigram serves also to distance Aper from excessive involvement in the irrelevant (and, worse, potentially negative) narrative implications of the myth (Meleager's love for Atalanta, his killing of his uncles and his mother's subsequent actions that caused his own death) by turning its theme to the pathos of sudden death's demolition of his youth. It thus helps to police the image's meanings by not only drawing verbal attention to its visual mythological references, but attempting also to limit them.

By contrast, take the epigram in eight elegiac couplets that survives in fragmentary form from the lid of probably the greatest sarcophagus carved in fourth-century Rome – that of the urban prefect Junius Bassus, who died in AD 359 (figures 21.3 and 21.4). The main imagery of the sarcophagus is a complex series of Christian scenes showing Old Testament and Passion narratives as well as images of the martyrdoms of Peter and Paul in the intercolumniations of a grand double-register frontage. An elegantly carved prose inscription runs along the upper rim identifying Bassus, the coffin's recipient, describing his place on the *cursus honorum* (as prefect of the city), his baptism as a Christian, and the precise date of his death (25 August, 359). The images on the lid, very poorly preserved, seem to have largely represented the traditional Roman themes of a funerary meal and perhaps a family scene, but neither necessarily or overtly Christian as in the images on the main part of the coffin (Malbon 1990: 104–14). What survives of the inscription (from line 7) reads, with restorations, as follows:

> hic moderans plebem patriae sedemque senatus,
>   urbis perpetuas occidit ad lacrimas.
> nec licuit famulis domini gestare feretrum,
>   certantis populi sed fuit illud onus.
> flevit turba omnis, matres puerique senesque,
>   flevit et abiectis tunc pius ordo togis.
> flere videbantur tunc et fastigia Romae
>   ipsaque tunc gemitus edere tecta viae.
> cedite, sublimes spirantum, cedite, honores!
>   celsius est culmen mors quod huic tribuit.

> The man who governed the people of city and the house of the Senate
> has died, to the everlasting tears of the city.
> His slaves were forbidden to bear their master's bier,
> but that was the burden of the Roman people, who vied for the task.
> The whole crowd wept – mothers, children and old men,
> the reverent Senate wept, their togas put aside for mourning,
> then even the rooftops of Rome seemed to weep,
> and the very arcades along the street to groan.
> Give way, highest honours of the living! Give way!
> Loftier still is the height assigned him in death.
>   (Corrected by Cameron 2002: 288–9)

Figure 21.3 The sarcophagus of Junius Bassus from Rome. Marble, AD 359. This is a grand double register sarcophagus with Old and New Testament scenes in the intercolumniations. St Peter's Basilica, Rome. Photograph: Conway Library, Courtauld Institute of Art

Here, far from directly relating to the elegantly executed imagery of an unusually grand sarcophagus in the way the Aper poem plays off the iconography of his monument, the two inscriptions (prose and verse) strike different but equally personal notes that contrast with the universal Christian message of the visual imagery. Bassus the man is given his curriculum vitae and his dates in the prose inscription on the rim, while the poem elevates him through its spectacular imagery of weeping into a paragon of the lamented deceased. The last two lines, elegantly alluding to Propertius 2.34.65 (on how all former writers should yield their place to Vergil) play on the pun in Bassus' name ('low' in colloquial Latin) by referring to the heights that must give way to him and the pinnacle he has achieved in death. Effectively, the personal and Rome-centred account of a dignitary who had proved a loyal servant to his city is used to supplement the Christian univer-salism of the main iconography. The literary genre of the epigram and its tropes, but also the very act of its epigraphic incision, work to provide a highly traditional

Figure 21.4 Detail of the fragment of the poetic inscription from the lid of the Bassus sarcophagus. After Apollonj Ghetti, Ferrua, Josi and Kirschenbaum (1951) fig. 171.

(even antiquarian) link to the pre-Christian past of the city. While the visual imagery promises what may be a rather impersonal salvation in the kind of eternity proclaimed by Christ's triumphant appearance between Peter and Paul, enthroned over a personification of the world, in the central scene of the upper tier, the text personalizes the pathos and particularity of Bassus' death, in an elegiac-metrical tradition going back to archaic Greek epigrams from ten centuries earlier. That traditionalism (as opposed to the innovative implications of Bassus' Christianity) is further enforced by what appears to have been the highly traditional and non-Christian imagery of the lid, in whose centre the inscription stood.

2 Art within Writing: the Rise of Illustration

While texts frequently made their way on to images, the reverse gesture – dramatic in its own way for the reader of a specific papyrus roll or a vellum codex – was the intrusion of images on to the written page. Early surviving examples in papyrus – such as the third century AD fragment from Oxyrhynchus of a comic Greek Heracles poem with parodic sketches of the hero's battles (Nisbet 2002) – give a hint of what may have been available in the written Latin tradition before the codex took over from the roll as the dominant form of book in the fourth century (figure 21.5). What is impossible to tell in the absence of surviving evidence is how extensive and high quality the illustration of rolls could be – as many as 700 separate illuminations have been estimated for the most lavish roll editions of the Homeric epics (Weitzmann 1959: 37, 41). Pliny records (at *Natural History* 35.11) that Varro's *Imagines* – an important text that appears to have influenced both Vergil's parade of heroes in *Aeneid* 6 and the rows of statues that adorned the Forum of Augustus – included 700 illuminated portraits of famous men, each described in a short epigram of which two survive in later florilegists (Horsfall 1983: 211). But with the rise of the codex – made of durable vellum folios rather than fragile scrolls of papyrus, its pages protected by being flat (unlike the permanently rolled format of papyrus) and out of the light, and its images or particular passages of text easily found by turning pages rather than scrolling through an entire roll – the fine art of illustration entered a new age. Of the non-Christian antique books that survive, it was the text of Vergil that received the finest decorative treatment, in two great fifth century AD manuscripts now in Rome – the Vatican Vergil of about 425 and the Roman Vergil of about 475. Ironically, Vergil's reflective passages on art itself (on which see below) are never chosen for illustration.

Figure 21.5 Illustrated fragment from a small-format or 'pocket' papyrus book-roll (*P. Oxy. XXII 2331*) with verses about the adventures of Heracles and sketches of the hero performing his labours. Photograph: Courtesy of the Egypt Exploration Society, London.

In relation to a lengthy set of diverse texts like Vergil's poems, illustrations perform a series of varying functions. They may inaugurate a poem – like a kind of frontispiece, giving cues to specific sections and divisions – for instance by illustrating the first portion of text, as in the first surviving image from the Roman Vergil (fol. 1r), above the opening lines of the First Eclogue (1–5), which renders Meliboeus speaking to Tityrus as the latter plays his pipe (Wright 2001: 14), or the first surviving miniature of the Vatican Vergil (fol. 1r), which is a full-page illumination in six scenes depicting the first fifteen lines of the Third Georgic, and serves to introduce both the poem and the second half of the *Georgics* as a whole (Wright 1993: 8–9). The pictorial inauguration may be in the form of a generalized author portrait, as in those eclogues that are mono-logues in the Roman Vergil (the second, fourth and sixth of the seven that survive, fols. 3v, 9r and 14r with Wright 2001: 16–18, 20) or in the lost author portrait from the front of *Aeneid* 7 in the Vatican Vergil (another halfway centre point, within a long poem), whose traces survive on the largely blank page that preceded it (fol. 57v, Wright 1993: 60–1). Introductory images may also serve to summarize texts in a general way, rather than illustrating any particular aspect – as in the Roman Vergil's illustration for the Fifth Eclogue, which shows the dialogue of Menalcas and Mopsus that is the substance of the poem (fol. 11r, Wright 2001: 19) or the same manuscript's great opening (fols. 44v, 45r) of standard bucolic imagery generally relating to the themes of the Third Georgic (Wright 2001: 21–3) (figure 21.6).

In a long narrative poem, like the *Aeneid*, the miniatures are much more directly illustrative of particular episodes and in this way form a kind of visual commentary, heightening particular passages (at the expense of others). In the Vatican Vergil, the pictures come thick and fast around the abandonment and death of Dido (fols. 39v, 40r – these two being a full opening of two pages – and 41r, Wright (1993: 38–43) and in Aeneas' trip to the Underworld (fols. 47v, 48v and 49r – another full opening, 52r and 53v, Wright (1993: 48–57). The emphasis of these subjects may indicate an effort to claim a classic for Christianity, by emphasizing issues of lust, temptation and sin in the Dido episode and the visualization of hell, but they may equally represent a pagan illustrative model for the kinds of illuminated manuscripts of the Bible produced around the same period. The images do more than alleviate the process of reading the text: they direct the reader to particular sections, as a kind of emblematic signal to the subject matter, through pictures.

Take, as an individual example, the Laocoon image from the Vatican Vergil (fol. 18v) that appears below the text of *Aeneid* 2.191–8 but illustrates 2.201–24, the bulk of which would have appeared on the now lost folio opposite (Wright 1984: 60–1; 1993: 22–3) (figure 21.7). Here three episodes within Vergil's Laocoon story are shown. On the left, he stands beside an altar as a beardless priest (naked to the waist, skirted and with an axe, in the traditional iconography of a *victimar-ius* or sacrificial slaughterer rather than a priest). Behind him is the temple of

Figure 21.6   The Roman Vergil (Vatican Library, Vat. Lat. 3867), fol. 44v. Full-page miniature of herdsmen and flocks, one of two that served as the frontispiece for *Georgics* 3. Last quarter of the fifth century AD. Photograph: Courtesy of the Biblioteca Apostolica Vaticana (Vatican)

Neptune whose statue can be seen in the doorway, and above this the temple of Minerva to which the snakes escape at 2.225–8. This imagery closely follows the text of 2.201–2, with the vividness of *mactabat* (he slaughtered) perhaps justifying the unusual choice of showing the priest as actual bull-slayer. In the upper left are the two snakes approaching from the sea (as described at 2.203–9), while in the right foreground – in heroic nudity, billowing cape and larger scale – a bearded and long-haired Laocoon and his two sons are killed by the snakes (as described at 2.209–24). The miniature closely follows the text (and its artist provides helpful labels for the figures, just in case) and yet it transforms it radically. We have two Laocoons now – bearded and beardless – rendering the narrative movement of the poem as a series of visual episodes, discrete from each other but united (i.e. discrete from other parts of the *Aeneid*'s text) by being in a single picture frame. Yet some parts even of Vergil's Laocoon account are

Figure 21.7   The Vatican Vergil (Vatican Library, Vat. Lat. 3225) fol. 18v. Full page with the text of *Aeneid* 2.191–8 and a miniature showing the story of Laocoon, described in *Aeneid* 2.201–24, which was written on the lost page opposite. First quarter of the fifth century AD. Photograph: Courtesy of the Biblioteca Apostolica Vaticana (Vatican)

conflated – such as the narrative of the snakes attacking the sons and Laocoon vainly attempting to rescue them, which has become a single iconic scene that may owe something iconographically to the famous marble group by Hagesander, Polydorus and Athenodorus mentioned by Pliny at *Natural History* 36.37 and either identical with or replicated by the statue found in 1506 and now in the Vatican.

3   Art Described: the Uses of Ecphrasis

While the direct alignment of images and words through inscription or illustration represents a potent strand in Roman culture's combination of art and text, the move from inscriptional epigram to what might be called purely literary epigram reflects what was to become a profound use of visual art as a trope within Roman writing (for some reflections on Greek origins see e.g. Zeitlin 1994 and Steiner 2001). Whether in poetry, in letters (e.g. Henderson 2002) or in the prose novels, the rhetorical technique known as ecphrasis, description, that came to be most characteristically associated with the description of works of art, was to be used for special, often self-reflexive, often vividly climactic purposes. In both Latin and Greek prose, the insertion of an ecphrasis of a painting whose subject had thematic resonances with the rest of the text was to have significant structural impact on the composition of fiction, particularly in the use of a work of art as a kind of descriptive frontispiece, not so different in its way perhaps from the frontispieces of early books. Sometimes, there is a striking resonance between such descriptive insertions in literary texts and in works of art. For instance, Catullus' great poem 64 (from the first half of the first century BC) on the marriage of Peleus and Thetis boasts a long ecphrasis describing the embroidered coverlet of the nuptial bed with its images of the (hardly happy) liaison of Ariadne and Theseus and the arrival of Dionysus (64.50–264). The famous roughly contemporary painted frieze in the Villa of the Mysteries at Pompeii also interjects into its main imagery (whose subject is still uncertain but is usually thought to reflect the *rite de passage* into marriage) an epiphanic scene of Dionysus and Ariadne. To argue for a direct connection is over-speculative, though the case for a strong visual element in Catullus' poem 64 has been well made (Fitzgerald 1995: 144–6). Likewise, the way in which the third-century sophist Philostratus begins and ends his two books of collected ecphraseis, written in Greek, with images of the seasons has been linked to the visual use of seasonal imagery as a framing device in contemporary mosaics and sarcophagi (Elsner 2000).

But beyond a potential interrelationship of formal structure between art and text, what proved especially attractive to Roman writers, in focusing on a de-scribed work of art, was the chance to reflect figuratively upon their own writing, whether prose or verse. In turning their attention to an apparently self-contained painting, sculpture or building within their texts, writers could effectively step outside their own work to picture it as a whole (what has been called the technique of *mise en abyme*, with Dällenbach 1989), or to draw out some of its less immediately obvious meanings, or to dramatize some potential responses to their art by depicting responses to the object described. The specific qualities of vividness (*enargeia*) and clarity (*sapheneia*) prescribed by the rhetorical hand-books (e.g. Webb 1997a; Dubel 1997) allowed ecphraseis to stand as brilliant show-pieces within a larger text. But the existence of a tradition of ecphrasis in Greek literature, reaching back to Homer's description of the shield of Achilles in the *Iliad*, meant that every such description was inevitably a highly self-conscious display of intertextuality and more-or-less subtle allusion (on the power of the Vergilian example for later writers like Statius, Silius Italicus and Valerius Flaccus see respectively Harrison 1992: 51–2, Fowler 1996 and Hershkowitz 1998: 20–3).

These general comments may be exemplified by reference to the ecphraseis in Vergil's *Aeneid* – not only among the most complex examples of the topos in all Latin literature but also certainly the most influential (e.g. Dubois 1982: 28–51; R. F. Thomas 1983; Ravenna 1985; Heffernan 1993: 22–36). Obviously I cannot here quote and translate long sections of Vergil's text. So what follows must necessarily be a description of the ancient art of description in the absence of the object described (which is no bad definition of ecphrasis itself!). There are numerous descriptions of works of art within the epic that in each case extend beyond the object into a narrative account of what its decoration depicts (detailed scholarly treatments of these are listed in the section on Further Reading below): the murals of Dido's temple in Carthage (1.453–93), the silver-gilt dishes chased with the deeds of Dido's ancestors (1.640–2), the cloak with the story of Ganymede given to the victor of the ship race (5.250–7), the bronze doors made by Daedalus for the temple at Cumae (6.20–37), the cedar statues of the ancestors of king Latinus (7.177–91), the shield of Turnus (7.789–92), the shield of Aeneas (8.630–728), and the sword-belt of Pallas (10.495–505).

It is worth noting that the poet is careful to vary the material forms and types of the (imaginary) objects he chooses to describe, creating a deliberate variation, except in the case of the two shields of the opposed heroes Aeneas and Turnus, which are paired in counterpoint (on the range of materials, see Simon 1982). The actual description is in several cases the result of a deliberate build-up in which the narrative pace has been slowed – so that in Book 1 Aeneas and Achates survey the great prospect of Dido's new Carthage under construction (1.418–52) before focusing on the temple paintings, while in Book 8, Venus brings her son his new arms (8.608–25), before the narrator turns the textual gaze on to the shield itself. The pause in the pace of epic narrative allows a description that is at the same time the insertion of different narratives – the Trojan war and Aeneas' past in Book 1, the tragedies of Crete and especially of Daedalus in Book 6, the future history of Rome culminating in Augustus himself on the shield in Book 8, the crimes of the Danaids on the baldric of Pallas. These new narratives – apparently works of art figured in words – are expounded in the very language of the rest of the poem, but with the special difference that the actors of the *Aeneid* can be portrayed as themselves responding to art. As a result the reader is provided with an admittedly highly complex, not to say ambiguous, paradigm of the range of responses he or she is potentially to feel (Leach 1988: 311–19; Barchiesi 1997a: 275–8; Bartsch 1998: 335–7; Putnam 1998b: 269–75). At the same time, by being the account of the *Aeneid's* narrator and not of any particular internal actor (like Aeneas himself) the ecphraseis allow the reader to learn what the epic's protagonists cannot know themselves, and thus to be aware both of the subjectivity of responses within the poem and of the likely subjectivity of the reader's own reactions to the poem (Boyd 1995: 78–80).

The first of the ecphraseis poses the problem of emotional response – something emphasized by the rhetorical handbooks (Webb 1997b) – with eloquent reiteration. Looking at the frescoes of the Trojan War, Aeneas weeps (*lacrimans*, 1.459) and pronounces some famous lines on the sorrows evoked by deeds (*rerum*, 1.462) – whether these be actual (the 'real' history of Troy and Aeneas' part in that war), literary (effectively the passage is a summary of the *Iliad*'s narrative) or painted (paintings being the immediate cause for Aeneas' wonder (*miratur*, 1.456) and his tears:

> sunt lacrimae rerum et mentem mortalia tangunt.
> solve metus; feret haec aliquam tibi fama salutem

> And our misfortunes human pity breed.
> This fame may help produce; suppress thy dread
> (1.462–3; Sandys, 1632, cited from Gransden 1996: 62)

The viewer's misery (and Aeneas is hardly an ordinary viewer of course, but rather an actor in what he is portrayed as viewing) is a repeated theme:

> multa gemens, largoque umectat flumine vultum

> His heart with sighs, his face with rivers fraught...
> (1.465; cf. 470 and 485; Sandys, 1632, cited from Gransden 1996: 62)

Yet the flood of emotion goes side by side with the theme of wonder at the handicraft of the artist (1.455–6, 494) and a gaze concentrated on the object (which contrasts explicitly with the averted gaze of Athena as she looks away from the supplications of the Trojan women within the description itself at 1.482):

> dum stupet obtutuque haeret defixus in uno

> ...while yet amaz'd,
> Dardan Aeneas on each object gaz'd...
> (1.495; Sandys, 1632, cited from Gransden 1996: 63)

The wonder of this wonder – and what might be called the great aesthetic problem raised by this ecphrasis about art in general (and about responding to epic narrative like the *Aeneid* itself in particular) – is that

> ...atque animum pictura pascit inani
> multa gemens

> ...his Tears a ready Passage find,
> Devouring what he saw so well design'd
> And with an empty Picture fed his Mind.
> (1.464–5, Dryden 1997: 19)

That emptiness recurs within the described images too where Troilus' chariot is presented as a *curru...inani* (1.476, 'an empty car') – empty because its chariot-eer is slain by Achilles and empty too because art is simply a poor imitation of what were to Aeneas real events. The opening ecphrasis of Book 6 reconfigures the dual thematics of sorrow (*dolor* 6.31) and absence. Here

> ...tu quoque magnam
> partem opere in tanto, sineret dolor, Icare, haberes.
> bis conatus erat casus effingere in auro,
> bis patriae cecidere manus.

> Here hapless Icarus had found his part;
> Had not the Father's Grief retrained his Art.
> He twice assay'd to cast his Son in Gold;
> Twice from his hands he drop'd the forming Mold.
> (6.30–3, Dryden 1997: 150)

This time it is the artist who weeps and the images' emptiness (of Icarus) is testament to that sorrow, while Vergil's own intervention as descriptive artist makes present (as text rather than gilded bronze or personal feeling) both Daedalus' pain and Icarus' fall. Arguably the supreme confrontation with this complex thematics of art's imitative fragility and yet its ability to signify so much within the *Aeneid*'s mounting crescendo of ecphrasis lies in 'the fabric of the shield beyond all words to describe' (*clipei non enarrabile textum*, 8.625). This unnarratable visual text is what Vergil spends the next hundred odd lines describing – at great length for an ecphrasis but with great brevity for the great history of Rome from Romulus to Augustus. This time Aeneas' wonder is at a future not understood rather than a past that one might prefer to forget, and the emotion is of joy rather than of sorrow:

> miratur rerumque ignarus imagine gaudet
> attollens umeroque famamque et fata nepotum

> Unknown the Names, he yet admires the Grace;
> And bears aloft the Fame and Fortune of his Race.
> (8.730–1, Dryden 1997: 237)

Even this brief account has shown that the *Aeneid*'s ecphraseis link together powerfully. As a group they offer a meta-reflection on art and its responses, on the difficulties of writing epic and its emotive challenges. But within the fabric of Vergil's text as a whole they build a progressive argument. The first two – the confrontation with the Trojan War at Carthage and the silver dishes with Dido's ancestors – render the genealogies of the epic's opening protagonists. Yet the pre-history of Dido is merely referred to and dismissed in a couple of lines – an ecphrastic signal that her narrative is but a stage on the Trojan's long journey beyond Carthage and her love to Italy. The third – the cloak with the tale of Ganymede – returns to the theme of Aeneas' Trojan past, some of which had been portrayed on Dido's temple paintings. The first ecphrasis, as we have seen, is replete with emotion (Aeneas' at his own history, the reader's through Aeneas at Homer's great poem retold by Vergil). The narrative on the cloak, by contrast – half-remembered as it were, so that Ganymede is not mentioned by name – renders the distance Aeneas has come from that past as his epic moves into its Italian future; indeed Aeneas gives the cloak away as a prize to Cloanthus. In Book 6 (where Icarus is not depicted but is named), Aeneas and his companions are explicitly called away from their absorption in art by the priestess:

> non hoc ista sibi tempus spectacula poscit

> Time suffers not, she said, to feed your Eyes
> With empty Pleasures.
> (6.37, Dryden 1997: 150)

As the time for action comes, the lures of art (and its descriptions) are to be resisted.

The cedar statues at Latinus' palace give a narrative of ancestry to the Latins at the opening of the epic's second half – longer than that accorded to Dido and announcing the past that Aeneas would acquire for his people through his marriage to Latinus' daughter Lavinia. The two shields placed at the ends of Books 7 and 8 pit Turnus against Aeneas, the former bearing a motif of his own ancestral mythology (Io, Argus and Inachus) immured in the past, the latter carrying the future of Rome and interjecting the climactic rhetoric of its ecphrasis into the Augustan present and the time of the poem's composition (rather as the Bassus sarcophagus' inscriptions firmly place the Christian mythologies of its imagery firmly into the contemporary context of the urban prefect's death). While the emblem on Turnus' shield looks back genealogically, that of Aeneas carries the epic action of the poem as a whole onwards into its Augustan future – a future that is not part of the epic's own narrative but is nonetheless incorporated as the decoration of a work of art and thus included within the *Aeneid*'s own art. Apart from this motif of panegyric through prophecy and teleology culminating in Augustus through the apparent description of art, the accounts of the shields have the effect of moving the *Aeneid*'s ecphrastic pattern from a materializing of genealogy (that is at the same time an allegory in the figure of Io of Turnus' own fate at the hands of Juno) and an aesthetics of response, to a direct involvement in epic action. The shields become – in different ways – emblems for the two protagonists, like the shields of the heroes in Aeschylus *Seven against Thebes* (with Zeitlin 1982).

It is the last of the ecphraseis, that of Pallas' baldric, which fully unites the description of art with epic action, the thematics of aesthetic response and emotion with the dynamic of a narrative plot. The image – an 'abominable crime' (*impressum nefas*, 10.497) – is sketchily described, its protagonists (like Ganymede) never named, but its artist (like Daedalus) firmly announced as (the unknown) Clonus, whose name, meaning 'Din-of-Battle, seems like a joke at the expense of the Homeric epithet (10.499). Turnus wrests it from the dead body of Pallas and Vergil warns us that he will rue the act (10.500–505). That time comes at the very end of the entire poem when Turnus pleads for his life before the triumphant Aeneas. Aeneas wavers – his eyes rolling (*volvens oculos*, 12.939) – and then he sees the sword-belt of Pallas that Turnus is wearing. In the poem's last moment of the viewing of art, Aeneas 'feasted his eyes on the sight of this spoil, this reminder of his own wild grief' (*ille, oculis postquam saevi monimenta doloris / exuviasque hausit . . .*, 12.945–6).

Again the thematics of personal suffering (cf. *dolor* at 6.31), identification and memory (cf. 6.26 for *monimenta*) arise in the face of a work of art, this time with the response postponed for two books from the initial description and its impact altered by the epic's intervening action – notably the death of Pallas and the defeat of Turnus. Where Aeneas had stood transfixed and tearful before Dido's paintings, and transfixed until the priestess called him away at Cumae, where Daedalus had been so moved by *dolor* that he could not complete the images planned for the temple door, now grief gives way to vengeful fury and Aeneas strikes. That mindful anger in Aeneas' response to the sword-belt is effectively an echo of Juno's anger at the opening of the epic, which initiated its action. As *monimentum*, and especially a *monimentum* that is active in stirring its audience to emotive response, the artwork of the sword-belt merges with the artwork that is the poem as a whole.

4 Conclusion

I have been highly selective in my examples of art and text – whether epigraphic, illustrative or ecphrastic, favouring instances of the highest culture above the less grand or ambitious, and in the case of ecphrasis giving scandalously short shrift to everything but Vergil (including the whole of elegy and especially Ovid's masterly and repeated turns to art in the *Metamorphoses*), let alone the prose examinations of art in the novels or such texts as Pliny's Letter 3.6, with Henderson (2002). But I hope that the general case has been made for a deep and persistent engagement of word and image in (Graeco-)Roman culture. In particular, the remarkable development of ecphrasis into a most complex meditation on the nature of the work of art and its reception has proved fundamental in shaping the Western tradition of reflecting on the nature of art itself.[1]

1 My thanks are due to the editor and to three other Latin 'H's for their very useful comments and advice – in alphabetical order, Philip Hardie, John Henderson and Nicholas Horsfall.

FURTHER READING

On the inscriptional culture of Greece and Rome see for example MacMullen (1982), Meyer (1990) and Woolf (1996). On the cinerary grave altar of Titus Statilius Aper see Kleiner (1987: 213–16) and Koortbojian (1996: 229–31); on the sarcophagus of Junius Bassus, Apollonj Ghetti et al. (1951: 220–2 and fig. 171), Malbon (1990: 3–90), Cameron (2002) and Elsner (2003: 82–7, 89). On ekphrasis in general and its uses in literature see for example Friedländer (1912: 83–103), Downey (1959), Pernice and Gross (1969), Ravenna (1974), Bartsch (1989), Fowler (1991), Laird (1996), Webb (1999), Harrison (2001a); on ekphrastic techniques in the Latin novels compare Schissel von Fleschenberg (1913), Slater (1990: 91–101), Elsner (1993), Conte (1996: 14–22), Laird (1997) and Slater (1998).

On the murals of Dido's temple in Carthage (*Aeneid* 1.453–93) see for example Williams (1960a), Clay (1988), Barchiesi (1994: 114–24) and Putnam (1998a: 23–54); on the Ganymede cloak (5.250–7) see Boyd (1995: 84–8), Putnam (1998a: 55–74) and Hardie (2002b); on the bronze doors of the temple at Cumae (6.20–37) see Fitzgerald (1984), Paschalis (1986), Sharrock (1994: 103–11) and Putnam (1998a: 75–96); on the shield of Turnus (7.789–92) see for example Breen (1986), Gale (1997); on the shield of Aeneas (VIII.630–728) see e.g. Hardie (1986: 97–109, 120–4, 336–76) and Putnam (1998a: 119–88); and on the sword-belt of Pallas (10.495–505) see for example Breen (1986), Conte (1986: 185–95), Putnam (1998a: 119–88) and Harrison (1998a).

On ekphrasis in Ovid's *Metamorphoses* see for example Leach (1974), Solodow (1988: 203–31) and Hardie (2002a: 146–50, 173–226).

CHAPTER TWENTY-TWO

The Passions

Robert A. Kaster

1 Introduction

Literature, at any rate Roman literature, is all about action in the material world, as it is prompted by the value placed on external things. Humans (and gods too, who are no different here) act because they seek to gain goods or avoid evils, or because they have already gained things they prize or have had things they decry thrust upon them. Literature merely (though not simply) clothes these patterns of motive and action in the forms and fabrics of language that tradition or fashion provides: comedy, epic, tragedy, history, lyric, romance . . . And as the Stoics warned, when we invest external things with value and act to secure or enhance that investment, our actions will inevitably be shaped by 'the passions': love, hate, fear, envy, shame, and their brothers.

In this obvious sense the story of the passions in Roman literature just is the story of Roman literature; and in that sense, any attempt to survey the subject in a brief essay must bite off much more than it can chew. My plan is not to attempt such a survey but instead to consider three topics that can provide some useful perspectives even when treated in the broad strokes needed here: what might be called the Romans' cultural intuitions about the passions; the role that these intuitions played in rhetoric; and the links between rhetoric and imaginative literature in representing and evoking the passions. Along the way we shall see how both rhetoric and literature start from much the same understanding of how the passions work – especially the passions' grounding in certain kinds of judgement and evaluation – and how both rhetoric and literature can create, through their appeals to the passions, the sense of shared understanding and sentiment that is integral to a common culture. 'Reading the passions' can then be seen to provide a valuable entry into texts and the culture they reflect and constitute.

2   Roman Concepts of Passion

The Romans' intuitions about the passions will look familiar, because they are largely ours; and our intuitions are what they are in no small part because the Romans came before us. Most important is the view – universal save for the Stoics – that the passions are 'natural' and so inevitable. As human beings (on this view) we are put together in such a way that the experience of *ira* (anger) or *metus* (fear) can no more be avoided than can hunger and headaches. Yet though the passions are at base a given, that does not mean that they are not 'up to us' in consequential ways. Most important, it is possible to experience a passion either appropriately or inappropriately – a statement that cannot be made of a purely bodily 'feeling' such as hunger. In Aristotelian terms congenial to the standard Roman view, the idea is to achieve the mean in your passions: to experience the right passion for the right reason (as a fitting response to the given state of affairs), for the right length of time, with the right intensity, and with the right combination of pragmatic and expressive behaviours.

With talk of 'right' the passions cease to be merely 'natural' and become a product and concern of culture. Coordinating all the vectors of rightness is one of the primary aims of proper socialization; or in more recognizably ancient terms, achieving the mean in your passions is one of the components of virtue. When Catullus depicts the Spaniard Egnatius wearing a broad smile at a funeral (39.4– 6), we understand that the man has at least failed to master the correct expressive behaviours: as a result, he is no better than an outlandish fool, and might well be a knave. Right behaviours could come only through extensive training and acculturation, of the sort that natives acquire mostly just by virtue of being natives (that is part of Catullus' point). But more fundamental than such behaviours, and so more important as an object of training, is the habit of experiencing the right passion for the right reason.

Your father has been assaulted: what is your response? The answer depends in the first instance on the value you attach to your father, which in the standard case will be both considerable and multifaceted: you will value your father highly, and for more than one reason (as a person to whom you owe your life, as a person who has shown you love, as a person who has instructed you, as a person whose role has symbolic importance in the culture you have integrated with your self...). You will, accordingly, feel *ira* – a painful desire for revenge – because someone whom you prize has been subjected to *iniuria*. This will be a fitting response to the given state of affairs (unless you are a Stoic: Sen. *Dial.* 3.12.1–2), and it is important to recognize its basis: your *ira* here will not be 'instinctive' but will result from a cognitive process – a chain of judgements and evaluations – that is both complex and culturally determined (if you doubt this, for 'your father has been assaulted' substitute 'your sister has been complimented by a stranger'). The passions, on this view, take their start from judgements and evaluations that are forms of reason shaped by culture; and learning to match up reasons and passions so that they fit is part of what we have come to call acculturation.

But were cognition the whole story, we would merely have *di*spassionate consideration of experience ('Someone is abusing that older gentleman, who is tied to me in various ways. Surely that is wrong, for various reasons'). What follows cognition was the hard part, for the Romans as it is for us. The *feelings* engaged in body and mind by certain judgements and evaluations are essential to the ways in which the passions are experienced; indeed, these feelings are the components of experience that give the 'passions' their English name, from Latin *passio*, which in turn corresponds to πάθη (*pathe*), the standard Greek term to denote what one simply experiences, helplessly or at any rate beyond intention. These are the feelings that 'come over' us, making our chests tighten and fists ball in anger or our hearts swell and tears well in joy. The non-cognitive components of passion that we call 'feelings', like other non-cognitive feelings such as hunger, seem least to be 'up to us': for this reason they caused the Romans (as they cause us) to speak of passion as a 'seizure' or even as a form of 'madness'.

Hence the fundamental mystery of the passions. They start in an exercise of reason, leading to relevant evaluations and judgements, but they are commonly experienced as opposed to reason: at best as phenomena that we wish reason would control – calibrating their intensity and duration and the behaviours they cue (so that not every episode of *ira* ends in murder) – or at worst as wholly beyond the control of reason (so that murder does sometimes ensue). In the moment of passion, the mind is often experienced as a thing divided against itself, and this intuition underlies the most common explanation of the passions in ancient psychology, as the consequences of a mind that is literally segmented into a reasoning 'part' that must struggle to exercise control over an appetitive 'part' in which the passions arise (see esp. Plato *Rep.* 4.435C ff.).

3 The Passions and Rhetoric

The division between the cognitive (judging, evaluating) and the non-cognitive (desiring, feeling) dimensions of the passions finds its way into Roman rhetorical theory, which seeks first of all to engage cognition, the better to profit from feeling. As we shall see, however, rhetoric prefers not to dwell on what I have called the passions' 'mystery'. As an *ars* – a technique built on reason – rhetoric is above all about creating reasoned judgements in the minds of its audience. It just happens that many of these reasoned judgements are the starting point of passions.

There are two primary reasons why rhetoric should be our next stop on this *tour d'horizon*. First, it is in rhetoric that we find the earliest comprehensive discussion of the passions, and one of the most penetrating. In the second book of his *Rhetoric* Aristotle surveys the psychological states that the orator might encounter, or wish to create, in his audience and in so doing stresses strongly the cognitive underpinnings of the passions: thus pity (*eleos*), 'a kind of pain caused by seeing an undeserving person suffer a destructive or painful harm' (2.8.2), and its opposite, indignation (*nemesis*) 'being pained at [another's] undeserved success' (2.9.1), both start from a reckoning of 'desert'. Whether or not the attention given the subject by Aristotle continued to be prominent in the (now lost) handbooks of Hellenistic rhetoric we do not know; but the attention is certainly present (if in somewhat different application) in the earliest works of formal rhetoric at Rome, from Cicero's *De inventione* (1.98–109) through his *De oratore* (2.185–211) and on to Quintilian's *Institutio* (6.1–2). The second reason for our attention here has to do with the background of those who wrote the texts to which the present volume is a 'companion'; for the vast majority of these (almost exclusively) men wrote after formal rhetoric was introduced to Roman culture and so knew the discipline as part of their education. Having been schooled in rhetoric, they inevitably based their own writings upon it, in the approach to the passions no less than in other ways.

Now there were nuances in the approach of different rhetorical doctrines to the passions, but uniting them all was one central supposition: the appeal to the passions was ethically unproblematic. Nowhere in Roman rhetorical writings do we find squarely addressed the concern that rousing the passions for argument's sake might be undesirable, either in itself – for example, because passion (as the Stoics believed) is a deformation of the right reason that is godlike in us – or in pursuit of some larger aim – for example, the accurate administration of justice (Quintilian barely glances in this direction at *Inst.* 6.1.7). This lack of concern is crucial both for rhetoric and for literature, and so it is worth lingering a moment over it, to consider its causes. Here I would stress two reasons, though there are certainly others.

First, there is the relation between rhetoric and life. Much of formal rhetoric did no more than systematize and analyse what people said and did as they went about their everyday affairs: crafting arguments (e.g.) according to the letter versus the spirit of an agreement, or vice versa, belonged to a particular province of rhetoric ('status-theory'), but arguments of that sort had presumably been used since the first agreement begat the first disagreement. So too with rousing the passions in order to press one's case. Any ancient city on any given day would have presented a lively theatre of passionate display and appeal, from the semi-ritualized institution of the *flagitatio* (in which an aggrieved party followed a tormentor through the streets, heaping on him abuse intended to shame him into repentance), through the occasions when mourning dress was assumed (e.g. by the family of a defendant in court) to gain onlookers' pity, to the ways in which (under the principate) the emperor's image could be used to arouse indignation and ill-will against a personal enemy. That life and rhetoric should be kept distinct in this regard would have seemed bizarre.

At the same time, formal rhetoric was cushioned against self-examination by what might be called its doubly cognitive orientation. If you commanded

rhetoric's tools, you were confident that you knew which judgements and evaluations were suited to arousing which passions, and you set about creating those
cognitions in the judges' minds. But your expertise did not end there: for you
were also confident that you knew which judgements and evaluations were suited
to *allaying* the passions as well. For this reason Roman *consolationes*, intended to
comfort the bereaved in their mourning, can seem downright chilly to a modern
reader. The orator is a man who can orchestrate the emotions of the court, now
mobilizing them, now calming them, much as a musical maestro calls on the reeds
or the brass arrayed before him to play now forte, now piano. That the 'instruments' might take on a life of their own and gallop away uncontrolled is a thought
that simply does not occur.

Rhetoric's very limited concern with the ethical dimension, combined with its
strongly cognitive orientation, also meant that it did not deeply probe an interesting question: why bother? If you wish the judges to find for a complainant who
alleges that he has suffered undeservedly, you will seek to arouse their *misericordia*, 'pity', which depends precisely on a recognition of undeserved suffering; in
the same way, if you wish the judges to find that the accused has behaved
outrageously by using his advantages to abuse one or another social norm, you
will seek to arouse their *invidia*, 'ill-feeling', which depends precisely on a finding
that personal advantages have been abused in this way (cf. Cic. *Inv. rhet.* 1.22 ~
Auct. ad Her. 1.8, sim. Quint. *Inst.* 4.1.14 and 6.1.14). But if you can bring the
judges to conclude that A has suffered undeservedly or that B has abused his
advantages, why is that not sufficient? What added value is derived from having
the psychosomatic experience of pity or indignation ride piggy-back on these
judgements?

I assume that anyone reading this chapter has experienced passion in an argumentative setting and so will be able to propose reasons why the tactic worked,
starting with the fact that our psychosomatic feelings, having once supervened
upon judgement, tend to strengthen that judgement even in the face of good
evidence and arguments to the contrary (Quintilian suggests a variant of this at
Inst. 6.2.6). But I will round off this stage of our discussion by suggesting a less
obvious reason, and a less obvious sort of work that the passions performed, thanks
to the social context in which rhetoric operated. When a speaker sought to arouse
misericordia or *invidia* or *ira*, there was often at least one other passion that he
tacitly sought to engage as well: the *pudor*, 'sense of shame', of the judge himself,
the desire to see oneself being seen in a creditable light, and to avoid being seen
otherwise. Being persuaded to judge that the person before you has suffered
undeservedly will cause you to experience the feelings associated with *misericordia*;
and experiencing those feelings tends to confirm not only the judgement itself, in a
kind of cognitive loop (if I feel this way, the person before me must have suffered
undeservedly), but also your own identity as the sort of person who feels pity or
indignation *appropriately*. Indeed, given the group setting in which persuasion
typically operated – in the court, from the rostra, in the senate or council chamber

– and the sensitivity of the human face and body as media of passionate expression, you would have ample opportunity to confirm the appropriateness of your response merely by remarking the faces and the postures of your peers. In this way the successful speaker produced in his audience the shared sense that they were both 'right-thinkers' *and* 'right-feelers': evoking passions in speech served as a way not only of confirming judgements but of creating a community compounded jointly of reason and sentiment.

Consider, for example, the peroration of Cicero's speech of 80 BC defending Sex. Roscius of Ameria against the charge of patricide, in the case often credited with making Cicero's early reputation. It is Cicero's strategy throughout not only to argue that Roscius could not have committed the crime, and to shift the blame on to plausible others, but especially to implicate the former dictator Sulla's henchman, the freedman Chrysogonus, who (we are to believe) schemed to frame Roscius in order to acquire his property. In the peroration (143–54) Cicero draws these threads together by presenting the judges with contrasting images of the defenceless Roscius and his powerful tormentor. He begins by asserting that his entire oration has had three motive forces (143): the common good (*res publica*), the wrong done by 'those awful people' (*istorum iniuria*), and his own *dolor* – the psychic pain that is the common element of several 'negative' emotions. Cicero will make us feel this pain too, as he invites us – in part explicitly, in part by implication – to entertain at least four specific passions.

Two of these passions are immediate and complementary. Roscius, not only innocent but assailed and defenceless (*nudus*: 144, 150), is deserving of *misericordia*. That would be obvious even if his advocate did not cue us explicitly by using the word three separate times (145, 150, 154) or twice adopt the first-person singular to speak in Roscius' character (145, 150), thereby making the plea more vivid and reminding us that the ability to see oneself in the other's suffering is at the core of pity. Just as obviously, Chrysogonus merits indignation. He is vastly more powerful than his victim, he is using his power beyond the law and against the common good to gain his personal ends, and he is doing all this with cold-blooded cruelty (*crudelitas*), attacking someone for whom he feels neither the hatred (*odium*) nor the fear (*metus*) that might explain the attack (146–7). The two passions, and the perceptions that Cicero creates to stir them, are of course mutually entailing and reinforcing: if we feel indignation for one who causes another undeserved suffering, we will feel pity for the victim, and if we feel pity for the victim of undeserved suffering, we will feel indignation for the person who caused it.

Or rather, we *ought* to feel these complementary passions. And to ensure that we do, Cicero brings into play two other complementary passions – pride and shame – that depend on our seeing ourselves as being perceived in creditable or discreditable terms. Accepting Cicero's framing of the issues, and sharing in his pity and indignation, confirms our 'goodness' as individuals and as members of the community (150 *unum perfugium, iudices, una spes reliqua est Sex. Roscio eadem quae rei publicae, vestra pristina bonitas et misericordia*: 'Sextus Roscius has only one refuge remaining, the same as the state itself has, your undiminished virtue and pity'), whereas failure to see things in Cicero's terms, and therefore to feel the pain he feels, would simply be shameful: in that respect, pride and shame function here as second-order passions, experience of which depends on our sharing or failing to share the first two passions that Cicero seeks to arouse. The only alternative that Cicero leaves us is to align ourselves with Chrysogonus in his cruelty and to see ourselves being seen as accomplices in his crimes – and again, this would be perfectly plain even if Cicero did not make it explicit (150 *sin ea crudelitas…vestros quoque animos…duriores acerbioresque reddit, actum est, iudices*: 'but if that cruelty makes your minds, too, harder and harsher, it is all over, men of the jury').

The young Cicero's evocation of the passions here is not without its power, and it is evident how the orator gains by forming a community of sentiment around his cause. To gain its ends in persuasion, oratory both stirs the passions of its audience and represents the experience of passion in others (Cicero, e.g., must manifest his own pain and indignation and cause the judges to 'see' all the sadness suffered by Roscius). In this respect oratory is no different from imaginative literature in the effects it seeks to achieve. To those effects we can now turn.

4 The Passions in Roman Imaginative Literature

We can start with 'pure' representation, and a text in which the author wishes us clearly to see – but not to share – a character's passion. The *Aeneid*, like the *Iliad*, begins with anger, though not the protagonist's (that, most famously, comes at the end), as Vergil presents us with the multidimensional and richly imagined *ira* of Juno: 'I sing of arms and the man…much buffetted on land and sea…on account of the mindful anger of fierce Juno' (*saevae memorem Iunonis ob iram*):

> Muse, bring to my mind the reasons – her godhead harmed,
> the thing that caused her pain: why did the queen of the gods make
> a man of signal devotion unfurl so many misfortunes?…
> Do the minds of the heaven-dwellers know such anger?
> There was an ancient city (colonists from Tyre possessed it),
> Carthage…,
> which Juno (it's said) cherished beyond all lands…:
> that this place hold sway over the nations (should the fates
> allow) was even then the goddess' warm intent.
> But there was a line descended from Trojan blood (she had heard)
> that would one day overturn the Tyrians' citadel; from this line
> would come a people, wide-ruling and proud in war,
> to bring destruction to Africa: so the Fates spun the skein.

In fear of this, and mindful of the old war that she
first and foremost had waged at Troy for dear Argos' sake –
indeed not yet had the causes of her anger and her fierce pain
slipped from her mind, in her thought there stayed deep-set
the judgement of Paris and the wrong done her spurned beauty
and the hateful race and the honours paid to ravished Ganymede:
inflamed by all this too she kept the Trojans, the leavings of the Greeks
and of ungentle Achilles, tossed over all the sea,
far away from Latium.

(Aeneid 1.7–32)

The narrator names the passion, then asks its causes (*causas*): the question
assumes that her anger is about something, and that the 'aboutness' comprises
some injury done to her (*numine laeso*) and some pain she feels (*quidve dolens*).
The muse (we must assume) gives a careful reply, for in a scrupulous sequence we
learn that Juno comes to her anger from a certain disposition, her favour for
Carthage and her attachment to it (15–18); that a perception supervenes upon
this disposition, knowledge of the fact (for it is 'fated') that the city she favours
will come to harm (19–22); and that her value-laden disposition, combined with
this perception, prompts a prospective passion, fear of the harm to come (23–4).

But here Vergil's imagining takes its most perceptive turn: for one painful
passion, the *fear* of *future harm* implicating the Trojans, is represented as leading
immediately to the *memory* of *past harm* involving the same people. Even the
syntax ruptures at this point, as though to suggest the wave of sudden memory
that breaks over the goddess: what flashes through the next few lines is simply
what flashes through her thoughts as she relives the hurts. In quick order we are
given:

(a)   the *causes* (25–6), whose cognitive character is emphasized by repeated
      reference to Juno's mind (*animus, mens*), and
(b)   the concomitant *feelings*, her 'pains' (*dolores*);
(c)   an elaboration of the *causes* (26–8), in a catalog of the wrong (*iniuria*) done
      to her through the judgement of Paris, with its tincture of shame (the
      thought of her 'beauty spurned'), through Zeus' infidelity with Electra
      (condensed in reference to the 'hateful race' thereby engendered through
      Dardanus, first lord of Troy), and through the 'honour' paid by Zeus to the
      fair boy Ganymede (whose *honores* contrast with the *inuria* suffered by
      Juno); and
(d)   the *response* (29–31), comprising both Juno's embodied feeling (the 'heat of
      anger': *accensa*) and her acts of vengeance.

We can understand Juno's passion – her *ira*, with its prelude in fear and its overlay
of shame – intimately and fully, because Vergil has meticulously represented it to
us. We can even understand, by implication, how the passion that has cognitively

'reasonable' causes will have completely unreasonable consequences; for her passion will cause Juno to try to keep the Trojans from Italy, even though she knows that their establishment in Italy, and the eventual destruction of Carthage, are destined and unalterable. But however much we are meant to understand Juno's passion, we are surely not meant to feel it ourselves.

Nor, I think, are we meant to feel any other passion of our own in response to Juno's wrath, save perhaps a touch of pity for the sea-tossed Trojans: Vergil at this point aims primarily to make us see how the divine *ira* sets the story in motion, and so aims just to represent it as clearly as he can. For an example of the opposite effect – a passion that is meant to be evoked in the reader though it is not quite represented in the text – we can turn to a very different kind of text, and a passion more subtle than rage.

In his 'Love-Cures' (*Remedia amoris*) Ovid adopts the character of the 'teacher of love' first assumed in the *Ars amatoria*, though now with the opposite intent (see Gibson, chapter 11 above). Among the strategies he recommends is a set of 'aversion-therapies' meant to make you regard your beloved with one form of revulsion or another: for example, by forcing yourself to see her as often as possible, you will soon come to feel *taedium* – the sense of 'having had it up to here' (cf. 537–42). One of these therapies involves the feeling expressed by the verb *piget* – an especially interesting case because it denotes a passion that in its full-blown form corresponds to no single English label. When you experience *pig-* (as we can put it, to preserve the strangeness), you feel an overwhelming lassitude of body and mind, the sense that any further action would be too much (this feeling predominates in the cognate adjective and noun *piger/pigritia* = 'slug-gish(ness), lazy(-ness)'). This feeling, furthermore, is accompanied by a certain cognitive orientation toward your present state: a repugnance for where you find yourself and a regret for the actions that brought you there.

With these elements of the passion in mind, then, consider the blunt (and deeply misogynistic) use to which the 'teacher' puts them as he sketches a bout of love-making:

> Then too I bid you open wide the windows and
> in the full flood of light remark the base body-parts.
> But as soon as your pleasure has reached its goal and come to an end,
> when body and mind are drained and drooping –
> while you feel *pig-* and would rather not have touched any girl,
> and think you won't touch one again for a good long while –
> then carefully catalogue all her blemishes
> and keep your eyes fixed on her flaws.
>
> (*Remedia Amoris*, 411–18)

The 'teacher' is obviously trading on the associations that can be formed between various forms of sight-induced aversion (cf. 429–32) and post-coital tristesse, in the expectation that the former will reinforce the latter to produce a lasting repugnance. Two other points, perhaps less obvious, are worth drawing out. First, we can appreciate the way in which Ovid neatly suggests both the psycho-somatic and the cognitive components of the passion by lodging the statement of the feeling ('while you feel *pig-*': *dum piget*) between, on the one hand, the lassitude of body and mind (414 'when body and mind are drained and drooping') and, on the other, the judgements and evaluations associated with regret (415–16 'and would rather not have touched any girl / and think you won't touch one again for a good long while'). The second point is this: the evocation of *pig-* is meant to be evocative in fact, to arouse in the reader at least some of the same feeling. The 'teacher' assumes that the reader has known *pig-* not just in general terms but in these circumstances: the insinuating second-person singular guarantees this, and the very fact that 'you' are looking for a cure for love means that you have 'been there'. And so you are encouraged to think, 'Oh Lord, I know just what you mean.' To persuade you that this therapy will work, the teacher invites you to slip into the feeling again and try it on for size.

    Now consider a final example of the passions put to work in literature, a text in which both representation and evocation are balanced with great beauty. It is the point at which, near the end of *Aeneid* 10, the renegade tyrant Mezentius is about to meet his deserved end, as he withdraws wounded before Aeneas' onslaught – but before Aeneas can close for the death blow Mezentius' devoted son, Lausus, enters the frame, weeping:

> He groaned heavily (*ingemuit graviter*), out of love for his dear begetter,
> did Lausus when he saw, and tears rolled down his cheeks.
> (*Aeneid* 10.789–90)

At the same time the narrator too steps forward, as he does when other splendid youths die (cf. 9. 446–9; 10. 501–9), now to foreshadow what we know must happen:

> Here the calamity of harsh (*acerbae*) death and your excellent (*optima*) deeds...
> I for my part shall not pass in silence, no, nor you, o memorable (*memorande*) youth.
> (*Aeneid* 10.791–3)

The epithets – 'harsh', 'excellent', 'memorable' – guide our judgement, prompting us to view Lausus' acts as noble and his death as undeserved, as he slips between his father and his attacker, holding the latter off long enough to allow the former to withdraw. Then the end:

> Aeneas bears up under the storm of war..., taunting Lausus,
> threatening Lausus: 'Why do you rush to your death, daring things

beyond your strength? Your devotion (*pietas*) makes you careless
and leads you astray.' Still Lausus leaps about in a frenzy (*exsultat demens*),
and now feelings of fierce anger (*saevae irae*) mount higher
in the Trojan leader: the Fates pluck the final strands of Lausus' life.
(*Aeneid* 10.809–15)

So Lausus dies in an ecstasy of mad aggression brought on by love and rage. Aeneas too feels great anger; yet in the midst of that anger is an awareness of virtue – *fallit te incautum pietas tua* – that both corroborates the judgement the narrator has already provided and prepares us for what happens next:

> But as he saw the expression on his face as he died,
> his face as it turned uncanny pale, the son of Anchises
> groaned heavily (*ingemuit graviter*), taking pity (*miserans*), and held out
> his right hand, and there stole upon his mind an image of a son's devotion
> for his father: 'What now, pitiable youth, will *pius* Aeneas give you to balance
> the praise you are due, what worthy of so noble a character?'
(*Aeneid* 10.821–6)

Aeneas' groan of pity (823) balances Lausus' earlier groan of love (789) to round the episode off; and by this point Vergil has done everything within his power to insure that we understand – and share – these groans. Not only has the narrator intervened in his own voice to mould our judgements; not only has Aeneas reinforced those judgements by expressly acknowledging Lausus' virtue, even at the peak of his fury; but because the moment of Lausus' death is presented through Aeneas' eyes ('But as he saw...'), we see only what he sees and, more important, we see it *as* he sees it, *Anchisiades*, 'the son of Anchises' himself once greatly devoted to his father, in whose mind the image of *pietas* is still alive and who can accordingly see himself in the dying youth before him. Not to share this pity would require a detachment so austere as to place the reader outside the community of sentiment that the text works to create. But then, the poet might ask, why bother to read at all?

To be sure, being swept up in literature's passions is not without its dangers, as readers from Plato to St Augustine, and beyond, have pointed out. But reading with an eye to the passions – with an understanding of their basis and the means used to represent and evoke them – is one of the most useful tools for grasping the play of values, virtues, and vices that makes literature most like life. And insofar as reading with understanding is itself an enjoyment, keeping an alert eye on the passions can be said to be one of the chief pleasures of the text.

FURTHER READING

The passions (or 'emotions': for present purposes the terms can be regarded as synonymous) have been much studied in the past twenty-five years, in a range of academic disciplines: Lewis and Haviland-Jones (2000) is a useful starting point, offering essays in several broad categories (e.g., 'Interdisciplinary Foundations', 'Social Processes Related to Emotion', 'Select Emotions'), with each essay supplemented by an up-to-date bibliography. Other valuable general studies, with varied conceptual frameworks, include Solomon (1976), Rorty (1980), Harré (1986), Shweder (1991), Ekman and Davidson (1994), Damasio (1995), Elster (1999), Katz (1999), Ben Ze'ev (2000), Nussbaum (2001); on the cognitive basis of the passions emphasized in this essay, especially useful are Lyons (1980), Taylor (1985), Gordon (1987), De Sousa (1987), Ortony et al. (1988).

The cognitivist approach has ancient roots, and it is therefore not surprising that much useful recent work has been done on the passions in ancient psychology and philosophy, including Fortenbaugh (1975), Frede (1986), Annas (1989), Brunschwig and Nussbaum (1993), Nussbaum (1994), Sihvola and Engberg-Pedersen (1998), Cooper (1999), Sorabji (2000). Several studies of specific passions in their ancient social and cultural context have also recently appeared, again with varied conceptual frameworks: see especially Cairns (1993) and Barton (2001) on 'shame' and 'honour' in (respectively) Greece and Rome; Barton (1993) on 'despair' and 'envy'; Harris (2001) on 'anger'; Konstan (2001) on 'pity'; Kaster (2001) on 'disgust'; Toohey (2004) on 'melancholy'. Wisse (1989) rigorously discusses the place of the passions in rhetorical theory from Aristotle to Cicero, and Fortenbaugh (1988) comments helpfully on the latter in particular; Graver (2002) is an excellent guide to Cicero's *Tusculan Disputations* 3–4, the most important overview of the passions in Latin. Finally, the contributors to Braund and Gill (1997) offer a far richer array of studies on the passions in, specifically, Roman literature than this brief essay has been able even to suggest.

CHAPTER TWENTY-THREE

Sex and Gender

A. M. Keith

1   Introduction

Throughout its history, Latin literature was produced and consumed largely by men of the Roman upper classes (Habinek 1998). Latin literature therefore exhibits a class and gender bias that tells us a great deal about how the Roman governing elites, by definition male, viewed themselves in relation to society. Of particular concern in my discussion will be the ways in which this literature codifies relations between the sexes. I shall argue that Latin letters were, from the outset, harnessed to the didactic project of training the (male) children of the Roman aristocracy in the codes and conventions of elite Roman masculinity. Formal Roman education centred on training in public speaking, which the elite male needed to master for use in the law-courts, Senate and military camps, not only among his peers but also among his social superiors and inferiors. This rhetorical education played an early role in shaping the elite Roman man's understanding of the world he was socially destined to govern, by naturalizing and legitimating social hierarchies of class, nationality, age and gender.

2   The Didactic Impulse: Fathers and Sons

Suetonius identifies the earliest teachers of Latin at Rome as Livius Andronicus and Ennius, whom he notes were both poets and half-Greeks (Suet. *Gram.* 1). Livius was the author of an *Odyssia*, adapted from Homer's *Odyssey*, which was still taught in Horace's youth (*Epist.* 2.1.69–71). Like its Homeric model, Livius' poem seems to have opened with a statement of an avowedly gendered subject: 'the man full of stratagems, goddess, tell me of him' (fr. 1, adapting Hom. *Od.* 1.1). Livius' translation of Homer's *andra* by the Latin *uirum* is faithful to the dual class and gender bias of the Homeric epics and implicitly encodes those foci at the foundation of Latin literature, which emerges as written for and about an elite (rather than base-born) and male (rather than female) audience. This is the audience addressed by Ennius in his *Annales*, which took as its subject 'the greatest deeds of the fathers' (Enn. *epigr.* 45.2 Courtney) and attributed the pre-eminence of the Roman state to her ancient traditions and men (*Ann.* 156 Sk), in a line whose first four words begin with the letters that spell out the name of Mars, the Roman god of war.

Implicit in the design of these early Latin epics (see also Goldberg, Chapter 1) is the characteristically Roman social project of celebrating moral exempla in a 'poetry that trains men' by inculcating the 'values, examples of behavior, [and] cultural models' with which Rome won and governed her Mediterranean empire (Conte 1994b: 83). If this project necessarily entails an imperial narrative of foreign conquest and external expansion, it also requires a domestic narrative of internal hierarchy and social cohesion that documents the establishment and maintenance of orderly relations between generations, classes and sexes. Thus we find embedded in Ennius' record of foreign conquest passages that delimit the social contributions of the statesman's trusted confidant (*Ann.* 268–86 Sk) and the good woman (147 Sk), as well as passages that underscore the importance of military discipline even when it conflicts with intra-familial loyalties such as those between father and son (156 Sk) or brother and sister (132 Sk). Of particular importance is the emphasis in these poems on exemplary military courage and manly conduct in the context of their use as teaching texts for the sons of the Roman elite.

Early in the Principate the *Annales* and other early epics were displaced from a central place in the curriculum by Vergil's *Aeneid* (see also Hardie, Chapter 6 above). Like Livius' *Odyssia*, the *Aeneid* takes as its focus a singular man, Aeneas – 'arms and a man I celebrate' (*Aen.* 1.1) – while like Ennius' *Annales*, Vergil's poem displays a profound commitment not only to the generational succession of father by son but also to the instruction of son by father. Mercury appeals to Aeneas' love for his own son when instructing him to quit Carthage: 'if no glory of so great an empire moves you, consider growing Ascanius, Iulus' expectation as your heir, to whom the kingdom of Italy and the Roman land are due' (4.272–6). The paternal love Aeneas demonstrates for his son by leaving North Africa in book four is paralleled by the filial love he shows for his father in his descent to the underworld in book six.

In this context, it is especially significant that the three great prophetic set-pieces in Books 1, 6 and 8, are founded on orderly sequences of genealogical descent deriving the Julians from Ascanius/Iulus (1.267–88) and the Romans from Anchises (6.679–83, 754–886) and Aeneas respectively (8.626–731). All three scenes, moreover, enact the principle of generational succession in their context as well as in their content: Jupiter instructs his daughter Venus in the future hegemony of his grandson's descendants in Book 1; Anchises instructs his son Aeneas in the exploits of their progeny in Book 6; and Vulcan forges a shield for Aeneas (at Venus' request) that documents Rome's warrior heroes. In its celebration of Roman martial valour and the father–son relationship, the *Aeneid* also continues the tradition of self-reflexive attention to the pedagogical context in which Latin epic was first encountered. Aeneas relies on the advice and guidance of his father Anchises throughout the first half of the poem, and offers both to his own son Ascanius-Iulus:

> Learn courage, son, and true toil from me, luck from others. Now my right hand will keep you safe in war and lead you into the midst of great rewards. See to it that you remember my deeds, when adulthood comes upon you, and that your father Aeneas and your father's brother Hector inspire you to live up to the examples of your ancestors. (*Aeneid* 12.435–40)

Since the *Aeneid* came to occupy a central position in the Roman school curriculum, the exemplary exploits Aeneas instructs his son to remember were taught as those for emulation by Roman schoolboys, especially the sons of the Roman governing class.

Quintilian endorsed the pedagogical practice of his day, which introduced students to reading through instruction in the epics of Vergil and Homer, precisely for the perceived moral exemplarity of the genre:

> therefore the established practice, that reading should commence with Homer and Vergil is best…let the boy's mind be elevated by the sublimity of heroic verse, derive inspiration from the greatness of the subjects, and be imbued with the best sentiments. (*Inst.* 1.8.5)

The rich commentary tradition on Vergil that survives from late antiquity demonstrates the long *durée* that this principle enjoyed. Of particular interest are the *Interpretationes Vergilianae* dedicated by Tiberius Claudius Donatus to his son, a prose paraphrase of the entire poem with discussion 'which father passed on to son without deceit' (1.2.6).

It is very likely that the circulation of the early Latin epics was restricted to the upper classes and so these texts may only have represented elite concerns, although the wide dissemination of the *Aeneid* after its appearance in *circa* 19 BCE meant that anyone with the least education would in practice have been exposed to the poem. Nonetheless we are fortunate to possess several popular dramatic works of mid-Republican date (on such comedies in general see further Panayotakis, Chapter 9 above) that display a similar attention to the relationship between fathers and sons, especially in terms of the moral education of the latter by the former, and confirm the significance in Roman culture of the principles of paternal guidance and male generational succession. In Terence's comedy *Adelphoe*, for example, the two brothers Micio and Demea exemplify rival educational theories in the upbringing of their sons. The urban sophisticate Micio propounds a doctrine of indulgence towards his (adoptive) son Aeschinus (64–77), in contrast to his brother Demea's strictness with his son Ctesipho. For most of the play, Demea and his strictures are held up to mockery and derision by the other characters, but the final scenes stage his recovery of the moral high ground in the exposition of an ideal educational programme in which father checks son's waywardness but avoids the excesses of either severity or indulgence (986–95). This is a paternal educative code which all can endorse; as Micio himself says, 'that's the right way' (997).

Plautus too highlights the father's responsibility for educating his son in a number of his comedies. In *Trinummus*, for example, Lysiteles acknowledges his father's role in forming his character, in a passage that highlights the advantages he has received from following paternal precepts:

LYSITELES.   From the beginning of my adolescence to my present age I always obeyed
             your commands and precepts, father . . . . By my modesty I have ever held
             your precepts wind-tight and water-tight.
PHILTO.   Why are you reproaching me? What you did well you did for yourself, not for
             me; indeed my life is nearly over: this matters most for you.
                                                         (*Trinummus* 301–2, 314–19)

Here Plautus illustrates the pragmatic familial and social goals that led father to educate son. More frequently, however, he mocks and subverts the traditional paternal role in a son's education in his comedies. Thus in *Mostellaria* a wastrel son reflects on the responsibility of parents for their children's education:

> Parents are their children's builders: they construct their children's foundations;
> they raise them up, carefully make them strong, and neither spare material nor think
> outlay there an expense in order that their children be productive and attractive to
> the public and to themselves; they groom them: they teach them literature, statutes,
> laws, and strive by cost and labour to make others want similar children for
> themselves. (*Mostellaria* 118–28)

The comedy of the passage resides in the spendthrift character of the youth who enunciates these principles, since the play focuses on his efforts to conceal from his father the depradations he has made on the paternal estate in the course of his parent's absence.

Latin epic and comedy are not alone in displaying both a didactic impulse and a prominent emphasis on the generational transmission of the exemplary standards of Roman manliness from father to son. These features also characterize the earliest Latin prose writing, by Cato the Elder (see further Goldberg, Chapter 1 above). In the preface to his treatise on farming, for example, Cato declares that farmers make the bravest men and most energetic soldiers while their occupation is the most honourable (*Agr. pr.* 4). The association of farming with the core values of exemplary Roman masculinity – bravery and military service – both underlies and authorizes this didactic treatise on farming. Moreover Cato seems to have promoted the same principles in other works no longer extant. In the *Origines*, for example, he expounded the origins of Rome and other Italian cities and documented her rise to domination of the Mediterranean through the collective accomplishments, primarily in warfare, of the Roman people (defined as the male citizen body). We also hear of a series of works addressed to his son Cato Licinianus on agriculture, medicine, and rhetoric (sometimes referred to compendiously under the title 'Precepts to his Son'), which exemplify the Roman father's special role in educating his son. Plutarch records that Cato himself not only taught his son to read but even wrote histories for him in large characters in order to instruct him in the exemplary exploits of their ancestors and fellow-countrymen (*Cat. Mai.* 20.7).

At the end of the Republic Cicero produced an even more voluminous body of prose-writing in rhetoric and oratory, philosophy and letters (see also Levene, Chapter 2 above). Like Cato in his agricultural and historical works, moreover, Cicero seems to have been moved by a didactic impulse in the composition of his numerous rhetorical and philosophical treatises. In *Brutus*, for example, he traces for his young protégé Brutus (the tyrannicide) the history of oratory at Rome from its origins to his own day. As a record of the evolution of oratory in ancient Rome, the dialogue contains a chronological series of biographical sketches of famous Roman politicians, culminating in Cicero's autobiographical account of his own rhetorical training. With its teleological schema celebrating successive generations of prominent Roman orators along with its paternalistic dedication, the *Brutus* reads like the rhetorical equivalent of the pageant of military heroes reviewed by Anchises in *Aeneid* 6. Unfortunately Brutus proved an unsatisfactory 'son', resisting Cicero's 'Asianist' teleology to remain firmly in the 'Atticist' camp.

Cicero seems to have been more successful in instilling his rhetorical and moral principles into his own son, whose education he supervised and to whom he dedicated his last treatise, the three books 'On Duties'. In the proem Cicero asserts the rhetorical utility of both his philosophical treatises and his speeches:

> you will make your Latin discourse fuller by reading my works indeed . . . . Therefore I encourage you especially, my son, to read carefully not only my speeches but even those books on philosophy which are now nearly equal in number to them – for the force of speaking is greater in the former, but an even and moderate style of discourse must also be practised. (*Off.* 1.1–3)

Of particular interest is Cicero's advice to his son to immerse himself in his literary, which is to say rhetorical, style. For Cicero here undertakes to train his son in rhetoric by harnessing retrospectively all his speeches, forensic and political, to the project of young Marcus' education. But it is not only as a stylistic model that Cicero claims value for this work. At the end of the preface he emphasizes the utility for his son's education of the theme of duty:

> But when I had decided to write something for you … I wanted especially to start with something most suitable for your age and my authority. For although many weighty and useful subjects in philosophy have been treated carefully and fully by the philosophers, those precepts which have been handed down concerning duties seemed to have the widest significance. For no part of life – neither in public nor private, neither in legal work nor domestic, neither if you are transacting business by yourself nor if you are contracting with another – can be free of duty; every honourable pursuit of life lies in its cultivation, every disgrace in its neglect. (*Off.* 2.1)

The younger Cicero seems to have learned his father's precepts well. Although he was in Athens studying philosophy at the time of Cicero's murder in 43 BCE, he went on to enjoy a distinguished political career under Octavian, serving as his colleague in the consulship in 30 BCE and was eventually appointed governor of the province Syria and proconsul of Asia.

3   Between Men: Homosocial Intercourse in Latin Literature

The intimate connection between fathers' education of their sons and Roman rhetorical training recurs in the writings of the elder Seneca, who dedicated to his three sons, ostensibly at their request, his ten books of *Controversiae* celebrating the declamatory culture of the early principate (*Contr.* 1 *pr.* 1, 4, 6, 10). Seneca *pater* self-consciously cites the elder Cato in his preface, implicitly taking the Republican censor as his own model for educating his sons in rhetoric: 'What then did that famous man say? "An orator, Marcus my son, is a good man, skilled in speaking" ' (*Contr.* 1 *pr.* 9). Like Cato and Cicero, the elder Seneca asserts the social value of rhetoric in his history of Roman declamation:

> But, my young men, you are pursuing an important and useful matter because, not content with the examples of your own day, you wish also to know those of an earlier generation. First since the more examples one examines, the greater the benefit to one's own eloquence. (*Contr.* 1 *pr.* 6)

In the dedication to his sons, moreover, Seneca explictly includes a broader (elite Roman male) audience for his reminiscences: 'So much the more happily shall I do what you ask, and I shall dedicate to the public whatever eloquent sayings of illustrious men I remember, so that they do not belong to anyone privately' (*Contr.* 1 *pr.* 10). Seneca envisions his work in circulation among the Roman political elite (Bloomer 1997: 120), which enjoyed privileged access to rhetorical education and gained political office through competitive displays of eloquence

(Gleason 1995: xx–xxiv). Seneca thus makes explicit the paternal role in initiating sons into the male homosocial network central to Latin political, rhetorical, and literary culture.

The adjective 'homosocial' describes social bonds between members of the same sex in such arenas as 'friendship, mentorship, entitlement, rivalry, and … sexuality' (Sedgwick 1985: 1). Seneca's handbooks can be seen to articulate male homosocial bonds along all of these axes. Thus in broadening his prospective audience from his sons to the public, Seneca assumes the role of mentor to the sons of the Roman elite. In recalling the declaimers of a previous generation, moreover, he privileges the performances of his Spanish friends Latro and Gallio in the private halls of Roman aristocrats while ignoring a host of Greek teachers and practitioners (Bloomer 1997: 115–35); his work thereby exemplifies the homosocial bonds of elite Hispano-Roman male friendship and implicitly documents the social and political entitlement of that class. Finally the format of the treatises, in which Seneca lists seriatim the interventions of the declaimers on each side of a given theme, exposes the social and professional alliances and rivalries that animated declamatory teaching and practice in the early Principate.

Declamation, like its nobler counterpart oratory, was an exercise in masculine co-operation and competition. The co-operative aspect of rhetoric is almost wholly lost to our view since we lack complete speeches by anyone other than Cicero. We know nonetheless that in the law courts the senior advocate could be supported by junior counsel in both prosecution and defence. Similarly, more than one speech on either side of a political issue would be heard in both senate and assembly. More visible to us is the competitive nature of rhetorical culture. We possess, for example, a matched set of political invectives, school exercises, in the form of a pseudo-Sallustian 'Invective against Cicero' and a pseudo-Ciceronian 'Invective against Sallust'. Rhetorical competition is most clearly illustrated in Roman historical literature. In his *Bellum Catilinae*, for example, Sallust selects for verbatim report from the debate in the Senate on the punishment of the captured Catilinarian conspirators the speeches of Julius Caesar and the younger Cato since senatorial opinion was swayed by each in turn. Caesar's speech invokes ancestral custom, which he characterizes as deliberation and daring (*Cat.* 51.37), to educate his fellow senators in the duties of the Roman political elite and advocate confiscation of the conspirators' property and their imprisonment. Cato likewise appeals to *mos maiorum* in his speech in support of the consul's proposal to execute the conspirators, but for him hard work and the ideal of liberty constitute ancestral custom (*Cat.* 52.21) and he contrasts the degeneracy of his contemporaries with the manliness of the ancestors: 'in their place we have luxury and greed, public want, private opulence . . . . Between good and bad men there is no distinction, and ambition holds all the rewards of courage' (*uirtus*, literally 'manliness', *Cat.* 52.22).

Such rhetorical set-pieces are common in Latin literature, and as instances of elite male homosocial competition often appeal to clichés of masculinity even as they

enact elite male solidarity. Livy furnishes a particularly lively example in his report of
the debate in 195 BCE about the repeal of the Oppian law, which limited the display
of wealth by Roman matrons. In this debate the consuls, the elder Cato and L.
Valerius, spoke for and against the law respectively. Livy's Cato opens with an appeal
to male solidarity in the face of the women's seditious demonstrations in favour of
the law's repeal: 'if each of us, Roman citizens, had decided to retain a husband's
right and power over his own wife, we should have less trouble with the mass of
them' (34.2.1). Invoking ancestral custom, Cato emphasizes Roman men's long-
standing authority over their womenfolk in a formulation that vividly documents
male social and financial power: 'our ancestors allowed no woman to transact
business, not even privately, without a guardian and wanted women to be under
the control of fathers, brothers, husbands' (34.2.11). If the law were to be
repealed, Cato argues, individual men's power – and therefore collective male
authority – would be dangerously compromised. Indeed, for Livy's Cato, yielding
to the women's pressure will inevitably result in the complete overthrow of male
authority: 'as soon as they begin to be our equals, they will be our superiors'
(34.3.3). Cato's appeal to male solidarity thus enlists the ideological support of
ancestral custom in a battle over legislative authority between the sexes.

In a debate concerning the repeal of a women's sumptuary law, it is hardly
surprising that the speakers rehearse the clichés of femininity, and Cato's opponent also appeals to feminine stereotypes in his speech in support of the law's
repeal: 'This could wound the feelings of men; what do you think it does to
foolish women, whom even small things move?' (34.7.7). Valerius, like the elder
Cato, presses ancestral custom into the service of his argument, but he scoffs at
the idea that repeal of the Oppian law will release women from male authority:

> daughters, wives, even sisters will be less in the power (*in manu*, literally in the
> hand') of some men – but never will women's slavery be shaken off while their men
> are alive; and they themselves hate the freedom which loss of husband and father
> causes. They prefer their dress to be at your discretion than the law's; and you ought
> to hold them in power and guardianship, not in slavery, and to prefer to be called
> fathers or husbands than masters. (Valerius, 34.7.11–14)

Since under the stricter law of Republican Rome women were subject throughout
their lives to male authority, either of father in *patria potestas* or of husband if
married *in manu*, Livy's Valerius implies that with the repeal of the Oppian law
Roman men should in fact recover full domestic authority over their womenfolk.

4   The Traffic in Women

The feminine clichés to which Livy's consuls appeal in their speeches not only
strengthen male social bonds and elite authority – over foreigner, female and slave

– but also naturalize the hierarchy of the sexes on display throughout Latin literature. For like Latin speeches and texts, women are conceptualized as circulating among men. Since, as we have seen, women are in the hands of father, husband or brother, their exchange – from father or brother to husband – can cement good relations between natal and marital families. Thus Suetonius comments that in 70 BCE Julius Caesar secured the political recall of his wife Cornelia's brother, L. Cinna (*Iul.* 5). Caesar's loyalty to Cornelia had already incurred the wrath of the dictator Sulla when he took Rome from the Marians in the late 80s BCE, for it implied his continuing political loyalty to her father Cinna, Marius' colleague:

> He took to wife Cornelia, daughter of the Cinna who was consul four times . . . nor could he be persuaded in any way by the dictator Sulla to divorce her. Therefore he was stripped of his priesthood, his wife's dowry, and his family inheritances, and was considered to be a member of the opposing faction. (*Iul.* 1.1–2)

His loyalty to Cornelia was such that on her death he delivered in her honour a funeral oration in the Forum, which Suetonius connects with one Caesar delivered for his aunt Julia (*Iul.* 6.1). Suetonius reports that Caesar used his aunt's ancestry to trace his familial lineage back to the king Ancus Marcius and the goddess Venus in order to enhance his political prestige and authority, and it is likely that he used the opportunity of Cornelia's death similarly, to associate himself with his father-in-law's politics. In this regard, it is significant that Suetonius sets Caesar's funeral orations for his dead womenfolk in the context of his quaestorship, a junior political office en route to the consulship, for it implies that Caesar made political capital out of these speeches.

The textualization of women and their circulation among men is a central gender dynamic of Roman lyric and love elegy (cf. Harrison, Chapter 13 above and Gibson, Chapter 11 above). Catullus, for example, invites his friend and fellow-poet Caecilius on a visit to Verona to discuss the progress of his friend's unfinished poem on Cybele, which he calls both 'Mistress of Dindymus' (35.13–14) and 'Great Mother' (35.18). Catullus' poem constitutes particularly interesting evidence about the reception of a textual woman, because it sets into literary circulation a second female figure, whom Catullus treats at even greater length than Caecilius' Cybele:

> And so, if [Caecilius] is clever, he'll eat up the road, even if a beautiful girl calls him back a thousand times, casts both hands round his neck and asks him to linger; who now, if the report I hear is true, loves him hopelessly with an ungovernable passion. For from the time when she read the unfinished 'Mistress of Dindymus', the tender flames of love have consumed her to the core. I forgive you, girl more learned than Sappho's Muse; for Caecilius has begun his 'Great Mother' charmingly. (Cat. 35.7–18)

Catullus thus responds to Caecilius' textual woman by composing another: one literary 'mistress' is exchanged for another.

Catullus addresses some of his most passionate love lyrics to a woman he names 'Lesbia' (5, 7, 51), usually identified as a Clodia (see Wiseman 1985: 130–7), but he sets these poems in a collection dedicated to Cornelius Nepos:

> To whom shall I give my slender new book, freshly polished with dry pumice? To you, Cornelius: for you were accustomed to think my trifles something . . . . Therefore have for yourself whatever this little book is, such as it is . . . (Cat. 1)

The Lesbia lyrics are thereby subsumed into the gift presented to a literary patron. Even within the collection, moreover, Lesbia circulates between Catullus and his friends (Fitzgerald 1995). In Poem 11, for example, Catullus asks Furius and Aurelius to inform Lesbia of his repudiation of her, while in Poem 58 he tells Caelius of Lesbia's sexual degradation:

> Caelius, our Lesbia, that Lesbia, infamous Lesbia, whom alone Catullus loved more than himself and all his relations, now peels great-souled Remus' grandsons at crossroads and in alleys.

Most critics have interpreted this obscene lyric more or less literally, to the effect that Lesbia abandons herself to a succession of degenerate lovers (though it is frequently allowed that she is perhaps not actually working as a prostitute) after throwing over Catullus and his friend Caelius. Certainly the poem explicitly sets Lesbia in circulation among Roman nobles in general, and between Caelius and Catullus in particular. But its placement so close to the end of the polymetric part of the collection as a whole, invites interpretation in metaliterary terms, as a meditation on the circulation of Catullus' 'Lesbia' lyrics among the Roman reading public.

This reading receives some support by analogy with elegiac poetry. Propertius, for example, wrote elegies about a woman he calls 'Cynthia', and opened his first book with a description of how he fell in love: 'Cynthia first captivated me – alas! – with her eyes, though I had been untouched by desire before' (Prop. 1.1.1–2). The first word of the first poem in the book, 'Cynthia', will have functioned as the title of the work as Propertius himself implies, in a later reference to his 'Cynthia read in the whole forum' (Prop. 2.24.2) that recalls Caesar's delivery of a funeral oration for his dead wife and aunt from the Rostra. But the public circulation of Propertius' Cynthia – both elegiac mistress and text – redounds in this instance to the speaker's discredit, for it reveals his essentially frivolous lifestyle in avoiding the political career laid out for upper-class Roman men to publish instead literary trifles about a courtesan (24.3–10). If Propertius here accepts Cynthia's circulation as a source of disgrace for himself, Ovid both accuses his mistress of prostitution (like Catullus) and accepts a measure of responsibility (like Propertius) for her circulation among men:

She who just now was called my own, whom I alone began to love, I fear I must share with many. Am I mistaken, or did she become known in my little books? So it is – she prostituted herself through my talent. And I deserve it! For what did I do but auction her beauty? My mistress was put up for sale through my fault. (*Am.* 3.12.5–8)

Ovid thus literalizes the trope that figures the publication of poetry about an elegiac mistress as the mistress' sexual circulation among men (Fear 2000b).

5   Among Women

We look in vain for women writing to, for or about women in extant Roman literature. Archaeology, however, has unearthed an invitation to a birthday party from a Roman matron named Claudia Severa, whose husband was an army-officer stationed in Britain early in the second century CE, to her close friend (or sister) Sulpicia Lepidina, whose husband was the prefect of a cohort of Batavians at Vindolanda. The invitation was written by a scribe, but contains a postscript added by Claudia Severa herself: 'I shall expect you, sister. Farewell, sister, my dearest soul, as I hope to prosper, and hail.' This tantalizing artefact offers us a rare glimpse into the personal lives of two women living in Roman Britain and illustrates the close bonds of affection among women that for the most part elude us in our scrutiny of the dynamics of gender in Latin literature.

The best-known female author of classical Rome is probably the elegiac poet Sulpicia, either the daughter or the granddaughter of Cicero's friend, the jurist Ser. Sulpicius Rufus, and the niece of Augustus' senior statesman, the orator and literary patron M. Valerius Messalla Corvinus. Her poetry could be said to 'traffic in men', or at least in one man since she publishes her love for a certain Cerinthus in her verse. And indeed recent scholarship has found her to be a subtle reader of the gender clichés of contemporary Augustan epic and elegy, adapting them in her poetry in such a way as to articulate a female perspective on love and love elegy (Santirocco 1979; Parker 1994; Keith 1997; see also Gibson, Chapter 11 above). There is, however, no evidence for the circulation of her poetry among women. Quite the contrary, in fact, for she addresses individual poems exclusively to men – Messala (3.14.5) and Cerinthus (3.17.1; presumably also the addressee of 3.15, 16 and 18). Whatever the context in which her poetry circulated, however, and this remains unclear, she herself explicitly invites others to rehearse the details of her passion:

At last has come a love which it would disgrace me more to hide out of shame than expose to someone. Prevailed upon by my Camenae the Cytherean delivered him into my arms on trust. Venus has kept her promise. My joys can be the talk of all who are said to have none of their own. I would not wish to send a message under seal so

no one could read it before my man. But I'm glad to sin and tired of wearing
reputation's mask. The world shall know I've met my match. ([Tib.] 3.13)

Stephen Hinds (1987a) has observed that at least one of her readers met this
challenge – the author of some, or all, of the poems of the so-called 'Garland of
Sulpicia' ([Tib.] 3.8–12). There is considerable controversy over the identity of
the *auctor de Sulpicia* (interested readers should consult Parker 1994 for the
debate), but it seems clear that the reason her poetry is still extant is its inclusion
in the manuscripts of Tibullus, a context that sets her poetry in a framework
consistent with the sociological conventions of gender in Latin literary culture
and thereby facilitates her assimilation to an elegiac *puella*. Thus in the opening
couplet of (Tib.) 3.8, the first poem in the sequence, Mars is invited to enjoy the
sight of Sulpicia adorned on the occasion of the first day of his month, March
([Tib.] 3.8 1–2): 'Great Mars, on your Kalends Sulpicia's dressed for you; if
you're wise, you'll come from heaven to see her.' The couplet, and by implication
the sequence that follows, thus engage the conventionally male 'gaze' of elegiac
poetry to objectify a *puella* named Sulpicia for our delectation. Indeed the
opening poem celebrates Sulpicia's beauty at some length and concludes with
an exhortation to the Muses and Apollo to make her the subject of their song on
this day every year ([Tib.] 3.8.21–4): 'Of her on the holiday Kalends sing,
Pierides and Phoebus, proud of your tortoiseshell lyre. May she celebrate this
solemn rite for many years; no girl is worthier of your choir.' Sulpicia and her
poetry are thereby framed from the outset as circulating among men.

   Although we look in vain for female intimacy such as we find in Sappho in the
elegidia of Sulpicia, there are some notable instances elsewhere in Latin literature.
Towards the end of Trimalchio's dinner party in Petronius' *Satyricon*, for
example, with the arrival of Habinnas and his wife, Trimalchio's wife Fortunata
joins the party and reclines with Scintilla on her couch. While the two women
compare jewellery their husbands mock this feminine interest in baubles (Petron.
Sat. 67): ' "You see women's chains," Trimalchio said. "Thus we fools are
plundered" .... Then Habinnas said, "If women didn't exist, we'd rate everything dirt cheap." ' Ignoring their husbands' mockery, the women drink wine and
cuddle as Fortunata complains about her household responsibilities and Scintilla
about her husband's affairs. This comic scene illuminates Roman clichés of
feminine nature in its focus on the pair's interest in gold and trinkets, household
duties and love. But it also testifies to the emotional intimacy of women's
relations with one another, for their absorption in conversation allows Habinnas
to sneak over unnoticed and play a practical joke on Fortunata.

   Perhaps surprisingly, the genre in which bonds among women are most fully
explored and elaborated in Latin literature is epic. Ennius, for example, describes
Aeneas' daughter Ilia reporting a dream which has frightened her to her half-
sister and their old nurse (*Ann.* 34–50 Sk). The exclusively feminine audience for
Ilia's story contrasts with the male figures in her dream: Mars, who ravishes her,

and Aeneas, who reassures her. It is her sister, however, whom Ilia seeks in the confusion of her dream (38–42 Sk): 'For a handsome man seemed to drag me through pleasant willow-thickets, along river banks and new places; and then, dear sister, I seemed to wander alone, walking slowly and seeking you; nor could I embrace you.' Yet although Ennius emphasizes Ilia's affection for her sister, he also implies Ilia's erotic interest in the 'handsome man'.

Love stories are frequently represented as the subject of women's narratives in the mostly male-authored texts of antiquity, and Ilia's report of her dream-encounter finds a suggestive parallel in the love stories Clymene tells her sister river-nymphs in Vergil's fourth *Georgic* (345–7): 'in their midst Clymene was telling the story of Vulcan's vain care, the tricks and sweet thefts of Mars, and was recounting the frequent loves of the gods from Chaos on'. In the *Aeneid* too, Vergil includes a scene in which sisters exchange amatory confidences, when Dido discloses her love for the handsome stranger, Aeneas, to Anna. Ovid in the *Metamorphoses* admits several scenes of female intimacy, but his women also discuss erotic subjects. In the third book, for example, Juno visits the Theban princess Semele in the guise of her aged nurse Beroë and turns their talk to Semele's lover: 'I wish that he may be Jupiter,' she said, 'but I fear all things: many men have entered chaste bed-chambers under the name of the gods' (3.280–2). Moreover in the fourth book, the daughters of Minyas beguile their wool-working with a series of mythological love stories while they spurn the rites of Bacchus. The wool-working context is itself quintessentially feminine, an activity that enjoyed particular esteem in Augustan Rome where the emperor boasted that his wife, daughter, and granddaughters wove his clothing (Suet. *Aug.* 64.2, 73). The Minyads implicitly assert their exemplary feminine virtue by drawing a contrast between their own service to the 'better' goddess, Minerva, and the Theban women's misguided worship of the false god Bacchus (4.37–8). Yet the stories they tell reveal the excessive interest in love of even the most virtuous women: the forbidden love of Pyramus and Thisbe; Venus' punishment of the Sun for betraying her adulterous liaison with Mars; and Salmacis' rape of Hermaphroditus.

FURTHER READING

The sociopolitical implications of Latin literature have been well discussed recently by Bloomer (1997) and Habinek (1998), who emphasize the upper-class bias and aristocratic invention respectively of this literature; see also Habinek's chapter in this volume. Lee (1979) is a comprehensive introduction to the theme of fathers and sons in the *Aeneid*, while Starr (1991) analyses an exemplary case of father–son instruction in the context of reading Vergil's epic. The standard discussion of male homosocial relations is Sedgwick (1985), on English literature:

the subject is treated in connection with classical rhetorical culture by Gleason (1995), who examines the construction of masculinity in the period of the second Sophistic, and Bloomer (1997), who analyses the assertion of class privilege by declaimers in early imperial Rome; in connection with Catullan lyric by Fitzgerald (1995) and Wiseman (1985); and in connection with Ovidian elegy by Fear (2000b). The Vindolanda writing tablets were comprehensively edited by Bowman and Thomas (1994). Hemelrijk (1998) investigates what is known and what can be surmised about women's writing in Latin. The literary qualities of Sulpicia's poetry are discussed by Santirocco (1979) and Keith (1997); Hinds (1987a) examines the literary achievement of the 'Garland'-poet, while Parker (1994) analyses the misogynistic scholarly tradition that attributes Sulpicia's work to him. Keith (2000) discusses the public roles of women in Latin epic.

CHAPTER TWENTY-FOUR

Friendship and Patronage

David Konstan

1 Introduction

Ancient Rome was a deeply stratified society. From the time when Latin literature first began to be produced in the third century BC (see Goldberg, Chapter 1 above), and indeed well before then, the Roman census divided citizens according to wealth and status, with the senatorial order at the top and proletarians, that is, those whose wealth consisted solely in their children, at the bottom rung. In these circumstances, the poor depended for security and well being on powerful families, who in turn relied on them for political support. Such relations, largely informal in the historical period but sanctioned by custom, were what the Romans understood by the terms 'patron' (*patronus*) and 'client' (*cliens*). In the late Republic, clients were expected to vote for their patron if he ran for office, while he in turn undertook to represent them, if necessary, in legal proceedings (Deniaux 1993: 2–12, with bibliography; on judicial patronage, David 1992).

Friendship, in turn, was ideally a relationship between equals: *philotēs isotēs* went the Greek jingle (Aristotle *EN* 8.5.1157b36; *EE* 7.8.1241b13): 'amity is parity'. This does not mean that bonds of mutual affection could not develop across class boundaries; there is abundant evidence that they did, and that such relations were recognized as true friendships. And yet, class lines are not so easily erased, and there are indications that attitudes of deference and condescension often persisted among such friends. One sign of this self-consciousness is the practice of referring to friends of higher social standing as 'powerful friends' (*amici potentes*), 'great friends' (*magni amici*) and the like. Indeed, among cultivated people the terms 'patron' and 'client' seem to have been avoided, and polite usage insisted on the term 'friend' (*amicus*) even where the inequality of the relationship seems to us glaring (Nauta 2002: 14–18).

This convention does not in and of itself mean that the friendships in question were purely formal, with no element of reciprocal fondness. Many scholars today, however, hold that even among equals, *amicitia* was basically a matter of services rather than affection. Thus, Michael Peachin (2001b: 135 n. 2) observes that 'the standard modern view...tends to reduce significantly the emotional aspect of the relationship among the Romans, and to make of it a rather pragmatic business.' Some go so far as to treat Roman friendship as a formal, institutionalized relation involving reciprocal obligations and established on specific terms (Caldelli 2001: 22). On this view, hierarchical friendships differ from those between equals chiefly in respect to the kinds of services due. This surely overstates the business-like character of friendship (see Konstan 1997 and 2002): there are numerous passages in Roman literature that reveal the core of *amicitia* to be love or *amor*, as Cicero maintained (*De Amicitia* 26; cf. *Partitiones oratoriae* 88). Undoubtedly, personal interests might compromise friendships, and differences in power opened the way to exploitation of the relationship whether by the richer or the poorer party. But such behaviour, then as now, was an abuse of friendship, not its essence.

Nevertheless, the association between friendship and patronage may have blurred to some extent the distinction between genuine intimacy and more pragmatic connections. If a humble man spoke of social superior as his 'friend,' was he merely using a euphemistic formula for 'benefactor,' or was he pretending to a mutuality beyond and above the difference of station? Richard Saller affirms:

> To discuss bonds between senior aristocrats and their aspiring juniors in terms of 'friendship' seems to me misleading, because of the egalitarian overtones that the word has in modern English. Though willing to extend the courtesy of the label *amicus* to some of their inferiors, the status-conscious Romans did not allow the courtesy to obscure the relative social standings of the two parties. (1989: 57)

I should rather say that, just because the notion of friendship or *amicitia* retained the sense of a voluntary affective tie, the ambiguity cannot be eliminated. Cicero, writing in the persona of Laelius, the intimate friend of Scipio Aemilianus, gives the right nuance:

> in a friendship, it is crucial to be a peer to one's inferior. For there are often certain outstanding cases, like Scipio in our bunch, if I may put it so: never did he put himself above Philus, or Rupilius or Mummius, or friends of lower rank (*ordo*). (*De Amicitia* 19.69)

Laelius adds that

> just as those who are superior in a relationship of friendship and association should make themselves equal to their inferiors, so too inferiors ought not to take it ill that they are surpassed in ability or fortune or station. (20.71)

Class differences are taken for granted, but Cicero does not on that account dismiss such friendships as inauthentic. Roman friendship was thus a loaded concept: it designated a selfless, loving bond, but it might also connote a reciprocal expectation of services, whether between equals or unequals, such as true friendship too afforded, albeit on the basis of generosity and love rather than practical considerations (Raccanelli 1998: 19–40).

Finally, we may note that Roman social relations were governed by a refined sense of etiquette that enabled men to preserve their face or *dignitas* in the intensely competitive and status-conscious world of the Roman aristocracy. The elaborate expressions of good will and affection in which these courtesies were encoded are not signs of insincerity, but rather forms of civility that were 'a necessary prelude to social transactions' (Hall, forthcoming; cf. Hall 1996 and 1998). Politeness was, indeed, so integral to Roman conversation that even the most intimate expression of affection necessarily made use of the same coinage. Thus, Cicero writes to Atticus:

> I imagine you are the one person less ingratiating (*blandus*) than I am, or else, if we are both so from time to time toward someone, at least we never are among ourselves. So listen when I tell you this matter-of-factly: may I cease to live, dear Atticus, if not just Tusculum, where I am otherwise content, but even the Isles of the Blessed mean so much to me that I would be whole days without you. (*Ad Atticum* 12.3.1)

Cicero employs the formulas of gracious hyperbole even as he fears that his affirmation 'may appear indistinguishable from the polite effusions conventionally exchanged between aristocrats' (Hall, forthcoming). Nor were such courtesies confined to exchanges between members of the upper classes; the young Marcus Cicero, while studying in Athens, employs the same conventions in a letter written to his father's freedman and secretary Tiro (*Ad Familiares* 16.21; Hall, forthcoming).

The preceding discussion indicates the complex context in which literary relationships of friendship and patronage must be understood. To this we must add the further consideration that these relations changed to some degree over time, and especially with the transformation in Roman social life that accompanied the shift from Republic to Empire. The best procedure, accordingly, is to respect chronology and follow the evolution of literary patronage and friendship, beginning with the earliest Roman writers.

2 Patronage and Friendship in Early Roman Literature

The first author of whom we hear (see Goldberg, Chapter 1 above) is Livius Andronicus, who composed tragedies and comedies and translated Homer's *Odyssey* into the archaic Saturnian metre. Information concerning Livius' social status is largely late and contradictory, but it seems he had been a prisoner of war, was subsequently freed, and worked as a schoolteacher in Rome. It is conceivable that he was a client of the Livius clan. The historian Livy reports (27.37) that Livius was chosen to compose a choral poem for girls in the year 207, a critical moment during the Second Punic War. Livius Salinator was one of the consuls in that year, and it is plausible that he acted in the role of patron to the poet, at least to the extent of granting him the commission.

It is remarkable that not just Livius but all poets active in Rome in the century following him appear to have been foreigners, with none belonging to the highest level of the aristocracy. Gnaeus Naevius, who composed an annalistic epic on the first Punic War as well as tragedies and comedies, came from Campania to the south of Rome (Aulus Gellius 1.24.2). He seems to have mocked the Metellus family, one of whom was consul and another praetor in 206, and to have paid for this indiscretion with a stint in prison (Plautus *Miles Gloriosus* 209–12 may allude to this episode). Evidently, his social position was precarious; whether he had a patron on his side is moot.

Ennius, who, like Naevius, wrote an epic history of Rome along with tragedies and comedies (and works in various other genres), was born in Calabria and brought to Rome by Cato the Elder, according to Cornelius Nepos (*Cato* 1.4). Ennius accompanied Marcus Fulvius Nobilior on his campaign to Aetolia (189), perhaps with a view to celebrating his achievements, and he acquired Roman citizenship thanks to Fulvius' son, Quintus. Aulus Gellius (12.4) quotes some verses from the seventh book of Ennius' *Annales* for their depiction of the ideal relationship between a man of lesser station and an upper-class friend (*hominis minoris erga amicum superiorem*), which he regards as constituting veritable laws of friendship. The passage had been taken by the first century BC antiquarian Aelius Stilo to reflect Ennius' own relationship with Fulvius:

> He summons a man with whom he often shares his table and conversation and takes counsel on his affairs, after having spent the better part of the day deliberating on the highest matters of state in the wide forum and hallowed senate . . . . A learned, loyal, gentle man, pleasant, content with his station, happy, cultivated, saying the right thing at the right time, amenable, of few words . . . (see Goldberg 1995: 120–3).

Were the Fulvii, then, Ennius' patrons? Yet Ennius was also on intimate terms with the Scipios. Cicero (*De Oratore* 2.276) records an anecdote in which Scipio Nasica once knocked at Ennius' door and was told by the maid that Ennius wasn't at home; when Ennius dropped by at Nasica's a few days later, Nasica himself answered that he was out. Ennius protested that he recognized Nasica's voice, and the latter replied, 'Insolent fellow: when I was looking for you I believed your maid that you weren't home, and you don't believe me in person?' Whatever the truth of this story, Cicero thought it plausible, and it presupposes an easy comradeship between the poet and the patrician.

Plautus, the earliest Roman writer whose works, or at least some of them, survive entire, came to Rome from Umbria. According to Varro (cited in Aulus Gellius 3.3.14), he made money in the theatre, lost it in commerce, and earned it back again by writing comedies, which were so successful that he could live off the proceeds of his art. There is no mention of a patron or other personal relations in the biographical tradition, which in any case is of dubious value. With Terence, however, the case is different. His cognomen, Afer, makes it at least plausible that he was brought to Rome as a slave from the area round Carthage, as Suetonius claimed (*Vita Terenti* 1). Later, he was on intimate terms with Scipio Aemilianus, Laelius, and their crowd, and was selected to present a play at the funeral celebration for Aemilius Paulus, Scipio's father (one sees the importance of individual sponsorship). What is more, malicious rumour had it that powerful friends helped Terence compose his comedies (Suetonius *De Poetis* 11; other references in Courtney 1993: 88). In the prologue to *Adelphoe* (15–19), Terence himself affirms (via one of his actors):

> As to what those spiteful fellows say, that noblemen help him and in fact constantly write together with him, they may consider this a terrible insult, but he [Terence] deems it the greatest praise if he pleases men who please all of you and Rome. (cf. *Heautontimoroumenos* 22–6; on their identities, see Gruen 1993: 197–202).

In Cicero's *De Amicitia*, moreover, Laelius speaks of Terence as his *familiaris* (24.89), which suggests that (in Cicero's view) he regarded the playwright as an intimate.

Of other comic writers, it is known that Caecilius Statius came to Rome as a slave and prisoner of war, and lived for a time with Ennius. Among tragic poets, Pacuvius, the nephew of Ennius, was born in Brindisi, and Accius, who first performed in Rome in 140 and wrote also annals and other works, hailed from Pisaurum in Umbria and was a client of Decimus Junius Brutus.

Evidently, the Roman aristocracy of this period disdained to write poetry, at least in the popular forms of drama, epic, and commissioned lyrics. As Cicero puts it (*Tusc.* 1.1.3), 'poets, then, were recognized or received among us late, even though it is stated in [Cato's] *Origines* that guests at feasts used to sing to the flute about the virtues of distinguished men; yet a speech of Cato's asserts that there was no honour accorded even to this kind [of poetry]' (1.2.3; cf. Aulus Gellius 11.2.5; Krostenko 2001: 22–31). I cannot help wondering whether the insinuation that powerful friends helped Terence compose his comedies was more a slur against aristocrats who stooped to writing poetry than the literary incompetence of their protégé (contra Gruen 1993: 202).

In contrast to the foreign and relatively humble origins of the earliest playwrights and epic poets, Cato himself inaugurated the publication of history and speeches in Latin (see Kraus, Chapter 17 above, and Berry, Chapter 18 above), and these genres remained the province of the highest echelon of society; as

Cicero says, 'we quickly embraced oratory' (*Tusc.* 1.3.5; cf. Sciarrino 2004). While the powerful might patronize professional poets, they distanced themselves from them by composing a different kind of literature.

Surviving Roman comedies (see Panayotakis, Chapter 9 above) are based on Greek models, and tend to reflect Greek social relations. Friendships are generally respected in the plays; the few cases where a friend is suspected of a doublecross (Plautus' *Bacchides* and *Epidicus*, Terence's *Andria*) turn out to have rested on a misapprehension. It also looks as though the Roman playwrights themselves created or amplified these scenes (on *Bacchides*, Raccanelli 1998: 79; on *Andria*, Donatus ad 997), which may suggest that tension between friends was a more congenial theme to Roman dramatists than to Greek.

It is generally agreed that Plautus expanded the roles of clever slaves and wily parasites over his Greek models, sometimes adapting them to the pattern of Roman clientship. Conceivably, the scene in the *Miles Gloriosus* in which the wealthy bachelor Periplectomenus describes his slave in the throes of thinking up a plot (200–17) evoked for a Roman audience the relation between a patron and a client poet. True friendship between a master and slave was also a possibility; in Plautus' *Captivi*, the slave Tyndarus, who has switched roles with his master Philocrates, reminds the latter: 'be faithful to one who is faithful: keep me as your friend forever, be not less faithful to me than I have been to you, for you are now my master, my patron, my father' (439–44, abridged). Terence is more of a purist in this as in other respects, although he too imports Roman customs into his plays; in *Adelphoe*, for example, a character inquires in a scene clearly inspired by Roman legal conventions: 'have you no client, friend, or guest-relation (*hospes*)?' (529).

3   Patronage and Friendship in the Literature of the Later Republic

Toward the end of the second century BC, members of the upper classes began to dabble in new forms of poetry, though not yet epic or drama (one exception perhaps proves the rule: Gaius Julius Caesar Strabo produced tragedies, but seems to have been disdained by his potential associates in the collegium poetarum; Valerius Maximus 3.7.11; cf. Asconius on Cicero *Pro Scauro* 22). Most notable among them was Lucilius, who was credited with the invention of satire (see Goldberg, Chapter 1 above, and Morgan, Chapter 12 above). Lucilius was a friend of the Scipios; though he kept out of politics himself, he was independently wealthy and his brother became a Roman senator. There are no references to patrons or clients in the 1300 verses that survive of his work, but Lucilius does observe that 'a friend should give good advice and take good care' (quoted by Nonius 372M.26), and he contrasts the friend, who is interested in the other's mind or self (*animum*), with the parasite, who cares only about his wealth

(Nonius 331M.27). Mario Citroni (1995: 44) argues that, unlike the writers of dramatic, lyric, and epic poetry who composed for a broad public, 'the author of a "new" genre like satire is . . . free to establish the scope of his own readership,' and could now address himself to an aristocratic audience whose level of literary culture had expanded enormously since the time of Ennius (some scholars suppose that epic poems were recited at aristocratic *convivia* [Rüpke 2001b: 49–53], though I am inclined to believe, with Leo 1913: 73, that they were disseminated principally in schools: cf. the career of Livius Andronicus, above). Several members of the nobility also tried their hand at epigrammatic verse, including Quintus Lutatius Catulus, who was consul in 102; as Courtney (1993: 75) remarks, 'the willingness of a member of the highest aristocracy to toss off imitations of Hellenistic sentimental erotic poetry. . . is a new phenomenon in Roman culture at this time'. Lyric, epigram and other miniature genres of poetry became a serious avocation among the Roman aristocracy, however, only with the so-called 'neoteric' movement in the mid-first century BC, whose chief representative was Catullus (see also Levene, Chapter 2 above).

The 'new' poets adopted a Callimachean aesthetic of brevity and learned wit. Catullus congratulated his friend Cinna on his miniature epic, *Smyrna* (Poem 95), and admired the three-volume universal history of Cornelius Nepos for its concision. In turn, he lambasted turgid poets like Volusius (Poem 36), who composed verse annals. The sophisticated Suffenus, who was unrefined only in his poetry, wrote tens of thousands of lines of verse, according to Catullus, but perhaps these consisted of many short poems rather than one or more of epic length (the same may be true of Hortensius, in Catullus' Poem 95; cf. Cameron (1995: 460–1)). When his friend Calvus sent him as a joke a short collection (*libellus*) of bad verse, Catullus assumed that Calvus had received it from a client of his, or else from a schoolteacher (Poem 14). Perhaps we may detect, behind the partiality for an urbane muse, a lingering prejudice against the traditionally popular genres of national epic and drama (cf. Citroni 1995: 57–60).

Friendship is at the heart of Catullus' poetry: even love was ideally modelled on *amicitia* (poem 109), and nothing offends Catullus more than betrayal (e.g. poem 30). His friendship with the orator and poet, Gaius Licinius Calvus, was legendary (poem 50; cf. Ovid *Amores* 3.9.61–2), and in general his poems project a comfortable familiarity with the most prominent figures of his day. In these verses, as also in Cicero's letters to his friends, one glimpses how friendships based on shared tastes bound together the Roman elite (Citroni 1995: 185 compares Cicero's *Ad Fam.* 7.22, in which Cicero describes an evening he spent with the jurist Trebatius Testa, to Catullus poem 50 on Calvus). Catullus' family was distinguished enough to have played host to Caesar in Verona. Nevertheless, as a newcomer to Rome, Catullus may have felt the need for a patron; hence the dedication of his book to Cornelius Nepos as *patronus* in poem 1, on the reading adopted by Goold (1983). Yet he freely attacked such powerful men as Caesar and Pompey. Whereas Naevius was humbled for an affront to the Metellus clan,

Catullus carried on an affair with the wife (if it was she) of the leading Metellus of his day (Quintus Metellus Celer).

In this period, some poets consented to celebrate the achievements of great men in hexameter verse, sometimes on what seems like a commission, other times as a favour to friends. Publius Terentius Varro, who came from Atax in Gaul, wrote a poem on Caesar's conquests in that province, as well as an adaptation of Apollonius of Rhodes' *Argonautica*, an Alexandrian composition that would have commended itself to the 'neoterics' (on such combinations, cf. Courtney 1993: 199–200). Gnaeus Matius, who rendered the *Iliad* into Latin and was the first to compose *mimiambi* at Rome, also wrote an historical epic on Caesar in at least two books, very possibly as a gesture of friendship. Furius Bibaculus, also from the north, composed annals on Caesar's Gallic wars in at least eleven books (Macrobius *Saturnalia* 6.1.34; cf. Courtney 1993: 197), but was evidently unafraid to assail Octavian much as Catullus had maligned Julius Caesar (Tacitus *Annales* 4.34). Atticus himself had commemorated Cicero's consulship in Greek (presumably in prose), though the result was not entirely to Cicero's liking (*Ad Atticum* 2.1.1). Cicero also put pressure on the Greek poet Archias (and perhaps on Thyillus), who evidently failed to produce, even though Cicero had assumed the role of *patronus* and defended him in court (*Ad Atticum* 1.16.15). In desperation, Cicero, who had himself translated Aratus' *Phaenomena* in the neoteric manner, celebrated his own consulship in verse. Perhaps such works on living subjects were regarded as the poetic equivalent of a prose historical mono-graph, of the sort that Cicero had attempted to exact from his friend Lucceius (*Ad Fam.* 5.12; cf. Hall 1998), or else a kind of panegyric rather than narrative epic proper (Cameron 1995: 463–71).

4 Patronage and Friendship in the Literature of the Augustan Age

It is, however, with the Augustan principate, and the emergence of powerful sponsors of poetry such as Maecenas, Messalla, and Augustus himself, that something like formal, state-centred literary patronage first appears (see Farrell, Chapter 3 above). While recognizing their vast power, one must be careful to determine what role these men played in the literary activity they encouraged, without importing anachronistic notions of political censorship and control in evaluating their role.

None of the major poets of this epoch was of the senatorial class. The two greatest were of relatively humble origin. Horace was the son of an ex-slave, or maligned as such (Williams 1995), and Virgil, who came from Mantua in the north, was helped out by Asinius Pollio after his property was confiscated in the civil wars. Horace, indeed, addresses a certain Virgil as a 'client of noble youths' (*Odes* 4.12.15). Some scholars have hesitated to identify this figure with the famous poet, despite apparent allusions to his verses (Putnam 1986: 205 n. 13; cf. Mayer 1995: 288–9), but it is not implausible that Horace is referring here to the dead Virgil at an early stage of his career (Johnson 1994: 51–5, 62–4). It is these two who undertook to compose a national epic (the *Aeneid*) and an officially sponsored lyric poem (Horace's *Carmen saeculare*), genres associated particularly with the professional poets of the third and second centuries BC.

How did such men gain access to the privileged literary circles in Augustus' court? Horace gives us the following description:

> I now come back to myself, son of a freedman father, whom they all run down as son of a freedman father . . . . I couldn't say that I was lucky in that it was an accident which allotted you to me as a friend, because it was certainly not chance that set you in my path; some time ago the good Virgil and after him Varius told you what I was. When I came face to face, I gulped out a few words, because tongue-tied shyness stopped me speaking out further, and told you not that I was the son of a distinguished father, not that I rode round my country estates on a Tarentine nag, but the facts about myself. Your reply, after your fashion, was brief; I left, and nine months later you called me back and bade me be numbered amongst your friends. I consider it a great distinction to have found favour with you – who can tell the honourable from the base – not because of an eminent father but because of integrity of life and character. (*Satires* 1.6.45–64, trans. Brown 1993: 65)

The complexity of the term *amicus* is apparent here. It has been suggested that Maecenas literally inscribed Horace's name in a list of welcome visitors, and that admission to his circle was no more a matter of affection than achieving membership in an exclusive club. Brown (1993: 156) notes that '*amicus* is here also appropriate in its technical application to either party in the patron/client relationship'. Horace was certainly aware of the price to be paid for connections to secure political advancement. He warns a bold young man just entering upon such a career: 'Cultivating a powerful friend seems nice to those who have not experienced it; one who has fears it' (*Epistles* 1.18.86–7). As Mayer (1995: 291) puts it, 'Lollius seemed to need advice on treading the narrow path of true independence within a hierarchical aristocracy now transforming itself into a royal court.' Only when he has achieved the psychological independence that Epicurean philosophy confers will Lollius be ready to engage in true friendships with the rich and powerful, although even then, tact will be essential (*Satires* 1.3).

And yet, Horace's relationship with Maecenas, like that with his fellow poets, was or soon became one of genuine friendship. Horace's own poems indicate the quality of the bond, as in his description of the trip he took with Maecenas and others to Brindisi:

> Meanwhile Maecenas and Cocceius arrive and together with them Fonteius Capito, a character of tailored perfection, second to none in his friendship with Antony . . . . The next day's dawn was easily the most welcome, because at Sinuessa Plotius,

Varius and Virgil met us – no fairer spirits has the earth produced, and no one's attachment to them is closer than mine. How we embraced and how great was our joy! While I'm in my right mind, there's nothing I'd compare with the pleasure of friendship (*Satires* 1.5.31–44, trans. Brown 1993: 55–7).

Some critics have seen a difference in tone between Horace's formal mention of the political grandees and the warmth he expresses in respect to his fellow poets (Estafanía 1994a, citing Fedeli 1992). But no doubt his friendship with Maecenas 'soon transcended a relation of clientship and was transformed into a mutual and sincere affection' (Estafanía 1994a: 9). When Horace came to publishing his *Odes*, it is significant that the first three were so arranged as to address in turn Maecenas, Augustus and Virgil.

Friendship as a theme is pervasive in Horace's verse, as one might expect of an adherent of Epicureanism, the philosophical school that most prized this bond (for the attitude of Roman Epicureans to friendship, cf. Cicero *De finibus* 1.20.65; *De officiis* 1.66–70). This was a notion of friendship predicated on autonomy and self-sufficiency. In a letter almost certainly addressed to his fellow poet Albius Tibullus, Horace writes:

In a world torn by hope and worry, dread and anger,
imagine every day that dawns is the last you'll see;
the hour you never hoped for will prove a happy surprise.
Come and see me when you want a laugh. I'm fat and sleek,
in prime condition, a porker from Epicurus' herd.
                    (*Epistles* 1.4.12–16, trans. Rudd 1979: 138)

Horace projects a life of private ease, which he invites his friend to share (cf. *Odes* 2.18). No doubt he brought a similar attitude to his relationship with Augustus and Maecenas.

The elegiac poets Cornelius Gallus, Tibullus, Propertius and Ovid, along with some lesser figures such as Lygdamus, were of the equestrian class, the census rank below that of senator. Rather than compose epic or drama, they limited themselves (with the exception of Ovid) to short, Callimachean compositions, that were new to Rome and dealt largely with personal erotic themes (see Gibson, Chapter 11 above), sometimes even pointing up the tension between servitude to a mistress and service to the state (Tibullus 1.1.1–6; Propertius 2.7). Nevertheless, Augustus and his ministers enlisted Tibullus and Propertius, as they had Virgil and Horace, in support of their political and social programme. In this context, a new subgenre of Latin poetry came into being: the *recusatio*, or 'refusal,' in which a poet protested his incapacity to write epic eulogies of Augustus' achievements in war and peace (Virgil *Eclogues* 6.3–8; Horace *Odes* 1.6; 2.12; 4.2; Propertius 2.1; 2.10; 3.1; 3.3; 3.9; Ovid *Amores* 1.1). Though the device goes back to Callimachus, who declined to treat the hackneyed themes of mythology, the 'Augustan poets . . . give this a completely new twist', professing that their talents are insufficient for 'the great affairs of contemporary Roman history and, in particular, the deeds of Augustus' (Williams 1968: 46–7; cf. Cameron 1995: 454–83). Propertius finally lent his voice in support of the regime (4.6), while Tibullus squared the circle by commending the peace that Augustus had made possible as the condition for the harmonious relationship between lovers (1.7; 1.10). The extreme case was Ovid, who was punished with exile for the licentious character of his early poems; not his divinization of Julius Caesar in the *Metamorphoses*, nor his half-finished poem on Rome's sacred calendar, nor again his tearful verse epistles to influential friends and acquaintances (of whose loyalty he often despaired) sufficed to have the sentence repealed (see Grebe 1998).

Apart, perhaps, from Ovid, the coin in which these patrons exerted their pressure on the poets was not direct coercion, nor again the overt purchase of their services, just as the poetry they demanded or inspired was not mere flattery or propaganda. The ties of friendship on which patronage rested entailed subtler forms of commerce, more analogous to the exchange of gifts than to hired labour (Bowditch 2001). These poets wrote for an elite public, and their aim was not so much to doctor history as to articulate a vision of the principate in which they and their peers might believe. It is here that the modern 'conceptual separation of "literature" and "politics" is most misleading' (Kennedy 1992: 37).

Outside the court, Gaius Asinius Pollio, who was sympathetic to Augustus' regime, also patronized good poets. Pollio himself was famous as a historian and orator, but he too composed erotic poems in the Catullan manner (Virgil *Eclogues* 3.86: *Pollio et ipse facit nova carmina*) as well as tragedies, as did Ovid, Varius and others, though whether they were intended for the popular stage is moot. Pollio held readings in his house, anticipating the vogue for recitals both public and private in the following century.

5   Patronage and Friendship in the Literature of the Empire

After the death of Augustus, the emperor remained, or was perceived to be, the chief source of poetic patronage (see Mayer, Chapter 4 above, and Gibson, Chapter 5 above). Juvenal goes so far as to affirm that only the emperor was prepared to support poets, whereas the aristocracy had turned its back on them. Juvenal notes that Lucan was wealthy and independent (*Satires* 7.79–80), but Statius is treated as an impoverished poet who failed to obtain gifts, despite the enormous popularity of his *Thebaid* (7.82–90; see Nauta 2002: 3–4). In his *Silvae*, Statius wrote occasional poems for various members of the aristocracy, with whom he was on intimate terms (Nauta 2002: 193–248). Lucan, on the contrary, wrote a bold epic on the civil wars that was critical of Julius Caesar (see Hardie, Chapter 6 above); despite the inclusion of a eulogy to Nero, he was condemned to death by the emperor for his ostensible part in a conspiracy. In the hands of an aristocrat, epic was a potentially subversive genre (so too, perhaps, were the tragedies composed by Lucan's uncle, Seneca). For Juvenal, Lucan's high status is a figure for his poetic daring. Poets of lesser station, like Statius and Silius Italicus (made consul by Nero), were poor but safe: conventional epic was still a client's genre.

Juvenal, writing under Trajan, was looking back at an age that seemed dominated by tyrannical emperors such as Tiberius, Nero, and Domitian, where writers feared to speak openly. Pliny the Younger, in his *Panegyricus* to Trajan composed in the year 100 (when Pliny shared the consulship with Tacitus), placed an unusual emphasis on the new ruler's capacity for friendship (44.7; 85.5; cf. Dio of Prusa's third *Oration on Kingship*; Konstan 1977). Like Juvenal (*Satire* 4), Pliny was insisting on the right relationship between patron and dependent as one of amity rather than domination. Pliny prided himself on his friendships, and his correspondence breathes a spirit of affection for his intimates (*Epistles* 1.14.10; 2.7.6; de Blois 2001: 130). He describes to Trajan how a friendship between a superior and inferior party evolves:

> My lord, Nymphidius Lupus served with me as chief centurion, and when I was tribune he was prefect; that is when I began to feel a warm affection for him. Afterwards, there developed a love based on the very duration of our mutual friendship. (*Epistles* 10.87.1)

His letters to Trajan, composed chiefly while he was governor in Bithynia, betray an obsequious dependency on the emperor's judgement, but his deference does not entirely smother the personal warmth that evidently obtained between the two, while Trajan, for his part, calls him 'My dearest Pliny' (*mi Secunde carissime*, 10.16.1, cf. 10.21.1; 10.41.1 etc.). As a poet, Pliny limited himself to lyric poems in the style of Catullus.

Pliny enjoyed encouraging the literary activities of others, including Martial (see Watson, Chapter 14 above), whose expenses he helped defray for his trip back to his native Spain (Pliny *Epistles* 3.21). Martial unashamedly adopted the pose of a poor poet, economically dependent on the generosity of wealthy benefactors:

> What Maecenas, a knight sprung from ancient kings [cf. Horace *Odes* 1.1.1], was to Horace and Varius and the great Virgil, loquacious fame and ancient records will declare to all races and peoples that you, Priscus Terentius, have been to me. You create inspiration for me; you make possible whatever I seem able to accomplish; you give me the leisure that belongs to a free man .... To give, to provide, to increase modest wealth and grant what gods when they are generous have scarcely bestowed, now one may do lawfully. But you, under a harsh ruler and in evil times, dared to be a good man. (Martial 12.3)

Martial traced his literary ancestry to Catullus (10.78.16), but he does not imitate Catullus' easy interaction with the powerful, whether for good or ill. Barbara Gold (2002: 591) observes (with a little exaggeration): 'there is not a single subject that receives more attention in Martial's epigrams than the troubled relations between *amici* ("friends") or patrons and their clients'. Martial not only writes for or under patrons; he makes patronage the theme of much of his verse.

The role of friendship in patronage is central to Martial's thoughts. On his ascent up the Esquiline hill to visit the rich Paulus, who had already gone out for the day, Martial complains (5.22.13–14): 'shall the faithful client ever be cultivating unconscionable friends? Unless you stay abed, you can be no patron of mine' (trans. Shackleton Bailey 1993, vol.1: 375). *Amicus* here is all but a euphemism for patron (cf. 10.19). Or again (3.36): 'You bid me, Fabianus, to provide you with what a new, recently made friend provides you' (1–2), upon which Martial enumerates the services he performs, such as waiting outside his patron's house at the crack of dawn. He next protests: 'Have I earned this over thirty Decembers, to be forever a new recruit to your friendship?' (7–8). The final couplet suggests he should be granted a veteran's discharge. The point is that after so long an acquaintance, the demeaning routine of a client is inappropriate; there is thus a subtle hit at the hypocrisy of patronizing friends (cf. 3.37 on rich 'friends' who get angry so as not to have to compensate their poor acquaintances; also 2.74.6; 3.41). In 3.46, however, Martial contrasts the services of a client, which he proposes sending his freedman to perform, with those of a friend, which, he says, is all that the freedman cannot perform (11–12). So too he exclaims (2.55), 'You want to be toadied to (*coli*), Sextus; I wanted to love you. I must obey you: you shall be toadied to, as you order. But if I toady to you, Sextus, I shan't love you.' Again (9.14): 'Do you believe that this man, whom your table, your dinners have made your friend, is the soul of faithful friendship (*fidae pectus amicitiae*)? He loves your boar and mullets and udder and oysters, not you. If I should dine that well, he'll be my friend' (on the value of a true friend, cf. 9.52; 9.99; 10.44). Martial distinguishes (4.56.7) between giving unconditionally (*largiri*) and giving with a view to gaining or receiving in return (*donare*; cf. 10.11; 10.15). John Sullivan (1991: 120) observes that the picture of Roman patronage as a system of duties and benefits is blurred because it 'is forced to overlap with the concept of friendship'; but Martial is clear that the two ideas are 'theoretically distinct' and may simultaneously describe his relationship to a single individual.

Sometimes Martial laments the lack of a generous Maecenas (11.3; cf. 1.107; 4.40; 8.55; 12.36); at other times he claims to be indifferent to whether his poems profit him (5.15.5–6). Most often his complaints of poverty have nothing to do with poetry at all (e.g. 12.53.1–5; see Holzberg 2002: 74–85). In all, Martial's pose is that of a gossip columnist whose livelihood depends on access to the rich and famous; that is why he needs to be invited to aristocratic dinner parties – for material, so that he can expose their petty avarice and sexual deviance (cf. 10.4). Martial explicitly distances himself from learned Alexandrian poetry like Callimachus' *Aetia*, part of which his own Catullus translated (poem 68). Catullus too could represent himself as poor (e.g. poem 10), but he is the equal of the aristocrats to whom he addresses his verses. Martial, however, writes as an interloper, who must constantly seek entry to the world whose foibles he amusingly reveals. It is from this self-conscious posture that Martial teases out the values of friendship and patronage, as he adapts the traditionally haughty Roman epigram, as cultivated by poets since Catulus and Catullus, to a poor man's lampoon.

I conclude this survey of attitudes toward patrons and friends with a cynical epigram ascribed to Seneca, though in all likelihood written a century or so after the time of Martial:

> 'Live and avoid all friendships': this is more true
>   Than just 'avoid friendships with patrons'.
> My fate bears witness: my high-ranking friend ruined me,
>   My humble one abandoned me. Shun the whole pack alike.
> For those who had been my equals fled the crash
>   And abandoned the house even before it collapsed.
> Go then and avoid only patrons! If you know how to live,
>   Live for yourself only – for you'll die for yourself.
>   (*Anthologia Latina* I.404 SB)

FURTHER READING

In treating patronage and friendship, this chapter brings together two themes that are in reality distinct, though related. Konstan (1997) provides a survey of ancient friendship in general, and argues that it was conceived as a bond based on mutual affection rather than obligation. This view has not won universal acceptance; for criticism of it, see (among others) the essays in Peachin (2001b), with the review by Konstan (2002). For friendship as a political relationship in Rome, see the chapter on *amicitia* in Brunt (1988).

Patronage is a different kind of relationship, based on the reciprocal obligation between a superior and inferior party. At an early stage, the dependency of clients upon their patrons was probably compulsory, but in the historical period it was largely customary; for the evolution, see Deniaux (1993), and for the special sense of patron as legal counsellor, David (1992). The best introduction to Roman patronage is Saller (1989); see also Saller (1982), White (1993).

Literary patronage in the modern sense is a distinct issue; for general discussion, see Gold (1987) (on Greece and Rome). Bowditch (2001) discusses Horace's relationship to his imperial patrons; White (1993) treats patronage in the Augustan period generally; while White (1978) and Nauta (2002) provide a detailed account of patronage in the early imperial period, with special attention to Statius and Martial.

A further issue is the role of friendship within poetry; for friendship in Plautus' comedies, see Raccanelli (1998), who offers a balanced discussion of affection and duty in Roman friendship generally; for Horace and his friends, see Kilpatrick (1986); and for Pliny, de Blois (2001).

How patronage and friendship interacted remains a disputed question. Were both characterized more by obligation than by affection, or were they radically distinct? If so, could patron and client be true friends? The above studies indicate the nature of the problem, but work remains to be done.

CHAPTER TWENTY-FIVE

Romans and Others

Yasmin Syed

1 Introduction

The purpose of this chapter is to survey modes of representation of foreign peoples in Roman literature. Roman ethnographic writing takes such representations as its explicit purpose. Other modes of representation of the ethnic 'other', less neatly bundled than ethnographies, include literary depictions of individual foreigners, be they historical, mythical or fictional figures. These tell us much about Roman conceptions of their nations. Additionally, Romans held some ethnic stereotypes about foreign peoples that contributed to Roman views about them.

Roman representations of other nations or individual foreigners are informed at least as much by the genre of the text, its intended target audience and the aims of the author, as they are by knowledge of the actual people portrayed. In some sense, all we get when Roman authors describe non-Romans is information about Roman views of non-Romans, rather than information about the non-Romans themselves. This point is not obvious. The temptation to seek information about non-Romans in Roman texts is great in cases when all the literary evidence we have of a given nation is Roman (or Greek) literature. But because Greek and Roman accounts of foreigners must be seen within their own Greek or Roman cultural context and its influence on the representation of others, it is perilous to take them at face value (Wells 1999: 99–104).

2 Roman Authors, Audiences and Texts

Before turning to the different modes of representing ethnic otherness in Roman literary texts it is instructive to question the term 'Roman'. By 'Roman texts' I mean texts from antiquity written in Latin before the third century AD; by

'Roman views of other cultures' I mean the views embodied in these texts. But by no means does it follow that the authors of such texts were Romans in the sense of holding Roman citizenship or being born in Rome. It is a topos among historians of Roman literature that most authors commonly designated Roman were not Roman citizens born in Rome. Many of the earliest authors of Roman literature were non-Romans, such as Livius Andronicus, Ennius, Plautus and Terence (see Goldberg, Chapter 1 above). How justified are we in regarding the views represented in their texts as Roman views?

In this regard ancient literature is very different from modern literature. Literary discussions of the works of ancient authors rarely take into account the author's ethnic identity. The case of Terence is here particularly interesting because, as a native of Carthage who came to Rome as a slave, he belonged to a nation hostile to and at war with Rome before Terence's birth and after his death. Going on the analogy of modern literature, one might expect to find some reflection of this fact in his works. It is customary in modern critical approaches to literature, for instance feminist and post-colonial theory, to view the gender, cultural and ethnic identity of authors as determining whether they can be regarded as representing the perspectives of the dominant discourse or that of a marginalized group.

But in the case of Terence it would be wrong to assume that his works in any way reflect Carthaginian world views or the viewpoint of a foreigner from a hostile nation writing in and for Roman culture. Not only did Terence rise to fame as an author of Roman literature; he even became a classic of Roman literature. The language of his comedies, far from being regarded as the efforts of a non-native speaker of Latin, became a model of correct Latinity in Roman school education, to be emulated by Roman schoolboys for centuries. To all intents and purposes, Terence is a Roman author.

From a modern perspective one might wonder how this came to pass. It is possible to account for this in several ways, such as speculation about his Roman upbringing from early childhood, or his association with elite Roman aristocratic literary circles. Nevertheless, the question is worth raising, because it makes us aware of the cultural gap between Roman culture and the modern world, and it helps us understand the cultural specificity of Roman literary and cultural conceptualizations of ethnicity.

When we speak of Roman views as they are embodied in a Roman text, it is also necessary to consider in what ways the target audience of this text influences the views expressed in the text. As an example of texts in which the target audience is a vital factor in assessing their representations of other cultures, consider the works of Cicero. In his trial speeches Cicero often exploits ethnic stereotypes to discredit his opponent's provincial witnesses, drawing on the predisposition of his Roman audiences to be influenced by commonly held prejudices against the ethnic group involved. This rhetorical strategy is at work in several speeches. In *Pro Fonteio* he calls Gauls savage and untrustworthy, in *Pro Scauro* the Sardinians are presented as deceptive, and in *Pro Flacco* he portrays Greeks as either trust-worthy or untrustworthy, depending on whether the individual Greeks involved are on his side or that of his opponent (Vasaly 1993: 191–243).

In addition to authors and audiences as factors in the representation of ethnic others we should also consider how certain properties of the text itself, such as the conventions of its genre and the influence exerted by literary models, contributes to determining its representation of ethnic others.

I shall demonstrate the relevance of these factors in the final section of this chapter, a discussion of Plautus' *Poenulus*. There I shall consider in some detail how competing discourses such as the conventions of the comic genre, the depictions of characters in Greek model plays, and Roman ethnic stereotyping contribute to the construction of Punic identity in the depictions of individual fictional Carthaginian characters. The remaining sections are case studies of some forms of representation of ethnic others, beginning with a brief overview of Roman ethnography. There follows a discussion of Cicero's representations of Greeks and Greek culture and a survey of Roman stereotypes about the Cartha-ginians that leads into the final section on the *Poenulus*.

3   Roman Ethnography

Most work on Roman representations of ethnic others has been done in the field of Roman ethnography. Following in the tradition of Greek ethnography, Roman writers often drew on past ethnographers for descriptions of the same foreign nations, or applied established topoi from other ethnographies to the descriptions of new nations. Their accuracy depends not only on the problem of repetition of traditional motifs, but also on the varying degrees in which they contain para-doxographic, marvellous or utopian elements. I shall here limit myself to a brief survey of important primary texts and refer the interested reader to secondary works for further study.

Roman ethnographies of foreign peoples could serve various functions and address themselves to various audiences. They are most commonly found as digressions in historical works. Caesar's *Bellum Gallicum* contains ethnographies of the Gauls, the Germans and Britain (4.1–4; 5.12–14; 6.11–28), Sallust de-scribes Africa in the *Bellum Iugurthinum* (17–19), and Tacitus has ethnographies of Britain in the *Agricola* (10–12), and of the Jews in the *Histories* (5.2–8). Tacitus' *Germania* is the only extant example of an ethnographic monograph in Latin literature (Rives 1999: 11–21).

Ethnographies are also often found in ancient geographies in such Roman authors as Pomponius Mela and Pliny the Elder. Pliny's encyclopedic work *Naturalis Historia* contains several ethnographies in his geographic survey of the world in Books 3–6, written as two voyages (*periplus*) along the coastlines of the Mediterranean, the Black Sea and the Ocean. Pliny also has ethnographies in other parts of the *Naturalis Historia*, such as his account of the Chauci (a German tribe dwelling by the shores of the North Sea) in his book on forest trees, where the ethnography serves to illustrate life in a region without forests or trees (*NH* 16.1–4). Pliny's description of India in his book about mankind (*NH* 7) greatly influenced later ethnographic writing about India and the East. But his ethnography of India serves to set normal human beings apart from monstrous races, people with deformed bodies or superhuman strength. Pliny treats India as a repository of such marvellous nations, rather than pursuing ethnographic interests such as relating the customs of these nations (*NH* 7.21–32) (Murphy 2004).

Some ethnographies can be found in poetry: Vergil's *Georgics* contain some ethnographic digressions (e.g. the excursus on Libya and Scythia in *Georg.* 3.339–83), and in Lucan's *Pharsalia* we find an ethnographic description of Libya (*Phars.* 9.411–44). Indeed, the *Georgics* as a whole are strongly influenced by the ethnographic tradition, and even Italy is described there according to the conventions of ethnography (*Georg.* 2.136–76) (Thomas 1982: 35–92, 108–23).

But Vergil's ethnographic depiction of Italy is an exception; in general ethnographies depict only certain kinds of foreign nations, those that are far away, whose customs are strange to the Roman reader, or those the Romans and Greeks would have designated as barbarians. There are, for instance, no ethnographies of Greeks, nor do the Romans depict the Carthaginians in the ethnographic format. Yet, Roman representations of Greeks and Carthaginians are numerous and can be found in many contexts. As examples of non-ethnographic conceptualizations of foreigners the following two sections will consider ethnic stereotypes in Roman literary representations of Greeks and Carthaginians.

4 Cicero and the Greeks

The most significant intellectual of the Republic (see Levene, Chapter 2 above), Cicero displays a range of Roman attitudes to foreigners, some of which have been mentioned above. His professed attitudes to Greeks are instructive because they vary in different contexts in accordance with expediency. We have already observed that Cicero accomplishes a remarkable feat of oratorical skill in the *Pro Flacco* when he uses ethnic stereotypes about the Greeks to both discredit his opponents' Greek witnesses and bolster the credibility of his own (Vasaly 1993: 198–205). But the reason he can do this lies in a general ambivalence towards Greek culture among Romans. Admiration for the cultural achievements of classical Greece was one side of this ambivalent attitude. The other was a feeling of superiority towards their Greek contemporaries who were, after all, their provincial subjects and whom they often regarded with contempt.

Cicero often expresses a Roman sense of superiority over the Greeks. In a letter to his brother Quintus he warns him to be careful in his choice of Greek friends;

many Greeks are untrustworthy and have a tendency, because of their long servitude, to sycophancy (*Q Fr.* 1.1.16). This attitude to contemporary Greeks is also evident to a certain degree in his depiction of the Greek poet and philosopher Philodemus in *In Pisonem* (55 BC). Throughout this speech, which he delivered before the senate in response to an invective directed against him by Piso, Cicero ridicules Piso for his Epicurean sympathies and links them to accusations of debauchery and licentiousness. Cicero attributes Piso's alleged licentiousness to Piso's faulty understanding of Epicurean doctrines. The Epicurean philosopher Philodemus is introduced as a friend and client of Piso whose philosophical teachings Piso is unable to understand because of his mediocre intellect (*Pis.* 68). Cicero introduces Philodemus because the Greek had written licentious poetry for Piso in which, Cicero claims, he had depicted his patron's licentious behaviour.

Cicero's portrait of Philodemus himself is not entirely negative. He refers to Philodemus' licentious poetry not so much to criticize the poet himself but to prove Piso's licentiousness. He even says that Philodemus was quite gentlemanly and could have been a far more respectable man had he not fallen in with Piso (*Pis.* 68–71). But even as he acknowledges Philodemus' respectable qualities, he attributes the philosopher's willingness to write such poetry for such a patron to the fact that he is Greek. He asks his audience to show forbearance with Philodemus because he is, after all, just a *Graeculus* (a term Cicero most likely uses here in a disparaging sense) and a sycophant (*Pis.* 70).

To denigrate Piso himself Cicero exploits his Epicurean leanings rather than his association with Philodemus. Depicting Piso's banquets as licentious affairs where Piso surrounds himself with foul-smelling and drunken Greeks (*Pis.* 22) Cicero argues that Piso felt encouraged to indulge in such licentious behaviour by a Greek philosophical doctrine (*Pis.* 69). Cicero follows a similar strategy in his defence speech *Pro Murena* (63 BC), where he makes fun of Cato, the prosecutor of the court case and therefore Cicero's opponent, for his Stoic convictions (*Mur.* 3; 61). Amusingly enough, in this speech Cicero defends the very practices, banqueting and other displays of lavish spending, he will later condemn in his attack on Piso.

The parallel between the rhetorical strategies of the two speeches lies in their reliance on basic prejudices the Romans held about Greek intellectuals and those at Rome who showed interest in such pursuits. In both speeches Greek philosophical doctrines are blamed for having a detrimental effect on Cicero's opponents whose behaviour he wants to represent as aberrant or undesirable. While Epicurean philosophy is to blame for Piso's licentious banqueting in *In Pisonem*, Cicero depicts Cato's unyielding condemnation of Murena's lavish spending as a misguided application of Stoic doctrine to well-established and traditional Roman practices (*Mur.* 74). Whereas Piso's feasts are excessive and inappropriate for a Roman because of Epicureanism, Cato's severity towards Murena's feasts is excessive and inappropriate for a Roman because of Stoicism.

In view of Cicero's groundbreaking work in articulating philosophical ideas in Latin and his towering achievements in forging a Latin philosophical vocabulary (see Powell 1995), it is ironic that Cicero should use Greek philosophy to attack his opponents in public speeches. Of course, Cicero's professed attitude to Greek culture always takes into account the audience he addresses and the effect he wants his words to have on his audience. It is often useful for Cicero to exploit Roman suspicions of philhellenic tendencies. To this purpose Cicero professes ignorance of Greek culture and art in the speech *In Verrem* where he pretends not to remember the name of the sculptor Polyclitus in order not to appear too philhellenic to the audience of the court case (*Verr.* 2.4.5). But his philosophical and rhetorical works, which address themselves to those with an interest in these pursuits, show his intimate knowledge of and familiarity with Greek culture, as do his letters (Vasaly 1993: 108–9).

Cicero expressed a more positive attitude to Greek culture not only in his theoretical works or private correspondence. Even in a public speech Cicero could turn the Romans' respect for the cultural achievements of the Greeks to the advantage of a Greek client. In his defence speech for the poet Archias, Cicero entered into a panegyric of the Greek poet's genius and the usefulness of his, as well as of other Greek and Roman, poetry. But even here Cicero had to forestall objections to a line of argument that took its departure from a positive view of Greek culture. His first move was to assure his audience that he was going to discuss his client's learnedness only because his listeners were themselves so accomplished in the liberal arts (*Arch.* 3). Since the audience included a large body of merely curious observers of the trial, it is doubtful whether all of them deserved to be called *literatissimi* by Cicero.

Another strategy Cicero pursued in this speech was to play down his client's Greek provenance by designating him with his Roman citizen name Aulus Licinius (*Arch.* 1), thus also asserting the poet's citizen status, the main point contested by the opposition. In a similar vein he stated his client's age at his arrival in Rome by referring to a Roman custom: he was still wearing the *toga praetexta*, the garb of a youth of no more than 17 (*Arch.* 5). It is doubtful whether Archias who, coming from Antioch in Syria, had arrived in Rome after travels in Asia, Greece and *Magna Graecia* actually did follow the Roman custom of clothing, especially since he was not then a Roman citizen.

Cicero's main line of defence was that Archias deserved Roman citizenship because as a poet he was useful to Rome as one who could praise the deeds of famous contemporary Romans and the Roman state. For this Cicero had to make a case that literature – and Greek learning as a whole – had at least some use. He argued that by depicting the deeds of great men as models of excellence, literature could give incentives for noble action to its readers. Far from the frivolous pursuit of bookish intellectuals his listeners might consider it, the study of literature was useful to the state (*Arch.* 12–14). Cicero did not expect such an argument to go unchallenged. He immediately himself raised the objection his listeners might feel:

did the exemplary figures depicted in literature act as they did because they themselves were learned or because of an innate excellence? This objection pointed to the essence of the Romans' suspiciousness about Greek culture, namely that Greek excellence lay in learning, not in doing, as Roman excellence did. Cicero himself expressed this dichotomy in another speech where he distinguished between the accomplishments of the ancient Romans and Greeks as accomplishments of deeds as opposed to words (*Cael.* 40). Even as Cicero took a positive view of the Greeks and Greek culture his praise came in a muted and qualified form.

5   The Carthaginians

The Carthaginians were a subject in Latin literature almost from its beginning (see Goldberg, Chapter 1 above). The central theme of Naevius' *Bellum Poenicum* (written between 218 BC and 204/201 BC) was the First Punic War, in which the author himself had fought. In Plautus' comedy *Poenulus* (dated to between 195 to 189 BC by Maurach 1988: 32–3), four of the main characters are Carthaginians. Ennius dealt with the Second Punic War in Books 7–10 of the *Annales* (written before 169 BC). And Cato dealt with the First and Second Punic Wars in Books 4 and 5 of his *Origines*, the first Roman historical work written in Latin (written before 149 BC). Representations of the Carthaginians in subsequent Roman literature are too numerous to list here, but among them the accounts of Hannibal in Livy and Nepos, very different in tendency, stand out. Of course, the most famous Carthaginian character in Roman literature is Vergil's Dido in Books 1, 4 and 6 of the *Aeneid*, also portrayed by Ovid in *Heroides* 7.

Roman literary depictions of Carthaginians were shaped by a number of ethnic stereotypes. Most prominent among them was the topos of *Punica fides* (Punic (un)trustworthiness), the claim that Carthaginians were untrustworthy and apt to break treaties, oaths and all manner of promises, a stereotype attested throughout Roman literature (Prandi 1979). The idea that Carthaginians were apt to break treaties was associated with events leading up to the First Punic War, when the Romans justified their own breaking of a treaty with reference to treaties previously broken by the Carthaginians (Prandi 1979: 90–2).

The earliest reference in Roman literature to Carthaginian duplicity is in Plautus' *Poenulus* (see further §6, 'Plautus' *Poenulus*', below; on Roman comedy in general see Panayotakis, Chapter 9 above). From the beginning, the play draws on the ethnic stereotypes of the cunning and deceitful Carthaginian for its characterization of Hanno, the title character. The prologue says that Hanno knows every language but conceals this knowledge from others. It is then implied that such behaviour is typical of Carthaginians:

> omnis linguas scit, sed dissimulat sciens
> se scire: Poenus plane est. Quid verbis opust?

He knows all languages, but although he does, he hides this knowledge from others:
clearly he is a Carthaginian. What need is there for words?

(Plaut. *Poen.* 112–13)

In fact, although all the Carthaginian characters in this play are portrayed perfectly sympathetically, the humour of many scenes is fuelled by preconceptions
that Carthaginians are deceitful and cunning.

This second stereotype of the cunning Carthaginian, closely connected to that
of deceitfulness, could occasionally be turned into praise, as when Cicero called a
certain philosopher 'shrewd as a Carthaginian' (*Ac.* 2.98: *acutus ut Poenus*). It
could denote cleverness, as it does in the *Poenulus*, where Hanno is depicted as
clever and knowledgeable. But it could also be understood negatively, as cunning
in the service of deceit.

Cruelty and arrogance were among some other stereotypes the Romans had
about Carthaginians. These, too, are well attested throughout Roman literature
(Burck 1943). Ennius is our earliest testimony for these stereotypes. One *Annales*
fragment states that the Carthaginians are accustomed to sacrificing their children
to the gods (*Ann.* 7, fr. 237 Warmington 1936–8 = fr. 215 Skutsch 1968).
Another reports of mutilations of dead enemy soldiers' bodies by Carthaginians
and attributes these actions to arrogance (*Ann.* 8, fr. 282 Warmington 1936–8
= fr. 287 Skutsch 1968).

6 Plautus' *Poenulus*

The ethnic stereotypes surveyed above are not the only determinants of Roman
constructions of the Carthaginians. Plautus' *Poenulus* depicts its four Carthaginian characters in a very sympathetic light. Hanno, a rich man from Carthage, is a
devoted father searching for his two daughters who, abducted as children, are
now in danger of being sold as courtesans. Agorastocles, also abducted from
Carthage as a child, is the requisite young lover of the play who pines for one of
the two girls, who live next door in a pimp's house.

The portrayals of all four Carthaginian main characters is in no way any more or
less sympathetic than what the conventions of the genre require. If we were to
look for denigrating portraits of Carthaginians as former enemies of Rome, we
would not find them here. But we have already had occasion to observe that the
Poenulus is our earliest witness for the Roman stereotype of the cunning and
deceitful Carthaginian. How can we account for this seeming contradiction?

To answer this question it is necessary to approach the representation of Carthaginians in the *Poenulus* as an aggregate of several converging discourses, which
contribute various elements to the construction of the Carthaginian characters of
the play. One of these discourses is that of ethnic stereotyping. That Carthaginians
were cunning and deceitful may have been a current preconception at Rome

because of war-time animosities. It is assumed that the play was performed only a few years after the end of the Second Punic War. But the stereotypes of cunning and deceitfulness do not originate with Rome's conflict with Carthage. These are literary topoi associated with Phoenicians already in Homer (Prandi 1979: 93–6). Their presence in the *Poenulus* may be due to war-time animosities at Rome, but they may already have formed a vital part of the humour in Plautus' Greek model, the (lost) *Karchedonius*, probably written by Alexis. In any case, the Greek model certainly informed Plautus' characterizations of his Carthaginian characters, an influence that can, of course, no longer be gauged.

Moreover, as in Roman comedies generally, the characterizations of all figures in this play must be seen in the context of the stock character types of Roman and Greek New Comedy. The depiction of Hanno's relationship with his daughters conforms to the character type of the 'devoted father' (*pater pius*), and towards his nephew he behaves like the standard old man as helpful friend (Duckworth 1952: 242–9). These conventions of stock characterization ensure that Hanno is depicted sympathetically and as one of the heroes of the comedy. Furthermore, the play articulates Hanno's ethnicity through more than ethnic stereotypes. Hanno's first words on the stage are in Punic or what purports to be Punic (930–49). The speech is followed by a translation into Latin, a prayer for success in his search for his daughters. It introduces Hanno as a devoted father who wants to find his children.

This speech is remarkable for two reasons, first because the *Poenulus* is the only work of Greek or Latin literature to contain passages in this foreign language, and secondly because it shows no signs of the ethnic stereotyping found in the prologue. It does continue the prologue's depiction of Hanno as a devoted father and as bilingual. How authentically Plautus' Punic passages reflect actual Punic is an open question, but although linguists consider them as a source for the reconstruction of the Punic language, they have suffered extensive corruption in the manuscript transmission, which has rendered their meaning doubtful (Friedrich and Röllig 1999: 2–3; Krahmalkov 1988).

The inclusion of Punic in the play signals a mode of representing the ethnic other, which engages the issue of cultural difference in a completely different register from other modes of representation discussed so far. If Plautus' Punic is authentic, then a Roman literary text for once conveyed actual information about another culture, not just an articulation of Roman culture by means of contrast with the representation of ethnic otherness.

The Punic of Hanno's first speech, then, articulates his foreignness and his ethnic identity without reference to stereotyping. In the next scene Hanno speaks Punic again, but here Hanno's bilingual abilities become a means of depicting him according to the stereotypes of the cunning and deceitful Carthaginian. Overhearing a conversation between Agorastocles and his slave Milphio, Hanno resolves to pretend to them that he speaks only Punic. When they address him, Hanno greets and speaks to them in Punic, while Milphio, pretending to know

Punic but not understanding a word, makes up translations for his master that are surely cued for comic effect. Hanno's deception here, while serving the purpose of creating the comic situation of Milphio's inept translations, also highlights his Punic character: there is no good reason for Hanno to pretend not to speak Latin.

When Hanno switches to Latin, Milphio violently abuses him for making a fool of him. He accuses Hanno of cunning and deceit in terms reminiscent of later Roman stereotypes of Carthaginians (1032: *sycophans, subdolus, bisulci lingua*). The expression *bisulci lingua* (with a double tongue) is a pun because it suggests deceit with the image of a double (or forked) tongue, and Hanno's deceit lies exactly in concealing that he is bilingual, master of two tongues.

On discovering that Agorastocles is his nephew, Hanno is recruited by Milphio for a plot to steal his master's beloved from the pimp. He asks Hanno if he can be 'cunning' (l.1089: *subdolus*), using the same word he had earlier used in abusing him. Milphio wants Hanno to pretend that the two girls next door are his abducted daughters and claim them from the pimp as freeborn. Hanno agrees to this proposal with excitement, because he hopes and suspects that the girls really are his daughters, having overheard Milphio tell his master that they were abducted from Carthage with their nurse. But Milphio thinks that Hanno is already playing the part he had asked him to play, and admires his powers of deception. Milphio assumes that Hanno's excitement cannot be genuine and explains it to himself as the result of typical Punic deceitfulness. But Hanno is not pretending; he is really moved by Milphio's suggestion.

Hanno is again depicted as acting deceitfully for no good reason when he approaches his daughters to tell them that he is their father. Instead of telling them directly, Hanno plays a joke on his daughters for his own and Agorastocles' amusement, pretending that he wants to summon them to court for the theft of his lost daughters (1224–48). But after the situation is explained, all four Carthaginians fall into each others' arms in their joy of being reunited.

The happy ending is brought about when Hanno tells the pimp that the girls are his abducted daughters. This is exactly what the clever slave Milphio had planned as a scheme to steal his master's beloved from the pimp, but it is Hanno's rightful claim to his daughters, not Milphio's scheme of deception that wins the victory over the pimp. In this, then, there is an inversion of the Roman stereotype of the deceitful Carthaginian, as it turns out that this Carthaginian is perfectly honest and justified in his claim.

In terms of stock character types Hanno is not only a devoted father to his daughters and a helpful friend to his nephew, but he also brings about the resolution of the play by following the scheme Milphio, the clever slave, had planned. In fact, once Hanno takes over the scheme of recovering the girls from the pimp, Milphio drops out of the plot. But Hanno's resolution is not the result of deception, as was the case with Milphio. His claim to the girls is genuine. While replacing the clever slave in the function of solving the problem posed in the beginning, Hanno fulfils this function in a manner diametrically opposed to the methods of the clever slave.

Nevertheless, the play takes pains to depict Hanno as a 'clever Carthaginian' (*Poenus callidus*), and what is more, it does so in several places where the deceit is required by the plot. The play simultaneously asserts and denies the stereotype of the *Poenus callidus*, because Hanno's own deceptions and the assumptions of Milphio about his cunning establish him in these terms, but then his victory over the pimp turns out to result from a genuine claim rather than a clever scheme.

Both the title of the play and the list of *dramatis personae* at the beginning make much of Hanno's ethnic identity. Hanno is the 'little Carthaginian' of the title, and the list of *dramatis personae* introduces him as 'Hanno the Carthaginian', although it is far more common in these lists to designate characters with stock character types. So Agorastocles is designated as 'young man' and Milphio as 'slave'. 'The Carthaginian' is not a recognized stock character, and Hanno fulfils the roles of several stock characters in this play that could have been used as a designation in the list of *dramatis personae*, such as 'father', 'paternal uncle' and 'old man'. The text's insistence on Hanno's ethnic identity as a stock character type suggests that the play exploits the conventions of stock characterization to establish Punic identity as a character type, while Plautus' depiction of Hanno tends towards exploding the ethnic stereotype of Punic duplicity. Hanno never uses deceit to accomplish his objectives. His deceptions are either a means of creating farce, as in his first encounter with Milphio, or a vehicle for overturning audience expectations, by revealing a person set up as duplicitous to be truthful, genuine, upright and a force that drives the plot towards a happy ending.

7   Conclusion

In this chapter I have aimed to demonstrate the multitude of registers in which representations of ethnic others can be articulated in Roman texts. Discussion of Cicero's attitudes to Greeks in different contexts has shown that ethnic stereotypes and other commonly held conceptions about foreign cultures can be used to argue diametrically opposed positions. Discussion of Plautus' *Poenulus* showed that a literary text can both construct an ethnic identity and problematize its own construction. Roman representations of ethnic others can be found in numerous different contexts, and they depend on factors that have more to do with the Roman cultural context within which they are found than with the foreigners depicted. In assessing such representations it is important to understand what we mean by designating them as 'Roman'. In the case of Terence we have seen that this may not be unproblematic. Furthermore we should consider several factors that may contribute to their construction, such as the target audience of a text and the conventions of its genre. Even within a given text, representations of ethnic others are always an aggregate of converging discourses that contribute various elements. We have seen this clearly in the case of Roman comedy, whose characterizations of individual figures depend on comic stock characters, on the depictions of characters in the Greek plays from which the Roman comedy is adapted, and on Roman conceptions of the foreigners depicted in the plays.

FURTHER READING

A good starting point for research into Roman views of foreigners is Balsdon (1979). See also Veyne (1993) and Sherwin-White (1967). The volume edited by Sordi (1979) contains several individual studies about Greek and Roman views of foreigners. Vasaly (1993) discusses some representations of foreign peoples in Cicero's speeches. Thomas (1982) discusses ethnographic material in Roman poetry. A good introduction to the ancient ethnographic tradition can be found in Rives (1999: 11–21), the introduction to his commentary on Tacitus' *Germania*. Rives is especially good on Roman ethnographies in historical works. For Roman ethnography in geographic contexts and for the ethnographies in Pliny the Elder's *Naturalis Historia* see Murphy (2004). Wells (1999) puts Roman literary accounts of non-literate peoples into perspective by examining the archaeological record they left behind. This study focuses on the native peoples of temperate Europe, referred to in Roman authors as Germans, Gauls and Celts.

On Roman views of the Greeks see the monograph by Petrochilos (1974). Burck (1943) has a general overview of Roman literary representations of the Carthaginians. Prandi (1979) is a specialized study of the stereotype of Carthaginian treachery (*Punica fides*), addressing its association with the causes of the Punic Wars and its Greek literary precedents in representations of treacherous Phoenicians. Henderson (1999: 3–37) is a suggestive discussion of Plautus' *Poenulus*, which reads the ethnic identity of the main character as a means of articulating Roman cultural expectations and fantasies. Horsfall (1973–4) discusses the Dido episode in Vergil's *Aeneid* in the light of Roman stereotypes about the Carthaginians. Syed (forthcoming) contains studies of the representations of various ethnicities in Vergil's *Aeneid*.

CHAPTER TWENTY-SIX

Marriage and Family

Susan Treggiari

1 Introduction

This chapter attempts to explain what Romans took for granted in thinking of and writing about family life, and what was especially praised and valued. To look at values in any society, we examine ideas and practice. In looking at Rome, we switch between theory (attested especially in philosophical writing, derived from Greece, but also in literary sources; e.g. Vergil's *Aeneid* or Horace's *Odes*); prescription/prohibition (e.g. customary and statute law); convention and fashion (reflected in visual arts and 'the epigraphic habit' as well as in literature); representation (what people say about what they or others do and think, including tendentious/moralizing sources, such as Cicero in his courtroom speeches, Valerius Maximus or Juvenal); practice (what people *do*, which might be documented by historiography, private letters, jurists' description of cases or problems, tomb-inscriptions). We would like to see how all these change over time.

But development is often difficult to document because of the disparity of sources for different periods. Is it true that idealization of family life increased when the Principate limited aristocratic power (Veyne 1978, demolished by Saller and Shaw 1984: 134–6; Dixon 1991)? Or is it just that it shows up more in our sources? Did the lower classes have different values? Can we get at them through what they put on their tombstones or their appeals to the emperor? How can we distinguish the Roman part of a man's thinking when he might be a Greek aristocrat like Plutarch or a Parthian freedman (*CIL* 11.137 = *ILS* 1980)? The discussion that follows focuses on Roman citizens, the period from the late Republic to the early third century AD, husband–wife and parent–child relationships.

Where I have not given a reference to bibliography, the reader may find it in *OCD*. Some of the material is further explored in Treggiari (1991).

2　Prefatory

Fewer people marry and rear children than in the old days; more married people divorce. You can read it now or in writings of the Roman upper classes:

> If we could manage without wives ... we would all do without the annoyance they cause, but since nature has taught us we cannot live comfortably with them, nor live at all without them, we must take thought for our eternal welfare rather than our temporary pleasure. (Q. Caecilius Metellus Macedonicus, censor 131 BC, or Q. Caecilius Metellus Numidicus, censor 102–101 BC, quoted by Gell. *NA* 1.6)

Augustus read the whole of Metellus' speech to the Senate when he in his turn was trying to pressure people into marriage.

Or take this, Cicero's remark about his brother to the ex-wife's brother after a divorce that ended about a quarter-century of marriage:

> He's far from having any idea of marrying again. He says he finds it much pleasanter to have his bed to himself. (Cic. *Att.* 14.13.5, 26 April 44 BC)

Or a husband commemorating his wife and pleased with their record of a marriage that lasted over forty years:

> Such long unions, ended by death, not interrupted by divorce, are uncommon. (*Laudatio 'Turiae'* 1.27)

In dealing with such sources, in various genres, we should ask, 'Are such perceptions accurate? What are people's motives in saying this? How did they expect their hearers to react?' Cicero, who had just divorced twice in two years, may have been sympathetic to his brother's disillusionment. But Atticus, who married late, seems to have been happy with his wife and daughter and had loyally supported his own sister, may have been less inclined to smile. (We cannot tell if the Cicerones would have remained unmarried from choice, for both died in December 43.) Similarly, let us ask what statistics the happy husband had to back his generalization. He will have known divorced people, but surely his statement is impressionistic. The censor, and, later, Augustus, will have had census evidence for thinking Roman men did not marry (early enough and often enough).

3　Theory and Prescription

In his treatise on the Republic, which was circulated to acclaim during his absence as a provincial governor (51–50 BC), Cicero shows a predictable liking for the pairing of the individual and the community to which he belongs and of the family and the city. While Ennius (*ap.* Cic. *Rep.* 5.1) makes Rome depend on traditions and *viri* (males), Cicero, though he pays deference to the series of Roman heroes, has an eye to the role of women such as Lucretia (*Rep.* 2.46; cf. *Leg.* 2.10). The comparison of family and state is a continuing theme (e.g. *Rep.* 1.8, 61; 1 fr. 2; 3.45; 4.7; 5.4). Cicero presents the standard Greek view that the family developed before the wider community (*Rep.* 1.38; cf. Arist. *Eth. Nic.* 1162a 16–22). This view is forcefully restated at the very end of his life in the book on duty addressed to his son:

> Because the urge to reproduce is an instinct common to all animals, society origin-ally consists of the pair, next of the pair with their children, then one house and all things in common. This is the beginning of the city and the seed-bed of the state. (Cic. *Off.* 1.54)

The doctrine that marriage is based on natural law was juristic orthodoxy (e.g. *Dig.* 1.1.1.3, Ulp. i *inst.*). Secondly, Cicero believes that the health of the state depends on the family and that the education of children and self-control of grown men, are vital (e.g. *Leg.* 1.57; 3.29–30). Senators set an example (*Leg.* 3.10, 28). Good states depend on the family:

> For the sake of life and the practice of living, a prescription has been made for recognized marriages, legitimate children and the sacred homes of the household gods and family Lares, so that everyone should enjoy common and individual blessings. For living well is impossible without a good community and there is nothing happier than a well-set-up polity. (Cic. *Rep.* 5.7)

The family, religion and the wider community are inextricable. The state, however large, for instance all Roman citizens, is constructed on couples who obey their animal instinct to mate and reproduce. Justice and law emerge from Nature. Justice is to give each individual what belongs to him and this principle is as true for peoples as for individuals. In a good community, all its members have a share in the common good: 'a commonwealth', or *res publica*, is one in which everything belongs to 'the people', *res populi*. A Roman theorist would not make a state and its citizens into opposites: the state *is* the Roman People. Anyone reviewing the rise and fall of cities inevitably sought the cause in the nature of their organization and lifestyle (Polyb.1.1; cf. Sall. *Cat.* 5.9; 6.3; Livy *Praef.* 9). Imperial expansion brought worries about a change in Roman morality, which included unease with the idea and reality of the well-dowered wife who might control her husband (e.g. Malcovati 1967, *ORF*[3] Cato 158; Plaut. *Asin.* 87). 'All men rule their wives; we rule all men, our wives rule us' (Plut. *Apophth.* 198D3) is attributed, aptly, to Cato the Censor, who opposed the repeal of the Oppian law and later sponsored a law limiting inheritance-rights, which Cicero characterizes as full of injustice to women (*Rep.* 3.17; Dixon 1985).

4   Roman Peculiarities

What, in the ancient view, made the Romans 'top nation'? Piety, a mixed constitution or features of their family life? Dionysius of Halicarnassus, who chose the
third answer, idealized the ancient sacramental marriage that put the wife under
her husband's control (*Ant. Rom.* 2.24–26.1). Cicero considers it right and
Roman that no public official should keep women in order, but

> There should be a censor to teach husbands to guide their wives. (*Rep.* 4.6)

Philosophers conceived the household as a monarchy. The father might consult
his opposite numbers from other households. He answered to the law, custom
and opinion of his community, but, as Cicero's Scipio puts it to Laelius, 'Isn't it
true that no-one but you rules your entire house?' (*Rep.* 1.61) This concept had
long been enshrined in the practically unique (Gai. *Inst.* 1.55) 'paternal power'
(*patria potestas*) held by a 'head of household' (*paterfamilias*), any male who was
not himself under the power of a male ascendant. A grandfather might have in his
power his sons (*filiifamilias*), daughters (*filiaefamilias*), and grandchildren
through sons. If the grandfather died, his sons automatically each became *paterfamilias*. If a son predeceased his father and himself had a son, that grandson
would similarly become an independent household-head on his grandfather's
death. Women who on marriage passed into the husband's family because he
obtained 'control' over them, *manus*, came under something like a paternal
power of the husband or his *paterfamilias*. Originally, the power of the *paterfamilias* was absolute. He could put those in his power to death (very rare: Harris
1986), and any property they acquired was his, but it was, as it were, held in trust
and if the father died without a will, then all dependants took equal shares. Since
filiifamilias could not act independently, the father's will was necessary for their
marriage or divorce. The 'household' (*familia*) included slaves. What we
would call the family might be the group of *liberi* or 'free persons' (a word that
comes to mean descendants in the male line) under one *paterfamilias*, plus his
wife. *Uxor liberique* (wife and children) was the usual expression for a man's
nuclear family.

The legal structure dictated emphasis on agnates, kin through males (who
shared the gentile name). In the extended family, agnates had a claim on inheritance and male agnates would be guardians to fatherless children. But emotional
ties to the female-line asserted themselves (e.g. Saller 1997). Sisters might maintain strong ties, so the word for cousins who are the children of sisters became the
word for 'cousins' in general (*consobrini* [Gai. *Inst.* 3.10]). By Augustus' time,
descent in the 'female line' (*maternum genus*) was valued in sentiment, appraisal
of status and inheritance-practices (Gardner 2001). Members of the upper
classes, at least, would try to make a will and to take all close kin into account

(Champlin 1991: 103–30). Demography affected the number who might qualify. For instance, Cicero had been close to a patrilineal cousin, L. Cicero, but he died young (68 BC; Cic. *Fin.* 5.1; *Verr.* 2.3.170; 4.25, 137, 145; *Att.* 1.5.1). His own daughter died in 45 BC. The close kin who were left in 43 BC were a son, brother and nephew, but the latter two perished, like Cicero, in the proscriptions of that year. Being divorced from two women, Cicero had no moral obligation to name a wife in his will.

We do not know whether marriage in which the wife did not enter the control of her husband was as old as *manus*, but we know that it was well established by the fifth century (Gai. *Inst.* 1.111 citing *XII Tables*). The two continued to exist as options, but by Cicero's time it was relatively rare for a wife to be in her husband's control, *in manu mariti* (Treggiari 1991: 20–1). So her *legal* ties were to her family of birth, with the curious consequence that her legal connection with her own children was played down and only slowly asserted by the emperors. Moral duties and emotional ties cut across this (Dixon 1988).

Although *patria potestas* shaped relationships, it is hard to find historic fathers using it to coerce: neither of the Cicerones seems to have appealed to it in difficulties with their sons.

Like moderns, Romans could think of who constituted 'family' in ways that changed according to the individual's circumstances (Dixon 1992: 1–11). Although *pietas* mandated especial attention to children/parents (reflected in epigraphic practice), and husband/wife commemoration is the commonest type (Saller and Shaw 1984), which confirms that the nuclear family was the usual *household* unit, siblings might be important (Bradley 1991: 177–204; Bannon 1997) and cousins, uncles and so on had claims on loyalty and affection. Nor must we forget that the nuclear or extended family provided scope for conflict as well as affection (Dixon 1997b).

5   Marriage

A man took a wife in order to produce legitimate children, *liberorum quaerendorum causa*. *Matrimonium*, the usual word for marriage, means an institution for making mothers. If the couple were married according to Roman law – that is, if they were qualified to marry each other and the necessary consents were given – then the children took the status and family name of their father. The wife took the social status of her husband.

The general rules on who could marry whom were not unduly restrictive. A Roman could marry any other Roman of the opposite sex who was not a close relation or under age (12 for a girl; perhaps 14 for a boy). Incest taboos ruled out ascendants and descendants, siblings and so on. Augustus added further regulations based on social class and also (probably) ruled that soldiers could not marry (*Lex Julia de maritandis ordinibus* and *Lex Papia Poppaea*; Phang 2001).

The Romans expressed the right of A to marry B by the term *conubium*. It was fundamental that this capacity existed between Romans and citizens of other Latin cities, but not (unless specifically granted) with 'foreigners' (*peregrini*) and not between a free person and a slave, or between two slaves. *Peregrini* formed marriages according to their own customs; Rome did not legislate for them. Valid Roman marriages involved transmission of citizenship to the children, an increasingly valuable privilege vis-à-vis other citizenships. Slaves might, with owners' permission or encouragement, form comparatively lasting 'relationships', *contubernia*. It is possible to trace such unions at various stages: when both partners were slaves and any child born a slave; when the man had been freed but the woman had not and any child was born a slave; when the woman had been freed and the man had not and any child was born free but illegitimate; when both had been freed and become legally married citizens, so that a child was freeborn and legitimate.

It was normal to assess the success of matches by socio-economic compatibility: birth, wealth, male talent, female beauty. Philosophers added virtue, medical men fertility. Yet, when friends suggested to Cicero a lady whom they thought suitable for an aging divorcee, he rejected her outright: 'I've never seen anything uglier' (Cic. *Att*. 12.11, 46 BC).

Older kin, particularly the *paterfamilias*, might claim to decide on behalf of young people. But the father's power was modified by the expectation that he would take no major decisions without consulting kinsmen. By the late Republic, it was apparently normal for him to consult his wife and other women. Also by the late Republic the father could not engage or marry off a child without his or her technical consent. Girls might be allowed a veto on individual candidates. More than that, we can find Cicero's nephew Quintus negotiating a marriage for himself without obtaining his father's approval (Cic. *Att*. 15.29.2; 16.2.5). When it came to a woman's second marriage, when she had already participated in social events as a wife, she could claim more independence. Cicero mentions one candidate whom he thinks his daughter Tullia could not be persuaded to accept (*Att*. 5.4.1), and left the decision on her third husband to her and her mother:

> Since I was going to be so far away, I instructed them not to consult me but to do what they thought proper. (*Fam*. 3.12.2)

The man she picked turned out disastrously.

So individual taste could cut across the utilitarian motives for choosing a husband or wife which society approved, and the future husband or wife, particularly if the *paterfamilias* and other kin were dead, might act for himself or herself. What of love? Critics sometimes say people marry because of passion. This may not be true of the individual instance, but it suggests that the motive was seen as possible. The best confirmation is Augustus' law, *Lex Aelia Sentia*, of AD 4 (Gai. *Inst*. 1.18–19), which laid down that a male slave-owner, under the age of

20, who needed to apply for permission if he wanted to manumit, could free a woman in order to marry her. There was no social advantage for anyone in marrying his own ex-slave, so the motive must be personal attraction. Augustus recognizes it as a valid reason. (There was a strong sociolegal prejudice, however, against matches between a free woman and her ex-slave, unless they had previously been fellow-slaves: Evans Grubbs 1993.)

Consent was necessary in classical law for engagement (*Dig.* 23.1.7.1, Paulus *xxxv ad edictum*) and marriage:

> A marriage cannot exist unless everyone consents, that is, those who come together and those in whose power they are. (*Dig.* 23.2.2, Paulus, *xxxv ad edictum*)

Engagements could be made simply, by letters or verbal statements (*Dig.* 23.1.4, 5, 7 *pr.*, 18). In the second century AD a great lawyer held, and others agreed, that if a *filiafamilias* acted by herself, her father's consent was to be taken for granted unless there was contrary evidence (*Dig.* 23.1.7.1, Paulus *xxxv ad edictum*, citing Iulianus).

A daughter or son in power could not be betrothed if she or he refused consent (*Dig.* 23.1.11, 13). But a daughter's non-opposition, like a father's, implied her consent, and it was thought improper for her to refuse betrothal except for strong reasons (*Dig.* 23.1.12). Engagement, however, did not always lead to marriage.

What made a marriage was the consent of the bride, bridegroom and the *paterfamilias* of each (if there was one). Consent – for the couple – was a mental resolve to be married, each to the other. Various ceremonies were practised and several verbal formulae are attested, but none was essential, although the resolve had to be made clear. Usually bride and bridegroom went through a ceremony before kin and friends. Some sarcophagi show the most important moment: the clasping of right hands (*dextrarum iunctio*) as the couple faced each other. Literary sources stress sacrifice, feasting, the bride's toilette, her procession to the bridegroom's house. Some participants had ritual roles. Parents handed over the bride. Guests wished the couple harmony. But no priest or public official ratified the marriage and no register was signed. The protagonists bilaterally made the marriage (with the *paterfamilias* of either or both). Sexual consummation was not necessary to make the marriage valid (*Dig.* 50.17.30, Ulp. *xxxvi ad Sabinum*).

How did a Roman know he was married? It is clearer if we look first at divorce.

Divorce, always an option for the husband (or his *paterfamilias*) if the wife committed a serious fault or was childless, was, by Cicero's time, available to either partner. A divorce could be brought about by either husband or wife and unilaterally. This made it shortsighted for parents to force children into an unwanted marriage:

> 'You are not marrying the wife I want you to marry,' says my father. What is that to the point? Are you not aware that marriages are at our own choice? Our affections are not

at your beck and call; you cannot make us love or hate whom you want by giving an order. Marriage is only eternal if it is a union brought about by mutual consent. When a wife is sought for me, the companion of my bed, the partner of my life, I must choose her for all eternity. In any case, what is the good of compelling me against my will? If you do that, I will simply divorce her. (*Quint. Decl. Min.* 376.2)

In theory, it was enough for one partner in the marriage to cease to regard the other as husband or wife. In practice, it was sensible and no doubt usual to inform the other partner, though not, in principle, necessary (Cic. *De or.* 1.183, 238; *Dig.* 24.2.4, Ulp. *xxvi ad Sabinum*).

Divorce might happen because both husband and wife agreed on it. Such a bilateral divorce was said to happen *bona gratia*, 'with a good grace'. Again, no public authority had to ratify divorce.

Marriage and divorce were 'free'. No one could be compelled to marry, to stay married or to divorce. The principle is unaffected by the possibility that families or the state might try to make people marry. What makes a marriage is the joint consent of two qualified individuals. The marriage lasts as long as both continue to consent. If one withdraws consent, there is a unilateral divorce.

the word 'divorce' derives from the fact that those who separate go different ways. (*Dig.* 50.16.191, Paulus *xxxv ad edictum*)

Continued consent is described as *maritalis affectio*, the attitude of regarding the other as one's husband or wife (e.g. *Dig.* 24.3.32.13, Ulp. *xxxiii ad Sabinum*). Contracts and ceremonies might be evidence of this, but were inessential. So other sexual relationships might turn into marriage, without a public marking of the fact. Slave mates (*contubernales*) who continued their relationship after manumission, when they became citizens and capable of Roman marriage provide one frequent instance. The same might happen between a concubine and her (usually socially superior) man.

Supposing legal Roman marriage was open to a couple, for instance neither was a slave and their marriage would not be invalid under the Augustan laws, then it was usually to be assumed that they were married. In such a context, the misunderstandings of Dido and Aeneas become comprehensible. A sovereign viewed her guest as a husband; he did not reciprocate (Verg. *Aen.* 4.171–2, 337–9).

6   Ideals

A philosopher might hold lofty views:

In marriage there must be above all perfect companionship (*symbiosis*) and mutual love (*kedemonia*) of husband and wife, both in health and in sickness and under all conditions, since it was with desire for this as well as for having children that both entered upon marriage. Where, then, this love for each other is perfect and the two share it completely, each striving to outdo the other in devotion, the marriage is ideal and worthy of envy, for such a union is beautiful. But where each looks only to his own interests and neglects the other, or, what is worse, when one is so minded and lives in the same house but fixes his attention elsewhere and is not willing to pull together with his yoke-mate nor to agree, then the union is doomed to disaster and though they live together, yet their common interests fare badly; eventually they separate entirely or they remain together and suffer what is worse than loneliness. (Musonius 13 A. 'What is the chief end of marriage?' trans. Lutz 1947: 88–9)

That ordinary people had a high ideal of marriage is confirmed by people who divorced, not for 'sensible reasons' such as getting children, but because they were unhappy. An anonymous Roman divorced a wife everyone else thought was ideal: virtuous, beautiful and fertile. But he said he was the only one who knew where his shoe pinched (Plut. *Aem.* 5). Some divorced because they wanted to marry someone else, perhaps for love.

There are two paradoxes here. One is that the theoretical availability of divorce, which need not have happened frequently, could be an incentive for each partner to try to make the other happy. The other is that divorcing because of unhappiness is evidence for the ideal of happy family life, a literary commonplace. The conventional list of a man's most precious possessions was wife, house, children and country (e.g. Lucr. 3. 894–6; Ov. *Tr.* 1.3.62–4). So Crassus praised Cicero for having saved everything he loved: 'every time he beheld his wife, his home, his country, he beheld a gift from me' (Cic. *Att.* 1.14.3)

The sentimental ideal is a theme for poets, even Horace (e.g. *Odes* 2.14.21–2 [trans. West]: 'we must leave the earth, our home / and the wife we love'). It also occurs in prosaic contexts, addressed to more closely identified audiences (e.g. *P Oxy.* 2435 trans. Kokkinos 1992: 82; Tac. *Ann.* 3.34).

The speech the third-century Greek senator Dio put in the mouth of Augustus could equally well have been written in the first century AD:

For is there anything better than a wife who is chaste, domestic, a good house-keeper, a rearer of children; one to gladden you in health, to tend you in sickness; to be your partner in good fortune, to console you in misfortune; to restrain the mad passion of youth and to temper the unseasonable harshness of old age? And is it not a delight to acknowledge a child who shows the endowments of both parents? (Cass. Dio 56.3.3–4, trans. Cary [Loeb])

7   Husband and Wife

At a wedding, the couple was wished 'long-lasting harmony', *longa concordia*. Romans saw marriage as a partnership. *Coniunx*, the word for 'husband' or 'wife', means a yoke-mate. A wife may be termed 'partner' (Dixon 1991: 106–7; Treggiari 1991: 248–51). Although philosophers and others stressed the sharing of property and the good and evil life brought, when a wife did not enter *manus*, she retained independence as a property-owner, and the law safeguarded separation of the property of both *coniuges* (Crook 1990).

The virtues and vices of wives had long been subjected to scrutiny. The most famous Roman eulogy says that the wife shared with all reputable married ladies her wool-working, observance of religion, quiet way of dressing (cf. Pliny *Pan.* 83.7), equal care for her own relatives and her husband's, and four abstract virtues, *pudicitia*, *obsequium*, *comitas* and *facilitas* (*Laud. Tur.* 1.30–4). This gives an overview of the conventional virtues. *Pudicitia*, inadequately translated 'chastity', connotes in a wife sexual fidelity and love towards her husband. The abstraction was worshipped by women who had been married only once, *univirae*. These receive special praise on tombstones and in literature. It was no virtue (though it might be good fortune) in a man to have only one wife in his lifetime, and sexual exclusivity during a marriage was less prescribed for him, although it was thought to occur (Val. Max. 4.3.3, *Cons. ad Liviam* 305). Concubinage with a woman of inferior status was acceptable for unmarried young or old men (Treggiari 1981), though cavorting with a number of sexual partners of either sex (*concubinae/concubini*) is a commonplace of invective and biographies of bad emperors. Adultery (extramarital intercourse with a married woman), a sin earlier dealt with by families, for example by divorce, became a crime for both sexes under Augustus (McGinn 1998). The incidence of adultery is irrecoverable.

Comitas and *facilitas*, graciousness and being easy-going, were appreciated by a man at the receiving end and sometimes criticized by third parties (e.g. Tac. *Ann.* 5.1). *Obsequium*, co-operativeness, was said to win back an erring husband (Publilius 492, [Sen.] *Octavia* 84–5, 177, 213; Williams 1958: 25). These qualities which made a marriage run smoothly were equally appropriate for a husband to show to his wife (e.g. Cic. *Att.* 6.6.1; Hor. *Epist.* 2.2.133; cf. Livy 33.21.4). Respect, *reverentia*, was also to be reciprocal (Columella 12 pr. 7; Pliny *Ep.* 8.5.1; *Dig.* 25.2.3.2), as was *fides*, 'good faith', the quality demanded in any friendly relationship. It is *fides* when a wife rescues her proscribed husband (Val. Max. 6.7.2–3); it is *fides* when the anonymous heroine's husband refuses to divorce her for sterility (*Laud. Tur.* 2.45; cf. Val. Max. 2.1.4). A husband shows faith in administering the dowry, the wife in looking after the house (Treggiari 1991: 238). *Pietas*, 'affectionate dutifulness', prescribed between all family members (Saller 1994) is attributed to both husbands and wives in epitaphs. Romans might classify as *pietas* the self-sacrifice of a husband who volunteered to die instead of his wife, or of one who pined to death for love (Saller 1994: 400, citing Plin. *HN* 7.122). Less heroic devotion in Augustus:

> All of a sudden he died with Livia's kisses on his lips and with these words: 'Livia, live remembering our marriage, and farewell!' (Suet. *Aug.* 99.1)

8   Parents and Children

Duties between parents and children were similarly defined: reciprocal *obsequium* (dutifulness) and reverence (e.g. Ter. *Haut.* 152; Cic. *QFr.* 1.3.3; *CIL* 6.3150, 28888); 'indulgence' (*indulgentia*), chiefly from parent to child (Cic *Verr.* 2.1.112; *De orat.* 2.168); love and concern for children (e.g. Cic. *Inv.*1.107–9). It was natural to desire and love children (Cic. *Att.* 7.2.4; *Fin.* 3.62–8; 4.17; 5.65), a gift from the gods (Cic. *Red. pop.* 5), dear and delightful (*cari, iucundi*) (Cic. *Dom.* 98; *Cael.* 79). Cicero and Atticus enjoyed their small children:

> Tulliola ['Little Tullia'] my darling [then perhaps around 8], is demanding that you pay over the little present; she is dunning me as your guarantor ....Tulliola is serving a summons on you, she is not calling on the guarantor to pay. (Cic. *Att.* 1.8.3; 10.6)

The poor might hope that children would support them in their old age, the rich that their sons would perpetuate their name, wealth and distinction (Parkin 1997). Nevertheless, statesmen often perceived upper-class men as reluctant to do their patriotic duty. Augustus attempted to encourage marriage and reproduction through legislation.

It was a commonplace that children ought not to die before their parents (e.g. Sigismund Nielsen 1997: 198–202), but there was a high risk that they would, and ancient literature contains pathetic testimony (Bradley 2001). Children also ran the risk of being orphaned: Roman lawyers were concerned with guardianship for those who lost a father before puberty (Saller 1994: 181–203). Eventually, emperors took measures to support some children (Rawson 2001). Rejection of a child or of a parent, for instance ignoring either in one's will, was a serious step. Children were normally the preferred heirs (Champlin 1991: 103–30). Violence to parents was a sin, parallel to sacrilege or treason (Cic. *Sex. Rosc.* 63; *Fin.* 3.32; 4.76; *Rhet. ad Her.* 4.19, 38, 46). Ideally, violent punishment of children was avoided (Saller 1994: 133–53). *Pietas* to blood-kin is a theme in all kinds of text (Saller 1994: 102–32; Nielsen 1997, 2001).

Scholars have asked whether childhood was seen as a separate stage of life. The consensus is that it was, vague though Latin is on age (Dixon 1992: 98–132; Harlow and Laurence 2002). Vergil observed the socialization of babies:

> Incipe, parve puer, risu cognoscere matrem.

> Begin, little child, to recognize your mother with a smile.
> (*Ecl.* 4.60)

Scholars worry about who smiles; surely they both do. Later development (walking, speech, formal education) was also carefully observed. Girls marked a transition at marriage. Boys exchanged the *toga praetexta* for a white toga and were received into the father's tribe as full citizens when their families considered them mature. Children were also a recognized group within the citizen body: Augustus gave freeborn boys a bloc of seats at the games (Suet. *Aug.* 44.2; Rawson 1991b: especially 518–19); Horace names young unmarried people among those who welcomed Augustus home in 24 BC (*Odes* 3.14.5–12). Horace accepts that children can and should be trained in virtue and good citizenship (e.g. *Sat.* 1.6.62–99; *Ep.* 1.2.64–70; *Odes* 3.6.17–44; 3.24.54–62; 4.4.25–36): they are the addressees of the Roman Odes (3.1.1–4). They had a role in cult, both as members of a family and, sometimes, outside their own household (Mantle 2002). They are prominent both on the Altar of Augustan Peace and in the Centennial Games of 17 BC (Hor. *Odes* 4.6.31–44; *Carmen Saeculare*, Braund 1985: 769 p. 295 = EJ 32).

A second area of interest is the emotional relationship between parents and children. Specialists in later epochs have suggested that parents resisted parental love. Despite the high rate of infant mortality, there is evidence that Romans allowed themselves to love their babies and grieved when they died (Golden 1988). The ideal parent of either sex was, nevertheless, strict (Dixon 1988). The upper classes delegated routine care to slaves, including wetnursing (despite philosophical approval for mothers' milk). Abortion, usually dangerous for the mother, was an offence against an unwitting husband, but not generally seen as violence to the foetus. 'Exposure' (*expositio*) of newborn infants (who might be raised by others) was not unthinkable (Corbier 2001).

On legitimacy, Roman ideas differed from the norms of Western societies before the twentieth-century sexual revolution (Rawson 1989). Although being the offspring of a marriage recognized in law was important for succession to the father's property and status, no stigma attached to lower-class people born outside marriage. Their parents might have been disqualified from marrying. For example, an imperial freedman commemorated three 'natural' children, but proudly named his one freeborn and legitimate son Ingenuus (born free). There was no shame in putting the adjective *naturalis* three times on an epitaph (*Année Epigraphique* 1939: 10). Similarly, many people on epitaphs stress their lack of a legal father with the formula *Sp. f., spurius/spuria filius/filia*, 'illegitimate child', in place of the usual mention of a father, as in *Marci filius/filia*.

Childless men who wanted an heir might have recourse to adoption (*adoptio* of a *filiusfamilias/filiafamilias* or *adrogatio* of an independent man), normally of an adult. Both men and women might also by will name someone heir, on condition he took their family name, as Julius Caesar artificially made the future Augustus his 'son'.

Even humble people were anxious to perpetuate themselves through their descendants. Testators took care that their tomb should 'not go out of the name'.

Slaves legally had no parents. Freed slaves, whose monuments assert their citizenship, had themselves portrayed with their children.

Susan Treggiari

FURTHER READING

I have concentrated on giving references to recent scholarship in English, which will allow the reader to work backwards to earlier bibliography, but have also included some pioneering work where this has not become dated.

The history of scholarship on the Roman family can best be traced in B. M. Rawson (1986: 1–57; 1991: 1–5), Bradley (1993 and 1998a), Dixon (1994 and 1997a), Rawson and Weaver (1997: 1–5). Studies on the family have roots in Roman law, upper-class prosopography, work on Roman women and on slavery and the lower classes. The legal material has been illuminated by scholars such as Crook (1967 and 1990), Gardner (1986, 1992 and 1998), Evans Grubbs (1995 and 2002), Arjava (1996) and McGinn (1998). There are influences from the study of classical literature, mediaeval and modern history, anthropology, gender studies. French scholarship has had a particular impact, especially Corbier. Close study of inscriptions (e.g. Wilkinson/Rawson 1966; Saller 1987; Shaw 1987; Weaver 1972) has been important. Word usage is used to illuminate *mentalité*. Critical interrogation of disparate sources is seen as vital (e.g. Corbier 2001); a wide variety of texts is mined (e.g. Bradley 1999 and 2001). The visual arts play an increasing role (e.g. Rawson 1997; Bradley 1998b). Theory plays a role, but is prudently deployed. The complexity of the Roman world is recognized: work has until recently focused on Roman citizens and the central period of the late Republic and Principate, but now the regions of Italy (Gallivan and Wilkins 1997), the provinces (Bradley 2000; Cherry 1998; Phang 2001), later periods (Evans Grubbs 1995; Arjava 1996), non-Roman cultures are increasingly receiving attention.

CHAPTER TWENTY-SEVEN

Slavery and Class

Thomas Habinek

1   Introduction

Slaves made Latin literature possible. In a broad sense, the productive energies of slaves and other dependent labourers generated the surplus that sustained the leisure, or *otium*, necessary (in the Roman view) for the production and consumption of literary texts. In a narrower sense, slaves and ex-slaves, functioning as readers, researchers, amanuenses, tutors, librarians, copyists, referees and critics were integral to the creation and circulation of texts and to the transmission of the various kinds of knowledge that informed them. Indeed, for all we know, a Roman author was no more responsible for the literary works attributed to him than a modern fashion designer can be said to have 'made' the clothing sold under his or her label. The Roman ego was expandable, not limited by the boundaries of a single body. Just as the pronouns 'I' and 'you' could signify 'my slaves and I' or 'you and your slaves', so in practice a slave performed as a prosthesis of his master, even when that master was an esteemed writer (Reay 2002).

Given the indispensability of slaves to Roman literature (and to Roman culture more generally), we might expect surviving works of literature to display some anxiety with respect to slaves' capabilities and their role in literary production. We will not be disappointed. From the clever slave of Plautine comedy, who often plays the part of theatrical impresario, to the slave who lectures the philosophical satirist Horace on commonplaces of philosophy (*Satires* 2.7), to the servile or all-but-servile shepherds of Virgil's *Eclogues*, whom the ancient commentators regarded, not without reason, as allegories of the author and other poets, to the freedwoman conspirator (*Annals* 15.57) whose silence under torture mimes the silence of the young Tacitus (but he, unlike she, 'survived himself') – over and over again, slaves or freedmen serve as distorted counterparts of the author as creator. Even the term that Latin writers use for playful rehearsal of serious composition, *ludus*, otherwise describes the activity of slaves and of children, the two categories of human beings expected always to modulate their actions to the rhythms of others.

It is something of a truism that freedom is an absolute value only in societies that are or have been dependent on slaves (Patterson 1991). The possibility of its loss makes freedom seem dear. And rivalry between slaves and poor free citizens leads the latter to place a rhetorical and psychological premium on the one possession that distinguishes their condition from that of slaves. In a similar vein, Roman writers privilege precisely the characteristics that differentiate themselves from slaves as literary producers: authoritative voice, potential to speak truth to power, and male potency, both literally (Ovid boasted of nine acts of sexual intercourse in a single night, *Amores* 3.7.25) and figuratively in the aspiration to poetic immortality.

What a slave could not do is speak for himself, contradict a superior (except under specific circumstances, as in the case of a house-slave trained to be impertinent), or represent his life and labour as embedded in an unbroken chain of predecessors and descendants. No slave could hope, in so far as he remained a slave, through production and reproduction, of texts or anything else, to be 'sung throughout the whole world forever' (*in toto ut semper orbe canar*, *Am.* 1.15.8). He was, qua slave, both 'socially dead' (a phrase made famous by Patterson 1982) and socially unborn, deprived even of a name that would situate him within a family line and legitimate him as a discrete, autonomous member of the community. Slaves had names, but these referred to ethnic background or occupation, not to the family ties that guaranteed legitimacy and determined status. How must a slave, separated forever from home and kin, have heard Horace's boast to 'have heaped up a monument more lasting than bronze', his claim to be able to escape death at Rome through poetic production and return to the land from which he came? (*C.* 3.30).

And yet the experience of individual poets and writers may have offered at least some slaves something to look forward to. After all, many of the Roman writers whose names did come to matter, whose voices carried at least literary authority, who procreated within the literary tradition, were freed slaves or sons of slaves: Livius Andronicus, Plautus, Terence, Horace, Phaedrus as well as less familiar figures such as Tiro, Parthenius, and Remmius Palaemon. Their experience points to a critical difference between Roman slavery and the more familiar chattel slavery of the Americas, namely the relative frequency of manumission in the Roman world, at least among educated, urban slaves, and, more generally, the embeddedness of Roman slavery within a complex system of greater and lesser degrees of honour and shame, or abjection and elevation. At the risk of oversimplification we might say that Roman slavery was, at least potentially, a rung on a ladder or a stage in reintegration into the community of the free, whereas New World slavery was an attempted rending of the human species into separate races. Ancient slavery was a misfortune that could be visited on anyone of any natal status who had been captured in war or by slavers; New World slavery was a policy of racial subjugation for purposes of economic exploitation. Such differences hardly constitute an apology for or amelioration of Roman slavery, but they must be kept in mind if we are to understand the place of slaves in the Roman literary imagination, especially in the creators' representation of the processes and conditions of creation. At any given moment, a slave was radically other with respect to a free person; yet it was at least possible to imagine a slave as some day becoming free.

2   Slavery and Honour

The hierarchical, as opposed to strictly categorical, nature of the Roman slave system reminds us that Roman literature could be implicated in the distribution of power among and between groups ranged across a broad spectrum of (dis)-empowerment. Through their literary efforts Roman writers sought to enhance their own honour, that of their patrons and allies, and that of the Roman elite more generally (however that elite might be defined at a given point in history). In so doing they participated in the distribution of a key constituent of social power, namely honour. Honour was not an incidental asset, as it sometimes seems to be in contemporary society; rather it was the means through which individuals and groups were motivated to take action and a measurable indicator of status. For example, Cicero argued that it was his prestige as a speaker that allowed him to triumph over the Catilinarian conspirators, while under the empire we hear of emperors taking action to forestall potential rivals' accumulation of honour, including honour from literary production (Habinek 2000). Indeed, the role of literature in the acquisition of honour seems to expand, rather than diminish over time, as certain political and military positions come to be defined as off-limits to the senatorial aristocracy.

By continually emphasizing its role in the creation of honour, literature implicitly accepts and reinforces a system that is ultimately dependent on the radical dishonour of the slave. This nexus of ideas is perhaps most clearly expressed in the idea of *servitium amoris*, or slavery of love, that characterizes the genre of Augustan elegy. It is through celebration in poetry of his willing enslavement to the elegiac 'mistress', *domina*, that the poet hopes to achieve eternal renown. Propertius goes so far as to imagine a tombstone inscription that, in describing him as 'the slave of a single love' will make his fame outstrip that even of Achilles (Prop. 2.13.34–8). What is more, the elegist's renown stands in opposition to that of his rivals, such as the soldier (e.g. Ov. *Am.* 1.9) or the businessman (e.g. Prop. 1.6; 1.14) In other words, the poet seeks not only to maximize his honour within the rules of the game, but also to reinforce honour as the basis of social authority at the expense of potential competing systems of distribution of power. In particular, the poet resists the appeal of commerce or commodification, which would, in effect, undermine the importance of honour. Here again, elegy provides a ready illustration with its repeated denunciation of both rich male rivals and money-grubbing mistresses. For the mistress to prefer expensive gifts over poetry, or a rich rival to the allegedly resourceless poet, is a repudiation not just of the poet-lover's love for her, but of the whole system of honour and shame that structures their relationship. It turns her, in Ovid's harsh language (e.g. *Am.* 1.10.42), into a prostitute, that is to say a figure, like the slave, who lacks honour altogether. That such concerns are not unique to the Augustan period is suggested by the poetry of Martial, composed during the reign of Domitian. While Martial represents himself as slave to no one, nonetheless his work is rife with anxiety over his status as a relative newcomer in the social and literary elite at Rome. In its coarsest sense, it is Martial's ability to penetrate others – whether slaves and social subordinates with his phallus or rivals and peers with his witty invective – that secures his honour. Not surprisingly, this set of attitudes coincides with a disdain for the financial necessities of life in the imperial capital and the attempt to dishonour others precisely through publicization of their fondness for money.

In effect, its ability to convey honour may well be literature's most important social role. Mastery of the literary tradition was an important means through which relative newcomers established their legitimacy as Romans; and the cultural authority that literature vested in honour helped to sustain both the polarity of slave and free and the hierarchical distribution of honour and shame that characterized Roman society.

3   Slaves in Latin Literature

While representations of slaves and other dependents abound throughout the entire history of Latin literature, a few examples taken from the chronological midsection of the tradition give some sense of the challenge they pose to the reader and of the need for nuanced interpretation attentive to the specifics of historical circumstance and the complexity of Roman social relations.

Consider first Virgil's *Eclogues* – ten short poems, in extraordinarily refined language, seeking to adapt the conventions of Theocritean pastoral to the social and literary conditions of post-civil-war Rome (see Heyworth, Chapter 10 above). The *Eclogues* speak of dispossession and loss, of forced migration, of the vagaries of fortune, of unrequited longing, of the ultimately futile solidarity of the oppressed. Many of the speakers in the poems are slaves, or likely to be understood as slaves by ancient audiences. Like slaves to slave-owners, the characters in the *Eclogues* are both highly individualized and virtually interchangeable: the lack of detailed characterization that is sometimes held against Latin literature more generally is really just another way of saying that it is a product of a slave-owning, feudalistic society, one long predating the invention of Enlightenment subjectivity. Within the *Eclogues*, the selection of slaves as the focalizers for meditations on historical developments that affect all society (civil war, proscription, the spectacular growth of the city of Rome, Hellenization, emperor-cult etc.) may be a way in which the elite poet and audience negotiate their own relations of dependency (slaves evidently being 'good to think with').

But the poems may also really be about slaves. One of the striking aspects of the opening poem in the collection is its indirect yet clear reference to the treatment of Octavian as a god. According to the historian Appian, this novel welcome of the returning strongman was due in part to his success in clearing Italy of bandits – that is, groups of shepherds, herdsmen and runaway slaves who preyed upon the free. In the light of such information, the *Eclogues* can be read as, among other things, an attempt to reassure an urban(e) audience of the passivity of the rural oppressed and/or a plea for the inclusion of the latter in the energizing vision of a unified Italy – not a call to liberation, to be sure, but a movement of the cultural discourse in the direction, we might say, of the hierarchical as opposed to the bipolar model of slavery discussed above.

Indeed, there is some reason to believe that the material condition of slaves, like that of other marginalized groups, did improve with the transition from aristocratic republic to hegemonic principate. And certainly the empire's need for a more reliable commercial and administrative bureaucracy than privilege-obsessed senators could provide was a factor in the growth and influence of the freedman sector of the population. Literature reflects the growing influence of freedmen as well as other aspects of the evolving status-system of Roman society, but again it does so through the distorting perspective of elite authors and audiences with their own particular interests and anxieties. For example, Horace, in his verse epistle to Florus (*Epist.* 2.2), constructs a kind of allegorical autobiography by way of explaining his purported retreat from literary competition, one that evinces a disturbing ambivalence toward the condition of slaves. Within the poem, Horace manages to describe himself (in sequence) as both slave and slave vendor, as heroic and cowardly soldier, as cooperative dinner guest who sings for his supper, as victim of the distractions and obligations of life at Rome, and finally as lyric poet trapped in an unsought competition with an unnamed elegist. The movement of examples follows the chronological movement of Horace's own life story, at least as represented elsewhere in his poetry: from son of freedman to slave owner, from cowardly soldier at Philippi to social striver, from deferential satirist to envied and attacked lyric poet, and beyond. Yet the end result is not a celebration of upward mobility or even a compassionate commemoration of the youthful slave who started the chain of events, but a narrowing of the definition of freedom. For the second half of the poem turns out to be a denunciation of enslavement to desire, property, luxury goods, exaggerated fears and so on. The poem thus looks forward to a widespread tendency in imperial literature to insist on liberation of the spirit alongside legal and social liberation.

The Greek notion that condition equals character (discussed by Just 1985) can't quite be made to fit the Roman circumstances of manumission, mobility, and integration, and so the character of the free man, his refusal to let aspects of himself (such as desire) control himself, comes to be understood as constructed by a never-ending process of personal discipline. Hence the appeal to Latin authors of philosophical sects such as Epicureanism and Stoicism, which offer what one scholar has described as a 'therapy of desire' (Nussbaum 1994) – not a quick fix, but a lifelong process of self-regulation. As Seneca advises his corres-pondent at the very beginning of his moral epistles, composed several generations after the Horatian prototype, 'take possession of yourself for yourself' (*Ep.* 1.1) The term he uses for 'self-possession' is *vindicatio*, which describes the legal process whereby an owner lays claim to property (such as a slave) that has been wrongfully alienated from him. As examples of escape from real slavery multiply, elite authors promulgate a new set of criteria for membership in the club of the 'truly' free. In so doing they may be seen as commending the achievements and efforts of at least some slaves, who are in fact represented as being freer, due to character, than those who possess legal freedom. But they are also raising the bar for membership in the elite and, perhaps too, seeking to cleanse themselves of any taint of slavish dishonour in their personal or familial past.

The obsession with differentiating slave from free, with removing traces of servile origin, spills over from concern with ethical comportment to a re-evaluation of the resources of the Latin language itself. Linguistic formalization had long been used as a means of differentiating elite from non-elite, insider from outsider, newcomer from old-time Roman. The Hellenization of Latin verbal performance, it might be argued, was in part an attempt to create a type of speech that had to be learned, and thus was less accessible to those with fewer material resources (Habinek 1998: 60–8). And the privileging of certain features of style was a means of differentiating the urbane from the non-urbane, the in from the out, by republican writers as different in temperament as Catullus and Cicero. But with the emergence of the principate, and the social changes effected thereby, concern over linguistic propriety comes to be expressed in terms of real or imagined linguistic boundaries between slave, freedman, and free, or between 'the mob' (*vulgus*) and the better sort.

For example, the freedman Phaedrus, it has been argued, seeks acceptance in the literary society of Rome precisely by conveying a sense that he knows and observes the limits of freedman discourse (Bloomer 1997: 73–109). Phaedrus' choice of genre is the iambic animal fable – a type of communication that he and others attribute to the slave's need to disguise his true opinions through 'made-up jests' (*fictis iocis*, Phaedrus 3 prol. 37; see discussion by Marchesi 2002, and also Harrison, Chapter 13 above). Phaedrus presents these fables in Latin verse, the accuracy of which he himself represents as unassailable. Yet the content of the fables, rather than acknowledging or promoting social mobility through educa-tion, in fact seems to criticize those who use language to rise above their assigned station: frogs are punished for abusing their king (Phaedrus 1.2); a jackdaw suffers for disparaging his peers (Phaedrus 1.3). Indeed, the emphasis Phaedrus places on correctness of language and loyal use of voice seems to build upon the more widespread association of bodiliness with slaves, voice with free citizens. Is Phaedrus then a traitor to his former class, revealing to the master the self-protective strategies of the slave and co-opting potentially resistant slave discourse (of the sort some scholars find in the Greek Aesopic tradition) to elite ends? Or is he a reformer of sorts, asserting the right of participation in Latin literary culture by members of an otherwise marginal or transitional class? And to what extent is his concentration on animal fables to be understood in psychological terms, perhaps as a conflicted working out of the consequences of enslavement, which forced a slave to speak of himself and his fellow-sufferers as beasts in order to exercise the human faculty of speech at all?

Freedman psychology and the social valence of language are important factors as well in one of the most memorable literary passages to deal with relations among classes, namely the banquet of Trimalchio in Petronius' *Satyrica* (on this novel see Harrison, Chapter 15 above). The language of the freedman Trimalchio and his dinner guests has been extensively discussed, yet in the final analysis, as Bloomer suggests, it is not possible to maintain a strict distinction between the speech of freedmen and the speech of those born free (Bloomer 1997: 196–231). Just as Phaedrus, Seneca the Elder, and countless students at rhetoric schools presuppose that mastery of speech can grant freedmen or provincials social authority, even among their betters, so Petronius illustrates how the free may be disconnected from cultural and linguistic tradition to the same extent as the freed slaves they despise. But Trimalchio is much more than just a foil for his free dinner guests, even though they, not he, are the main characters of the fragmentary novel. He constitutes an elite author's use of literary realism to depict the character of a freedman *as if* taken from everyday life (D'Arms 1981: 97–120; Boyce 1991). Language, setting and characterization conspire to make Trimalchio seem like the kind of person one might actually encounter, in contrast to the slaves of Plautine comedy who constantly call attention to their own theatricality or the shepherds of Virgil's *Eclogues* who illustrate situations rather than creating them.

This realism, paradoxically, should put us on guard against reading the *Satyrica* as a source for social mores or aspects of everyday life. It may well be more appropriate to regard it as an artistic strategy through which the author strives to make his own view of class relations appear inevitable. As Erich Auerbach argued long ago, the realism of classical literary texts, in which characters of lower social status are consigned to the realm of the comic or satiric, was not the only realism available, even in the Roman era. In contrast to classical texts, biblical stories written in the same era allow for the possibility that a tragic, self-reflective character can emerge from the lower orders. While Auerbach's specific claims about the text of Petronius' *Satyrica* have been modified by more recent scholars and critics, his larger social-historical point bears repeating: namely, that the

limited realism of classical literature, which by and large denies complex subjectivity to lower-class characters, corresponds to a limited historical consciousness
that fails to probe 'the social forces underlying the facts and conditions' presented
in literature (Auerbach 1953: 31).

Yet in one respect, at least, Petronius does seem to illuminate a genuine, class-
specific practice attested by other sources. I am referring to his depiction of
Trimalchio's concern with the circumstances of his own funeral and postmortem
commemoration (*Sat.* 71–2, 78). For, as it turns out, besides animal fables, funeral
epitaphs for freedmen and women, and to a lesser extent slaves, provide precious
access to what might be called subaltern subjectivity (for examples of such epitaphs,
see Joshel 1992). These texts themselves are of course conditioned by the expectations of elite practice and discourse, and thus in no sense constitute unmediated
access to the thoughts and feelings of the oppressed. But their very existence gives
us some sense of what aspects of elite culture slaves and freedmen found it most
important to claim for themselves. As indicated above, the experience of the slave
was one of uprooting from connections of place and community over time. To this
situation slaves and ex-slaves responded with the shared, coded discourse of fable
and with ritual commemoration in the form of funerary monuments and epitaphs.
Petronius indicates awareness of both practices by introducing animal fables into
the discourse of his freedmen and by having Trimalchio design his own monument
and epitaph. The epitaph parodies those of the elite, referring to honours accepted
and rejected, and listing personal characteristics: external and internal indicators of
a life well led. There is a final joke – 'he never listened to a philosopher' – that is not
so funny after all if we consider that philosophers might well have told Trimalchio
that he wasn't truly free. And there is a heading for the whole monument, to be
placed, as Trimalchio puts it, 'before everything else', namely 'this monument is
not to pass to an heir' (*hoc monumentum heredem non sequatur, Sat.* 71.7)

What are we to make of Trimalchio as end of his own line? Of his request for
depictions of a puppy and a dove where children might have been expected to
appear? Is Petronius mocking the greed and selfishness of this multimillionaire,
who cannot bear the thought of 'suffering injury' (*Sat.* 71.8) even after he is
dead? Are we to laugh at his misapprehension of the conventions he seeks to
appropriate? Do we list Trimalchio with other examples of a supposed world-
weariness brought on by the decadent luxury of Neronian Rome? Or is it just
possible that his life experience is something Trimalchio wants no heir to replicate? That his final act of self-assertion is to deny the connection between
reproduction and freedom, to rewrite the script that would equate condition
with character? For all that literature as a system reinforces the strongly hierarchical nature of Roman society and seeks to reproduce the conditions of its own
production (i.e. dependence on slave labour), it can never fully contain the
contradictory impulses and conflicting discourses that go into its creation.
Thus, now as always, it is the reader who is at least partially responsible for the
ethics of the text as she or he decides what aspects to observe and value.

FURTHER READING

For background information on the legal and social conditions of slaves see Bradley (1987 and 1994). On the involvement of slaves and freedmen in the circulation of literary texts see Horsfall (1995) and Houston (2002). Kaster (1988) examines the social status of teachers of literature. The role of slaves in the Roman literary imagination is the subject of Fitzgerald (2000). Also relevant are the essays gathered in Murnaghan and Joshel (1998). McCarthy (2000) is a careful consideration of the figure of the slave in relation to various forms of domination within the works of a single author, the comic playwright Plautus. So too Garrido-Hory (1981 and 1984) on Martial. Essays in Giardina and Schiavone (1981) specifically relate texts by Cicero, Valerius Maximus and others, to the tension between commerce and landowning as sources of wealth in the Roman world. Roller (2001) provides an excellent account of elite authors' use of slavery as a way of comprehending and constructing their own relationship to the emperor.

The role of honour in the distribution of power at Rome is considered by Lendon (1997); its place in the psychology of Roman authors is the subject of Barton (2001). Barton rightly notes that the slave himself may have felt honour or shame; but this does not change the fact that from the vantage point of ideology (not to mention law) the slave was without honour. For more detailed discussion of the interconnection of literary form and social status throughout the history of Latin literature see Habinek (1998) as well as the essays in Habinek and Schiesaro (1997), especially those pertaining to the topic of 'status anxiety'. Bloomer (1997) discusses the politics of proper Latinity, while Habinek (2000) provides a case study of the role of literary prestige in the reproduction of social power. Joshel (1992) considers non-elite perspectives as presented in inscriptions. Holzberg (2002) provides the raw material for a re-evaluation of the social dynamics of animal fable in the Graeco-Roman world – a topic that has attracted much attention lately from widely differing perspectives; for example Hopkins (1993), Bloomer (1997) and Henderson (2001). Williams (1995) makes an interesting (but in this author's view, unsuccessful) attempt to remove Horace from the list of low-status authors. In general it seems fair to say that scholars are only beginning to clarify the degree to which anxiety about status and class permeates Latin literature and to understand the role of literature in the maintenance and distribution of power in the Roman world.

CHAPTER TWENTY-EIGHT

Centre and Periphery

Alessandro Barchiesi

1   Introduction: the Roman Miracle

The difference between core and periphery in cultural studies can be understood in terms of attention, attention being a basic type of power-relationship: the core receives compulsory attention from the periphery, and can in its turn afford to ignore the periphery. When this dynamic shifts, we will have a different core. In terms of culture, broadly understood, the city of Rome is very clearly, and with impressive stability, the core of the Roman Empire, and literary production follows suit. Yet Rome also has a more surprising characteristic: if we focus on literary traditions and forms, Rome is for a long time a self-avowed periphery. It is the site of production and the marketplace for a typically peripheral, contact-zone literature, one in which forms imported from the Greek South and East are being used for local content. In the middle Republic, the imprint of the Greek matrix is so profound that for some time we cannot even identify the local content except at the level of social reception: the theatre is not only Greek-style, but Greek in subject matter, and the true *local* content is the social communication that binds together different levels of the Latin-speaking audience – people who watch comedy *à la grecque* and receive a refracted message about Roman family and its morality, people who meditate on Greek-style tragic action and therefore are invited to reconsider their social and political links within Roman society. A long process then leads to generations who develop, in the late Republic and Augustan periods, more autonomous forms for more local contents: not by chance the emerging genres, more independent from Greek models, such as love elegy and satire, are not only set in the growing metropolis of Rome, but obsessed with it.

In the meantime, we see the rise of a generational approach to literature – the Catullan generation is the first self-conscious 'generational group' in Roman letters (see Levene, Chapter 2 above) – and a shift from Greek genres which had been naturalized through a long process (epic, the theatre) towards 'elitist'

Greek genres that are being reinvented ad hoc in the post-revolutionary climate of Augustan Rome: lyric, pastoral, didactic, aetiology, epistles. In the Imperial age this dynamic freezes, and the core transmits to the periphery a closed canon of Latin-speaking authors and genres, while Christianity begins to undermine the traditional communication system; only a few authors, like the tantalizing Petronius and Apuleius, seem to suggest a different role for the Imperial periphery, but they do not establish a tradition. And in any case we have some access to following the traces left by schools and especially armies (readers of Gallus in Egypt, of Virgil in Vindolanda), but almost no material evidence when it comes to private reading for entertainment.

The interplay of a strong centralized control (as seen for example in the strategy of colony building and methodical military expansion) and of a 'peripheral' approach to literature and even cultural identity is arresting and remains a very specific feature of Roman culture for a long time. If there was ever a Roman miracle, it is this mix of imperial autonomy and aesthetic importation.

2   The Provincial

One main reason why the Roman world is still popular in contemporary culture is that it tells a story of a widening Empire with various forms of competing cultural, military and economic hegemony, and diverse rhythms of accommodation and assimilation among ethnic groups. This is still a thrilling story to rehearse for many of us, but it was not always the same story in the Western reception of Roman antiquity. For some time the Roman world has been read as a model of a nation state, a model for European nation states: therefore its literature and culture have been interpreted in different ways. We can see the alternative if we start from a passage written in the heyday of the multicultural Empire, the second century CE (clearly the rising period in the study of classical antiquity as I write, and there is a clear link with the atmosphere of globalization, 'end of history', post-colonial imperialism and cosmopolitanism that has been prevalent in Western ideology since the 1980s):

> Tum infit ad me Byrrhena: 'Quam commode uersaris in nostra patria? Quod sciam, templis et lauacris et ceteris operibus longe cunctas ciuitates antecellimus, utensilium praeterea pollemus adfatim. Certe libertas otiosa, et negotioso quidem aduenae Romana frequentia, modesto uero hospiti quies uillatica: omni denique prouinciae uoluptarii secessus sumus.'

> Byrrhena turned to me, at this point, and asked, 'How do you like your stay here in our home town? As far as I know, we are ahead of all other communities in terms of temples, baths and all the other public venues, and besides we are very well equipped with the necessities of life. In fact we are able to offer freedom for the

leisure-oriented person, the bustle of Rome for the business traveller, and resort-like
buen retiro for the restrained tourist. In short, we are the pleasure retreat for the
entire province.'

Here a secondary character in Apuleius' narrative work, *The Metamorphoses* or *The
Golden Ass* (see Harrison, chapter 15 above) introduces herself (2.19) as the aunt
of the narrator, and offers what is for us in the twenty-first century a glimpse of a
tantalizing alternative. But let us review the text briefly.

   She is talking about her 'homeland' within the Empire, Hypata in Thessaly, a
marginal city for a reader located in Rome, yet a significant centre in the periphery
of the Roman Empire. According to this upper-class lady, a descendant of the
Greek dignitary Plutarch (who was also a famous author in Greek literature, and
therefore a significant influence on Apuleius as a Roman man of letters), Hypata
has it all: leisure and freedom, the basic requirements for Greek *paideia* (culture)
and Roman *humanitas* (humane values), temples, thermal amenities and monuments. It offers the sorely missed mediation between the quiet but uncivilized
countryside and the dangerous mess of the metropolis. Of course this may be a
little too modern as a reaction, but it is difficult for us not to feel identification
with Byrrhena's perspective. Provincial sophistication – this is our slightly anachronistic impression – is the precondition for a national literature and a growing
market for authors and genres. Byrrhena is not just a character in Apuleius; she is
an ideal reader for the entire work – except that Roman letters do not have a true
market in the Greek East by the time of Apuleius, and in the end never will.
Apuleius will not be able to compete with Byrrhena's Greek lineage on her own
turf, and the extension of the Roman Empire will not create a unified literature,
ousting the likes of Plutarch and Lucian. This is a pity because the civilized but
slightly boring Hypata is perhaps the ideal audience (as well as the physical
setting) for the adventurous project of Lucius, the nephew of Byrrhena: he is
fascinated ('worried', he will prudently say to his aunt) by the existence of a 'dark
side' to Hypata, he wants to discover the nocturnal and magical side of the
provincial capital: 'the best of Thessalian towns' now resonates with the top
tourist attraction that makes Thessaly famous, witchcraft. And here of course
the advantage is all for a wide audience of Roman and provincial readers who will
never visit Thessaly, but are learning how to enjoy a good tale of magic in a
Romanized Greek setting.

   And now we can experiment with our two alternative reactions. If we read the
text in its historical context, it is an interesting and uncommon testimony for
what it was like to live in a Roman provincial town. If we read the text from a
future perspective, it is a prophecy of the modern European novel: a genre that
takes shape in a rich osmosis from the development of vast nation states, whose
identities require the idea of a centre and a periphery (see Moretti 1998). The
periphery attracts a lot of attention, and it is different from the centre but also
from the boundary areas: it is internal to the nation, far from the capital, yet

related to it. Cervantes' La Mancha, Jane Austen's Britain (more than a day trip from London, yet excluding Scotland, Ireland, Wales and the industrial North), Chekhov's Not-Moscow. Without this idea of 'the provincial', defined by sentiments of longing for the metropolis and pride in local identity, we would not have the modern novel, Stendhal, Goethe, Thackeray and Turgenev, or Proust and the rise of postcolonial narrative.

Yet this second perspective is unhistorical. Roman literature did not develop its own equivalent of the European Novel. Trimalchio in Petronius and Byrrhena in Apuleius look like distant prophecies of the atmosphere of modern 'provincial' fictions, but the definitive breakthrough never arrived, not in Latin, not even in Greek. Greek fictional narratives, which were more lasting and successful than those written in Latin, look backwards and eastwards: the plot is regularly set before Roman conquest, the action develops in the eastern hemisphere of the Mediterranean sea, the part that stretches from Syracuse to Babylon.

More generally, very few genres of literary production in Latin take into account what is for us the most striking change in Roman social history: the growth of an Imperial community in Western Europe and the Mediterranean, the spread of homogeneous cultural practices ('Romanization', 'Hellenization', urbanization), the diaspora and mobility of people. The literary work that seems most germane to this historical evolution is isolated and (not by chance) very mysterious to us: Petronius' *Satyrica* (see Harrison, Chapter 15 above). A literary evolution like that which took place in early modern and modern Europe, or like that of the post-colonial planetary culture, should have taken into account clashes and mergers of cultures, pidgin and hybridization in contact zones, polyglossia and local resistance, imperialism and fashions. Most of all, this evolution would have required a very vital exchange between Rome and the provinces, and its representation and performance in and through literary activity. The effect on readers of the twenty-first century is sometimes exasperating. We are obviously unable to access our own blind spots, and very sensitive to their limitations: no narrative of colonial encounters, even granted that we accept the perspective of the Roman elite, is what we would like to read. Cicero in Cilicia and Pliny the Younger in Bithynia do not match our expectations; people who grew up in a still multicultural landscape like first century BCE Spain or second century CE North Africa or fourth century CE Gaul do not say enough to bring out the interaction of cultures and languages. We are never going to find the ancient equivalent of Joseph Conrad, nor, for that matter, of Amitav Ghosh.

Yet we should never forget that processes of acculturation can be recovered from the background noise, if not from the explicit message, of ancient texts. Byrrhena's hospitable house, for example, has one significant implication in its material layout: the impressive atrium (2.4) with mythological statues, winged Victories, and reflecting pools, spells out Romanization, the imposition of a

Roman architectural order and lifestyle over the traditional cityscape of Hellenic Hypata. So there is something to learn for a classicist, after all, from the multicultural sensitivity and from the link between material culture and ethnicity that is so important in contemporary writing about the Roman Empire – and here I mean fictional writing, fed by the experience of living in South London or California. So, for example, the narrator of the multicultural English novel in verse, Bernardine Evaristo's *The Emperor's Babe* (2001), puts into sharp focus the cultural misery of Romanization in Britain. Being a semi-insider within Roman provincial elites – a Nubian girl co-opted through marriage into the Roman elite of early third-century Londinium, Britannia – the narrator ironically comments on the downside of Roman architecture in colonial Britain. Now that she has turned into the trophy wife of the vulgar Roman businessman Felix, she is the sub-elite observer who will identify neither with native barbarism nor with Roman imperialism:

> I walk into the atrium, gaze up
> at the square hole of the sky. You see, our villa
>
> is built in the fashionable style of the Med,
> as Felix always boasts,
>
> 'Great for British winters' I once replied
> as snow fell on the frozen fountain
>
> its centrepiece a statue of snarling Medusa
> (a strange choice, but Felix believed
>
> low-class intruders would fear
> they'd be turned to stone, and backtrack)
>
> Water poured out of her open mouth,
> and her flying dreadlocks, which normally
>
> produced fine sprays,
> had grown icicle extensions.
>   (Evaristo 2001: 64–5)

But what about ancient works that have been composed and read from a Roman-metropolitan perspective? There is also the possibility that great works of the classical canon need to be defamiliarized and revisited, now that the model of the nation state is not the only implicit parameter. Few works are so enmeshed in the idea of empire as the *Aeneid*, yet we can see that the poem was effective not only in enforcing the concept of imperial control, but also in addressing an audience of displaced people in search of a new identity: the poem is very much about teaching people how to bond with new places, and continues the discourse of mobility that had been so important for the *Eclogues* and the *Georgics*: the herdsman Meliboeus of *Eclogue* 1, leaving Italy for the distant provinces, and the Corycian old man of *Georgic* 4, displaced from his Cilician home to his garden near Tarentum, are implicitly present in the new epic.

3 National and Local

The study of classics as still practised in education and academic research was shaped by the emergence of European nation states. The ideology and the identity of those states were wildly different from what can be reconstructed about ancient Rome, but the cultural context of the new nation states has influenced modern perceptions: in many cases it is evident that the Roman state and/ or the Roman Empire have been assimilated, more or less subtly, to the rising powers of, for example, Britain, Germany and France (see e.g. Hingley 2000). Classical scholarship has striven to limit this assimilation, but even more important is the transformation of nationhood, ethnicity and citizenship that is taking place as I write. As in other historical circumstances, it is likely that present transformations will have an impact on our understanding of the past, both revealing and occluding some issues.

In this evolving context, it can be argued that studies of Roman literature, or Latin literature (and the terminology is not a trivial choice here), should pay more attention to polarities like localism and universalism, centre and periphery, and more generally, to spaces and places. This is a salutary strategy not only as a response to contemporary culture, a culture in which issues of identity and globalization are arguably central (arguably, even too central and excessively bandied about), but also as a corrective to a permanent danger: the discipline of Classics has framed itself by isolating 'Rome' and 'Greece' as unitary constructs, severing links with other cultures, ignoring local differences, and generalizing shared elements in a process of self-justification. The construction of Greece in nineteenth-century Europe can be traced in Bernal (1987) and the ensuing dossier of polemics, while the importance of identifying many Greek cultures within our construction of Classical Greece can be seen in Kurke and Dougherty (2003).

4 Mobility and Writing

One of the most curious facts about Roman literary production is that no famous author until the late Empire is known to have been born in Rome, except (by inference) for Julius Caesar. Whenever we can check, and for most of the famous authors we are in a position to know, the attested birthplaces are in Italy and, as the Empire widens, in various places scattered across the Romanized Mediterranean. What this fact or, better, factoid can mean, is controversial, because we should not mistake birthplace for cultural identity, yet it is impressive as a quantitative datum demanding interpretation. Note also that even Caesar, the one who is centrally located, the true Roman of them all, is said by his correspondent Oppius to have 'been the first to invent a form of conversation with his friends through letter-writing: he could not wait to see them face to face on urgent matters, because of the excess of his duties and the great size of the city of Rome' (Plutarch, *Life of Caesar* 17.7–9). So even within Rome, being Roman is increasingly a matter of writing and reading. Writing letters, in particular, transforms human interaction into *exempla*, reputation, text to be analysed by third parties. This production can be accommodated to the overachieving, multitasking lifestyle of Roman leading circles: the composition was normally composition in performance, through dictating.

The rise of letter-writing in the elite (see Edwards, Chapter 19 above) is important in keeping together prose and poetry, official and private, domestic and exotic, literature and politics. At the end of this process, the epistolary collection of Pliny the Younger, capitalizing on the very different examples of Cicero and Seneca, straddles most of those distinctions. Publication of letters, in this context, means that individuals are not only displaying their own lives as a topic worthy of attention, but also offering a template for the various levels of long-distance communication that were holding together the Empire. When we talk about prominent Romans, it is always easy to exaggerate their urban location: Augustus, for example, spent relatively little of his time in Rome, and this is even more true of many other emperors; the world of Roman citizenship was rich in people who spent their lives between two or three provinces without having to base themselves in the capital. By the end of the Republic, Rome is still in part a 'face-to-face society', but a number of political and cultural practices are based on transactions involving absence and distance. Caesar, according to Suetonius, not only writes an impressive amount of correspondence, but is the first Roman officer to transfer his epistolary texts from the format of messages to some kind of booklike format, and to offer a textual image of his political as well as private relationships (*Life of Caesar*, 56.6): 'we can access his Letters to the Senate, since he appears to be the first author who converted those letters into the book-columns and the textual shape of a notebook . . . we also have his letters to Cicero as well as his intimate letters about private issues'. So Cicero is not the first citizen to be represented by a collected corpus of epistles, nor the most important Roman to gather one; and Caesar is of course emphatically a case of the Roman abroad, even (as we saw) when he is at home. A few years later, Caesar Augustus, away from Rome, fighting the Cantabrians in Spain, writes to Virgil 'insisting with pleas and even humorous threats that he be sent "just the preliminary sketch or just a chunk" of the *Aeneid*' (Donatus *Vita Vergilii* 31 Hardie). Did he want the travels of Aeneas, or the tale of Hercules, just arrived from Spain, fighting monsters in the wilderness of the Roman Palatine? In any case, what he ended up receiving is a poem about being abroad and the clashes of nations, about the need for unification and the endless variety of Mediterranean history and geography.

5 Authorial Self-positioning

And the authors themselves? One typical avenue has been to study authorial identities as 'local' voices, the Cisalpine in Catullus, the citizen of North Africa in Apuleius. But for our purposes it is also important to look at how those authors accommodate different 'levels of address' (Citroni 1995) in their works. Instead of insisting only on local affiliations (the Northerners, the Spaniards, the Africans) it is best to trace patterns of Roman-provincial negotiation, and imagine readers of Catullus in Roman Asia and readers of Apuleius in Italy. On the other hand, it is also true that local identities can be all too easily forgotten in the study of more 'objective' kinds of writers. If one takes as an example the work on geography by the little-known early Imperial writer Pomponius Mela, it takes quite some time to work out where he comes from. The detail is buried (very wittily, for a geographer) in his account of the most famous landmark and boundary of ancient geography and cosmology, the Pillars of Heracles: the sea becomes very narrow, he reports; then we have coastal places inhabited by Phoenicians who crossed over from Africa, among them 'Tingentera, where I come from' (2.96 *unde nos sumus Tingentera*); then, as we follow the shoreline, the contours of Europe are over. In a different tradition, the author would not have resisted the opportunity of inscribing himself into the progress of the textual geography of the work: suggestively enough, Mela was born exactly where his image of the Romanized West has to stop, and in an area marked by the very name of 'Deportation' (Tingentera is identical or close to Traducta Iulia, a settlement of Phoenicians relocated to Spain under Roman control). It has been shown recently (Batty 2000) that being from a boundary area in a territory that had been colonized by Phoenicians is not irrelevant to Mela's voice as an author. There are signs that his geography is intended for readers who know what it means to be a Roman outside Rome. Yet it is not only the law of the genre; it is the tradition of writing in the Roman world that prevents more direct forms of expression. Roman imperialism has colonized Mela long before he starts writing about the entire universe of the Mediterranean.

Other early Imperial authors, more ambitious and closer to the Imperial centre than Mela, conspire in constructing a unified image of the Roman world, and even a cosmology. Most of them develop a polarity between Rome as a cosmic city of consumption and decadence and the margins as places of curiosity and marvel. This is a fruitful construction in terms of future imperial ideologies in the West and elsewhere, but it could be argued that this double focus has a negative effect on the perception of what lies in between the cosmopolis and the margins: many writers in Latin, for different reasons, end up offering a reductive vision of the normal life of the provinces. The dominant fictional writers of the Neronian age, Seneca (in his plays) and Lucan (see Mayer, Chapter 4 above), build on Stoic cosmology and represent the universe as a unified place, even sometimes a claustrophobic, suffocating space. However, some of the works where the

Romanization of the world is being celebrated are in fact less than canonical, not a secondary paradox in the formation of a Roman literature: those texts are, for example, the encyclopedia of Pliny, Martial's holiday epigrams and circus epigrams, and some are even written in Greek, as in Strabo and some Greek historians. Between Nero and the Flavians, the growing favourite boom is paradoxography (see Schepens and Delcroix 1996), a prose genre that hypes frontier *mirabilia*, 'wonder literature', and of course centralized control over those freakish items of nature. People like Pliny the Elder and his forerunner Licinius Mucianus are writing *mirabilia*, *because* they are Imperial functionaries: the act of collecting information on the borders has strong political and moral implications. Ocean shells, prodigious fountains, domesticated elephants, the effects of the moon on monkeys: these are delightful and curious, but also morally justified by the imposition of the *pax Romana*, which creates at the same time the indispensable leisure and the spatial control necessary to the pursuit of discovery and acquisition. They aim at pleasure for their readers, but they also implicitly declare that Roman power enables knowledge of nature, as well as *humanitas*. The Romanocentric perspective looks indispensable for writers on geography, natural questions and surprise findings, yet as we have seen in Mela's case this does not always preclude the expression of a self-conscious and oblique 'provincial' marginality.

Some of the leading voices in poetry and prose also elaborate various nostalgias, another important approach to the widening horizons of Imperial life (see Harrison, Chapter 20 above). Horace uses understatement, and limits the span of nostalgia to the alternation between the unbearable megalopolis of Rome and the protective *angulus*, the 'neck of the woods' in the Italic heartland. Some of the other surviving approaches include Martial's return to small-town Spain, Ovid's exile, Juvenal and his bitter stories of mobility, Senecan epigrams from Corsica, and the construction of private life in villas versus public Roman life in Pliny the Younger. All those genres have their own specific traditions and the writers do have distinctive personal agendas, but one cumulative effect was that people actually learned about different lifestyles and locations, and used literature to imagine themselves in unfamiliar settings.

6 Peripheral Readers

In spite of the absolute centrality of Rome at every moment of Latin literature, mentions of readership located in the outside world are by no means uncommon, and should encourage critics to take the issue seriously. The problem is of course that it is not always easy to evaluate every single occurrence without paying attention to contextual factors and to (for example) ironies or other underpinnings. One declaration that emerges with some force from the context of early and mid-Republican literature results from a couple of fragments (unfortunately indirect and without context) by the satiric poet Lucilius, the first poet in Latin of high social status (see Goldberg, Chapter 1, and Morgan, Chapter 12 above). He is known to have had many aristocratic connections, but he is reported as saying that he is not writing for the most learned, nor for the ignorant, and that his favourite audience consists of the people of Tarentum, Consentia and Sicily (cf. Cic. *de orat.* 2,25; *fin.* 1,7; Lucilius frs 594 and 596 Krenkel, 632–5 Warmington 1936–8). There is a very good chance that all this is to be taken with a heap of salt: the strategy could be to mock other people's pretensions to learning while promoting his own work as both accessible and deeply civilized, and we should not be too optimistic in imagining wide readership in the recently Latinized provinces of Southern Italy. And yet, the very presence of those constituents of readership should not be underrated. This is the same poet who introduces Italic vocabulary into his Latin verse, and perhaps reflects not just contact between various linguistic groups but even – more crucially for the future of Italy and Rome – contact between various groups in the Roman colonies and miltary service abroad; for example in the new frontier of the second century BCE, Spain. The poet wants readers in Rome to be aware of other potential readers, and readers in the provinces are of course being drawn into the circle of literary awareness. This is important because from now on we can start imagining a double register even in literary production that looks very Romanocentric and centred on the Urbs. It is possible that writers and poet take their chances and calculate their odds in representing the Roman capital of culture to the provinces.

From Horace, a poet who fashions himself, at least in important parts of his work, as a modern, reconstructed Lucilius for a post-Republican Rome, we have two assertions in different generic frames. In the *Odes* he mentions 'cultivated provincial readership' (Mayer 1994: 271) at 2.20.19–20, 'the well-educated Hiberian and the one who drinks from the Rhone will learn me', in a context of global pride; in the *Epistles*, in a different key, the future of his epistle-book is to be sent to the edges of the Empire to become a school text after having been a success in Rome. The marginal destinations (1.20.13) are Utica in Africa and Ilerda in Spain. The tone is sarcastic but again we cannot discount the importance of export from Rome as a possibility: Utica and Ilerda may be surprising choices, but the only shared factor between the two place-names is that they had been two of the bloodiest battlefields of the civil wars. Horace has survived the civil wars, is a favourite of the Roman elite (an important theme in *Ep.* 1.20, itself based on models of Republican literature, like Terence) and now his text – one debased copy of it – will reach those marginal places that had become Roman through the catastrophe of a world conflict.

Even more difficult would be to neglect indications of provincial readership in the works of Martial. Martial is one of Rome's most 'metropolitan' authors, and when he ends up composing epigrams in his hometown of Bilbilis in Spain he complains about his separation from the capital. Yet, in his Roman period, he also suggests that people in Spain are able to recognize his compositions (9.84;

12.2,17–18). On the other hand, being a writer in Rome has become synonymous with proximity to the Emperor (no matter whether fictional or real): Book 3 of Martial, published from Gallia Cisalpina, is the only volume by Martial without any reference to the Emperor.

Ovid builds on a tradition of pro-Augustan poets linking the future of their work with the perennial greatness of Rome, but in his coda to the *Metamorphoses* he decides to shift the emphasis slightly: he will be read wherever Roman domination extends (*Met.* 15.877) over conquered lands, a prodigious success in space, not time. It is probably excessive to interpret this as a bitter prophecy of his own exile to the Danube area (although some critics take this step), but the hyperbole does suggest that the creation of the Roman Empire, one of the biggest metamorphoses of this poem, finds a parallel in the publication of a truly Imperial epic, one that exceeds previous epic poems in space, timeline and bilingual learning.

The related phenomenon to which we should pay attention is the tendency in Roman epic to develop plots of travel, conquest and Mediterranean/cosmic progression. This phenomenon has no equivalent in canonic Greek epic, except for some aspects of the project of Apollonius' *Argonautica*, a poem whose plot journeys across all the continents of the inhabited earth. Naevius and Ennius, both writing about epic deeds in Asia and Africa as well as in the Roman world, celebrate the transference of Troy into Latium. Ennius narrates the rippling expansion of Roman power until he reaches the Greek territories of the Muses, Ambracia and Parnassus. The plot of the *Annales* is therefore reinforced by its poetics: a poetics of Hellenization for an epic that actually celebrates the appropriation of the Greek East. The ensuing vogue for Argonautic poems in the Triumviral and Flavian ages can be seen in the context of Eastern and Western explorations and confrontations with barbarian powers. The *Aeneid* and Lucan's *Bellum Civile* are poems of universal geography; both feature action in all the main corners of the Mediterranean, of course with a very different (but related) teleology and vision of history. Even the learned epics of Statius, while representing a return to more localized Hellenic myths, participate in the discourse of Romanization: the very absence of a Roman reference is a bold statement that literature in Latin can now claim to have replaced Greek traditions on their own home turf.

We can see this tradition of universalism as an aggressive manifesto for Roman Imperialism. Yet it is also true that multiple readerships, still provided with their own claims to ethnicity and local autonomy, can turn to those texts and find some value in the literary transactions and linkages. There were readers of Latin in Carthage, Asia Minor, Britannia, Alexandria and Gaul: they read Virgil on Dido and Priam, or Lucan on Cleopatra and the Druids, and were led to think about the binding links and staggering differences of the Empire. Even more important, readers in various parts of the Empire thought about readers in other parts of the Empire, and saw them refracted in the texts, including the texts that were so narrowly about Rome, Rome as a cultural hub. The process had many serious shortcomings: in random order, the limits in the diffusion of Latin in the East; the early and in a sense precocious canonization of late Republican and Early Imperial writers, which created a rigid barrier against newer literary production; the absence of a genuine investment in the creation of a 'colonial' or 'post-colonial' culture. In hindsight, we see those shortcomings as more important than what was accomplished. It remains helpful, nevertheless, to think about Rome and the provinces as interactive matrices and energizing forces in literary communication. Texts produced and performed in Rome would acquire new meanings through circulation and reperformance in the provinces: they would represent to the periphery the myth of Rome as the City of Letters (Woolf and Edwards 2003). Other texts aimed at the power of offering access to the margins for the metropolitan audience: they took various and for us sometimes devious forms, paradoxography, epistolary collections, exile literature, fictional narrative. All of these literary activities, through their social and historical constraints and in spite of them, have contributed to the Western tradition of literature as a habitat for the desire and mental experience of being somewhere else.

FURTHER READING

It is difficult to suggest basic secondary reading for the topic of this chapter. We do not have comprehensive works addressing issues of centre and periphery in literary production. Some of the contributions to Cavallo et al. (1993), in particular the piece by Isabella Gualandri, are perhaps the best starting point in terms of coverage; in English, Woolf and Edwards (2003) is a collection that brings the discussion up to speed with contemporary debates in comparative literature and post-colonial studies. Important introductions to space perception in the ancient world are Nicolet (1991) and Romm (1992); highly suggestive on the relationship of literary production to geography in the modern world is Moretti (1998).

There is of course a vast literature on all the separate questions touched upon in my text. I limit myself to a few references, especially to recent work: multiple levels of audience and address in Roman poetry (Citroni 1995); identity in the Roman Empire (Citroni 2003); provincial identity in Mela (Batty 2000); localism in Apuleius (S. J. Harrison 2000); Caesar and letter-writing (Ebbeler 2003); nationalism, racism and Classics (Bernal 1987); Panhellenism and local identities (Kurke and Dougherty 2003). (Benton and Fear 2003 came out too late for me to refer to, but contains relevant material.)

Bibliography

The abbreviations used here for journals and major reference works (see also List of Abbreviations on p. xvii) are largely those of the *Oxford Classical Dictionary* (3rd edn) [Hornblower and Spawforth 1996]; a fuller index of journal abbreviations is to be found in the standard bibliographical annual journal *L'année philologique* (see http://www.annee-philologique.com/aph [subscription needed]).

Acosta-Hughes, B. 2002. *Polyeideia: the Iambi of Callimachus and the Archaic Iambic Tradition*. Berkeley.

Adams, J. N. 1995. *Pelagonius and Latin Veterinary Terminology in the Roman Empire*. Leiden.

Adams, J. N. and Mayer, R. G. (eds.) 1999. *Aspects of the Language of Latin Poetry*. Oxford.

Ahl, F. 1976. *Lucan: an Introduction*. Ithaca, N.Y.

Ahl, F. 1984. The art of safe criticism in Greece and Rome. *AJP* 105: 174–208.

Ahl, F. M., Davis, M. A., Pomeroy, A. 1986. Silius Italicus. *ANRW* II.32.4: 2492–561.

Albrecht, M. von 1964. *Silius Italicus: Freiheit und Gebundenheit römischer Epik*. Amsterdam.

Albrecht, M. von 1989. *Masters of Roman Prose from Cato to Apuleius*. Leeds

Albrecht, M. von 1992. *Geschichte der römischen Literatur*. Bern.

Albrecht, M. von 1997. *A History of Roman Literature*. Leiden (English trans. of Von Albrecht 1992).

Allen, A. W. 1962. *Sunt qui Propertium malint*. In Sullivan 1962: 107–48.

Alpers, P. 1979. *The Singer of the* Eclogues*: a Study of Virgilian Pastoral*. Berkeley.

Altman, J. G. 1982. *Epistolarity: Approaches to a Form*. Columbus, Ohio.

Anderson, G. 1990. The Second Sophistic: some problems of perspective. In Russell 1990: 91–110.

Anderson, R. D., Parsons, P. J., Nisbet, R. G. M. 1979. Elegiacs by Gallus from Qasr Ibrîm. *JRS* 69: 125–55.

Anderson, W. S. 1972. *Ovid's Metamorphoses Books 6–10*. Norman, Okla.

Anderson, W. S. 1982. *Essays on Roman Satire*. Princeton.

Anderson, W. S. 1993. *Barbarian Play: Plautus' Roman Comedy.* Toronto.

Anderson, W. S. 1997. *Ovid's Metamorphoses Books 1–5.* Norman, Okla.

André, J. M. 1987. La rhétorique dans les préfaces de Vitruve: le statut culturel de la science. In Anon. (ed.), *Studi Della Corte.* Vol. 3. Urbino: 265–98.

Andreassi, M. 1997. Osmosis and contiguity between 'low' and 'high' literature: *Moicheutria* and Apuleius. *GCN* 8: 1–21.

Andreassi, M. 2001. *Mimi greci in Egitto: Charition e Moicheutria.* Bari.

Andreau, Jean and Bruhns, H. (eds). 1990. *Parenté et stratégies familiales dans l'antiquité romaine.* Rome.

Andrieu, J. 1954. *Le Dialogue antique: structure et presentation.* Collection d'études latines, série scientifique, 29. Paris.

Annas, J. 1989. Epicurean emotions. *GRBS* 30: 145–64.

Annas, J. 2001. *Cicero: On Moral Ends.* Cambridge.

Apollonj Ghetti, B., Ferrua, A., Josi, E., Kirschenbaum, E. 1951. *Esplorazioni sotto la confessione di San Pietro in Vaticano.* Vatican City.

Arjava, Antti 1996. *Women and Law in Late Antiquity.* Oxford.

Armstrong, D. 1986. *Horatius Eques et Scriba*: Satires 1.6 and 2.7. *TAPA* 116: 255–88.

Arnott, W. G. 1975. *Menander, Plautus, Terence.* Oxford.

Arrowsmith, W. 1966. Luxury and death in the *Satyricon.* *Arion* 5: 304–31.

Asmis, E. 1992. Crates on poetic criticism. *Phoenix* 46: 138–69.

Astbury, R. 1977. Petronius, *P.Oxy.* 3010, and Menippean satire. *CPh* 72: 22–31 (repr. in Harrison 1999: 74–84).

Astin, A. E. 1978. *Cato the Censor.* Oxford.

Astin, A.E., Walbank, F.W., Fredriksen, M.W., Ogilvie, R.M. (eds). 1989. *The Cambridge Ancient History VIII : Rome and the Mediterranean to 133 B.C.* Cambridge.

Atti del convegno. 1986. *Atti del convegno internazionale di studi su Albio Tibullo.* Rome.

Auerbach, E. 1953. *Mimesis.* Princeton.

Austin, C. and Bastianini, G. 2002. *Posidippi Pellaei quae supersunt omnia.* Milan.

Austin, R. G. 1955. *P.Vergili Maronis Aeneidos Liber IV.* Oxford.

Austin, R. G. 1960. *Cicero: Pro Caelio.* 3rd edn. Oxford.

Austin, R. G. 1964. *P.Vergili Maronis Aeneidos Liber II.* Oxford.

Austin, R. G. 1971. *P.Vergili Maronis Aeneidos Liber I.* Oxford.

Austin, R. G. 1977. *P.Vergili Maronis Aeneidos Liber VI.* Oxford.

Badian, E. 1966. The early historians. In Dorey 1966: 1–38.

Bagnall, R. S. and Harris, W. V. (eds). 1986. *Studies in Roman Law in Memory of A. Arthur Schiller.* Leiden.

Bain, D. 1979. *PLAVTVS VORTIT BARBARE*: Plautus, *Bacchides* 526–61 and Menander, *Dis exapaton* 102–12. In West and Woodman 1979: 17–34.

Bakhtin, M. 1981. *The Dialogic Imagination: Four Essays.* Austin.

Balsdon, J. P. V. D. 1979. *Romans and Aliens.* London.

Bannon, C. 1997. *The Brothers of Romulus: Fraternal* Pietas *in Roman Law, Literature, and Society.* Princeton.

Barchiesi, A. 1986. Tracce di narrativa greca e romanzo latino: una rassegna. In *Semiotica della novella latina,* 219–36 (trans. as 'Traces of Greek narrative and the Roman novel' in Harrison 1999: 124–41).

Barchiesi, A. 1993a. L'epos. In Cavallo et al. 1993: 115–41.

Barchiesi, A. 1993b. Future reflexive: two modes of allusion and Ovid's *Heroides. HSCP* 37:1–21.

Barchiesi, A. 1994. Rappresentazioni del dolore e interpretazione nell' *Eneide. AuA* 40: 109–24.

Barchiesi, A. 1997a. Ekphrasis. In Martindale 1997: 271–81.

Barchiesi, A. 1997b. *The Poet and the Prince: Ovid and Augustan Discourse.* Berkeley.

Barchiesi, A. 2000. Rituals in ink: Horace on the Greek lyric tradition. In Depew and Obbink 2000: 167–82.

Barchiesi, A. 2001. Horace and Iambos: the poet as literary historian. In Cavarzere et al. 2001: 141–64.

Barchiesi, A. 2002. The uniqueness of the *Carmen Saeculare* and its tradition. In Woodman and Feeney 2002: 107–23.

Barnes, J. and Griffin, M. (eds). 1997. *Philosophia Togata II: Plato and Aristotle at Rome.* Oxford.

Barsby, J. 1986. *Plautus: Bacchides.* Warminster.

Barsby, J. 1999. *Terence: Eunuchus.* Cambridge.

Barsby, J. 2001. *Terence.* 2 vols. Cambridge, Mass.

Barton, C. 1993. *The Sorrows of the Ancient Romans.* Princeton.

Barton, C. 2001. *Roman Honor: the Fire in the Bones.* Berkeley.

Bartsch, S. 1989. *Decoding the Ancient Novel.* Princeton.

Bartsch, S. 1994. *Actors in the Audience: Theatricality and Doublespeak from Nero to Hadrian.* Cambridge, Mass.

Bartsch, S. 1997. *Ideology in Cold Blood: a Reading of Lucan's Civil War.* Cambridge, Mass.

Bartsch, S. 1998. Ars and the man: the politics of art in Vergil's *Aeneid. CPh* 93: 322–42.

Barwick, K. 1959. *Martial und die zeitgenössische Rhetorik.* Berlin.

Batty, R. 2000. Mela's Phoenician geography. *JRS* 90: 70–94.

Beacham, R. C. 1991. *The Roman Theatre and its Audience.* London.

Beagon, M. 1992. *Roman Nature: the Thought of Pliny the Elder.* Oxford.

Beare, W. 1964. *The Roman Stage.* 3rd edn. London.

Beck, H. and Walter, U. 2001. *Die fruehen Roemischen Historiker I.* Darmstadt.

Beck, R. 1973. Some observations on the narrative technique of Petronius. *Phoenix* 27: 42–61 (repr. in Harrison 1999: 50–73).

Becker, E. 1938. *Technik und Szenerie des ciceronischen Dialogs.* Osnabrück.

Ben Ze'ev, A. 2000. *The Subtlety of Emotions.* Cambridge, Mass.

Benton, C. and Fear, T. (eds). 2003 *Center and Periphery in the Roman World. Arethusa* 36.3. Baltimore.

Bernal, M. 1987. *Black Athena.* 2 vols. New Brunswick, N.J.

Bernini, F. 1915. *Studi sul mimo.* Pisa.

Bernstein, F. 1998. *Ludi publici: Untersuchungen zur Entstehung und Entwicklung der öffentlichen Spiele im republikanischen Rom.* Historia Einzelschriften 119. Stuttgart.

Berry, D. H. 1996. *Cicero: Pro Sulla Oratio.* Cambridge.

Berry, D. H. 2000. *Cicero: Defence Speeches.* Oxford.

Berry, D. H. and Heath, M. 1997. Oratory and declamation. In Porter 1997: 393–420.

Bettini, M. 1991. *Anthropology and Roman Culture: Kinship, Time, Images of the Soul.* Baltimore.

Bianchini, E. 2001. *Carmina Priapea.* Rome.

Bieber, M. 1961. *The History of the Greek and Roman Theatre.* 2nd edn. Princeton.

Bing, P. 1988. *The Well-Read Muse : Present and Past in Callimachus and the Hellenistic Poets.* Göttingen.

Bing, P. 1993. Aratus and his audiences. In Schiesaro et al. 1993: 99–109.

Binns, J. W. (ed.). 1973. *Ovid.* London.

Blois, L. de 2001. The political significance of friendship in the letters of Pliny the Younger. In Peachin 2001b: 129–34.

Bloomer, W. M. 1997. *Latinity and Literary Society at Rome.* Philadelphia.

Bonaria, M. (ed.). 1965. *Romani Mimi.* Rome.

Bonfante, G. 1967. La lingua delle Atellane e dei mimi. *Maia* 19: 3–21.

Bonner, S. F. 1949. *Roman Declamation in the Late Republic and Early Empire.* Liverpool.

Boriaud, J.-Y. 1997. *Hyginus: Fabulae.* Paris.

Bowditch, P. L. 2001. *Horace and the Gift Economy of Patronage.* Berkeley.

Bowie, E. L. 2000. Literature and sophistic. In Bowman et al. 2000: 898–921.

Bowman, A. K. and Thomas, J. D. 1994. *The Vindolanda Writing-Tablets (Tabulae Vindolandenses II).* London.

Bowman, A. K., Champlin, E., Lintott, A. (eds). 1996. *The Cambridge Ancient History X: The Augustan Empire, 43 B.C.- A.D. 69.* Cambridge.

Bowman, A. K., Garnsey, P., Rathbone, D. (eds). 2000. *The Cambridge Ancient History XI: The High Empire, A.D. 70–192.* 2nd edn. Cambridge.

Boyce, B. C. 1991. *The Language of the Freedmen in Petronius'* Cena Trimalchionis. Leiden.

Boyd, B. W. 1995. *Non enarrabile textum:* ecphrastic trespass and narrative ambiguity in the *Aeneid. Vergilius* 41: 71–92.

Boyd, B. W. 1997. *Ovid's Literary Loves: Influence and Innovation in the Amores.* Ann Arbor.

Boyd, B. W. (ed.). 2002. *Brill's Companion to Ovid.* Leiden.

Boyle, A. J. 1979. *In medio Caesar:* paradox and politics in Virgil's *Georgics. Ramus* 8: 65–86.

Boyle, A. J. 1986. *The Chaonian Dove.* Leiden.

Boyle, A. J. 1987. *Seneca's Phaedra.* Liverpool.

Boyle, A. J. 1994. *Seneca's Troades.* Leeds.

Boyle, A. J. 1997. *Tragic Seneca: an Essay on the Theatrical Tradition.* London.

Boyle, A. J. (ed.). 1983. *Seneca Tragicus: Ramus Essays on Senecan Drama.* Bendigo.

Boyle, A. J. (ed.). 1993. *Roman Epic.* London.

Boyle, A. J. and Dominik, W. D. (eds). 2002. *Flavian Rome: Culture, Image, Text.* Leiden.

Bradley, K. R. 1978. *Suetonius' 'Life of Nero': an Historical Commentary.* Brussels.

Bradley, K. R. 1987. *Slaves and Masters in the Roman Empire: a Study in Social Control,* Oxford.

Bradley, K. R. 1991. *Discovering the Roman Family: Studies in Roman Social History.* New York.

Bradley, K. R. 1993. Writing the history of the Roman family. *CPh* 88: 237–50.

Bradley, K. R. 1994. *Slavery and Society at Rome*, Cambridge.

Bradley, K. R. 1998a. The Roman family: new directions. *EMC/CV* n.s. 17: 129–37.

Bradley, K. R. 1998b. The sentimental education of the Roman child: the role of pet-keeping. *Latomus* 57: 523–57.

Bradley, K. R. 1999. Images of childhood: the evidence of Plutarch. In Pomeroy 1999: 183–96.

Bradley, K. R. 2000. Fictive families: family and household in the *Metamorphoses* of Apuleius. *Phoenix* 54: 282–308.

Bradley, K. R. 2001. Children and dreams. In Dixon 2001: 43–51.

Bramble, J. C. 1974. *Persius and the Programmatic Satire*. Cambridge.

Bramble, J. C. 1982a. Lucan. In Kenney and Clausen 1982: 533–57.

Bramble, J. C. 1982b. Martial and Juvenal. In Kenney and Clausen 1982: 597–623.

Branham, R. B. and Kinney, D. 1996. *Petronius: Satyrica*. London.

Braun, M., Mutschler, F.-H., Haltenhoff, A. (eds). 2000. *Moribus antiquis res stat Romana. Römische Werte und römische Literatur im 3. und 2. Jh. v. Chr.* Leipzig.

Braund, D. 1985. *Augustus to Nero: a Sourcebook on Roman History 31 BC – AD 68.* London.

Braund, D. and Gill, C. (eds). 2003. *Myth, History and Culture in Republican Rome: Studies in honour of T. P. Wiseman*. Exeter.

Braund, S. 1988. *Beyond Anger: a Study of Juvenal's Third Book of Satires*. Cambridge.

Braund, S. 1992. *Roman Verse Satire*. Greece and Rome, New Surveys in the Classics 23. Oxford.

Braund, S. 1996. *Juvenal Satires Book 1*. Cambridge.

Braund, S. 2002. *Latin Literature*. London.

Braund, S. and Gill, C. (eds). 1997. *The Passions in Roman Thought and Literature*. Cambridge.

Breen, C. 1986. The shield of Turnus, the sword-belt of Pallas and the wolf. *Vergilius* 32: 63–71.

Bright, D. F. and Ramage, E. S. (eds). 1984. *Classical Texts and their Traditions: Studies in Honor of C. R. Trahman*. Chico, Calif.

Brink, C. O. 1963–82. *Horace on Poetry*. 3 vols. Cambridge.

Briscoe, J. 1973. *A Commentary on Livy Books XXXI–XXXIII*. Oxford.

Briscoe, J. 1981. *A Commentary on Livy Books XXXIV–XXXVII*. Oxford.

Brothers, A. J. 1988. *Terence: the Self-tormentor*. Warminster.

Brothers, A. J. 2000. *Terence: the Eunuch*. Warminster.

Brown, P. M. 1993. *Horace: Satires I*. Warminster.

Brown, S. A. 1999. *The Metamorphosis of Ovid: From Chaucer to Ted Hughes*. London.

Brown, S. A. and Martindale, C. A. 1998. *Lucan: the Civil War*. London (Nicholas Rowe's trans., *Pharsalia*, 1718).

Brunschwig, J. and M. C. Nussbaum (eds). 1993. *Passions and Perceptions: Studies in Hellenistic Philosophy of Mind*. Cambridge.

Brunt, P. A. 1988. *The Fall of the Roman Republic and Related Essays*. Oxford.

Bubel, F. 1992. *Bibliographie zu Plautus 1976–1989*. Bonn.

Burck, E. 1943. Das Bild der Karthager in der römischen Literatur. In Vogt 1943: 297–345.

Burck, E. 1971. *Vom römischen Manierismus.* Darmstadt.

Burnikel, W. 1980. *Untersuchungen zur Struktur des Witzepigramms bei Lukillius und Martial.* Wiesbaden.

Burridge, R. A. 1992. *What Are the Gospels? A Comparison with Greco-Roman Biography.* Cambridge.

Butler, H. M. and Owen, S. G. 1914. *Apuleius: Apologia.* Oxford (repr. Hildesheim, 1983).

Butrica, J. L. 1996. Hellenistic erotic elegy: the evidence of the papyri. *PLLS* 9: 297–322.

Cairns, D. 1993. *AIDÓS: The Psychology and Ethics of Honour and Shame in Ancient Greek Literature.* Oxford.

Cairns, F. 1979. *Tibullus: a Hellenistic Poet at Rome.* Cambridge.

Cairns, F. 1989. *Virgil's Augustan Epic.* Cambridge.

Caldelli, M.L. 2001. *Amicus/-a* nelle iscrizioni di Roma: l'apporto dell'epigrafia al chiarimento di un sentimento sociale. In Peachin 2001b: 21-30.

Callebat, L. 1982. La prose du *De Architectura* de Vitruve. *ANRW* II.30.1: 696–722.

Cameron, Alan. 1993. *The Greek Anthology from Meleager to Planudes.* Oxford.

Cameron, Alan. 1995. *Callimachus and his Critics.* Princeton.

Cameron, Alan. 2002. The funeral of Junius Bassus. *ZPE* 139: 288–92.

Cameron, Averil. 1969. Petronius and Plato. *CQ* n.s. 19: 367–70.

Campbell, B. 1987. Teach yourself how to be a Roman general. *JRS* 77: 13–29.

Campbell, B. 2000. *The Writings of the Roman Land Surveyors.* JRS Monographs 9. London.

Campbell, D. A. 1982–93. *Greek Lyric.* 5 vols. Cambridge, Mass.

Camps, W. A. 1961. *Propertius Book I.* Cambridge.

Camps, W. A. 1965. *Propertius Book IV.* Cambridge.

Camps, W. A. 1966a. *Propertius Book II.* Cambridge.

Camps, W. A. 1966b. *Propertius Book III.* Cambridge.

Carne-Ross, D. S. 1996. *Horace in English.* Harmondsworth.

Carter, M. A. S. 2002. Ve*rgilium Vestigare: Aeneid* 12.587–8. *CQ* 52: 615–17.

Cartledge, P. and Harvey, F. (eds). 1985. *Crux: Essays in Greek History Presented to G. E. M. de Ste. Croix on his 75th birthday.* London.

Cavallo, G. et al. (eds). 1993. *Lo spazio letterario di Roma antica I.* Rome.

Cavarzere, A., Aloni, A., Barchiesi, A. (eds). 2001. *Iambic Ideas.* Lanham, Md.

Chadwick, H. 1981. *Boethius.* Oxford.

Champlin, E. 1974. The chronology of Fronto. *JRS* 64: 136–59.

Champlin, E. 1980. *Fronto and Antonine Rome.* Cambridge, Mass.

Champlin, E. 1991. *Final Judgments: Duty and Emotion in Roman Wills 200 B.C.–A.D. 250.* Berkeley.

Chaplin, Jane D. 2000. *Livy's Exemplary History.* Oxford.

Chassignet, M. 1996–. *L'annalistique romaine.* Paris.

Cherry, D. 1998. *Frontier and Society in Roman North Africa.* Oxford.

Chilver, G. E. F. 1979. *A Historical Commentary on Tacitus' Histories I and II.* Oxford.

Chilver, G. E. F. and Townend, G. B. 1985. *A Historical Commentary on Tacitus' Histories IV and V.* Oxford.

Christenson, D. M. 2000. *Plautus: Amphitruo.* Cambridge.

Cicu, L. 1988. *Problemi e strutture del mimo a Roma.* Sassari.

Citroni, M. 1968. Motivi di polemica letteraria negli epigrammi di Marziale. *DArch* 2: 259–301.

Citroni, M. 1969. La teoria lessinghiana dell'epigramma e le interpretazioni moderne di Marziale. *Maia* 21: 215–43.

Citroni, M. 1975. *M. Valerii Martialis Epigrammaton Liber I*. Florence.

Citroni, M. 1991. L'epigramma. In Montanari 1991: 171–89, 203–7.

Citroni, M. 1995. *Poesia e lettori in Roma antica: forme della comunicazione letteraria*. Rome.

Citroni, M. 1996. Sulpicia. In Spawforth and Hornblower 1996: 1454.

Citroni, M. (ed.). 2003. *Memoria e identità*. Florence.

Clarke, K. 1999. Universal perspectives in historiography. In Kraus 1999: 249–79.

Clarke, M. L. 1956. *The Roman Mind*. London.

Clarke, M. L. (rev. D. H. Berry) 1996. *Rhetoric at Rome: a Historical Survey*. London.

Classen, C. J. 1985. *Recht-Rhetorik-Politik: Untersuchungen zu Ciceros rhetorischer Strategie*. Darmstadt.

Classen, C. J. 2003. *Antike Rhetorik im Zeitalter des Humanismus*. Munich.

Clausen, W. V. 1964. Callimachus and Roman poetry. *GRBS* 5: 181–96.

Clausen, W. V. 1987. *Virgil's* Aeneid *and the Tradition of Hellenistic Poetry*. Berkeley.

Clausen, W. V. 1994. *Virgil: Eclogues*. Oxford.

Clay, D. 1988. The archaeology of the temple to Juno at Carthage. *CPh* 83: 195–205.

Coffey, M. 1976. *Roman Satire*. London (repr. Bristol, 1989).

Colace, P. R. and Zumbo, A. (eds). 2000. *Atti del seminario internazionale di studi: letteratura scientifica e tecnica greca e latina (Messina 29–31 ottobre 1997)*. Messina.

Cole, T. 1991. In response to Nevio Zorzetti, 'Poetry and the Ancient City'. *CJ* 86: 377–82.

Coleman, K. M. 1990. Fatal charades: Roman executions staged as mythological enactments. *JRS* 80: 44–73.

Coleman, K. M. 2000. Latin literature after AD 96: change or continuity. *AJAH* 15 [formal date 1990]: 19–39.

Coleman, R. G. (ed.). 1977. *Virgil*, Eclogues. Cambridge.

Connors, C. 1998. *Petronius the Poet*. Cambridge.

Conte, G. B. 1986. *The Rhetoric of Imitation*. Ithaca, NY.

Conte, G. B. 1994a. *Genres and Readers: Lucretius, Love Elegy, Pliny's Encyclopedia*. Baltimore.

Conte, G. B. 1994b. *Latin Literature: A History*. Baltimore.

Conte, G. B. 1996. *The Hidden Author: an Interpretation of Petronius' Satyricon*. Berkeley.

Conybeare, C. 2000. *Paulinus Noster*. Oxford.

Cooper, J. 1999. *Reason and Emotion: Essays on Ancient Moral Psychology and Ethical Theory*. Princeton.

Corbett, P. B. 1970. *Petronius*. New York.

Corbier, M. 2001. Child exposure and abandonment. In Dixon 2001: 52–73.

Cornell, T. J. 1991. The tyranny of the evidence: a discussion of the possible uses of literacy in Etruria and Latium in the archaic age. In Humphrey 1991: 7–33.

Costa, C. D. N. (ed.). 1974. *Seneca*. London.

Coulston, J. C. and Dodge, H. (eds). 2000. *Ancient Rome: the Archaeology of the Eternal City*. Oxford.

Courtney, E. 1980. *A Commentary on the Satires of Juvenal*. London.

Courtney, E. 1993. *The Fragmentary Latin Poets*. Oxford.

Courtney, E. 1995. *Musa Lapidaria: a Selection of Latin Verse Inscriptions*. Atlanta.

Courtney, E. 1999. *Archaic Latin Prose*. APA American Classical Studies 42. Atlanta.

Courtney, E. 2001. *A Companion to Petronius*. Oxford.

Cox, A. 1969. Didactic poetry. In Higginbotham 1969: 134–45.

Craig, C. P. 1993. *Form as Argument in Cicero's Speeches: a Study of Dilemma*. Atlanta.

Crawford, M.H. (ed.). 1983. *Sources for Ancient History*. Cambridge.

Crawford, M. H. and Ligota, C. R. (eds). 1995. *Ancient History and the Antiquarian*. London.

Crook, J. A. 1967. *Law and Life of Rome*. London.

Crook, J. A. 1990. 'His and hers': what degree of financial responsibility did husband and wife have for the matrimonial home and their life in common, in a Roman marriage? In Andreau and Bruhns 1990: 153–72.

Crook, J. A. 1995. *Legal Advocacy in the Roman World*. London.

Crook, J. A., Lintott, A., Rawson, E. (eds.) 1994. *The Cambridge Ancient History IX : The Last Age of the Roman Republic 146–43 B.C.* Cambridge.

Crowther, N. B. 1970. ΟΙ ΝΕΩΤΕΡΟΙ, *Poetae Novi* and *Cantores Euphorionis*. *CQ* 20: 322–7.

Cugusi, P. 1983. *Evoluzione e forme dell'epistolografia latina*. Rome.

Cupaiolo, G. 1984. *Bibliografia Terenziana (1470–1983)*. Napoli.

Cupaiolo, G. 1992. Supplementum Terentianum. *Bollettino di Studi Latini* 22: 32–57.

D'Anna, G. 1967. *M. Pacuvii fragmenta*. Rome.

D'Arms, J.H. 1981. *Commerce and Social Standing in Ancient Rome*. Cambridge, Mass.

Dahlmann, H. 1954. Die Bienenstaat in Vergils *Georgica*. *AAWM* 10: 547–62 (= Hardie 1999: 2.253–67).

Dällenbach, L. 1989. *The Mirror in the Text*. Cambridge.

Dalzell, A. 1996. *The Criticism of Didactic Poetry: Essays on Lucretius, Virgil, and Ovid*. Toronto.

Damasio, A. 1995. *Descartes' Error: Emotion, Reason, and the Human Brain*. New York.

Dangel, J. 1995. *Accius – Oeuvres: Fragments*. Paris.

Dauge, Y. 1981. *Le Barbare: recherches sur la conception romaine de la barbarie et de la civilisation*. Brussels.

Daviault, A. 1981. *Comoedia Togata: Fragments*. Paris.

David, J.-M. 1992. *Le patronat judiciaire au dernier siècle de la république romaine*. Rome.

Davis, G. 1991. *Polyhymnia: the Rhetoric of Horatian Literary Discourse*. Berkeley.

Davis, J. T. 1989. *Fictus Adulter: Poet as Actor in the Amores*. Amsterdam.

Day, A. A. 1938. *The Origins of Latin Love-Elegy*. Oxford.

Day Lewis, C. 1940. *The Georgics of Virgil*. London (repr. with his *Eclogues*, Oxford, 1983).

De Graff, T. 1940. Plato in Cicero. *Classical Philology* 35: 143–53.

Deniaux, E. 1993. *Clientèles et pouvoir à l'époque de Cicéron*. Rome.

Depew, M. and Obbink, D. (eds). 2000. *Matrices of Genre*. Cambridge, Mass.

Deroux, C. (ed.). 2000. *Studies in Latin Literature* X. Brussels.

Derrida, J. 1980. *The Postcard: From Socrates to Freud and Beyond*. Chicago.

De Sousa, R. 1987. *The Rationality of Emotion*. Cambridge, Mass.

Dewar, M. 1994. Laying it on with a trowel: the proem to Lucan and related texts. *CQ* 44: 199–211.

Dilke, O. A. W. 1971. *The Roman Land Surveyors: an Introduction to the Agrimensores*. Newton Abbot.

Dillery, J. 2002. Quintus Fabius Pictor and Greco-Roman historiography at Rome. In Miller et al. 2002: 1–23.

Dixon, S. 1985. Breaking the law to do the right thing: the gradual erosion of the Voconian Law in Ancient Rome. *Adelaide Law Review* 9: 519-34.

Dixon, S. 1988. *The Roman Mother*. London.

Dixon, S. 1991. The sentimental ideal of the Roman family. In Rawson 1991: 99–113.

Dixon, S. 1992. *The Roman Family*. Baltimore.

Dixon, S. 1994. Rewriting the family: a review essay. *CJ* 89: 395–407.

Dixon, S. 1997a. Continuity and change in Roman social history: retrieving 'family feeling(s)' from Roman law and literature. In Golden and Toohey 1997: 79–92.

Dixon, S. 1997b. Conflict in the Roman family. In Rawson and Weaver 1997: 149–67.

Dixon, S. (ed.). 2001. *Childhood, Class and Kin in the Roman World*. London.

Dominik, W. J. 1994. *The Mythic Voice of Statius: Power and Politics in the Thebaid*. Leiden.

Dominik, W. J. (ed.). 1997. *Roman Eloquence: Rhetoric in Society and Literature*. London.

Dorey, T. A. (ed.). 1964. *Cicero*. London.

Dorey, T. A (ed.). 1966. *Latin Historians*. London.

Dorey, T. A. (ed.). 1967. *Latin Biography*. London.

Dorey, T. A. (ed.). 1971. *Livy*. London.

Dorey, T. A. (ed.). 1975. *Empire and Aftermath: Silver Latin II*. London.

Dougan, T. W. 1905. *M. Tulli Ciceronis Tuscularum Disputationum libri quinque*. Vol. 1. Cambridge.

Douglas, A. E. 1966. *Cicero: Brutus*. Oxford.

Downey, G. 1959. Ekphrasis. *RAC* 4: 921–44.

Dryden, J. 1997. *Vergil's Aeneid*. London (originally 1697).

Dubel, S. 1997. *Ekphrasis* et *enargeia*: la description antique comme parcours. In Lévy and Pernot 1997: 249–64.

Dubois, P. 1982. *History, Rhetorical Description and the Epic: from Homer to Spenser*. Cambridge.

Duckworth, G. E. 1952. *The Nature of Roman Comedy: a Study in Popular Entertainment*. Princeton (repr. Bristol, 1994).

Due, O. S. 1974. *Changing Forms: Studies in the Metamorphoses of Ovid*. Copenhagen.

Duff, J. W. and Duff, A. M. 1934. *Minor Latin Poets*. Cambridge, Mass.

Dupont, F. 1999. *The Invention of Literature: from Greek Intoxication to the Latin Book*. Baltimore.

DuQuesnay, I. M. Le M. 1973. The *Amores*. In Binns 1973: 1–48.

DuQuesnay, I. M. Le M. 1979. From Polyphemus to Corydon. In West and Woodman 1979: 35–69.

DuQuesnay, I. M. Le M. 1984. Horace and Maecenas: the Propaganda Value of *Sermones* I. In Woodman and West 1984: 19–58.

Duret, L. 1982. Dans l'ombre des plus grands I: Poètes et prosateurs mal connus de l'époque augustéenne. *ANRW* II.30.3: 1447–560.

Dyck, A. R. 1996. *A Commentary on Cicero De Officiis*. Ann Arbor.

Earl, D. C. 1961. *The Moral and Political Tradition of Rome*. London.

Easterling, P. and Hall, E. (eds). 2002. *Greek and Roman Actors: Aspects of an Ancient Profession*. Cambridge.

Ebbeler, J. 2003. Caesar's letters and the ideology of literary history. *Helios* 30: 3–19.

Eden, P. T. 1964. Faba mimus. *Hermes* 92: 251–5.

Eden, P. T. 1975. *A Commentary on Virgil Aeneid VIII*. Leiden.

Eden, P. T. 1984. *Seneca: Apocolocyntosis*. Cambridge.

Edmunds, L. 1992. *From a Sabine Jar: Reading Horace* Odes *1.9*. Chapel Hill.

Edmundson, J., Mason, S., Rives, J. (eds). Forthcoming. *Flavius Josephus in Flavian Rome*. Leiden.

Edwards, C. 1993. *The Politics of Immorality in Ancient Rome*. Cambridge.

Edwards, C. 1997. Self-scrutiny and self-transformation in Seneca's letters. *Greece and Rome* 44: 23–38.

Edwards, C. 2000. *Suetonius: Lives of the Caesars*. Oxford.

Edwards, C. and Woolf, G. (eds). 2003. *Rome the Cosmopolis*. Cambridge.

Edwards, J. 1984. *The Roman Cookery of Apicius*. London.

Edwards, M. J. and Swain, S. (eds). 1997. *Portraits: Biographical Representation in the Greek and Latin Literature of the Roman Empire*. Oxford.

Effe, B. 1977. *Dichtung und Lehre: Untersuchungen zur Typologie des antiken Lehrgedichts*. Munich.

Ekman, P. and Davidson, R. J. (eds). 1994. *The Nature of Emotions: Fundamental Questions*. Oxford.

Elsner, J. 1993. Seductions of art: Encolpius and Eumolpus in a Neronian picture gallery. *PCPS* 39: 30–47.

Elsner, J. 2000. Making myth visual: the Horae of Philostratus and the dance of the text. *Römische Mitteilungen* 207: 253–76.

Elsner, J. 2003. Inventing Christian Rome: the role of early Christian art. In Edwards and Woolf 2003: 71–99.

Elsner, J. (ed.). 1996. *Art and Text in Roman Culture*. Cambridge.

Elster, J. 1999. *Alchemies of the Mind: Rationality and the Emotions*. Cambridge.

Estafanía, D. 1994a. Horacio, la amistad y los amigos. In Estafanía 1994: 10–20.

Estafanía, D. (ed.). 1994b. *Horacio, el poeta y el hombre*. Madrid.

Evans Grubbs, J. 1993. 'Marriage more shameful than adultery': slave–mistress relationships, 'mixed marriages', and late Roman law. *Phoenix* 47: 125–54.

Evans Grubbs, J. 1995. *Law and Family in Late Antiquity*. Oxford.

Evans Grubbs, J. 2002. *Women and the Law in the Roman Empire*. London.

Evaristo, B. 2001. *The Emperor's Babe*. London.

Ewbank, W. W. 1933. *The Poems of Cicero*. London.

Fairweather, J. 1981. *Seneca the Elder*. Cambridge.

Faller, S. and Manuwald, G. (eds). 2002. *Accius und seine Zeit*. Würzburg.

Fantham, E. 1982. *Seneca: Troades*. Princeton.

Fantham, E. 1988. Mime: the missing link in Roman literary history. *CW* 82: 153–63.

Fantham, E. 1996. *Roman Literary Culture: from Cicero to Apuleius*. Baltimore.

Fantham, E. 1997. Images of the city: Propertius' New-old Rome. In Habinek and Schiesaro 1997: 122–35.

Fantham, E. 2000. Production of Seneca's Trojan women, ancient ? and modern. In G. W. M. Harrison 2000: 13–26.

Fantham, E. 2003. Pacuvius: recognition, reversal and melodrama. In Braund and Gill 2003: 98–188.

Farrell, J. 1991. *Virgil's Georgics and the Traditions of Ancient Epic: the Art of Allusion in Literary History.* Oxford.

Farrell, J. 1992. Dialogue of genres in Ovid's 'Lovesong of Polyphemus' (*Met.* 13.719–897). *AJPh* 113: 235–68.

Farrell, J. 1998. Reading and writing the *Heroides. HSCP* 98: 307–38.

Favro, D. 1996. *The Urban Image of Augustan Rome.* Cambridge.

Fear, T. (ed.) 2000a. *Fallax Opus: Approaches to Reading Roman Elegy* (= *Arethusa* 33.2). Baltimore.

Fear, T. 2000b. The poet as pimp: elegiac seduction in the time of Augustus. In Fear (ed.) 2000a, 217–40.

Fedeli, P. 1980. *Sesto Properzio: il primo libro delle elegie.* Florence.

Fedeli, P. 1985. *Sesto Properzio: il libro terzo delle elegie.* Bari.

Fedeli, P. 1992. In viaggio con Orazio da Roma a Brindisi. *Aufidus* 17: 37–54.

Feeney, D. C. 1991. *The Gods in Epic.* Oxford.

Feeney, D. C. 1992. 'Shall I compare thee … ?': Catullus 68b and the limits of analogy. In Woodman and Powell 1992: 33–44.

Feeney, D. C. 1993. Horace and the Greek lyric poets. In Rudd 1993: 41–63.

Feldherr, A. 1998. *Spectacle and Society in Livy's History.* Berkeley.

Ferguson, J. 1963. Catullus and Martial. *PACA* 6: 3–15.

Ferguson, J. 1979. *Juvenal: the Satires.* London (repr. Bristol, 1999).

Ferri, R. 2003. *Octavia Praetexta.* Cambridge.

Finkelpearl, E. 1990. Psyche, Aeneas and an ass: Apuleius *Met.* 6.10–6.21. *TAPA* 120: 333–48 (repr. in Harrison 1999: 290–306).

Finkelpearl, E. 1998. *Metamorphosis of Language in Apuleius.* Ann Arbor.

Fisher, R. S. 1982. Conon and the poet: a solution to *Eclogue* 3.40–2. *Latomus* 41: 803–14.

Fitch, J. G. 1987. *Seneca: Hercules Furens.* Ithaca, N.Y.

Fitch, J. G. 2000. Playing Seneca. In G. W. M. Harrison 2000: 1–12.

Fitch, J. G. 2002 and 2004. *Seneca: Tragedies I, II.* Cambridge, Mass.

Fitzgerald, W. 1984. Aeneas, Daedalus and the labyrinth. *Arethusa* 17: 51–61.

Fitzgerald, W. 1995. *Catullan Provocations: Lyric Poetry and the Drama of Position.* Berkeley.

Fitzgerald, W. 2000. *Slavery and the Roman Literary Imagination.* Cambridge.

Flamant, J. 1969. La technique du banquet dans les *Saturnales* de Macrobe. *REL* 46: 303–19.

Flintoff, E. 1974. The setting of Virgil's *Eclogues. Latomus* 33: 814–46.

Flintoff, E. 1975–6. Characterisation in Virgil's *Eclogues. PVS* 15: 16–26.

Flower, H. I. 1995. *Fabulae praetextae* in context: when were plays on contemporary subjects performed in Republican Rome? *CQ* 45: 170–90.

Fordyce, C. J. 1961. *Catullus: a Commentary.* Oxford.

Fortenbaugh, W. 1975. *Aristotle on Emotion: a Contribution to Philosophical Psychology, Rhetoric, Poetics, Politics, and Ethics.* New York.

Fortenbaugh, W. 1988. *Benevolentiam conciliare* and *animos permovere*: some remarks on Cicero's *De oratore* 2. 178–216. *Rhetorica* 6: 259–73.

Foster, B. O. et al. 1919–59. *Livy.* 14 vols. Cambridge, Mass.

Foucher, A. 2000. *Historia proxima poetis: L'influence de la poésie épique sur le style des historiens latins, de Salluste à Ammien Marcellin.* Brussels.

Fowler, D. 1991. Narrate or describe: the problem of Ekphrasis. *JRS* 81, 25–35.

Fowler, D. 1995. Horace and the aesthetics of politics. In Harrison 1995: 248–66.

Fowler, D. 1996. Even better than the real thing: a tale of two cities. In Elsner 1996: 57–74.

Fowler, D. 2000. *Roman Constructions: Readings in Postmodern Latin.* Oxford.

Fraenkel, E. 1922. *Plautinisches im Plautus.* Berlin (rev. Ital. trans. [1960] *Elementi Plautini in Plauto.* Florence).

Fraenkel, E. 1932. Selbstmordwege. *Philologus* 87: 470–3.

Fraenkel, E. 1956. Eine Form römischer Kriegsbulletins. *Eranos* 54: 189–94.

Fraenkel, E. 1957. *Horace.* Oxford.

Frank, M. 1995. *Seneca's* Phoenissae. Leiden.

Fränkel, H. 1945. *Ovid, a Poet between Two Worlds.* Berkeley.

Frassinetti, P. 1967. *Atellanae fabulae.* Rome.

Frede, M. 1986. The Stoic doctrine of the affections of the soul. In Schofield and Striker 1986: 93–110.

Freudenburg, K. 1993. *The Walking Muse: Horace on the Theory of Satire.* Princeton.

Freudenburg, K. 2001. *Satires of Rome.* Cambridge.

Freudenburg, K. (ed.). Forthcoming. *The Cambridge Companion to Roman Satire.* Cambridge.

Friedländer, P. 1912. *Johannes von Gaza und Paulus Silentiarius: Kunstbeschreibungen Justinianischer Zeit.* Berlin.

Friedrich, J. and Röllig, L. 1999. *Phönizisch-punische Grammatik.* Rome.

Frier, B. 1985. *The Rise of the Roman Jurists: Studies in Cicero's Pro Caecina.* Princeton.

Fuhrmann, M. 1960. *Das systematische Lehrbuch: Ein Beitrag zur Geschichte der Wissenschaften in der Antike.* Göttingen.

Furneaux, H., Fisher, C. D., Pelham, H. F. 1896. *The Annals of Tacitus. Volume I: Books 1–6.* Oxford.

Furneaux, H., Fisher, C. D., Pelham, H. F. 1907. *The Annals of Tacitus. Volume II: Books 11–16.* Oxford.

Fusillo, M. 1996. Modern critical theories and the ancient novel. In Schmeling 1996: 277–305.

Fyfe, W. H. (rev. D. S. Levene). 1997. *Tacitus: the Histories.* Oxford.

Gabba, E. 1984. The historians and Augustus. In Millar and Segal 1984: 61–88.

Gaisser, J. H. 1993. *Catullus and his Renaissance Readers.* Oxford.

Gaisser, J. H. 2001. *Catullus in English.* Harmondsworth.

Gale, M. R. 1994. *Myth and Poetry in Lucretius.* Cambridge.

Gale, M. R. 1997. The shield of Turnus (*Aen.* 7.783–92). *G&R* 44: 176–96.

Gale, M. R. 2000. *Virgil on the Nature of Things: the* Georgics, *Lucretius and the Didactic Tradition.* Cambridge.

Gale, M. R. 2001. *Lucretius and the Didactic Epic*. London.

Galinsky, G. K. 1975. *Ovid's* Metamorphoses: *an Introduction to the Basic Aspects*. Oxford.

Galinsky, G. K. 1989. Was Ovid a silver Latin poet? *ICS* 14: 69–88.

Galinsky, G. K. 1996. *Augustan Culture: an Interpretive Introduction*. Princeton.

Gallivan, P. and Wilkins, P. 1997. Familial structures in Roman Italy: a regional approach. In Rawson and Weaver 1997: 239–79.

Garbarino, G. 1973. *Roma e la filosofia greca della origini alle fine del ii secolo A. C.* 2 vols. Turin.

Gardner, J. F. 1986. *Women in Roman Law and Society*. London.

Gardner, J. F. 1992. *Being a Roman Citizen*. London.

Gardner, J. F. 1998. *Family and* Familia *in Roman Law and Life*. Oxford.

Gardner, J. F. 2001. Nearest and dearest: liability to inheritance tax in Roman families. In Dixon 2001: 205–20.

Garrido-Hory, M. 1981. *Martial et l'esclavage*, Paris.

Garrido-Hory, M. 1984. *Martial: Index thematique de la dépendance*. Paris.

Gee, E. 2000. *Ovid, Aratus and Augustus: Astronomy in Ovid's* Fasti. Cambridge.

Geiger, J. 1975. *Cornelius Nepos and Ancient Political Biography*. Stuttgart.

George, E.V. 1974. *Aeneid VIII and the Aitia of Callimachus*. Leiden.

Gerber, D. E. 1997. *A Companion to the Greek Lyric Poets*. Leiden.

Gerber, D. E. 1999. *Greek Iambic Poetry*. Cambridge, Mass.

Giancotti, F. 1967. *Mimo e Gnome*. Messina.

Giardina, A. (ed.). 1993. *The Romans*. Chicago.

Giardina, A. and Schiavone, A. (eds). 1981. *Societa romana e produzione schiavistica, III: modelli etici, diritto e trasformazioni sociali*. Rome-Bari.

Gibson, R. K. 1995. How to win girlfriends and influence them: *Amicitia* in Roman love elegy. *PCPS* 41: 62–82.

Gibson, R. K. 2003. *Ovid: Ars Amatoria Book 3*. Cambridge.

Ginsburg, J. 1993. *In maiores certamina*: past and present in the *Annals*. In Luce and Woodman 1993: 86–103.

Gleason, M. W. 1995. *Making Men*. Princeton.

Glucker, J. 1995. *Probabile, veri simile* and related terms. In Powell 1995: 115–144.

Gold, B. K. 1987. *Literary Patronage in Greece and Rome*. Chapel Hill.

Gold, B. K. 2002. *Accipe Divitias et Vatum Maximus Esto*: money, poetry, mendicancy and patronage in Martial. In Boyle and Dominik 2002: 591–612.

Goldberg, C. (ed.). 1992. *Carmina Priapea*. Heidelberg.

Goldberg, S. M. 1986. *Understanding Terence*. Princeton.

Goldberg, S. M. 1995. *Epic in Republican Rome*. Oxford.

Goldberg, S. M. 1998. Plautus on the Palatine. *JRS* 78: 1–20.

Golden, M. 1988. Did the ancients care when their children died? *G&R* 35: 152–63.

Golden, M. and Toohey, P. (eds). 1997. *Inventing Ancient Culture: Historicism, Periodization, and the Ancient World*. London.

Goldhill, S. 1994. The naïve and knowing eye: ecphrasis and the culture of viewing in the Hellenistic world. In Goldhill and Osborne 1994: 197–223.

Goldhill, S. 1999. Literary history without literature: reading practices in the ancient world. *Substance* 88: 57–89.

Goldhill, S. (ed.). 2001. *Being Greek under Rome*. Cambridge.

Goldhill, S. and Osborne, R. (eds). 1994. *Art and Text in Ancient Greek Culture*. Cambridge.

Goldschmidt, R. 1940. *Paulinus' Churches at Nola*. Amsterdam.

Goodyear, F. R. D. 1972. *The Annals of Tacitus: Volume 1: Annals 1.1–1.54*. Cambridge.

Goodyear, F. R. D. 1981. *The Annals of Tacitus: Volume 1: Annals 1.55–81 and Annals 2*. Cambridge.

Goodyear, F. R. D. 1982. Various entries in Kenney and Clausen 1982: 639–41 (Velleius Paterculus), 641–2 (Curtius), 667–8 (Mela), 668–70 (Columella), 629–30 (*Aetna*).

Goold, G. P. 1977. *Manilius: Astronomica*. Cambridge, Mass.

Goold, G. P. 1983. *Catullus*. London.

Gordon, R. M. 1987. *The Structure of Emotions: Investigations in Cognitive Philosophy*. Cambridge.

Gowers, E. 1993a. *The Loaded Table: Representations of Food in Roman Literature*. Oxford.

Gowers, E. 1993b. Horace, *Satires* 1.5: an inconsequential journey. *PCPS* 39: 48–66.

Gowing, A. M. Forthcoming. *Empire and Memory: the Representation of the Roman*.

Granarolo, J. 1973. L'époque néotérique ou la poésie romaine d'avant-garde au dernier siècle d'la République (Catulle excepté). *ANRW* I.3: 278–360.

Gransden, K. W. 1984. *Virgil's Iliad*. Cambridge.

Gransden, K. W. 1996. *Vergil in English*. Harmondsworth.

Gratwick, A.S. 1973. 'Titus Maccius Plautus'. *CQ* 23 : 78-84.

Gratwick, A. S. 1982. Drama. In Kenney and Clausen 1982: 77–137.

Gratwick, A. S. 1993. *Plautus: Menaechmi*. Cambridge.

Gratwick, A. S. 1999. *Terence: the Brothers*. 2nd edn. Warminster.

Graver, M. 2002. *Cicero on the Emotions: 'Tusculan Disputations' 3 and 4*. Chicago.

Grebe, S. 1998. Ovids *Tristia* und *Epistulae ex Ponto* unter ausgewählten Aspekten des Freundschaftsthemas. In Schubert 1998: 737–54.

Green, R. P. H. 1988. Review of H. J. Williams 1986. *CR* 38: 30–2.

Greenblatt, S. 1980. *Renaissance Self-Fashioning: from More to Shakespeare*. Chicago.

Grewing, F. 1997. *Martial, Buch VI. Ein Kommentar*. Göttingen.

Grewing, F. (ed.). 1998. *Toto notus in orbe: Perspektiven der Martial-Interpretationen*. Stuttgart.

Griffin, J. 1979. The fourth Georgic, Virgil and Rome. *G&R* 26: 61–80 (repr. in Hardie 1999: 2.268–88).

Griffin, J. 1985. *Latin Poets and Roman Life*. London.

Griffin, J. 1992. Theocritus, the *Iliad*, and the east. *AJP* 113: 189–211.

Griffin, M. 1976. *Seneca: a Philosopher in Politics*. Oxford.

Griffin, M. 1997. The composition of the *Academica*: motives and versions. In B. Inwood and J. Mansfeld (eds), *Assent and Argument: Studies in Cicero's Academic Books*. Philosophia Antiqua 76. Leiden.

Griffin, M. and Atkins, M. 1991. *Cicero: De Officiis*. Oxford.

Griffin, M. and Barnes J. (eds). 1989. *Philosophia Togata I: Essays on Philosophy and Roman Society*. Oxford.

Gruen, E. 1984. *The Hellenistic World and the Coming of Rome*. 2 vols. Berkeley.

Gruen, E. 1990. *Studies in Greek Culture and Roman Policy*. Leiden.

Gruen, E. 1993. *Culture and National Identity in Republican Rome*. Ithaca, N.Y.

Gryzar, C. J. 1854. Der römische Mimus. *Sitzungsberichte der Wiener Akademie der Wissenschaften* 12: 237–337.

Guardi, T. 1985. *Fabula togata: i frammenti*. Milano.

Gunderson, E. 1997. Catullus, Pliny and love-letters. *TAPA* 127: 201–31.

Gutzwiller, K. 1996. The evidence for Theocritean poetry books. In Harder et al. 1996: 119–48.

Gutzwiller, K. 1998. *Poetic Garlands: Hellenistic Epigrams in Context*, Berkeley.

Gutzwiller, K. 2001. Art's echo: the tradition of the Hellenistic ekphrastic epigram. In Harder et al. 2001: 85–112.

Gwyn Griffiths, J. 1975. *Apuleius of Madauros: the Isis-Book*. Leiden.

Habinek, T. 1998. *The Politics of Latin Literature: Writing, Identity, and Empire*. Princeton.

Habinek, T. 2000. Seneca's renown: *Gloria, Claritudo*, and the replication of the Roman elite. *ClAnt* 19: 264–303.

Habinek, T. and Schiesaro, A. (eds). 1997. *The Roman Cultural Revolution*. Cambridge.

Haight, E. L. 1927. *Apuleius and his Influence*. London (repr. New York, 1963).

Hall, J. 1996. Cicero *Fam.* 5.8 and *Fam.* 15.5 in the light of modern politeness theory. *Antichthon* 30: 19–33.

Hall, J. 1998. Cicero to Lucceius (*Fam.* 5.12) in its social context: *Valde Bella? CPh* 93: 308–21.

Hall, J. Forthcoming. Cicero *Fam.* 16.21, Roman politeness, and the socialization of Marcus Cicero the Younger. In Welch and Hillard forthcoming.

Hallett J. P. 1997. *Ego mulier* : The Construction of Male Sexuality in Catullus. In Hallett and Skinner, 129–150.

Hallett J. P. and Skinner, M. B. (eds). 1997. *Roman Sexualities*. Princeton.

Hammond, C. 1996. *Caesar: the Gallic War*. Oxford.

Handley, E. W. 1968. *Menander and Plautus: a Study in Comparison*. London.

Harder, M. A., Regtuit, R., Wakker, G. (eds). 1996. *Theocritus*. Groningen.

Harder, M. A., Regtuit, R., Wakker, G. (eds). 2001. *Hellenistic Epigrams*. Groningen.

Hardie, A. 1983. *Statius and the Silvae: Poets, Patrons and Epideixis in the Graeco-Roman World*. Liverpool.

Hardie, P. R. 1986. *Vergil's Aeneid: Cosmos and Imperium*. Oxford.

Hardie, P. R. 1993. *The Epic Successors of Virgil: a Study in the Dynamics of a Tradition*. Cambridge.

Hardie, P. R. 1998. *Virgil*. Greece and Rome, New Surveys in the Classics 28. Oxford.

Hardie, P. R. 2002a. *Ovid's Poetics of Illusion*. Cambridge.

Hardie, P. R. 2002b. Another look at Virgil's Ganymede. In Wiseman (ed.) 2002: 333–61.

Hardie, P. R. (ed.). 1999. *Virgil: Critical Assessments*. 4 vols. London.

Hardie, P. R. (ed.). 2002. *The Cambridge Companion to Ovid*. Cambridge.

Hardwick, L. 2003. *Reception Studies. G&R* New Surveys in the Classics 33. Oxford.

Harlow, M. and Laurence, R. 2002. *Growing Up and Growing Old in Ancient Rome*. London.

Harré, R. (ed.). 1986. *The Social Construction of Emotions*. Oxford.

Harris, W. V. 1986. The Roman father's power of life and death. In Bagnall and Harris 1986: 81–95.

Harris, W. V. 2001. *Restraining Rage: the Ideology of Anger Control in Classical Antiquity.* Cambridge, Mass.

Harrison, G. W. M. 1987. The confessions of Lucilius (Horace, *Sat.* 2.1.30–4): a defense of autobiographical satire? *ClAnt.* 6: 38–52.

Harrison, G. W. M. (ed.). 2000. *Seneca in Performance.* London.

Harrison, S. J. 1991. *Vergil: Aeneid 10.* Oxford.

Harrison, S. J. 1992. The arms of Capaneus: Statius *Thebaid* 4.165–77. *CQ* 42: 247–52.

Harrison, S. J. 1995. Poetry, philosophy and letter-writing in Horace, *Epistles* I. In Innes et al. 1995: 47–61.

Harrison, S. J. 1996. Apuleius' *Metamorphoses.* In Schmeling 1996: 491–516.

Harrison, S. J. 1997. From Epic to Novel : Apuleius as Reader of Vergil. *MD* 39: 53–74.

Harrison, S. J. 1998a. The sword-belt of Pallas: moral symbolism and political ideology. *Aeneid* 10.495–505. In Stahl 1998: 223–42.

Harrison, S. J. 1998b. The Milesian tales and the Roman novel. *GCN* 9: 61–74.

Harrison, S. J. 2000. *Apuleius: a Latin Sophist.* Oxford.

Harrison, S. J. 2001a. Picturing the future: the proleptic ekphrasis from Homer to Vergil. In Harrison 2001c: 70–90.

Harrison, S. J. 2001b. Some generic problems in Horace's *Epodes*: or, on (not) being Archilochus. In Cavarzere et al. 2001: 165–86.

Harrison, S. J. (ed.). 2001c. *Texts, Ideas and the Classics.* Oxford.

Harrison, S. J. 2002a. Ovid and genre: evolutions of an elegist. In Hardie 2002: 79–94.

Harrison, S. J. 2002b. Constructing Apuleius: the emergence of a literary artist. *Ancient Narrative* 2: 143–71.

Harrison, S. J. (ed.). 1990. *Oxford Readings in Vergil's Aeneid.* Oxford.

Harrison, S. J. (ed.). 1995. *Homage to Horace: a Bimillenary Celebration,* Oxford.

Harrison, S. J. (ed.) 1999. *Oxford Readings in the Roman Novel.* Oxford.

Harrison, S. J., Hilton, J. L., Hunink, V. 2001. *Apuleius: Rhetorical Works.* Oxford.

Hausmann, U. (ed.). 1969. *Allgemeine Grundlagen der Archäologie.* Munich.

Havelock, E. A. 1939. *The Lyric Genius of Catullus.* Oxford.

Heaney, S. 2001. *Electric Light.* London.

Heffernan, J. A. W. 1993. *Museum of Words: the Poetics of Ekphrasis from Homer to Ashbery.* Chicago.

Heinze, R. 1899. Petron und der griechische Roman. *Hermes* 34: 494–519 (repr. in Heinze 1960: 417–39).

Heinze, R. 1960. *Vom Geist des Römertums.* Stuttgart.

Heinze, R. 1993. *Virgil's Epic Technique.* Bristol.

Hemelrijk, E. A. 1999. *Matrona Docta: Educated Women in the Roman Elite from Cornelia to Julia Domna.* London.

Henderson, A. A. R. 1979. *P.Ovidi Nasonis Remedia Amoris.* Edinburgh.

Henderson, J. 1982. P.L.I.N.Y.'s letters: portrait of the artist as a figure of style. *Omnibus* 4: 31–2.

Henderson, J. 1991. Statius' *Thebaid*/form premade. *PCPS* 37: 30–80.

Henderson, J. 1998a. *Fighting for Rome: Poets and Caesars, History, and Civil War.* Cambridge.

Henderson, J. 1998b. Virgil's Third *Eclogue*: how do you keep an idiot in suspense? *CQ* 48: 213–28.

Henderson, J. 1999. *Writing down Rome: Satire, Comedy, and Other Offences in Latin Poetry.* Oxford.

Henderson, J. 2001. *Telling Tales on Caesar: Roman Stories from Phaedrus.* Oxford.

Henderson, J. 2002. *Pliny's Statue: the* Letters, *Self-portraiture and Classical Art.* Exeter.

Herbert-Brown, G. 1994. *Ovid and the* Fasti: *a Historical Study.* Oxford.

Herbert-Brown, G. (ed.). 2002. *Ovid's* Fasti: *Historical Readings at its Bimillennium.*

Herington, C. J. 1961. O*ctavia Praetexta*: a survey. *CQ* 11: 18–30.

Herington, C. J. 1966. Senecan tragedy. *Arion* 5: 422–71 (repr. in Rudd 1972: 170–219).

Herington, C. J. 1982. Excursus: the *Octavia.* In Kenney and Clausen 1982: 530–32.

Herrmann, L. 1985. Laureolus. In Renard and Laurens 1985: 225–34.

Hershkowitz, D. 1995. Pliny the poet. *G&R* 42: 168–81.

Hershkowitz, D. 1998. *Valerius Flaccus'* Argonautica. *Abbreviated Voyages in Silver Latin Epic.* Oxford.

Herzog, R. and Schmidt, P. L. (eds). 1997. *Handbuch der lateinischen Literatur der Antike* IV: *Die Literatur des Umbruchs von der römischen zur christlichen Literatur.* Munich.

Herzog, R. and Schmidt, P. L. (eds). 2002. *Handbuch der lateinischen Literatur der Antike* I: *Die Archaische Literatur von den Anfängen bis Sullas Tod.* Munich.

Heyworth, S. J. 2001. Catullian iambics, Catullian *iambi.* In Cavarzere et al. 2001: 117–40.

Higginbotham, J. (ed.). 1969. *Greek and Latin Literature: a Comparative Study.* London.

Highet, G. 1954. *Juvenal the Satirist.* Oxford.

Hijmans, B. L., Jr and van den Paardt, R. Th. (eds). 1978. *Aspects of Apuleius' Golden Ass.* Groningen.

Hinds, S. 1985. Booking the return trip: Ovid and *Tristia* 1. *PCPS* 31:13–32.

Hinds, S. 1987a. The poetess and the reader: further steps towards Sulpicia. *Hermathena* 143: 29–46.

Hinds, S. 1987b. *The Metamorphosis of Persephone: Ovid and the Self-conscious Muse.* Cambridge.

Hinds, S. 1988. Generalising about Ovid. *Ramus* 16: 4–31.

Hinds, S. 1993. Medea in Ovid: scenes from the life of an intertextual heroine. *MD* 30: 9–47.

Hinds, S. 1998. *Allusion and Intertext: Dynamics of Appropriation in Roman Poetry.* Cambridge.

Hine, H. M. 2000. *Seneca: Medea.* Warminster.

Hingley, R. 2000. *Roman Officers and English Gentlemen.* London.

Hirzel, R. 1895. *Der Dialog.* 2 vols. Leipzig (repr. Hildesheim, 1963).

Hoffer, S. E. 1999. *The Anxieties of Pliny the Younger.* New York.

Hofmann, H. (ed.). 1999. *Latin Fiction.* London.

Holford-Strevens, L. 1988. *Aulus Gellius.* London.

Hollis, A. S. 1970. *Ovid: Metamorphoses VIII.* Oxford.

Hollis, A. S. 1977. *Ovid: Ars Amatoria I.* Oxford.

Holloway, R. R. 1994. *The Archaeology of Early Rome and Latium.* London.

Holzberg, N. 1986. Neuansatz zu einer Martial-Interpretation. *WJA* 12: 197–215.

Holzberg, N. 2001. *Die Antike Fabel: eine Einführung.* Darmstadt.

Holzberg, N. 2002. *Martial und das antike Epigramm*. Heidelberg.

Hopkins, K. 1978. *Conquerors and Slaves*. Cambridge.

Hopkins, K. 1983. *Death and Renewal*. Cambridge.

Hopkins, K. 1993. Novel evidence for Roman slavery. *Past and Present* 138: 3–27.

Hornblower, S. and Spawforth, A. J. 1996. *The Oxford Classical Dictionary*. 3rd edn. Oxford.

Horsfall, N. M. 1973–4. Dido in the light of history. *PVS* 13: 1–13 (repr. in Harrison 1990: 127–44).

Horsfall, N. M. 1974. Labeo and Capito. *Historia* 23: 253.

Horsfall, N. M. 1982. The literary mime. In Kenney and Clausen 1982: 119–20.

Horsfall, N. M. 1983. The origins of the illustrated book. *Aegyptus* 63: 199–216.

Horsfall, N. M. 1989. *Cornelius Nepos: a Selection*. Oxford.

Horsfall, N. M. 1994. The prehistory of Latin poetry: some problems of method. *RFIC* 122: 50–75.

Horsfall, N. M. 1995. Rome without spectacles. *G&R* 42: 49–56.

Horsfall, N. M. 1997. Criteria for the dating of Calpurnius Siculus. *RFIC* 125: 166–96.

Horsfall, N. M. 2000. *Virgil Aeneid 7: a Commentary*. Leiden.

Horsfall, N. M. 2003. *Virgil Aeneid 11: a Commentary*. Leiden.

Horster, M. and Reitz, C. (eds). 2003. *Antike Fachschriftsteller: Literarischer Diskurs und sozialer Kontext*. Wiesbaden.

Housman, A. E. 1926. *Lucanus*. Oxford.

Houston, G. W. 2002. The slave and freedmen personnel of public libraries in ancient Rome. *TAPA* 132: 139–76.

Howell, P. 1980. *A Commentary on Book One of the Epigrams of Martial*. London.

Hubbard, M. 1974. *Propertius*. London.

Hubbard, T. K. 1995. Allusive artistry and Vergil's revisionary program: *ecl.* 1–3. *MD* 34: 37–67.

Hubbard, T. K. 1996. Calpurnius Siculus and the unbearable weight of tradition. *Helios* 23: 67–89.

Hubbard, T. K. 1998. *The Pipes of Pan: Intertextuality and Literary Filiation in the Pastoral Tradition from Theocritus to Milton*. Ann Arbor.

Hughes, J. D. 1975. *A Bibliography of Scholarship on Plautus*. Amsterdam.

Hughes, T. 1997. *Tales from Ovid*. London.

Humphrey, J. H. (ed.). 1991. *Literacy in the Roman World*. Ann Arbor.

Hunink, V. 1992. *Lucanus, Bellum Civile III*. Amsterdam.

Hunink, V. 1997. *Apuleius of Madauros: Pro Se De Magia*. Amsterdam.

Hunink, V. 2001. *Apuleius of Madauros: Florida*. Amsterdam.

Hunter, R. L. 1985. *The New Comedy of Greece and Rome*. Cambridge.

Hunter, R. L. 1994. Bibliographical appendix. In Duckworth 1952, 465–71.

Hunter, R. L. 1999. *Theocritus: a selection*. Cambridge.

Huss, W. 1985. *Geschichte der Karthager*. Munich.

Hutchinson, G. O. 1993. *Latin Literature from Seneca to Juvenal*. Oxford.

Hutchinson, G. O. 1998. *Cicero's Correspondence: a Literary Study*. Oxford.

Hutchinson, G. O. 2002. The publication and individuality of Horace's *Odes* Books 1–3. *CQ* 52: 517–37.

Innes, D., Hine, H., Pelling, C. (eds). 1995. *Ethics and Rhetoric: Classical Essays for Donald Russell on his Seventy-fifth Birthday.* Oxford.

Iodice, M. G. 2002. *Appendix Vergiliana.* Milan.

Ireland, S. 1990. *Terence: the Mother in Law.* Warminster.

Jackson, J. 1937. *Tacitus: the Annals.* Cambridge, Mass.

Jacobson, H. 1974. *Ovid's Heroides.* Princeton.

Jal, P. 1963. *La guerre civile à Rome.* Paris.

Janko, R. 2000. *Philodemus On Poems, Book 1.* Oxford.

Janson, T. 1964. *Latin Prose Prefaces: Studies in Literary Conventions.* Stockholm.

Jenkyns, R.H.A. 1989. Virgil and Arcadia. *JRS* 79: 26–39

Jenkyns, R. H. A. 1992. Pastoral. In Jenkyns (ed.) 1992: 151–76.

Jenkyns, R. H. A. (ed.). 1992. *The Legacy of Rome: a New Appraisal.* Oxford.

Jenkyns, R. H. A. 1999. *Virgil's Experience.* Oxford.

Jocelyn, H. D. 1967. *Ennius: the Tragedies.* Cambridge.

Jocelyn, H. D. 1985. The new chapters of the ninth book of Celsus' *Artes.* *PLLS* 5: 299–336.

Jocelyn, H. D. 1995. Horace and the reputation of Plautus in the late first century B.C. In Harrison 1995: 228–47.

Johnson, T. S. 1994. Horace, C. IV.12: Vergilius at the Symposion. *Vergilius* 40: 49–66.

Johnson, W. R. 1976. *Darkness Visible: a Study of Vergil's Aeneid.* Berkeley.

Johnson, W. R. 1982. *The Idea of Lyric.* Berkeley.

Johnson, W. R. 1987. *Momentary Monsters: Lucan and his Heroes.* Ithaca, N.Y.

Jones, R. E. (1939) Cicero's accuracy of characterization in his dialogues. *AJP* 60: 307–25.

Joshel, S. 1992. *Work, Identity, and Legal Status at Rome: a Study of the Occupational Inscriptions.* Norman, Okla.

Just, R. 1985. Freedom, slavery and the female psyche. In Cartledge and Harvey 1985: 169–88.

Kahane, A. and Laird, A. J. W. (eds). 2001. *A Companion to the Prologue to Apuleius' Metamorphoses.* Oxford.

Kaimio, J. 1979. *The Romans and the Greek Language.* Helsinki.

Kaster, R. A. 1988. *Guardians of Language: the Grammarian and Society in Late Antiquity.* Berkeley.

Kaster, R. A. 1995. *Suetonius: De grammaticis et rhetoribus.* Oxford.

Kaster, R. A. 2001. The dynamics of *Fastidium* and the ideology of disgust. *TAPA* 131: 143–89.

Katz, J. 1999. *How Emotions Work.* Chicago.

Kauer, R., Lindsay, W. M., Skutsch, O. 1958. *P. Terenti Afri Comoediae.* Oxford.

Kauffman, L. 1986. *Discourses of Desire: Genders, Genre and Epistolary Fiction.* Ithaca, N.Y.

Kauffman, L. 1992. *Special Delivery: Epistolary Modes in Modern Fiction.* Chicago.

Kay, N. 1985. *Martial, Book XI: a Commentary.* London.

Kay, N. 2002. *The Epigrams of Ausonius.* London.

Kehoe, P. E. 1984. The adultery mime reconsidered. In Bright and Ramage 1984: 89–106.

Keitel, E. 1992. *Foedum Spectaculum* and related motifs in Tacitus' Histories II–III. *RhM* 135: 342–51.

Keith, A. M. 1997. *Tandem Venit Amor:* a Roman woman speaks of love. In Hallett and Skinner (eds) 1997: 295–310.

Keith, A. M. 2000. *Engendering Rome: Women in Latin Epic.* Cambridge.

Kelsey, F. W. 1905. The title of Caesar's work on the Gallic and Civil Wars. *TAPA* 36: 211–38.

Kennedy, D. F. 1983. Shades of meaning: Vergil, *ecl.* 10.75–7. *LCM* 8: 124.

Kennedy, D. F. 1984. The epistolary mode and the first of Ovid's *Heroides. CQ* 34: 413–22.

Kennedy, D. F. 1987. *Arcades ambo:* Virgil, Gallus and Arcadia. *Hermathena* 143: 47–59.

Kennedy, D. F. 1992. 'Augustan' and 'Anti-Augustan': reflections on terms of reference. In Powell 1992: 26–58.

Kennedy, D. F. 1993. *The Arts of Love: Five Studies in the Discourse of Roman Love Elegy.* Cambridge.

Kennedy, D. F. 2002. Epistolarity: the *Heroides.* In Hardie 2002: 217–32.

Kennedy, G. A. 1972. *The Art of Rhetoric in the Roman World, 300 BC–AD 300.* Princeton.

Kenney, E. J. 1962. The First Satire of Juvenal. *PCPS* 8: 29–40.

Kenney, E. J. 1970. Doctus Lucretius. *Mnemosyne* (ser. 4) 23: 366–92.

Kenney, E. J. 1990. *Apuleius: Cupid and Psyche.* Cambridge.

Kenney, E. J. 1996. *Ovid, Heroides XVI–XXI.* Cambridge.

Kenney, E. J. 1998. *Apuleius: the Golden Ass: a New Translation.* Harmondsworth.

Kenney, E. J. and Clausen, W. (eds). 1982. *The Cambridge History of Classical Literature.* Vol. II: *Latin Literature.* Cambridge.

Kerkhecker, A. 1999. *Callimachus' Book of Iambi.* Oxford.

Keulen, A. J. 2001. *L.Annaeus Seneca: Troades.* Leiden.

Kiaulehn, W. 1914. *De Scaenico Dialogorum Apparatu Capita Tria.* Halle.

Kilpatrick, R. S. 1986. *The Poetry of Friendship: Horace, Epistles I.* Edmonton.

Kilpatrick, R. S. 1990. *The Poetry of Criticism: Horace, Epistles II and Ars Poetica.* Edmonton.

Kissel, W. 1994. Ovid und das Corpus Priapeorum. *RhM* 137: 299–311.

Klebs, E. 1889. Zur Komposition von Petronius Satirae. *Philologus* 47: 623–55.

Kleiner, D. 1987. *Roman Funerary Altars with Portraits.* Rome.

Knauer, G. N. 1964a. *Die Aeneis und Homer.* Göttingen.

Knauer, G. N. 1964b. Vergil's *Aeneid* and Homer. *GRBS* 5: 61–84 (repr. in Harrison 1990: 390–412).

Knox, P. E. 1986. *Ovid's Metamorphoses and the Traditions of Augustan Poetry.* Cambridge.

Knox, P. E. 1993. Philetas and Roman poetry. *PLLS* 7: 61–83.

Knox, P. E. 1995. *Ovid,* Heroides: *Select Epistles.* Cambridge.

Koch, G. and Sichtermann, H. 1982. *Römische Sarkophage.* Munich.

Kokkinos, N. 1992. *Antonia Augusta: Portrait of a Great Roman Lady.* London.

Konstan, D. 1977. Friendship and monarchy: Dio of Prusa's third oration on kingship. *SO* 72: 124–43.

Konstan, D. 1997. *Friendship in the Classical World.* Cambridge.

Konstan, D. 2001. *Pity Transformed.* London.

Konstan, D. 2002. Review of Peachin 2001b, *BMCR* 29th April 2002.

Koortbojian, M. 1996. *In Commemorationem Mortuorum*: text and image along the Street of the Tombs. In Elsner 1996: 210–33.

Krahmalkov, C. R. 1988. Observations on the Punic passages of Hanno in the *Poenulus*. *Orientalia* 57: 55–66.

Kraus, C. S. 2000. The path between truculence and servility: prose literature from Augustus to Hadrian. In Taplin 2000: 438–67.

Kraus, C. S. Forthcoming. From *exempla* to *exemplar*? Writing history around the emperor in imperial Rome. In Edmundson et al. forthcoming.

Kraus, C. S. (ed.). 1999. *The Limits of Historiography*. Leiden.

Kroll, W. 1924. *Studien zur Verständnis der römischen Literatur*. Stuttgart.

Kroll, W. 1929. *C. Valerius Catullus*. 2nd edn. Leipzig.

Krostenko, B. A. 2001. *Cicero, Catullus, and the Language of Social Performance*. Chicago.

Kurke, L. and Dougherty, C. (eds). 2003. *Cultural Poetics II*. Cambridge.

Kyriakidis, S. (ed.). Forthcoming. *Middles in Latin Poetry*. Bari.

Lacey, W. K. 1996. *Augustus and the Principate: the Evolution of the System*. Leeds.

Laird, A. 1993. Sounding out ecphrasis: art and text in Catullus 64. *JRS* 83: 18–30.

Laird, A. 1996. *Ut figura poesis*: writing art and the art of writing in Augustan poetry. In Elsner 1996: 75–102.

Laird, A. 1997. Description and divinity in Apuleius' *Metamorphoses*. *GCN* 8: 59–86.

Laird, A. 1999. *Powers of Expression, Expressions of Power: Speech Presentation and Latin Literature*. Oxford.

Langslow, D. 2000. *Medical Latin in the Roman Empire*. Oxford.

La Penna, A. 1968. *Sallustio e la 'rivoluzione' romana*. Milan.

Laughton, E. 1960. Observations on the style of Varro. *CQ* 10: 1–28.

Laurens, P. 1965. Martial et l'épigramme grecque du 1er siècle ap. J.-C. *REL* 43: 315–41.

Laurens, P. 1989. *L'abeille dans l'ambre. Célébration de l'épigramme de l'époque alexandrine à la fin de la Renaissance*. Paris.

Lausberg, M. 1982. *Das Einzeldistichon: Studien zum antiken Epigramm*. Munich.

Leach, E. W. 1964. Georgic imagery in the *Ars Amatoria*. *TAPA* 95: 142–54.

Leach, E. W. 1974. Ekphrasis and the theme of artistic failure in Ovid's *Metamorphoses*. *Ramus* 3: 102–42.

Leach, E. W. 1988. *The Rhetoric of Space*. Princeton.

Leach, E. W. 1990. The politics of self-presentation: Pliny's 'Letters' and Roman portrait sculpture. *ClAnt* 9:14–39.

Leary, T. J. 1996. *Martial Book XIV: the Apophoreta*. London.

Lee, G. 1968. *Ovid's Amores*. London.

Lee, G. 1977. A reading of Virgil's fifth *Eclogue*. *PCPhS* n.s. 23: 62–70.

Lee, G. 1984. *Virgil: the* Eclogues. Harmondsworth.

Lee, G. 1990. *Tibullus: Elegies*. 3rd edn. Leeds.

Lee, G. 1994. *Propertius: the Poems*. Oxford.

Lee, G. and Barr, W. 1987. *The Satires of Persius*. Liverpool.

Lee, M.O. 1979. *Fathers and Sons in Virgil's Aeneid*. Albany, N.Y.

Lee, M. O. 1989. *Death and Rebirth in Virgil's Arcadia*. Albany, N.Y.

Leeman, A. D. 1963. *Orationis Ratio: the Stylistic Theories and Practice of the Roman Orators, Historians and Philosophers*. 2 vols. Amsterdam.

Leeman, A. D. et al. 1981–96. *M.Tullius Cicero De Oratore Libri. Kommentar.* 4 vols. Heidelberg.

Lee-Stecum, P. 1998. *Powerplay in Tibullus.* Cambridge.

Lefèvre, E. 1970. Die Bedeutung des Paradoxen in der römischen Literatur der frühen Kaiserzeit. *Poetica* 3: 59–82.

Lefèvre, E. (ed.). 1978. *Das römische Drama.* Darmstadt.

Lefkowitz, M. 1991. *First-Person Fictions: Pindar's Poetic 'I'.* Oxford.

Leigh, M. 1997. *Lucan: Spectacle and Engagement.* Oxford.

Lendon, J. 1997. *Empire of Honour.* Oxford.

Leo, F. 1913. *Geschichte der römischen Literatur. 1: Die archaische Literatur.* Leipzig (repr. Darmstadt, 1967).

Leo, F. 1895–6. *Plauti Comoediae.* 2 vols. Berlin.

Leonhardt, J. (1999) *Ciceros Kritik der Philosophenschulen.* Zetemata 103. Munich.

Lerer, S. 1985. *Boethius and Dialogue: Literary Method in* The Consolation of Philosophy. Princeton.

Lessing, G. E. 1895. Verstreute Anmerkungen über das Epigramm. In his *Sämtliche Schriften* (ed. K. Lachmann). Vol. 11. Stuttgart: 214–315.

Levene, D. S. 2000. Sallust's Catiline and Cato the Censor. *CQ* 50: 170–91.

Levene, D. S. and Nelis, D. P. (eds). 2002. *Clio and the Poets. Mnem.* Supplement 224. Leiden.

Lévy, C. and L. Pernot (eds). 1997. *Dire l'evidence.* Paris.

Lewis, M. and Haviland-Jones, J. M. (eds). 1993. *Handbook of Emotions.* New York.

Liebeschuetz, W. 1968. The cycle of growth and decay in Lucretius and Virgil. *PVS* 7: 30–40.

Lightfoot, J. L. 1999. *Parthenius of Nicaea.* Oxford.

Lindsay, W. M. 1903–10. *T. Macci Plauti Comoediae.* Oxford.

Lodge, G. 1904–33. *Lexicon Plautinum.* Leipzig.

Londey, D. and Johanson, C. 1987. *The Logic of Apuleius.* Leiden.

Loomis, J. W. 1972. *Studies in Catullan Verse.* Leiden.

Lorenz, S. 2002. *Erotik und Panegyrik: Martials epigrammatische Kaiser.* Tübingen.

Lovejoy, A. O. and Boas, G. 1935. *Primitivism and Related Ideas in Antiquity.* Baltimore (repr. 1997).

Lowe, N. J. 1988. Sulpicia's syntax. *CQ* 38: 193–305.

Lowrie, M. 1995. A parade of lyric predecessors: Horace *C.*1.12–18. *Phoenix* 49: 33–48.

Lowrie, M. 1997. *Horace's Narrative Odes.* Oxford.

Luce, T. J. 1977. *Livy: The Composition of His History.* Princeton.

Luce, T. J. 1990. Livy, Augustus and the *Forum Augustum.* In Raaflaub and Toher 1990: 123–38.

Luce, T. J. and Woodman, A. J. (eds). 1993. *Tacitus and the Tacitean Tradition.* Princeton.

Lutz, C. 1947. Musonius Rufus: the Roman Socrates. *YCS* 10: 88–9.

Lyne, R. O. A. M. 1978. The Neoteric poets. *CQ* 28: 167–87.

Lyne, R. O. A. M. 1980. *The Latin Love Poets from Catullus to Horace.* Oxford.

Lyne, R. O. A. M. 1987. *Further Voices in Vergil's Aeneid.* Oxford.

Lyne, R. O. A. M. 1995. *Horace: behind the Public Poetry.* New Haven.

Lyons, W. E. 1980. *Emotion.* Cambridge.

MacCary, W. T. and Willcock, M. M. 1976. *Plautus: Casina*. Cambridge.

MacCormack, S. 1975. Latin prose panegyrics. In Dorey 1975: 143–205.

Machor, J. L. and Goldstein, P. (eds). 2001. *Reception Study*. London.

Mack, S. 1988. *Ovid*. New Haven.

MacMullen, R. 1982. The epigraphic habit in the Roman Empire. *AJP* 103: 233–46.

Malbon, E. 1990. *The Sarcophagus of Junius Bassus*. Princeton.

Malcovati, E. 1967. *Oratorum Romanorum Fragmenta Liberae Rei Publicae*. 4th edn. Turin.

Malherbe, A. J. 1988. *Ancient Epistolary Theorists*. Atlanta, Ga.

Maltby, R. 1999. Tibullus and the language of Latin elegy. In Adams and Mayer 1999: 377–98.

Maltby, R. 2002. *Tibullus: Elegies*. Leeds.

Mankin, D. 1995. *Horace: Epodes*. Cambridge.

Mantle, I. C. 2002. The roles of children in Roman religion. *G&R* 49: 85–106.

Manuwald, G. 2001. *Fabulae praetextae: Spuren einer literarischen Gattung der Römer*. Munich.

Marchesi, I. 2002. When animals talk: Horace, Petronius, and the servile origin of fables. Lecture, University of California at Berkeley, 2 November.

Marincola, J. M. 1997. *Authority and Tradition in Ancient Historiography*. Cambridge.

Marincola, J. M. 1999a. Genre, convention, and innovation in Greco-Roman historiography. In Kraus 1999: 281–324.

Marincola, J. M. 1999b. Tacitus' Prefaces and the decline of imperial historiography. *Latomus* 58: 391–404.

Martin, R. H. 1976. *Terence: Adelphoe*. Cambridge.

Martin, R. H. 1981. *Tacitus*. London.

Martindale, C. A. 1997. Green politics: the *Eclogues*. In Martindale 1997: 107–24.

Martindale, C. A. (ed.). 1988. *Ovid Renewed*. Cambridge.

Martindale, C. A. (ed.). 1993. *Horace Made New*. Cambridge.

Martindale, C. A. (ed.). 1997. *The Cambridge Companion to Virgil*. Cambridge.

Mason, H. J. 1978. *Fabula Graecanica*: Apuleius and his Greek sources. In Hijmans and Van der Paardt 1978: 1–15 (repr. in Harrison 1999: 217–36).

Massaro, M. 1992. *Epigrafia metrica latina di età repubblicana*. Bari.

Masters, J. 1992. *Poetry and Civil War in Lucan's 'Bellum Civile'*. Cambridge.

Maurach, G. 1988. *Der Poenulus des Plautus*. Heidelberg.

May, J. M. 1988. *Trials of Character: the Eloquence of Ciceronian Ethos*. Chapel Hill.

May, J. M. (ed.). 2002. *Brill's Companion to Cicero: Oratory and Rhetoric*. Leiden.

May, J. M. and Wisse, J. (eds and trans.) 2001. *Cicero: On the Ideal Orator*. Oxford.

Mayer, R. G. 1980. Calpurnius Siculus: technique and style. *JRS* 70: 175–6.

Mayer, R. G. 1983. Neronian classicism. *AJP* 103: 305–18.

Mayer, R. G. 1990. The epic of Lucretius. *PLLS* 6: 35–43.

Mayer, R. G. 1994. *Horace, Epistles I*. Cambridge.

Mayer, R. G. 1995. Horace's Moyen de Parvenir. In Harrison (ed.) 1995: 279–95.

Mayer, R. G. 2001. *Tacitus: Dialogus*. Cambridge.

Mayer, R. G. Forthcoming. The impracticability of Latin 'Kunstprosa'. In T. Reinhardt and C. Rauer (eds), *Aspects of the Language of Latin Prose*. Oxford.

Mazzoli, G. 1991. La prosa filosofica, scientifica, epistolare. In F. Montanari (ed.), *La Prosa Latina*. Rome: 198–214.

McCarthy, K. 2000. *Slaves, Masters, and the Art of Authority in Plautine Comedy.* Princeton.

McGinn, T. A. J. 1998. *Prostitution, Sexuality and the Law in Ancient Rome.* New York.

McGlynn, P. 1963–7. *Lexicon Terentianum.* 2 vols. London.

McGushin, P. 1977. *C. Sallustius Crispus: Bellum Catilinae. A Commentary.* Leiden.

McGushin, P. 1992. *Sallust: the Histories. Volume 1: Books I–II.* Oxford.

McKeown, J. C. 1979. Augustan elegy and mime. *PCPS* 25: 71–84.

McKeown, J. C. 1987. *Ovid: Amores. Volume 1: Text and Prolegomena.* Liverpool.

McKeown, J. C. 1989. *Ovid: Amores. Volume 2: a Commentary on Book One.* Leeds.

McKeown, J. C. 1998. *Ovid: Amores. Volume 3: a Commentary on Book Two.* Leeds.

Meissner, B. 1999. *Die technologische Fachliteratur der Antike: Struktur, Überlieferung und Wirkung technischen Wissens in der Antike (ca. 400 v. Chr. – ca. 500 n. Chr.).* Berlin.

Merkelbach, R. 1962. *Roman und Mysterium in der Antike.* Berlin.

Meyer, E. 1990. Explaining the epigraphic habit in the Roman Empire: the evidence of epitaphs. *JRS* 80: 74–96.

Meyer, W. 1880. *Publilii Syri Mimi Sententiae.* Leipzig.

Miles, G. B. 1980. *Virgil's Georgics: a New Interpretation.* Berkeley.

Miles, G. B. 1995. *Livy: Reconstructing Early Rome.* Ithaca, N.Y.

Millar, F. 1983. Epigraphy. In Crawford 1983: 80–136.

Millar, F. 1993. Ovid and the *Domus Augusta*: Rome seen from Tomoi. *JRS* 83: 1–17.

Millar, F. and Segal, E. (eds). 1984. *Caesar Augustus: Seven Aspects.* Oxford.

Miller, J. F., Damon, C., Myers, K. S. (eds). 2002. *Vertis in Vsum: Studies in Honor of Edward Courtney.* Munich.

Minadeo, R. 1965. The formal design of *De Rerum Natura. Arion* 4: 444–61.

Minyard, J. D. 1985. *Lucretius and the Late Republic.* Leiden.

Moles, J. L. 1993. Livy's Preface. *PCPS* 39: 141–68.

Momigliano, A. 1957. Perizonius, Niebuhr and the character of early Roman tradition. *JRS* 47: 104–14.

Momigliano, A. 1971. *The Development of Greek Biography: Four Lectures.* Cambridge, Mass.

Montanari, F. (ed.). 1991. *La poesia latina.* Rome.

Moore, T. 1998. *The Theater of Plautus: Playing to the Audience.* Austin.

Morelli, A. M. 2000. *L'epigramma latino prima di Catullo.* Cassino.

Morello, R. 2002. Livy's Alexander digression (9. 17–19): counterfactuals and apologetics. *JRS* 92: 62–85.

Morello, R. and Gibson, R. K. (eds). 2003. *Re-imagining Pliny the Younger. Arethusa* 36.2. Baltimore.

Moretti, F. 1998. *Atlas of the European Novel.* London.

Morford, M. P. O. 2002. *The Roman Philosophers.* London.

Morgan, L. 2000a. Creativity out of chaos: poetry between the death of Caesar and the death of Vergil. In Taplin 2000: 75–112.

Morgan, L. 2000b. Metre matters: some higher-level metrical play in Latin poetry. *PCPS* 46: 99–120.

Muecke, F. 1993. *Horace, Satires II.* Warminster.

Munari, F. 1965. *Epigrammata Bobiensia*. Rome.

Murgatroyd, P. 1975. *Militia Amoris* and the Roman elegists. *Latomus* 34: 59–79.

Murgatroyd, P. 1980. *Tibullus I*. Pietermaritzburg (repr. Bristol, 1991).

Murgatroyd, P. 1981. *Servitium Amoris* and the Roman elegists. *Latomus* 40: 589–606.

Murgatroyd, P. 1994. *Tibullus: Elegies II*. Oxford.

Murgia, C. E. 1985. Pliny's Letter and the *Dialogus*. *HSCP* 89: 171–206.

Murnaghan, S. and Joshel, S. (eds). 1998. *Women and Slaves in Greco-Roman Culture*. London.

Murphy, T. M. 2004. *Pliny the Elder's Natural History: the Empire in the Encyclopedia*. Oxford.

Murray, O. (ed.). 1990. *Sympotica: a Symposium on the Symposium*. Oxford.

Myerowitz, M. 1985. *Ovid's Games of Love*. Detroit.

Myers, K. S. 1994. *Ovid's Causes: Cosmogony and Aetiology in the* Metamorphoses. Ann Arbor.

Mynors, R. A. B. 1990. *Virgil: Georgics*. Oxford.

Nagle, B. R. 1980. *The Poetics of Exile*. Brussels.

Narducci, E. (ed.). 2002. *Interpretare Cicerone: Percorsi della critica contemporanea*. Florence.

Nauta, R. R. 2002. *Poetry for Patrons: Literary Communication in the Age of Domitian*. Leiden.

Nelis, D. 2001. *Vergil's* Aeneid *and the* Argonautica *of Apollonius Rhodius*. Leeds.

Newlands, C. 1995. *Playing with Time: Ovid and the* Fasti. Ithaca, NY.

Newlands, C. 2002. *Statius'* Silvae *and the Poetics of Empire*. Cambridge.

Newman, J. K. 1990. *Roman Catullus and the Modification of the Alexandrian Sensibility*. Hildesheim.

Nicolet, C. 1991. *Space, Geography and Politics in the Early Roman Empire*. Ann Arbor.

Nicolet, C. et al. 1995. *Les littératures techniques dans l'antiquité romaine*. Fondation Hardt, Entretiens 42. Geneva.

Nicoll, A. 1931. *Masks, Mimes and Miracles: Studies in the Popular Theatre*. London.

Nicoll, W.S.M. 1980. Cupid, Apollo and Daphne (Ovid *Met*. 1.452ff). *CQ* 30 : 174-82.

Nicolosi, C. et al. (eds). 1972. *Studi classici in onore di Quintino Cataudella* III. Univ. di Catania.

Nielsen, H. S. 1997. Interpreting epithets in Roman epitaphs. In Rawson and Weaver 1997: 169–204.

Nielsen, H.S. 2001. The value of epithets in pagan and Christian epitaphs from Rome. In Dixon 2001: 165-77.

Nisbet, G. 2002. 'Barbarous verses': a mixed media narrative from Greco-Roman Egypt. *Apollo* 156 (July): 15–19.

Nisbet, G. 2004. *Greek Epigram in the Roman Empire: Martial's Forgotten Rivals*. Oxford.

Nisbet, R. G. M. 1961. *Cicero: In L. Calpurnium Pisonem Oratio*. Oxford.

Nisbet, R. G. M. 1964. The speeches. In Dorey 1964: 47–79.

Nisbet, R. G. M. 1978. Virgil's fourth eclogue: Easterners and Westerners. *BICS* 25: 59–78.

Nisbet, R. G. M. 1984. Horace's *Epodes* and History. In Woodman and West 1984: 1–18.

Nisbet, R. G. M. and Hubbard, M. 1970. *A Commentary on Horace's Odes: Book I*. Oxford.

Nisbet, R. G. M. and Hubbard, M. 1978. *A Commentary on Horace's Odes: Book II*. Oxford.

Nisbet, R. G. M. and Rudd, N. 2004. *A Commentary on Horace's Odes: Book III*. Oxford.

Norwood, G. 1923. *The Art of Terence*. Oxford.

Nussbaum, M. C. 1994. *The Therapy of Desire: Theory and Practice in Hellenistic Ethics*. Princeton.

Nussbaum, M. C. 2001. *Upheavals of Thought: the Intelligence of Emotions*. Cambridge.

O'Connor, E. M. 1989. *Symbolum Salacitatis: a Study of the God Priapus as a Literary Character*. Frankfurt am Main.

O'Connor, J. F. 1976. The conflict of rhetoric in the *Octavius* of Minucius Felix. *Classical Folia. Studies in the Christian Perpetuation of the Classics*. Catholic Classical Association of Greater New York. 30: 165–73.

O'Gorman, E. 1993. No place like home: identity and difference in the *Germania* of Tacitus. *Ramus* 22: 135–54.

Oakley, S. P. 1997. *A Commentary on Livy, Books VI–X*. Volume 1. Oxford.

Oakley, S. P. 1998. *A Commentary on Livy, Books VI–X*. Volume 2. Oxford.

Ogilvie, R. M. 1965. *A Commentary on Livy Books I–V*. Oxford.

Ogilvie, R. M. 1980. *Roman Literature and Society*. London.

Ogilvie, R. M. and Richmond, I. 1967. *Tacitus: Agricola*. Oxford.

Oliensis, E. 1998. *Horace and the Rhetoric of Authority*. Cambridge.

Ortony, A., Clore, G. L., Collins, A. 1988. *The Cognitive Structure of Emotions*. Cambridge.

Otis, B. 1964. *Virgil: a Study in Civilized Poetry*. Oxford.

Otis, B. 1970. *Ovid as an Epic Poet*. 2nd edn. Cambridge.

Page, D. L. (ed.). 1962. *Select Papyri*. Vol. III: *Literary Papyri*. London.

Panayotakis, C. 1995. *Theatrum Arbitri: Theatrical Elements in the* Satyrica *of Petronius*. Leiden.

Panayotakis, C. 1997. Baptism and crucifixion on the mimic stage. *Mnem.* 50: 302–19.

Parker, H. N. 1994. Sulpicia, the *Auctor de Sulpicia* and the authorship of 3.9 and 3.11 of the *Corpus Tibullianum*. *Helios* 21: 39–62.

Parker, W. H. 1988. *Priapea: Poems for a Phallic God*. London.

Parkin, T. 1997. Out of sight, out of mind: elderly members of the Roman family. In Rawson and Weaver 1997: 123–48.

Parry, A. 1963. The two voices of Virgil's *Aeneid*. *Arion* 2: 66–80.

Paschalis, M. 1986. The unifying theme of Daedalus' sculptures on the Temple of Apollo Cumaeus (*Aen.* 6.20–33). *Vergilius* 32: 33–41.

Patterson, O. 1982. *Slavery and Social Death: a Comparative Study*, Cambridge, Mass.

Patterson, O. 1991. *Freedom in the Making of Western Civilization*. New York.

Paukstadt, R. 1876. *De Martiale Catulli imitatore*. Halle.

Paul, G. M. 1984. *A Historical Commentary on Sallust's Bellum Jugurthinum*. Liverpool.

Peachin, M. 2001a. Friendship and abuse at the dinner table. In Peachin 2001b: 135–44.

Peachin, M. (ed.). 2001b. *Aspects of Friendship in the Graeco-Roman World*. Portsmouth, R.I.

Pecere, O. and Stramaglia, A. (eds). 1996. *La letteratura di consumo nel mondo greco-latino*. Cassino.

Pelling, C. B. R. 1997. Biographical history? Cassius Dio on the Early Principate. In Edwards and Swain 1997: 117–44.

Pelling, C. B. R. 2000. *Literary Texts and the Greek Historian*. London.

Pelling, C. B. R. 2002. *Plutarch and History*. Swansea.

Perkell, C. G. 1989. *The Poet's Truth: a Study of the Poet in Virgil's Georgics*. Berkeley.

Pernice, E and W. Gross 1969. Beschriebungen von Kunstwerken in der Literatur. Rhetorische Ekphrasis. In Hausmann 1969: 433–47.

Perrin, B. 1914–26. *Plutarch's Lives*. 11 vols. Cambridge, Mass.

Perry, B. E. 1967. *The Ancient Romances*. Berkeley.

Peter, H. 1914. *Historicorum Romanorum Reliquiae*. Vol. 1. Leipzig.

Petersmann, H. 1985. Umwelt, Sprachsituation und Stilschichten in Petrons *Satyrica*. *ANRW* II.32.3: 1687–1705 (trans. as 'Environment, linguistic situation and levels of style in Petronius' *Satyrica*' in Harrison 1999: 105–23).

Petrochilos, N. K. 1974. *Roman Attitudes to the Greeks*. Athens.

Pfeiffer, R. 1968. *History of Classical Scholarship*. Vol. 1. Oxford.

Phang, S. E. 2001. *The Marriage of Roman Soldiers (13 B.C. – A.D. 235): Law and Family in the Imperial Army*. Leiden.

Philips, C. R., III. 1991. Poetry before the ancient city: Zorzetti and the case of Rome. *CJ* 86: 382–9.

Pöhlmann, E. 1973. Charakteristika des römischen Lehrgedichts. *ANRW* I.3: 813–901.

Pomeroy, S. B. (ed.). 1999. *Plutarch's Advice to the Bride and Groom and a Consolation to his Wife*. Oxford.

Poole, A. and Maule, J. (eds). 1995. *The Oxford Book of Classical Verse in Translation*. Oxford.

Porter, S. E. (ed.). 1997. *Handbook of Classical Rhetoric in the Hellenistic Period 330 BC–AD 400*. Leiden.

Posch, S. 1969. *Beobachtungen zur Theokritnachwirkung bei Vergil*. Innsbruck.

Pöschl, V. 1962. *Virgil's Poetic Art*. Ann Arbor (original German edn 1950).

Poucet, J. 1989. Réflexions sur l' écrit et l' écriture dans la Rome des premières siècles. *Latomus* 48: 285–311.

Powell, A. (ed.). 1992. *Roman Poetry and Propaganda in the Age of Augustus*. London.

Powell, J. G. F., 1988. *Cicero: Cato Maior De Senectute*. Oxford.

Powell, J. G. F., 1992. Persius' First Satire. In Woodman and Powell 1992: 150–72.

Powell, J. G. F. 1994. The *rector rei publicae* of Cicero's *de Republica*. *Scripta Classica Israelica* 13: 19–29.

Powell, J. G. F. 1996. Second thoughts on the dream of Scipio. *Proceedings of the Leeds International Latin Seminar* 9: 13–27.

Powell, J. G. F. (ed.). 1995. *Cicero the Philosopher: Twelve Papers*. Oxford.

Prandi, L. 1979. La 'fides Punica' e il pregiudizio anticartaginese. In Sordi 1979: 90–7.

Prato, C. 1964. *Gli epigrammi attribuiti a L. Anneo Seneca*. Rome.

Pretis, A. de 2002. *Epistolarity in the First Book of Horace's Epistles*. Piscataway, N.J.

Puelma, M. 1996. ΕΠΙΓΡΑΜΜΑ / epigramma. Aspekte einer Wortgeschichte. *MH* 53: 123–39.

Putnam, M. C. J. 1965. *The Poetry of the Aeneid*. Cambridge, Mass. (2nd edn, Ithaca, N.Y., 1988).

Putnam, M. C. J. 1970. *Virgil's Pastoral Art*. Princeton.

Putnam, M. C. J. 1979. *Virgil's Poem of the Earth: Studies in the Georgics*. Princeton.

Putnam, M. C. J. 1986. *Artifices of Eternity: Horace's Fourth Book of Odes*. Ithaca, NY.

Putnam, M. C. J. 1995. *Virgil's Aeneid: Interpretation and Influence*. Chapel Hill.

Putnam, M. C. J. 1998a. *Virgil's Epic Designs: Ekphrasis in the Aeneid*. New Haven.

Putnam, M. C. J. 1998b. Dido's murals and Virgilian ekphrasis. *HSCP* 98: 243–75.

Quinn, K. F. 1970. *Catullus: the Poems*. London.

Quinn, K. F. 1972. *Catullus: an Interpretation*. London.

Raaflaub, K. and Samons, L. 1990. Opposition to Augustus. In Raaflaub and Toher 1990: 417–54.

Raaflaub, K. and Toher, M. (eds). 1990. *Between Republic and Empire: Interpretations of Augustus and his Principate*. Berkeley.

Raby, F. J. E. 1927. *A History of Christian Latin Poetry*. Oxford.

Raccanelli, R. 1998. *L'amicitia nelle commedie de Plauto: un' indagine antropologica*. Bari.

Radice, B. 1976. *Terence: the Comedies*. Harmondsworth.

Rambaud, M. 1953. *L'art de la déformation historique dans les Commentaires de César*. Paris.

Ramsey, J. T. and Licht, A. L. 1997. *The Comet of 44 B.C. and Caesar's Funeral Games*. Atlanta.

Ravenna G. 1974. L'Ekphrasis poetica di opere d'arte: Temi e problemi. *Quaderni dell' Istituto Filologica Latina di Padova* 3: 1–52.

Ravenna, G. 1985. Ekphrasis. *Enciclopedia Virgiliana* II: 183–5.

Rawson, B. M. 1966 (writing as B. M. Wilkinson). Family life among the lower classes in Rome at the first two centuries of the empire. *CPh* 61: 71–83.

Rawson, B. M. 1989. *Spurii* and the Roman view of illegitimacy. *Antichthon* 23: 10–41.

Rawson, B. M. 2001. Children as cultural symbols: imperial ideology in the second century. In Dixon 2001: 21–42.

Rawson, B. M. 1997. The iconography of Roman childhood. In Rawson and Weaver 1997: 205–38.

Rawson, B. M. (ed.). 1986. *The Family in Ancient Rome: New Perspectives*. London.

Rawson, B. M. (ed.). 1991. *Marriage, Divorce and Children in Ancient Rome*. Canberra.

Rawson, B. M. and Paul Weaver (eds). 1997. *The Roman Family in Italy: Status, Sentiment, Space*. Canberra.

Rawson, E. 1972. Cicero the historian and Cicero the antiquarian. *JRS* 62: 33–45 (repr. in Rawson 1991a: 58–79).

Rawson, E. 1975. *Cicero*. London.

Rawson, E. 1978. The introduction of logical organisation in Roman prose literature. *PBSR* 46: 12–34 (repr. in Rawson 1991a: 324–51).

Rawson, E. 1985. *Intellectual Life in the Late Roman Republic*. London.

Rawson, E. 1991a. *Roman Culture and Society: Collected Papers*. Oxford.

Rawson, E. 1991b. *Discrimina ordinum*: the *Lex Julia Theatralis*. In Rawson 1991a: 508–45.

Reay, B. 2002. Seeing the *Georgics*' slaves. Unpublished lecture, University of California at Berkeley, 2 November 2002.

Reeve, M. D. 2003. Review of Meissner 1999. *CR* 53: 331–4.

Reich, H. 1903. *Der Mimus*. Berlin.

Reitzenstein, R. 1907. Epigramm. *RE* 6: 70–111.

Renard, M. and Laurens, P. (eds). 1985. *Hommages à Henry Bardon*. Brussels.

Reynolds, R. W. 1946. The adultery mime. *CQ* 40: 77–84.

Ribbeck, O. (ed.). 1898. *Scaenicae Romanorum Poesis Fragmenta*. 3rd edn. *Volumen II Comicorum Fragmenta*. Leipzig.

Rieks, R. 1978. Mimus und Atellanae. In Lefèvre 1978: 348–77.

Riffaterre, M. 1972. Système d'un genre descriptif. *Poétique* 3: 15–30.

Riggsby, A. M. 1995. Pliny on Cicero and oratory: self- fashioning in the public eye. *AJP* 116: 123–35.

Riggsby, A. M. 1998. Self and community in the Younger Pliny. *Arethusa* 31: 75–98.

Riggsby, A. M. 1999. *Crime and Community in Ciceronian Rome*. Austin.

Rigney, A. 1992. Review of L. Gossman, *Between Literature and History*. *History and Theory* 31: 208–22.

Rives, J. B. 1999. *Tacitus: Germania*. Oxford.

Robert, L. 1989. Épigraphie. In idem, *Opera Minora Selecta* 5. Amsterdam: 65–109.

Roberts, G. 2001. *The History and Narrative Reader*. London.

Roller, M. 1998. Pliny's Catullus: the politics of literary appropriation. *TAPA* 128: 265–304.

Roller, M. 2001. *Constructing Autocracy: Aristocrats and Emperors in Julio-Claudian Rome*. Princeton.

Romm, J. S. 1992. *The Edges of the Earth in Ancient Thought*. Princeton.

Rorty, A. O. (ed.). 1980. *Explaining Emotions*. Berkeley.

Rosati, G. 1983. Trimalchione in scena. *Maia* 35: 213–27 (trans. as 'Trimalchio on stage' in Harrison 1999: 85–104).

Rose, H. J. 1966. *A Handbook of Latin Literature from the Earliest Times to the Death of Saint Augustine*. 3rd edn. London.

Rosenblum, M. 1961. *Luxorius*. New York.

Rosenmeyer, P. 1997. Ovid's *Heroides* and *Tristia*: voices from exile. *Ramus* 26.1: 29–56.

Ross, D. O. 1969. *Style and Tradition in Catullus*. Cambridge, Mass.

Ross, D. O. 1975. *Backgrounds to Augustan Poetry: Gallus, Elegy and Rome*. Cambridge.

Ross, D. O. 1987. *Virgil's Elements: Physics and Poetry in the Georgics*. Princeton.

Rossi, A. 2000. The camp of Pompey: strategy of representation in Caesar's *Bellum Ciuile*. *CJ* 95: 239–56.

Rudd, N. 1966. *The Satires of Horace*. Cambridge (repr. Bristol, 1985).

Rudd, N. 1976. Architecture: Theories about Virgil's *Eclogues*. In idem, *Lines of Enquiry*. Cambridge: 119–144.

Rudd, N. 1979. *Horace: Satires and Epistles, Persius: Satires*. Harmondsworth.

Rudd, N. 1986. *Themes in Roman Satire*. London.

Rudd, N. 1991. *Juvenal: the Satires*. Oxford.

Rudd, N. (ed.). 1972. *Essays on Classical Literature*. Cambridge.

Rudd, N. (ed.). 1993. *Horace 2000: a Celebration*. London.

Rüpke, J. 2000. Räume literarischer Kommunikation in der Formierungsphase römischer Literatur. In Braun et al. 2000: 31–52.

Rüpke, J. 2001a. Kulturtransfer als Rekodierung: zum literaturgeschichtlichen und sozialen Ort der frühen römischen Epik. In Rüpke 2001b: 42–64.

Rüpke, J. (ed.). 2001b. *Von Göttern und Menschen erzählen: Formkonstanzen und Funktionswandel vormoderner Epik.* Stuttgart.

Russell, D. A. 2001. *Quintilian: the Orator's Education.* Loeb Classical Library. 5 vols. Cambridge, Mass.

Russell, D. A. (ed.). 1990. *Antonine Literature.* Oxford.

Russell, D. A. and Winterbottom, M. 1972. *Ancient Literary Criticism.* Oxford.

Russo, A. 2001. Iambic Presences in Ennius' *Saturae.* In Cavarzere et al.: 99–116.

Rutherford, R. B. 1995. Authorial rhetoric in Virgil's *Georgics.* In Innes et al. 1995: 19–29.

Saller, R. P. 1982. *Personal Patronage under the Early Empire.* Cambridge.

Saller, R. P. 1987. Men's age at marriage and its consequences in the Roman family. *CPh* 82: 21–34.

Saller, R. P. 1989. Patronage and friendship in early imperial Rome: drawing the distinction. In Wallace-Hadrill 1989: 49–62.

Saller, R. P. 1994. *Patriarchy, Property and Death in the Roman Family.* Cambridge.

Saller, R. P. 1997. Roman kinship: structure and sentiment. In Rawson and Weaver 1997: 7–34.

Saller, R. P. and Shaw, B. D. 1984. Tombstones and Roman family relations in the principate: civilians, soldiers and slaves. *JRS* 74: 124–56.

Salmon, E. T. 1956. The evolution of the Augustan principate. *Historia* 5: 456–78.

Sandbach, F. H. 1977. *The Comic Theatre of Greece and Rome.* London.

Sanders, G. 1991. *Lapides Memores.* Faenza.

Sandy, G. 1997. *The Greek World of Apuleius.* Leiden.

Santini, C. and Scivoletto, N. (eds). 1990. *Prefazioni, prologhi, proemi di opere tecnico-scientifiche latine.* 3 vols. Rome.

Santirocco, M. S. 1979. Sulpicia reconsidered. *CJ* 74: 229–39.

Scanlon, T. F. 1980. *The Influence of Thucydides on Sallust.* Heidelberg.

Schechter, S. 1975. The aetion and Virgil's *Georgics.* *TAPA* 105: 347–91.

Schepens, G. and Delcroix, K. 1996. Ancient paradoxography: origins, evolution, production and reception. In Pecere and Stramaglia 1996: 373–460.

Schiesaro, A. 1990. *Simulacrum et imago: gli argomenti analogici nel De rerum natura.* Pisa.

Schiesaro, A. 1993. Il destinatario discreto: funzioni didascaliche e progetto culturale nelle Georgiche. In Schiesaro et al. 1993: 129–47.

Schiesaro, A., Mitsis, P., Clay, J. S. (eds). 1993. *Mega Nepios: il destinatario nell' epos didascalico. MD* 31. Pisa.

Schissel von Fleschenberg, O., 1913. Die Technik des Bildeinsatzes. *Philologus* 72: 83–4.

Schlam, C. C. 1992. *The Metamorphoses of Apuleius: on Making an Ass of Oneself.* Chapel Hill.

Schlunk, R. R. 1974. *The Homeric Scholia and the Aeneid.* Ann Arbor.

Schmal, S. 2001. *Sallust.* Hildesheim.

Schmeling, G. L. (ed.). 1996. *The Novel in the Ancient World.* Leiden.

Schmidt, E. A. (ed.). 2001. *L'histoire littéraire immanente dans la poésie latine. Entretiens Hardt* 47. Geneva.

Schmidt, P. L. 1989. *Postquam ludus in artem paulatim verterat.* Varro und die Frühgeschichte des römischen Theaters. In Vogt-Spira 1989: 77–134.

Schmidt, P. L. 2001. The original version of the *De Re Publica* and the *De Legibus.* In J. G. F. Powell and J. A. North (eds), *Cicero's Republic. BICS* Supplement 76: 7–16.

Schofield, M. and Striker, G. (eds). 1986. *The Norms of Nature: Studies in Hellenistic Ethics.* Cambridge.

Schubert, W. (ed.). 1998. *Ovid: Werk und Wirkung. Festgabe für Michael von Albrecht zum 65. Geburtstag.* 2 vols. Frankfurt.

Schulz, F. 1953. *History of Roman Legal Science.* 2nd edn. Oxford (first published 1946).

Schulze, K. P. 1887. Martials Catullstudien. *JKPh* 135: 637–40.

Schwindt, J. P. 2001. Literatursgeschichtsschreibung und immanente Literaturgeschichte. Bausteine literarhistorischen Bewusstseins in Rom. In Schmidt 2001: 1–49.

Sciarrino, E. 2004. Putting Cato the censor's *Origines* in its place. *ClAnt* 32.2 (forthcoming).

Sedgwick, E. K. 1985. *Between Men: English Literature and Male Homosocial Desire.* New York.

Sedley, D. N. 1998. *Lucretius and the Transformation of Greek Wisdom.* Cambridge.

Seel, O. 1961. Ansatz zu einer Martial-Interpretation. *AA* 10: 53–76.

Segal, C. P. 1966. Orpheus and the Fourth *Georgic*: Virgil on nature and civilization. *AJP* 87: 307–25 (repr. in idem, *Orpheus: the Myth of the Poet.* Baltimore, 1989: 36–53).

Segal, E. 1987. *Roman Laughter: the Comedy of Plautus.* 2nd edn. Oxford.

Segal, E. 1996. *Plautus: Four Comedies.* Oxford.

Serban, G. 1973. *Les fonctions du fantastique dans la Pharsale.* Bucharest.

Shackleton Bailey, D. R 1965–70. *Cicero Ad Atticum.* 7 vols. Cambridge.

Shackleton Bailey, D. R. 1977. *Cicero Ad familiares.* 2 vols. Cambridge.

Shackleton Bailey, D. R. 1980. *Ad Quintum fratrem* and *Ad Brutum.* Cambridge.

Shackleton Bailey, D. R. 1986. *Cicero: Philippics.* Chapel Hill.

Shackleton Bailey, D. R. 1990. *M. Valerii Martialis Epigrammata.* Stuttgart.

Shackleton Bailey, D. R. 1991. *Cicero: Back from Exile: Six Speeches upon his Return.* Chicago.

Shackleton Bailey, D. R. 1993. *Martial: Epigrams.* 3 vols. Cambridge, Mass.

Shackleton Bailey, D. R. 1999. *Letters to Atticus.* 4 vols plus index vol. Cambridge, Mass.

Shackleton Bailey, D. R. 2001. *Letters to his friends.* 3 vols. Cambridge, Mass.

Share, D. 1998. *Seneca in English.* Harmondsworth.

Sharrock, A. R. 1994. *Seduction and Repetition in Ovid's Ars Amatoria II.* Oxford.

Sharrock, A. R. 2000. Constructing characters in Propertius. *Arethusa* 33: 263–84.

Shaw, B. D. 1987. The age of Roman girls at marriage: some reconsiderations. *JRS* 77: 30–46.

Sherwin-White, A. N. 1966. *The Letters of Pliny: an Historical and Social Commentary.* Oxford.

Sherwin-White, A. N. 1967. *Racial Prejudice in Imperial Rome.* Cambridge.

Shipley, F. W. 1924. *Velleius Paterculus.* Loeb Classical Library. Cambridge, Mass.

Shulmann, J. 1981. *Te quoque falle tamen*: Ovid's anti-Lucretian didactics. *CJ* 76: 242–53.

Shweder, R. A. (ed.). 1991. *Thinking through Cultures: Expeditions in Cultural Psychology.* Cambridge, Mass.

Sickle, J. van 1978. *The Design of Virgil's* Bucolics. Rome.

Sider, R. D. 1972. *Ancient Rhetoric and the Art of Tertullian*. Oxford.

Sihvola, J. and Engberg-Pedersen, T. (eds). 1998. *The Emotions in Hellenistic Philosophy.* Dordrecht.

Simon, E. 1982. Vergil und die Bildkunst. *Maia* 34: 203–17.

Skoie, M. 2002. *Reading Sulpicia: Commentaries 1475 to 1990*. Oxford.

Skutsch, O. 1968. *Studia Enniana*. London.

Skutsch, O. 1985. *The Annals of Quintus Ennius*. Oxford.

Slater, N. W. 1985. *Plautus in Performance: the Theatre of the Mind*. Princeton.

Slater, N. W. 1990. *Reading Petronius*. Baltimore.

Slater, N. W. 1998. Passion and petrifaction: the gaze in Apuleius. *CPh* 93: 18–48.

Slavitt, D. R. and Bovie, S. P. 1974. *Terence: the Comedies*. Baltimore.

Slavitt, D. R. and Bovie, S. P. 1995. *Plautus: the Comedies*. 3 vols. Baltimore.

Slavitt, D. R. (ed.). 1992, 1995. *Seneca: the Tragedies*. 2 vols. Baltimore.

Smith, M. F. 1975. *Lucretius: De Rerum Natura*. Cambridge, Mass.

Smith, M. S. 1975. *Petronius: Cena Trimalchionis*. Oxford.

Smith, P. L. 1991. *Plautus: Three Comedies*. Ithaca, N.Y.

Solodow, J. B. 1977a. Ovid's *Ars Amatoria*: the Lover as cultural ideal. *WS* 11: 106–27.

Solodow, J. B. 1977b. *Poeta impotens*: the last three *eclogues*. *Latomus* 36: 757–71.

Solodow, J. B. 1979. Livy and the story of Horatius, I.24–26. *TAPA* 109: 251–68.

Solodow, J. B. 1988. *The World of Ovid's Metamorphoses*. Chapel Hill.

Solomon, R. C. 1976. *The Passions: the Myth and Nature of Human Emotions*. New York.

Sorabji, R. 2000. *Emotion and Peace of Mind: from Stoic Agitation to Christian Temptation*. Oxford.

Sordi, M. (ed.). 1979. *Conoscenze etniche e rapporti di convivenza nell'antichità*. Milan.

Soubiran, J. 1988. *Essai sur la versification dramatique des Romains: sénaire iambique et septénaire trochaïque*. Paris.

Spawforth, A. and Hornblower, S. (eds). 1996. *Oxford Classical Dictionary.* 3rd edn. Oxford.

Spencer, D. 2002. *The Roman Alexander: Reading a Cultural Myth*. Exeter.

Speyer, W. 1963. *Epigrammata Bobiensia*. Leipzig.

Springer, C. 1983–4. Aratus and the cups of Menalcas: a note on *Eclogue* 3.42. *CJ* 79: 131–4.

Stace, C. 1981. *Plautus: Rudens, Curculio, Casina*. Cambridge.

Stahl, H.-P. 1985. *Propertius: 'Love' and 'War'*. Berkeley.

Stahl, H.-P. (ed.). 1998. *Vergil's* Aeneid: *Augustan Epic and Political Context*. London.

Stahl, W. H. 1962. *Roman Science: Origins, Development and Influence*. Madison.

Starr, R. J. 1991. Explaining Dido to your son: Tiberius Claudius Donatus on Vergil's Dido. *CJ* 87: 25–34.

Steel, C. E. W. 2001. *Cicero, Rhetoric and Empire*. Oxford.

Steiner, D. T. 2001. *Images in Mind: Statues in Archaic and Classical Greek Literature and Thought*. Princeton.

Steinmetz, P. 1982. *Untersuchungen zur römischen Literatur des zweiten Jahrhunderts nach Christi Geburt*. Wiesbaden.

Stemplinger, E. 1918. Der Mimus in der horazischen Lyrik. *Philologus* 75: 466–9.

Stoppard, T. 1997. *The Invention of Love*. London.

Stroh, W. 1971. *Die römische Liebeselegie als werbende Dichtung*. Amsterdam.

Stroh, W. 1975. *Taxis und Taktik: die advokatische Dispositionskunst in Ciceros Gerichtsreden*. Stuttgart.

Suerbaum, W. 1980. Hundert Jahre Vergil-Forschung. *ANRW* II.31.1: 3–358.

Sullivan, J. P. 1964. *Ezra Pound and Sextus Propertius: a Study in Creative Translation*. Austin (repr. London, 1965).

Sullivan, J. P. 1965. *Petronius: the Satyricon and the Fragments*. Harmondsworth (rev. 1977).

Sullivan, J. P. 1968. *The Satyricon of Petronius: a Literary Study*. London.

Sullivan, J. P. 1985. *Literature and Politics in the Age of Nero*. Ithaca, N.Y.

Sullivan, J. P. 1991. *Martial: the Unexpected Classic*. Cambridge.

Sullivan, J. P. and Boyle, A. J. 1996. *Martial in English*. Harmondsworth.

Sullivan, J. P. (ed.). 1962. *Critical Essays on Roman Literature: Elegy and Lyric*. London.

Sullivan, J. P. (ed.). 1993. *Martial*. New York.

Summers, W. C. 1910. *Select Letters of Seneca*. London (repr. Bristol, 1990).

Summers, W. C. 1920. *The Silver Age of Latin Literature*. London.

Sumner, G. V. 1973. *The Orators in Cicero's* Brutus: *Prosopography and Chronology*.

Süß, W. 1952. Die dramatische Kunst in den philosophischen Dialogen Ciceros. *Hermes* 80: 419–36.

Sutton, D. F. 1986. *Seneca on Stage*. Leiden.

Swain, S. 1996. *Hellenism and Empire*. Oxford.

Swann, B. W. 1994. *Martial's Catullus*. Hildesheim.

Syed, Y. Forthcoming. *Vergil's Aeneid and the Roman Self: Subject and Nation in Literary Discourse*. Ann Arbor.

Syme, R. 1939. *The Roman Revolution*. Oxford.

Syme, R. 1958a. *Imperator Caesar*: a study in nomenclature. *Historia* 1: 361–77, 7: 172–88 (repr. in Syme 1979–91, 1: 361–77).

Syme, R. 1958b. *Tacitus*. 2 vols. Oxford.

Syme, R. 1964. *Sallust*. Berkeley.

Syme, R. 1974. History or biography: the case of Tiberius Caesar. *Historia* 23: 481–96 (repr. in Syme 1979–91, 3: 937–52).

Syme, R. 1978. Mendacity in Velleius. *AJP* 99: 45–63.

Syme, R. 1979–91. *Roman Papers*. 7 vols. Ed. E. Badian (vols 1–2) and A. R. Birley (vols 3–7). Oxford.

Syme, R. 1986. *The Augustan Aristocracy*. Oxford.

Taplin, O. (ed.). 2000. *Literature in the Greek and Roman Worlds: A New Perspective*. Oxford.

Tarrant, R. J. 1976. *Seneca: Agamemnon*. Cambridge.

Tarrant, R. J. 1978. Senecan drama and its antecedents. *HSCP* 82: 214–64.

Tarrant, R. J. 1985. *Seneca: Thyestes*. Atlanta, Ga.

Tarver, T. 1994. Varro, Caesar, and the Roman calendar: a study in late Republican religion. In A. H. Sommerstein (ed.), *Religion and Superstition in Latin Literature*. Nottingham Classical Literature Studies 3. Bari.

Tarver, T. 1997. Varro and the Antiquarianism of Philosophy. In Barnes and Griffin 1997: 130–64.

Tatum, J. 1969. The tales in Apuleius' *Metamorphoses*. *TAPA* 100: 487–527 (repr. in Harrison 1999: 157–94).

Tatum, J. 1979. *Apuleius and the Golden Ass.* Ithaca, N.Y.

Tatum, J. 1983. *Plautus. The Darker Comedies: Bacchides, Casina, Truculentus.* Baltimore.

Taylor, G. 1985. *Pride, Shame, and Guilt: Emotions of Self-Assessment.* Oxford.

Taylor, L. R. 1937. The opportunities for dramatic performance in the age of Plautus and Terence. *TAPA* 68: 284–304.

Theodorakopoulos, E. 1997. The book of Vergil. In Martindale 1997: 155–65.

Thomas, R. 1983. *The Latin Masks of Ezra Pound.* Ann Arbor.

Thomas, R. F. 1982. *Lands and Peoples in Roman Poetry: the Ethnographic Tradition.* Cambridge.

Thomas, R. F. 1983. Virgil's ekphrastic centrepieces. *HSCP* 87: 175–84.

Thomas, R. F. 1987. Prose into poetry: tradition and meaning in Virgil's *Georgics. HSCP* 91: 229–60.

Thomas, R. F. 1988. *Virgil: Georgics.* Cambridge.

Thomas, R. F. 2001. *Virgil and the Augustan Reception.* Cambridge.

Tietze-Larson, V. 1994. *The Role of Description in Senecan Tragedy.* Frankfurt.

Timpe, D. 1973. Fabius Pictor und die Anfänge der römischen Historiographie. *ANRW* I.2: 928–69.

Tipping, B. Forthcoming. Middling epic: Silius Italicus' *Punica.* In Kyriakidis (ed.), *Middles in Latin Poetry.* Bari.

Tissol, G. 1997. *The Face of Nature: Wit, Narrative, and Cosmic Origins in Ovid's Metamorphoses.* Princeton.

Toohey, P. 1996. *Epic Lessons: an Introduction to Ancient Didactic Poetry.* London.

Toohey, P. 2004. *Melancholy, Love, and Time: Boundaries of the Self in Ancient Literature.* Ann Arbor.

Townend, G. B. 1980. Calpurnius Siculus and the *munus Neronis. JRS* 70: 166–74.

Traglia, A. 1950–2. *Ciceronis Poetica Fragmenta.* 2 vols. Rome.

Traglia, A. 1972. Sulla lingua dei frammenti delle *Atellane* e dei *mimi.* In Nicolosi et al. 1972: 7–20.

Treggiari, S. 1981. *Concubinae. PBSR* 49: 59–81.

Treggiari, S. 1991. *Roman Marriage*: Iusti Coniuges *from the Time of Cicero to the Time of Ulpian.* Oxford.

Tuplin, C. 2000. Nepos and the origins of political biography. In Deroux 2000: 124–61.

Van Mal-Maeder, D. and Zimmerman, M. 1998. The many voices in *Cupid and Psyche.* In Zimmerman et al. 1998: 83–102.

Vance, N. 1997. *The Victorians and Ancient Rome.* Oxford.

Vasaly, A. 1993. *Representations: Images of the World in Ciceronian Oratory.* Berkeley.

Verducci, F. 1985. *Ovid's Toyshop of the Heart: Epistulae Heroidum.* Princeton.

Vessey, D. W. T. C. 1973. *Statius and the* Thebaid. Cambridge.

Veyne, P. 1978. La famille et l'amour sous le Haut-Empire romain. *Annales ESC* 33: 35–63.

Veyne, P. 1980. *Bread and Circuses: Historical Sociology and Political Pluralism.* Harmondsworth.

Veyne, P. 1988. *Roman Erotic Elegy: Love, Poetry and the West.* Chicago.

Veyne, P. 1993. Humanitas: Romans and non-Romans. In Giardina 1993: 342–69.

Vogt, J. (ed.). 1943. *Rom und Karthago.* Leipzig.

Vogt-Spira, G. (ed.). 1989. *Studien zur vorliterarischen Periode im frühen Rom.* Tübingen.

Volk, K. 2001. Pious and impious approaches to cosmology in Manilius. *MD* 47: 85–117.

Volk, K. 2002. *The Poetics of Latin Didactic: Lucretius, Vergil, Ovid and Manilius.* Oxford.

Voss, B. R. 1970. *Der Dialog in der frühchristlichen Literatur.* Munich.

Walbank, F. W., Astin, A. E., Fredriksen, M. W., Ogilvie, R. M. (eds). 1989. *The Cambridge Ancient History VII.2: The Rise of Rome to 220 B.C.* Cambridge.

Walker, A. D. 1993. Enargeia and the spectator in Greek historiography. *TAPA* 123: 353–78.

Walker, B. 1960. *The Annals of Tacitus.* Manchester.

Wallace-Hadrill, A. 1982. The golden age and sin in Augustan ideology. *Past and Present* 95: 19–36.

Wallace-Hadrill, A. 1983. *Suetonius, the Scholar and his Caesars.* London.

Wallace-Hadrill, A. 1986. Time for Augustus: Ovid, Augustus, and the *Fasti.* In Whitby et al. 1986: 221–30.

Wallace-Hadrill, A. (ed.). 1989. *Patronage in Ancient Society.* London.

Walsh, P. G. 1961. *Livy: His Historical Aims and Methods.* Cambridge.

Walsh, P. G. 1970. *The Roman Novel: The Satyricon of Petronius and the Metamorphoses of Apuleius.* Cambridge (repr. with addenda Bristol, 1995).

Walsh, P. G. 1978. Petronius and Apuleius. In Hijmans and Van der Paardt 1978: 17–24.

Walsh, P. G. 1994. *Apuleius: the Golden Ass.* Oxford.

Walsh, P. G. 1996. *Petronius: the Satyricon.* Oxford.

Warmington, E. H. 1936–8. *Remains of Old Latin.* 4 vols. Cambridge, Mass.

Watling, E. F. 1964. *Plautus: the Rope and Other Plays.* London.

Watling, E. F. 1965. *Plautus: the Pot of Gold and Other Plays.* London.

Watson, L. C. 1995. Horace's *Epodes*: the impotence of Iambos? In Harrison 1995: 188–202.

Watson, L. C. 2003. *A Commentary on Horace's Epodes.* Oxford.

Watson, L. C. and Watson, P. 2003. *Martial: Select Epigrams.* Cambridge.

Weaver, P. R. C. 1972. Familia Caesaris: *A Social Study of the Emperor's Freedmen and Slaves.* Cambridge.

Webb, R. 1997a. Mémoire et imagination: Les limites de l'*enargeia* dans la théorie rhétorique grecque. In Lévy and Pernot 1997: 229–48.

Webb, R. 1997b. Imagination and the arousal of the emotions in Greco-Roman rhetoric. In Braund and Gill 1997: 112–27.

Webb, R. 1999. Ekphrasis ancient and modern: the invention of a genre. *Word and Image* 15: 7–18.

Weitzmann, K. 1959. *Ancient Book Illustration.* Cambridge, Mass.

Welch, K. and Hillard, T. (eds). Forthcoming. *Roman Crossings: Theory and Practice in the Roman Republic.* Swansea.

Welch, K. and Powell, A. (eds). 1998. *Julius Caesar as Artful Reporter.* London.

Wellesley, K. 1972. *Cornelius Tacitus: the Histories Book III.* Sydney.

Wells, P. S. 1999. *The Barbarians Speak: how the Conquered Peoples Shaped Roman Europe.* Princeton.

West, D. 1969. *The Imagery and Poetry of Lucretius.* Edinburgh.

West, D. 1974. Of mice and men: Horace, *Satires* 2.6.77–117. In Woodman and West 1974: 67–80.

West, D. 1995. *Horace Odes I:* Carpe Diem. Oxford.

West, D. 1997. *Horace: the Complete Odes and Epodes.* Oxford.

West, D. 1998. *Horace Odes II:* Vatis Amici. Oxford.

West, D. 2002. *Horace Odes III:* Dulce Periculum. Oxford.

West, D. and Woodman, T. (eds). 1979. *Creative Imitation and Latin Literature.* Cambridge.

West, M. L. 1978. *Hesiod: Works and Days.* Oxford.

West, M. L. 1982. *Greek Metre.* Oxford.

West, M. L. 1992. *Iambi et Elegi Graeci.* 2nd edn. 2 vols. Oxford.

West, M. L. 1997. *The East Face of Helicon: West Asiatic Elements in Greek Poetry and Myth.* Oxford.

Westendorp Boerma, R. E. H. 1949, 1963. *P. Vergili Maronis Catalepton.* 2 vols. Assen.

Wheeler, A. L. 1934. *Catullus and the Traditions of Ancient Poetry.* Berkeley.

Wheeler, S. M. 1999. *A Discourse of Wonders: Audience and Performance in Ovid's Metamorphoses.* Philadelphia.

Wheeler, S. M. 2000. *Narrative Dynamics in Ovid's Metamorphoses.* Tübingen.

Whitby, M., Hardie, P. R., Whitby, M. (eds). 1986. *Homo Viator: Classical Essays for John Bramble.* Bristol.

White, K. D. 1973. Roman agricultural writers I: Varro and his predecessors. *ANRW* I.4: 439–97.

White, P. 1978. *Amicitia* and the profession of poetry in early imperial Rome. *JRS* 68: 74–92.

White, P. 1991. Maecenas' retirement. *CPh* 86: 130–38.

White, P. 1993. *Promised Verse: Poets in the Society of Augustan Rome.* Cambridge, Mass.

Whitmarsh, T. 2001. *Greek Literature and the Roman Empire: the Politics of Imitation.* Oxford.

Wiemken, H. 1972. *Der griechische Mimus.* Bremen.

Wilkes, J. 1972. Julio-Claudian historians. *CW* 65: 177–203.

Wilkinson, B. M. (Rawson, B. M.). 1966. Family life among the lower classes at Rome in the first two centuries of the empire. *CPh* 61: 71–83.

Wilkinson, L. P. 1975. *The Roman Experience.* London.

Williams, G. D. 1994. *Banished Voices: Readings in Ovid's Exile Poetry.* Cambridge.

Williams, G. D. 1996. *The Curse of Exile: A Study of Ovid's* Ibis. Cambridge.

Williams, G. D. 2002. Ovid's exile poetry. In Hardie 2002: 233–45.

Williams, G. W. 1958. Some aspects of Roman marriage ceremonies and ideals. *JRS* 48: 16–29.

Williams, G. W. 1968. *Tradition and Originality in Roman Poetry.* Oxford.

Williams, G. W. 1978. *Change and Decline: Roman Literature in the Early Empire.* Berkeley.

Williams, G. W. 1990. Did Maecenas 'fall from favor'? Augustan literary patronage. In Raaflaub and Toher 1990: 258–75.

Williams, G. W. 1995. *Libertino Patre Natus:* true or false? In Harrison 1995: 296–313.

Williams, H. J. 1986. *The* Eclogues *and* Cynegetica *of Nemesianus.* Leiden.

Williams, J. H. C. 2001. *Beyond the Rubicon: Romans and Gauls in Republican Italy.* Oxford.

Williams, R. D. 1960a. The pictures on Dido's temple. *CQ* 10: 145–51.

Williams, R. D. 1960b. *P. Vergili Maronis Aeneidos Liber V.* Oxford.

Williams, R. D. 1962. *P. Vergili Maronis Aeneidos Liber III.* Oxford.

Williams, R. D. 1972. *Virgil: Aeneid I–VI.* London.

Williams, R. D. 1973. *Virgil: Aeneid VII–XII.* London.

Wilson, M. 2001. Seneca's *Epistles* reclassified. In Harrison 2001: 164–87.

Winkler, J. J. 1985. Auctor *and* Actor: *a Narratological Reading of Apuleius'* Golden Ass. Berkeley.

Winterbottom, M. 1975. Quintilian and rhetoric. In Dorey 1975: 79–97.

Wiseman, T. P. 1969. *Catullan Questions.* Leicester.

Wiseman, T. P. 1974. *Cinna the Poet and Other Roman Essays.* Leicester.

Wiseman, T. P. 1979. *Clio's Cosmetics.* Leicester.

Wiseman, T. P. 1985. *Catullus and his World.* Cambridge.

Wiseman, T. P. 1987. *Roman Studies: Literary and Historical.* Liverpool.

Wiseman, T. P. 1994. *Historiography and Imagination.* Exeter.

Wiseman, T. P. 1995. *Remus: A Roman Myth.* Cambridge.

Wiseman, T. P. 1998. *Roman Drama and Roman History.* Exeter.

Wiseman, T. P. 2002. Ovid and the stage. In Herbert-Brown 2002: 275–99.

Wiseman, T. P. (ed.). 2002. *Classics in Progess: Essays on Ancient Greece and Rome.* Oxford.

Wisse, J. 1989. *Ethos and Pathos from Aristotle to Cicero.* Amsterdam.

Wistrand, E. 1976. *The So-called* Laudatio Turiae. *Introduction, Text, Translation and Commentary.* Göteborg.

Wood, N. 1988. *Cicero's Social and Political Thought.* Berkeley.

Woodman, A. J. 1977. *Velleius Paterculus: the Tiberian Narrative.* Cambridge.

Woodman, A. J. 1988. *Rhetoric in Classical Historiography.* London.

Woodman, A. J. 1998. *Tacitus Reviewed.* Oxford.

Woodman, A. J. and Martin, R. H. 1996. *Tacitus Annals Book 3.* Cambridge.

Woodman, T. (A. J.) and Feeney, D. (eds). 2002. *Traditions and Contexts in the Poetry of Horace.* Cambridge.

Woodman, T. (A. J.) and Powell, J. (eds). 1992. *Author and Audience in Latin Literature.* Cambridge.

Woodman, T. (A. J.) and West, D. (eds). 1974. *Quality and Pleasure in Latin Poetry.* Cambridge.

Woodman, T. (A. J.) and West, D. (eds). 1984. *Poetry and Politics in the Age of Augustus.* Cambridge.

Woolf, G. 1996. Monumental writing and the expansion of Roman society in the early empire. *JRS* 86: 22–39.

Woolf, G. and Edwards, C. (eds). 2003. *Rome the Cosmopolis.* Cambridge.

Wray, D. 2001. *Catullus and the Poetics of Roman Manhood.* Cambridge.

Wright, D. 1984. *Vergilius Vaticanus: Commentarius.* Graz.

Wright, D. 1993. *The Vatican Vergil.* Berkeley.

Wright, D. 2001. *The Roman Vergil and the Origins of Medieval Book Design.* London.

Wright, J. 1974. *Dancing in Chains: the Stylistic Unity of the Comoedia Palliata.* Rome.

Wright, J. 1983. Virgil's pastoral programme: Theocritus, Callimachus and *Eclogue* 1. *PCPhS* n.s. 29: 107–60.

Wüst, E. 1932. Mimos. *RE* 15.2: 1727–64.

Wyke, M. 2002. *The Roman Mistress*. Oxford.

Yardley, J. C. 1973. Comic influences in Propertius. *Phoenix* 27: 134–9.

Zanker, G. 1987. *Realism in Alexandrian Poetry: a Literature and its Audiences*. London.

Zanker, P. 1988. *The Power of Images in the Age of Augustus*. Ann Arbor.

Zeitlin, F. 1971. Petronius as paradox: anarchy and artistic integrity. *TAPA* 102: 631–84 (repr. in Harrison 1999: 1–49).

Zeitlin, F. 1982. *Under the Sign of the Shield: Semiotics and Aeschylus' Seven against Thebes*. Rome.

Zeitlin, F. 1994. The artful eye: vision, ecphrasis and spectacle in Euripidean theatre. In Goldhill and Osborne 1994: 138–96.

Zetzel, J. E. G. 1980. Horace's *Liber Sermonum*: the structure of ambiguity. *Arethusa* 13: 59–77.

Zimmermann, M. et al. (eds). 1998. *Aspects of Apuleius' Golden Ass II: Cupid and Psyche*. Groningen.

Ziolkowski, T. 1993. *Virgil and the Moderns*. Princeton.

Zoll, G. 1962. *Cicero Platonis Aemulus: Untersuchung über die Form von Ciceros Dialogen, besonders von De Oratore*. Zurich.

Zorzetti, N. 1980. *La pretesta e il teatro latino arcaico*. Naples.

Zorzetti, N. 1990. The *Carmina Convivalia*. In Murray 1990: 289–307.

Zorzetti, N. 1991. Poetry and ancient city: the case of Rome. *CJ* 86: 311–29.

Index

Roman names are usually given in the most easily recognizable version: thus 'Cicero, M. Tullius', rather than the conventional 'Tullius Cicero, M.'; and 'Virgil (P. Vergilius Maro)', not 'Vergilius Maro, P'. The topics named in chapter titles are not generally indexed unless they are important elsewhere; there is extensive cross-referencing between chapters in the text of the volume, but this index will be especially useful for finding material on a particular author when it is divided between more than one chapter.